SOUTH-WESTERN
CENGAGE Learning

MKTG8

Charles W. Lamb
Texas Christian University

Joseph F. Hair, Jr.
Kennesaw State University

Carl McDaniel
University of Texas–Arlington

General Manager, 4LTR Press:
    Neil Marquardt

Product Director, 4LTR Press:
    Steven E. Joos

Marketing Director, 4LTR Press:
    Caroline Concilla

Sr. Product Manager: Jason Fremder

Marketing Manager: Jeff Tousignant

Developmental Editor: Colin Grover,
    B-books, Ltd.

Marketing Coordinator: Christopher Walz

Production Director: Amy McGuire,
    B-books, Ltd.

Sr. Content Project Managers:
    Tammy Moore, Jennifer Ziegler

Sr. Media Developer: John Rich

Manufacturing Planner: Ron Montgomery

Vice President, General Manager, Social
    Science & Qualitative Business:
    Erin Joyner

Product Director: Mike Schenk

Production Service: B-books, Ltd.

Sr. Rights Acquisitions Specialist:
    Deanna Ettinger

Photo Researcher: Padmapriya
    Soundararajan

Text Permissions Researcher: Anjana
    Ragavendran

Sr. Art Director: Stacy Shirley

Internal Designer: KeDesign, Mason, OH

Cover Designer: KeDesign, Mason, OH

For product information and technology assistance, contact us at **Cengage Learning Customer & Sales Support, 1-800-354-9706**.

For permission to use material from this text or product, submit all requests online at **www.cengage.com/permissions**. Further permissions questions can be emailed to **permissionrequest@cengage.com**.

Library of Congress Control Number: 2013954309

Student Edition ISBN-13: 978-1-285-43268-7
Student Edition ISBN-10: 1-285-43268-1
Student Edition with PAC ISBN-13: 978-1-285-43262-5
Student Edition with PAC ISBN-10: 1-285-43262-2

South-Western
5191 Natorp Boulevard
Mason, OH 45040
USA

Cengage Learning products are represented in Canada by Nelson Education, Ltd.

For your course and learning solutions, visit **www.cengage.com**. Purchase any of our products at your local college store or at our preferred online store **www.CengageBrain.com**.

Cover and Page i Photography Credits:
Cover Image: © Peshkova/Shutterstock.com
Inside Front Cover: © iStockphoto.com/CostinT;
© iStockphoto.com/photovideostock; © iStockphoto.com/Leontura
Back Cover: © iStockphoto.com/René Mansi

Printed in the United States of America
2 3 4 5 6 7 18 17 16 15 14

MKTG8
Lamb | Hair | McDaniel

BRIEF CONTENTS

© iStockPhoto.com/GlobalStock

CONTENTS

© iStockPhoto.com/LincolnRogers

© Vitaly Titov & Maria Sidelnikova/Shutterstock.com

© iStockPhoto.com/Ashok Rodrigues

© iStockphoto.com/james steidl

Contents   V

Part 2
ANALYZING MARKETING OPPORTUNITIES

6 CONSUMER DECISION MAKING   91

7 BUSINESS MARKETING   121

Part 3 PRODUCT DECISIONS

Mike Lawrie/Getty Images

Part 4
DISTRIBUTION DECISIONS

© iStockphoto.com/dem10

© fStop/Alamy

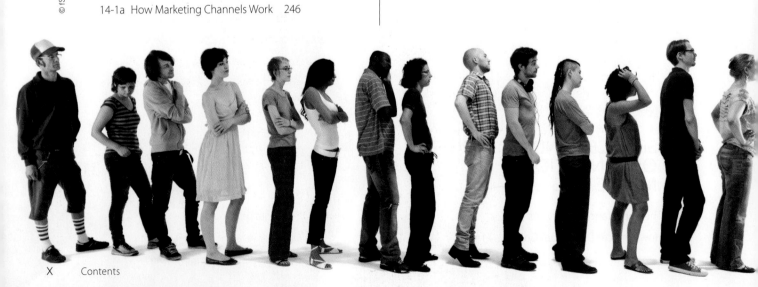

Part 5
PROMOTION AND COMMUNICATION STRATEGIES

© iStockPhoto.com/Murat Giray Kaya

© iStockPhoto.com/Vladimir Volkov

© Vasiliy Koval/Shutterstock.com

Image Source/Jupiterimages

Part 6
PRICING
DECISIONS

19 PRICING CONCEPTS 353

20 SETTING THE RIGHT PRICE 373

1-1 WHAT IS MARKETING?

What does the term *marketing* mean to you? Many people think it means personal selling. Others think marketing means advertising. Still others believe marketing has to do with making products available in stores, arranging displays, and maintaining inventories of products for future sales. Actually, marketing includes all of these activities and more.

> "Marketing is too important to be left only to the marketing department." David Packard, cofounder of Hewlett-Packard

marketing the activity, set of institutions, and processes for creating, communicating, delivering, and exchanging offerings that have value for customers, clients, partners, and society at large

Marketing has two facets. First, it is a philosophy, an attitude, a perspective, or a management orientation that stresses customer satisfaction. Second, marketing is an organization function and a set of processes used to implement this philosophy.

The American Marketing Association's definition of marketing focuses on the second facet. **Marketing** is the activity, set of institutions, and processes for creating, communicating, delivering, and exchanging offerings that have value for customers, clients, partners, and society at large.[1]

Marketing involves more than just activities performed by a group of people in a defined area or department. In the often-quoted words of David Packard, cofounder of Hewlett-Packard, "Marketing is too important to be left only to the marketing department." Marketing entails processes that focus on delivering value and benefits to customers, not just selling goods, services, and/or ideas. It uses communication, distribution, and pricing strategies to provide customers and other stakeholders with the goods, services, ideas, values, and benefits they desire when and where they want them. It involves building long-term, mutually rewarding relationships when these benefit all parties concerned. Marketing also entails an understanding that organizations have many connected stakeholder "partners," including employees, suppliers, stockholders, distributors, and others.

Research shows that companies that consistently reward employees with incentives and recognition are those that perform best, while disgruntled, disengaged workers cost the United States economy upward of $350 billion a year in lost productivity.[2] Google captured the number one position in *Fortune*'s "100 Best Companies to Work For in 2012." The company pays 100 percent of employees' health care premiums, offers paid sabbaticals, and provides bocce courts, a bowling alley, and twenty-five cafés—all for free. Google has also never had a layoff. One so-called Googler reported that "employees are never more than 150 feet away from a well-stocked pantry."[3]

Chapter 1

An Overview of Marketing

Learning Outcomes

1-1 *Define the term* marketing 2–4

1-2 *Describe four marketing management philosophies* 4–7

1-3 *Discuss the differences between sales and market orientations* 7–12

1-4 *Describe several reasons for studying marketing* 12–13

After you finish this chapter go to
p13 *for* **STUDY TOOLS** ⟶

exchange people giving up something in order to receive something else they would rather have

production orientation a philosophy that focuses on the internal capabilities of the firm rather than on the desires and needs of the marketplace

Google offers many amenities to its employees, part of the reason *Fortune* ranked it as the best company to work for in 2012.

One desired outcome of marketing is an **exchange**, people giving up something in order to receive something else they would rather have. Normally, we think of money as the medium of exchange. We "give up" money to "get" the goods and services we want. Exchange does not require money, however. Two (or more) people may barter or trade such items as baseball cards or oil paintings. An exchange can take place only if the following five conditions exist:

1. **There must be at least two parties.**
2. **Each party has something that might be of value to the other party.**
3. **Each party is capable of communication and delivery.**
4. **Each party is free to accept or reject the exchange offer.**
5. **Each party believes it is appropriate or desirable to deal with the other party.[4]**

Exchange will not necessarily take place even if all these conditions exist, but they must exist for exchange to be possible. For example, suppose you place an advertisement in your local newspaper stating that your used automobile is for sale at a certain price. Several people may call you to ask about the car, some may test-drive it, and one or more may even make you an offer. All five conditions that are necessary for an exchange to occur exist in this scenario. But unless you reach an agreement with a buyer and actually sell the car, an exchange will not take place.

Notice that marketing can occur even if an exchange does not occur. In the example just discussed, you would have engaged in marketing by advertising in the local newspaper even if no one bought your used automobile.

1-2 MARKETING MANAGEMENT PHILOSOPHIES

Four competing philosophies strongly influence an organization's marketing processes. These philosophies are commonly referred to as production, sales, market, and societal marketing orientations.

1-2a Production Orientation

A **production orientation** is a philosophy that focuses on the internal capabilities of the firm rather than on the desires and needs of the marketplace. A production orientation means that management assesses its resources and asks these questions: "What can we do best?" "What can our engineers design?" "What is easy to produce, given our equipment?" In the case of a service organization, managers ask, "What services are most convenient for the firm to offer?" and "Where do our talents lie?" Some have referred to this orientation as a *Field of Dreams* orientation, from the well-known movie line, "If we build it, they will come." The furniture industry is infamous for its disregard of customers and for its slow cycle times. For example, most traditional furniture stores (think Ashley or Haverty's) carry the same styles and varieties of furniture that they have carried for many years. They always produce and stock sofas, coffee tables, arm chairs, and end tables for the living room. Master bedroom suites always include at least a queen- or king-sized bed, two dressers, and two side tables. Regardless of what customers may actually be looking for, this is what they will find at these stores—and they have been so long-lived because what they produce has matched up with customer expectations. This has always been a production-oriented industry.

There is nothing wrong with assessing a firm's capabilities; in fact, such assessments are major considerations in strategic marketing planning (see Chapter 2). A production orientation falls short because it does not consider whether the goods and services that the firm produces most efficiently also meet the needs of the marketplace. Sometimes what a firm can best produce is exactly what the market wants. Apple has a history of production orientation, creating computers, operating systems, and other gadgetry because it can and hoping to sell the result. Some items have found a waiting market (early computers, iPod, iPhone). Other products, like the Newton, one of the first versions of a PDA, were simply flops.

In some situations, as when competition is weak or demand exceeds supply, a production-oriented firm can survive and even prosper. More often, however, firms that succeed in competitive markets have a clear understanding that they must first determine what customers want and then produce it, rather than focus on what company management thinks should be produced and hope that the product is something customers want.

1-2b Sales Orientation

A **sales orientation** is based on the belief that people will buy more goods and services if aggressive sales techniques are used and that high sales result in high profits. Not only are sales to the final buyer emphasized, but intermediaries are also encouraged to push manufacturers' products more aggressively. To sales-oriented firms, marketing means selling things and collecting money.

The fundamental problem with a sales orientation, as with a production orientation, is a lack of understanding of the needs and wants of the marketplace. Sales-oriented companies often find that, despite the quality of their sales force, they cannot convince people to buy goods or services that are neither wanted nor needed.

1-2c Market Orientation

The **marketing concept** is a simple and intuitively appealing philosophy that articulates a market orientation. It states that the social and economic justification for an organization's existence is the satisfaction of customer wants and needs while meeting organizational objectives. What a business thinks it produces is not of primary importance to its success. Instead, what customers think they are buying—the perceived value—defines a business. The marketing concept includes the following:

» **Focusing on customer wants and needs so that the organization can distinguish its product(s) from competitors' offerings**

» **Integrating all the organization's activities, including production, to satisfy customer wants**

» **Achieving long-term goals for the organization by satisfying customer wants and needs legally and responsibly**

The recipe for success is to develop a thorough understanding of your customers and your competition, your distinctive capabilities that enable your company to execute plans on the basis of this customer understanding,

sales orientation the belief that people will buy more goods and services if aggressive sales techniques are used and that high sales result in high profits

marketing concept the idea that the social and economic justification for an organization's existence is the satisfaction of customer wants and needs while meeting organizational objectives

A THUNDERBOLT TO YOUR SALES

One of the dangers of a sales orientation is failing to understand what is important to the firm's customers. When that occurs, sales-oriented firms sometimes use aggressive incentives to drive sales. For example, after Apple received complaints about the $49 selling price of its Thunderbolt cable, the company reduced the cable's price to $39 and introduced a shorter $29 version. The company hoped to spark sales of the optical data transfer cable, compatible only with Apple's newest line of computers and laptops.[5]

market orientation a philosophy that assumes that a sale does not depend on an aggressive sales force but rather on a customer's decision to purchase a product; it is synonymous with the marketing concept

societal marketing orientation the idea that an organization exists not only to satisfy customer wants and needs and to meet organizational objectives but also to preserve or enhance individuals' and society's long-term best interests

and how to deliver the desired experience using and integrating all of the resources of the firm.[6]

Firms that adopt and implement the marketing concept are said to be **market oriented**, meaning they assume that a sale does not depend on an aggressive sales force but rather on a customer's decision to purchase a product. Achieving a market orientation involves obtaining information about customers, competitors, and markets; examining the information from a total business perspective; determining how to deliver superior customer value; and implementing actions to provide value to customers.

Some firms are known for delivering superior customer value and satisfaction. J. D. Power and Associates listed Hampton Hotels, Virgin America, Kohl's, Jaguar, and L.L.Bean among its 2012 Customer Service Champions.[7]

Understanding your competitive arena and competitors' strengths and weaknesses is a critical component of a market orientation. This includes assessing what existing or potential competitors might intend to do tomorrow and what they are doing today. For example, BlackBerry (formerly Research in Motion) failed to realize it was competing against computer companies as well as telecom companies, and its wireless handsets were quickly eclipsed by offerings from Google, Samsung, and Apple. Had Black-Berry been a market-oriented company, its management might have better understood the changes taking place in the market, seen the competitive threat, and developed strategies to counter the threat. Instead, it reentered the market after a five-year slump with the wholly redesigned BlackBerry 10 operating system, which launched alongside two new handsets on January 30, 2013. By contrast, American Express's success has rested largely on the company's ability to focus on customers and adapt to their changing needs over the past 160 years.[8]

1-2d Societal Marketing Orientation

The **societal marketing orientation** extends the marketing concept by acknowledging that some products that customers want may not really be in their best interests or the best

interests of society as a whole. This philosophy states that an organization exists not only to satisfy customer wants and needs and to meet organizational objectives but also to preserve or enhance individuals' and society's long-term best interests. Marketing products and containers that are less toxic than normal, are more durable, contain reusable materials, or are made of recyclable materials is consistent with a societal marketing orientation. The American Marketing Association's definition of marketing recognizes the importance of a societal marketing orientation by including "society at large" as one of the constituencies for which marketing seeks to provide value.

Although the societal marketing concept has been discussed for more than thirty years, it did not receive widespread support until the early 2000s. Concerns such as climate change, the depleting of the ozone layer, fuel shortages, pollution, and health issues have caused consumers and legislators to become more aware of the need for companies and consumers to adopt measures that conserve resources and cause less damage to the environment.

Studies reporting consumers' attitudes toward, and intentions to buy, environmentally friendly products show widely varying results. A Nielsen study found that while 83 percent of consumers worldwide believe companies should have environmental programs, only 22 percent would pay more for an eco-friendly product. The key to consumer purchasing lies beyond labels proclaiming sustainability, natural ingredients, or "being green." Customers want sustainable products that perform better than their unsustainable counterparts.[9]

1-2e Who's In Charge?

The Internet and the widespread use of social media have accelerated the shift in power from manufacturers and retailers to consumers and business users. This shift began when customers began using books, electronics, and the Internet to access information, goods, and services. Customers use their widespread knowledge to shop smarter, leading executives such as former Procter & Gamble CEO A. G. Lafley to conclude that "the customer is boss."[10] Founder of Walmart and Sam's Club Sam Walton echoed this sentiment when he reportedly once said, "There is only one boss. The customer. And he can fire everybody in the company from the chairman on down, simply by spending his money somewhere else."[11] The

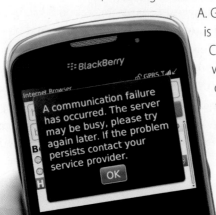

© iStockphoto.com/Scott Mangham

following quotation, attributed to everyone from L.L.Bean founder Leon Leonwood Bean to Mahatma Gandhi, has been a guiding business principle for more than 70 years: "A customer is the most important visitor on our premises. He is not dependent on us. We are dependent on him. He is not an interruption in our work. He is the purpose of it. He is not an outsider in our business. He is part of it. We are not doing him a favor by serving him. He is doing us a favor by giving us an opportunity to do so."[12] And as Internet use and mobile devices become increasingly pervasive, that control will continue to grow. This means that companies must create strategy from the outside in by offering distinct and compelling customer value.[13] This can be accomplished only by carefully studying customers and using deep market insights to inform and guide companies' outside-in view.[14] Jeff Bezos, founder and chairman of Amazon.com calls this a "working backward" mentality.[15]

1-3 DIFFERENCES BETWEEN SALES AND MARKET ORIENTATIONS

The differences between sales and market orientations are substantial. The two orientations can be compared in terms of five characteristics: the organization's focus, the firm's business, those to whom the product is directed, the firm's primary goal, and the tools used to achieve the organization's goals.

1-3a The Organization's Focus

Personnel in sales-oriented firms tend to be inward looking, focusing on selling what the organization makes rather than making what the market wants. Many of the historic sources of competitive advantage—technology, innovation, economies of scale—allowed companies to focus their efforts internally and prosper. Today, many successful firms derive their competitive advantage from an external, market-oriented focus. A market orientation has helped companies

such as Zappos.com and Bob's Red Mill Natural Foods outperform their competitors. These companies put customers at the center of their business in ways most companies do poorly or not at all.

CUSTOMER VALUE The relationship between benefits and the sacrifice necessary to obtain those benefits is known as **customer value**. Customer value is not simply a matter of high quality. A high-quality product that is available only at a high price will not be perceived as a good value, nor will bare-bones service or low-quality goods selling for a low price. Price is a component of value (a $4,000 handbag is perceived as being more luxurious and of higher quality than one selling for $100), but low price is not the same as good value. Instead, customers value goods and services that are of the quality they expect and that are sold at prices they are willing to pay.

Value can be used to sell a Mercedes-Benz as well as a Tyson frozen chicken dinner. In other words, value is something that shoppers of all markets and at all income levels look for. Lower-income consumers are price sensitive, but they will pay for products if they deliver a benefit that is worth the money.[16] Conversely, wealthy customers with money to spend may value the social message of their purchases above all else. These shoppers are being courted by a new breed of social shopping sites. The basic premise is that a well-known fashion name (be it a fashion editor, elite socialite, or celebrity) moderates sites by hand-picking pieces from favorite retailers, such as Barneys New York or Saks Fifth Avenue. Shoppers then purchase the curated items, and the site receives commission for each purchase. There are many of these sites; Moda Operandi has highlighted (and sold out of) woven skirts for $4,000 each, Motilo focuses on French fashion (including couture pieces), and *Fino File* is an online, shopable magazine, with pieces ranging from $80 tops to $1,000 boots. With reports of growing subscribers and sold-out merchandise, it is clear that these sites are attracting customers who value curated style.[17]

Marketers interested in customer value:

▸ **OFFER PRODUCTS THAT PERFORM: This is the bare minimum requirement. After grappling with the problems associated with its Vista operating system, Microsoft listened to its customers and made drastic changes for Windows 7, which received greatly improved reviews. Microsoft's subsequent release, Windows 8, performed even better than**

customer value the relationship between benefits and the sacrifice necessary to obtain those benefits

Windows 7, but consumers were much slower to embrace the operating system's incremental improvements.

▸ **EARN TRUST:** A stable base of loyal customers can help a firm grow and prosper. To attract customers, online eyewear company Coastal.com offers a First Pair Free program, whereby new customers receive their first pair of prescription eyeglass for free. Moreover, Coastal.com offers 366-day returns and encourages its staff members to do whatever it takes to ensure that customers are delighted by a smooth and stress-free experience. Coastal.com's dedication to earning customers' trust is evident—in 2013, the company received the STELLAService elite seal for excellence in outstanding customer service.[18]

▸ **AVOID UNREALISTIC PRICING:** E-marketers are leveraging Internet technology to redefine how prices are set and negotiated. With lower costs, e-marketers can often offer lower prices than their brick-and-mortar counterparts. The enormous popularity of auction sites such as eBay and the customer-bid model used by Priceline and uBid.com illustrates that online customers are interested in bargain prices. In fact, as smartphone usage grows, brick-and-mortar stores are fighting customers who compare prices using their smartphone and purchase items for less online while standing in the store.

▸ **GIVE THE BUYER FACTS:** Today's sophisticated consumer wants informative advertising and knowledgeable salespeople. It is becoming very difficult for business marketers to differentiate themselves from competitors. Rather than trying to sell products, salespeople need to find out what the customer needs, which is usually a combination of products, services, and thought leadership.[19] In other words, salespeople need to start with the needs of the customer and work toward the solution.

▸ **OFFER ORGANIZATION-WIDE COMMITMENT IN SERVICE AND AFTER-SALES**

SUPPORT: Upscale fashion retailer Nordstrom is widely known for its company-wide support system. If a customer finds that a competitor has reduced the price of an item also sold at Nordstrom, Nordstrom will match the other retailer's price and credit the customer's account—even long after the sale is made. Customer service agents at each of Nordstrom's 117 locations are knowledgeable and eager to assist customers before, during, or after a sale, and strive to make the return process as painless as possible. This attention to customer service is carried through to Nordstrom's online store as well: every order receives free shipping, as well as free return shipping. However and wherever they place their orders, customers know that Nordstrom will support them throughout—and long after—the checkout process.[20]

▸ **COCREATION:** Some companies and products allow customers to help create their own experience. For example, Case-Mate, a firm that makes formfitting cases for cell phones, laptops, and other personal devices, allows customers to design their own cases by uploading their own photos. Customers who don't have designs of their own can manipulate art from designers using the "design with" feature at case-mate.com. Either way, customers produce completely unique covers for their devices.

CUSTOMER SATISFACTION The customers' evaluation of a good or service in terms of whether that good or service has met their needs and expectations is called **customer satisfaction**. Failure to meet needs and expectations results in dissatisfaction with the good or service. Some companies, in their passion to drive down costs, have damaged their relationships with customers. Comcast, Wells Fargo, and Sprint Nextel are examples of companies where executives lost track of the delicate balance between efficiency and service.[21] Firms that have a reputation for delivering high levels of customer satisfaction do things differently from their competitors. Top management is obsessed with customer satisfaction, and employees throughout the organization understand the link between their job and satisfied customers. The culture of the organization is to focus on delighting customers rather than on selling products.

Coming back from customer dissatisfaction can be tough, but there are some key ways that companies begin to improve customer satisfaction. Forrester Research discovered that when companies experience gains in the firm's Customer Experience Index (CxPi), they have implemented one of two major changes. Aetna, a major health insurance provider, executed the first type of change—changing its decentralized, part-time customer service group into a full-time, centralized customer service team. Aetna's CxPi score rose six points in one year. Office Depot executed the second type of change—addressing customer "pain points" and making sure that what customers need is always available to them. By streamlining its supply chain and adding more stylish office products, Office Depot satisfied business customers and female shoppers, increasing its CxPi by nine points.[22]

BUILDING RELATIONSHIPS Attracting new customers to a business is only the beginning. The best companies view new-customer attraction as the launching point for developing and enhancing a long-term relationship. Companies can expand market share in three ways: attracting new customers, increasing business with existing customers, and retaining current customers. Building relationships with existing customers directly addresses two of the three possibilities and indirectly addresses the other.

Relationship marketing is a strategy that focuses on keeping and improving relationships with current customers. It assumes that many consumers and business customers prefer to have an ongoing relationship with one organization rather than switch continually among providers in their search for value. In early 2013, legal information and consulting firm Manzama, Inc. reported a 100 percent retention rate among existing clients in 2012, as well as an expanding base of new clients that included many of the country's top law firms. Manzama's flagship data analysis platform provides law firms with personalized, long-term information about their own businesses and the legal industry at large. Discussing the record year, Manzama CEO Peter Ozolin said, "Our clients recognize that stakeholders within the firm need business intelligence that's personalized. Manzama is the only Listening Platform that enables firms to quickly configure and personalize each individual's profile so they receive the customized intelligence they need." This long-term focus on customer needs is a hallmark of relationship marketing.[23]

Most successful relationship marketing strategies depend on customer-oriented personnel, effective training programs, employees with the authority to make decisions and solve problems, and teamwork.

CUSTOMER-ORIENTED PERSONNEL For an organization to be focused on building relationships with customers, employees' attitudes and actions must be customer oriented. An employee may be the only contact a particular customer has with the firm. In that customer's eyes, the employee *is* the firm. Any person, department, or division that is not customer oriented weakens the positive image of the entire organization. For example, a potential customer who is greeted discourteously may well assume that the employee's attitude represents the whole firm.

Customer-oriented personnel come from an organizational culture that supports its people. Southwest Airlines has been operating with high levels of customer satisfaction for forty years (forty years of love, as the airline quips). Not only does the airline have low fares, charge few fees (first two bags fly free!), and apologize via e-mail or phone for any delays or mishaps, it also receives tons of fan mail about its employees. The secret? Executives say they "hire nice people" and "empower employees to make decisions, and we support them."[24] Listed on several customer service "Best of" lists, Southwest's nice people are definitely popular with their customers.

Some companies, such as Coca-Cola, Delta Air Lines, Hershey, Kellogg, Nautilus, and Sears, have appointed chief

HOW DO YOU GET ALL THE MOISTURE WITHOUT THE MUCK?

BEESWAX   VS.   PETROLATUM

BURT'S BEES REPLENISHING LIP BALM

Burt's Bees, a popular beauty brand, assures each customer that "Your well-being is important to us." Such commitment helps retain existing customers.

customer officers (CCOs). These customer advocates provide an executive voice for customers and report directly to the CEO. Their responsibilities include ensuring that the company maintains a customer-centric culture and that all company employees remain focused on delivering customer value.

THE ROLE OF TRAINING Leading marketers recognize the role of employee training in customer service and relationship building. Sales staff at the Container Store receive more than 240 hours of training and generous benefits compared to an industry average of 8 hours of training and modest benefits.

EMPOWERMENT In addition to training, many market-oriented firms are giving employees more authority to solve customer problems on the spot. The term used to describe this delegation of authority is **empowerment**. Employees develop ownership attitudes when they are treated like part-owners of the business and are expected to act the part. These employees manage themselves, are more likely to work hard, account for their own performance and that of the company, and take prudent risks to build a stronger business and sustain the company's success. In order to empower its workers, the Ritz-Carlton chain of luxury hotels developed a set of 12 Service Values guidelines. These brief, easy-to-understand guidelines include statements such as "I am empowered to create unique, memorable and personal experiences for our guests" and "I own and immediately resolve guest problems." The 12 Service Values are printed on cards distributed to employees, and each day a particular value is discussed at length in Ritz-Carlton team meetings. Employees talk about what the value means to them and offer examples of how the value can be put into practice that day.[25]

Empowerment gives customers the feeling that their concerns are being addressed and gives employees the feeling that their expertise matters. The result is greater satisfaction for both customers and employees.

TEAMWORK Many organizations that are frequently noted for delivering superior customer value and providing high levels of customer satisfaction, such as Southwest Airlines and Walt Disney World, assign employees to teams and teach them team-building skills. **Teamwork** entails collaborative efforts of people to accomplish common objectives. Job performance, company performance, product value, and customer satisfaction all improve when people

An emphasis on cooperation over competition can help a company's performance improve. That's why many companies have moved to using teams to get jobs done.

© kristian sekulic/Shutterstock.com

in the same department or work group begin supporting and assisting each other and emphasize cooperation instead of competition. Performance is also enhanced when cross-functional teams align their jobs with customer needs. For example, if a team of telecommunications service representatives is working to improve interaction with customers, back-office people such as computer technicians or training personnel can become part of the team, with the ultimate goal of delivering superior customer value and satisfaction.

1-3b The Firm's Business

A sales-oriented firm defines its business (or mission) in terms of goods and services. A market-oriented firm defines its business in terms of the benefits its customers seek. People who spend their money, time, and energy expect to receive benefits, not just goods and services. This distinction has enormous implications. As Michael Mosley, director of office operations at health care provider Amedisys Home Health, notes, "We're in the business of making people better."[26] Answering the question "What is this firm's business?" in terms of the benefits customers seek, instead of goods and services, offers at least three important advantages:

▸▸ It ensures that the firm keeps focusing on customers and avoids becoming preoccupied with goods, services, or the organization's internal needs.

▸▸ It encourages innovation and creativity by reminding people that there are many ways to satisfy customer wants.

> ▸▸ It stimulates an awareness of changes in customer desires and preferences so that product offerings are more likely to remain relevant.

Because of the limited way it defines its business, a sales-oriented firm often misses opportunities to serve customers whose wants can be met through a wide range of product offerings instead of through specific products. For example, in 1989, 220-year-old Britannica had estimated revenues of $650 million and a worldwide sales force of 7,500. Just five years later, after three consecutive years of losses, the sales force had collapsed to as few as 280 representatives. How did this respected company sink so low? Britannica managers saw that competitors were beginning to use CD-ROMs to store huge masses of information but chose to ignore the new computer technology as well as an offer to team up with Microsoft. In 2012, the company announced that it would stop printing its namesake books and instead focus on selling its reference works to subscribers through its Web site and apps for tablets and smartphones.[27]

Having a market orientation and a focus on customer wants does not mean offering customers everything they want. It is not possible, for example, to profitably manufacture and market automobile tires that will last for 100,000 miles for twenty-five dollars. Furthermore, customers' preferences must be mediated by sound professional judgment as to how to deliver the benefits they seek. As Henry Ford once said, "If I had listened to the marketplace, I would have built a faster, cheaper horse."[28] Consumers have a limited set of experiences. They are unlikely to request anything beyond those experiences because they are not aware of benefits they may gain from other potential offerings. For example, before the Internet, many people thought that shopping for some products was boring and time-consuming but could not express their need for electronic shopping.

1-3c Those to Whom the Product Is Directed

A sales-oriented organization targets its products at "everybody" or "the average customer." A market-oriented organization aims at specific groups of people. The fallacy of developing products directed at the average user is that relatively few average users actually exist. Typically, populations are characterized by diversity. An average is simply a midpoint in some set of characteristics. Because most potential customers are not "average," they are not likely to be attracted to an average product marketed to the average customer. Consider the market for shampoo as one simple example. There are shampoos for oily hair, dry hair, and dandruff. Some shampoos remove the gray or color hair. Special shampoos are marketed for infants and elderly people. There are even shampoos for people with average or normal hair (whatever that is), but this is a fairly small portion of the total market for shampoo.

A market-oriented organization recognizes that different customer groups want different features or benefits. It may therefore need to develop different goods, services, and promotional appeals. A market-oriented organization carefully analyzes the market and divides it into groups of people who are fairly similar in terms of selected characteristics. Then the organization develops marketing programs that will bring about mutually satisfying exchanges with one or more of those groups. For example, Toyota developed a series of tongue-in-cheek videos and interactive Web pages featuring comedian Michael Showalter to advertise the 2013 Yaris subcompact sedan. Toyota used absurdist humor and an ironic slogan ("It's a car!") to appeal to Internet-savvy teens and young adults—a prime market for inexpensive subcompact cars.[29]

CUSTOMER RELATIONSHIP MANAGEMENT Beyond knowing to whom they are directing their products or services, companies must also develop a deeper understanding of their customers. One way of doing this is through *customer relationship management*. **Customer relationship management (CRM)** is a company-wide business strategy designed to optimize profitability, revenue, and customer satisfaction by focusing on highly defined and precise customer groups. This is accomplished by organizing the company around customer segments, establishing and tracking customer interactions with the company, fostering customer-satisfying behaviors, and linking all processes of the company from its customers through its suppliers. The difference between CRM and traditional mass marketing can be compared to shooting a rifle versus a shotgun. Instead of scattering messages far and wide across the spectrum of mass media (the shotgun approach), CRM marketers now are homing in on ways to effectively communicate with each customer (the rifle approach).

Companies that adopt CRM systems are almost always market oriented, customizing product and service offerings based on data generated through interactions between the customer and the company. This strategy transcends all functional areas of the business, producing an internal system where all of the company's decisions and actions are a direct result of customer information. We will examine specific applications of CRM in several chapters throughout this book.

1-3d The Firm's Primary Goal

A sales-oriented organization seeks to achieve profitability through sales volume and tries to convince potential customers to buy, even if the seller knows that the customer and product are mismatched. Sales-oriented organizations place a higher premium on making a sale than on developing a long-term relationship with a customer. In contrast, the ultimate goal of most market-oriented organizations is to make a profit by creating customer value, providing customer satisfaction, and building long-term relationships with customers. The exception is so-called nonprofit organizations that exist to achieve goals other than profits. Nonprofit organizations can and should adopt a market orientation. Nonprofit organization marketing is explored further in Chapter 12.

1-3e Tools the Organization Uses to Achieve Its Goals

Sales-oriented organizations seek to generate sales volume through intensive promotional activities, mainly personal selling and advertising. In contrast, market-oriented organizations recognize that promotion decisions are only one of four basic marketing mix decisions that must be made: product decisions, place (or distribution) decisions, promotion decisions, and pricing decisions. A market-oriented organization recognizes that each of these four components is important. Furthermore, market-oriented organizations recognize that marketing is not just a responsibility of the marketing department. Interfunctional coordination means that skills and resources throughout the organization are needed to create, communicate, and deliver superior customer service and value.

1-3f A Word of Caution

This comparison of sales and market orientations is not meant to belittle the role of promotion, especially personal selling, in the marketing mix. Promotion is the means by which organizations communicate with present and prospective customers about the merits and characteristics of their organization and products. Effective promotion is an essential part of effective marketing. Salespeople who work for market-oriented organizations are generally perceived by their customers to be problem solvers and important links to supply sources and new products. Chapter 18 examines the nature of personal selling in more detail.

1-4 WHY STUDY MARKETING?

Now that you understand the meaning of the term _marketing_, why it is important to adopt a marketing orientation, and how organizations implement this philosophy, you may be asking, "What's in it for me?" or "Why should I study marketing?" These are important questions whether you are majoring in a business field other than marketing (such as accounting, finance, or management information systems) or a nonbusiness field (such as journalism, education, or agriculture). There are several important reasons to study marketing: Marketing plays an important role in society, marketing is important to businesses, marketing offers outstanding career opportunities, and marketing affects your life every day.

Using the correct tool for the job will help an organization ACHIEVE ITS GOALS. *Marketing tools are covered throughout this book!*

1-4a Marketing Plays an Important Role in Society

The total population of the United States exceeds 314 million people.[30] Think about how many transactions are needed each day to feed, clothe, and shelter a population of this size. The number is huge. And yet it all works quite well, partly because the well-developed U.S. economic system efficiently distributes the output of farms and factories. A typical U.S. family, for example, consumes 2.5 tons of food a year.[31] Marketing makes food available when we want it, in desired quantities, at accessible locations, and in sanitary and convenient packages and forms (such as instant and frozen foods).

1-4b Marketing Is Important to Businesses

The fundamental objectives of most businesses are survival, profits, and growth. Marketing contributes directly to achieving these objectives. Marketing includes the following activities, which are vital to business organizations: assessing the wants and satisfactions of present and potential customers, designing and managing product offerings, determining prices and pricing policies, developing distribution strategies, and communicating with present and potential customers.

All businesspeople, regardless of specialization or area of responsibility, need to be familiar with the terminology and fundamentals of accounting, finance, management, and marketing. People in all business areas need to be able to communicate with specialists in other areas. Furthermore, marketing is not just a job done by people in a marketing department. Marketing is a part of the job of everyone in the organization. Therefore, a basic understanding of marketing is important to all businesspeople.

1-4c Marketing Offers Outstanding Career Opportunities

Between one-fourth and one-third of the entire civilian workforce in the United States performs marketing activities. Marketing offers great career opportunities in such areas as professional selling, marketing research, advertising, retail buying, distribution management, product management, product development, and wholesaling. Marketing career opportunities also exist in a variety of nonbusiness organizations, including hospitals, museums, universities, the armed forces, and various government and social service agencies.

1-4d Marketing in Everyday Life

Marketing plays a major role in your everyday life. You participate in the marketing process as a consumer of goods and services. About half of every dollar you spend pays for marketing costs, such as marketing research, product development, packaging, transportation, storage, advertising, and sales expenses. By developing a better understanding of marketing, you will become a better-informed consumer. You will better understand the buying process and be able to negotiate more effectively with sellers. Moreover, you will be better prepared to demand satisfaction when the goods and services you buy do not meet the standards promised by the manufacturer or the marketer.

STUDY TOOLS 1

LOCATED AT BACK OF THE TEXTBOOK
- ☐ *Rip out Chapter Review Card*

LOCATED AT WWW.CENGAGE.COM/LOGIN
- ☐ *Review Key Terms Flashcards*
- ☐ *Watch visual summaries to review key concepts*
- ☐ *Complete Practice Quizzes to prepare for tests*
- ☐ *Complete "Crossword Puzzle" to review key terms*
- ☐ *Watch Video "Geoffrey B. Small" for a real company example*

Strategic planning is the managerial process of creating and maintaining a fit between the organization's objectives and resources and the evolving market opportunities. The goal of strategic planning is long-run profitability and growth. Thus, strategic decisions require long-term commitments of resources.

> "There are a lot of great ideas that have come and gone in [the digital advertising] industry. Implementation many times is more important than the actual idea." David Moore, CEO of 24/7 Real Media

strategic planning
the managerial process of creating and maintaining a fit between the organization's objectives and resources and the evolving market opportunities

A strategic error can threaten a firm's survival. On the other hand, a good strategic plan can help protect and grow the firm's resources. For instance, if the March of Dimes had decided to focus only on fighting polio, the organization would no longer exist because polio is widely viewed as a conquered disease. The March of Dimes survived by making the strategic decision to switch to fighting birth defects.

Strategic marketing management addresses two questions: (1) What is the organization's main activity at a particular time? (2) How will it reach its goals? Here are some examples of strategic decisions:

▸▸ At the 2013 Consumer Electronics show, computer graphics hardware manufacturer Nvidia unveiled Project Shield, an Android-based portable gaming and media console that allows users to stream games directly from compatible computers. Project Shield is Nvidia's first foray into mobile gaming, a field dominated by Nintendo and Sony—and more recently, smartphones of all varieties.[1]

▸▸ Disney is trying to capture the two- to seven-year-old demographic, hoping to steal viewership from Viacom, which owns powerhouse shows *Dora the Explorer* and *SpongeBob SquarePants*. To do so, Disney is shuttering its twelve-year-old SOAPnet channel, which was devoted to soap operas, to create the new Disney Junior channel. The channel will feature shows such as *Doc McStuffins*, an animated show about a young girl who fixes up ailing stuffed animals.[2]

▸▸ Target plans to open 100 to 150 retail locations in Canada by the end of 2014—the company's first expansion outside of the United States. According to Target Corp. CEO Gregg Steinhafel, 70 percent of Canadians are already familiar with the brand. With the move into Canada, Target projects annual revenue growth of more than 4.5 percent—nearly double that of the previous five years.[3]

All these decisions have affected or will affect each organization's long-run course, its allocation of resources, and ultimately its financial success. In contrast, an operating decision, such as changing the package design for Post Grape-Nuts cereal

Chapter 2

Strategic Planning for Competitive Advantage

Learning Outcomes

After you finish this chapter go to
p31 *for* **STUDY TOOLS**

or altering the sweetness of a Kraft salad dressing, probably won't have a big impact on the long-run profitability of the company.

2-2 STRATEGIC BUSINESS UNITS

Large companies may manage a number of very different businesses, called strategic business units (SBUs). Each SBU has its own rate of return on investment, growth potential, and associated risks, and requires its own strategies and funding. When properly created, an SBU has the following characteristics:

- **A distinct mission and a specific target market**
- **Control over its resources**
- **Its own competitors**
- **A single business or a collection of related businesses**
- **Plans independent of the other SBUs in the total organization.**

In theory, an SBU should have its own resources for handling basic business functions: accounting, engineering, manufacturing, and marketing. In practice, however, because of company tradition, management philosophy, and production and distribution economies, SBUs sometimes share manufacturing facilities, distribution channels, and even top managers.

2-3 STRATEGIC ALTERNATIVES

There are several tools available that a company, or SBU, can use to manage the strategic direction of its portfolio of businesses. Three of the most commonly used tools are Ansoff's strategic opportunity matrix, the Boston Consulting Group model, and the General Electric model. Selecting which strategic alternative to pursue depends on which of two philosophies a company maintains

about when to expect profits—right away or after increasing market share. In the long run, market share and profitability are compatible goals. For example, Amazon lost hundreds of millions of dollars for its first few years as a company. The important goal early on, however, was market share—not profit. Amazon was sacrificing short-term profit for long-term market share, and thus larger long-term profits.[4]

2-3a Ansoff's Strategic Opportunity Matrix

One method for developing alternatives is Ansoff's strategic opportunity matrix (see Exhibit 1), which matches products with markets. Firms can explore these four options:

- **MARKET PENETRATION: A firm using the market penetration alternative would try to increase market share among existing customers. FTR Energy Services, a division of Frontier Communications, introduced a Green-e certified energy service into New York, Ohio, and Indiana markets served by Frontier's telephone and broadband services. Though these markets were already served by separate well-established energy companies, FTR Energy hoped to penetrate the energy market by allowing customers to lock in competitive rates and offering 5 percent cash back on energy usage.[5] Customer databases, discussed in Chapter 9, would help managers implement this strategy.**

- **MARKET DEVELOPMENT: Market development means attracting new customers to existing products. Ideally, new uses for old products stimulate additional sales among existing customers while also bringing in new buyers. McDonald's, for example, has opened restaurants in Russia, China, and Italy and is**

Exhibit 1

ANSOFF'S STRATEGIC OPPORTUNITY MATRIX

	Present Product	New Product
Present Market	*Market Penetration* Starbucks sells more coffee to customers who register their reloadable Starbucks cards.	*Product Development* Starbucks develops powdered instant coffee called Via.
New Market	*Market Development* Starbucks opens stores in Brazil and Chile.	*Diversification* Starbucks launches Hear Music and buys Ethos Water.

© Cengage Learning

Courtesy Daisy Brand LLC.

This ad for Daisy Brand cottage cheese shows ten different ingredients to use with the product. Daisy is hoping to increase market share among existing customers by encouraging them to try its product in many different ways.

eagerly expanding into Eastern European countries. In the nonprofit arena, the growing emphasis on continuing education and executive development by colleges and universities is a market development strategy.

▸▸ **PRODUCT DEVELOPMENT:** A **product development** strategy entails the creation of new products for present markets. In November 2012, Nintendo launched Wii U, a successor to the incredibly successful Wii video game console. Though the Wii U features all new hardware, a new operating system, and a tablet-like touch screen–based controller, the Wii U uses several types of Wii controllers and can even play Wii games. Nintendo hopes that the Wii U's new connectivity features, high-definition graphics, and increased processing power will attract Wii users who already own a library of readily compatible games and controllers.[6]

▸▸ **DIVERSIFICATION:**
Diversification is a strategy of increasing sales by introducing new products into new markets. For example, UGG, a popular footwear brand known for its casual boots, has introduced an upscale men's footwear collection. The shoes are inspired by rock'n'roll legends such as Jimi Hendrix and Jim Morrison, and are meant to appeal to new customers. "There are some UGG customers that will be interested in the Collection product, but it will also bring in new customers for us," says Leah Larson, UGG's vice president and creative director.[7] A diversification strategy can be risky when a firm is entering unfamiliar markets. However, it can be very profitable when a firm is entering markets with little or no competition.

Critics of Ansoff's matrix mention that the matrix doesn't reflect the reality of how businesses grow—that modern businesses plan growth in a more fluid manner based on current capabilities rather than the clear-cut sectors outlined by the opportunity matrix. To reflect this, Bansi Nagji and Geoff Tuff, global innovation managers at Monitor Group, have recently developed a system that enables a company to see exactly what types of assets need to be developed and what types of markets are possible to grow into (or create) based on the company's core capabilities, as shown in Exhibit 2.

The layout of the innovation matrix demonstrates that as a company moves away from its core capabilities (the lower left) it traverses a range of change and innovation rather than choosing one of the four sectors in Ansoff's matrix. These ranges are broken down into three levels:

1. **CORE INNOVATION:** Represented by the yellow circle in Exhibit 2, these decisions implement changes that use existing assets to provide added convenience to existing customers and potentially entice customers from other brands. Packaging changes, such as Tide's laundry detergent pods, fall into this category.

2. **ADJACENT INNOVATION:** Represented by the orange arc in Exhibit 2, these decisions are designed to take company strengths into new markets. This space uses existing abilities in new ways. For example, Botox, the popular cosmetic drug, was originally developed to treat intestinal problems and to treat crossed eyes. Leveraging the drug into cosmetic medicine has dramatically increased the market for Botox.

3. **TRANSFORMATIONAL INNOVATION:** Represented by the red arc in Exhibit 2, these decisions result in brand-new markets, products, and often new businesses. The company must rely on new, unfamiliar assets to develop the type of breakthrough decisions that fall in this category. The wearable, remote-controlled GoPro documentary video camera is a prime example of developing an immature market with a brand-new experience.[8]

2-3b The Boston Consulting Group Model

Management must find a balance among the SBUs that yields the overall organization's desired growth and profits with an acceptable level of risk. Some SBUs generate large amounts of cash, and others need cash to foster growth. The challenge is to balance the organization's portfolio of SBUs for the best long-term performance.

To determine the future cash contributions and cash requirements expected for each SBU, managers can use the Boston Consulting Group's portfolio matrix. The **portfolio matrix** classifies each SBU by its present or forecast growth and market share. The underlying assumption is that market share and profitability are strongly linked. The measure of market share used in the portfolio approach is *relative market share*, the ratio between the company's share and the share of the largest competitor. For example, if a firm has a 50 percent share and the competitor has 5 percent, the ratio is 10 to 1. If a firm has a 10 percent market share and the largest competitor has 20 percent, the ratio is 0.5 to 1.

Exhibit 3 is a hypothetical portfolio matrix for a computer manufacturer. The size of the circle in each cell of the matrix represents dollar sales of the SBU relative to dollar sales of the company's other SBUs. The portfolio matrix breaks SBUs into four categories:

▸ **STARS:** A **star** is a fast-growing market leader. For example, the iPad is Apple's current star. Star SBUs usually have large profits but need lots of cash to finance rapid growth. The best marketing tactic is to protect existing market share by reinvesting earnings in product improvement, better distribution, more promotion, and production efficiency. Management must capture new users as they enter the market.

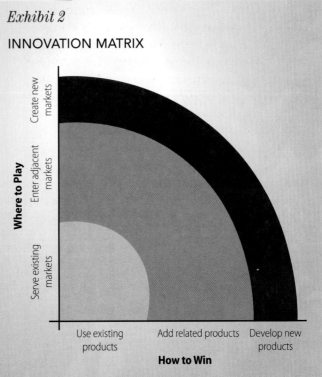

Exhibit 2

INNOVATION MATRIX

Source: Bansi Nagji and Geoff Tuff, "Managing Your Innovation Portfolio," *Harvard Business Review*, May 2012, http://hbr.org/2012/05/managing-your-innovation-portfolio/ar/1 (Accessed June 1, 2012).

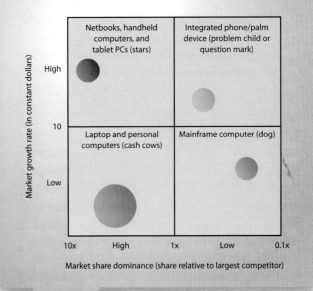

Exhibit 3

PORTFOLIO MATRIX FOR A LARGE COMPUTER MANUFACTURER

© Cengage Learning

CASH COWS: A cash cow is an SBU that generates more cash than it needs to maintain its market share. It is in a low-growth market, but the product has a dominant market share. Personal computers and laptops are categorized as cash cows in Exhibit 3. The basic strategy for a cash cow is to maintain market dominance by being the price leader and making technological improvements in the product. Managers should resist pressure to extend the basic line unless they can dramatically increase demand. Instead, they should allocate excess cash to the product categories where growth prospects are the greatest. For example, Heinz has two cash cows: ketchup and Weight Watchers frozen dinners.

PROBLEM CHILDREN: A problem child, also called a question mark, shows rapid growth but poor profit margins. It has a low market share in a high-growth industry. Problem children need a great deal of cash. Without cash support, they eventually become dogs. The strategy options are to invest heavily to gain better market share, acquire competitors to get the necessary market share, or drop the SBU. Sometimes a firm can reposition the products of the SBU to move them into the star category. Elixir guitar strings, made by W. L. Gore & Associates, maker of Gore-Tex and Glide floss, were originally tested and marketed to Walt Disney theme parks to control puppets. After trial and failure, Gore repositioned and marketed heavily to musicians, who have loved the strings ever since.

DOGS: A dog has low growth potential and a small market share. Most dogs eventually leave the marketplace. In the computer manufacturer example, the mainframe computer has become a dog. Another example is BlackBerry's smartphone line, which started out as a star for its manufacturer. Over time, the BlackBerry moved into the cash cow category, and then more recently, to a question mark, as the iPhone and Android-based phones captured market share. Recall from Chapter 1 that BlackBerry is hoping to reinvigorate its smartphone line with its new operating system, and perhaps even turn it into a star again. Until then, BlackBerry has moved into other geographic markets to sell its devices; it currently holds the dominant share in Nigeria and South Africa.[9]

While typical strategies for dogs are to harvest or divest, sometimes companies—like BlackBerry—are successful with this class of product in other markets. Other companies may revive products that were abandoned as dogs. Pantene, a division of Procter & Gamble, brought back three hair care products that had been discontinued (Anti-Dandruff, Ice Shine, and Silver Expressions) using a "Back by Popular Demand" promotional campaign.[10]

After classifying the company's SBUs in the matrix, the next step is to allocate future resources for each. The four basic strategies are to:

BUILD: If an organization has an SBU that it believes has the potential to be a star (probably a problem child at present), building would be an appropriate goal. The organization may decide to give up short-term profits and use its financial resources to achieve this goal. Apple postponed further work on the iPad to pursue the iPhone. The wait paid off when Apple was able to repurpose much of the iOS software and the iPhone's App Store for the iPad, making development less expensive and getting the product into the marketplace more quickly.[11]

HOLD: If an SBU is a very successful cash cow, a key goal would surely be to hold or preserve market share so that the organization can take advantage of the very positive cash flow. Fashion-based reality series *Project Runway* is a cash cow for the Lifetime cable television channel and parent companies Hearst and Disney. New seasons and spin-off editions of the long-running series are expected for years to come.[12]

HARVEST: This strategy is appropriate for all SBUs except those classified as stars. The basic goal is to increase the short-term cash return without too much concern for the long-run impact. It is especially worthwhile when more cash is needed from a cash cow with long-run prospects that are unfavorable because of a low market growth rate. For instance, Lever Brothers has been harvesting Lifebuoy soap for a number of years with little promotional backing.

cash cow in the portfolio matrix, a business unit that generates more cash than it needs to maintain its market share

problem child (question mark) in the portfolio matrix, a business unit that shows rapid growth but poor profit margins

dog in the portfolio matrix, a business unit that has low growth potential and a small market share

© Comstock/Thinkstock

▸ **DIVEST:** Getting rid of SBUs with low shares of low-growth markets is often appropriate. Problem children and dogs are most suitable for this strategy. Procter & Gamble dropped its entire snack food division—an entire SBU—because of its low growth potential.[13]

2-3c The General Electric Model

The third model for selecting strategic alternatives was originally developed by General Electric. The dimensions used in this model—market attractiveness and company strength—are richer and more complex than those used in the Boston Consulting Group model but are harder to quantify.

Exhibit 4 presents the GE model. The horizontal axis, Business Position, refers to how well positioned the organization is to take advantage of market opportunities. Business position answers questions such as: Does the firm have the technology it needs to effectively penetrate the market? Are its financial resources adequate? Can manufacturing costs be held down below those of the competition? Can the firm cope with change? The vertical axis measures the attractiveness of a market, which is expressed both quantitatively and qualitatively. Some attributes of an attractive market are high profitability, rapid growth, a lack of government regulation, consumer insensitivity to a price increase, a lack of competition, and availability of technology. The grid is divided into three overall attractiveness zones for each dimension: high, medium, and low.

Dr. Dre (right) stands with Jimmy Lovine, cofounder of Interscope Records, at a 2012 Beats by Dr. Dre event in London, England.

Those SBUs (or markets) that have low overall attractiveness (indicated by the red cells in Exhibit 4) should be avoided if the organization is not already serving them. If the firm is in these markets, it should either harvest or divest those SBUs. The organization should selectively maintain markets with medium attractiveness (indicated by the yellow cells in Exhibit 4). If attractiveness begins to slip, then the organization should withdraw from the market.

Conditions that are highly attractive—a thriving market plus a strong business position (the green cells in Exhibit 4)—are the best candidates for investment. For example, when Beats Electronics launched a new line of over-the-ear headphones in 2008, the consumer headphone market was strong but steady, led by inexpensive, inconspicuous earbuds. Four years later, the heavily branded and premium-priced Beats by Dr. Dre—helmed by legendary hip-hop producer Dr. Dre—captured 40 percent of all U.S. headphone sales, fueling market growth from $1.8 billion in 2011 to $2.4 billion in 2012. In 2013, Beats announced that it was launching Daisy, a streaming music service to compete with services like Rdio and Spotify. This new market is growing quickly and is highly competitive, and will surely take Beats' strong business position to penetrate.[14]

2-3d The Marketing Plan

Based on the company's or SBU's overall strategy, marketing managers can create a

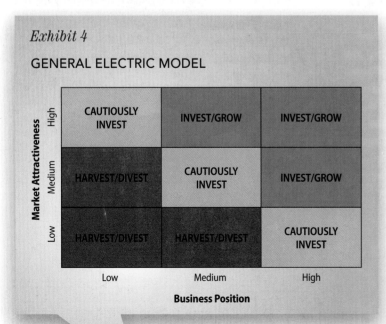

Exhibit 4

GENERAL ELECTRIC MODEL

		Low	Medium	High
Market Attractiveness	High	CAUTIOUSLY INVEST	INVEST/GROW	INVEST/GROW
	Medium	HARVEST/DIVEST	CAUTIOUSLY INVEST	INVEST/GROW
	Low	HARVEST/DIVEST	HARVEST/DIVEST	CAUTIOUSLY INVEST

Business Position

© Cengage Learning

marketing plan for individual products, brands, lines, or customer groups. **Planning** is the process of anticipating future events and determining strategies to achieve organizational objectives in the future. **Marketing planning** involves designing activities relating to marketing objectives and the changing marketing environment. Marketing planning is the basis for all marketing strategies and decisions. Issues such as product lines, distribution channels, marketing communications, and pricing are all delineated in the **marketing plan**. The marketing plan is a written document that acts as a guidebook of marketing activities for the marketing manager. In this chapter, you will learn the importance of writing a marketing plan and the types of information contained in a marketing plan.

2-3e Why Write a Marketing Plan?

By specifying objectives and defining the actions required to attain them, you can provide in a marketing plan the basis by which actual and expected performance can be compared. Marketing can be one of the most expensive and complicated business activities, but it is also one of the most important. The written marketing plan provides clearly stated activities that help employees and managers understand and work toward common goals.

Writing a marketing plan allows you to examine the marketing environment in conjunction with the inner workings of the business. Once the marketing plan is written, it serves as a reference point for the success of future activities. Finally, the marketing plan allows the marketing manager to enter the marketplace with an awareness of possibilities and problems.

2-3f Marketing Plan Elements

Marketing plans can be presented in many different ways. Most businesses need a written marketing plan because a marketing plan is large and can be complex. Details about tasks and activity assignments may be lost if communicated orally. Regardless of the way a marketing plan is presented, some elements are common to all marketing plans. Exhibit 5 shows these elements, which include defining the business mission, performing a situation analysis, defining objectives, delineating a target market, and establishing components of the marketing mix. Other elements that may be included in a plan are budgets, implementation timetables, required marketing research

efforts, or elements of advanced strategic planning. Log in to the CourseMate for *MKTG* at cengagebrain.com for a marketing plan outline and an example of a marketing plan.

2-3g Writing the Marketing Plan

The creation and implementation of a complete marketing plan will allow the organization to achieve marketing objectives and succeed. However, the marketing plan is only as good as the information it contains and the effort, creativity, and thought that

planning the process of anticipating future events and determining strategies to achieve organizational objectives in the future

marketing planning designing activities relating to marketing objectives and the changing marketing environment

marketing plan a written document that acts as a guidebook of marketing activities for the marketing manager

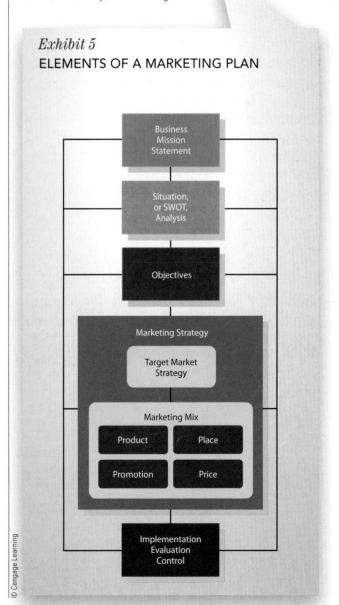

Exhibit 5
ELEMENTS OF A MARKETING PLAN

- Business Mission Statement
- Situation, or SWOT, Analysis
- Objectives
- Marketing Strategy
  - Target Market Strategy
  - Marketing Mix
    - Product
    - Place
    - Promotion
    - Price
- Implementation Evaluation Control

© Cengage Learning

went into its creation. Having a good marketing information system and a wealth of competitive intelligence (covered in Chapter 9) is critical to a thorough and accurate situation analysis. The role of managerial intuition is also important in the creation and selection of marketing strategies. Managers must weigh any information against its accuracy and their own judgment when making a marketing decision.

Note that the overall structure of the marketing plan (Exhibit 5) should not be viewed as a series of sequential planning steps. Many of the marketing plan elements are decided simultaneously and in conjunction with one another. Further, every marketing plan has different content, depending on the organization, its mission, objectives, targets, and marketing mix components. There is not one single correct format for a marketing plan. Many organizations have their own distinctive format or terminology for creating a marketing plan. Every marketing plan should be unique to the firm for which it was created. Remember, however, that although the format and order of presentation should be flexible, the same types of questions and topic areas should be covered in any marketing plan.

2-4 DEFINING THE BUSINESS MISSION

The foundation of any marketing plan is the firm's mission statement, which answers the question "What business are we in?" The way a firm defines its business mission profoundly affects the firm's long-run resource allocation, profitability, and survival. The mission statement is based on a careful analysis of benefits sought by present and potential customers and an analysis of existing and anticipated environmental conditions. The firm's mission statement establishes boundaries for all subsequent decisions, objectives, and strategies.

A mission statement should focus on the market or markets the organization is attempting to serve rather than on the good or service offered. Otherwise, a new technology may quickly make the good or service obsolete and the mission statement irrelevant to company functions. Business mission statements that are stated too narrowly suffer from **marketing myopia**—defining a business in terms of goods and services rather than in terms of the

benefits customers seek. In this context, *myopia* means narrow, short-term thinking. For example, Frito-Lay defines its mission as being in the snack-food business rather than in the corn chip business. The mission of sports teams is not just to play games but also to serve the interests of the fans.

Alternatively, business missions may be stated too broadly. "To provide products of superior quality and value that improve the lives of the world's consumers" is probably too broad a mission statement for any firm except Procter & Gamble. Care must be taken when stating what business a firm is in. For example, the mission of Ben & Jerry's centers on three important aspects of its ice cream business: (1) Product: "To make, distribute and sell the finest quality all natural ice cream and euphoric concoctions with a continued commitment to incorporating wholesome, natural ingredients and promoting business practices that respect the Earth and the Environment"; (2) Economic: "To operate the Company on a sustainable financial basis of profitable growth, increasing value for our stakeholders and expanding opportunities for development and career growth for our employees"; and (3) Social: "To operate the Company in a way that actively recognizes the central role that business plays in society by initiating innovative ways to improve the quality of life locally, nationally, and internationally."[15] By correctly stating the business mission in terms of the benefits that customers seek, the foundation for the marketing plan is set. Many companies are focusing on designing more appropriate mission statements because these statements are frequently displayed on the companies' Web sites.

Just as myopia negatively affects how people see, marketing myopia negatively affects how businesses see themselves and their environment.

© Vitaly Titov & Maria Sidelnikova/Shutterstock.com

2-5 CONDUCTING A SITUATION ANALYSIS

Marketers must understand the current and potential environment in which the product or service will be marketed. A situation analysis is sometimes referred to as a **SWOT analysis**—that is, the firm should identify its internal strengths (**S**) and weaknesses (**W**) and also examine external opportunities (**O**) and threats (**T**).

When examining internal strengths and weaknesses, the marketing manager should focus on organizational resources such as production costs, marketing skills, financial resources, company or brand image, employee capabilities, and available technology. For example, when Dell's stock fell sharply throughout the late 2010s, management needed to examine strengths and weaknesses in the company and its competition. Dell had a $6 billion server business (strength), but the shrinking PC market accounted for a significant 24 percent of sales (weakness). Competitors like IBM and Hewlett-Packard (HP) were moving heavily into software and consulting, so to avoid them, Dell moved into the enterprise IT and services market. The shift wasn't enough to offset poor sales in other areas, however, and in 2013, the company entered buyout talks with private investors such as Blackstone and company founder Michael S. Dell.[16] Another issue to consider in this section of the marketing plan is the historical background of the firm—its sales and profit history.

When examining external opportunities and threats, marketing managers must analyze aspects of the marketing environment. This process is called **environmental scanning**—the collection and interpretation of information about forces, events, and relationships in the external environment that may affect the future of the organization or the implementation of the marketing plan. Environmental scanning helps identify market opportunities and threats and provides guidelines for the design of marketing strategy. The six most often studied macroenvironmental forces are social, demographic, economic, technological, political and legal, and competitive. These forces are examined in detail in Chapter 4. Powerful electronic retailers like Best Buy, GameStop, and RadioShack are fighting to survive against online competitors like Valve Corporation's Steam software and Amazon.com, which can offer low prices and downloadable products. Consumers can also buy quality electronics products at discount retailers like Walmart and Target. Electronics chains were built to let consumers browse competing innovations, but competitive factors and the fact that consumers have become comfortable buying electronics online have altered the environment for these stores. Paul Raines, GameStop's chief executive, says, "In order to survive, our internal rate of change has to be greater than the external rate of change."[17]

2-6 COMPETITIVE ADVANTAGE

Performing a SWOT analysis allows firms to identify their competitive advantage. A competitive advantage is a set of unique features of a company and its products that are perceived by the target market as significant and superior to those of the competition. It is the factor or factors that cause customers to patronize a firm and not the competition. There are three types of competitive advantage: cost, product/service differentiation, and niche.

2-6a Cost Competitive Advantage

Cost leadership can result from obtaining inexpensive raw materials, creating an efficient scale of plant operations, designing products for ease of manufacture, controlling overhead costs, and avoiding marginal customers. Hydraulic fracturing (or fracking) is a controversial mining technique used to release petroleum, natural gas, and other valuable chemicals from layers of rock in the earth's crust. In the United States, fracking has revealed a vast supply of natural gas locked in shale rock, greatly reducing the cost of energy across the country and making the United States a primary player in the global natural gas market. According to George Blitz, vice president of energy and climate change at Dow Chemical Company, the shale gas boom has given the United States the biggest competitive advantage the industry has seen in several decades.[18] Having a **cost competitive advantage** means being

Hydraulic fracturing is a competitive advantage for the United States in the global natural gas market. Here, Universal Well Service engineer Mike Michaelson (right) talks with technician Sean Cline before they start the sixteen-cylinder diesel engine that pumps millions of gallons of water, sand, and chemicals down a well to break apart tight sands that trap natural gas.

AP Images/Keith Srakocic

the low-cost competitor in an industry while maintaining satisfactory profit margins. Costs can be reduced in a variety of ways:

▸▸ **EXPERIENCE CURVES:** Experience curves tell us that costs decline at a predictable rate as experience with a product increases. The experience curve effect encompasses a broad range of manufacturing, marketing, and administrative costs. Experience curves reflect learning by doing, technological advances, and economies of scale. Firms like Boeing use historical experience curves as a basis for predicting and setting prices. Experience curves allow management to forecast costs and set prices based on anticipated costs as opposed to current costs.

▸▸ **EFFICIENT LABOR:** Labor costs can be an important component of total costs in low-skill, labor-intensive industries such as product assembly and apparel manufacturing. Many U.S. publishers and software developers send data entry, design, and formatting tasks to India, where skilled engineers are available at lower overall cost.

▸▸ **NO-FRILLS GOODS AND SERVICES:** Marketers can lower costs by removing frills and options from a product or service. Southwest Airlines, for example, offers low fares but no seat assignments or meals. Low costs give Southwest a higher load factor and greater economies of scale, which, in turn, mean lower prices.

experience curves curves that show costs declining at a predictable rate as experience with a product increases

▸▸ **GOVERNMENT SUBSIDIES:** Governments can provide grants and interest-free loans to target industries. Such government assistance enabled Japanese semiconductor manufacturers to become global leaders.

▸▸ **PRODUCT DESIGN:** Cutting-edge design technology can help offset high labor costs. BMW is a world leader in designing cars for ease of manufacture and assembly. Reverse engineering—the process of disassembling a product piece by piece to learn its components and obtain clues as to the manufacturing process—can also mean savings. Reverse engineering a low-cost competitor's product can save research and design costs. The Chinese military has for years copied foreign hardware.[19]

▸▸ **REENGINEERING:** Reengineering entails fundamental rethinking and redesign of business processes to achieve dramatic improvements in critical measures of performance. It often involves reorganizing functional departments such as sales, engineering, and production into cross-disciplinary teams.

▸▸ **PRODUCTION INNOVATIONS:** Production innovations such as new technology and simplified production techniques help lower the average cost of production. Technologies such as computer-aided design (CAD) and computer-aided manufacturing (CAM) and increasingly sophisticated robots help companies such as Boeing, Ford, and General Electric reduce their manufacturing costs.

NEW METHODS OF SERVICE DELIVERY: Medical expenses have been substantially lowered by the use of outpatient surgery and walk-in clinics. Online-only magazines deliver great savings, and even some print magazines are exploring ways to go online to save material and shipping costs.

2-6b Product/Service Differentiation Competitive Advantage

Because cost competitive advantages are subject to continual erosion, product/service differentiation tends to provide a longer-lasting competitive advantage. The durability of this strategy tends to make it more attractive to many top managers. A **product/service differentiation competitive advantage** exists when a firm provides something that is unique and valuable to buyers beyond simply offering a lower price than that of the competition. Examples include brand names (Lexus), a strong dealer network (Caterpillar for construction work), product reliability (Maytag appliances), image (Neiman Marcus in retailing), or service (Zappos). Though its membership fees often eclipse those of traditional gyms, the CrossFit strength and conditioning program has grown exponentially since its founding in 2000. CrossFit gyms typically feature predetermined daily workouts combining Olympic-style weightlifting, interval training, and other effective forms of exercise. Like yoga and Pilates, CrossFit is organized into a series of classes, each led by a certified instructor who pays personal attention to members' technique. Beyond the high-intensity workouts, community, teamwork, and inter-gym competition play a large part in

Athletes compete in a CrossFit competition at the George R. Brown Convention Center in Houston, Texas.

Mike Roach/Zuffa LLC via Getty Images

CrossFit—all of which differentiate it from traditional gyms.[20]

2-6c Niche Competitive Advantage

A **niche competitive advantage** seeks to target and effectively serve a single segment of the market (see Chapter 8). For small companies with limited resources that potentially face giant competitors, niche targeting may be the only viable option. A market segment that has good growth potential but is not crucial to the success of major competitors is a good candidate for developing a niche strategy.

Many companies using a niche strategy serve only a limited geographic market. Stew Leonard's is an extremely successful but small grocery store chain found only in Connecticut and New York. Blue Bell Ice cream is available in only about 26 percent of the nation's supermarkets, but it ranks as one of the top three best-selling ice creams in the country.[21]

The Chef's Garden, a 225-acre Ohio farm, specializes in growing and shipping rare artisan vegetables directly to its customers. Chefs from all over the world call to order or request a unique item, which is grown and shipped by the Chef's Garden. The farm provides personal services and specialized premium vegetables that aren't available anywhere else and relies on its customers to supply it with ideas for what they would like to be able to offer in their restaurants. The excellent service and feeling of contribution keep chefs coming back.[22]

2-6d Building Sustainable Competitive Advantage

The key to having a competitive advantage is the ability to sustain that advantage. A **sustainable competitive advantage** is one that cannot be copied by the competition. For example, Netflix, the online movie subscription service, has a steady hold over the movie rental market. No company has come close to the incomparable depth of titles available to be sent directly to homes or streamed online. Blockbuster tried to set up a similar online subscription service tied to new releases and Amazon.com offers

product/service differentiation competitive advantage the provision of something that is unique and valuable to buyers beyond simply offering a lower price than that of the competition

niche competitive advantage the advantage achieved when a firm seeks to target and effectively serve a small segment of the market

sustainable competitive advantage an advantage that cannot be copied by the competition

free streaming to Prime members, but so far neither has been able to compete with the convenience and selection offered by Netflix. Netflix's 27.5 million subscribers have a twenty-eight-day delay on most of the latest movies, but Netflix says that only a couple hundred customers have complained about the delay. Redbox Instant, an up-and-coming streaming service from Verizon and Coinstar, builds on the popular Redbox kiosk-based rental service, allowing customers to stream movies *and* rent up to four physical DVDs for just $8 a month. Redbox Instant does not offer television shows, however—a key advantage of Netflix's service.[23] In contrast, when Datril was introduced into the pain-reliever market, it was touted as being exactly like Tylenol, only cheaper. Tylenol responded by lowering its price, thus destroying Datril's competitive advantage and ability to remain on the market. In this case, low price was not a sustainable competitive advantage. Without a competitive advantage, target customers don't perceive any reason to patronize an organization instead of its competitors.

The notion of competitive advantage means that a successful firm will stake out a position unique in some manner from its rivals. Imitation by competitors indicates a lack of competitive advantage and almost ensures mediocre performance. Moreover, competitors rarely stand still, so it is not surprising that imitation causes managers to feel trapped in a seemingly endless game of catch-up. They are regularly surprised by the new accomplishments of their rivals.

Rather than copy competitors, companies need to build their own competitive advantages. The sources of tomorrow's competitive advantages are the skills and assets of the organization. Assets include patents, copyrights, locations, equipment, and technology that are superior to those of the competition. Skills are functions such as customer service and promotion that the firm performs

The ability to stream movies *and* rent up to four physical DVDs for just $8 a month is a compelling competitive advantage for Redbox Instant.

better than its competitors. Marketing managers should continually focus the firm's skills and assets on sustaining and creating competitive advantages.

Remember, a sustainable competitive advantage is a function of the speed with which competitors can imitate a leading company's strategy and plans. Imitation requires a competitor to identify the leader's competitive advantage, determine how it is achieved, and then learn how to duplicate it.

2-7 SETTING MARKETING PLAN OBJECTIVES

Before the details of a marketing plan can be developed, objectives for the plan must be stated. Without objectives, there is no basis for measuring the success of marketing plan activities.

A **marketing objective** is a statement of what is to be accomplished through marketing activities. To be useful, stated objectives should be:

▸ **REALISTIC:** Managers should develop objectives that have a chance of being met. For example, it may be unrealistic for start-up firms or new products to command dominant market share, given other competitors in the marketplace.

- ▸ **MEASURABLE:** Managers need to be able to quantitatively measure whether or not an objective has been met. For example, it would be difficult to determine success for an objective that states, "To increase sales of cat food." If the company sells 1 percent more cat food, does that mean the objective was met? Instead, a specific number should be stated, "To increase sales of Purina brand cat food from $300 million to $345 million."

- ▸ **TIME SPECIFIC:** By what time should the objective be met? "To increase sales of Purina brand cat food between January 1, 2014, and December 31, 2014."

- ▸ **COMPARED TO A BENCHMARK:** If the objective is to increase sales by 15 percent, it is important to know the baseline against which the objective will be measured. Will it be current sales? Last year's sales? For example, "To increase sales of Purina brand cat food by 15 percent over 2012 sales of $300 million."

Therefore, a successful marketing objective would include all four elements. For example, a strong marketing objective for Purina might be: "To increase sales of Purina brand cat food between January 1, 2014 and December 31, 2014 by 15 percent, compared to 2012 sales of $300 million."

Objectives must also be consistent with and indicate the priorities of the organization. Specifically, objectives flow from the business mission statement to the rest of the marketing plan.

Carefully specified objectives serve several functions. First, they communicate marketing management philosophies and provide direction for lower-level marketing managers so that marketing efforts are integrated and pointed in a consistent direction. Objectives also serve as motivators by creating something for employees to strive for. When objectives are attainable and challenging, they motivate those charged with achieving the objectives. Additionally, the process of writing specific objectives forces executives to clarify their thinking. Finally, objectives form a basis for control: the effectiveness of a plan can be gauged in light of the stated objectives.

2-8 DESCRIBING THE TARGET MARKET

Marketing strategy involves the activities of selecting and describing one or more target markets and developing and maintaining a marketing mix that will produce mutually satisfying exchanges with target markets.

2-8a Target Market Strategy

A market segment is a group of individuals or organizations who share one or more characteristics. They therefore may have relatively similar product needs. For example, parents of newborn babies need formula, diapers, and special foods.

The target market strategy identifies the market segment or segments on which to focus. This process begins with a **market opportunity analysis (MOA)**—the description and estimation of the size and sales potential of market segments that are of interest to the firm and the assessment of key competitors in these market segments. After the firm describes the market segments, it may target one or more of them. There are three general strategies for selecting target markets.

Target markets can be selected by appealing to the entire market with one marketing mix, concentrating on one segment, or appealing to multiple market segments using multiple marketing mixes. The characteristics, advantages, and disadvantages of each strategic option are examined in Chapter 8. Target markets could be eighteen- to twenty-five-year-old females who are interested in fashion (*Vogue* magazine), people concerned about sugar and calories in their soft drinks (Diet Pepsi), or parents without the time to

marketing strategy the activities of selecting and describing one or more target markets and developing and maintaining a marketing mix that will produce mutually satisfying exchanges with target markets

market opportunity analysis (MOA) the description and estimation of the size and sales potential of market segments that are of interest to the firm and the assessment of key competitors in these market segments

potty train their children (Booty Camp classes where kids are potty trained).

Any market segment that is targeted must be fully described. Demographics, psychographics, and buyer behavior should be assessed. Buyer behavior is covered in Chapters 6 and 7. If segments are differentiated by ethnicity, multicultural aspects of the marketing mix should be examined. If the target market is international, it is especially important to describe differences in culture, economic and technological development, and political structure that may affect the marketing plan. Global marketing is covered in more detail in Chapter 5.

2-9 THE MARKETING MIX

The term marketing mix refers to a unique blend of product, place (distribution), promotion, and pricing strategies (often referred to as the four Ps) designed to produce mutually satisfying exchanges with a target market. The marketing manager can control each component of the marketing mix, but the strategies for all four components must be blended to achieve optimal results. Any marketing mix is only as good as its weakest component. For example, the first pump toothpastes were distributed over cosmetics counters and failed. Not until pump toothpastes were distributed the same way as tube toothpastes did the products succeed. The best promotion and the lowest price cannot save a poor product. Similarly, excellent products with poor placing, pricing, or promotion will likely fail.

Successful marketing mixes have been carefully designed to satisfy target markets. At first glance, McDonald's and Wendy's may appear to have roughly identical marketing mixes because they are both in the fast-food hamburger business. However, McDonald's has been most successful at targeting parents with young children for lunchtime meals, whereas Wendy's targets the adult crowd for lunches and dinner. McDonald's has playgrounds, Ronald McDonald the clown, and children's Happy Meals. Wendy's has salad bars, carpeted restaurants, and no playgrounds.

Variations in marketing mixes do not occur by chance. Astute marketing managers devise marketing strategies to gain advantages over competitors and best serve the needs and wants of a particular target market segment.

By manipulating elements of the marketing mix, marketing managers can fine-tune the customer offering and achieve competitive success.

2-9a Product Strategies

Of the four Ps, the marketing mix typically starts with the product. The heart of the marketing mix, the starting point, is the product offering and product strategy. It is hard to design a place strategy, decide on a promotion campaign, or set a price without knowing the product to be marketed.

The product includes not only the physical unit but also its package, warranty, after-sale service, brand name, company image, value, and many other factors. A Godiva chocolate has many product elements: the chocolate itself, a fancy gold wrapper, a customer satisfaction guarantee, and the prestige of the Godiva brand name. We buy things not only for what they do (benefits) but also for what they mean to us (status, quality, or reputation).

Products can be tangible goods such as computers, ideas like those offered by a consultant, or services such as medical care. Products should also offer customer value. Product decisions are covered in Chapters 10 and 11, and services marketing is detailed in Chapter 12.

2-9b Place (Distribution) Strategies

Place, or distribution, strategies are concerned with making products available when and where customers want them. Would you rather buy a kiwi fruit at the 24-hour grocery store within walking distance or fly to Australia to pick your own? A part of this P—place—is physical distribution, which involves all the business activities concerned with storing and transporting raw materials or finished products. The goal is to make sure products arrive in usable condition at designated places when needed. Place strategies are covered in Chapters 13 and 14.

2-9c Promotion Strategies

Promotion includes advertising, public relations, sales promotion, and personal selling. Promotion's role in the marketing mix is to bring about mutually satisfying exchanges with target markets by informing, educating, persuading, and reminding them of the benefits of an organization or a product. A good promotion strategy, like using a beloved cartoon character such as SpongeBob SquarePants to sell gummy snacks, can dramatically increase sales. Each

THE GAME OF ORGANIZING E-MAIL

E-mail has become a necessity for students and business professionals, as well as an integral part of many personal lives. With so much riding on e-mail, inboxes can overflow, and important e-mails can fall by the wayside. One company is out to change that. Baydin is a software developer that sells Boomerang, a product that allows users to "snooze" e-mails. The user sets the time for the e-mail to reappear in the inbox, and Boomerang moves it into a folder out of the inbox until the specified time. To promote their e-mail management products for Outlook, Baydin also developed *The Email Game*. The game sets a timer for each message and accrues points for decisions made in a timely manner. Baydin guarantees the game will get you through your e-mail 40 percent faster or your money back.[24]

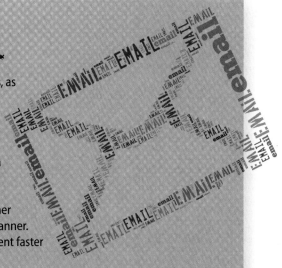

element of this P—promotion—is coordinated and managed with the others to create a promotional blend or mix. These integrated marketing communications activities are described in Chapters 15, 16, and 17. Technology-driven and social media aspects of promotional marketing are covered in Chapter 18.

2-9d Pricing Strategies

Price is what a buyer must give up in order to obtain a product. It is often the most flexible of the four Ps—the quickest element to change. Marketers can raise or lower prices more frequently and easily than they can change other marketing mix variables. Price is an important competitive weapon and is very important to the organization because price multiplied by the number of units sold equals total revenue for the firm. Pricing decisions are covered in Chapters 19 and 20.

2-10 FOLLOWING UP ON THE MARKETING PLAN

One of the keys to success overlooked by many businesses is to actively follow up on the marketing plan. The time spent researching, developing, and writing a useful and accurate marketing plan goes to waste if the plan is not used by the organization. One of the best ways to get the most out of a marketing plan is to correctly implement it. Once the first steps to implementation

are taken, evaluation and control will help guide the organization to success as laid out by the marketing plan.

2-10a Implementation

Implementation is the process that turns a marketing plan into action assignments and ensures that these assignments are executed in a way that accomplishes the plan's objectives. Implementation activities may involve detailed job assignments, activity descriptions, time lines, budgets, and lots of communication. Implementation requires delegating authority and responsibility, determining a time frame for completing tasks, and allocating resources. Sometimes a strategic plan also requires task force management. A *task force* is a tightly organized unit under the direction of a manager who, usually, has broad authority. A task force is established to accomplish a single goal or mission and thus works against a deadline.

Implementing a plan has another dimension: gaining acceptance. New plans mean change, and change creates resistance. One reason people resist change is that they fear they will lose something. For example, when new-product research is taken away from marketing research and given to a new-product department, the director of marketing research will naturally resist this loss of part of his or her domain. Misunderstanding and lack of trust also create opposition to change, but effective communication through open

implementation
the process that turns a marketing plan into action assignments and ensures that these assignments are executed in a way that accomplishes the plan's objectives

evaluation gauging the extent to which the marketing objectives have been achieved during the specified time period

control provides the mechanisms for evaluating marketing results in light of the plan's objectives and for correcting actions that do not help the organization reach those objectives within budget guidelines

marketing audit a thorough, systematic, periodic evaluation of the objectives, strategies, structure, and performance of the marketing organization

discussion and teamwork can be one way of overcoming resistance to change.

Although implementation is essentially "doing what you said you were going to do," many organizations repeatedly experience failures in strategy implementation. Brilliant marketing plans are doomed to fail if they are not properly implemented. These detailed communications may or may not be part of the written marketing plan. If they are not part of the plan, they should be specified elsewhere as soon as the plan has been communicated. Strong, forward-thinking leadership can overcome resistance to change, even in large, highly integrated companies where change seems very unlikely.

2-10b Evaluation and Control

After a marketing plan is implemented, it should be evaluated. **Evaluation** entails gauging the extent to which marketing objectives have been achieved during the specified time period. Four common reasons for failing to achieve a marketing objective are unrealistic marketing objectives, inappropriate marketing strategies in the plan, poor implementation, and changes in the environment after the objective was specified and the strategy was implemented.

Once a plan is chosen and implemented, its effectiveness must be monitored. **Control** provides the mechanisms for evaluating marketing results in light of the plan's objectives and for correcting actions that do not help the organization reach those objectives within budget guidelines. Firms need to establish formal and informal control programs to make the entire operation more efficient.

Perhaps the broadest control device available to marketing managers is the **marketing audit**—a thorough, systematic, periodic evaluation of the objectives, strategies, structure, and performance of the marketing organization. A marketing audit helps management allocate marketing resources efficiently.

Although the main purpose of the marketing audit is to develop a full profile of the organization's marketing effort and to provide a basis for developing and revising the marketing plan, it is also an excellent way to improve communication and raise the level of marketing consciousness within the organization. It is a useful vehicle for selling the

FOUR CHARACTERISTICS OF A MARKETING AUDIT:

▸▸ **COMPREHENSIVE:** The marketing audit covers all the major marketing issues facing an organization—not just trouble spots.

▸▸ **SYSTEMATIC:** The marketing audit takes place in an orderly sequence and covers the organization's marketing environment, internal marketing system, and specific marketing activities. The diagnosis is followed by an action plan with both short-run and long-run proposals for improving overall marketing effectiveness.

▸▸ **INDEPENDENT:** The marketing audit is normally conducted by an inside or outside party that is independent enough to have top management's confidence and has the ability to be objective.

▸▸ **PERIODIC:** The marketing audit should be carried out on a regular schedule instead of only in a crisis. Whether it seems successful or is in deep trouble, any organization can benefit greatly from such an audit.

philosophy and techniques of strategic marketing to other members of the organization.

2-10c Postaudit Tasks

After the audit has been completed, three tasks remain. First, the audit should profile existing weaknesses and inhibiting factors, as well as the firm's strengths and the new opportunities available to it. Recommendations have to be judged and prioritized so that those with the potential to contribute most to improved marketing performance can be implemented first. The usefulness of the data also depends on the auditor's skill in interpreting and presenting the data so decision makers can quickly grasp the major points.

The second task is to ensure that the role of the audit has been clearly communicated. It is unlikely that the suggestions will require radical change in the way the firm operates. The audit's main role is to address the question "Where are we now?" and to suggest ways to improve what the firm already does.

The final postaudit task is to make someone accountable for implementing recommendations. All too often, reports are presented, applauded, and filed away to gather dust. The person made accountable should be someone

© iStockphoto.com/Bill Noll

Before being ousted as CEO of JCPenney (JCP), Ron Johnson collaborated with brands to create mini-boutiques within each store. Here, Johnson (right) stands with Joe Fresh Creative Director Joe Mimran at a Joe Fresh at JCP launch event on March 7, 2013.

who is committed to the project and who has the managerial power to make things happen.

2-11 EFFECTIVE STRATEGIC PLANNING

Effective strategic planning requires continual attention, creativity, and management commitment. Strategic planning should not be an annual exercise in which managers go through the motions and forget about strategic planning until the next year. It should be an ongoing process because the environment is continually changing and the firm's resources and capabilities are continually evolving.

Sound strategic planning is based on creativity. Managers should challenge assumptions about the firm and the environment and establish new strategies. For example, major oil companies developed the concept of the gasoline service station in an age when cars needed frequent and rather elaborate servicing. These major companies held on to the full-service approach, but independents were quick to respond to new realities and moved to lower-cost self-service and convenience store operations. Major companies took several decades to catch up.

Perhaps the most critical element in successful strategic planning is top management's support and participation. For example, when Ron Johnson, the man behind the Apple stores, took over JCPenney, he wanted to turn it into "America's favorite store." His plan was to transform all of the merchandise, the pricing, and the retail locations themselves. Johnson collaborated with brands to create mini-boutiques within each store. His new pricing strategy entailed modifying "everyday" prices, in many cases reducing retail prices by as much as 40 percent. Each location was renovated so that sections were laid out in pathways, with a square in the center offering fun experiences, such as free ice cream in the summer. While Johnson was ousted as CEO in April 2013, his participation in JCPenney's strategic planning set the course for a period of innovation and evolution at the struggling retailer.[25]

STUDY TOOLS 2

LOCATED AT BACK OF THE TEXTBOOK
☐ *Rip out Chapter Review Card*

LOCATED AT WWW.CENGAGE.COM/LOGIN
☐ *Review Key Terms Flashcards*
☐ *Watch visual summaries to review key concepts*
☐ *Complete Practice Quizzes to prepare for tests*
☐ *Complete "Crossword Puzzle" to review key terms*
☐ *Watch Video "The Nederlander Organization" for a real company example*

Have you ever stopped to think about the social glue that binds society together? That is, what factors keep people and organizations from running amok and doing harm, and what factors create order in a society like ours? The answer lies in the six modes of social control.[1] These modes are:

> If you have ever resented a line-cutter, then you understand ethics and have applied ethical standards in life.

ethics the moral principles or values that generally govern the conduct of an individual or a group

1. **ETHICS:** Ethics are the moral principles or values that generally govern the conduct of an individual or a group. Ethical rules and guidelines, along with customs and traditions, provide principles of right action.

2. **LAWS:** Often, ethical rules and guidelines are codified into law. Laws created by governments are then enforced by governmental authority. This is how the dictum "Thou shall not steal" has become part of formal law throughout the land. Law, however, is not a perfect mechanism for ensuring good corporate and employee behavior. This is because laws often address the lowest common denominator of socially acceptable behavior. In other words, just because something is legal doesn't mean that it is ethical. For example, an individual goes to Barnes & Noble every day and spends the afternoon reading books and magazines in the store. The store has big comfortable chairs and the clerks never bother him or ask him to leave. He even takes his own lunch if he plans to spend the day there. He does this at least twenty days per month. The bookstore allows this practice, and it is not against the law. It is, however, not ethical. If everyone who read books followed this individual's behavior, Barnes & Noble would soon be bankrupt!

3. **FORMAL AND INFORMAL GROUPS:** Businesses, professional organizations (such as the American Marketing Association and the American Medical Association), and clubs (such as Shriners and Ducks Unlimited) all have codes of conduct. These codes prescribe acceptable and desired behaviors of their members.

4. **SELF-REGULATION:** Self-regulation involves the voluntary acceptance of standards established by nongovernmental entities, such as the American Association of Advertising Agencies (AAAA) or the National Association of Manufacturers. The AAAA has a self-regulation arm that deals with deceptive advertising. Other associations have regulations relating to child labor, environmental issues, conservation, and a host of other issues.

5. **THE MEDIA:** In an open, democratic society, the media play a key role in informing the public about the actions of individuals and organizations—both

Chapter **3**

Ethics and Social Responsibility

Learning Outcomes

After you finish this chapter go to
p46 *for* **STUDY TOOLS**

good and bad. The Children's Online Privacy Protection Act requires Web site operators to obtain verifiable consent from parents before collecting personal information about children under age thirteen. When the Federal Trade Commission (FTC) reported that six popular Web sites aimed at children violated that law by encouraging children who play brand-related games to provide friends' e-mail addresses without seeking parental consent, the media quickly picked up the story. "It really shows that companies are doing an end run around a law put in place to protect children's privacy," said Laura Moy, a lawyer for the Center for Digital Democracy.[2]

6. **AN ACTIVE CIVIL SOCIETY:** An informed and engaged society can help mold individual and corporate behavior. The last state in the union to get a Walmart store was Vermont. Citizen campaigns against the big-box retailer were deciding factors in management's decision to avoid the state. And when the state of Arizona passed an immigration law that many felt was discriminatory, a grass roots campaign sprang up to "boycott Arizona."[3]

All six of the preceding factors—individually and in combination—are critical to achieving a socially coherent, vibrant, civilized society. These six factors (the social glue) are more important today than ever before due to the increasing complexity of the global economy and the melding of customs and traditions within societies.

3-2 THE CONCEPT OF ETHICAL BEHAVIOR

It has been said that ethics is something everyone likes to talk about but nobody can define.

Others have suggested that defining ethics is like trying to nail Jell-O to a wall. You begin to think that you understand it, but that's when it starts squirting out between your fingers.

Simply put, ethics can be viewed as the standard of behavior by which conduct is judged. Standards that are legal may not always be ethical, and vice versa. Laws are the values and standards enforceable by the courts. Ethics, then, consists of personal moral principles. For example, there is no legal statute that makes it a crime for someone to "cut in line." Yet, if someone doesn't want to wait in line and cuts to the front, it often makes others very angry.

If you have ever resented a line-cutter, then you understand ethics and have applied ethical standards in life. Waiting your turn in line is a social expectation that exists because lines ensure order and allocate the space and time needed to complete transactions. Waiting your turn is an expected but unwritten behavior that plays a critical role in an orderly society.

So it is with ethics. Ethics consists of those unwritten rules we have developed for our interactions with one another. These unwritten rules govern us when we are sharing resources or honoring contracts. "Waiting your turn" is a higher standard than the laws that are passed to maintain order. Those laws apply when physical force or threats are used to push to the front of the line. Assault, battery, and threats are forms of criminal conduct for which the offender can be prosecuted. But the law does not apply to the stealthy line-cutter who simply sneaks to the front, perhaps using a friend and a conversation as a decoy. No laws are broken, but the notions of fairness and justice are offended by one individual putting himself or herself above others and taking advantage of others' time and position.

Ethical questions range from practical, narrowly defined issues, such as a businessperson's obligation to be honest with customers, to broader social and philosophical questions, such as whether a company is responsible for preserving the environment and protecting employee rights. Many ethical dilemmas develop from conflicts between the differing interests of company owners and their workers, customers, and surrounding community. Managers must balance the ideal against the practical—that is, the need to produce a reasonable profit for the company's shareholders against honesty in business practices and concern for environmental and social issues.

HEY! THAT JERK JUST CUT IN FRONT OF ME!

Carl Court/AFP/Getty Images

3-2a Ethical Theories

People usually base their individual choice of ethical theory on their life experiences. The following are some of the ethical theories that apply to marketing.[4]

DEONTOLOGY The **deontological theory** states that people should adhere to their obligations and duties when analyzing an ethical dilemma. This means that a person will follow his or her obligations to another individual or society because upholding one's duty is what is considered ethically correct. For instance, a deontologist will always keep his promises to a friend and will follow the law. A person who follows this theory will produce very consistent decisions because they will be based on the individual's set duties.

Note that deontological theory is not necessarily concerned with the welfare of others. For example, suppose a salesperson has decided that it is her ethical duty (and very practical!) to always be on time to meetings with clients. Today she is running late. How is she supposed to drive? Is the deontologist supposed to speed, breaking the law to uphold her duty to society, or is the deontologist supposed to arrive at her meeting late, breaking her duty to be on time? This scenario of conflicting obligations does not lead us to a clear, ethically correct resolution, nor does it protect the welfare of others from the deontologist's decision.

UTILITARIANISM The **utilitarian ethical theory** is founded on the ability to predict the consequences of an action. To a utilitarian, the choice that yields the greatest benefit to the most people is the choice that is ethically correct. One benefit of this ethical theory is that the utilitarian can compare similar predicted solutions and use a point system to determine which choice is more beneficial for more people. This point system provides a logical and rational argument for each decision and allows a person to use it on a case-by-case context.

There are two types of utilitarianism: act utilitarianism and rule utilitarianism. *Act utilitarianism* adheres exactly to the definition of utilitarianism as just described. In act utilitarianism, a person performs the acts that benefit the most people, regardless of personal feelings or societal constraints such as laws. *Rule utilitarianism*, however, takes into account the law and is concerned with fairness. A rule utilitarian seeks to benefit the most people but through the fairest and most just means available. Therefore, added benefits of rule utilitarianism are that it

values justice and doing good at the same time.

As is true of all ethical theories, however, both act and rule utilitarianism contain numerous flaws. Inherent in both are the flaws associated with predicting the future. Although people can use their life experiences to attempt to predict outcomes, no human being can be certain that his predictions will be true. This uncertainty can lead to unexpected results, making the utilitarian look unethical as time passes because his choice did not benefit the most people as he predicted.

Another assumption that a utilitarian must make is that he has the ability to compare the various types of consequences against each other on a similar scale. However, comparing material gains such as money against intangible gains such as happiness is impossible because their qualities differ so greatly.

CASUIST The **casuist ethical theory** compares a current ethical dilemma with examples of similar ethical dilemmas and their outcomes. This allows one to determine the severity of the situation and to create the best possible solution according to others' experiences. Usually, one will find examples that represent the extremes of the situation so that a compromise can be reached that will include the wisdom gained from the previous situations.

One drawback to this ethical theory is that there may not be a set of similar examples for a given ethical dilemma. Perhaps that which is controversial and ethically questionable is new and unexpected. Along the same line of thinking, this theory assumes that the results of the current ethical dilemma will be similar to results in the examples. This may not be necessarily true and would greatly hinder the effectiveness of applying this ethical theory.

MORAL RELATIVISM **Moral relativism** is a belief in time-and-place ethics, that is, that ethical truths depend on the individuals and groups holding them.[5] According to a moral relativist, for example, arson is not always wrong—if you live in a neighborhood where drug dealers are operating a crystal meth lab or crack house, committing arson by burning down the meth lab may

deontological theory ethical theory that states that people should adhere to their obligations and duties when analyzing an ethical dilemma

utilitarian ethical theory ethical theory that is founded on the ability to predict the consequences of an action

casuist ethical theory ethical theory that compares a current ethical dilemma with examples of similar ethical dilemmas and their outcomes

moral relativism an ethical theory of time-and-place ethics; that is, the belief that ethical truths depend on the individuals and groups holding them

virtue   a character trait
valued as being good

morals   the rules people
develop as a result of cultural
values and norms

be ethically justified. If you are a parent and your child is starving, stealing a loaf of bread is ethically correct. The proper resolution to ethical dilemmas is based upon weighing the competing factors at the moment and then making a determination to take the lesser of the evils as the resolution. Moral relativists do not believe in absolute rules. Their beliefs center on the pressure of the moment and whether the pressure justifies the action taken.

VIRTUE ETHICS Aristotle and Plato taught that solving ethical dilemmas requires training—that individuals solve ethical dilemmas when they develop and nurture a set of virtues.[6] A **virtue** is a character trait valued as being good. Aristotle taught the importance of cultivating virtue in his students and then having them solve ethical dilemmas using those virtues once they had become an integral part of his students' being through their virtue training.

Some modern philosophers have embraced this notion of virtue and have developed lists of what constitutes a virtuous businessperson. Some common virtues for business people are self-discipline, friendliness, caring, courage, compassion, trust, responsibility, honesty, determination, enthusiasm, and humility. You may see other lists of virtues that are longer or shorter, but here is a good start for core business virtues.

3-3 ETHICAL BEHAVIOR IN BUSINESS

Depending upon which, if any, ethical theory a businessperson has accepted and uses in his or her daily conduct, the action taken may vary. For example, faced with bribing a foreign official to get a critically needed contract or shutting down a factory and laying off a thousand workers, a person following a deontology strategy would not pay the bribe. Why? A deontologist always follows the law. However, a moral relativist would probably pay the bribe.

While the boundaries of what is legal and what is not are often fairly clear (for example, don't run a red light, don't steal money from a bank, and don't kill anyone), the boundaries of ethical decision making are predicated on which ethical theory one is following. The law typically relies on juries to determine if an act is legal or illegal.

Society determines whether an action is ethical or unethical. Sometimes, society decides that a person acted unethically—recall the shooting of unarmed teen Trayvon Martin by neighborhood watch coordinator George Zimmerman—but a jury may decide that no illegal act was committed. In a business-related case, the United States Department of Justice filed a fraud lawsuit against Bank of America in 2012 for knowingly selling thousands of toxic mortgage loans to Fannie Mae and Freddie Mac, costing taxpayers more than $1 billion. In a strange turn of events, American International Group (AIG) filed a lawsuit against the U.S. government a few months later for the right to sue Bank of America itself—a right forfeited by AIG when it accepted assistance from the government following a bankruptcy in 2008.[7]

Morals are the rules people develop as a result of cultural values and norms. Culture is a socializing force that dictates what is right and wrong. Moral standards may also reflect the laws and regulations that affect social and economic behavior. Thus, morals can be considered a foundation of ethical behavior.

Morals are usually characterized as good or bad. "Good" and "bad" have many different connotations. One such connotation is "effective" and "ineffective." A good salesperson makes or exceeds the assigned quota. If the salesperson sells a new computer system or HDTV to a disadvantaged consumer—knowing full well that the person can't keep up the monthly payments—is that still a good salesperson? What if the sale enables the salesperson to exceed his or her quota?

"Good" and "bad" can also refer to "conforming" and "deviant" behaviors. A doctor who runs large ads offering discounts on open-heart surgery would be considered bad, or unprofessional, because he or she is not conforming to the norms of the medical profession. "Good" and "bad" also express the distinction between law-abiding and criminal behavior. And finally, different religions define "good" and "bad" in markedly different ways. A Muslim who eats pork would be considered bad by other Muslims, for example. Religion is just one of the many factors that affect a businessperson's ethics.

3-3a Morality and Business Ethics

Today's business ethics actually consist of a subset of major life values learned since birth. The values businesspeople use to make decisions have been acquired through family, educational, and religious institutions.

In this 2013 courtroom sketch, former Detroit Mayor Kwame Kilpatrick (left) appears before U.S. District Judge Nancy Edmunds after being convicted of corruption charges. Jurors found Kilpatrick guilty of a raft of crimes, including racketeering conspiracy, which carries a maximum punishment of twenty years behind bars. During the trial, Kilpatrick was portrayed as an amoral politician who took bribes, rigged contracts, and lived far beyond his means.

Ethical values are situation specific and time oriented. Everyone must have an ethical base that applies to conduct in the business world and in personal life. One approach to developing a personal set of ethics is to examine the consequences of a particular act. Who is helped or hurt? How long do the consequences last? What actions produce the greatest good for the greatest number of people? A second approach stresses the importance of rules. Rules come in the form of customs, laws, professional standards, and common sense. "Always treat others as you would like to be treated" is an example of a rule.

A third approach to personal ethics emphasizes the development of moral character within individuals. In this approach, ethical development is thought to consist of three levels:[8]

▸ *Preconventional morality*, the most basic level, is childlike. It is calculating, self-centered, and even selfish, based on what will be immediately punished or rewarded. Fortunately, most businesspeople have progressed beyond the self-centered and manipulative actions of preconventional morality.

▸ *Conventional morality* moves from an egocentric viewpoint toward the expectations of society. Loyalty and obedience to the organization (or society) become paramount. A marketing decision maker operating at this level of moral development would be concerned only with whether a proposed action is legal and how it will be viewed by others.

▸ *Postconventional morality* represents the morality of the mature adult. At this level, people are less concerned about how others might see them and more concerned about how they see and judge themselves over the long run. A marketing decision maker who has attained a postconventional level of morality might ask, "Even though it is legal and will increase company profits, is it right in the long run? Might it do more harm than good in the end?"

3-3b Ethical Decision Making

Ethical questions rarely have cut-and-dried answers. Studies show that the following factors tend to influence ethical decision making and judgments:[9]

▸ **EXTENT OF ETHICAL PROBLEMS WITHIN THE ORGANIZATION:** Marketing professionals who perceive fewer ethical problems in their organizations tend to disapprove more strongly of "unethical" or questionable practices than those who perceive more ethical problems. Apparently, the healthier the ethical environment, the more likely it is that marketers will take a strong stand against questionable practices.

▸ **TOP MANAGEMENT'S ACTIONS ON ETHICS:** Top managers can influence the behavior of marketing professionals by encouraging ethical behavior and discouraging unethical behavior. Researchers found that when top managers develop a strong ethical culture, there is reduced pressure to perform unethical acts, fewer unethical acts are performed, and unethical behavior is reported more frequently. [10]

▸ **POTENTIAL MAGNITUDE OF THE CONSEQUENCES:** The greater the harm done to victims, the more likely that marketing professionals will recognize a problem as unethical.

▸ **SOCIAL CONSENSUS:** The greater the degree of agreement among managerial peers that an action is harmful, the more likely that marketers will recognize a problem as unethical. Research has found that a strong ethical culture among coworkers decreases observations of ethical misconduct. In companies with strong ethical cultures, 8 percent of employees observed misconduct, compared with 31 percent in companies with weaker cultures. [11]

▸ **PROBABILITY OF A HARMFUL OUTCOME:** The greater the likelihood that an action will result in a harmful outcome, the more likely that marketers will recognize a problem as unethical.

▸ **LENGTH OF TIME BETWEEN THE DECISION AND THE ONSET OF CONSEQUENCES:** The shorter the length of time between the action and the onset of negative consequences, the more likely that marketers will perceive a problem as unethical.

▸ **NUMBER OF PEOPLE TO BE AFFECTED:** The greater the number of persons affected by a negative outcome, the more likely that marketers will recognize a problem as unethical.

As you can see, many factors determine the nature of an ethical decision. Consider the following scenario: In a remote Amazon village a full day's travel by canoe from the nearest road in western Brazil, Yawanawá Indians gather around a pile of urukum, a spiky fruit they use to make body paint, and pose for two photographers from U.S. beauty firm Aveda. The images will help Aveda, a unit of Estée Lauder, sell its popular Uruku line of lipsticks, eye shadows, and facial bronzers that use the plant as coloring. The company can charge a premium for products that look good, and at the same time, help save the rain forest by giving the tribe a sustainable livelihood.

Images of the Yawanawá Indians help Aveda sell its popular Uruku line of lipsticks, eye shadows, and facial bronzers, but the actual involvement of the Yawanawá in the production of these products may be less impactful than Aveda suggests.

But there's something wrong with this picture. The Yawanawá don't produce much urukum, and the plant itself isn't as exotic as Aveda portrays it in a documentary-style video on its Web site. Best known as annatto, an inexpensive food-coloring agent, urukum is grown commercially around the world. You've likely come across it yourself—annatto gives Kraft Macaroni & Cheese its distinctive orange hue.

There is little doubt that Aveda has helped the tribe in many important ways, such as improving access to health care, education, and government services. But the venture has failed to make the Yawanawá self-sufficient. The market value of its crop in an average year is around $500—not enough to sustain a population of 700—and the tribe has no other customers besides Aveda. Today, the project is basically a form of philanthropy, wherein the tribe gets aid in exchange for providing small amounts of annatto and an uplifting storyline. [12]

3-3c Ethical Guidelines and Training

In recent years, many organizations have become more interested in ethical issues. One sign of this interest is the increase in the number of large companies that appoint ethics officers—from virtually none several years ago to between 35 and 40 percent of large corporations today. [13] In addition, many companies of various sizes have developed a **code of ethics** as a guideline to help marketing managers and other employees make better decisions. Creating ethics guidelines has several advantages:

- **A code of ethics helps employees identify what their firm recognizes as acceptable business practices.**

- **A code of ethics can be an effective internal control of behavior, which is more desirable than external controls such as government regulation.**

- **A written code helps employees avoid confusion when determining whether their decisions are ethical.**

- **The process of formulating the code of ethics facilitates discussion among employees about what is right and wrong and ultimately leads to better decisions.**

Businesses, however, must be careful not to make their code of ethics too vague or too detailed. Codes that are too vague give little or no guidance to employees in their day-to-day activities. Codes that are too detailed encourage employees to substitute rules for judgment. For instance, if employees are involved in questionable behavior, they may use the absence of a written rule as a reason to continue behaving that way, even though their conscience may be telling them to stop. Following a set of ethical guidelines will not guarantee the "rightness" of a decision, but it will improve the chances that the decision will be ethical.

Although many companies have issued policies on ethical behavior, marketing managers must still put the policies into effect. They must address the classic "matter of degree" issue. For example, marketing researchers often resort to deception to obtain unbiased answers to their research questions. Asking for a few minutes of a respondent's time is dishonest if the researcher knows the interview will last forty-five minutes. Unless there are examples of ethical and unethical behavior relating to each item in the code, an employee may not apply a certain item to the appropriate situation. Moreover, top management must stress to all employees the importance of adhering to the company's code of ethics. Without an appropriately detailed code of ethics and top management's support, creating ethical guidelines becomes an empty exercise.

Ethics training is an effective way to help employees put good ethics into practice. Because of various scandals, such as Bernard Madoff's financial trickery that cost investors billions, more and more companies are offering ethics

PEPSI'S CODE OF ETHICS

Like virtually all major corporations, PepsiCo has a code of ethics, sometimes referred to as a "code of conduct." PepsiCo has a single code of conduct for Pepsi and all of its subsidiaries around the world. Their guiding principles are to:

- **Care for our customers, consumers, and the world we live in**
- **Sell only products we can be proud of**
- **Speak with truth and candor**
- **Balance the short term and the long term**
- **Win with diversity and inclusion**
- **Respect others and succeed together[14]**

AirTran Airways flight attendant Vincent Johnson (left) sneaks up on coworker Linda Winn during a Close Quarter Defense training class, a two-day program customized for flight attendants. In the interest of avoiding negative feedback and potential lawsuits from customers, flight attendants undergo rigorous training to deal with dangerous situations quickly—and ethically.

Erik S. Lesser/Stringer/Getty Images

© iStockphoto.com/billnoll

training to their employees. Today, about 70 percent of all large employers (more than 500 employees) provide ethics training.[15] But simply giving employees a long list of "dos and don'ts" does not really help employees navigate the gray areas or adapt to a changing world market. In Carson City, Nevada, all governmental lobbyists are required to attend a course on ethics and policy before they can meet with lawmakers. The training outlines exactly how and when lobbyists are allowed to interact with lawmakers and how to report any money they spend. A clear understanding of ethical expectations is essential to an industry like lobbying, where illicit—often illegal—actions are taken to promote individual causes.[16]

Do ethics training programs work? The National Business Ethics Survey (NBES) found that in 2011, misconduct witnessed by U.S. workers was the lowest it had ever been and that reporting of violations was at an all-time high. However, the number of employees who said they had felt pressure to commit an ethics violation—to cut corners or worse—rose from 8 to 13 percent in 2011.[17] The NBES suggests that working with employees who avidly use social networks may be the next big step in ethics training. The survey found that despite a tendency to be tolerant of questionable activities, most social network users are more likely to report violations than non-social media users. Social network users are also more likely to post positive statements about coworkers and employers.[18]

THE MOST ETHICAL COMPANIES Each year, *Ethisphere* magazine (targeted toward top management and focused on ethical leadership) examines more than 5,000 companies in thirty separate industries, seeking the world's most ethical companies. It then lists the top 100. The magazine uses a rigorous format to identify true ethical leadership. A few of the selected winners are shown in Exhibit 1.

3-3d Ethics in Other Countries

Studies suggest that ethical beliefs vary little from culture to culture. Certain practices, however, such as the use of illegal payments and bribes, are far more acceptable in some places than in others, though enforced laws are increasingly making the

practice less accepted. One such law, the **Foreign Corrupt Practices Act (FCPA)**, was enacted because Congress was concerned about U.S. corporations' use of illegal payments and bribes in international business dealings. This act prohibits U.S. corporations from making illegal payments to public officials of foreign governments to obtain business rights or to enhance their business dealings in those countries. The act has been criticized for putting U.S. businesses at a competitive disadvantage. Many contend that bribery is an unpleasant but necessary part of international business, especially in countries such as China, where business gift giving is widely accepted and expected. But, as prosecutions under the FCPA have increased worldwide, some countries are implementing their own anti-bribery laws. For example, even though China is among the three countries with the most international corruption cases prosecuted under the FCPA, the country is working to develop its own anti-bribery laws.

Exhibit 1
SELECTED WINNERS OF THE WORLD'S MOST ETHICAL COMPANIES

Company	Industry
Rockwell Collins	Aerospace and Defense
The Aerospace Corporation	Aerospace and Defense
Ethical Fruit Company, Ltd.	Agriculture
Gap, Inc.	Apparel
H & M Hennes & Mauritz AB	Apparel
Ford Motor Company	Autos
Old National Bank	Banking
Accenture	Business Services
Intel Corporation	Computer Hardware
Microsoft Corporation	Computer Software
Colgate-Palmolive Company	Consumer Products
Kimberly-Clark Corporation	Consumer Products
General Electric Company	Diversified
Ebay	E-commerce
Kellogg Company	Food and Beverage
PepsiCo	Food and Beverage
L'OREAL	Health and Beauty
Honeywell International Inc.	Industrial Manufacturing
Marriott International	Leisure and Hospitality
UPS	Transportation and Logistics

Source: "2012 World's Most Ethical Companies," *Ethisphere*, http://ethisphere.com/wme/ (Accessed April 3, 2013).

© Cengage Learning

3-4 CORPORATE SOCIAL RESPONSIBILITY

Corporate social responsibility (CSR) is a business's concern for society's welfare. This concern is demonstrated by managers who consider both the long-range best interests of the company and the company's relationship to the society within which it operates.

3-4a Stakeholders and Social Responsibility

An important aspect of social responsibility is **stakeholder theory**. Stakeholder theory says that social responsibility is paying attention to the interest of every affected stakeholder in every aspect of a firm's operation.[27] The stakeholders in a typical corporation are shown in Exhibit 2.

▸▸ *Employees* have their jobs and incomes at stake. If the firm moves or closes, employees often face a severe hardship. In return for their labor, employees expect wages, benefits, and meaningful work. In return for their loyalty, workers expect the company to carry them through difficult times.

▸▸ *Management* plays a special role, as they also have a stake in the corporation. Like employees, managers have their jobs and incomes at stake. On the other hand, management must safeguard the welfare of the organization. Sometimes this means balancing the multiple claims of conflicting stakeholders. For example, stockholders want a higher return on investment and perhaps lower costs by moving factories overseas. This naturally conflicts with the interests of employees, the local community, and perhaps suppliers.

▸▸ *Customers* generate the revenue for the organization. In exchange, they expect high-quality goods and services delivered in a timely manner. Customer satisfaction leads to higher revenues and the ability to enhance the satisfaction of other stakeholders.

▸▸ *The local community*, through its government, grants the firm the right to build facilities. In turn, the community benefits directly from local taxes paid by the corporation and indirectly by property and sales taxes paid by the workers. The firm is expected to be a good citizen by paying a fair wage, not polluting the environment, and so forth.

▸▸ *Suppliers* are vital to the success of the firm. For example, if a critical part is not available for an assembly line, then production grinds to a halt. The materials supplied determine the quality of the product produced and create a cost floor, which helps determine the retail price. In turn, the firm is the customer of the supplier and is therefore vital to the success and survival of the supplier. Small firms that sold most of their production to Walmart and were subsequently dropped by Walmart have sometimes gone bankrupt.[19]

▸▸ *Owners* have a financial stake in the form of stock in a corporation. They expect a reasonable return based upon the amount of inherent risk on their investment. Often managers and employees have a portion of their retirement funds in company stock—a financial strategy that proved perilous during the Great Recession. Between 2007 and 2008, the price of one share of AIG stock plummeted from nearly $1,500 to less than $40, causing many workers to lose their retirement savings. The likelihood of an AIG recovery remains slim, with a share of AIG stock consistently trading at less than $40 into 2013.[20]

One theorist suggests that total corporate responsibility has four components: economic, legal, ethical,

corporate social responsibility (CSR) a business's concern for society's welfare

stakeholder theory ethical theory stating that social responsibility is paying attention to the interest of every affected stakeholder in every aspect of a firm's operation

Exhibit 2

STAKEHOLDERS IN A TYPICAL CORPORATION

© Cengage Learning

pyramid of corporate social responsibility a model that suggests corporate social responsibility is composed of economic, legal, ethical, and philanthropic responsibilities and that the firm's economic performance supports the entire structure

sustainability the idea that socially responsible companies will outperform their peers by focusing on the world's social problems and viewing them as opportunities to build profits and help the world at the same time

and philanthropic. The **pyramid of corporate social responsibility** portrays economic performance as the foundation for the other three responsibilities (see Exhibit 3). At the same time that it pursues profits (economic responsibility), however, a business is expected to obey the law (legal responsibility); to do what is right, just, and fair (ethical responsibilities); and to be a good corporate citizen (philanthropic responsibility). These four components are distinct but together constitute the whole. Still, if the company doesn't make a profit, then the other three responsibilities are moot.

3-5 ARGUMENTS FOR AND AGAINST SOCIAL RESPONSIBILITY

CSR can be a divisive issue. Some analysts believe that a business should focus on making a profit and leave social and environmental problems to nonprofit organizations and government. Economist Milton Friedman believed that the free market, not companies, should decide what is best for the world.[21] Friedman argued that when business executives spend more money than necessary—to purchase delivery vehicles with hybrid engines, pay higher wages in developing countries, or even donate company funds to charity—they are spending shareholders' money to further their own agendas. It would be better to pay dividends and let the shareholders give the money away if they choose.

On the other hand, CSR has an increasing number of supporters based on several compelling factors. One is that it is simply the right thing to do. Some societal problems, such as pollution and poverty-level wages, have been brought about by corporations' actions; it is the responsibility of business to right these wrongs. Businesses also have the resources, so businesses should be given the chance to solve social problems. For example, businesses can provide a fair work environment, safe products, and informative advertising.

Another, more pragmatic, reason for being socially responsible is that if businesses don't act responsibly, then

government will create new regulations and perhaps levy fines against them.

Finally, social responsibility can be profitable. Smart companies can prosper and build value by tackling social problems. In 2013, Starbucks rolled out a reusable plastic tumbler that customers could buy for $1 instead of using a disposable cardboard cup for each coffee they buy. Not only does the reusable tumbler reduce energy use, landfill waste, and litter, it saves Starbucks the cost of the disposable cups and encourages customers to buy their daily cup of coffee from the company.[22]

3-5a Sustainability

The newest theory in social responsibility—embodied by the Starbucks example—is called **sustainability**. This refers to the idea that socially responsible companies will outperform their peers by focusing on the world's social and environmental problems and viewing them as

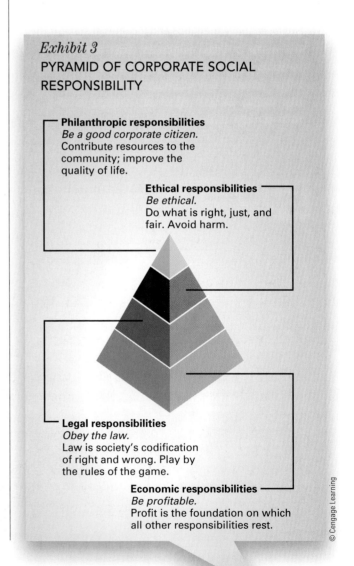

Exhibit 3
PYRAMID OF CORPORATE SOCIAL RESPONSIBILITY

Philanthropic responsibilities
Be a good corporate citizen.
Contribute resources to the community; improve the quality of life.

Ethical responsibilities
Be ethical.
Do what is right, just, and fair. Avoid harm.

Legal responsibilities
Obey the law.
Law is society's codification of right and wrong. Play by the rules of the game.

Economic responsibilities
Be profitable.
Profit is the foundation on which all other responsibilities rest.

© Cengage Learning

RICHARD B. LEVINE/Newscom

This reusable tumbler was purchased from a Starbucks location in the Chelsea neighborhood of New York City. Consumers have long criticized Starbucks's use of disposable containers, so the introduction of the reusable cup benefited both the company and its customers.

3-5b Growth of Social Responsibility

The social responsibility of businesses is growing around the world. One survey found that companies around the globe are coming under increasing pressure from governments, advocacy groups, investors, prospective employees, current employees, and consumers to make their organizations more socially responsible. In turn, firms are seeing social responsibility as an opportunity. According to Forrester Research, social responsibility and sustainability practices have led to profit increases of more than 35 percent within large corporations.[26]

opportunities to build profits and help the world at the same time. The movement has enough momentum that many companies are hiring chief sustainability officers (CSOs) to ensure that the company saves energy, meets standards, and qualifies for federal stimulus money.[23] A recent survey of CEOs found that 96 percent thought that sustainability should be fully embedded into a company's strategy and operations.[24]

When an organization focuses on sustainability, it is acting with long-term consequences in mind and managing its business so that its processes or overall state can be maintained indefinitely. A company that believes in sustainability will integrate long-term economic, environmental, and social factors into its business strategies while maintaining its competitiveness and brand reputation. To do so, a company must have effective planning for long-run economic growth. This requires focusing on product and service innovation and building customer loyalty. It also means having the highest ethical standards and a meaningful code of conduct. Sustainability also demands that human resources be managed in a way that maintains workforce capabilities and employee satisfaction. Some companies that excel in their sustainability philosophies include Adidas, Samsung, Procter & Gamble, IBM, and Unilever.[25]

Sustainability is not simply "green marketing," though environmental sustainability is an important component of the sustainability philosophy. An environmentally sustainable process contributes to keeping the environment healthy by using renewable resources and by avoiding actions that depreciate the environment.

UNITED NATIONS GLOBAL COMPACT One way that U.S. firms can do more is by joining the United Nations Global Compact (UNGC). The UNGC, the world's largest global corporate citizenship initiative, has seen its ranks swell over the past few years. In 2001—the first full year after its launch—just sixty-seven companies joined, agreeing to abide by ten principles covering, among other things, human rights, labor practices, and the environment. In its tenth-anniversary Annual Review, the UNGC boasts more than 8,000 participants in 135 countries.[27]

Dimitrios Kambouris/Getty Images for Avon

Executive Director of the United Nations Global Compact Georg Kell addresses global women's rights leaders at the United Nations Headquarters on March 7, 2013.

Firms realize that CSR isn't easy or quick. It doesn't work without a long-term strategy, effort, and coordination throughout the enterprise. It doesn't always come cheap, either. And the pay-off, both to society and to the business itself, isn't always immediate. Today, only 77 percent of the Global Compact members are in full compliance with Global Compact policies. Firms that have been members the longest perform at significantly higher levels of sustainability than more recent joiners.[28]

3-5c Green Marketing

An outgrowth of the social responsibility and sustainability movements is green marketing. **Green marketing** is the development and marketing of products designed to minimize negative effects on the physical environment or to improve the environment.[29] According to NASA, average global temperatures have risen by 0.53°C since 1975, largely because of industrial pollution and other human activities. The United Nations Intergovernmental Panel on Climate Change predicts that an increase of 3.5°C could drive 40 to 70 percent of the world's species into extinction. For these—and many other—reasons, environmentalism has become a pressing concern for many businesses and consumers alike.[30]

Not only can a company aid the environment through green marketing, but it can often help its bottom line as well. The problem, however, is one of credibility. Eight of ten Americans don't believe companies are addressing all of their environmental impacts, and only 44 percent trust companies' green claims. Also, 43 percent of consumers actively seek out environmental information on the products they buy. When purchasing an environmental product, 81 percent are likely to be swayed by an ecolabel such as Energy Star or WaterSense. And 80 percent would choose a product if its packaging features specific data detailing, for instance, how much plastic was saved over an earlier version.

In general, green consumers are getting more savvy about products' environmental claims. Just 36 percent of consumers thought that products labeled "environmentally friendly" have a positive impact on the environment—rather than just being less damaging than non-green products. Forty-two percent of Americans have been discouraged from buying a green product because they believed it cost more than the traditional product,

THE PRACTICAL SIDE OF GREEN MARKETING

Some green products have practical benefits that are readily apparent to consumers. A few examples are energy-efficient appliances (cut electric bills), heat-reflective windows (cut air-conditioning costs), and organic foods (no pesticides poisoning the food or the planet). Every month, Windsor Rubber Processing shreds more than 50,000 used tires into rubber mulch. Some of the mulch is shipped to companies that make rubber tiles and carpet padding, but the majority is distributed to playgrounds across Canada. The shredded rubber is softer than sand or gravel, looks good, and saves the tires from landfills.[31]

© iStockphoto.com/walrusmail / © iStockphoto.com/diephosi

and one-third believed the environmentally preferred product would not be of equal quality.[32]

PROACTIVE SOCIAL RESPONSIBILITY AND GREEN MARKETING Two very different companies that are often lauded for their social responsibility and green marketing are ice cream company Ben & Jerry's and TOMS Shoes.

BEN & JERRY'S Ben & Jerry's was founded and built on the concept of sustainability before the term became a business buzzword.[33] The firm's dedication to society and its stakeholders is exemplified by the three components of its mission statement:

➤ **SOCIAL MISSION:** To operate the company in a way that actively recognizes the central role that business plays in society by initiating innovative ways to improve the quality of life locally, nationally, and internationally.

➤ **PRODUCT MISSION:** To make, distribute, and sell the finest-quality all-natural ice cream and

cause-related marketing the cooperative marketing efforts between a for-profit firm and a nonprofit organization

euphoric concoctions with a continued commitment to incorporating wholesome, natural ingredients and promoting business practices that respect the earth and the environment.

▸▸ **ECONOMIC MISSION:** To operate the company on a sustainable financial basis of profitable growth, increasing value for our stakeholders and expanding opportunities for development and career growth for our employees.

The mission statement also discusses eliminating injustices in the world through the company's day-to-day business activities. Ben & Jerry's strives to create economic opportunities for people around the globe. The firm recognizes that manufacturing creates waste, and it tries to minimize its impact on the environment. Making ice cream requires a number of raw ingredients. The firm supports sustainable and safe methods of food production that reduce environmental degradation, maintain the productivity of the land over time, and support the economic viability of family farms and rural communities.

Ben & Jerry's has created a large number of initiatives and programs to make social responsibility a reality. The Ben & Jerry's Foundation gives more than $2 million a year to nonprofit, grassroots organizations working for progressive social change. The company buys eggs only from cage-free farms. Working with Yoko Ono, Ben & Jerry's launched the flavor Whirled Peace, named in honor of John Lennon. The firm then kicked off a search for modern-day peace pioneers on its Web site. Two winners were named and each organization was awarded $10,000.

Recently, Ben & Jerry's announced its commitment to fair trade across its entire global flavor portfolio, meaning that producers in developing countries would be paid fairly for their products and not exploited. From Cherry Garcia to Chocolate Fudge Brownie, all of the flavors in all of the countries where Ben & Jerry's is sold were converted to Fair Trade Certified ingredients by the end of 2013. Globally, this involved converting up to 121 different chunks and swirls, working across eleven different ingredients, such as cocoa, banana, vanilla and other flavorings, fruits, and nuts. It also meant working with fair-trade cooperatives with a combined membership of more than 27,000 farmers. Ben & Jerry's was the first ice cream company in the world to use Fair Trade Certified ingredients, starting in 2005, and it's the first ice cream company to make such a significant commitment to fair trade across its global portfolio. Company cofounder Jerry Greenfield said, "Fair trade is about making sure people get their fair share of the pie.

The whole concept of fair trade goes to the heart of our values and sense of right and wrong. Nobody wants to buy something that was made by exploiting somebody else."

TOMS SHOES In 2006, Blake Mycoskie took off from his online driver's education school business and went to Argentina.[34] There he met a few people involved in a shoe drive for children outside of Buenos Aires. He learned that the children were not allowed to go to school unless they wore shoes, which many families could not afford. So touched by the experience, Mycoskie grew determined to help more kids on a long-term basis. When he returned to California, his revolutionary business model was created and named simply: TOMS Shoes.

TOMS' premise is simple. With every pair of shoes a customer buys, TOMS gives a pair of shoes to a child in need—one for one. All TOMS Shoes products are made in environmentally friendly factories, in various countries, that pay a fair wage. Since its beginning, TOMS has given away more than 2 million pairs of shoes. TOMS now gives away shoes in forty-four countries, ranging from Angola to Zambia.

Mycoskie spends about twenty-five days a month traveling around the world, speaking to companies and universities about his business model. His goal is to inspire the next generation of entrepreneurs to help make the world a better place.

Ben & Jerry's and TOMS Shoes are models of social responsibility, with the inspiration coming from their founders. Other, long-established corporations were created before social responsibility was a business mantra. Their success in becoming socially responsible has moved forward at varying paces.

3-6 CAUSE-RELATED MARKETING

A sometimes controversial subset of social responsibility is cause-related marketing. Sometimes referred to as simply "cause marketing," it is the cooperative efforts of a for-profit firm and a nonprofit organization for mutual benefit. Any marketing effort for social or other charitable causes can be referred to as cause-related marketing. Cause marketing differs from corporate giving (philanthropy), as the latter generally involves a specific donation that is tax deductible, whereas cause marketing is a marketing relationship not based on a straight donation.

Cause-related marketing is very popular and is estimated to generate about $7 billion a year in revenue. It creates good public relations for the firm and will often stimulate sales of the brand. Nevertheless, the huge growth of cause-related marketing can lead to *consumer cause fatigue*. Researchers have found that businesses need to guard against being perceived as exploiting a cause simply to sell more of a product.[35]

Examples of cause-related marketing used by large companies are abundant. Arby's asked customers for a $1 donation to help Big Brothers Big Sisters. In turn, the customer received a coupon valued at $1. Whirlpool donated a range and refrigerator to every home built by Habitat for Humanity for a year. Nike and the Livestrong Foundation have sold more than 80 million Livestrong bracelets for cancer research. However, companies also participate on a smaller, more local scale. For example, Nantucket Bookworks, an independent bookstore in Nantucket, Massachusetts, ran "Love Month" in February 2012. Throughout the month, the bookstore donated 10 percent of its sales to a nonprofit pulled from a hat each day. The twenty-nine participating nonprofits promoted the event through their mailing lists. The extra word of mouth and advertising benefitted the store by increasing sales during a traditionally slow month and showing the store's dedication to community.[36]

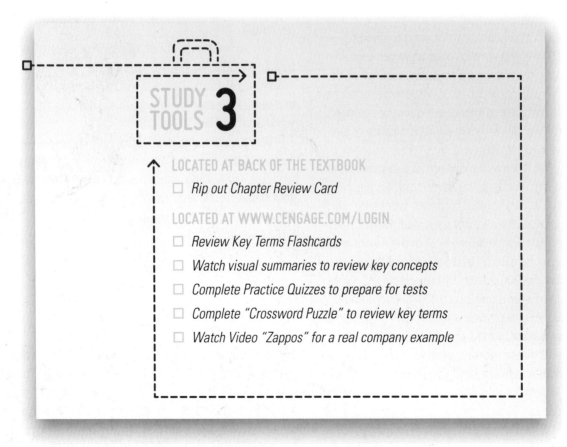

STUDY TOOLS 3

LOCATED AT BACK OF THE TEXTBOOK

☐ *Rip out Chapter Review Card*

LOCATED AT WWW.CENGAGE.COM/LOGIN

☐ *Review Key Terms Flashcards*

☐ *Watch visual summaries to review key concepts*

☐ *Complete Practice Quizzes to prepare for tests*

☐ *Complete "Crossword Puzzle" to review key terms*

☐ *Watch Video "Zappos" for a real company example*

4LTR Press solutions are designed for today's learners through the continuous feedback of students like you. Tell us what you think about **MKTG** and help us improve the learning experience for future students.

YOUR FEEDBACK MATTERS.

THE EXTERNAL MARKETING ENVIRONMENT

Perhaps the most important decisions a marketing manager must make relate to the creation of the marketing mix. Recall from Chapters 1 and 2 that a marketing mix is the unique combination of product, place (distribution), promotion, and price strategies. The marketing mix is, of course, under the firm's control and is designed to appeal to a specific group of potential buyers, or target market. A **target market** is a group of people or organizations for which an organization designs, implements, and maintains a marketing mix intended to meet the need of that group, resulting in mutually satisfying exchanges.

Although managers can control the marketing mix, they cannot control elements in the external environment.

target market a group of people or organizations for which an organization designs, implements, and maintains a marketing mix intended to meet the need of that group, resulting in mutually satisfying exchanges

Managers must alter the marketing mix because of changes in the environment in which consumers live, work, and make purchasing decisions. Also, as markets mature, some new consumers become part of the target market; others drop out. Those who remain may have different tastes, needs, incomes, lifestyles, and buying habits than the original target consumers. Technology, and the resulting change in buying habits, meant that consumers no longer have those "Kodak Moments" when taking pictures of a birthday party or an exceptional sunset. Digital photography has sent thirty-five-millimeter film the way of the horse and buggy. Unfortunately, shifting technology ultimately led to the bankruptcy of Eastman Kodak.

Although managers can control the marketing mix, they cannot control elements in the external environment that continually mold and reshape the target market. Controllable and uncontrollable variables affect the target market, whether it consists of consumers or business purchasers. The uncontrollable elements in the center of the environment continually evolve and create changes in the target market. In contrast, managers can shape and reshape the marketing mix to influence the target market. That is, managers react to changes in the external environment and attempt to create a more effective marketing mix.

Chapter *4*

The Marketing Environment

Learning Outcomes

After you finish this chapter go to
p66 *for* **STUDY TOOLS**

© iStockPhoto.com/Robert Churchill

4-1a Understanding the External Environment

Unless marketing managers understand the external environment, the firm cannot intelligently plan for the future. Thus, many organizations assemble a team of specialists to continually collect and evaluate environmental information, a process called *environmental scanning*. The goal in gathering the environmental data is to identify future market opportunities and threats.

UNDERSTAND CURRENT CUSTOMERS You must first understand how customers buy, where they buy, what they buy, and when they buy. For example, in 2008, Stephen Quinn, Walmart's chief marketing officer, dropped the firm's iconic smiley face in a sweeping act of change. This move stemmed from thorough marketing research to understand Walmart customers better. Walmart always knew it served the bottom half of America's household income distribution, but research showed that during the 2008–2009 recession (called the Great Recession by some), higher income consumers also began shopping at Walmart for certain items. These consumers are very value-oriented. Quinn realized that Walmart served value-oriented customers from a wide spectrum of income groups. This had an impact on Walmart's image and the items it stocked on its shelves. Along with the end of the smiley face, Walmart developed a new slogan to reflect its wider audience: "Save money, live better."[1]

UNDERSTAND WHAT DRIVES CONSUMER DECISIONS American Express call center agents used to use a scripted message when answering customer calls. Recently, American Express dropped the script in an attempt to use each customer call as an opportunity to build a relationship. Because it tracks customer spending, American Express possesses a staggering amount of data and a deep knowledge about each customer's life. If a representative can use that information to uncover an underlying customer need and address it using an American Express product or service, "that has the most powerful marketing benefit to us of any marketing communication or marketing channel," says Jim Bush, executive vice president of World Services.[2]

IDENTIFY THE MOST VALUABLE CUSTOMERS AND UNDERSTAND THEIR NEEDS Often, 20 percent of a firm's customers produce 80 percent of the firm's revenue. Jim Hilt, vice president of E-books at Barnes & Noble, calls the 20 percent of readers who drive the digital market

"power readers." Hilt says that the "explosion of players in the tablet marketplace has fundamentally changed the way we sell books." With so many businesses competing for customers, maintaining loyalty among the power readers is paramount to success.[3] An organization must understand what drives that loyalty and then take steps to ensure that those drivers are maintained and enhanced.

UNDERSTAND THE COMPETITION Successful firms know their competitors and attempt to forecast those competitors' future moves. Competitors threaten both a firm's market share and its profitability. Procter & Gamble (P&G) has faced growing questions about the effectiveness of its competitive strategy. In a recent quarter, it lost market share across more than half of its business around the globe. As one analyst notes, "There's no question P&G

Understanding the competition means knowing the competition and attempting to forecast their future moves. How does Olay demonstrate that it understands its competitors with this advertisement?

used to be miles ahead of their competitors. And now their competitors have caught up because Procter has not executed well." P&G may already be well on its way to regaining its lead, however. In January 2013, the company reported quarterly earnings and revenues that beat analyst expectations.[4]

4-1b Environmental Management

No single business is large or powerful enough to create major change in the external environment. Thus, marketing managers are basically adapters rather than agents of change. For example, despite the huge size of firms like General Electric, Walmart, Apple, and Caterpillar, they don't control social change, demographics, or other factors in the external environment.

Just because a firm cannot fully control the external environment, however, doesn't mean that it is helpless. Sometimes a firm can influence external events. For example, extensive lobbying by FedEx has enabled it to acquire virtually all the Japanese routes it has sought. When a company implements strategies that attempt to shape the external environment within which it operates, it is engaging in **environmental management**. The factors within the external environment that are important to marketing managers can be classified as social, demographic, economic, technological, political and legal, and competitive.

4-2 SOCIAL FACTORS

Social change is perhaps the most difficult external variable for marketing managers to forecast, influence, or integrate into marketing plans. Social factors include our attitudes, values, and lifestyles. Social factors influence the products people buy; the prices paid for products; the effectiveness of specific promotions; and how, where, and when people expect to purchase products.

4-2a American Values

A *value* is a strongly held and enduring belief. During the United States' first 200 years, four basic values strongly influenced attitudes and lifestyles:

▸ **SELF-SUFFICIENCY:** Every person should stand on his or her own two feet.

▸ **UPWARD MOBILITY:** Success would come to anyone who got an education, worked hard, and played by the rules.

▸ **WORK ETHIC:** Hard work, dedication to family, and frugality were moral and right.

▸ **CONFORMITY:** No one should expect to be treated differently from anybody else.

environmental management when a company implements strategies that attempt to shape the external environment within which it operates

component lifestyles the practice of choosing goods and services that meet one's diverse needs and interests rather than conforming to a single, traditional lifestyle

These core values still hold for a majority of Americans today. A person's values are key determinants of what is important and not important, what actions to take or not to take, and how one behaves in social situations.

People typically form values through interaction with family, friends, and other influencers such as teachers, religious leaders, and politicians. The changing environment can also play a key role in shaping one's values.

Values influence our buying habits. Today's consumers are demanding, inquisitive, and discriminating. No longer willing to tolerate products that break down, they are insisting on high-quality goods that save time, energy, and often calories. U.S. consumers rank the characteristics of product quality as (1) reliability, (2) durability, (3) easy maintenance, (4) ease of use, (5) a trusted brand name, and (6) a low price. Shoppers are also concerned about nutrition and want to know what's in their food; many have environmental concerns as well.

4-2b The Growth of Component Lifestyles

People in the United States today are piecing together **component lifestyles**. A lifestyle is a mode of living; it is

THE POWER OF PARTY

The Pew Research Center's 2012 American Values Survey found that political party affiliation has become the single largest fissure in American society—differences in values are greater between Democrats and Republicans than they are between different genders, ages, races, or classes. The most divisive issues include the scope of the social safety net, environmental issues, the role of labor unions, and equal opportunity provisions.[5]

the way people decide to live their lives. With component lifestyles, people are choosing products and services that meet diverse needs and interests rather than conforming to traditional stereotypes.

In the past, a person's profession—for instance, banker—defined his or her lifestyle. Today, a person can be a banker and also a gourmet, fitness enthusiast, dedicated single parent, and Internet guru. Each of these lifestyles is associated with different goods and services and represents a target audience. Component lifestyles increase the complexity of consumers' buying habits. Each consumer's unique lifestyle can require a different marketing mix.

4-2c How Social Media Have Changed Our Behavior

Social media are Web-based and mobile technologies that allow the creation and exchange of user-generated content. Social media encompasses a wide variety of content formats—you have most likely used sites such as Facebook, YouTube, Twitter, Tumblr, Instagram, and Pinterest, each of which serves a different function (see Chapter 18). These media have changed the way we communicate, keep track of others, browse for products and services, and make purchases. Social networking is part of regular life for people of all ages—people ages fifty-five to sixty-four spend more than eleven hours on social media per month, while people over the age of sixty-five spend eight hours per month. The most active users—those ages eighteen to twenty-four—spend more than twenty-one hours on social networking sites every month.[6]

By the beginning of 2012, one minute out of every five spent on the Internet worldwide was dedicated to social networking. This statistic is based upon data from 1.2 billion people around the globe, or 82 percent of the world's Internet population.[7] Facebook, YouTube, and Twitter are the most-used social networking sites worldwide. Facebook, by far, is the world's most popular, with more than 1 billion users. Ninety-two percent of all social networkers have Facebook accounts. Fifteen percent of Facebook users update their own statuses, 22 percent comment on other users' posts or statuses, 20 percent comment on other users' photos, 26 percent like other users' content, and 10 percent send other users a private message.[8]

Social networking has changed the game when it comes to opinion sharing. Now, consumers can reach many people at once with their views—and can respond to brands and events in real time. Each day, Facebook processes 2.76 billion "likes."[9] Are likes important? One recent study found that 54 percent of Facebook users who "liked" a company's or brand's Facebook page were much more likely to purchase that brand.[10] Teenagers and young adults are more likely to view social networks as a valuable source of information. In a recent survey, more than half of respondents between the ages of thirteen and thirty-four said the information on social networking sites was very valuable or extremely valuable to them. In contrast, only about 20 percent of those forty-five and older put the same high value on social network information.[11]

HOW FIRMS USE SOCIAL MEDIA If Facebook were a country, it would be the world's third largest behind China and India. How can marketing managers use Facebook and other fast-growing social media to influence buyer behavior? A starting point is to monitor what is being said about the brand. Gatorade has been working toward its goal of becoming the "largest participatory brand in the world." It has created a Chicago-based "war room" within its marketing department to monitor the brand in real time across social media. Team members track custom-built data dashboards (including information on terms related to the brand, sponsored athletes, and competitors) and run sentiment analyses (feelings toward the brand) around promotional campaign launches. A data dashboard, like an auto dashboard, is a series of graphs, charts, and gauges that give signs about how a business strategy or tactic is performing. This feedback is then integrated into products and marketing. For example, a spike in interest in one product might push that product to the front of the company's Web site. Since the war room's

© iStockphoto.com/DanielBendjy

FACEBOOK AND BRAND AWARENESS

Social media can be used to increase brand awareness. Here are two examples from Facebook:

» Corona put the faces of its Facebook fans onto a Times Square billboard, generating 1.5 million impressions per day and feeding into 200,000 more likes for the brand.

» Bacardi created a promotion on Facebook called "Like It Live, Like It Together." In a six-week period, Bacardi fans liked randomly featured items on the brand's Facebook page (for example, one promotion asked people to "like" a pizza truck or a taco truck). The promotion gained Bacardi more than 145,000 fans in the United States and boosted its YouTube channel views by 67 percent.[12]

Roz Woodward/Photodisc/Getty Images

creation, the average traffic to Gatorade's online sites, the length of visitor interactions, and viral sharing from campaigns have all more than doubled.[13]

In addition to monitoring, firms must respond to both positive and negative buzz about a company or brand. In recent years, American Airlines has been in a lengthy labor dispute with its pilots and other employees; in 2012, a bankruptcy judge allowed American to impose its contract terms on pilots. In retaliation, pilots began reporting maintenance items shortly before takeoff. This resulted in flight delays, cancellations, and unhappy passengers. There were also several instances of seats coming loose. American used e-mail and various social media to explain to its customers the various steps the airline was taking to solve the crises.

Social media can also be used to amplify a promotional campaign by inviting consumers to join the conversation about a brand. In turn, consumers (hopefully) share their positive experiences with others. When Starbucks wanted to increase awareness of its brand, for example, it launched a competition challenging its Twitter followers to be the first to tweet a photograph of one of the new advertising posters that the company had placed in six major U.S. cities. The fastest tweeters received a $20 Starbucks gift card. This social media effort delivered a marketing punch that significantly outweighed its budget. Starbucks said that the effort was "the difference between launching an advertising campaign with millions of dollars versus millions of fans."[14]

4-3 DEMOGRAPHIC FACTORS

Another uncontrollable variable in the external environment—also extremely important to marketing managers—is demography, the study of people's vital statistics, such as age, race and ethnicity, and location. Demographics are significant because the basis for any market is people. Demographic characteristics are strongly related to consumer buyer behavior in the marketplace.

4-3a Population

People are directly or indirectly the basis of all markets, making population the most basic statistic in marketing. The world's population hit 7 billion in 2012. China has the largest population with 1.34 billion persons; India is second with 1.24 billion.[15] Census data put the U.S. population at 315 million in January 2013. The country grew by 27 million from 2000 to 2010. But growth was unevenly distributed. Metropolitan areas, defined as the collection of small cities and suburbs that surround an urban core with at least 50,000 people, accounted for most of the gain, growing 10.8 percent over the decade to 257.7 million people.[16]

Rural areas, meanwhile, grew just 4.5 percent to 51 million. Many regions—from the Great Plains to the Mississippi delta to rural New England—saw population declines. About 46 percent of rural counties lost population in the decade, including almost 60 percent of rural counties that aren't adjacent to a metro area.[17] In many parts of the country, multigenerational households are increasingly common. More than 5 million households contain at least two adult generations.[18]

Population is a broad statistic that is most useful to marketers when broken into smaller, more specific increments. For example, age groups present opportunities to focus on a section of the population and offer opportunities for marketers. These groups are called tweens, teens, Generation Y, Generation X, and baby boomers. Each cohort has its own needs, values, and consumption patterns.

demography the study of people's vital statistics, such as age, race and ethnicity, and location

4-3b Tweens

America's tweens (ages eight to twelve) are a population of more than 20 million. With access to information, opinions, and sophistication well beyond their years (and purchasing power to match), these young consumers are directly or indirectly responsible for sales of over $180 billion annually. Tweens themselves spend about $30 billion per year, and the remainder is spent by parents and family members for them.[19] For example, the average family budget for back-to-school clothes is $688.62.[20]

Kaci Tamburro gives tea to her American Girl doll while having lunch at the American Girl store in Los Angeles.

With such spending power, this age group is very attractive to many markets. One of the fastest growing tween markets is home décor. Both boys and girls want their rooms to be more than just rooms, and retailers such as Pottery Barn, Pier 1 Imports, and other home goods retailers sell bedding, furniture, and wall art designed specifically for tweens. By introducing tweens to home furnishings at a younger age, these firms hope to keep their business as they change their fashion sense and need to furnish dorms or apartments for college.[21]

Tweens are also making an effort to look more mature at a younger age. Sixty-one percent of tween girls would like to wear more makeup than their parents allow. Covering tweens and most teens, 37 percent of girls ages nine to seventeen say they use lip gloss or lipstick every day, while 33 percent report applying mascara on a daily basis. Twenty-seven percent stencil on eyeliner every day, and 16 percent use foundation every day. Tweens are most likely to rely on their mothers to help with purchasing decisions (73 percent).[22]

Tweens have grown up with mobile technology and social media and begin using it at an early age. For example, 15 percent of tweens have a smartphone or mobile phone.[23] And although they are too young to participate on social media sites such as Facebook and Twitter, tweens have their own social media outlets, such as Walt Disney's Club Penguin. Recently, tweens have moved to new sites such as FashionPlaytes.com, a meeting place aimed at girls ages five to twelve who are interested in designing clothes. Everloop, a social network for kids under the age of thirteen, and Viddy, a video-sharing site that functions similarly to Instagram, are also popular with tweens.

Tweens respond very favorably to having control over, or being able to create, their own experiences. Two companies that do an excellent job of this are Build-A-Bear and American Girl. Targeted to tween girls, American Girl stores sell dolls, accessories, books, and more. Located in major markets, such as New York, Chicago, and Dallas, the stores offer a unique experience for the child. After purchasing one of the dolls (around $80), the child can shop for accessories and visit the dining room or birthday party area. Each area of the store features a specific doll and associated merchandise. A doll named Molly, for example, not only offers the obligatory clothes but also six books about the character, camping equipment and a tent, and a bedtime set. Many outfits are also offered in tween sizes so the doll and child can match. Finally, the purchaser can bring the doll to the

American Girl store to have the doll's hair washed and set and, if so inclined, get the doll's ears pierced.[24]

4-3c Teens

There are approximately 25 million teenagers in the United States, and they spend approximately seventy-two hours per week tuned in electronically to television, the Internet, music, video games, and cell phones. About 95 percent of U.S. teens use the Internet, 77 percent own a cell phone, and 74 percent say they text. Seventy-five percent of teens in the United States are into social networking. Among those, 93 percent have Facebook accounts, while just 12 percent have Twitter accounts and 2 percent have Tumblr accounts. These figures may soon be changing, however. A 2013 survey found that social media newcomers Snapchat, Instagram, and Tumblr are growing in popularity among teens. Currently, twenty-seven percent of teens record and upload video, while 37 percent participate in video chats.[25]

For teens, shopping has become a social sport whether online or at the mall, though most teens prefer to shop in stores instead of online.[26] They patronize big box retailers such as Best Buy and luxury boutiques such as Michael Kors—with little room for retailers in between. Teens love Taco Bell and Coca-Cola as much as they love Gucci and Coach.[27] On average, just over $156 is spent on or by every American teen each week. A teen's average annual income is $3,095, while 21 percent of teens qualify themselves as unemployed.[28] Thirty-one percent of teen spending goes toward clothing, shoes, and accessories, and the biggest purchase influence comes from friends.[29] There are two key strategies to effectively market to teens:

▸ **MAKE THE PRODUCT MODERN AND CONVENIENT.** When it first launched, Apple's iPod addressed a timeless teen activity: listening to music. Apple made a device that was easy to use, compact, and held a large library. Suffice to say, the original iPod was a huge hit with teens, as have been many versions released since. Electronic book readers, such as the Kindle, have not yet had the same level of success with teens.

▸ **ENGAGE TEENS THROUGH PROMOTIONS THAT GET THEM INVOLVED.** Teens want to be a part of the action. On YouTube, there are millions of teens posting videos touting their lifestyles, wants, needs, and emotions. It is important to engage teens with interactive contests and voting challenges, and to empower the teen audience with

the opportunity to help develop new ideas, commercials, and brand names. Companies have set up online communities with the sole purpose of getting feedback and ideas from teens.

4-3d Generation Y

Generation Y, also called the millennial generation, is made up of people born between 1979 and 1994. Initially, Generation Y was a smaller cohort than baby boomers. However, due to immigration and the aging of the boomer generation, the 77 million Gen Yers in the United States passed the boomers in total population in 2010. Millennials are currently in two different stages of the life cycle. The youngest members of Gen Y, born in 1994, are just entering young adulthood. In contrast, the oldest Gen Yers, born in 1979, turned thirty-five years old in 2014. They have started their careers, and many have become parents for the first time, leading to dramatic lifestyle changes. They care for their babies rather than go out, and they spend money on baby products. Gen Yers already spend more than $200 billion annually; over their lifetimes, they will likely spend about $10 trillion. No group was hit harder by the Great Recession of 2008–2009 than the Millennials. Many found their newly launched careers stalled or their jobs eliminated. The lucky ones have been able to keep their jobs during the difficult economic times and are making major purchasing decisions such as cars and homes; at the very least, they are buying computers, MP3 players, smartphones, tablet computers, and sneakers.

Millennials may be the most tech-savvy generation yet, spending more time surfing the Web and on social media than they do watching television, listening to radio, or reading newspapers, but they still use and value traditional media. Gen Yers expect brands to be on social media. Two-thirds say a brand being on social media shows it cares about their generation, and 56 percent think social media sites are a great way to find out what's new with brands they like. That may be why 64 percent have liked a brand on Facebook and follow an average of ten brands or companies.[30]

4-3e Generation X

Generation X—people born between 1965 and 1978—consists of 50 million U.S. consumers. It was the first generation of latchkey children—products of dual-career households or, in roughly half of the cases, of divorced or separated parents. Gen Xers often spent more time without adult support and guidance than any other age cohort. This experience made them independent, resilient, adaptable, cautious, and skeptical.[31]

Gen Xers, like the Millennials, have also been hit hard by the Great Recession. As one Gen Xer noted, "I don't know anyone in my age group who's 'where they want to be' from a financial perspective." Many Gen Xers face stagnant careers, growing debt, and a 59 percent decline in net worth from 2005 to 2010—the largest drop of all age groups.[32] Difficult financial times have made Gen Xers big spenders at discounters such as Walmart. Gen Xers' annual income dropped about 11 percent from 2000 to 2010. This was partially due to baby boomers delaying retirement and keeping high-paying jobs and Gen Yers moving up and being willing to work for less. Gen Xers' home ownership rates declined more than any other group during the Great Recession.[33]

The good economic news regarding Gen Xers is that they are entering their peak earning and spending years. By far, Xers spend more on food than any other generational demographic. Xers also spend 62 percent more on housing, 50 percent more on apparel, and 27 percent more on entertainment than average, likely because many Xers are in their child-rearing years. Xers constitute 45 percent of households with children, making this generation a primary target for marketers promoting family-oriented products and services.[34]

4-3f Baby Boomers

In 2012, there were approximately 75 million **baby boomers** (persons born between 1946 and 1964) in the United States. With average life expectancy at an all-time high of 77.4 years, more and more Americans over fifty consider middle age a new start on life. Boomers are carrying substantial financial burdens, including mortgages, health care expenses, and their children's educations. Many are postponing retirement to pay these debts.[35] Still, they control about 70 percent of America's net worth—approximately $7 trillion—and they spend disproportionately more money than other

age group.[36] Boomers spend $1.8 trillion annually on food, cars, personal care, and other personal products.

Unfortunately, some marketers believe that boomers are set in their ways and figured out what to buy many years ago, so there is no point in marketing to them. In fact, the opposite is true. Research has found that boomers are willing to change brands and try new things, making them an ideal group—affluent, experienced, and flexible.[37] For example, an analysis of consumers who bought P&G's Swiffer Sweeper found that boomers bought more Swiffers than any other age bracket. They were also more likely to try not just the original product, but four newer versions.[38]

Boomers' ability and willingness to spend have prompted marketers to develop new advertisement campaigns that they will find relatable. Because of this trend,

WHEN ONE HEART GOES HEART HEALTHY, TWO HEARTS CELEBRATE.

This advertisement for Campbell's soup appeals to baby boomers' desire for new experiences, rewarding relationships, and healthy living.

demand for models and actors in their forties and fifties has increased. Casting agent Kristy Martin's most-booked client is in her forties, while professional fashion photographer and baby boomer Liz Garza has noticed more and more of her contemporaries coming in front of her camera. "Even though we have a little gray in our hair, our money is green," said Garza.[39]

Since 2010, Walgreens has been gradually adapting its 7,655 stores to be friendlier to aging boomers. Subtle changes make it easier to navigate stores. Many stores have positioned magnifying glasses in aisles that carry products with lots of fine print, such as household cleaners, hair color, and cold medicine. The chain is also redesigning its reading glasses styles and releasing newer models more often. "This customer is focused not just on function but on fashion," says Robert Tompkins, Walgreens' divisional vice president and general merchandise manager. Walgreens has also introduced easier-to-open packages on its private-label painkillers and other products and expanded its vitamin aisles.[40]

4-4 GROWING ETHNIC MARKETS

The United States Hispanic consumer market is now larger than all but 13 world economies. African American buying power increased 73 percent between 2000 and 2012, while Asian American buying power increased a whopping 165 percent over the same period—both eclipsing the 60 percent increase among Caucasians.[41]

The minority population of the United States reached 115 million in 2013. About one in three U.S. residents is a member of a minority group. By 2050, about one in three U.S. residents will be Hispanic. Currently, nonwhite minorities account for 50.4 percent of the children born in the United States.[42] Hawaii (77.1 percent), the District of Columbia (64.7 percent), New Mexico (59.8 percent), California (60.3 percent), and Texas (55.2 percent) are all majority-minority areas in the United States.[43] The United States will flip to majority-minority completely in 2041, meaning whites of European ancestry will make up less than 50 percent of the total population. Today there are more Hispanics living in the United States than there are Canadians in Canada. Hispanics accounted for most of the population growth in the 2010 census. Without Hispanics, America's under-eighteen population would have actually declined.[44]

As you'll see in the following sections, minority populations embrace other cultures while continuing to patronize companies that understand their native cultural preferences. Smart marketers are reaching out and tapping these dynamic, growing markets with a wide range of products and targeted advertising. For example, an increasing number of companies are meeting the Association of Hispanic Advertising Agencies (AHAA) Best-In-Class requirement, meaning that they spend more than 11.8 percent of their total advertising budget on Hispanic media. As of 2013, the forty companies receiving the AHAA's Best-In-Class recognition averaged a budgetary allotment of 21.4 percent.[45]

4-4a Marketing to Hispanic Americans

The term *Hispanic* encompasses people of many different backgrounds. Nearly 60 percent of Hispanic Americans are of Mexican descent. Puerto Ricans, the next largest group, make up just under 10 percent of Hispanics. Other groups, including Central Americans, Dominicans, South Americans, and Cubans, each account for less than 5 percent of all Hispanics.

The diversity of the Hispanic population and the language differences create many challenges for those trying to target this market. Hispanics, especially recent immigrants, often prefer products from their native country. Therefore, many retailers along the southern U.S. border import goods from Mexico. If the brands found in their homeland are not available, Hispanics will choose brands that reflect their native values and culture.

Kraft Foods has realized that the Internet is a good way to connect with Hispanics. The company launched Comida Kraft (**www.comidakraft.com**), where Hispanics can share or post their recipes online, through the specialized Recipe Connection page. This page encourages Hispanic consumers to submit their favorite recipes containing at least one Kraft food product, "perhaps one that has been passed down in your family or an original creation from your own kitchen." Many of the recipes later appear in *Comida y Familia*, a Spanish-language recipe index published by Kraft.

Kleenex, the tissue brand of Kimberly-Clark Corp., is a top seller among consumers, but a smaller percentage of Hispanics buy Kleenex compared to the general market. To amend this, Kleenex decided to orchestrate its first marketing campaign targeted exclusively at Hispanic consumers. Kleenex approached Miami-based marketing agency MASS

THE CHANGING HISPANIC MARKET

For many years, broadcast media have assumed that immigrants, as they settled into the United States, would move away from Hispanic channels to mainstream media. However, there are key changes in the Hispanic market that are challenging that assumption. Over the last decade, the largest growth in the Hispanic population has come from births, not immigration. With such a large number of children being raised inside the United States, it should come as little surprise to researchers that 80 percent of the Latino population prefers English or bilingual programming. Univision and Telemundo, the largest Hispanic broadcast television networks, both have English subtitles on their prime-time telenovelas, and Univision broke its all-Spanish programming tradition by interviewing Republican presidential hopefuls in English with a Spanish translation. The new assumption seems to be that Hispanics have acculturated and are maintaining the best parts of their cultures while adapting some aspects of American culture.[46]

© iStockphoto.com/billnoll

Hispanic Inc. for help. According to MASS, more than twice as many Hispanics make their purchase decisions based on package and design compared to the general population, so Kleenex and MASS decided to create limited-time custom packaging to attract Hispanic consumers. To increase potential sales, Kleenex wanted the customized packages to be distributed during National Hispanic Heritage Month.

The resulting campaign, *"Con Kleenex, Expresa Tu Hispanidad,"* gave amateur artists the chance to submit work to be considered for Kleenex package designs. Consumers voted on the submissions and the three top designs were sold in stores nationwide. The three winning artists each received $5,000, while nine runner-ups netted $500 apiece. Not only was the campaign a way for Kleenex to communicate with Hispanics directly, it also celebrated Hispanic artists and culture.[47]

4-4b Marketing to African Americans

African Americans are nearly six years younger on average than other American consumers; 47 percent are between eighteen and forty-nine years old, which is considered the top-spending age demographic by marketers. Although their population is smaller, there are more African American households in the United States than Hispanic households because the latter tend to have larger families.[48] Fifty-four percent of African American children are raised exclusively by their mothers—that number jumps to 88 percent below the poverty line.[49]

Several companies owned by African Americans—such as SoftSheen-Carson and Pro-Line—target the African American market for health and beauty aids. Huge corporations like Revlon, Gillette, and Alberto Culver have either divisions or major product lines for this market as

well. The promotional dollars spent on African Americans continue to rise, as does the number of black media choices. BET, the Black Entertainment Television network, has more than 80 million viewers. The forty-five-year-old *Essence* magazine reaches one-third of all black females aged eighteen to forty-nine. African Americans spend considerable time with radio (an astounding 4 hours a day versus 2.8 hours for other groups), and urban audiences have an intensely personal relationship with the medium. ABC Radio Networks' Tom Joyner reaches an audience of more than 8 million in 115 markets, and Doug Banks is heard by 1.5 million listeners in 36 markets. Recent research shows that more African Americans than ever before are achieving the American dream. In 2012, there were 2.8 million African Americans earning more than $75,000 annually.[50]

4-4c Marketing to Asian Americans

The Asian American population is the fastest growing among minority groups. It quadrupled to about 17 million between 1980 and 2012.[51] Asian Americans, who represent only 6 percent of the U.S. population, have the highest average family income of all groups. At $68,780, it exceeds the average U.S. household income by roughly $15,000. Fifty-two percent of Asian Americans over age twenty-five have at least a bachelor's degree.[52] Because Asian Americans are younger (the average age is thirty-four), better educated, and have higher incomes than average, they are sometimes called a "marketer's dream." Asian Americans are heavy users of technology. Moreover, they are early adopters of the latest digital gadgets. They visit computer and consumer electronics Web sites 36 percent more often and spend 72 percent more time at these sites than the total population.[53] Because of their high level

In addition to social and demographic factors, marketing managers must understand and react to the economic environment. The three economic areas of greatest concern to most marketers are consumers' incomes, inflation, and recession.

4-5a Consumers' Incomes

As disposable (or after-tax) incomes rise, more families and individuals can afford the "good life." In recent years, however, average U.S. incomes have actually fallen. The annual median household income in the United States in 2012 was approximately $50,000, though the median household income varies widely from state to state. This means half of all U.S. households earned less, and the other half earned more. Census data shows that average family incomes, when adjusted for inflation (discussed later in the chapter), fell around 8 percent between 2007 and 2011.[54] Income fell the most in the South, West, and Florida.[55] These areas also had the largest declines in home values and housing construction. With jobs scarce, many people have accepted pay cuts to keep their current jobs or have taken less-paying—but available—jobs.[56]

Education is the primary determinant of a person's earning potential. For example, just 1 percent of workers with only a high school education earn over $100,000 annually. By comparison, 13 percent of college-educated workers earn six figures or more. People with a bachelor's degree take home an average of 38 percent more than those with just a high school diploma. Over a lifetime, an individual with a bachelor's degree will earn more than twice as much total income as a nondegree holder.[57]

Today's business headlines discuss "the demise of the middle class" and "the shrinking middle class." The Great Recession, and resulting slow growth, have indeed squeezed the middle class, which, with annual household incomes between $50,000 and $140,000, comprises about 40 percent of all households.[58]

AP Images/Shiho Fukada

Women shop for symbolic Chinese New Year flowers at a New York City Chinatown flower market.

of education, Asian Americans are thriving in America's technology sector.

Although Asian Americans embrace the values of the larger U.S. population, they also hold on to the cultural values of their particular subgroup. Consider language: many Asian Americans, particularly Koreans and Chinese, speak their native tongue at home (though Filipinos are far less likely to do so). Cultural values are also apparent in the ways different groups make big-ticket purchases. In Japanese American homes, husbands alone make large purchase decisions nearly half the time; wives decide only about 6 percent of the time. In Filipino families, however, wives make these decisions a little more often than their husbands do, although, by far, most decisions are made by husbands and wives jointly or with the input of other family members.

Asian Americans like to shop at stores owned and managed by other Asian Americans. Small businesses such as flower shops, grocery stores, and appliance stores are often best equipped to offer the products that Asian Americans want. For example, at first glance, the Hannam Chain supermarket in Los Angeles's Koreatown seems like any other grocery store. But next to the Kraft American singles and the State Fair corn dogs are jars of whole cabbage kimchi. A snack bar in another part of the store cooks up aromatic mung cakes, and an entire aisle is devoted to dried seafood.

In recent years, stores that cater to lower-income consumers—like Family Dollar and Dollar General—have done well. P&G has found that its typical middle-class customers are increasingly unwilling to spend their money on household staples with extra features, such as Tide with bleach. Many customers have switched to cheaper brands while P&G brands like Bounce fabric softener and Bounty paper towels suffered. To regain market share, P&G has launched its bargain-priced Gain dish soap. The firm has also reduced some package sizes of Tide in order to sell them at Walmart for less than ten dollars.[59]

4-5b Purchasing Power

Even when incomes rise, a higher standard of living does not necessarily result. Increased standards of living are a function of purchasing power. **Purchasing power** is measured by comparing income to the relative cost of a standard set of goods and services in different geographic areas, usually referred to as the *cost of living*. Another way to think of purchasing power is income minus the cost of living (i.e., expenses). In general, a cost of living index takes into account housing, food and groceries, transportation, utilities, health care, and miscellaneous expenses such as clothing, services, and entertainment. HomeFair.com's salary calculator uses these metrics when it determines that the cost of living in New York City is almost three times the cost of living in Youngstown, Ohio. This means that a worker living in New York City must earn nearly $279,500 to have the same standard of living as someone making $100,000 in Youngstown.

When income is high relative to the cost of living, people have more discretionary income. That means they have more money to spend on nonessential items (in other words, on wants rather than needs). This information is important to marketers for obvious reasons. Consumers with high purchasing power can afford to spend more money without jeopardizing their budget for necessities like food, housing, and utilities. They also have the ability to purchase higher-priced necessities—for example, a more expensive car, a home in a more expensive neighborhood, or a designer handbag versus a purse from a discount store.

4-5c Inflation

Inflation is a measure of the decrease in the value of money, generally expressed as the percentage reduction in value since the previous year, which is the rate of inflation. Thus, in simple terms, an inflation rate of 5 percent means you will need 5 percent more units of money than you would have needed last year to buy the same basket of products. If inflation is 5 percent, you can expect that, on average, prices have risen by about 5 percent since the previous year. Of course, if pay raises are matching the rate of inflation, then employees will be no worse off in terms of the immediate purchasing power of their salaries.

In times of low inflation, businesses seeking to increase their profit margins can do so only by increasing their efficiency. If they significantly increase prices, no one will purchase their goods or services. The Great Recession brought inflation rates to almost zero.

In creating marketing strategies to cope with inflation, managers must realize that, regardless of what happens to the seller's cost, the buyer is not going to pay more for a product than the subjective value he or she places on it. No matter how compelling the justification might be for a 10 percent price increase, marketers must always examine its impact on demand. Many marketers try to hold prices level for as long as is practical.

4-5d Recession

A **recession** is a period of economic activity characterized by negative growth. More precisely, a recession is defined as occurring when the gross domestic product falls for two consecutive quarters. Gross domestic product is the total market value of all final goods and services produced during a period of time. The official beginning of the Great Recession of 2008–2009 was December 2007. While the causes of the recession are very complex, this one began with the collapse of inflated housing prices. Those high prices led people to take out mortgages they couldn't afford from banks that should have known the money would not be repaid. By 2008, the recession had spread around the globe. A very slow economic recovery began in July 2009 and continues to this day.

The Great Recession was the largest economic downturn since the Great Depression, which spanned 1929 to 1939. Unemployment rose from slightly over 4 percent to over 10 percent.[60] The unemployment rate has been slowly falling since mid-2010 due to job creation and people leaving the workforce entirely. Uncertain economic times have caused many consumers to shift to store brands. Upscale Australian clothing and home goods chain Myer saw a 5.5 percent growth in private brands over the fiscal year 2012, compared to a 1.3 percent decline in overall sales. Private brands now account for more than 19 percent of Myer's overall sales—up from 7 percent ten years earlier.[61] Wary of economic uncertainty and still burdened by massive credit card debts, more consumers have begun using coupons, cutting out frivolous purchases, putting fewer charges on their credit cards, and paying down their balances.[62]

4-6 TECHNOLOGICAL FACTORS

The recent economic downturn and slow recovery have had an impact on research and development (R&D) spending. In order to cut costs and boost short-term profits, many companies, particularly in the auto and drug industries, slashed R&D, product design, and laboratory spending. Other firms have taken a different track and either increased or held R&D spending steady, hoping that they will be able to compete more effectively when the economy improves. Companies such as 3M, Microsoft, Google, Intel, and Cisco Systems have followed this strategy. Without investment in R&D, the United States cannot compete in a knowledge-based global economy.

4-6a Research

The United States, historically, has excelled at both basic and applied research. **Basic research** (or *pure research*) attempts to expand the frontiers of knowledge but is not aimed at a specific, pragmatic problem. Basic research aims to confirm an existing theory or to learn more about a concept or phenomenon. For example, basic research might focus on high-energy physics. **Applied research**, in contrast, attempts to develop new or improved products. The United States has dramatically improved its track record in applied research. For example, the United States leads the world in applying basic research to aircraft design and propulsion systems.

4-6b Stimulating Innovation

Companies attempting to innovate often limit their searches to areas they are already familiar with. This can help lead to incremental progress but rarely leads to a dramatic breakthrough. For the past decade, P&G has focused on reformulating products instead of inventing new ones.[63] Thus, it hasn't had a blockbuster new product in over a decade and sales have suffered. Companies are now using several approaches to keep innovation strong. These include:

▸ **BUILDING SCENARIOS:** Some firms use teams of writers to imagine detailed opportunities and threats for their companies, partners, and collaborators in future markets.

▸ **ENLISTING THE WEB:** A few companies have created Web sites that act as literal marketplaces of ideas where they can go to look for help with scientific and business challenges.

▸ **TALKING TO EARLY ADOPTERS:** Early adopters tend to be innovators themselves. They are risk takers and look for new things or wish for something better to help in daily tasks at home and work.

▸ **USING MARKETING RESEARCH:** Firms find out what customers like and dislike about their products and competitors' products.

▸ **CREATING AN INNOVATIVE ENVIRONMENT:** Companies let employees know that they have the "freedom to fail." They create intranets to encourage sharing ideas. Most importantly, top management must lead by example to create an atmosphere where innovation is encouraged and rewarded.

▸ **CATERING TO ENTREPRENEURS:** Policies that reserve blocks of time for scientists or engineers to explore their own ideas have worked well at some companies. At 3M, scientists can spend 15 percent of their time on projects they dream up themselves—a freedom that led to the development of the yellow Post-It note. Google is well known in the tech industry for its "20% time" policy, which grants employees a day a week to follow their entrepreneurial passions.[64]

Although developing new technology internally is a key to creating and maintaining a long-term competitive advantage, external technology is also important to managers for two reasons. First, by acquiring the technology,

basic research
pure research that aims to confirm an existing theory or to learn more about a concept or phenomenon

applied research
research that attempts to develop new or improved products

© iStockphoto.com/james steidl

the firm may be able to operate more efficiently or create a better product. Second, a new technology may render existing products obsolete.

Recently, China has been rolling out an array of interlocking regulations and state spending aimed at making their country a global technology powerhouse by 2020. The new initiatives—shaped by rising nationalism and a belief that foreign companies unfairly dominate key technologies—range from big investments in national industries to patent laws that favor Chinese companies and mandates that essentially require foreign companies to transfer technology to China if they hope to sell in that market. The U.S. Chamber of Commerce, a business trade group, called China's actions, "an intricate web of new rules considered by many international technology companies to be a blueprint for technology theft on a scale the world has never seen before."[65] This issue promises to dominate relations between the two countries for years to come.

The Chinese government has money to spend on innovation—the problem is knowing *how* to spend it. Even in the United States, the biggest spenders on research and development, such as Pfizer, Ford, Johnson & Johnson, and IBM, have not been the most innovative. Those honors go to Apple, Google, Exxon, and Tenneco.[66]

Business needs government regulation to protect innovators of new technology, the interests of society in general, one business from another, and consumers. In turn, government needs business because the marketplace generates taxes that support public efforts to educate our youth, pave our roads, protect our shores, and the like.

Every aspect of the marketing mix is subject to laws and restrictions. It is the duty of marketing managers or their legal assistants to understand these laws and conform to them, because failure to comply with regulations can have major consequences for a firm. Sometimes just sensing trends and taking corrective action before a government agency acts can help avoid regulation.

4-7a Federal Legislation

Federal laws that affect marketing fall into several categories of regulatory activity: competitive environment, pricing, advertising and promotion, and consumer privacy. The key pieces of legislation in these areas are summarized in Exhibit 1. The primary federal laws that protect consumers are shown in Exhibit 2. It should also be noted that the Patient Protection and Affordable Care Act, commonly called Obamacare, will have a significant impact on marketing. One provision, for example, says that any restaurant chain with more than twenty stores must post its nutrition details for every item on the menu. An H&R Block commercial released in early 2013 highlighted the effect of Obamacare on personal tax filing: "The Affordable Care Act means big changes this year when you file your taxes," says the commercial's spokesperson, "I know the law, I have the solution, and I can help you figure it out."[67]

In 2010, Congress passed the Restoring American Financial Stability Act that brought sweeping changes to bank and financial market regulations. The legislation created the Consumer Financial Protection Bureau to oversee checking accounts, private student loans, mortgages, and other financial products. The agency deals with unfair, abusive, and deceptive practices.

4-7b State Laws

Legislation that affects marketing varies state by state. Oregon, for example, limits utility advertising to 0.5 percent of the company's net income. California has forced industry to improve consumer products and has enacted legislation to lower the energy consumption of refrigerators, freezers, and air conditioners. Several states, including California and North Carolina, are considering levying a tax on all in-state commercial advertising.

Many states and cities are attempting to fight obesity by regulating fast-food chains and other restaurants. For example, California and New York have passed a law banning trans fats in restaurants and bakeries, New York City chain restaurants must now display calorie counts on menus, and Boston has banned trans fats in restaurants. New York City recently enacted a law prohibiting restaurants from selling soft drinks larger than 16 ounces, but the ban was overturned a day before it was to go into effect.

4-7c Regulatory Agencies

Although some state regulatory bodies actively pursue violators of their marketing statutes, federal regulators generally have the greatest clout. The Consumer Product Safety Commission, the Federal Trade Commission, and the Food and Drug Administration are the three federal agencies most directly and actively involved in marketing affairs. These agencies, plus others, are discussed throughout the book, but a brief introduction is in order at this point.

The sole purpose of the **Consumer Product Safety Commission (CPSC)** is to protect the health and safety of consumers in and around their homes. The CPSC has the power to set mandatory safety standards for almost all products consumers use (about 15,000 items) and can fine offending firms up to $500,000 and sentence their officers to up to a year in prison. It can also ban dangerous products from the marketplace. The CPSC oversees about 400 recalls per year. In 2008, Congress passed the Consumer Product Safety Improvement Act. The law is aimed primarily at children's products, which are defined as those used by individuals twelve years old or younger. The law addresses items such as cribs, electronics and video games, school supplies, science kits, toys, and pacifiers. The law requires mandatory testing and labeling and increases fines and prison time for violators.

The **Food and Drug Administration (FDA)**, another powerful agency, is charged with enforcing regulations against selling and distributing adulterated, misbranded, or hazardous food and drug products. In 2009, the Tobacco Control Act was passed. This act gave the FDA authority to regulate tobacco products, with a special emphasis on

Consumer Product Safety Commission (CPSC) a federal agency established to protect the health and safety of consumers in and around their homes

Food and Drug Administration (FDA) a federal agency charged with enforcing regulations against selling and distributing adulterated, misbranded, or hazardous food and drug products

---

Exhibit 1

PRIMARY U.S. LAWS THAT AFFECT MARKETING

Legislation	Impact on Marketing
Sherman Act of 1890	Makes trusts and conspiracies in restraint of trade illegal; makes monopolies and attempts to monopolize misdemeanors.
Clayton Act of 1914	Outlaws discrimination in prices to different buyers; prohibits tying contracts (which require the buyer of one product to also buy another item in the line); makes illegal the combining of two or more competing corporations by pooling ownership of stock.
Federal Trade Commission Act of 1914	Created the Federal Trade Commission to deal with antitrust matters; outlaws unfair methods of competition.
Robinson-Patman Act of 1936	Prohibits charging different prices to different buyers of merchandise of like grade and quantity; requires sellers to make any supplementary services or allowances available to all purchasers on a proportionately equal basis.
Wheeler-Lea Amendments to FTC Act of 1938	Broadens the Federal Trade Commission's power to prohibit practices that might injure the public without affecting competition; outlaws false and deceptive advertising.
Lanham Act of 1946	Establishes protection for trademarks.
Celler-Kefauver Antimerger Act of 1950	Strengthens the Clayton Act to prevent corporate acquisitions that reduce competition.
Hart-Scott-Rodino Act of 1976	Requires large companies to notify the government of their intent to merge.
Foreign Corrupt Practices Act of 1977	Prohibits bribery of foreign officials to obtain business.

Exhibit 2
PRIMARY U.S. LAWS PROTECTING CONSUMERS

Legislation	Impact on Marketing
Federal Food and Drug Act of 1906	Prohibits adulteration and misbranding of foods and drugs involved in interstate commerce; strengthened by the Food, Drug, and Cosmetic Act (1938) and the Kefauver-Harris Drug Amendment (1962).
Federal Hazardous Substances Act of 1960	Requires warning labels on hazardous household chemicals.
Kefauver-Harris Drug Amendment of 1962	Requires that manufacturers conduct tests to prove drug effectiveness and safety.
Consumer Credit Protection Act of 1968	Requires that lenders fully disclose true interest rates and all other charges to credit customers for loans and installment purchases.
Child Protection and Toy Safety Act of 1969	Prevents marketing of products so dangerous that adequate safety warnings cannot be given.
Public Health Smoking Act of 1970	Prohibits cigarette advertising on television and radio and revises the health hazard warning on cigarette packages.
Poison Prevention Labeling Act of 1970	Requires safety packaging for products that may be harmful to children.
National Environmental Policy Act of 1970	Established the Environmental Protection Agency to deal with various types of pollution and organizations that create pollution.
Public Health Cigarette Smoking Act of 1971	Prohibits tobacco advertising on radio and television.
Consumer Product Safety Act of 1972	Created the Consumer Product Safety Commission, which has authority to specify safety standards for most products.
Child Protection Act of 1990	Regulates the number of minutes of advertising on children's television.
Children's Online Privacy Protection Act of 1998	Empowers the FTC to set rules regarding how and when marketers must obtain parental permission before asking children marketing research questions.
Aviation Security Act of 2001	Requires airlines to take extra security measures to protect passengers, including the installation of stronger cockpit doors, improved baggage screening, and increased security training for airport personnel.
Homeland Security Act of 2002	Protects consumers against terrorist acts; created the Department of Homeland Security.
Do Not Call Law of 2003	Protects consumers against unwanted telemarketing calls.
CAN-SPAM Act of 2003	Protects consumers against unwanted e-mail, or spam.
Credit Card Act of 2009	Provides many credit card protections.
Restoring American Financial Stability Act of 2010	Created the Consumer Financial Protection Bureau to protect consumers against unfair, abusive, and deceptive financial practices.

© Cengage Learning

Federal Trade Commission (FTC) a federal agency empowered to prevent persons or corporations from using unfair methods of competition in commerce

preventing their use by children and young people and reducing the impact of tobacco on public health. Another recent FDA action is the "Bad Ad" program. It is geared toward health care providers to help them recognize misleading prescription drug promotions and gives them an easy way to report the activity to the FDA.

The **Federal Trade Commission (FTC)** is empowered to prevent persons or corporations from using unfair methods of competition in commerce. The FTC consists of five members, each holding office for seven years. Over the years, Congress has greatly

expanded the powers of the FTC. Its responsibilities have grown so large that the FTC has created several bureaus to better organize its operations. One of the most important is the Bureau of Competition, which promotes and protects competition. The Bureau of Competition:

➤➤ reviews mergers and acquisitions, and challenges those that would likely lead to higher prices, fewer choices, or less innovation;

➤➤ seeks out and challenges anti-competitive conduct in the marketplace, including monopolization and agreements between competitors;

➤➤ promotes competition in industries where consumer impact is high, such as health care, real estate, oil and gas, technology, and consumer goods; and

- provides information and holds conferences and workshops for consumers, businesses, and policy makers on competition issues for market analysis.[68]

The FTC's Bureau of Consumer Protection works for the consumer to prevent fraud, deception, and unfair business practices in the marketplace. The Bureau of Consumer Protection claims that it:

- enhances consumer confidence by enforcing federal laws that protect consumers;

- empowers consumers with free information to help them exercise their rights and to spot and avoid fraud and deception; and

- wants to hear from consumers who want to get information or file a complaint about fraud or identity theft.[69]

Another important FTC bureau is the Bureau of Economics. It provides economic analysis and support to antitrust and consumer protection investigations. Many consumer protection issues today involve the Internet.

CONSUMER PRIVACY The popularity of the Internet for direct marketing, for collecting consumer data, and as a repository for sensitive consumer data has alarmed privacy-minded consumers. In 2003, the U.S. Congress passed the CAN-SPAM Act in an attempt to regulate unsolicited e-mail advertising. The act prohibits commercial e-mailers from using false addresses and presenting false or misleading information, among other restrictions.

Internet users who once felt fairly anonymous when using the Web are now disturbed by the amount of information marketers collect about them and their children as they visit various sites in cyberspace. The FTC, with jurisdiction under the Children's Online Privacy Protection Act, requires Web site operators to post a privacy policy on the home page and a link to the policy on every page where personal information is collected. An area of growing concern to privacy advocates is called *behavioral targeting*, which is discussed in more detail in Chapters 9 and 16. Behavioral targeting is used by researchers to better target advertising to Web surfers and users of search engines and social media.

In 2012, the FTC called for online data collectors to adopt better privacy policies and asked Congress to pass comprehensive privacy legislation. The FTC wants data collectors to implement a "Do Not Track" button in Web browsers. "No one has the right to put anything on [your

computer] that you don't want," said Jon Leibowitz, chairman of the FTC.[70]

The agency also turned its attention to off-line data brokers—which buy and sell names, addresses, and other personal information—calling on them to create a centralized Web site providing consumers with better access to their data. The agency also wants legislation requiring data brokers to give consumers the right to see and make corrections to their information.[71]

Despite federal efforts, online tracking has become widespread and pervasive. A vast amount of personal data is collected through application software, commonly called *apps*. For example, some widely used apps on Facebook gather volumes of information when they are downloaded. A Wall Street Journal analysis of the 100 most popular Facebook apps found that some seek e-mail addresses, current locations, and even sexual preferences. Information is collected not only from app users but also from their Facebook friends.[72] One app gathered forty pieces of data about the user and twenty-one data points about friends.[73]

Companies that serve advertisements within mobile apps have started using new identifiers that collect information like location and preferences as the user moves across apps. One of the newest mobile tracking systems is based on a unique identifier located in a smartphone's wireless networking hardware—a system known as Open Device Identification Network, or ODIN. The other prominent tracking alternative, called OpenUDID, uses the device's built-in copy-and-paste function.[74] The mobile ad networks employ the new tracking system to place ads for thousands of companies, including Mazda, Nikon, and eHarmony.[75]

Successful tracking has created a $31 billion online-advertising business that is growing rapidly. In 2012, there were more than 300 companies collecting data about users.[76] More than half the time, data collectors piggyback on each other. When a user visits a Web site that has a code for one type of tracking technology, the data collection triggers other tracking technologies that

aren't embedded on the site. Piggybacking means that Web sites really don't know how much data are being gathered about their users.

4-8 COMPETITIVE FACTORS

The competitive environment encompasses the number of competitors a firm must face, the relative size of the competitors, and the degree of interdependence within the industry. Management has little control over the competitive environment confronting a firm.

4-8a Competition for Market Share and Profits

As U.S. population growth slows, global competition increases, costs rise, and available resources tighten, firms find that they must work harder to maintain their profits and market share, regardless of the form of the competitive market. Sometimes technology advances can usher in a whole new set of competitors that can change a firm's business model. For example, online learning took a leap forward when Harvard, Stanford, and other prestigious universities began offering free online courses to anyone who wanted to enroll. High-speed Internet, streaming video, and other Web-based technologies allowed students to experience instructor-led college education without investing in an expensive degree. In early 2013, forty public universities took the online learning platform a step further, announcing that they would be offering massive open online courses (MOOCs) for free—and for full credit. Developed in partnership with commercial company Academic Partnerships, the MOOC2Degree program serves as a recruitment program. Said Michael Tanner, vice president of academic affairs at the Association of Public and Land-Grant Universities, "Give them a free sample, and maybe they'll find they have an appetite for it. It's hard to say how well it will work. The MOOC business will become crowded over time."[77]

4-8b Global Competition

Boeing is a very savvy international business competitor. Now EADS, Boeing's primary competitor, is going to start assembling planes in the United States. Many foreign competitors also consider the United States to be a ripe target market. Thus, a U.S. marketing manager can no longer focus only on domestic competitors. In automobiles, textiles, watches, televisions, steel, and many other areas, foreign competition has been strong. In the past, foreign firms penetrated U.S. markets by concentrating on price, but the emphasis has switched to product quality. Nestlé, Sony, and Rolls-Royce are noted for quality, not cheap prices. Global competition is discussed in much more detail in Chapter 5.

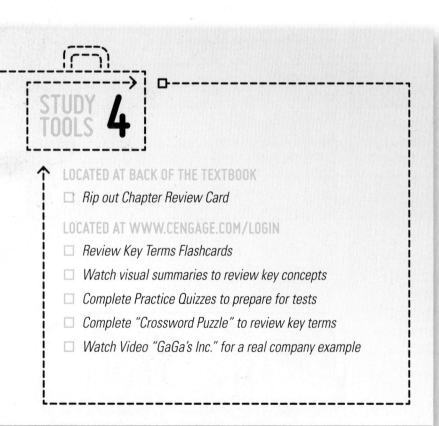

STUDY TOOLS 4

LOCATED AT BACK OF THE TEXTBOOK

☐ *Rip out Chapter Review Card*

LOCATED AT WWW.CENGAGE.COM/LOGIN

☐ *Review Key Terms Flashcards*

☐ *Watch visual summaries to review key concepts*

☐ *Complete Practice Quizzes to prepare for tests*

☐ *Complete "Crossword Puzzle" to review key terms*

☐ *Watch Video "GaGa's Inc." for a real company example*

USE THE TOOLS.

• Rip out the Review Cards in the back of your book to study.
Or Visit CourseMate to:
• Read, search, highlight, and take notes in the Interactive eBook
• Review Flashcards (Print or Online) to master key terms
• Test yourself with Auto-Graded Quizzes
• Bring concepts to life with Games, Videos,
  and Animations!

Go to CourseMate for **MKTG** to begin using these tools.
Access at **www.cengagebrain.com**

Complete the Speak Up
survey in CourseMate at
www.cengagebrain.com

f Follow us at
www.facebook.com/4ltrpress

5-1 REWARDS OF GLOBAL MARKETING

Today, global revolutions are underway in many areas of our lives: management, politics, communications, and technology. The word *global* has assumed a new meaning, referring to a boundless mobility and competition in social, business, and intellectual arenas. **Global marketing**—marketing that targets markets throughout the world—has become an imperative for business.

Over the past two decades, world trade has climbed from $200 billion a year to more than $13 trillion.

global marketing
marketing that targets markets throughout the world

global vision
recognizing and reacting to international marketing opportunities, using effective global marketing strategies, and being aware of threats from foreign competitors in all markets

U.S. managers must develop a global vision not only to recognize and react to international marketing opportunities but also to remain competitive at home. Often a U.S. firm's toughest domestic competition comes from foreign companies. Moreover, a global vision enables a manager to understand that customer and distribution networks operate worldwide, blurring geographic and political barriers and making them increasingly irrelevant to business decisions. In summary, having a **global vision** means recognizing and reacting to international marketing opportunities, using effective global marketing strategies, and being aware of threats from foreign competitors in all markets.

Over the past two decades, world trade climbed from $200 billion a year to more than $17.8 trillion in 2011. There was a 45.7 percent growth from 2009 as the world began to pull out of the global economic crisis.[1]

Today's marketers face many challenges to their customary practices. Product development costs are rising, the life of products is getting shorter, and new technology is spreading around the world faster than ever. But marketing winners relish the pace of change instead of fear it.

Adopting a global vision can be very lucrative for a company. Caterpillar, one of the world's largest manufacturers of construction and mining equipment, diesel and natural gas engines, and industrial turbines, has sales of more than $33 billion annually. Almost $21 billion comes from sales outside the United States.[2]

Despite the increasing availability of foreign customers, small businesses still account for only approximately 34 percent of U.S. exporting volume. Whether global business is daunting because of the various trade laws or tariffs, or because the markets are unfamiliar, small businesses are taking only slow, hesitant steps into the global market.[3]

Of course, global marketing is not a one-way street whereby only U.S. companies sell their wares and services throughout the world. Foreign competition in the domestic

Developing a Global Vision

Learning Outcomes

After you finish this chapter, go to
p88 *for* **STUDY TOOLS** ------->

gross domestic product (GDP) the total market value of all final goods and services produced in a country for a given time period

job outsourcing sending U.S. jobs abroad

market was once relatively rare but now is found in almost every industry. In fact, in many industries, U.S. businesses have lost significant market share to imported products. In electronics, cameras, automobiles, fine china, tractors, leather goods, and a host of other consumer and industrial products, U.S. companies have struggled at home to maintain their market shares against foreign competitors.

5-1a Importance of Global Marketing to the United States

Many countries depend more on international commerce than the United States does. For example, France, the United Kingdom, and Germany derive 27, 32, and 50 percent of their respective gross domestic products from world trade—considerably more than the United States' 14 percent.[4] **Gross domestic product (GDP)** is the total market value of all final goods and services produced in a country for a given time period (usually a year or a quarter of a year). *Final* in the definition refers to final products that are sold, not to intermediate products used in the assembly of a final product. For example, if the value of a brake (an intermediate product) and that of a car (the final product) were both counted, the brake would be counted twice. Therefore, GDP counts only the final goods and services to get the true value of a country's production.

Traditionally, only very large multinational companies have seriously attempted to compete worldwide, so most U.S. exports are shipped by large companies. Although

THE IMPACT OF EXPORTS

Although some countries depend more on international commerce than the United States does, the impact of international business on the U.S. economy is still impressive:

» The United States exports about 13 percent of its industrial production.[5]

» More than 10 million Americans hold jobs that are supported by exports.[6]

» Every U.S. state has realized net employment gains directly attributed to foreign trade.

» The United States exports more than $2.1 trillion in goods and services each year.[7]

most small- and medium-sized firms are essentially non-participants in global trade and marketing, more and more small companies have begun pursuing international markets. To increase U.S. exports, the federal government created the National Export Initiative (NEI). The NEI's goal is to double U.S. exports by 2017 and support 2 million U.S. jobs.[8] The government has also made $30 million in grants available to small businesses to begin exporting.[9]

5-1b The Impact of Trade and Globalization

Protests staged during meetings of the World Trade Organization, the World Bank, and the International Monetary Fund (the three organizations are discussed later in the chapter) have demonstrated that many people fear world trade and globalization. What do they fear? The negatives of global trade are as follows:

» **Millions of Americans have lost jobs due to imports, production shifts abroad, or outsourcing of tech jobs. Some find new jobs, but they often pay less.**

» **Millions of others fear losing their jobs, especially at those companies operating under competitive pressure.**

» **Employers often threaten to outsource jobs if workers do not accept pay cuts.**

» **Service and white-collar jobs are increasingly vulnerable to operations moving offshore.**

JOB OUTSOURCING The notion of **job outsourcing** (sending U.S. jobs abroad) has been highly controversial for several decades. Many executives say that it leads to corporate growth, efficiency, productivity, and revenue growth. Most companies see cost savings as a key driver in outsourcing. But outsourcing also has its negative side. For instance, Detroit has suffered as many factories in the auto industry have been shut down and relocated around the world. As just one example, Ford's newly reintroduced line of compact sedans and hatchbacks, called the Fiesta, is being built in several countries, including Mexico—but no Fiestas are being built in the United States.

BENEFITS OF GLOBALIZATION Traditional economic theory says that globalization relies on competition to drive down prices and increase product and service quality. Business goes to the countries that operate most efficiently and/or have the technology to produce what is needed. In summary, globalization expands economic freedom, spurs competition, and raises the productivity and living standards

Roz Woodward/Photodisc/Getty Images

© Max Earey/Shutterstock.com

multinational corporation a company that is heavily engaged in international trade, beyond exporting and importing

THE MANUFACTURE OF FORD'S FIESTA REPRESENTS ONE EXAMPLE OF NUMEROUS OUTSOURCED JOBS.

of people in countries that open themselves to the global marketplace. For less developed countries, globalization also offers access to foreign capital, global export markets, and advanced technology while breaking the monopoly of inefficient and protected domestic producers. Faster growth, in turn, reduces poverty, encourages democratization, and promotes higher labor and environmental standards. Though government officials in developing countries may face more difficult choices as a result of globalization, their citizens enjoy greater individual freedom. In this sense, globalization acts as a check on governmental power by making it more difficult for governments to abuse the freedom and property of their citizens.

Globalization deserves credit for helping lift many millions out of poverty and for improving standards of living of low-wage families. In developing countries around the world, globalization has created a vibrant middle class that has elevated the standard of living for hundreds of millions of people.

5-2 MULTINATIONAL FIRMS

The United States has a number of large companies that are global marketers. Many of them have been very successful. A company that is heavily engaged in international trade, beyond exporting and importing, is called a **multinational corporation**. A multinational corporation moves resources, goods, services, and skills across national boundaries without regard to the country in which its headquarters is located.

Multinationals often develop their global business in stages. In the first stage, companies operate in one

country and sell into others. Second-stage multinationals set up foreign subsidiaries to handle sales in one country. In the third stage, multinationals operate an entire line of business in another country. The fourth stage has evolved primarily due to the Internet and involves mostly high-tech companies. For these firms, the executive suite is virtual. Their top executives and core corporate functions are in different countries, wherever the firms can gain a competitive edge through the availability of talent or capital, low costs, or proximity to their most important customers.

A multinational company may have several worldwide headquarters, depending on where certain markets or technologies are located. Britain's APV, a maker of food-processing equipment, has a different headquarters for each of its worldwide businesses.

Many U.S.-based multinationals earn a large percentage of their total revenue abroad. Exhibit 1 shows revenue abroad for

Exhibit 1
INDUSTRIAL COMPANIES WITH THE LARGEST OVERSEAS REVENUE

Company	Percent Foreign Revenue	Percent Growth of International Exposure (April 2008–April 2009)
Caterpillar	67	120
General Electric	54	64
United Technologies	46	59
Deere	35	57
Honeywell	39	58

Source: David MacDougall, "Caterpillar Makes the Case for Going Abroad," *TheStreet*, April 27, 2010.

some industrial companies. Caterpillar, the construction-equipment company, receives 67 percent of its revenue from overseas markets, and General Electric earns 54 percent of its revenue abroad.

5-2a Are Multinationals Beneficial?

Although multinationals comprise far less than 1 percent of U.S. companies, they account for about 19 percent of all private jobs, 25 percent of all private wages, 48 percent of total exports of goods, and a remarkable 74 percent of nonpublic research and development (R&D) spending.[10] For decades, U.S. multinationals have driven an outsized share of U.S. productivity growth, the foundation of rising standards of living for everyone. They are responsible for 41 percent of the increase in private labor productivity since 1990.[22]

Some multinationals have shifted income to low-tax countries, which has reduced corporate income tax payments in America. The multinationals claim that this was necessary because the United States has a very complicated tax structure, with one of the highest corporate income tax rates among industrialized nations. It is estimated that U.S. multinationals have more than $1 trillion in profits held in overseas subsidiaries.[12]

A few examples of profits held abroad are Merck ($40 billion), Johnson & Johnson ($37 billion), IBM ($31 billion), PepsiCo ($26 billion), and Coca-Cola ($20 billion).[13] Money sitting overseas brings in no revenue for the U.S. Treasury. Thus, there are many proposals on how to bring all this money home. One proposal is to let the multinationals bring the money to the U.S. tax-free if they will use it for R&D or facilities expansion.

The role of multinational corporations in developing nations is a subject of controversy. The ability of multinationals to tap financial, physical, and human resources from all over the world and combine them economically and profitably can benefit any country. They also often possess and can transfer the most up-to-date technology. Critics, however, claim that often the wrong kind of technology is transferred to developing nations. Usually, it is **capital intensive** (requiring a greater expenditure for equipment than for labor) and thus does not substantially increase employment. A "modern sector" then emerges in the nation, employing a small proportion of the labor force with relatively high productivity and income levels

and with increasingly capital-intensive technologies. In addition, multinationals sometimes support reactionary and oppressive regimes if it is in their best interests to do so. Other critics say that the firms take more wealth out of developing nations than they bring in, thus widening the gap between rich and poor nations. The petroleum industry in particular has been heavily criticized in the past for its actions in some developing countries.

To counter such criticism, more and more multinationals are taking a proactive role in being good global citizens. Sometimes companies are spurred to action by government regulation; in other cases, multinationals are attempting to protect their good brand names.

5-2b Global Marketing Standardization

Traditionally, marketing-oriented multinational corporations have operated somewhat differently in each country. They use a strategy of providing different product features, packaging, advertising, and so on. However, Ted Levitt, a former Harvard professor, has described a trend toward what he refers to as "global marketing," with a slightly different meaning.[14] He contends that communication and technology have made the world smaller so that almost all consumers everywhere want all the things they have heard about, seen, or experienced. Thus, he sees the emergence of global markets for standardized consumer products on a huge scale, as opposed to segmented foreign markets with different products. In this book, *global marketing* is defined as individuals and organizations using a global vision to effectively market goods and services across national boundaries. To make the distinction, we can refer to Levitt's notion as **global marketing standardization**.

Global marketing standardization presumes that the markets throughout the world are becoming more alike. Firms practicing global marketing standardization produce "globally standardized products" to be sold the same way all over the world. Uniform production should enable companies to lower production and marketing costs and increase profits. Levitt has cited Coca-Cola, Colgate-Palmolive, and McDonald's as successful global marketers. His critics point out, however, that the success of these three companies is really based on variation, not on offering the same product everywhere. McDonald's, for example, changes its salad dressings and provides self-serve espresso for French tastes. It sells bulgogi burgers in South Korea and falafel burgers in Egypt. Further, the fact

multidomestic strategy when multinational firms enable individual subsidiaries to compete independently in domestic markets

A couple orders pastries at a Cinnabon shop in Dubai, United Arab Emirates. Rising wealth is fueling new markets for American companies in the Middle East as rising oil prices have opened the door to unique (often expensive) American cultural experiences.

that Coca-Cola and Colgate-Palmolive sell some of their products in more than 160 countries does not signify that they have adopted a high degree of standardization for all their products globally. Only three Coca-Cola brands are standardized, and one of them, Sprite, has a different formulation in Japan.

Companies with separate subsidiaries in other countries can be said to operate using a multidomestic strategy. A **multidomestic strategy** occurs when multinational firms enable individual subsidiaries to compete independently in domestic markets. Simply put, multidomestic strategy is how multinational firms use strategic business units (see Chapter 2). Colgate-Palmolive uses both strategies: Axion paste dishwashing detergent, for example, was formulated for developing countries, and La Croix Plus detergent was custom made for the French market—examples of multidomestic strategies.

Nevertheless, some multinational corporations are moving beyond multidomestic strategies toward a degree of global marketing standardization. Colgate toothpaste is marketed the same way globally, using global marketing standardization. Leading up to the 2012 Summer Olympics held in London, England, Coca-Cola unveiled a series of four television commercials that ran all around the world. Featuring the music of Mark Ronson and Katy B., the ads used universally understood visuals to tell the stories of five inspirational Olympic hopefuls.[15]

5-3 EXTERNAL ENVIRONMENT FACED BY GLOBAL MARKETERS

A global marketer or a firm considering global marketing must consider the external environment. Many of the same environmental factors that operate in the domestic market also exist internationally. These factors include culture, economic and technological development, political structure and actions, demographic makeup, and natural resources.

5-3a Culture

Central to any society is the common set of values shared by its citizens that determines what is socially acceptable. Culture underlies the family, the educational system, religion, and the social class system. The network of social organizations generates overlapping roles and status positions. These values and roles have a tremendous effect on people's preferences and thus on marketers' options. A company that does not understand a country's culture is doomed to failure in that country. Cultural blunders lead to misunderstandings and often perceptions of rudeness or even incompetence. For example, when people in India shake hands, they sometimes do so rather limply. This isn't a sign of weakness or disinterest; instead, a soft handshake conveys respect. Avoiding eye contact is also a sign of deference in India.

American culture often fascinates other countries. A mainstay of food courts across the United States, Cinnabon has made inroads into several unlikely international markets. "We've got a strong presence in Saudi Arabia and the United Arab Emirates and Egypt and Jordan," said company President Kat Cole. In fact, Cinnabon was the first U.S. franchise to open in Libya after the fall of Muammar Gaddafi. You might not associate the grand, American decadence of Cinnabon with the Middle East, but Cole explains, "They love sweets. If I showed you a picture of how their eat their cinnamon rolls, you would get a cavity just looking at it."[16]

Language is another important aspect of culture that can create problems for marketers. Marketers must take care in translating product names, slogans, instructions, and promotional messages so as not to convey the wrong meaning. Free translation software, such as babelfish.com or Google Translate, allows users to input text in one language and output in another language. But marketers must take care using the software, as it can have unintended results—the best being unintelligible, the worst being insulting.

Each country has its own customs and traditions that determine business practices and influence negotiations with foreign customers. In many countries, personal relationships are more important than financial considerations. For instance, skipping social engagements in Mexico may lead to lost sales. Negotiations in Japan often include long evenings of dining, drinking, and entertaining, and only after a close personal relationship has been formed do business negotiations begin.

Making successful sales presentations abroad requires a thorough understanding of the country's culture. Germans, for example, don't like risk and need strong reassurance. A successful presentation to a German client will emphasize three points: the bottom-line benefits of the product or service, that there will be strong service support, and that the product is guaranteed. In southern Europe, it is an insult to show a price list. Without negotiating, you will not close the sale. The English want plenty of documentation for product claims and are less likely to simply accept the word of the sales representative. Scandinavian and Dutch companies are more likely to approach business transactions as Americans do than are companies in any other country.

5-3b Economic Factors

A second major factor in the external environment facing the global marketer is the level of economic development in the countries where it operates. In general, complex and sophisticated industries are found in developed countries, and more basic industries are found in less developed nations. Average family incomes are higher in the more developed countries compared to the less developed countries. Larger incomes mean greater purchasing power and demand, not only for consumer goods and services, but also for the machinery and workers required to produce consumer goods.

According to the World Bank, the average *gross national income (GNI)* per capita for the world is $11,614.[17] GNI is a country's GDP (defined earlier) together with its income received from other countries (mainly interest and dividends) less similar payments made to other countries. The United States' GNI per capita is $48,620, but it is not the world's highest. That honor goes to Norway at $88,890. Of course, there are many very poor countries: Rwanda, $570; Nepal, $540; Afghanistan, $470; Ethiopia, $370; Liberia, $330; and Democratic Republic of Congo, $190.[18] GNI per capita is one measure of the ability of a country's citizens to buy various goods and services. A marketer with a global vision can use these data to aid in measuring market potential in countries around the globe.

Not only is per capita income a consideration when going abroad, but so is the cost of doing business in a country. Although it is not the same as the cost of doing business, we can gain insights into expenses by examining the cost of living in various cities. The most expensive cities in the world are Luanda, Angola; Tokyo, Japan; and N'Djamena, Chad. N'Djamena is mired in unrest and violence, and appropriately secure accommodations for both employees and businesses are very hard to come by. Such instability makes N'Djamena a place where it is very expensive to do business. Conditions are similar in Luanda, where a one-bedroom apartment rents for $11,800 a month.[19]

5-3c The Global Economy

A global marketer today must be fully aware of the intertwined nature of the global economy. In the past, the size of the U.S. economy was so large that global markets tended to move up or down depending on its health. It was said, "If America sneezes, then the rest of the world catches a cold." This is still true today. The U.S. housing market collapse and speculative financing led to a major global recession in 2008. It was, in fact, America's deepest decline in economic activity since the Great Depression. As the world slowly pulled itself out of the recession, the possibility of Greece defaulting on its national debt nearly stifled global economic recovery. The Greek crisis was followed by concern about other debt crises in Spain and Portugal. Moreover, the world now looks to economies such as China, India, and Brazil to help jump-start economic growth. The lesson for the global marketer is clear: forecasting global demand and economic growth requires an understanding of what is happening economically in countries around the globe.

5-3d Doing Business in China and India

Because of their huge economic potential, India and China are of growing interest to many multinationals. They have some of the highest growth rates in the world and are emerging as megamarkets. China and India also have the world's two largest populations, two of the world's largest geographic areas, greater linguistic and sociocultural diversity than any other countries, and among the highest levels of income disparity in the world—some people are extremely poor whereas others are very rich. Given this scale and variety, there is no "average Chinese customer" or "average Indian customer."

Both India and China have exploded in spending power, particularly in the upper classes. By 2015, China will likely surpass Japan as the largest luxury market in the world, with sales exceeding $27 billion.[20] Driving this growth are residents below the age of 45, a demographic that constitutes 73 percent of China's luxury buyers. Chinese luxury shoppers love to travel and buy things—the Chinese account for 15 percent of all luxury items purchased in France, but fewer than 2 percent of the visitors.[21]

While the luxury market is attractive to manufacturers of expensive clothes, watches, and jewelry, the growing Chinese and Indian middle classes have been a target for many American companies. About 247 million Chinese are currently considered middle class. That number will grow to more than 607 million by 2020.[22] Already, General Motors, KFC, Nike, Coca-Cola, Whirlpool, H. J. Heinz, and others have experienced success in the Chinese market. However, earning profits in China is not a sure thing. Mattel shut its Barbie stores after learning that Chinese parents wanted their girls to model themselves after studious children, not flirts. Home Depot has closed about half of its stores after finding little interest among Chinese for do-it-yourself renovation.

Starbucks is hoping its success in China (where it plans to triple its stores) can be mimicked in India. Many affluent Indians have experienced Starbucks outside of India and would likely welcome the coffee giant. It is a burgeoning market: Coffee consumption is increasing dramatically because the Indian consumer enjoys the casual café atmosphere. Starbucks hopes to increase the distribution of its Indian coffee beans and to open premium locations in the Tata Group's superluxurious Taj hotels. In 2012, the Indian government agreed to open the country to foreign retailers. Walmart has already opened two stores and has plans for more.[23]

Relations between the United States and China have not always been smooth, however. China is committed to protecting its businesses and asserting new global strength, which has resulted in several legislative stalemates with the United States. China has the power and draw of a country with steadily increasing consumption and high growth potential, making it particularly attractive to U.S. firms. American exports to China rose 542 percent from 2000 ($16.2 billion) to 2012 ($103.9 billion), making it the third largest importer of U.S. goods behind Mexico and Canada. According to United States Committee of the Blue Shield Vice President Erin Ennis, "U.S. exports to China recovered faster after the recession than exports to anywhere else in the world. Clearly, China is a market that is important to U.S. companies' bottom lines, even in tough economic times."[24]

5-3e Political Structure and Actions

Political structure is a third important variable facing global marketers. Government policies run the gamut from no private ownership and minimal individual freedom to little central government and maximum personal freedom. As rights of private property increase, government-owned industries and centralized planning tend to decrease. But

a political environment is rarely at one extreme or the other. India, for instance, is a republic with elements of socialism, monopoly capitalism, and competitive capitalism in its political ideology.

A recent World Bank study found that the least amount of business regulation fosters the strongest economies.[25] The least regulated and most efficient economies are concentrated among countries with well-established common-law traditions, including Australia, Canada, New Zealand, the United Kingdom, and the United States. On a par with the best performers are Singapore and Hong Kong. Not far behind are Denmark, Norway, and Sweden, social democracies that recently streamlined their business regulation. India, infamous for infrastructure troubles and avoiding international investment, recently made some regulation changes that should help global companies enter the huge Indian market. The major change offers companies such as Walmart more options for establishing business. Before, the company could only launch wholesale joint ventures. Now, it can own up to 51 percent of joint ventures in India.[26]

LEGAL CONSIDERATIONS Closely related to and often intertwined with the political environment are legal considerations. In France, nationalistic sentiments led to a law that requires pop music stations to play at least 40 percent of their songs in French (even though French teenagers love American and English rock and roll).

Many legal structures are designed to either encourage or limit trade:

▸ **TARIFF:** a tax levied on the goods entering a country. Because a tariff is a tax, it will either reduce the profits of the firms paying the tariff or raise prices to buyers, or both. Normally, a tariff raises prices of the imported goods and makes it easier for domestic firms to compete. In 2012, the United States decided that the domestic ethanol industry no longer needed protection and dropped a three-decade-old tariff on imported ethanol.[27]

▸ **QUOTA:** a limit on the amount of a specific product that can enter a country. Several U.S. companies have sought quotas as a means of protection from foreign competition.

▸ **BOYCOTT:** the exclusion of all products from certain countries or companies. Governments use boycotts to exclude companies from countries with which they have a political dispute. Several Arab nations have boycotted products made in Israel.

▸ **EXCHANGE CONTROL:** a law compelling a company earning foreign exchange from its exports to sell it to a control agency, usually a central bank. A company wishing to buy goods abroad must first obtain a foreign currency exchange from the control agency. Some countries with foreign exchange controls are Argentina, Brazil, China, Iceland, India, North Korea, Russia, and Venezuela.

▸ **MARKET GROUPING** (also known as a common trade alliance): occurs when several countries agree to work together to form a common trade area that enhances trade opportunities. The best-known market grouping is the European Union (EU).

▸ **TRADE AGREEMENT:** an agreement to stimulate international trade. Not all government efforts are meant to stifle imports or investment by foreign corporations. The largest Latin American trade agreement is **Mercosur**, which includes Argentina, Bolivia, Brazil, Chile, Colombia, Ecuador, Paraguay, Peru, Uruguay, and Venezuela. The elimination of most tariffs among the trading partners has resulted in trade revenues of more than $16 billion annually. The economic boom created by Mercosur will undoubtedly cause other nations to seek trade agreements on their own or to enter Mercosur.

THE URUGUAY ROUND, THE FAILED DOHA ROUND, AND BILATERAL AGREEMENTS The **Uruguay Round** is a trade agreement that has dramatically lowered trade barriers worldwide. Adopted in 1994, the agreement has been signed by 157 nations. It is the most ambitious global trade agreement ever negotiated. The agreement has reduced tariffs by one-third worldwide—a move that has raised global income by $235 billion annually.[28] Perhaps most notable is the recognition of new global realities. For the first time, a trade agreement covers services, intellectual property rights, and trade-related investment measures such as exchange controls.

The Uruguay Round made several major changes in world trading practices:

▸ **ENTERTAINMENT, PHARMACEUTICALS, INTEGRATED CIRCUITS, AND SOFTWARE:** The rules protect patents, copyrights, and trademarks for twenty years. Computer programs receive fifty years of protection, and semiconductor chips receive ten years of protection. But many developing nations were given a decade to phase in patent protection for drugs. France, which limits the number of U.S. movies and television shows that can be shown, refused to liberalize market access for the U.S. entertainment industry.

» **FINANCIAL, LEGAL, AND ACCOUNTING SERVICES:** Services came under international trading rules for the first time, creating a vast opportunity for these competitive U.S. industries. Now it is easier for managers and key personnel to be admitted to a country. Licensing standards for professionals, such as doctors, cannot discriminate against foreign applicants. That is, foreign applicants cannot be held to higher standards than domestic practitioners.

» **AGRICULTURE:** Europe is gradually reducing farm subsidies, opening new opportunities for such U.S. farm exports as wheat and corn. Japan and Korea are beginning to import rice. But U.S. growers of sugar and citrus fruit have had their subsidies trimmed.

» **TEXTILES AND APPAREL:** Strict quotas limiting imports from developing countries are being phased out, causing further job losses in the U.S. clothing trade. But retailers are the big winners, because past quotas have added $15 billion a year to clothing prices.

» **A NEW TRADE ORGANIZATION:** The World Trade Organization (WTO) replaced the old General Agreement on Tariffs and Trade (GATT), which was created in 1948. The WTO eliminated the extensive loopholes of which GATT members took advantage. Today, all WTO members must fully comply with all agreements under the Uruguay Round. The WTO also has an effective dispute settlement procedure with strict time limits to resolve disputes.

The latest round of WTO trade talks began in Doha, Qatar, in 2001. For the most part, the periodic meetings of WTO members under the Doha Round have been very contentious. One of the most contentious goals of the round was for the major developing countries, known collectively as BRIC (Brazil, Russia, India, and China), to lower tariffs on industrial goods in exchange for European and American tariff and subsidy cuts on farm products. Concerned that lowering tariffs would result in an economically damaging influx of foreign cotton, sugar, and rice, China and India demanded a safeguard clause that would allow them to raise tariffs on those crops if imports surged. Unable to agree on what percentage increase constituted a surge in imports, the countries remain at an impasse.[29]

In addition to the slow progress of the Doha Round, many countries have moved toward protectionism after the global recession of 2008–2009. This movement discourages new trade agreements, which are designed to encourage international trade. Ecuador, for instance, has hiked tariffs on more than 600 categories of imports. Chinese companies like Huawei Technologies and ZTE Corp. have alleged that the United States is engaging in protectionism and blocking companies from participating in bids for work or companies for sale.[30]

However, the move toward protectionism has not reversed the agreements and organizations that arose from the period of increased globalization before the economic crisis in 2008: the North American Free Trade Agreement, the Central America Free Trade Agreement, the European Union, the World Bank, and the International Monetary Fund.

World Trade Organization (WTO) a trade organization that replaced the old General Agreement on Tariffs and Trade (GATT)

General Agreement on Tariffs and Trade (GATT) a trade agreement that contained loopholes enabling countries to avoid trade-barrier reduction agreements

The Doha Round suffers from fears of mass imports on agricultural goods that would economically stunt domestic producers.

© Jim Barber/Shutterstock.com

NORTH AMERICAN FREE TRADE AGREEMENT At the time it was instituted, the **North American Free Trade Agreement (NAFTA)** created the world's largest free trade zone. Ratified by the U.S. Congress in 1993, the agreement includes Canada, the United States, and Mexico, with a combined population of 450 million and an economy of $17 trillion.[31]

The main impact of NAFTA was to open the Mexican market to U.S. companies. When the treaty went into effect, tariffs on about half the items traded across the Rio Grande disappeared. The pact removed a web of Mexican licensing requirements, quotas, and tariffs that limited transactions in U.S. goods and services. For instance, the pact allowed U.S. and Canadian financial-services companies to own subsidiaries in Mexico.

In August 2007, the three member countries met in Canada to tweak NAFTA but not make substantial changes. For example, the members agreed to further remove trade barriers on hogs, steel, consumer electronics, and chemicals. They also directed the North American Steel Trade Committee, which represents the three governments, to focus on subsidized steel from China.

The real question is whether NAFTA can continue to deliver rising prosperity in all three countries. The U.S. has certainly benefited from cheaper imports and more investment opportunities abroad. According to the World Trade Organization, trade between the three countries comprised 51 percent of total trade of the three nations, whereas 49 percent of exports went to other countries.[32]

NAFTA has also created millions of jobs for all three nations. It is estimated that Canada has gained almost 5 million jobs, the United States has picked up 25 million jobs, and Mexico has created nearly 10 million jobs.[33]

DOMINICAN REPUBLIC-CENTRAL AMERICA FREE TRADE AGREEMENT The **Dominican Republic-Central America Free Trade Agreement (CAFTA-DR)** was instituted in 2005. Because it joined after the original agreement was signed, the Dominican Republic was amended to the original agreement title (Central America Free Trade Agreement, or CAFTA). Besides the United States and the Dominican Republic, the agreement includes Costa Rica, El Salvador, Guatemala, Honduras, and Nicaragua.

Between 2005 and 2007, trade between the United States and CAFTA-DR countries grew 18 percent. The United States exported $24 billion of goods and services to CAFTA-DR nations in 2010, up 43 percent since 2005. The United States imported $23.8 billion of goods and services from CAFTA-DR nations, up 31 percent since 2005.[34] CAFTA-DR has been an unqualified success. It has created new commercial opportunities for its members, has promoted regional stability, and is an impetus for economic development for an important group of U.S. neighbors.

EUROPEAN UNION The **European Union (EU)** is one of the world's most important free trade zones and now encompasses most of Europe. More than a free trade zone, it is also a political and economic community. As a free trade zone, it guarantees the freedom of movement of people, goods, services, and capital between member states. It also maintains a common trade policy with outside nations and a regional development policy. The EU represents member nations in the WTO. Recently, the EU also began venturing into foreign policy as well, getting involved in issues such as Iran's refining of uranium.

The European Union currently has twenty-eight member states: Austria, Belgium, Bulgaria, Croatia, Cyprus, the Czech Republic, Denmark, Estonia, Finland, France, Germany, Greece, Hungary, Ireland, Italy, Latvia, Lithuania, Luxembourg, Malta, the Netherlands, Poland, Portugal, Romania, Slovakia, Slovenia, Spain, Sweden, and the United Kingdom. There are currently five candidate countries: Iceland, the Republic of Macedonia, Montenegro, Serbia, and Turkey. In addition, the western Balkan countries of Albania, Bosnia and Herzegovina, and Kosovo are recognized as potential candidates.[35]

In early 2010, Greece entered a financial crisis that highlighted the challenges of a large currency union where member nations maintain responsibility for their own fiscal policies. Unable to devalue its currency to boost sales of products without injuring other member nations, Greece turned to member states for a bailout. The crisis has highlighted debt problems in other EU nations such as Spain, Italy, and Ireland. Ireland, after a burst property bubble, may also need a bailout, while Greece faces protests as it imposes austerity measures in order to receive continued bailout money.[36]

The European Union Commission and the courts have not always been kind to multinationals. For example, in 2011 the EU fined Procter & Gamble (P&G) and Unilever for running a cartel with competitor Henkel to fix laundry detergent prices. The EU investigated the three companies and found that they formed the cartel after joining in efforts to reduce packaging materials for Ariel and Tide (P&G), OMO and Radiant (Unilever), and Persil (Henkel). In that meeting, the three companies agreed on pricing and respective market share, which the EU determined unfairly limited competition and forced consumers to pay higher prices. All three companies cooperated with the investigation and P&G and Unilever agreed to pay their fines. Henkel was not fined as it alerted the EU Commission to the cartel and received immunity.[37]

The EU is the largest economy in the world (with the United States very close behind). The EU is also a huge market, with a population of nearly 500 million and a GDP of $15.6 trillion in 2011.[38] The United States and the EU have the largest bilateral trade and investment relationship in world history. Together, they account for almost half of the entire world GDP and nearly one-third of world trade flows. United States and EU companies have invested trillions of dollars in each other's economies, contributing to significant job growth on both sides of the Atlantic. The relationship between these two economic superpowers has also shaped the global economy as a whole—the U.S. and EU are primary trade partners for almost every other country in the world.[39]

The EU is a very attractive market for multinational firms. But the EU presents marketing challenges because, even with standardized regulations, marketers will not be able to produce a single European product for a generic European consumer. With more than fourteen different languages and individual national customs, Europe will always be far more diverse than the United States. Thus, product differences will continue to be necessary. Atag Holdings NV, a diversified Dutch company whose main business is kitchen appliances, was confident it could cater to both the "potato" and "spaghetti" belts—marketers' terms for consumer preferences in northern and southern Europe. But Atag quickly discovered that preferences vary much more than that. Ovens, burner shape and size, knob and clock placement, temperature range, and colors vary greatly from country to country. Although Atag's kitchenware unit has lifted foreign sales to 25 percent of its total from 4 percent in the mid-1990s, it now believes that its diversified products and speed in delivering them—rather than the magic bullet of a Europroduct—will keep it competitive.

An entirely different type of problem facing global marketers is the possibility of a protectionist movement by the EU against outsiders. For example, European automakers have proposed holding Japanese imports at roughly their current 10 percent market share. The Irish, Danes, and Dutch don't make cars and have unrestricted home markets; they would be unhappy about limited imports of Toyotas and Nissans. But France has a strict quota on Japanese cars to protect Renault and Peugeot. These local carmakers could be hurt if the quota is raised at all.

THE WORLD BANK, THE INTERNATIONAL MONETARY FUND, AND THE G-20 Two international financial organizations are instrumental in fostering global trade. The **World Bank** offers low-interest loans to developing nations. Originally, the purpose of the loans was to help these nations build infrastructure such as roads, power plants, schools, drainage projects, and hospitals. Now the World Bank offers loans to help developing nations relieve their debt burdens. To receive the loans, countries must pledge to lower trade barriers and aid private enterprise. In addition to making loans, the World Bank is a major source of advice and information for developing nations. The **International Monetary Fund (IMF)** was founded in 1945, one year after the creation of the World Bank, to promote trade through financial cooperation and eliminate trade barriers in the process. The IMF makes short-term loans to member nations that are unable to meet their budgetary expenses. It operates as a lender of last resort for troubled nations, such as Greece. In exchange for these emergency loans, IMF lenders frequently extract significant commitments from the borrowing nations to address the problems that led to the crises. These steps may include curtailing imports or even devaluing the currency. Greece, working with both the IMF and the EU, has raised taxes to unprecedented levels, cut government spending (including pensions), and implemented labor reforms such as reducing minimum wage as part of its austerity measures to receive loans from the IMF and the EU.[40]

The **Group of Twenty (G-20)** finance ministers and central bank governors was established in 1999 to bring together industrialized and developing economies to discuss key issues in the global economy. The G-20 is

World Bank an international bank that offers low-interest loans, advice, and information to developing nations

International Monetary Fund (IMF) an international organization that acts as a lender of last resort, providing loans to troubled nations, and also works to promote trade through financial cooperation

Group of Twenty (G-20) a forum for international economic development that promotes discussion between industrial and emerging-market countries on key issues related to global economic stability

Despite the country's dire financial situation, Greeks are protesting the austerity measures imposed by the government. Many of the measures directly impact huge portions of the population.

© LOUISA GOULIAMAKI/AFP/Getty Images

a forum for international economic development that promotes discussion between industrial and emerging-market countries on key issues related to global economic stability. By contributing to the strengthening of the international financial system and providing opportunities for discussion on national policies, international cooperation, and international financial institutions, the G-20 helps to support growth and development across the globe. The members of the G-20 are shown in Exhibit 2.

Members of the G-20 met in Mexico in June 2012. Much of the discussion centered on the Eurozone (countries that use the euro as currency) debt crisis. Europe was told that it needed to put up more money to help struggling Eurozone countries before the rest of the world would contribute extra money to the IMF's crises fund. The conference decided that world economic growth was spotty and that the possibility of another global recession was fairly high. It also noted that key emerging markets were generally growing much faster than advanced economies.

Exhibit 2

MEMBERS OF THE G-20

Argentina	European Union	Italy	Saudi Arabia
Australia	France	Japan	South Africa
Brazil	Germany	Mexico	Turkey
Canada	India	Republic of Korea	United Kingdom
China	Indonesia	Russia	United States

© Cengage Learning

5-3f Demographic Makeup

China, India, and Indonesia are three of the most densely populated nations in the world. But that fact alone is not particularly useful to marketers. They also need to know whether the population is mostly urban or rural, because marketers may not have easy access to rural consumers. Belgium, with about 90 percent of the population living in urban settings, is an attractive market.

Another key demographic consideration is age. There is a wide gap between the older populations of the industrialized countries and the vast working-age populations of developing countries. This gap has enormous implications for economies, businesses, and the competitiveness of individual countries. It means that while Europe and Japan struggle with pension schemes and the rising cost of health care, countries like Brazil, China, and Mexico can reap the fruits of a demographic dividend: falling labor costs, a healthier and more educated population, and the entry of millions of women into the workforce. The demographic dividend is a gift of falling birthrates, and it causes a temporary bulge in the number of working-age people. Population experts have estimated that one-third of East Asia's economic miracle can be attributed to a beneficial age structure. But the miracle occurred only because the governments had policies in place to educate their people, create jobs, and improve health.

5-3g Natural Resources

A final factor in the external environment that has become more evident in the past decade is the shortage of natural resources. For example, petroleum shortages have created huge amounts of wealth for oil-producing countries such as

Norway, Saudi Arabia, and the United Arab Emirates. Both consumer and industrial markets have blossomed in these countries. Other countries—such as Indonesia, Mexico, and Venezuela—were able to borrow heavily against oil reserves in order to develop more rapidly. On the other hand, industrial countries such as Japan, the United States, and much of Western Europe experienced an enormous transfer of wealth to the petroleum-rich nations. The high price of oil has created inflationary pressures in petroleum-importing nations. Now, however, new technologies like fracking are facilitating the economical recovery of oil and gas from the tar sands of Canada and shale rock of America. This will significantly reduce U.S. demand for foreign oil.

Petroleum is not the only natural resource that affects international marketing. Warm climate and lack of water mean that many of Africa's countries will remain importers of foodstuffs. The United States, on the other hand, must rely on Africa for many precious metals. Vast differences in natural resources create international dependencies, huge shifts of wealth, inflation and recession, export opportunities for countries with abundant resources, and even a stimulus for military intervention.

5-4 GLOBAL MARKETING BY THE INDIVIDUAL FIRM

A company should consider entering the global marketplace only after its management has a solid grasp of the global environment.

Companies decide to "go global" for a number of reasons. Perhaps the most important is to earn additional profits. Managers may believe that international sales will result in higher profit margins or more added-on profits. A second stimulus is that a firm may have a unique product or technological advantage not available to other international competitors. Such advantages should result in major business successes abroad. In other situations, management may have exclusive market information about foreign customers, marketplaces, or market situations not known to others. While exclusivity can provide an initial motivation for international marketing, managers must realize that competitors can be expected to catch up with the firm's information advantage. Finally, saturated domestic markets, excess capacity, and potential for economies of scale can also be motivators to go global. Economies of scale mean that average per-unit production costs fall as output is increased.

Many firms form multinational partnerships—called strategic alliances—to assist them in penetrating global markets; strategic alliances are examined in Chapter 7. Five other methods of entering the global marketplace are, in order of risk, exporting, licensing and franchising, contract manufacturing, joint venture, and direct investment (see Exhibit 3).

5-4a Exporting

When a company decides to enter the global market, exporting is usually the least complicated and least risky alternative. **Exporting** is selling domestically produced products to buyers in other countries. A company can sell

exporting selling domestically produced products to buyers in other countries

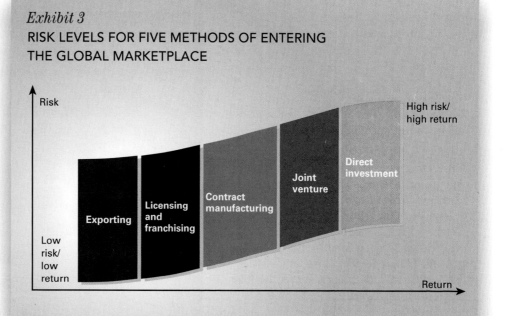

Exhibit 3

RISK LEVELS FOR FIVE METHODS OF ENTERING THE GLOBAL MARKETPLACE

Risk

Low risk/ low return

Exporting

Licensing and franchising

Contract manufacturing

Joint venture

Direct investment

High risk/ high return

Return

© Cengage Learning

buyer for export an intermediary in the global market that assumes all ownership risks and sells globally for its own account

export broker an intermediary who plays the traditional broker's role by bringing buyer and seller together

export agent an intermediary who acts like a manufacturer's agent for the exporter; the export agent lives in the foreign market

licensing the legal process whereby a licensor allows another firm to use its manufacturing process, trademarks, patents, trade secrets, or other proprietary knowledge

directly to foreign importers or buyers. The United States is the world's largest exporter.

Instead of selling directly to foreign buyers, a company may decide to sell to intermediaries located in its domestic market. The most common intermediary is the export merchant, also known as a **buyer for export**, which is usually treated like a domestic customer by the domestic manufacturer. The buyer for export assumes all risks and sells internationally for its own account. The domestic firm is involved only to the extent that its products are bought in foreign markets.

A second type of intermediary is the **export broker**, who plays the traditional broker's role by bringing buyer and seller together. The manufacturer still retains title and assumes all the risks. Export brokers operate primarily in agricultural products and raw materials.

Export agents, a third type of intermediary, are foreign sales agents/distributors who live in the foreign country and perform the same functions as domestic manufacturers' agents, helping with international financing, shipping, and so on. The U.S. Department of Commerce has an agent/distributor service that helps about 5,000 U.S. companies each year find an agent or distributor in virtually any country of the world. A second category of agents resides in the manufacturer's country but represents foreign buyers. This type of agent acts as a hired purchasing agent for foreign customers operating in the exporter's home market.

5-4b Licensing and Franchising

Another effective way for a firm to move into the global arena with relatively little risk is to sell a license to manufacture its product to someone in a foreign country. **Licensing** is the legal process whereby a licensor allows another firm to use its manufacturing process, trademarks, patents, trade secrets, or other proprietary knowledge. The licensee, in turn, pays the licensor a royalty or fee agreed on by both parties.

A licensor must make sure it can exercise sufficient control over the licensee's activities to ensure proper quality, pricing, distribution, and so on. Licensing may also create a new competitor in the long run, if the licensee decides to void the license agreement. International law is often ineffective in stopping such actions. Two common ways of maintaining effective control over licensees are shipping one or more critical components from the United States and locally registering patents and trademarks to the U.S. firm, not to the licensee. Garment companies maintain control by delivering only so many labels per day; they also supply their own fabric, collect the scraps, and do accurate unit counts.

Franchising is a form of licensing that has grown rapidly in recent years. More than 400 U.S. franchisors operate more than 40,000 outlets in foreign countries, bringing in sales of

LIGHTHEARTED LICENSING

In 2013, Hasbro launched two new face-to-face games based on the classic video game series Tetris. Expanding two of Hasbro's own massive brands, Jenga Tetris and Bop It Tetris utilize the enduring puzzle video game's name and design, licensed from The Tetris Company. Said Tetris Company Managing Director Henk Rogers, "We're thrilled to be teaming up with Hasbro to expand the Tetris brand and give our fans fun, challenging face-to-face formats to experience the 'Tetris Effect' in a unique way."[41]

© iStockphoto.com/walrusmail / AP Images/Jason DeCrow/Invision for Hasbro

more than $9 billion.[42] More than half of the international franchises are for fast-food restaurants and business services.

CONTRACT MANUFACTURING Firms that do not want to become involved in licensing or to become heavily involved in global marketing may engage in **contract manufacturing**, which is private label manufacturing by a foreign company. The foreign company produces a certain volume of products to specification, with the domestic firm's brand name on the goods. The domestic company usually handles the marketing. Thus, the domestic firm can broaden its global marketing base without investing in overseas plants and equipment. After establishing a solid base, the domestic firm may switch to a joint venture or direct investment.

5-4c Joint Venture

Joint ventures are somewhat similar to licensing agreements. In an international **joint venture**, the domestic firm buys part of a foreign company or joins with a foreign company to create a new entity. A joint venture is a quick and relatively inexpensive way to go global and to gain needed expertise. For example, Robert Mondavi Wines entered into a joint venture with Baron Philippe de Rothschild, owner of Bordeaux's Château, Mouton-Rothschild. Together, the powerhouse vineyards developed a California wine called Opus One. Benefiting from the experience of both winemakers, the new wine was immediately established as the American vanguard of quality and price (relatively speaking—each bottle retails for $365).[43]

While this collaboration was successful, joint ventures can also be very risky. Many fail. Others fall victim to a takeover in which one partner buys out the other. Sometimes joint venture partners simply can't agree on management strategies and policies.

5-4d Direct Investment

Active ownership of a foreign company or of overseas manufacturing or marketing facilities is called **direct foreign investment**. Direct foreign investment by U.S. firms is currently about $4.2 trillion.[44] Direct investors have either a controlling interest or a large minority interest in the firm. Thus, they have the greatest potential reward and the greatest potential risk. Because of problems with contract manufacturing and joint ventures in China, multinationals are going it alone. Today, nearly five times as much foreign direct investment comes into China in the form of stand-alone efforts as comes in for joint ventures.

A firm may make a direct foreign investment by acquiring an interest in an existing company or by building new facilities. It might do so because it has trouble transferring some resource to a foreign operation or getting that resource locally. One important resource is personnel, especially managers. If the local labor market is tight, the firm may buy an entire foreign firm and retain all its employees instead of paying higher salaries than competitors.

The United States is a popular place for direct investment by international companies. After falling off from a record high $320 billion in 2000, foreign investment in U.S. companies inched up to $234 billion in 2011.[45] Likewise, foreign investment is highly sought after by many state and local governments, which endured grave economic strain during the Great Recession. Direct investment increased in 2012, led by German software developer SAS's purchase of Ariba, Inc. and Switzerland technology corporation ABB's purchase of Thomas Betts, a U.S. manufacturer of electrical connectors.[46]

5-5 THE GLOBAL MARKETING MIX

To succeed, firms seeking to enter into foreign trade must still adhere to the principles of the marketing mix. Information gathered on foreign markets through research is the basis for the four Ps of global marketing strategy: product, place (distribution), promotion, and price. Marketing managers who understand the advantages and disadvantages of different ways of entering the global market and the effect of the external environment on the firm's marketing mix have a better chance of reaching their goals.

The first step in creating a marketing mix is developing a thorough understanding of the global target market. Often this knowledge can be obtained through the same types of marketing research used in the domestic market (see Chapter 9). However, global marketing research is conducted in vastly different environments. Conducting a survey can be difficult in developing countries, where telephone ownership is growing but is not always common and

contract manufacturing private label manufacturing by a foreign company

joint venture when a domestic firm buys part of a foreign company or joins with a foreign company to create a new entity

direct foreign investment active ownership of a foreign company or of overseas manufacturing or marketing facilities

mail delivery is slow or sporadic. Drawing samples based on known population parameters is often difficult because of the lack of data. In some cities in Africa, Asia, Mexico, and South America, street maps are unavailable, streets are unidentified, and houses are unnumbered. Moreover, the questions a marketer can ask may differ in other cultures. In some cultures, people tend to be more private than in the United States and will not respond to personal questions on surveys. For instance, in France, questions about one's age and income are considered especially rude.

5-5a Product Decisions

With the proper information, a good marketing mix can be developed. One important decision is whether to alter the product or the promotion for the global marketplace. Other options are to radically change the product or to adjust either the promotional message or the product to suit local conditions.

ONE PRODUCT, ONE MESSAGE The strategy of global marketing standardization, which was discussed earlier, means developing a single product for all markets and promoting it the same way all over the world. For instance, P&G uses the same product and promotional themes for Head & Shoulders in China as it does in the United States. The advertising draws attention to a person's dandruff problem, which stands out in a nation of black-haired people. Head & Shoulders is now the best-selling shampoo in China despite costing over 300 percent more than local brands. Rejecting global marketing standardization, Pizza Hut has reinvented itself in countries like India and China. Pizza Hut Casual Dining restaurants located across China resemble The Cheesecake Factory in terms of menu, décor, and promotion. Domino's Pizza, however, has maintained its American marketing mix throughout its push into emerging markets. For Domino's, a traditional menu and delivery service are enough to drive growth in China and beyond.[47]

Global media—especially satellite and cable television networks such as CNN International, MTV Networks, and British Sky Broadcasting—make it possible to beam advertising to audiences unreachable a few years ago. Eighteen-year-olds in Paris often have more in common with eighteen-year-olds in New York than with their own parents. Almost all of MTV's advertisers run unified English-language campaigns in the twenty-eight nations the firm reaches. The audiences buy the same products, go to the same movies, listen to the same music, and sip the same colas. Global advertising merely works on that premise. Although teens throughout the world prefer movies above all other forms of television programming, they are closely followed by music videos, stand-up comedy, and then sports.

Global marketing standardization can sometimes backfire. Unchanged products may fail simply because of cultural factors. Any type of war game tends to do very poorly in Germany, even though Germany is by far the world's biggest game-playing nation. A successful game in Germany is highly detailed and has a thick rulebook.

Sometimes the desire for absolute standardization must give way to practical considerations and local market dynamics. For example, because of the feminine connotations of the word *diet*, the European version of Diet Coke is Coca-Cola Light. Even if the brand name differs by market—as with Lay's potato chips, which are called Sabritas in Mexico—a strong visual relationship may be

One product, one message means developing a single product for all markets and promoting it the same way all over the world. This advertisement featuring Italian actress Monica Bellucci could easily be mistaken for an American ad—until one notices the Japanese text.

created by uniform application of the brandmark and graphic elements on packaging.

PRODUCT INVENTION In the context of global marketing, product invention can be taken to mean either creating a new product for a market or drastically changing an existing product. For example, more than 100 unique Pringles potato chip flavors have been invented for international markets. Prawn Cocktail (the United Kingdom), Seaweed (Japan), Blueberry (China), Cinnamon Sweet Potato (France), and Bangkok Grilled Chicken Wing (Thailand) are some of the many Pringles flavors available outside the United States.[48] Chinese consumers found Oreo cookies "too sweet," while Indian consumers said that they were "too bitter." In response, Kraft changed the recipe in each country and created a new Green Tea Oreo flavor for China.[49]

PRODUCT ADAPTATION Another alternative for global marketers is to alter a basic product slightly to meet local conditions. Unilever's Rexona brand deodorant sticks sell for sixteen cents and up. They are big hits in Bolivia, India, Peru, and the Philippines—where Unilever has grabbed 60 percent of the deodorant market. In many cases, the company makes smaller packages, often single-use packages, to accommodate lower income areas. McDonald's, long known for its foreign inventions and adaptations, ensures that all products sold in the Middle East are halal, meaning that they are permissible to eat according to Islamic law. Ingredients are inspected and approved by local halal officers before they are sold, and all meat can be traced back to trusted suppliers.[50]

5-5b Promotion Adaptation

Another global marketing strategy is to maintain the same basic product but alter the promotional strategy. For example, bicycles are mainly pleasure vehicles in the United States, but in many parts of the world, they are a family's main mode of transportation. Thus, promotion in these countries should stress durability and efficiency. In contrast, U.S. advertising may emphasize escaping and having fun.

Language barriers, translation problems, and cultural differences have generated numerous headaches for international marketing managers. For example, a toothpaste claiming to give users white teeth was especially inappropriate in many areas of Southeast Asia, where the well-to-do chew betel nuts and black teeth are a sign of higher social status.

5-5c Place (Distribution)

Solving promotional and product problems does not guarantee global marketing success. The product must still get adequate distribution. For example, Europeans don't play sports as much as Americans do, so they don't visit sporting-goods stores as often. Realizing this, Reebok started selling its shoes in about 800 traditional shoe stores in France. In just one year, the company doubled its French sales.

To combat distribution problems, companies are using creative strategies. A small company in India is setting up a unique distribution system that will allow large and small companies to distribute their goods to very small retailers in villages of 5,000 people or less. The company, Universal Village, uses a large sales staff, often from the villages they work with, to take orders from the small retailers. The staff then sends the orders through a mobile application to a warehouse. The warehouse packs the order into small boxes, and those boxes are delivered to each retailer. Not only does the system help distribute a wider range of products, but it also allows these small retailers to operate more efficiently by not having to leave their shop to travel large distances to restock the store.[51]

In many developing nations, channels of distribution and the physical infrastructure are inadequate. South Africa has perhaps the best infrastructure in all of Africa, but even there distributing products in a safe and cost-effective way is a monumental task. Though *spazas* (informal convenience stores) comprise approximately 30 percent of South Africa's national retail market, no formal distribution system exists—many shop owners cannot even afford delivery vans. To counter this distributional hurdle, Nestlé established eighteen distribution centers to deliver Nespray, a mineral-rich milk powder, directly to the spazas scattered across rural South Africa.[52]

American companies importing goods from overseas facilities to the United States are facing other problems. Logistics has been a growing challenge for U.S. companies seeking to cut costs by shifting more production to countries where manufacturing is cheaper. Now, however, the rising costs for shipping goods are adding to their profit pressures. The surge in global trade in recent years has added to strains and charges for all forms of transport. As a result, some manufacturers are developing costly buffer stocks—which can mean setting up days' or weeks' worth of extra components—to avoid shutting down production lines and failing to make timely deliveries. Others are shifting to more expensive but more reliable modes of transport, such as airfreight, which is faster and less prone to delays than ocean shipping.

5-5d Pricing

Once marketing managers have determined a global product and promotion strategy, they can select the remainder of the marketing mix. Pricing presents some unique problems in the global sphere. Exporters must not only cover their production costs but also consider transportation costs, insurance, taxes, and tariffs. When deciding on a final price, marketers must also determine how much customers are willing to spend on a particular product. Marketers also need to ensure that their foreign buyers will pay the price. Because developing nations lack mass purchasing power, selling to them often poses special pricing problems. Sometimes a product can be simplified in order to lower the price. The firm must not assume low-income countries are willing to accept lower quality, however. L'Oréal was unsuccessful selling cheap shampoo in India, so the company targets the rising class. It now sells a $17 Paris face powder and a $25 Vichy sunscreen. Both products are very popular.

EXCHANGE RATES The **exchange rate** is the price of one country's currency in terms of another country's currency. If a country's currency *appreciates*, less of that country's currency is needed to buy another country's currency. If a country's currency *depreciates*, more of that currency will be needed to buy another country's currency.

How do appreciation and depreciation affect the prices of a country's goods? If, say, the U.S. dollar depreciates relative to the Japanese yen, U.S. residents will need to pay more

IF A COUNTRY'S CURRENCY DEPRECIATES, MORE OF THAT CURRENCY WILL BE NEEDED TO BUY ANOTHER COUNTRY'S CURRENCY.

dollars to buy Japanese goods. To illustrate, suppose the dollar price of one yen is $0.012 and that a Toyota is priced at ¥2 million. At this exchange rate, a U.S. resident pays $24,000 for a Toyota ($0.012 x ¥2 million = $24,000). If the dollar depreciates to $0.018 to ¥1, then the U.S. resident will need to pay $36,000 for the same Toyota.

As the dollar depreciates, the prices of Japanese goods rise for U.S. residents, so they buy fewer Japanese goods—thus, U.S. imports may decline. At the same time, as the dollar depreciates relative to the yen, the yen appreciates relative to the dollar. This means prices of U.S. goods fall for the Japanese, so they buy more U.S. goods—and U.S. exports rise.

Currency markets operate under a system of **floating exchange rates**. Prices of different currencies "float" up and down based on the demand for and the supply of each currency. Global currency traders create the supply of and demand for a particular country's currency based on that country's investment, trade potential, and economic strength.

DUMPING Dumping is the sale of an exported product at a price lower than that charged for the same or a like product in the "home" market of the exporter. This practice is regarded as a form of price discrimination that can potentially harm the importing nation's competing industries. Dumping may occur as a result of exporter business strategies that include (1) trying to increase an overseas market share, (2) temporarily distributing products in overseas markets to offset slack demand in the home market, (3) lowering unit costs by exploiting large-scale production, and (4) attempting to maintain stable prices during periods of exchange rate fluctuations.

Historically, the dumping of goods has presented serious problems in international trade. As a result,

© Otna Ydur/Shutterstock.com

countertrade a form of trade in which all or part of the payment for goods or services is in the form of other goods or services

blog a publicly accessible Web page that functions as an interactive journal, where readers can post comments on the author's entries

dumping has led to significant disagreements among countries and diverse views about its harmfulness. Some trade economists view dumping as harmful only when it involves the use of "predatory" practices that intentionally try to eliminate competition and gain monopoly power in a market. They believe that predatory dumping rarely occurs and that antidumping rules are a protectionist tool whose cost to consumers and import-using industries exceeds the benefits to the industries receiving protection.

As the result of a complaint brought by the U.S. firm Solar World, anti-dumping duties have been placed on solar-energy cells imported from China. The U.S. Commerce Department found that 60 Chinese firms dumped the cells in the U.S. markets. Anti-dumping penalties range from 25 percent to 250 percent depending upon how far below cost the Chinese firms were selling the solar-energy cells.[53]

COUNTERTRADE Global trade does not always involve cash. Countertrade is a fast-growing way to conduct global business. In **countertrade**, all or part of the payment for goods or services is in the form of other goods or services. Countertrade is thus a form of barter (swapping goods for goods), an age-old practice whose origins have been traced back to cave dwellers. The U.S. Department of Commerce says that roughly 30 percent of all global trade is countertrade.[54] In fact, both India and China have made billion-dollar government purchasing lists, with most of the goods to be paid for by countertrade.

One common type of countertrade is straight barter. For example, PepsiCo sends Pepsi syrup to Russian bottling plants and in payment gets Stolichnaya vodka, which is then marketed in the West. Another form of countertrade is the compensation agreement. Typically, a company provides technology and equipment for a plant in a developing nation and agrees to take full or partial payment in goods produced by that plant. For example, General Tire Company supplied equipment and know-how for a Romanian truck tire plant. In turn, General Tire sold the tires it received from the plant in the United States under the Victoria brand name. Both sides benefit even though they don't use cash.

5-6 THE IMPACT OF THE INTERNET

In many respects, going global is easier than it has ever been before. Opening an e-commerce site on the Internet immediately puts a company in the international marketplace. Sophisticated language translation software can make any site accessible to people around the world. Global shippers such as UPS, FedEx, and DHL help solve international e-commerce distribution complexities. E4X Inc. offers software to ease currency conversions by allowing customers to pay in the currency of their choice. E4X collects the payment from the customer and then pays the site in U.S. dollars. Nevertheless, the promise of "borderless commerce" and the global "Internet economy" are still being restrained by the old brick-and-mortar rules, regulations, and habits. For example, Lands' End is not allowed to mention its unconditional refund policy on its e-commerce site in Germany because German retailers, which normally do not allow returns after fourteen days, sued and won a court ruling blocking mention of it.

5-6a Social Media in Global Marketing

Because Facebook, YouTube, and other social media are popular around the world, firms both large and small have embraced social media marketing. Tim Hortons, a Canadian fast-casual restaurant chain known for its coffee and donuts, has more than 3,000 stores. To engage its Facebook fans, the company will occasionally post a picture of one of its restaurants on Facebook, and its 1.4 million fans guess the location. Every time a fan makes a guess, Facebook posts a Tim Hortons branded message to that fan's and his or her friends' news feeds. The Sacred Ride is a bicycle shop in the small town of Nelson, British Columbia. The firm created a Facebook page, purchased Facebook ads, and targeted the ads to mountain bike enthusiasts. Within a short time, the Sacred Ride had more than $40,000 in incremental sales from outside its regular market.

Accor, a French company operating more than 4,400 hotels worldwide, uses a company called TrustYou to monitor online reviews, tweets (a comment posted on Twitter), and blog posts. A **blog** is a publicly accessible Web page that functions as an interactive journal, where readers can post comments on the author's entries. TrustYou continuously gathers information in fifteen different languages from travel review and social media sites, including Facebook, Foursquare, Google Places, TripAdvisor,

HolidayCheck, Twitter, Qype, Yelp, and blogs, for user-generated content pertaining to a particular hotel or restaurant. TrustYou takes opinions from all online reviews, tweets, and posts and creates a comprehensive Trust Score that reflects the global sentiment for a specific hotel or restaurant. By monitoring social media via TrustYou, Accor hotels can see where they stand against competitors in all its markets and identify strengths and weaknesses.[55]

Global marketers use social media not only for understanding consumers but also to build their brands as they expand internationally. Uniqlo is a Japanese retailer of low-cost, quality casual wear targeted to young adults that competes directly with Zara and H&M. In 2006, the company began to shift its promotional focus to the Internet and away from traditional media such as newspapers and television. The creative campaigns emphasize dance, music, and color rather than the spoken word. This enables Uniqlo to overcome language barriers as the firm expands globally.

When Uniqlo's e-commerce site went down in 2010, the company launched the Lucky Counter game on Twitter. This Web-based game lowered the prices of select items based on followers' tweets—the more people tweeted about Uniqlo, the lower the prices fell.[56] One of the company's most recent online campaigns flooded

social pinning site Pinterest with branded mosaics across multiple categories. When users scrolled down the giant, colorful blocks of images, they appeared to animate. Uniqlo created 100 dummy Pinterest accounts to pin the images simultaneously, so the giant mosaics were seen by Pinterest users whether they followed Uniqlo or not. This campaign represented the first attempt to use Pinterest to promote a brand or product in such a way.[57]

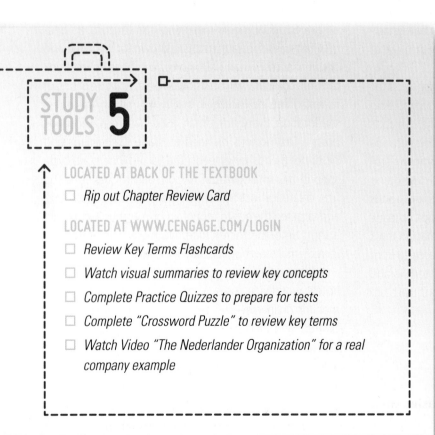

STUDY TOOLS 5

LOCATED AT BACK OF THE TEXTBOOK
☐ *Rip out Chapter Review Card*

LOCATED AT WWW.CENGAGE.COM/LOGIN
☐ *Review Key Terms Flashcards*
☐ *Watch visual summaries to review key concepts*
☐ *Complete Practice Quizzes to prepare for tests*
☐ *Complete "Crossword Puzzle" to review key terms*
☐ *Watch Video "The Nederlander Organization" for a real company example*

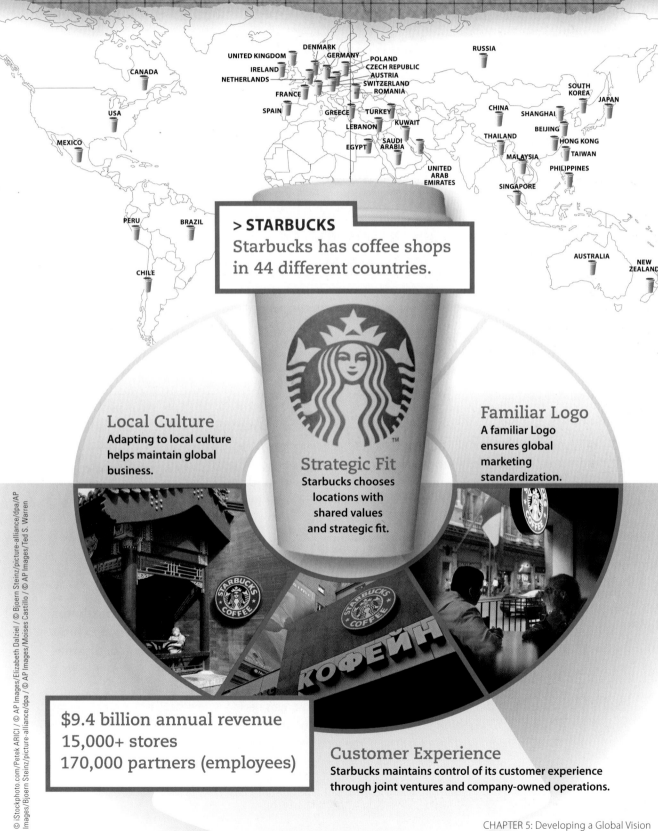

ANATOMY OF A MULTINATIONAL COMPANY: STARBUCKS

CANADA

USA

MEXICO

PERU

BRAZIL

CHILE

UNITED KINGDOM
IRELAND
NETHERLANDS
FRANCE
SPAIN

DENMARK
GERMANY
POLAND
CZECH REPUBLIC
AUSTRIA
SWITZERLAND
ROMANIA
GREECE
TURKEY
LEBANON
EGYPT
SAUDI ARABIA
KUWAIT
UNITED ARAB EMIRATES

RUSSIA

CHINA
SHANGHAI
BEIJING
THAILAND
MALAYSIA
SINGAPORE
HONG KONG
TAIWAN
PHILIPPINES

SOUTH KOREA
JAPAN

AUSTRALIA
NEW ZEALAND

> **STARBUCKS**
Starbucks has coffee shops in 44 different countries.

Strategic Fit
Starbucks chooses locations with shared values and strategic fit.

Local Culture
Adapting to local culture helps maintain global business.

Familiar Logo
A familiar Logo ensures global marketing standardization.

$9.4 billion annual revenue
15,000+ stores
170,000 partners (employees)

Customer Experience
Starbucks maintains control of its customer experience through joint ventures and company-owned operations.

6-1 THE IMPORTANCE OF UNDERSTANDING CONSUMER BEHAVIOR

Consumers' product and service preferences are constantly changing. Marketing managers must understand these desires in order to create a proper marketing mix for a well-defined market. So it is critical that marketing managers have a thorough knowledge of consumer behavior. **Consumer behavior** describes how consumers make purchase decisions and how they use and dispose of the purchased goods or services. The study of consumer behavior also includes factors that influence purchase decisions and product use.

> "You've got to be incredibly customer focused because the customer is in control." Steve Quinn, CEO, Walmart

consumer behavior processes a consumer uses to make purchase decisions, as well as to use and dispose of purchased goods or services; also includes factors that influence purchase decisions and product use

consumer decision-making process a five-step process used by consumers when buying goods or services

Understanding how consumers make purchase decisions can help marketing managers in several ways. For example, if a manager knows through research that gas mileage is the most important attribute for a certain target market, the manufacturer can redesign a car to meet that criterion. If the firm cannot change the design in the short run, it can use promotion in an effort to change consumers' decision-making criteria, for example, by promoting style, durability, and cargo capacity.

6-2 THE CONSUMER DECISION-MAKING PROCESS

When buying products, particularly new or expensive items, consumers generally follow the consumer decision-making process shown in Exhibit 1: (1) need recognition, (2) information search, (3) evaluation of alternatives, (4) purchase, and (5) postpurchase behavior. These five steps represent a general process that can be used as a guide for studying how consumers make decisions. It is important to note, though, that consumers' decisions do not always proceed in order through all of these steps. In fact, the consumer may end the process at any time or may not even make a purchase. The section on the types of consumer buying decisions later in the chapter discusses why a consumer's progression through these steps may vary. We begin, however, by examining the basic purchase process in greater detail.

Consumer Decision Making

Learning Outcomes

After you finish this chapter go to
p117 *for* **STUDY TOOLS**

6-2a Need Recognition

The first stage in the consumer decision-making process is need recognition. **Need recognition** is the result of an imbalance between actual and desired states. The imbalance arouses and activates the consumer decision-making process. A **want** is the recognition of an unfulfilled need and a product that will satisfy it. For example, have you ever gotten blisters from an old running shoe? Or maybe you have seen a television commercial for a new sports car and wanted to buy it. Need recognition is triggered when a consumer is exposed to either an internal or an external **stimulus**, which is any unit of input affecting one or more of the five senses: sight, smell, taste, touch, and hearing. *Internal stimuli* are occurrences you experience, such as hunger or thirst. For example, you may hear your stomach growl and then realize you are hungry. *External stimuli* are influences from an outside source, such as someone's recommendation of a new restaurant, the color of an automobile, the design of a package, a brand name mentioned by a friend, or an advertisement on television or radio.

The imbalance between actual and desired states is sometimes referred to as the *want-got gap*. That is, there is a difference between what a customer has and what he or she would like to have. This gap doesn't always trigger consumer action. The gap must be large enough to drive the consumer to do something. Just because your stomach growls once doesn't mean that you necessarily will stop what you are doing and go eat.

A marketing manager's objective is to get consumers to recognize this want-got gap. Advertising and sales promotion often provide this stimulus. Surveying buyer preferences provides marketers with information about consumer needs and wants that can be used to tailor products and services. Marketing managers can create wants on the part of the consumer. For example, when college students move into their own apartment or dorm room, they often need to furnish them and want new furniture rather than hand-me-downs from their parents. A want can be for a specific product, or it can be for a certain attribute or feature of a product. In this example, the college students not only need

home furnishings but also want items that reflect their personal sense of style. Similarly, consumers may want ready-to-eat meals, drive-through dry-cleaning service, and Internet shopping to fill their need for convenience.

UNDERSTANDING NEEDS AND WANTS If marketers don't properly understand the target market's needs, the right good or service will likely not be produced. An excellent way to understand needs is to view them as job statements or outcome statements. As economist Ted Levitt said, "People don't want to buy a quarter-inch drill. They want a quarter-inch hole."[1] A job is a fundamental goal that consumers are trying to accomplish or a problem they are trying to resolve; examples include preventing mildew in a shower, hanging a picture, or preparing income taxes. Desired outcome statements help marketers understand what consumers are seeking from a job. A desired outcome might be to minimize the time it takes to file an accurate income tax form that finds all possible legitimate deductions. People then can solve this problem several different ways: do the work themselves using government-provided information, do it themselves using software such as TurboTax, or hire a CPA to do it.

Marketers selling their products in global markets must carefully observe the needs and wants of consumers in various regions. Google was hit with massive shortages of the LG-manufactured

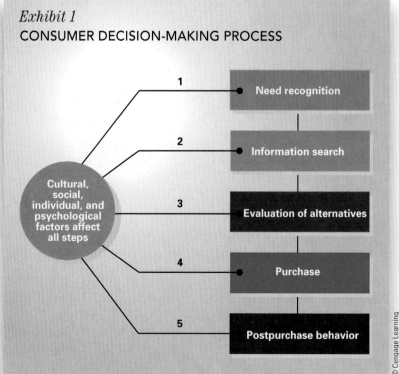

Exhibit 1
CONSUMER DECISION-MAKING PROCESS

1. Need recognition
2. Information search
3. Evaluation of alternatives
4. Purchase
5. Postpurchase behavior

Cultural, social, individual, and psychological factors affect all steps

© Cengage Learning

Nexus 4 smartphone after global demand proved to be far greater than anticipated. According to Cathy Robin of LG France, the shortage resulted from Google's inaccurate sales predictions, based on sales of previous Nexus models. "Predictions for the UK and Germany were ten times higher than for France," said Robin, "therefore we shipped a lot more to those markets than to France." Still, the handset sold out within minutes in the United Kingdom and the United States. The handset remained out of stock in the United States, Australia, and several European countries for months after its release.[2]

6-2b Information Search

After recognizing a need or want, consumers search for information about the various alternatives available to satisfy it. For example, you know you are interested in seeing a movie, but you aren't sure what to see. So you visit the Rotten Tomatoes Web site to see what is getting great reviews by both critics and your peers on Facebook. This is a type of information search, which can occur internally, externally, or both.

Kevin Thrash/Bloomberg/Getty Images

In an **internal information search**, the person recalls information stored in the memory. This stored information stems largely from previous experience with a product. For example, while traveling with your family, you may choose to stay at a hotel you have stayed in before because you remember that the hotel had clean rooms and friendly service.

In contrast, an **external information search** seeks information in the outside environment. There are two basic types of external information sources: nonmarketing-controlled and marketing-controlled. A **nonmarketing-controlled information source** is a product information source that is not associated with marketers promoting a product. These information sources include personal experiences (trying or observing a new product), personal sources (family, friends, acquaintances, and coworkers who may recommend a product or service), and public sources (such as Rotten Tomatoes, *Consumer Reports*, and other rating organizations that comment on products and services). Once you have read reviews on Rotten Tomatoes to decide which movie to see (public source), you may search your memory for positive theater experiences to determine where you'll go (personal experience). Or you might rely on a friend's recommendation to try out a new theatre (personal source). Marketers gather information on how these information sources work and use it to attract customers. For example, car manufacturers know that younger customers are likely to get information from friends and family, so they try to develop enthusiasm for their products via word of mouth.

Living in the digital age has changed the way consumers get nonmarketing-controlled information. It can be from blogs, bulletin boards, activists, Web sites, Web forums, or consumer opinion sites such as www.consumerreview .com, www.tripadvisor.com, or www.epinions.com. Eighty percent of U.S. consumers research electronics, computers, and media online before making an in-store purchase, and a quarter of shoppers utilize at least four sources for product information.[3] To give you an idea of the number of searches this implies, Google reported more than 4.7 billion searches *per day* in 2011.[4]

The latest research has examined how consumers use information picked up on the Internet. For example, in Web forums, the information seeker has normally never

marketing-controlled information source a product information source that originates with marketers promoting the product

evoked set (consideration set) a group of brands resulting from an information search from which a buyer can choose

met the information provider or ever interacted with the person before. Professor of economics Hui Chen found that online reviewers presenting full accounts of their entire online shopping experience influenced other shoppers to promote the company through word of mouth the most.[5] Reviews about pricing and quality of product influenced other shoppers the second most, and reviews discussing customer service by the company affected new consumers the least. Essentially, if other information seekers had found the provider trustworthy and kind, then the current seeker tended to believe the information, make a purchase, and then promote the company through other reviews.

A **marketing-controlled information source** is biased toward a specific product because it originates with marketers promoting that product. Marketing-controlled information sources include mass media advertising (radio, newspaper, television, and magazine advertising), sales promotion (contests, displays, premiums, and so forth), salespeople, product labels and packaging, and the Internet. Many consumers, however, are wary of the information they receive from marketing-controlled sources, believing that most marketing campaigns stress the product's positive attributes and ignore its faults. These sentiments tend to be stronger among better-educated and higher-income consumers. Some marketing-controlled information sources can shift out of marketers' control, however, when there is bad news to report. For example, in 2012, *Consumer Reports* dropped the Toyota Prius from its "recommended" list because of the car's "harsh ride, noisy engine and cabin, and slow acceleration." When the Honda Civic was dropped from *Consumer Reports'* list in 2011, Honda responded by completely redesigning the vehicle. Toyota has not yet responded to *Consumer Reports*, and may not ever, given the Prius's enduring popularity.[6]

The extent to which an individual conducts an external search depends on his or her perceived risk, knowledge, prior experience, and level of interest in the good or service. Generally, as the perceived risk of the purchase increases, the consumer enlarges the search and considers more alternative brands. For example, suppose that you want to purchase a surround-sound system for your home stereo. The decision is relatively risky because of the expense and technical nature of the stereo system, so you

are motivated to search for information about models, prices, options, compatibility with existing entertainment products, and capabilities. You may decide to compare attributes of many speaker systems because the value of the time expended finding the "right" stereo will be less than the cost of buying the wrong system.

A consumer's knowledge about the product or service will also affect the extent of an external information search. A consumer who is knowledgeable and well informed about a potential purchase is less likely to search for additional information. In addition, the more knowledgeable consumers are, the more efficiently they will conduct the search process, thereby requiring less time to search. For example, many consumers know that AirTran and other discount airlines have much lower fares, so they generally use the discounters and do not even check fares at other airlines.

The extent of a consumer's external search is also affected by confidence in one's decision-making ability. A confident consumer not only has sufficient stored information about the product but also feels self-assured about making the right decision. People lacking this confidence will continue an information search even when they know a great deal about the product. Consumers with prior experience in buying a certain product will have less perceived risk than inexperienced consumers. Therefore, they will spend less time searching and limit the number of products they consider.

A third factor influencing the external information search is product experience. Consumers who have had a positive experience with a product are more likely to limit their search to items related to the positive experience. For example, when flying, consumers are likely to choose airlines with which they have had positive experiences, such as consistent on-time arrivals, and avoid airlines with which they have had a negative experience, such as lost luggage.

Finally, the extent of the search is positively related to the amount of interest a consumer has in a product. A consumer who is more interested in a product will spend more time searching for information and alternatives. For example, suppose you are a dedicated runner who reads jogging and fitness magazines and catalogs. In searching for a new pair of running shoes, you may enjoy reading about the new brands available and spend more time and effort than other buyers in deciding on the right shoe.

The consumer's information search should yield a group of brands, sometimes called the buyer's **evoked set** (or **consideration set**), which are the consumer's most preferred alternatives. From this set, the buyer will further evaluate the alternatives and make a choice. Consumers do not consider all brands available in a product category, but they do seriously consider a much smaller set. For example, from the many brands of pizza available, consumers are likely to consider only the alternatives that fit their price range, location, take-out/delivery needs, and taste preferences. Having too many choices can, in fact, confuse consumers and cause them to delay the decision to buy, or in some instances, cause them not to buy at all.

6-2c Evaluation of Alternatives and Purchase

After getting information and constructing an evoked set of alternative products, the consumer is ready to make a decision. A consumer will use the information stored in memory and obtained from outside sources to develop a set of criteria. Recent research has shown that exposure to certain cues in your everyday environment can affect decision criteria and purchase. For example, when NASA landed the *Pathfinder* spacecraft on Mars, it captured media attention worldwide. The candy maker Mars also noted a rather unusual increase in sales. Although the Mars bar takes its name from the company's founder and not the planet, consumers apparently responded to news about the planet Mars by purchasing more Mars bars.

Further research also suggests that consumer reviews are influenced by existing reviews—if there are existing one-star ratings, even positive consumer reviews will have fewer stars. Additionally, if consumers see large variations in consumer reviews, they are more likely to purchase the item and make a postpurchase evaluation on that site.[7]

The environment, internal information, and external information help consumers evaluate and compare alternatives. One way to begin narrowing the number of choices in the evoked set is to pick a product attribute and then exclude all products in the set that don't have that attribute. For example, assume Jane and Jill, both college sophomores, are looking for their first apartment. They need a two-bedroom apartment, reasonably priced and located near campus. They want the apartment to have a swimming pool, washer and dryer, and covered parking. Jane and Jill begin their search with

all fifty apartments in the area and systematically eliminate complexes that lack the features they need. Hence, they may reduce their list to ten apartments that possess all of the desired attributes. Now they can use cutoffs to further narrow their choices. Cutoffs are either minimum or maximum levels of an attribute that an alternative must pass to be considered. Suppose Jane and Jill set a maximum of $1,000 per month for rent. Then all apartments with rent higher than $1,000 will be eliminated, further reducing the list of apartments from ten to eight. A final way to narrow the choices is to rank the attributes under consideration in order of importance and evaluate the products based on how well each performs on the most important attributes. To reach a final decision on one of the remaining eight apartments, Jane and Jill may decide proximity to campus is the most important attribute. As a result, they will choose to rent the apartment closest to campus.

If new brands are added to an evoked set, the consumer's evaluation of the existing brands in that set changes. As a result, certain brands in the original set may become more desirable. Suppose Jane and Jill find two apartments

THAT APARTMENT WAS IN A REALLY NICE PART OF TOWN AND HAD A BIG KITCHEN, BUT IT COST $1,800 A MONTH.

LET'S APPLY FOR THE ONE THAT COST $850— IT WAS CLOSE TO CAMPUS AND HAD A WASHING MACHINE!

located an equal distance from campus, one priced at $800 and the other at $750. Faced with this choice, they may decide that the $800 apartment is too expensive given that a comparable apartment is cheaper. If they add a $900 apartment to the list, however, then they may perceive the $800 apartment as more reasonable and decide to rent it.

The purchase decision process described above is a piecemeal process. That is, the evaluation is made by examining alternative advantages and disadvantages along important product attributes. A different way consumers can evaluate a product is according to a categorization process. The evaluation of an alternative depends upon the particular category to which it is assigned. Categories can be very general (motorized forms of transportation), or they can be very specific (Harley-Davidson motorcycles). Typically, these categories are associated with some degree of liking or disliking. To the extent that the product can be assigned membership in a particular category, it will receive an evaluation similar to that attached to the category. If you go to the grocery store and see a new organic food on the shelf, you may evaluate it on your liking and opinions of organic food.

So, when consumers rely on a categorization process, a product's evaluation depends on the particular category to which it is perceived as belonging. Given this, companies need to understand whether consumers are using categories that evoke the desired evaluations. Indeed, how a product is categorized can strongly influence consumer demand.

For example, what products come to mind when you think about the "morning beverages" category? To the soft drink industry's dismay, far too few consumers include sodas in this category. Several attempts have been made at getting soft drinks on the breakfast table, but with little success.

Brand extensions, in which a well-known and respected brand name from one product category is extended into other product categories, is one way companies employ categorization to their advantage. Brand extensions are a common business practice. For example, mixed martial arts promotional organization Ultimate Fighting Championship (UFC) has built its brand on pay-per-view events, cable and network television broadcasts, and merchandising. In 2013, the UFC launched a 24-hour full-service gym in Long Island, New York. In addition to martial arts–themed activities, the UFC Gym features standard fitness equipment, a café, and signature classes like Hot Hula and Hi-Octane Conditioning.[8]

TO BUY OR NOT TO BUY Ultimately, the consumer has to decide whether to buy or not buy. Specifically, consumers must decide:

1. **Whether to buy**
2. **When to buy**
3. **What to buy (product type and brand)**
4. **Where to buy (type of retailer, specific retailer, online or in store)**
5. **How to pay**

The UFC Gym extends the Ultimate Fighting Championship's combative nature and gritty aesthetic into a new product category.

When a person is buying an expensive or complex item, it is often a *fully planned purchase* based upon a lot of information. People rarely buy a new home simply on impulse. Often, consumers will make a *partially planned purchase* when they know the product category they want to buy (shirts, pants, reading lamp, car floor mats) but wait until they get to the store to choose a specific style or brand. Finally, there is the *unplanned purchase*, which people buy on impulse. The Great Recession has affected peoples' willingness to make unplanned purchases. In a recent study, 54 percent of consumers said they were buying fewer items on impulse. Fifty-nine percent reported that more than half of their purchases were bought on sale, and 65 percent reported that they would wait to purchase an item until it went on sale.[9]

6-3 POSTPURCHASE BEHAVIOR

When buying products, consumers expect certain outcomes from the purchase. How well these expectations are met determines whether the consumer is satisfied or dissatisfied with the purchase. For example, if a person bids on a used car stereo from eBay and wins, he may have fairly low expectations regarding performance. If the stereo's performance turns out to be of superior quality, then the person's satisfaction will be high because his expectations were exceeded. Conversely, if the person bids on a new car stereo expecting superior quality and performance, but the stereo breaks within one month, he will be very dissatisfied because his expectations were not met. Price often influences the level of expectations for a product or service.

For the marketer, an important element of any postpurchase evaluation is reducing any lingering doubts that the decision was sound. When people recognize inconsistency between their values or opinions and their behavior, they tend to feel an inner tension called **cognitive dissonance**. For example, suppose Angelika is looking to purchase an e-reader. After evaluating her options, she has decided to purchase an iPad, even though it is much more expensive than other dedicated e-readers. Prior to choosing the iPad, Angelika may experience inner tension or anxiety because she is worried that the current top-of-the-line technology, which costs much more than the middle-of-the-line technology, will be obsolete in a couple months. That feeling of dissonance arises as her worries over obsolescence battle her practical nature, which is focused on the lower cost of a NOOK HD and its adequate—but less fancy—technology.

Consumers try to reduce dissonance by justifying their decision. They may seek new information that reinforces positive ideas about the purchase, avoid information that contradicts their decision, or revoke the original decision by returning the product. In some instances, people deliberately seek contrary information in order to refute it and reduce dissonance. Dissatisfied customers sometimes rely on word of mouth to reduce cognitive dissonance by letting friends and family know they are displeased.

Marketing managers can help reduce dissonance through effective communication with purchasers. For example, a customer service manager may slip a note inside the package congratulating the buyer on making a wise decision. Postpurchase letters sent by manufacturers and dissonance-reducing statements in instruction booklets may help customers feel at ease with their purchase. Advertising that displays the product's superiority over competing brands or guarantees can also help relieve the possible dissonance of someone who has already bought the product. Apple's Genius Bar and customer service will ease cognitive dissonance for purchasers of an iPad because they know that the company is there to support them.

cognitive dissonance inner tension that a consumer experiences after recognizing an inconsistency between behavior and values or opinions

involvement the amount of time and effort a buyer invests in the search, evaluation, and decision processes of consumer behavior

routine response behavior the type of decision making exhibited by consumers buying frequently purchased, low-cost goods and services; requires little search and decision time

6-4 TYPES OF CONSUMER BUYING DECISIONS AND CONSUMER INVOLVEMENT

All consumer buying decisions generally fall along a continuum of three broad categories: routine response behavior, limited decision making, and extensive decision making (see Exhibit 2). Goods and services in these three categories can best be described in terms of five factors:

- ➡ **Level of consumer involvement**
- ➡ **Length of time to make a decision**
- ➡ **Cost of the good or service**
- ➡ **Degree of information search**
- ➡ **Number of alternatives considered**

The level of consumer involvement is perhaps the most significant determinant in classifying buying decisions. **Involvement** is the amount of time and effort a buyer invests in the search, evaluation, and decision processes of consumer behavior.

Frequently purchased, low-cost goods and services are generally associated with **routine response behavior**. These goods and services can also be called *low-involvement products* because consumers spend little time on search and decision before making the purchase. Usually, buyers are familiar with several different brands in the product category but stick with one brand. For example, a

limited decision making the type of decision making that requires a moderate amount of time for gathering information and deliberating about an unfamiliar brand in a familiar product category

extensive decision making the most complex type of consumer decision making, used when buying an unfamiliar, expensive product or an infrequently bought item; requires use of several criteria for evaluating options and much time for seeking information

person may routinely buy Tropicana orange juice. Consumers engaged in routine response behavior normally don't experience need recognition until they are exposed to advertising or see the product displayed on a store shelf. Consumers buy first and evaluate later, whereas the reverse is true for extensive decision making. A consumer who has previously purchased whitening toothpaste and was satisfied with it will probably walk to the toothpaste aisle and select that same brand without spending twenty minutes examining all other alternatives.

Limited decision making typically occurs when a consumer has previous product experience but is unfamiliar with the current brands available. Limited decision making is also associated with lower levels of involvement (although higher than routine decisions) because consumers expend only moderate effort in searching for information or in considering various alternatives. But what happens if the consumer's usual brand of whitening toothpaste is sold out? Assuming that toothpaste is needed, the consumer will be forced to choose another brand. Before making a final decision, the consumer will likely evaluate several other brands based on their active ingredients, their promotional claims, and the consumer's prior experiences.

Consumers practice **extensive decision making** when buying an unfamiliar, expensive product or an infrequently bought item. This process is the most complex type of consumer buying decision and is associated with high involvement on the part of the consumer. This process resembles the model outlined in Exhibit 1. These consumers want to make the right decision, so they want to know as much as they can about the product category and available brands. People usually experience the most cognitive dissonance when buying high-involvement products. Buyers use several criteria for evaluating their options and spend much time seeking information. Buying a home or a car, for example, requires extensive decision making.

The type of decision making that consumers use to purchase a product does not necessarily remain constant. For instance, if a routinely purchased product no longer satisfies, consumers may practice limited or extensive decision making to switch to another brand. And people who first use extensive decision making may then use limited or routine decision making for future purchases. For example, when a family gets a new puppy, they will spend a lot of time and energy trying out different toys to determine which one the dog prefers. Once the new owners learn that the dog prefers a bone to a ball, however, the purchase no longer requires extensive evaluation and will become routine.

© iStockphoto.com / Kenneth C. Zirkel

6-4a Factors Determining the Level of Consumer Involvement

The level of involvement in the purchase depends on the following factors:

Exhibit 2
CONTINUUM OF CONSUMER BUYING DECISIONS

	Routine	Limited	Extensive
Involvement	Low	Low to moderate	High
Time	Short	Short to moderate	Long
Cost	Low	Low to moderate	High
Information Search	Internal only	Mostly internal	Internal and external
Number of Alternatives	One	Few	Many

© Cengage Learning

- **PREVIOUS EXPERIENCE:** When consumers have had previous experience with a good or service, the level of involvement typically decreases. After repeated product trials, consumers learn to make quick choices. Because consumers are familiar with the product and know whether it will satisfy their needs, they become less involved in the purchase. For example, a consumer purchasing cereal has many brands to choose from—just think of any grocery store cereal aisle. If the consumer always buys the same brand because it satisfies his hunger, then he has a low level of involvement. When a consumer purchases cereal for the first time, however, it likely will be a much more involved purchase.

- **INTEREST:** Involvement is directly related to consumer interests, as in cars, music, movies, bicycling, or electronics. Naturally, these areas of interest vary from one individual to another. A person highly involved in bike racing will be more interested in the type of bike she owns and will spend quite a bit of time evaluating different bikes. If a person wants a bike only for recreation, however, he may be fairly uninvolved in the purchase and just look for a bike from the most convenient location.

- **PERCEIVED RISK OF NEGATIVE CONSEQUENCES:** As the perceived risk in purchasing a product increases, so does a consumer's level of involvement. The types of risks that concern consumers include financial risk, social risk, and psychological risk.

- **FINANCIAL RISK** is exposure to loss of wealth or purchasing power. Because high risk is associated with high-priced purchases, consumers tend to become extremely involved. Therefore, price and involvement are usually directly related: As price increases, so does the level of involvement. For example, someone who is purchasing a new car for the first time (higher perceived risk) will spend a lot of time and effort making this purchase. Financial risk may carry greater weight today because of the Great Recession. The loss of jobs and potential loss of jobs meant that prices did not necessarily have to be high to have high involvement. In 2013, 67 percent of consumers said they were buying more selectively and sticking to a strict budget.[10]

- **SOCIAL RISKS** occur when consumers buy products that can affect people's social opinions of them (for example, driving an old, beat-up car or wearing unstylish clothes).

- **PSYCHOLOGICAL RISKS** occur if consumers believe that making the wrong decision might cause some concern or anxiety. For example, some consumers feel guilty about eating foods that are not healthy, such as regular ice cream rather than fat-free frozen yogurt.

- **SOCIAL VISIBILITY:** Involvement also increases as the social visibility of a product increases. Products often on social display include clothing (especially designer labels), jewelry, cars, and furniture. All these items make a statement about the purchaser and, therefore, carry a social risk.

NOT ALL INVOLVEMENT IS THE SAME High involvement means that the consumer cares about a product category or a specific good or service. The product or service is relevant and important, and means something to the

Purchase involvement depends on level of interest. If this shopper is looking to use a bike as her main mode of transportation, then she is highly involved in this purchase decision.

© Cultura RM/Alamy

buyer. High involvement can take a number of different forms. The most important types are discussed below:

▸ **PRODUCT INVOLVEMENT** means that a product category has high personal relevance. Product enthusiasts are consumers with high involvement in a product category. The fashion industry has a large segment of product enthusiasts. These people are seeking the latest fashion trends and want to wear the latest clothes.

▸ **SITUATIONAL INVOLVEMENT** means that the circumstances of a purchase may temporarily transform a low-involvement decision into a high-involvement one. High involvement comes into play when the consumer perceives risk in a specific situation. For example, an individual might routinely buy low-priced brands of liquor and wine. When the boss visits, however, the consumer might make a high-involvement decision and buy more prestigious brands.

▸ **SHOPPING INVOLVEMENT** represents the personal relevance of the process of shopping. Modern shoppers tend to browse less and make fewer impulse buys because they shop on a mission. With armloads of research from the Internet, shoppers go into the store, buy what they came for, and get out. To these shoppers, the physical shopping is not as important as doing the research at home. Retailers must do their best to engage these mission shoppers in order to get them involved in the store and the shopping experience.[11]

▸ **ENDURING INVOLVEMENT** represents an ongoing interest in some product or activity. The consumer is always searching for opportunities to consume the product or participate in the activity. Enduring involvement typically gives personal gratification to consumers as they continue to learn about, shop for, and consume these goods and services. Therefore, there is often linkage between enduring involvement and shopping and product involvement.

▸ **EMOTIONAL INVOLVEMENT** represents how emotional a consumer gets during some specific consumption activity. Emotional involvement is closely related to enduring involvement because the things that consumers care most about will eventually create high emotional involvement. Sports fans typify consumers with high emotional involvement. The Olympics are one example of high emotional involvement in sporting outcomes.[12]

6-4b Marketing Implications of Involvement

Marketing strategy varies according to the level of involvement associated with the product. For high-involvement product purchases, marketing managers have several responsibilities. First, promotion to the target market should be extensive and informative. A good ad gives consumers the information they need for making the purchase decision and specifies the benefits and unique advantages of owning the product. For example, Ford has a vehicle with many custom options that is marketed to small business owners. One example of a recent print ad shows how one entrepreneur customized his Ford Transit Connect to help improve the efficiency of his home theater and electronics installation business. Ford highlights the fact that unique businesses need unique and customizable transportation. This ad not only demonstrates the customer's satisfaction, it also shows the hauling capacity of the vehicle.

For low-involvement product purchases, consumers may not recognize their wants until they are in the store. Therefore, in-store promotion is an important tool when promoting low-involvement products. Marketing managers focus on package design so the product will be eye-catching and easily recognized on the shelf. Examples of products that take this approach are Campbell's soups, Tide detergent, Velveeta cheese, and Heinz ketchup. In-store displays also stimulate sales of low-involvement products. A good display can explain the product's purpose and prompt recognition of a want. Displays of snack foods in supermarkets have been known to increase sales many times above normal. Coupons, cents-off deals, and two-for-one offers also effectively promote low-involvement items.

© Richard Levine/Alamy

Tide uses bright, eye-catching packaging to draw customers to what is otherwise a low-involvement product.

Linking a product to a higher-involvement issue is another tactic that marketing managers can use to increase the sales or positive publicity of a low-involvement product. For example, in 2012, Elevation Beer Company released Prostator, a smoked doppelbock beer that features a light blue ribbon and text about prostate cancer awareness on its label.[13]

It is important to understand that the consumer decision-making process does not occur in a vacuum. On the contrary, underlying cultural, social, individual, and psychological factors strongly influence the decision process. These factors have an effect from the time a consumer perceives a stimulus through postpurchase behavior. Cultural factors, which include culture and values, subculture, and social class, exert a broad influence over consumer decision making. Social factors sum up the social interactions between a consumer and influential groups of people, such as reference groups, opinion leaders, and family members. Individual factors, which include gender, age, family life cycle stage, personality, self-concept, and lifestyle, are unique to each individual and play a major role in the type of products and services consumers want. Psychological factors determine how consumers perceive and interact with their environments and influence the ultimate decisions consumers make. They include perception, motivation, learning, beliefs, and attitudes. Exhibit 3 summarizes these influences, and the following sections cover each in more detail.

6-5 CULTURAL INFLUENCES ON CONSUMER BUYING DECISIONS

Of all the factors that affect consumer decision making, cultural factors exert the broadest and deepest influence. Marketers must understand the way people's culture and its accompanying values, as well as their subculture and social class, influence their buying behavior.

6-5a Culture and Values

Culture is the set of values, norms, attitudes, and other meaningful symbols that shape human behavior and the artifacts, or products, of that behavior as they are transmitted from one generation to the next. It is the essential character of a society that distinguishes it from other cultural

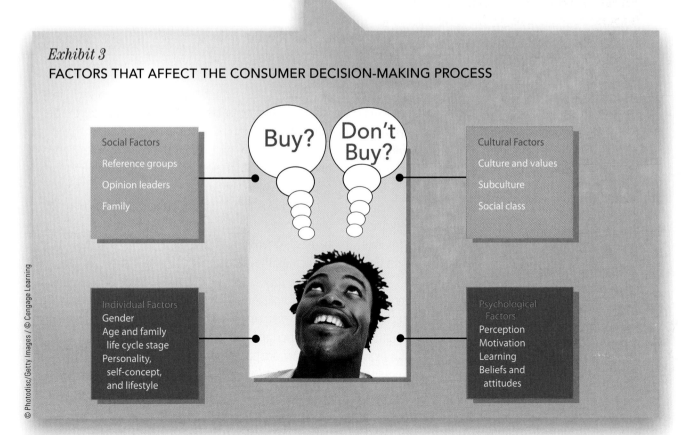

Exhibit 3
FACTORS THAT AFFECT THE CONSUMER DECISION-MAKING PROCESS

© Photodisc/Getty Images / © Cengage Learning

Social Factors
Reference groups
Opinion leaders
Family

Buy?

Don't Buy?

Cultural Factors
Culture and values
Subculture
Social class

Individual Factors
Gender
Age and family
life cycle stage
Personality,
self-concept,
and lifestyle

Psychological Factors
Perception
Motivation
Learning
Beliefs and
attitudes

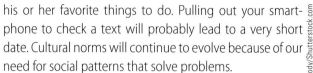

© bloody/Shutterstock.com

groups. The underlying elements of every culture are the values, language, myths, customs, rituals, and laws that guide the behavior of the people.

Culture is pervasive. Cultural values and influences are the ocean in which individuals swim, and yet most are completely unaware that it is there. What people eat, how they dress, what they think and feel, and what language they speak are all dimensions of culture. Culture encompasses all the things consumers do without conscious choice because their culture's values, customs, and rituals are ingrained in their daily habits.

Culture is functional. Human interaction creates values and prescribes acceptable behavior for each culture. By establishing common expectations, culture gives order to society. Sometimes these expectations are enacted into laws. For example, drivers in our culture must stop at a red light. Other times these expectations are taken for granted: grocery stores and hospitals are open twenty-four hours, whereas banks are open only during bankers' hours.

Culture is learned. Consumers are not born knowing the values and norms of their society. Instead, they must learn what is acceptable from family and friends. Children learn the values that will govern their behavior from parents, teachers, and peers. As members of our society, they learn to shake hands when they greet someone, to drive on the right-hand side of the road, and to eat pizza and drink Coca-Cola.

Culture is dynamic. It adapts to changing needs and an evolving environment. The rapid growth of technology in today's world has accelerated the rate of cultural change. Our culture is beginning to tell us when it is okay to send a text message and when it is considered impolite. Assume that you are on a first date with someone in a nice, romantic restaurant and your date is talking to you about

his or her favorite things to do. Pulling out your smartphone to check a text will probably lead to a very short date. Cultural norms will continue to evolve because of our need for social patterns that solve problems.

The most defining element of a culture is its values. A **value** is an enduring belief shared by a society that a specific mode of conduct is personally or socially preferable to another mode of conduct. People's value systems have a great effect on their consumer behavior. Consumers with similar value systems tend to react alike to prices and other marketing-related inducements. Values also correspond to consumption patterns. For example, Americans place a high value on convenience. This value has created lucrative markets for products such as breakfast bars, energy bars, and nutrition bars that allow consumers to eat on the go. Values can also influence consumers' television viewing habits or the magazines they read. For instance, people who strongly object to violence avoid crime shows, and those who oppose pornography do not buy *Hustler*.

6-5b Understanding Cultural Differences

As more companies expand their operations globally, the need to understand the cultures of foreign countries becomes more important. A firm has little chance of selling products in a culture that it does not understand. Like people, products have cultural values and rules that influence their perception and use. Culture, therefore, must be understood before the behavior of individuals within the cultural context can be understood. Colors, for example, may have different meanings in global markets than they do at home. In China, white is the color of mourning and brides wear red. In the United States, black is for mourning and brides wear white.

Language is another important aspect of culture that global marketers must consider. When translating product names, slogans, and promotional messages into foreign languages, they must be careful not to convey the wrong message. Coors encouraged its English-speaking customers to "Turn it loose," but the phrase in Spanish means "Suffer from diarrhea."

Although marketers expanding into global markets generally adapt their products and business formats to the local culture, some fear that increasing globalization, as well as the proliferation of the Internet, will result in a homogeneous world culture of the future. U.S. companies in particular, they fear, are Americanizing the world by exporting bastions of American culture, such as McDonald's fast-food restaurants, Starbucks coffeehouses, Microsoft software, and American movies and entertainment.

6-5c Subculture

A culture can be divided into subcultures on the basis of demographic characteristics, geographic regions, national and ethnic background, political beliefs, and religious beliefs. A **subculture** is a homogeneous group of people who share elements of the overall culture as well as cultural elements unique to their own group. Within subcultures, people's attitudes, values, and purchase decisions are even more similar than they are within the broader culture. Subcultural differences may result in considerable variation within a culture in what, how, when, and where people buy goods and services.

In the United States alone, countless subcultures can be identified. Many are concentrated geographically. People who belong to the Church of Jesus Christ of Latter-Day Saints, for example, are clustered mainly in Utah; Cajuns are located in the bayou regions of southern Louisiana. Many Hispanics live in states bordering Mexico, whereas the majority of Chinese, Japanese, and Korean Americans are found on the West Coast. Other subcultures are geographically dispersed. Computer hackers, people who are hearing or visually impaired, Harley-Davidson bikers, military families, and university professors may be found throughout the country. Yet they have identifiable attitudes, values, and needs that distinguish them from the larger culture.

6-5d Social Class

The United States, like other societies, has a social class system. A **social class** is a group of people who are considered nearly equal in status or community esteem, who regularly socialize among themselves both formally and informally, and who share behavioral norms.

A number of techniques have been used to measure social class, and a number of criteria have been used to define it. One view of contemporary U.S. status structure is shown in Exhibit 4.

As you can see from Exhibit 4, the upper and upper middle classes comprise the small segment of affluent and wealthy Americans. In terms of consumer buying patterns, the affluent are more likely to own their own homes and purchase new cars and trucks and are less likely to smoke. The very rich flex their financial muscles by spending more on vacation homes, vacations and cruises, and housekeeping and gardening services. The most affluent consumers are more likely to attend art auctions and galleries, dance performances, operas, the theater, museums, concerts, and sporting events. Marketers often pay attention to the superwealthy. While multi-thousand dollar wristwatches have long been seen as a sign of great wealth, luxury smartphones have only recently emerged as popular accessories among the affluent elite. The Porsche-designed BlackBerry P'9981 starts at $2,000, and the Android-based Lamborghini TL700 can be purchased for just $750 more. Diamond-encrusted iPhones designed by Continental Mobiles and Gresso can be purchased for $10,900 and $30,000 respectively. For the truly rich and fabulous, the Ulysse Nardin—an Android-based

subculture a homogeneous group of people who share elements of the overall culture as well as unique elements of their own group

social class a group of people in a society who are considered nearly equal in status or community esteem, who regularly socialize among themselves both formally and informally, and who share behavioral norms

¿HAY MUCHO DINERO? ¡QUE CHEVERE!

Once marketers identify subcultures, they can design special marketing to serve their needs. The United States' growing Hispanic population has made South and Central American subcultures a prime focus for many companies with large marketing budgets. The top four spenders on Spanish-language media in the United States are:

1. **Procter & Gamble ($226 million): Procter & Gamble (P&G) has been so successful in reaching Hispanic markets that instead of referring to diapers by the Spanish word *pañales*, many Hispanic parents simply use a P&G brand name—Pampers.**

2. **Bancorp Inc. ($193 million): Bancorp is the parent company of U.S. Bank, which has hundreds of locations across the West Coast and Southwest.**

3. **Dish Network ($161 million): Dish has captured a large swath of Hispanic viewers by offering a wide range of Spanish-language channels from all over Latin America.**

4. **McDonald's ($132 million): McDonald's has had success in Hispanic markets using a translation of its iconic "I'm Lovin' It" slogan—"Me Encanta."[14]**

The rising popularity of electronic dance music has fostered a burgeoning subculture among young concert-goers in the United States. Here, thousands of guests attend the 2013 Ultra Music Festival at Bayfront Park Amphitheater in Miami, Florida.

smartphone encrusted with 3,000 diamonds totaling seventeen carats—retails for $129,000.[15]

The majority of Americans today define themselves as middle class, regardless of their actual income or educational attainment. This phenomenon most likely occurs because working-class Americans tend to aspire to the middle-class lifestyle, while some of those who do achieve affluence may downwardly aspire to respectable middle-class status as a matter of principle.

The working class is a distinct subset of the middle class. Interest in organized labor is one of the most common attributes among the working class. This group often rates job security as the most important reason for taking a job. The working-class person depends heavily on relatives and the community for economic and emotional support.

Lifestyle distinctions between the social classes are greater than the distinctions within a given class. The most significant difference between the classes occurs between the middle and lower classes, where there is a major shift in lifestyles. Members of the lower class have annual incomes at or below the poverty level—$20,665 for individuals and $42,643 for families of four.[16]

Social class is typically measured as a combination of occupation, income, education, wealth, and other variables. For instance, affluent upper-class consumers are more likely to be salaried executives or self-employed professionals with at least an undergraduate degree. Working-class or middle-class consumers are more likely to be hourly service workers or blue-collar employees with only a high school education. Educational attainment, however, seems to be the most reliable indicator of a person's social and economic status. Those with college degrees or graduate degrees are more likely to fall into the upper classes, while those with some college experience fall closest to traditional concepts of the middle class.

Marketers are interested in social class for two main reasons. First, social class often indicates which medium to use for advertising. Suppose an insurance company seeks to sell its policies to middle-class families. It might advertise during the local evening news because middle-class families tend to watch more television than other classes do. If the company wanted to sell more policies to upscale individuals, it might place an ad in a business publication like the *Wall Street Journal*. The Internet, long the domain of more educated and affluent families, is becoming an increasingly important advertising outlet for advertisers hoping to reach blue-collar workers and homemakers. As the middle class rapidly adopts the medium, marketers have to do more research to find out which Web sites will reach their audience.

Second, knowing what products appeal to which social classes can help marketers determine where to best

Exhibit 4
U.S. SOCIAL CLASSES

Upper Classes		
Capitalist class	1%	People whose investment decisions shape the national economy; income mostly from assets, earned or inherited; university connections
Upper middle class	14%	Upper-level managers, professionals, owners of medium-sized businesses; well-to-do homemakers who decline occupational work by choice; college educated; family income well above national average
Middle Classes		
Middle class	33%	Middle-level white-collar, top-level blue-collar; education past high school typical; income somewhat above national average; loss of manufacturing jobs has reduced the population of this class
Working class	32%	Middle-level blue-collar, lower-level white-collar; income below national average; largely working in skilled or semi-skilled service jobs
Lower Classes		
Working poor	11–12%	Low-paid service workers and operatives; some high school education; below mainstream in living standard; crime and hunger are daily threats
Underclass	8–9%	People who are not regularly employed and who depend primarily on the welfare system for sustenance; little schooling; living standard below poverty line

Sources: Adapted from Richard P. Coleman, "The Continuing Significance of Social Class to Marketing," *Journal of Consumer Research*, December 1983, 267; Dennis Gilbert and Joseph A. Kahl, *The American Class Structure: A Synthesis* (Homewood, IL: Dorsey Press, 1982), ch. 11.

distribute their products. Affluent Americans, one-fifth of the U.S. population, have changed their buying habits since the Great Recession ended. They are now willing to spend more of their discretionary income on one-of-a-kind items. They are also spending more per item than in previous years. This trend will likely increase as the world pulls further out of recession—market research suggests that luxury goods sales will increase $74 billion by 2017.[17]

This shift has caused many full-priced and upscale retailers to demonstrate larger gains in revenue over discount chains. Because many lower-income consumers are still struggling to recover from job loss, retailers such as Walmart are selling smaller packages of items because customers do not have enough cash to buy more standard-size products. Even amid skyrocketing cotton prices, apparel stores that target the middle class, like H&M, are raising prices by only pennies for fear of driving away customers.[18]

6-6 SOCIAL INFLUENCES ON CONSUMER BUYING DECISIONS

Many consumers seek out the opinions of others to reduce their search and evaluation effort or uncertainty, especially as the perceived risk of the decision increases. Consumers may also seek out others' opinions for guidance on new products or services, products with image-related attributes, or products for which attribute information is lacking or uninformative. Specifically, consumers interact socially with reference groups, opinion leaders, and family members to obtain product information and decision approval.

6-6a Reference Groups

People interact with many reference groups. A **reference group** consists of all the formal and informal groups that influence the buying behavior of an individual. Consumers may use products or brands to identify with or become a member of a group. They learn from observing how members of their reference groups consume, and they use the same criteria to make their own consumer decisions.

Reference groups can be categorized very broadly as either direct or indirect (see Exhibit 5). Direct reference groups are face-to-face membership groups that touch people's lives directly. They can be either primary or secondary. A **primary membership group** includes all groups with

reference group all of the formal and informal groups in society that influence an individual's purchasing behavior

primary membership group a reference group with which people interact regularly in an informal, face-to-face manner, such as family, friends, and coworkers

secondary membership group a reference group with which people associate less consistently and more formally than a primary membership group, such as a club, professional group, or religious group

aspirational reference group a group that someone would like to join

norm a value or attitude deemed acceptable by a group

nonaspirational reference group a group with which an individual does not want to associate

opinion leader an individual who influences the opinions of others

which people interact regularly in an informal, face-to-face manner, such as family, friends, and coworkers. Today, they may also communicate by e-mail, text messages, Facebook, Skype, or other electronic means. In contrast, people associate with a **secondary membership group** less consistently and more formally. These groups might include clubs, professional groups, and religious groups.

Consumers also are influenced by many indirect, nonmembership reference groups to which they do not belong. An **aspirational reference group** is a group a person would like to join. To join an aspirational group, a person must at least conform to the norms of that group. (A **norm** consists of the values and attitudes deemed acceptable by the group.) Thus, a person who wants to be elected to public office may begin to dress more conservatively, as other politicians do. He or she may go to many of the restaurants and social engagements that city and business leaders attend and try to play a role that is acceptable to voters and other influential people.

Nonaspirational reference groups, or dissociative groups, influence our behavior when we try to maintain distance from them. A consumer may avoid buying some types of clothing or cars, going to certain restaurants or stores, or even buying a home in a certain neighborhood to avoid being associated with a particular group. For middle- and upper-middle-class professionals who take an interest in Harley-Davidson motorcycles, biker gangs serve as both an aspirational and a nonaspirational reference group. Though the professionals (derisively called RUBS—rich urban bikers—by hardcore Harley enthusiasts) aspire to the freedom, community, and tough posturing of biker gangs, they do not aspire to the perpetual life on the road, crime, or violence of gangs. Thus, a professional may buy a Harley because of the gangs, but he may intentionally buy a specific model not typically associated with those gangs.[19]

Reference groups are particularly powerful in influencing the clothes people wear, the cars they drive, the electronics they use, the activities they participate in, the foods they eat, and the luxury goods they purchase.[20] In short, the activities, values, and goals of reference groups directly influence consumer behavior. For marketers, reference groups have three important implications: (1) They serve as information sources and influence perceptions; (2) they affect an individual's aspiration levels; and (3) their norms either constrain or stimulate consumer behavior. However, marketers must also consider that people with well-formed networks of somewhat overlapping reference groups and those with strong personal values are less susceptible to reference group influences.[21]

6-6b Opinion Leaders

Reference groups frequently include an individual known as a group leader, or **opinion leader**—a person who influences others. Obviously, it is important for marketing managers to persuade such people to

Exhibit 5
TYPES OF REFERENCE GROUPS

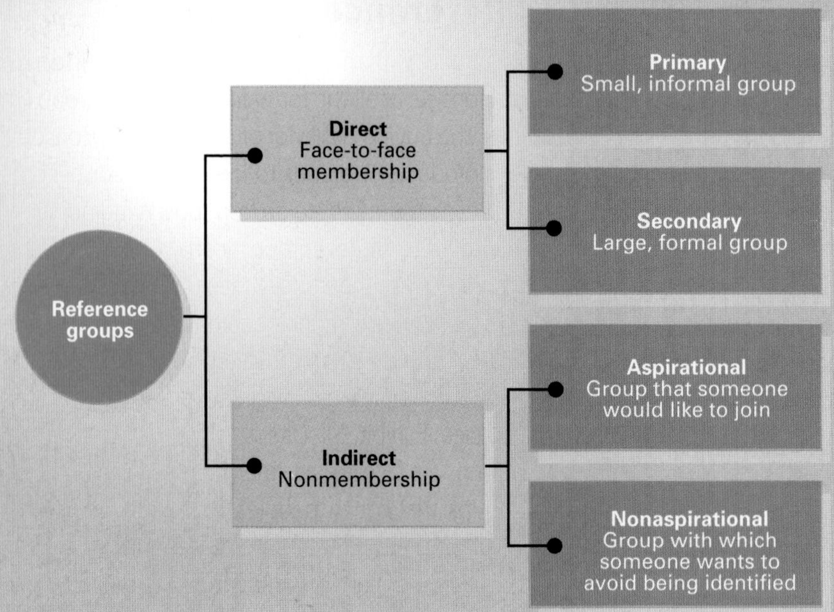

Reference groups

Direct — Face-to-face membership
- Primary — Small, informal group
- Secondary — Large, formal group

Indirect — Nonmembership
- Aspirational — Group that someone would like to join
- Nonaspirational — Group with which someone wants to avoid being identified

© Cengage Learning

Members of the Hell's Angels biker gang make their way to the funeral of Hell's Angels member Steve Tausan. Tausan was shot to death while attending the funeral of another Hell's Angel, Jeffrey "Jethro" Pettigrew.

purchase their goods or services. Many products and services that are integral parts of Americans' lives today got their initial boost from opinion leaders. For example, Kindles and iPads were purchased by opinion leaders well ahead of the general public.

Opinion leaders are often the first to try new products and services out of pure curiosity. They are often the most influential, informed, plugged-in, and vocal members of society.[22] Technology companies have found that teenagers, because of their willingness to experiment, are key opinion leaders for the success of new technologies.

Opinion leadership is a casual phenomenon and is usually inconspicuous, so locating opinion leaders can be a challenge. Thus, marketers often try to create opinion leaders. They may use high school cheerleaders to model new fall fashions or civic leaders to promote insurance, new cars, and other merchandise. On a national level, companies sometimes use movie stars, sports figures, and other celebrities to promote products, hoping they are appropriate opinion leaders. The effectiveness of celebrity endorsements varies, though, depending largely on how credible and attractive the spokesperson is and how familiar people are with him or her. Endorsements are most likely to succeed if a reasonable association between the spokesperson and the product can be established.

Respected organizations such as the American Heart Association and the American Cancer Society may also serve as opinion leaders. Marketers may seek endorsements from them as well as from schools, churches, cities, the military, and fraternal organizations as a form of group opinion leadership. Salespeople often ask to use opinion leaders' names as a means of achieving greater personal influence in a sales presentation.

Increasingly, marketers are looking to social media to find opinion leaders, but the sheer volume of posts and platforms makes determining true opinion leaders challenging. So, marketers are focusing their attention on platforms frequented by teens (such as Facebook, Pinterest, and Tumblr) because those sites better identify the social trends that are shaping consumer behavior. With their unprecedented ability to network and communicate with each other, young people rely on each other's opinions more than marketing messages when making purchase decisions. And social media are becoming a key way that teens communicate their opinions. Consequently, today's marketers are reading teen posts, developing products that meet the very specific needs that teens express there, and learning unique and creative ways to put key influencers in charge of marketing their brands for them. Some parents are made uneasy

Yes. She checks herself out in the mirror.

1 in 5 Americans will develop skin cancer in their lifetime. That's why Jennifer Garner made a promise to herself to examine her skin every month and see her dermatologist for a screening every year.

The Neutrogena Partnership for Skin Health, working with the American Academy of Dermatology (AAD), invites you to join them in their mission to stop skin cancer before it strikes. Empower their cause by wearing broad-spectrum sun protection, covering up and seeking shade between 10:00 am and 4:00 pm. Perform self-examinations regularly and report any changes in existing moles or birthmarks to your doctor. Because with early detection, skin cancer is 98% curable. And that's a statistic we love to share.

Protect yourself starting today.
The AAD and the Neutrogena Partnership for Skin Health encourage you to **get a free skin cancer screening** in May, June or July. Find one in your area by visiting aad.org or neutrogenaskinhealth.com. Mark the date of your screening on this slip as a healthy reminder.

Neutrogena®
PARTNERSHIP FOR SKIN HEALTH

Celebrity Jennifer Garner functions as an opinion leader for Neutrogena.

socialization process how cultural values and norms are passed down to children

by these marketing strategies. According to a Common Sense Media report, more than 90 percent of parents want the Federal Trade Commission to prohibit the behavioral profiling and mobile tracking of children.[23] Marketers are using other social networking and online media to determine and attract opinion leaders, which will be discussed in Chapter 18.

6-6c Family

The family is the most important social institution for many consumers, strongly influencing values, attitudes, self-concept, and buying behavior. For example, a family that strongly values good health will have a grocery list distinctly different from that of a family that views every dinner as a gourmet event. Moreover, the family is responsible for the **socialization process**, the passing down of cultural values and norms to children. Children learn by observing their parents' consumption patterns, so they tend to shop in similar patterns.

Decision-making roles among family members tend to vary significantly, depending on the type of item purchased. Family members assume a variety of roles in the purchase process. *Initiators* suggest, initiate, or plant the seed for the purchase process. The initiator can be any member of the family. For example, Sister might initiate the product search by asking for a new bicycle as a birthday present. *Influencers* are members of the family whose opinions are valued. In our example, Mom might function as a price-range watchdog, an influencer whose main role is to veto or approve price ranges. Brother may give his opinion on certain makes of bicycles. The *decision maker* is the family member who actually makes the decision to buy or not to buy. For example, Dad or Mom is likely to choose the final brand and model of bicycle to buy after seeking further information from Sister about cosmetic features such as color and then imposing additional criteria of his or her own, such as durability and safety. The *purchaser* (probably Dad or Mom) is the one who actually exchanges money for the product. Finally, the *consumer* is the actual user—in this case, Sister.

Marketers should consider family purchase situations along with the distribution of consumer and decision-maker roles among family members. Ordinary marketing views the individual as both decision maker and consumer. Family marketing adds several other

possibilities: sometimes more than one family member or all family members are involved in the decision, sometimes only children are involved in the decision, sometimes more than one consumer is involved, and sometimes the decision maker and the consumer are different people. In most households, when parental joint decisions are being made, spouses consider their partner's needs and perceptions to maintain decision fairness and harmony. This tends to minimize family conflict. When couples agree to narrow down their options before making a purchase, they are more likely to be satisfied with the eventual outcome and less likely to feel regret. Thus, in the event of conflict or stalemate, the best course of action is to eliminate options that do not at all appeal to one partner (even if they appeal greatly to the other). Immediately restricting the options to those that both partners see some merit in leads to the greatest degree of compromise.[24] This sort of balancing act is key in maintaining long-term family harmony.

Children can have great influence over the purchase decisions of their parents. In many families, with both parents working and short on time, children are encouraged to participate. In addition, children in single-parent households become more involved in family decisions at an earlier age. Children influence purchase decisions for many products and services. They are most influential in purchase decisions for products with which they will be directly involved or of which they will be the primary user. Children's involvement is greatest in decisions involving clothing and shoes (children participate in 85 percent of decisions made), fast-food (85 percent), vacations (56 percent), and mobile phones (49 percent).[25] Ninety-three percent of children accompanying their parents to drug stores ask for things, while 98 percent of children accompanying parents to clothing stores ask for things.[26] According to a 2012 Cartoon Network survey, nearly 40 percent of parents would consider their children's opinions, and 20 percent would definitely consider their children's opinions before making a purchase. For major appliances like refrigerators, those numbers increase to 46 and 21 percent, respectively.[27]

Traditionally, children learned about consumption from their parents. In today's technologically overloaded world, that trend is reversing for some topics. Teenagers and adult children often contribute information and influence the purchase of parents' technology products. For example, 70 percent of parents report that their teens influence their mobile phone purchases.[28] Often, they even help with installation and show the parents how to use the product!

6-7 INDIVIDUAL INFLUENCES ON CONSUMER BUYING DECISIONS

A person's buying decisions are also influenced by personal characteristics that are unique to each individual, such as gender; age and life cycle stage; and personality, self-concept, and lifestyle. Individual characteristics are generally stable over the course of one's life. For instance, most people do not change their gender, and the act of changing personality or lifestyle requires a complete reorientation of one's life. In the case of age and life cycle stage, these changes occur gradually over time.

By working with children to develop a drink they like, Innocent Smoothies for Kids can advertise kid-friendly flavors with healthy benefits, satisfying moms and kids.

6-7a Gender

Physiological differences between men and women result in many different needs, such as with health and beauty products. Just as important are the distinct cultural, social, and economic roles played by men and women and the effects that these have on their decision-making processes. Following the successful launch of low-calorie soft drink Dr Pepper Ten, Dr Pepper Snapple Group added five brands to the Ten line in 2013: 7Up Ten, A&W Ten, Canada Dry Ten, RC Ten, and Sunkist Ten. Following similar efforts by Coca-Cola (Zero) and PepsiCo (Max), Dr Pepper Snapple's Ten line targets men between the ages of twenty-five and thirty-nine. Because diet soft drinks are traditionally seen as feminine or "girly," men are less likely to purchase them. In an attempt to counter this image, the Ten line's advertising and packaging employs duct tape, riveted metal, bold fonts, and the none-too-subtle slogan, "It's not for women."[29]

Trends in gender marketing are influenced by the changing roles of men and women in society. For example, men used to rely on the women in their lives to shop for them. Today, however, more men are shopping for themselves. Seventy percent of men shopped online in 2012, up from 38 percent in 2006.[30] In 2010, 20 percent of fathers served as primary caretakers for children under the age of five, and 32 percent took care of their kids at least one day a week.[31] Whether because of the advent of online shopping or retailers becoming aware of the way men like to shop, today more men are comfortable shopping for themselves. An iProspect study found that 84 percent of men said they purchased their own clothes in 2012, up from 65 percent in 2002.[32]

Technology companies are working to develop new high-tech products that resonate with women. For example, Barnes & Noble markets everything about its e-reader, NOOK, to the ideal customer, whom they call "Julie." She is between twenty-five and forty-five years old, lives within fifteen minutes of a Barnes & Noble, enjoys family-friendly stores because she has a family, uses NOOK's apps because she doesn't have to worry about data consumption, and loves that NOOK has apps for her kids too. Based on this information, Barnes & Noble stores have short tables for kids to play with sample NOOKs, and the app store caters to topics that interest women, such as puzzles, fashion, health, fitness, and travel. The strategy is successful in that 70 percent of NOOK purchasers are women. [33]

6-7b Age and Family Life Cycle Stage

A consumer's age and family life cycle stage can have a significant impact on his or her behavior. How old a consumer is generally indicates what products he or she may be interested in purchasing. Consumer tastes in food, clothing, cars, furniture, and recreation are often age related.

Related to a person's age is his or her place in the family life cycle. As Chapter 8 explains in more detail, the *family life cycle* is an orderly series of stages through which consumers' attitudes and behavioral tendencies evolve through maturity, experience, and changing income and status. Marketers often define their target markets in terms of family life cycle, such as "young singles," "young married couples with children," and "middle-aged married couples without children." For instance, young singles spend more than average on alcoholic beverages, education, and entertainment. New parents typically increase their spending on health care, clothing, housing, and food and decrease their spending on alcohol, education, and transportation. Households with older children spend more on food, entertainment, personal care products, and education, as well as cars and gasoline. After their children leave home, spending by older couples on vehicles, women's clothing, health care, and long-distance calls typically increases. For instance, the presence of children in the home is the most significant determinant of the type of vehicle that's driven off the new car lot. Parents are the ultimate need-driven car consumers, requiring larger cars and trucks to haul their children and all their belongings. It comes as no surprise, then, that for all households with children, SUVs rank either first or second among new-vehicle purchases, followed by minivans.

Marketers should also be aware of the many nontraditional life cycle paths that are common today and provide insights into the needs and wants of such consumers as divorced parents, lifelong singles, and childless couples. Three decades ago, married couples with children under the age of 18 accounted for about half of U.S. households. Today, such families make up only 23 percent of all households, while people living alone or with nonfamily members represent more than 30 percent. Furthermore, according to the U.S. Census Bureau, the number of single-mother households grew by 25 percent over the last decade. The shift toward more single-parent households is part of a broader societal change that has put more women on the career track. Although many marketers continue to be wary of targeting nontraditional families, JCPenney targeted single mothers and lesbian couples with children in a 2012 Mother's Day-themed catalog. JCPenney received complaints from traditionalist advocacy groups like One Million Moms, but the clothing retailer stood behind the ads, saying, "We want to be a store for all Americans. In celebration of Mother's Day, we're proud that our May book honors women from diverse backgrounds who all share the heartwarming experience of motherhood."[34]

LIFE EVENTS Another way to look at the life cycle is to look at major events in one's life over time. Life-changing events can occur at any time. A few examples are death of a spouse, moving, birth or adoption of a child, retirement, job loss, divorce, and marriage. Typically, such events are quite stressful, and consumers will often take steps to minimize that stress. Many times, life-changing events will mean new consumption patterns. For example, a recently divorced person may try to improve his or her appearance by joining a health club and dieting. Someone moving to a different city will need a new dentist, grocery store, auto service center, and doctor, among other things. Marketers realize that life events often mean a chance to gain a new customer. The Welcome Wagon offers free gifts and services for area newcomers. Lowe's sends out a discount coupon to those moving to a new community. And when you put your home on the market, very quickly you start getting flyers from moving companies promising a great price on moving your household goods.

6-7c Personality, Self-Concept, and Lifestyle

Each consumer has a unique personality. **Personality** is a broad concept that can be thought of as a way of organizing and grouping how an individual typically reacts to situations. Thus, personality combines psychological makeup and environmental forces. It includes people's underlying dispositions, especially their most dominant characteristics. Although personality is one of the least useful concepts in the study of consumer behavior, some marketers believe personality influences the types and brands of products purchased. For instance, the type of car, clothes, or jewelry a consumer buys may reflect one or more personality traits.

Self-concept, or self-perception, is how consumers perceive themselves. Self-concept includes attitudes, perceptions, beliefs, and self-evaluations. Although self-concept may change, the change is often gradual. Through self-concept, people define their identity, which in turn provides for consistent and coherent behavior.

Self-concept combines the **ideal self-image** (the way an individual would like to be perceived) and the **real self-image** (how an individual actually perceives himself or herself). Generally, we try to raise our real self-image toward our ideal (or at least narrow the gap). Consumers seldom buy products that jeopardize their self-image. For example, someone who sees herself as a trendsetter wouldn't buy clothing that doesn't project a contemporary image.

Human behavior depends largely on self-concept. Because consumers want to protect their identity as individuals, the products they buy, the stores they patronize, and the credit cards they carry support their self-image. No other product quite reflects a person's self-image as much as the car he or she drives. For example, many young consumers do not like family sedans like the Honda Accord or Toyota Camry and say they would buy one for their mom but not for themselves. Likewise, younger parents may avoid purchasing minivans because they do not want to sacrifice the youthful image they have of themselves just because they have new responsibilities. To combat decreasing sales, marketers of the Nissan Quest minivan decided to reposition it as something other than a "mom mobile" or "soccer mom car." They chose the ad copy "Passion built it. Passion will fill it up," followed by "What if we made a minivan that changed the way people think of minivans?"

By influencing the degree to which consumers perceive a good or service to be self-relevant, marketers can affect consumers' motivation to learn about, shop for, and buy a certain brand. Marketers also consider self-concept important because it helps explain the relationship between individuals' perceptions of themselves and their consumer behavior.

Many companies now use psychographics to better understand their market segments. For many years, marketers selling products to mothers conveniently assumed that all moms were fairly homogeneous and concerned about the same things—the health and well-being of their children—and that they could all be reached with a similar message. But recent lifestyle research has shown that there are traditional, blended, and nontraditional moms, and companies like Procter & Gamble and Pillsbury are using strategies to reach these different types of mothers. Psychographics is also effective with other market segments. Psychographics and lifestyle segmentation are discussed in more detail in Chapter 8.

6-8 PSYCHOLOGICAL INFLUENCES ON CONSUMER BUYING DECISIONS

An individual's buying decisions are further influenced by psychological factors: perception, motivation, learning, and beliefs and attitudes. These factors are what consumers use to interact with their world. They are the tools consumers use to recognize their feelings, gather and analyze information, formulate thoughts and opinions, and take action. Unlike the other three influences on consumer behavior, psychological influences can be affected by a person's environment because they are applied on specific occasions. For example, you will perceive different stimuli and process these stimuli in different ways depending on whether you are sitting in class concentrating on the instructor, sitting outside of class talking to friends, or sitting in your dorm room watching television.

6-8a Perception

The world is full of stimuli. A stimulus is any unit of input affecting one or more of the five senses: sight, smell, taste,

---

self-concept how consumers perceive themselves in terms of attitudes, perceptions, beliefs, and self-evaluations

ideal self-image the way an individual would like to be perceived

real self-image the way an individual actually perceives himself or herself

touch, and hearing. The process by which we select, organize, and interpret these stimuli into a meaningful and coherent picture is called **perception**. In essence, perception is how we see the world around us and how we recognize that we need some help in making a purchasing decision.

People cannot perceive every stimulus in their environment. Therefore, they use **selective exposure** to decide which stimuli to notice and which to ignore. A typical consumer is exposed to nearly 3,000 advertising messages a day but notices only between 11 and 20.

The familiarity of an object, contrast, movement, intensity (such as increased volume), and smell are cues that influence perception. Consumers use these cues to identify and define products and brands. The shape of a product's packaging, such as Coca-Cola's signature contour bottle, can influence perception. Color is another cue, and it plays a key role in consumers' perceptions. Packaged foods manufacturers use color to trigger unconscious associations for grocery shoppers who typically make their shopping decisions in the blink of an eye. Ampacet, a world leader in color additives for plastics, reports that nature-inspired colors and organic values were becoming more popular as the economy and global focus shifted from the tech boom to the bio or eco boom. Ecological consequences and concerns have resulted in marketing initiatives such as "going green." Colors like natural greens, earthy browns, and strong yellows, as well as metallics such as steely silver, carbon black, gold, and copper, are popular for packaging. Color researchers speculate that technological overload has led to a resurgence in the appreciation of simple luxury. Color names for fabrics and makeup reflect that trend with names such as Grounded, Champagne Chic, and Serene Blue.[35]

What is perceived by consumers may also depend on the stimuli's vividness or shock value. Graphic warnings of the hazards associated with a product's use are perceived more readily and remembered more accurately than less vivid warnings or warnings that are written in text. "Sexier" ads excel at attracting the attention of younger consumers. According to researchers at Claremont Graduate University

in California, exposure to sexy alcohol advertisements is significantly correlated with teen alcohol use, especially among girls. For both boys and girls, the greater the exposure to alcohol advertisements, the greater the chance that alcohol use would increase from grades seven to ten.[36]

Two other concepts closely related to selective exposure are selective distortion and selective retention. **Selective distortion** occurs when consumers change or distort information that conflicts with their feelings or beliefs. For example, suppose a college student buys a Sony Vaio laptop. After the purchase, if the student gets new information about an alternative brand, such as an Apple MacBook Pro, he or she may distort the information to make it more consistent with the prior view that the Vaio is just as good as the MacBook Pro, if not better. Business travelers who fly often may distort or discount

Research suggests that exposure to sexy alcohol advertisements (such as this magazine ad for Moët & Chandon champagne) is significantly correlated with teen alcohol use, especially among girls.

Image Courtesy of the Advertising Archives

information about plane crashes because they must use air travel constantly in their jobs.

Selective retention is remembering only information that supports personal feelings or beliefs. The consumer forgets all information that may be inconsistent. After reading a pamphlet that contradicts one's political beliefs, for instance, a person may forget many of the points outlined in it. Similarly, consumers may see a news report on suspected illegal practices by their favorite retail store but soon forget the reason the store was featured on the news.

Which stimuli will be perceived often depends on the individual. People can be exposed to the same stimuli under identical conditions but perceive them very differently. For example, two people viewing a television commercial may have different interpretations of the advertising message. One person may be thoroughly engrossed by the message and become highly motivated to buy the product. Thirty seconds after the ad ends, the second person may not be able to recall the content of the message or even the product advertised.

MARKETING IMPLICATIONS OF PERCEPTION Marketers must recognize the importance of cues, or signals, in consumers' perception of products. Marketing managers first identify the important attributes, such as price or quality, that the targeted consumers want in a product and then design signals to communicate these attributes. For example, consumers will pay more for candy in expensive-looking foil packages. But shiny labels on wine bottles signify less expensive wines; dull labels indicate more expensive wines. Marketers also often use price as a signal to consumers that the product is of higher quality than competing products. Of course, brand names send signals to consumers. The brand names of Close-Up toothpaste, DieHard batteries, and Caress moisturizing soap, for example, identify important product qualities. Names chosen for search engines and sites on the Internet, such as Yahoo!, Amazon, and Excite, are intended to convey excitement, intensity, and vastness.

Consumers also associate quality and reliability with certain brand names. Companies watch their brand identity closely, in large part because a strong link has been established between perceived brand value and customer loyalty. Brand names that consistently enjoy high perceived value from consumers include Google, Disney, National Geographic, Mercedes-Benz, and Fisher-Price. Naming

a product after a place can also add perceived value by association. Brand names using the words Santa Fe, Dakota, or Texas convey a sense of openness, freedom, and youth, but products named after other locations might conjure up images of pollution and crime. Marketing managers are also interested in the *threshold level of perception*, the minimum difference in a stimulus that the consumer will notice. This concept is sometimes referred to as the "just-noticeable difference." For example, how much would Microsoft have to drop the price of its Surface Pro2 tablet before consumers recognize it as a bargain—$200? $500? Or more? One study found that the just-noticeable difference in a stimulus is about a 20 percent change. For example, consumers will likely notice a 20 percent price decrease more quickly than one of only 15 percent. This marketing principle can be applied to other marketing variables as well, such as package size or loudness of a broadcast advertisement.[37]

Besides changing such stimuli as price, package size, and volume, marketers can change the product or attempt to reposition its image. But marketers must be careful when adding features. How many new services will discounter Target need to add before consumers perceive it as a full-service department store? How many sporty features will General Motors have to add to a basic two-door sedan before consumers start perceiving it as a sports car?

Marketing managers who intend to do business in global markets should be aware of how foreign consumers perceive their products. For instance, in Japan, product labels are often written in English or French, even though they may not translate into anything meaningful. Many Japanese associate foreign words on product labels with the exotic, the expensive, and high quality.

Marketers have often been suspected of sending advertising messages subconsciously to consumers in what is known as *subliminal perception*. The controversy began when a researcher claimed to have increased popcorn and Coca-Cola sales at a movie theater after flashing "Eat popcorn" and "Drink Coca-Cola" on the screen every five seconds for 1/300th of a second, although the audience did not consciously recognize the messages. Almost immediately, consumer protection groups became concerned that advertisers were brainwashing consumers, and this practice was pronounced illegal in California and Canada. Although the researcher later admitted to making up the data and scientists have been unable to replicate the study since, consumers are still wary of hidden messages that advertisers may be sending.

6-8b Motivation

By studying motivation, marketers can analyze the major forces influencing consumers to buy or not buy products. When you buy a product, you usually do so to fulfill some kind of need. These needs become motives when they are aroused sufficiently. For instance, suppose this morning you were so hungry before class that you needed to eat something. In response to that need, you stopped at Subway for a breakfast sandwich. In other words, you were motivated by hunger to stop at Subway. A **motive** is the driving force that causes a person to take action to satisfy specific needs.

Why are people driven by particular needs at particular times? One popular theory is **Maslow's hierarchy of needs**, illustrated in Exhibit 6, which arranges needs in ascending order of importance: physiological, safety, social, esteem, and self-actualization. As a person fulfills one need, a higher-level need becomes more important.

The most basic human needs—that is, the needs for food, water, and shelter—are *physiological*. Because they are essential to survival, these needs must be satisfied first. Ads showing a juicy hamburger or a runner gulping down Gatorade after a marathon are examples of appeals to satisfy the physiological needs of hunger and thirst.

Safety needs include security and freedom from pain and discomfort. Marketers sometimes appeal to consumers' fears and anxieties about safety to sell their products. For example, aware of the aging population's health fears, the retail medical imaging centers Heart Check America and HealthScreen America advertise that they offer consumers a full body scan for early detection of health problems such as coronary disease and cancer. Some companies or industries advertise to allay consumer fears. For example, in the wake of the September 11, 2001, terrorist attacks, the airline industry found itself having to conduct an image campaign to reassure consumers about the safety of air travel.

After physiological and safety needs have been fulfilled, *social needs*—especially love and a sense of

belonging—become the focus. Love includes acceptance by one's peers, as well as sex and romantic love. Marketing managers probably appeal more to this need than to any other. Ads for clothes, cosmetics, and vacation packages suggest that buying the product can bring love. The need to belong is also a favorite of marketers, especially those marketing products to teens. Teens consider Apple to be not only their favorite brand but also something that defines their generation. Given the group's need for customization within a controlled environment, this love for Apple makes sense. Millennials' relationship with their parents is completely different from that of previous generations, and staying connected with family and friends is a priority. For marketers, this means understanding how to maximize crowdsourcing and peer-to-peer networks. For example, the open-source, Android-based Ouya video game console launched in 2013 after generating more than 8.5 million crowdsourced dollars on Kickstarter. With their money on the line, early backers eagerly spread the campaign on social media and news sites, creating a tidal wave of marketing (and preorders) for Ouya.[38]

Love is acceptance without regard to one's contribution. Esteem is acceptance based on one's contribution to the group. *Self-esteem needs* include self-respect and a sense of accomplishment. Esteem needs also include prestige, fame, and recognition of one's accomplishments. Montblanc pens, Mercedes-Benz automobiles, and Neiman Marcus stores all appeal to esteem needs.

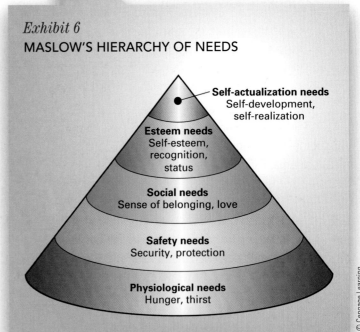

Exhibit 6
MASLOW'S HIERARCHY OF NEEDS

Self-actualization needs
Self-development, self-realization

Esteem needs
Self-esteem, recognition, status

Social needs
Sense of belonging, love

Safety needs
Security, protection

Physiological needs
Hunger, thirst

© Cengage Learning

The highest human need is *self-actualization*. It refers to finding self-fulfillment and self-expression, reaching the point in life at which "people are what they feel they should be." Maslow believed that very few people ever attain this level. Even so, advertisements may focus on this type of need. For example, American Express ads convey the message that acquiring its card is one of the highest attainments in life. Microsoft appealed to consumers' needs for self-actualization when it chose "I'm a PC and Windows 7 was my idea" as the slogan for Windows 7; similarly, the U.S. Army changed its slogan from "Be All You Can Be" to "Army of One."

6-8c Learning

Almost all consumer behavior results from **learning**, which is the process that creates changes in behavior through experience and practice. It is not possible to observe learning directly, but we can infer when it has occurred by a person's actions. For example, suppose you see an advertisement for a new and improved cold medicine. If you go to the store that day and buy that remedy, we infer that you have learned something about the cold medicine.

There are two types of learning: experiential and conceptual. *Experiential learning* occurs when an experience changes your behavior. For example, if the new cold medicine does not relieve your symptoms, you may not buy that brand again. *Conceptual learning*, which is not acquired through direct experience, is the second type of learning. Assume, for example, that you are standing at a soft drink machine and notice a new diet flavor with an artificial sweetener. Because someone has told you that diet beverages leave an aftertaste, you choose a different drink. You have learned that you would not like this new diet drink without ever trying it.

Reinforcement and repetition boost learning. Reinforcement can be positive or negative. If you see a vendor selling frozen yogurt (stimulus), buy it (response), and find the yogurt to be quite refreshing (reward), your behavior has been positively reinforced. On the other hand, if you buy a new flavor of yogurt and it does not taste good (negative reinforcement), you will not buy that flavor of yogurt again (response). Without positive or negative reinforcement, a person will not be motivated to repeat the behavior pattern or to avoid it. Thus, if a new brand evokes neutral feelings, some marketing activity, such as a price change or an increase in promotion, may be required to induce further consumption. Learning theory is helpful in reminding marketers that concrete and timely actions are what reinforce desired consumer behavior.

Repetition is a key strategy in promotional campaigns because it can lead to increased learning. Most marketers use repetitious advertising so that consumers will learn what their unique advantage is over the competition. Generally, to heighten learning, advertising messages should be spread out over time rather than clustered together.

A related learning concept useful to marketing managers is **stimulus generalization**. In theory, stimulus generalization occurs when one response is extended to a second stimulus similar to the first. Marketers often use a successful, well-known brand name for a family of products because it gives consumers familiarity with and knowledge about each product in the family. Such brand name families spur the introduction of new products and facilitate the sale of existing items. OXO relies on consumers' familiarity with its popular kitchen and household products to sell office and medical supplies; Sony's film division relies on name recognition from its home technology, such as the PlayStation. Clorox bathroom cleaner relies on familiarity with Clorox bleach, and Dove shampoo relies on familiarity with Dove soap. Branding is examined in more detail in Chapter 10.

Another form of stimulus generalization occurs when retailers or wholesalers design their packages to resemble well-known manufacturers' brands. Such imitation often confuses consumers, who buy the imitation thinking it's the original.

The opposite of stimulus generalization is **stimulus discrimination**, which means learning to differentiate among similar products. Consumers may perceive one product as more rewarding or stimulating, even if it is virtually indistinguishable from competitors. For example, some consumers prefer Miller Lite and others prefer Bud Light. Many insist they can taste a difference between the two brands.

With some types of products—such as aspirin, gasoline, bleach, and paper towels—marketers rely on promotion to point out brand differences that consumers would otherwise not recognize. This process, called *product differentiation*, is discussed in more detail in Chapter 8.

learning a process that creates changes in behavior, immediate or expected, through experience and practice

stimulus generalization a form of learning that occurs when one response is extended to a second stimulus similar to the first

stimulus discrimination a learned ability to differentiate among similar products

Usually, product differentiation is based on superficial differences. For example, Bayer tells consumers that it's the aspirin "doctors recommend most."

6-8d Beliefs and Attitudes

Beliefs and attitudes are closely linked to values. A **belief** is an organized pattern of knowledge that an individual holds as true about his or her world. A consumer may believe that Sony's Cyber-shot camera takes the best HD video, is easiest to use, and is the most reasonably priced. These beliefs may be based on knowledge, faith, or hearsay. Consumers tend to develop a set of beliefs about a product's attributes and then, through these beliefs, form a *brand image*—a set of beliefs about a particular brand. In turn, the brand image shapes consumers' attitudes toward the product.

An **attitude** is a learned tendency to respond consistently toward a given object, such as a brand. Attitudes rest on an individual's value system, which represents personal standards of good and bad, right and wrong, and so forth; therefore, attitudes tend to be more enduring and complex than beliefs.

For an example of the nature of attitudes, consider the differing attitudes of consumers around the world toward the practice of purchasing on credit. Americans have long been enthusiastic about charging goods and services and are willing to pay high interest rates for the privilege of postponing payment. To many European consumers, doing what amounts to taking out a loan—even a small one—to pay for anything seems absurd. Germans especially are reluctant to buy on credit. Italy has a sophisticated credit and banking system well suited to handling credit cards, but Italians prefer to carry cash, often huge wads of it. Although most Japanese consumers have credit cards, card purchases amount to less than 1 percent of all consumer transactions. The Japanese have long looked down on credit purchases but acquire cards to use while traveling abroad.

If a good or service is meeting its profit goals, positive attitudes toward the product merely need to be reinforced. If the brand is not succeeding, however, the marketing manager must strive to change target consumers' attitudes toward it. Changes in attitude tend to grow out of an individual's attempt to reconcile long-held values with a constant stream of new information. This change can be accomplished in three ways: changing beliefs about the brand's attributes, changing the relative importance of these beliefs, and adding new beliefs.

CHANGING BELIEFS ABOUT ATTRIBUTES The first technique is to turn neutral, negative, or incorrect beliefs about product attributes into positive ones. Imagine that 24 Hour Fitness conducts a survey among persons considering joining a health club. They find that most respondents believe that 24 Hour Fitness offers fewer classes and less variety than LA Fitness, Curves, and the YMCA. In fact, 24 Hour Fitness offers a greater variety and more classes than any other health and fitness center. Because target consumers have incorrect beliefs about 24 Hour Fitness's attributes (the number and variety of classes), the gym must advertise and do other forms of promotion (such as an open house) to correct the misimpressions.

Changing beliefs about a service can be more difficult because service attributes are usually intangible. Convincing consumers to switch hairstylists or lawyers or go to a mall dental clinic can be much more difficult than getting them to change brands of razor blades. Image, which is also largely intangible, significantly determines service patronage.

CHANGING THE IMPORTANCE OF BELIEFS The second approach to modifying attitudes is to change the relative importance of beliefs about an attribute. Due in part to a frumpy, behind-the-times persona and a disastrous logo change, clothing retailer the Gap suffered from plummeting sales throughout the 2000s. Recently, however, the Gap has risen to new profits by redesigning its store aesthetic and launching a "peppy and preppy" line of

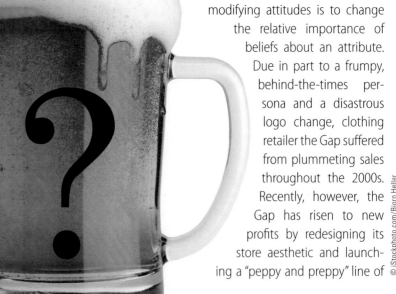

© iStockphoto.com/Bjorn Heller

colorful casualwear alongside restyled contemporary basics such as tailored dresses and cashmere sweaters.[39] Marketers can also emphasize the importance of some beliefs over others. For example, McDonald's has been fingered as the culprit for Americans' obesity. But the chain now offers a large line of salads and healthy meals and side options, hoping to demonstrate its ability to serve healthier options to customers who want them.[40]

ADDING NEW BELIEFS The third approach to transforming attitudes is to add new beliefs. Although changes in consumption patterns often come slowly, cereal marketers are betting that consumers will eventually warm to the idea of cereal as a snack. A print ad for General Mills' Cookie Crisp cereal features a boy popping the sugary nuggets into his mouth while he does his homework. Koch Industries, the manufacturer of Dixie paper products, is also attempting to add new beliefs about the uses of its paper plates and cups with an advertising campaign aimed at positioning its product as a "home cleanup replacement." Commercials pitch Dixie paper plates as an alternative to washing dishes after everyday meals and not just for picnics.

U.S. companies attempting to market their goods overseas may need to help consumers add new beliefs about a product in general. Coca-Cola and PepsiCo have both found it challenging to sell their diet cola brands to consumers in India partly because diet foods of any kind are a new concept in that country, where malnutrition was widespread until recently. Indians also have deep-rooted attitudes that anything labeled "diet" is meant for a sick person, such as a diabetic. As a general rule, most Indians are not diet conscious, preferring food prepared in the traditional manner that tastes good. Indians are also suspicious of the artificial sweeteners used in diet colas. India's Health Ministry has required warning labels on cans and bottles of Diet Coke and Diet Pepsi saying "Not Recommended for Children."[41]

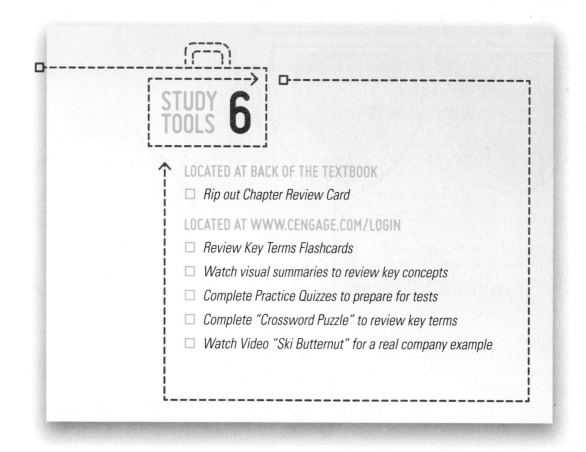

STUDY TOOLS 6

LOCATED AT BACK OF THE TEXTBOOK
☐ *Rip out Chapter Review Card*

LOCATED AT WWW.CENGAGE.COM/LOGIN
☐ *Review Key Terms Flashcards*
☐ *Watch visual summaries to review key concepts*
☐ *Complete Practice Quizzes to prepare for tests*
☐ *Complete "Crossword Puzzle" to review key terms*
☐ *Watch Video "Ski Butternut" for a real company example*

ANATOMY OF A BUYING DECISION: CAR

For a high-involvement purchase, such as buying a car, a consumer typically practices extensive decision making. Several factors ultimately affect her buying decision.

SOCIAL FACTORS:

Before deciding to buy a car, this woman may seek out others' opinions or observe what others purchase.

ADVICE FROM HER REFERENCE GROUP

EXAMPLE OF OPINION LEADER

INDIVIDUAL FACTORS:

LIFESTYLE

SELF-CONCEPT

Her buying decision will be influenced by her personality, self-concept, and lifestyle.

PSYCHOLOGICAL FACTORS:

The consumer's perception, motivation, learning, values, beliefs, and attitudes will influence her decision on which car to buy, too.

ATTITUDE

Should I try a new brand, or stick with the familiar one?

7-1 WHAT IS BUSINESS MARKETING?

Business marketing (also called industrial marketing) is the marketing of goods and services to individuals and organizations for purposes other than personal consumption. The sale of a PC to your college or university is an example of business marketing. Business products include those that are used to manufacture other products, become part of another product, or aid the normal operations of an organization. The key characteristic distinguishing business products from consumer products is intended use, not physical form.

> The key characteristic distinguishing business products from consumer products is intended use, not physical form.

business marketing (industrial marketing) the marketing of goods and services to individuals and organizations for purposes other than personal consumption

How do you distinguish between a consumer product and a business product? A product that is purchased for personal or family consumption or as a gift is a consumer good. If that same product, such as a PC or a cell phone, is bought for use in a business, it is a business product. Some common items that are sold as both consumer goods and business products are office supplies (e.g., pens, paper, staple removers). Some items, such as forklifts, are more commonly sold as business products than as consumer goods. According to FixCourse founder Brad Smith, the two primary marketing goals of U.S. business marketers' Web sites should be making sales and generating leads—that is, attracting customers, clients, and other new business.[1]

The size of the business market in the United States and most other countries substantially exceeds that of the consumer market. In the business market, a single customer can account for a huge volume of purchases. For example, IBM's purchasing department spends more than $40 billion annually on business products. Procter & Gamble, Apple, Merck, Dell, and Kimberly-Clark each spend more than half of their annual revenue on business products.[2]

Some large firms that produce goods such as steel, computer memory chips, or production equipment market exclusively to business customers. Other firms market to both businesses and to consumers. Hewlett-Packard marketed exclusively to business customers in the past but now markets laser printers and personal computers to consumers. Sony, traditionally a consumer marketer, now sells office automation products to businesses. Both companies have had to make organizational and marketing changes to expand into the new market categories.

Chapter 7

Business Marketing

After you finish this chapter go to
p138 *for* **STUDY TOOLS** ⬛┄┄┄┄→

7-2 BUSINESS MARKETING ON THE INTERNET

The use of the Internet to facilitate activities between organizations is called business-to-business electronic commerce (B-to-B or B2B e-commerce). This method of conducting business has evolved and grown rapidly throughout its short history. In 1995, there were few commercial Web sites, and those that did exist were static. Only a few had data-retrieval capabilities. Frames, tables, and advanced visual styles were not yet possible. Security of any sort was rare, and streaming video did not exist. Today, B-to-B sites look more like consumer sites with social media, valuable content, and community-building applications. Before the Internet became a commercial space, customers had to call Dow Chemical and request a specification sheet for the products they were considering. The information would arrive a few days later by mail. After choosing a product, the customer could then place an order by calling Dow (during business hours, of course). Now, such information is available through MyAccount@Dow, which provides information tailored to the customer's requirements, such as secure internal monitoring of a customer's chemical tank levels. When tanks reach a predetermined level, reordering can automatically be triggered.[3]

Companies selling to business buyers face the same challenges as all marketers, including determining who, exactly, the market is and how best to reach it. This is particularly difficult in business marketing because business has rapidly moved online. A recent study found that, in 2012, 32 percent of marketers were "very" or "fully" engaged in marketing through social channels, compared with 21 percent in 2011. The study authors forecasted that 53 percent of B-to-B marketers would be intensely engaged in social media marketing in 2013 and that 97 percent would be involved with social media to some extent.[4] Some of this growth can be attributed to companies looking to bypass more expensive offline tactics in favor of more measurable ones online. For example, 43 percent of B-to-B companies report that they have acquired new customers from Facebook alone.[5]

Content marketing is becoming more and more important to B-to-B marketing. Content marketing is based on the idea of developing valuable content for interested audience members—namely through videos, white papers, e-mail newsletters, webinars, and blog posts—and subsequently using e-mail marketing, search engine optimization, paid search, and display advertising to "pull" customers to the site. Just how important is content marketing? Kelly Outsourcing & Consulting Group spends about 60 percent of its B-to-B marketing budget on the creation and dissemination of content designed to provide useful information to executives about staffing and outsourcing. One recent study found that 91 percent of B-to-B marketers use content marketing, spending an average 33 percent of their total budgets on it.[6] Content marketing is clearly important—as long as marketers can make it valuable to users.

The reviews on social media are mixed. Some B-to-B marketers believe that social media are not as useful to them as to business-to-consumer (B-to-C) marketers. Indeed, compared to B-to-B's 43 percent, a whopping 77 percent of B-to-C companies have acquired new customers from Facebook.[7] But other experts see growth in social media use as B-to-B marketers use opportunities to generate quality leads. It is clear from some companies' Web sites that they are embracing new tools and applications. The tools most commonly used by B-to-B marketers are blogs, social networking sites, Twitter, video streaming sites, e-newsletters, and mobile marketing. Many B-to-B marketers are experimenting with how to use these media to build successful relationships with business customers, while others are already excelling. Newsletter platform developer Constant Contact won *BtoB Magazine*'s Best Use of Twitter and Best Use of Facebook awards in 2012, while McGraw-Hill won Best Use of Mobile, and tax software developer Intuit

Source: http://www.yelp.com/nyc

The reviews on social media are mixed for B-to-B marketing.

won Best Use of a Corporate Blog.[8] Some companies are using social media listening tools such as Twitter Search, Facebook Insights, and larger platforms such as Radian 6 to determine strategic topics to include in newsletters and videos. Listening tools are used primarily to gauge what topics are trending and to estimate consumer sentiment on social media platforms. There are many tools—some free or quite inexpensive, others larger and more expensive. The key to making social media effective is to combine it with other digital assets such as e-mail marketing and content marketing. For example, a marketer can drive e-mail subscriptions through Facebook or use Twitter to promote an upcoming e-mail newsletter that features an interview with an industry expert.

Exhibit 1 identifies ten B-to-B-oriented portals that are particularly good examples of how companies can use the Web to connect with business customers.[9] The key is to design Web sites with the user in mind. Many of these sites also share the following characteristics:

- **Simple, uncluttered design**
- **Use of bold colors and large text**
- **A central layout that is typically 960 pixels wide and works well on a variety of screen resolutions**
- **A separate top section**
- **Solid areas of screen real estate**
- **A strong visual hierarchy**

Exhibit 1
TEN GREAT B-TO-B WEB SITES

1.	Alibaba.com (www.alibaba.com)
2.	Global Sources (www.globalsources.com)
3.	Made-in-China.com (www.made-in-china.com)
4.	TradeKey (www.tradekey.com)
5.	Kompass (us.kompass.com)
6.	EC21 (www.ec21.com)
7.	IndiaMART (www.indiamart.com)
8.	GlobalMarket (www.globalmarket.com)
9.	HKTDC (www.hktdc.com)
10.	TradeFord (www.tradeford.com)

Source: "Top 10 B2B Websites," *TradeFord*, June 26, 2012, http://forum.tradeford .com/topic-354/top-10-b2b-websites.html (Accessed February 6, 2013).

7-2a Measuring Online Success

Most marketers use some sort of Web analytics (such as Google Analytics or an enterprise system like Omniture) to determine which activities generate leads and then use that information to make their Web sites more effective. Metrics include external search traffic, internal search engine analytics, and key word search results. Three of the most important measurements of online success are recency, frequency, and monetary value. *Recency* relates to the fact that customers who have made a purchase recently are more likely to purchase again in the near future than are customers who haven't purchased for a while. *Frequency* data help marketers identify frequent purchasers who are most likely to repeat their purchasing behavior in the future. The *monetary value* of sales is important because big spenders can be the most profitable customers for a business. As such, there are literally thousands of metrics that can then be utilized depending on the conversion task. The *conversion task* is the behavior that the marketer wants the visitor to take—such as signing up for e-mails, watching a video, calling for more information, signing up for a webinar, and/or a host of other activities. This sets up the conversion rate, which is another important metric for digital marketing. The *conversion rate* is defined as a ratio of the number of people who visited the site to the number of people who went on to complete the desired action.

One common way of evaluating a Web application, Web site, or other piece of interactive technology is to evaluate its **stickiness** factor by combining frequency data with the length of time a visitor spent on the Web site (duration) and the number of site pages viewed during each visit (total site reach). As competition within the smartphone market heats up, Apple is relying on the stickiness of iOS and its signature apps to retain—if not increase—its customer base. According to Barclays analysts, the iPhone's operating system and first-party apps (such as Siri and iCloud) serve as a long-term differentiator over competitors, enhancing loyalty and creating "a distinctive stickiness."[10]

$$\text{Stickiness} = \text{Frequency} \times \text{Duration} \times \text{Site Reach}$$

stickiness a measure of a Web site's effectiveness; calculated by multiplying the frequency of visits by the duration of a visit by the number of pages viewed during each visit (site reach)

By measuring the stickiness factor of a Web site before and after a design or function change, the marketer can quickly determine whether visitors embrace the change. By adding purchase information to determine the level of stickiness needed to provide a desired purchase volume, the marketer gains an even more precise understanding of how a site change affects business. An almost endless number of factor combinations can be created to provide a quantitative method for determining buyer behavior online. First, though, the marketer must determine what measures are required and which factors can be combined to arrive at those measurements.[11]

7-2b Trends in B-to-B Internet Marketing

Over the past decade, marketers have become more and more sophisticated in the use of the Internet. Companies have had to transition from "We have a Web site because our customer does" to having a site that attracts, interests, satisfies, informs, and retains customers. Every year, new applications that provide additional information about customers; lower costs; increase supply chain efficiency; or enhance customer retention, loyalty, and trust are developed. Increasingly, business customers expect suppliers to know them personally, monitor people's movement within their company, and offer personal interaction through social media, e-mail, and personal mailers.[12]

A few years ago, many people thought the Internet would eliminate the need for distributors. Why would customers pay a distributor's markup when they could buy directly from the manufacturer with a few mouse clicks? This has occurred less frequently than many expected because distributors often perform important functions such as providing credit, aggregating supplies from multiple sources, making deliveries, and processing returns. Many business customers, especially small firms, depend on knowledgeable distributors for information and advice that is not available to them online.

Social media usage in B-to-B marketing and B-to-C marketing has been the most pervasive marketing trend in the past five years. It requires vigilant adjustment to keep track of new applications and platforms, as well as constant evaluation to determine whether these new avenues are beneficial to (or used by) customers. Generally, B-to-C marketers were faster to adopt social media as part of the promotional mix. B-to-B marketers did not initially see the value in these tools. However, that has changed as social media has become more popular.

Many marketers use social media to create awareness and build relationships and community. As such, B-to-B marketers are more likely to use videos (especially those that teach or highlight something valuable that the company offers), e-newsletters to customers, and other tools like webinars, white papers, and e-books. The key to social media for B-to-B marketers is to create compelling and useful content for its customers. For example, HubSpot develops white papers and e-books on topics such as generating leads using social media for its customers and potential customers. While building community is important, B-to-B marketers are also using social media to gather leads. As platforms such as mobile and video grow, marketers must develop new ways to measure campaign effectiveness across those platforms. In late 2012, global information and measurement company Nielsen launched Nielsen Online Campaign Ratings, a "much-anticipated advertising measurement solution." According to data collected through this new platform, less than half of all online advertisement impressions reach their intended audiences. Depending on the medium used, customer targeting varies widely between a 15 percent and 80 percent success rate.[13] Some metrics that are particularly useful for increasing

Apple's iPhone has "a distinct stickiness."

the success of a social media campaign are awareness, engagement, and conversion. *Awareness* is the attention that social media attracts, such as the number of followers or fans. *Engagement* refers to the interactions between the brand and the audience, such as comments, retweets, and searches. *Conversions* occur when action is taken.[14] Each of these metrics affects the return on investment.

7-3 RELATIONSHIP MARKETING AND STRATEGIC ALLIANCES

As explained in Chapter 1, relationship marketing is a strategy that entails seeking and establishing ongoing partnerships with customers. Relationship marketing has become an important business marketing strategy as customers have become more demanding and competition has become more intense. Loyal customers are also more profitable than those who are price

sensitive and perceive little or no difference among brands or suppliers.

Relationship marketing is increasingly important as business suppliers use platforms like Facebook, Twitter, and other social networking sites to advertise themselves to businesses. Social networking sites encourage businesses to shop around and research options for all their needs. This means that, for many suppliers, retaining their current customers has become a primary focus, whereas acquiring new customers was the focus in the past. Maintaining a steady dialogue between the supplier and the customer is a proven way to gain repeat business.[16]

Building long-term relationships with customers offers companies a way to build competitive advantage that is hard for competitors to copy. For example, the FedEx PowerShip program includes a series of automated shipping, tracking, and invoicing systems that save customers time and money while solidifying their loyalty to FedEx. This produces a win-win situation.

> 13% OF B2B MKTRS <3 TWITTER!

7-3a Strategic Alliances

A **strategic alliance**, sometimes called a **strategic partnership**, is a cooperative agreement between business firms. Strategic alliances can take the form of licensing or distribution agreements, joint ventures, research and development consortia, and partnerships. They may be between manufacturers, manufacturers and customers, manufacturers and suppliers, and manufacturers and channel intermediaries.

Business marketers form strategic alliances to strengthen operations and better compete. eBay's popular online payment system, PayPal, has grown rapidly worldwide although adoption has been slow in Japan, where there are other more popular forms of electronic payment. However, eBay is partnering with Softbank to bring PayPal to Japan. The two companies are hoping to capitalize on the burgeoning mobile shopping movement and to increase credit card usage in Japan.[17]

Sometimes alliance partners are fierce competitors. For instance, sports and concert promotion company Anschutz Entertainment Group (AEG) announced plans in 2012 to partner with online ticket marketplace StubHub.

TOP SOCIAL MEDIA PLATFORMS FOR B-TO-B MARKETERS

BtoB Magazine surveyed 577 B-to-B marketers on their favorite social media platforms at work, and while LinkedIn, Facebook, and Twitter were used by nearly all of the marketers, LinkedIn was their favorite social media tool (chosen by 26 percent of respondents). Runners up were Facebook (20 percent), blogs (19 percent), customer communities (14 percent), Twitter, (13 percent), and YouTube (7 percent).

Those who didn't use social media marketing cited difficulty in convincing top management of its usefulness. This could be due in part to lack of measurable success metrics or simply poor understanding of the media.[15]

relationship commitment a firm's belief that an ongoing relationship with another firm is so important that the relationship warrants maximum efforts at maintaining it indefinitely

trust the condition that exists when one party has confidence in an exchange partner's reliability and integrity

On StubHub, event goers can bypass official ticket retailers like AEG and purchase tickets directly from other individuals—often scalpers—often at a much higher price than face value. Instead of trying to curtail the ticket resale market, AEG incorporated StubHub tickets into its own checkout system, collecting a commission on each StubHub order made through the site.[18] Other alliances are formed between companies that operate in completely different industries. For example, tax preparation company H&R Block partnered with Arizona's private Catholic school system in a marketing campaign highlighting the Private Education Tax Credit, which allows low-income students to attend the state's high-performing Catholic schools. The partnership generated good publicity for H&R Block while effectively serving the schools' customers (the students' parents). In the first year of the partnership, H&R Block clients generated $167,000 in tax credit gifts, sending ninety-two students to private Catholic schools.[19] Exhibit 2 demonstrates the benefits Starbucks and Green Mountain

Coffee receive from each other through their strategic alliance.

For an alliance to succeed in the long term, it must be built on commitment and trust. **Relationship commitment** means that a firm believes an ongoing relationship with some other firm is so important that it warrants maximum efforts at maintaining it indefinitely.[20] A perceived breakdown in commitment by one of the parties often leads to a breakdown in the relationship.

Trust exists when one party has confidence in an exchange partner's reliability and integrity.[21] Some alliances fail when participants lack trust in their trading partners. For example, the alliance between Volkswagen AG and Suzuki Motor Corp. was initially viewed as a win-win opportunity for both automobile companies. However, sharp differences between the corporate cultures of the two firms led to problems almost immediately after the $2.1 billion partnership was announced in 2009.[22] Suzuki accused Volkswagen of holding back technology it promised to share, while Volkswagen claimed that Suzuki breached its contract by buying an engine from rival manufacturer Fiat instead of first considering Volkswagen. After trying to salvage the alliance

Exhibit 2
STRATEGIC ALLIANCE: STARBUCKS AND GREEN MOUNTAIN

Gives		Gets	
	*Starbucks Branded Coffee* Starbucks ground coffee has worldwide recognition and a strong market share.		*Market Share* Starbucks's worldwide recognition allows Green Mountain to steal market share from other single-pod brands that don't carry Starbucks brand coffee.
	Starbucks Customers Starbucks customers are willing to brew at home and tend to be affluent.		*Stronger Brand Recognition* By offering the high-value Keurig brewing machine at Starbucks stores, Green Mountain is able to give its Keurig line stronger branding.
	Existing Green Mountain Customers Current Green Mountain customers own Keurig machines and brew single-pod coffee.		*Market Share* Focused access to Keurig machine users in homes and businesses increases Starbucks's presence in those markets.
	Technology Keurig machines and single-pod brewing technology		*Expanded Product Offering* By selling Keurig machines and coffee pods in retail stores, Starbucks can offer more products and more ways to drink Starbucks coffee.

© AP Images/Toby Talbot / © AP Images/Ted S. Warren

for three years, Suzuki turned to the ICC International Court of Arbitration in 2012 in an attempt to force Volkswagen to return its 19.9 percent stake in the company.[23]

7-3b Relationships in Other Cultures

Although the terms *relationship marketing* and *strategic alliances* are fairly new and popularized mostly by American business executives and educators, the concepts have long been familiar in other cultures. Businesses in China, Japan, Korea, Mexico, and much of Europe rely heavily on personal relationships.

In Japan, for example, exchange between firms is based on personal relationships that are developed through what is called *amae*, or indulgent dependency. *Amae* is the feeling of nurturing concern for, and dependence upon, another. Reciprocity and personal relationships contribute to *amae*. Relationships between companies can develop into a **keiretsu**—a network of interlocking corporate affiliates. Within a *keiretsu*, executives may sit on the boards of their customers or their suppliers. Members of a *keiretsu* trade with each other whenever possible and often engage in joint product development, finance, and marketing activity. For example, the Toyota Group *keiretsu* includes 14 core companies and another 170 that receive preferential treatment. Toyota holds an equity position in many of these 170 member firms and is represented on many of their boards of directors.

Many firms have found that the best way to compete in Asian countries is to form relationships with Asian firms. For example, Google Enterprise has allied with several Asian tech companies to introduce its mapping and location-based services in new Asian markets. Through these partnerships, Google will bring its Maps platform to Ramco Services' cloud-based resource planning services (India), Hyundai and Kia Motors' navigation systems (South Korea), HSR International Realtors' property comparisons (Singapore), and Nintendo's Wii U video game console (Japan).[24]

7-4 MAJOR CATEGORIES OF BUSINESS CUSTOMERS

The business market consists of four major categories of customers: producers, resellers, governments, and institutions.

7-4a Producers

The producer segment of the business market includes profit-oriented individuals and organizations that use purchased goods and services to produce other products, to incorporate into other products, or to facilitate the daily operations of the organization. Examples of producers include construction, manufacturing, transportation, finance, real estate, and food service firms. In the United States, there are more than 13 million firms in the producer segment of the business market. Some of these firms are small, and others are among the world's largest businesses.

Keiretsu entails a network of interlocking corporate affiliates.

© iStockPhoto.com/Urilux

Producers are often called **original equipment manufacturers**, or **OEMs**. This term includes all individuals and organizations that buy business goods and incorporate them into the products they produce for eventual sale to other producers or to consumers. Companies such as General Motors that buy steel, paint, tires, and batteries are said to be OEMs.

7-4b Resellers

The reseller market includes retail and wholesale businesses that buy finished goods and resell them for a profit. A retailer sells mainly to final consumers; wholesalers sell mostly to retailers and other organizational customers. There are approximately 1.5 million retailers and 500,000 wholesalers operating in the United States. Consumer product firms like Procter & Gamble, Kraft Foods, and Coca-Cola sell directly to large retailers and retail chains and through wholesalers to smaller retail units. Retailing is explored in detail in Chapter 14.

Business product distributors are wholesalers that buy business products and resell them to business customers. They often carry thousands of items in stock and employ sales forces to call on business customers. Businesses that wish to buy a gross of pencils or a hundred pounds of fertilizer typically purchase these items from local distributors rather than directly from manufacturers such as Empire Pencil or Dow Chemical.

7-4c Governments

A third major segment of the business market is government. Government organizations include thousands of federal, state, and local buying units. Collectively, these government units account for the greatest volume of purchases of any customer category in the United States.[25]

Marketing to government agencies can be an overwhelming undertaking, but companies that learn how the system works can position themselves to win lucrative contracts and build lasting, rewarding relationships.[26] Marketing to government agencies traditionally has not been an activity for companies seeking quick returns. The aphorism "hurry up and wait" is often cited as a characteristic of marketing to government agencies. Contracts for government purchases are often put out for bid. Interested vendors submit bids (usually sealed) to provide specified products during a particular time. Sometimes the lowest bidder is awarded the contract. When the lowest bidder is not awarded the contract, strong evidence must be presented to justify the decision. Grounds for rejecting the lowest bid include lack of experience, inadequate financing, or poor past performance. Bidding allows all potential suppliers a fair chance at winning government contracts and helps ensure that public funds are spent wisely.

Government spending is one of the most contentious issues in U.S. politics today. Here, Republican Ohio Representative Steve Chabot uses a chart to explain the U.S. budget deficit during a March 2013 town hall meeting in Montgomery, Ohio.

AP Images/Al Behrman

FEDERAL GOVERNMENT Name just about any good or service and chances are that someone in the federal government uses it. The U.S. federal government buys goods and services valued at more than $875 billion per year, making it the world's largest customer.[27]

Although much of the federal government's buying is centralized, no single federal agency contracts for all the government's requirements, and no single buyer in any agency purchases all that the agency needs. We can view the federal government as a combination of several large companies with overlapping responsibilities and thousands of small independent units. One popular source of information about government procurement is *FedBizOpps*. Until recently, businesses hoping to sell to the federal government found the document (previously called *Commerce Business Daily*) unorganized, and it often arrived too late to be useful. The online version (www.cbd-net.com) is timelier and allows contractors to find leads using key word searches. Other examples of publications designed to explain how to do business with the federal government include *Doing Business with the General Services Administration*, *Selling to the Military*, and *Selling to the U.S. Air Force*.

STATE, COUNTY, AND CITY GOVERNMENT Selling to states, counties, and cities can be less frustrating for both small and large vendors than selling to the federal government. Paperwork is typically simpler and more manageable than it is at the federal level. But vendors must decide which of the more than 89,000 government units are likely to buy their wares. State and local buying agencies include school districts, highway departments, government-operated hospitals, housing agencies, and many other departments and divisions.

7-4d Institutions

The fourth major segment of the business market consists of institutions that seek to achieve goals other than the standard business goals of profit, market share, and return on investment. This segment includes schools, hospitals, colleges and universities, churches, labor unions, fraternal organizations, civic clubs, foundations, and other so-called nonbusiness organizations. Some institutional purchasers operate similar to governments in that the purchasing process is influenced, determined, or administered by government units. Other institutional purchasers are organized more like corporations.[28]

7-5 THE NORTH AMERICAN INDUSTRY CLASSIFICATION SYSTEM

The North American Industry Classification System (NAICS) is an industry classification system introduced in 1997 to replace the standard industrial classification system (SIC). NAICS (pronounced *nakes*) is a system for classifying North American business establishments. The system, developed jointly by the United States, Canada, and Mexico, provides a common industry classification system for the North American Free Trade Agreement (NAFTA) partners. Goods- or service-producing firms that use identical or similar production processes are grouped together.

NAICS is an extremely valuable tool for business marketers engaged in analyzing, segmenting, and targeting markets. Each classification group is relatively homogeneous in terms of raw materials required, components used, manufacturing processes employed, and problems faced. The more digits in a code, the more homogeneous the group. Therefore, if a supplier understands the needs and requirements of a few firms within a classification, requirements can be projected for all firms in that category. The number, size, and geographic dispersion of firms can also be identified. This information can be converted to market potential estimates, market share estimates, and sales forecasts. It can also be used for identifying potential new customers. NAICS codes can help identify firms that may be prospective users of a supplier's goods and services. A sample of how NAICS codes function is listed in Exhibit 3. For a complete listing of all NAICS codes, see www.naics.com/search.htm.

7-6 BUSINESS VERSUS CONSUMER MARKETS

The basic philosophy and practice of marketing are the same whether the customer is a business organization or a

> **North American Industry Classification System (NAICS)** a detailed numbering system developed by the United States, Canada, and Mexico to classify North American business establishments by their main production processes

Exhibit 3
HOW NAICS WORKS

The more digits in the NAICS code, the more homogeneous the groups at that level.

NAICS Level	NAICS Code	Description
Sector	51	Information
Subsector	513	Broadcasting and telecommunications
Industry group	5133	Telecommunications
Industry	51332	Wireless telecommunications carriers, except satellite
Industry subdivision	513321	Paging

© Cengage Learning

consumer. Business markets do, however, have characteristics different from consumer markets.

7-6a Demand

Consumer demand for products is quite different from demand in the business market. Unlike consumer demand, business demand is derived, inelastic, joint, and fluctuating.

DERIVED DEMAND The demand for business products is called **derived demand** because organizations buy products to be used in producing their customers' products. For instance, the number of drills or lathes that a manufacturing firm needs is derived from, or based upon, the demand for products that are produced using these machines. Following the Great Recession, California timber harvests fell by over 50 percent due to dramatic reductions in building construction. Since hitting a record low in 2009, the industry has rebounded each year, due in part to increased exports of whole logs to China and a slowly recovering construction industry in the United States.[29] Because demand is derived, business marketers must carefully monitor demand patterns and changing preferences in final consumer markets, even though their customers are not in those markets. Moreover, business marketers must carefully monitor their customers' forecasts because derived demand is based on expectations of future demand for those customers' products.

Some business marketers not only monitor final consumer demand and customer forecasts but also try to influence final consumer demand. Aluminum producers use television and magazine advertisements to point out the convenience and recycling opportunities that aluminum offers to consumers who can choose to purchase soft drinks in either aluminum or plastic containers.

INELASTIC DEMAND The demand for many business products is inelastic with regard to price. *Inelastic demand* means that an increase or decrease in the price of the product will not significantly affect demand for the product. This will be discussed further in Chapter 19.

The price of a product used in the production of, or as part of, a final product is often a minor portion of the final product's total price. Therefore, demand for the final consumer product is not affected. If the price of automobile paint or spark plugs rises significantly, say, 200 percent in one year, do you think the number of new automobiles sold that year will be affected? Probably not.

JOINT DEMAND **Joint demand** occurs when two or more items are used together in a final product. For example, a decline in the availability of memory chips will slow production of microcomputers, which will in turn reduce the demand for disk drives. Likewise, the demand for Apple operating systems exists as long as there is demand for Apple computers. Sales of the two products are directly linked.

FLUCTUATING DEMAND The demand for business products—particularly new plants and equipment—tends to be less stable than the demand for consumer products. A small increase or decrease in consumer demand can produce a much larger change in demand for the facilities and equipment needed to make the consumer product. Economists refer to this phenomenon as the **multiplier effect** (or **accelerator principle**).

Cummins Inc., a producer of heavy-duty diesel engines, uses sophisticated surface grinders to make parts. Suppose Cummins is using twenty surface grinders. Each machine lasts about ten years. Purchases have been timed so two machines will wear out and be replaced annually.

derived demand the demand for business products

joint demand the demand for two or more items used together in a final product

multiplier effect (accelerator principle) phenomenon in which a small increase or decrease in consumer demand can produce a much larger change in demand for the facilities and equipment needed to make the consumer product

If the demand for engine parts does not change, two grinders will be bought this year. If the demand for parts declines slightly, only eighteen grinders may be needed, and Cummins won't replace the worn ones. However, suppose that next year demand returns to previous levels plus a little more. To meet the new level of demand, Cummins will need to replace the two machines that wore out in the previous year, the two that wore out in the current year, plus one or more additional machines. The multiplier effect works this way in many industries, producing highly fluctuating demand for business products.

7-6b Purchase Volume

Business customers tend to buy in large quantities. Just imagine the size of Kellogg's typical order for the wheat bran and raisins used to manufacture Raisin Bran. Or consider that in 2013, the Chicago Transit Authority (CTA) began accepting bids to fulfill a purchase order of 846 new rail cars to replace its aging fleet. The purchase budget was estimated at $2 billion—quite a bit larger than the CTA's $2.25 ride fare.[30]

7-6c Number of Customers

Business marketers usually have far fewer customers than consumer marketers. The advantage is that it is a lot easier to identify prospective buyers, monitor current customers' needs and levels of satisfaction, and personally attend to existing customers. The main disadvantage is that each customer becomes crucial—especially for those manufacturers that have only one customer. In many cases, this customer is the U.S. government.

7-6d Concentration of Customers

Manufacturing operations in the United States tend to be more geographically concentrated than consumer markets. More than half of all U.S. manufacturers concentrate the majority of their operations in the following eight states: California, New York, Ohio, Illinois, Michigan, Texas, Pennsylvania, and New Jersey.[32] Most large metropolitan areas host large numbers of business customers.

7-6e Distribution Structure

Many consumer products pass through a distribution system that includes the producer, one or more wholesalers, and a retailer. In business marketing, however, because of many of the characteristics already mentioned, channels of distribution for business marketing are typically shorter. Direct channels, where manufacturers market directly to users, are much more common. The use of direct channels has increased dramatically in the past decade with the introduction of various Internet buying and selling schemes. One such technique is called a **business-to-business online exchange**, which is an electronic trading floor that provides companies with integrated links to their customers and suppliers. The goal of B-to-B exchanges is to simplify business purchasing and to make it more efficient. For

business-to-business online exchange an electronic trading floor that provides companies with integrated links to their customers and suppliers

BOEING'S BIG BLUNDER

The success or failure of one bid can make the difference between prosperity and bankruptcy. By early 2013, Boeing had delivered fifty of the 848 orders placed for its new, top-of-the-line 787 Dreamliner aircraft. But when reports of onboard fires and emergency landings began to emerge, all fifty Dreamliners were grounded pending investigation of a potentially faulty lithium-ion battery. These events spelled potential disaster for Boeing. The 848 orders were placed by just fifty-six customers, some ordering as many as seventy-four units. Each Dreamliner costs approximately $225 million, so a loss of even one of the orders would be devastating. Boeing pledged to fix the problem as quickly as possible and resume production and delivery, but irreparable damage may have already been done to the company's sales and image.[31]

Crowds look on as a Boeing 787 Dreamliner taxies to the runway at the Air-Venture airshow in Oshkosh, Wisconsin.

example, Exostar was founded in 2000 to support the complex supply chains and security requirements of the global aerospace and defense industries. Its mission is to leverage the power of the Internet to assist 70,000 organizations worldwide in managing and coordinating business processes, including buying, selling, inventory control, logistics management, and communications. Exostar's primary goal is to reduce risk, complexity, and costs for member companies.[33]

7-6f Nature of Buying

Unlike consumers, business buyers usually approach purchasing rather formally. Businesses use professionally trained purchasing agents or buyers who spend their entire career purchasing a limited number of items. They get to know the items and the sellers well. Some professional purchasers earn the designation of Certified Purchasing Manager (CPM) after participating in a rigorous certification program.

7-6g Nature of Buying Influence

Typically, more people are involved in a single business purchase decision than in a consumer purchase. Experts from fields as varied as quality control, marketing, and finance, as well as professional buyers and users, may be grouped in a buying center (discussed later in this chapter).

7-6h Type of Negotiations

Consumers are used to negotiating price on automobiles and real estate. In most cases, however, American consumers expect sellers to set the price and other conditions of sale, such as time of delivery and credit terms. In contrast, negotiating is common in business marketing. Buyers and sellers negotiate product specifications, delivery dates, payment terms, and other pricing matters. Sometimes these negotiations occur during many meetings over several months. Final contracts are often very long and detailed.

7-6i Use of Reciprocity

Business purchasers often choose to buy from their own customers, a practice known as **reciprocity**. For example, General Motors buys engines for use in its automobiles and trucks from BorgWarner, which in turn buys many of the automobiles and trucks it needs from General Motors. This practice is neither unethical nor illegal unless one party coerces the other and the result is unfair competition. Reciprocity is generally considered a reasonable business practice. If all possible suppliers sell a similar product for about the same price, doesn't it make sense to buy from those firms that buy from you?

7-6j Use of Leasing

Consumers normally buy products rather than lease them. But businesses commonly lease expensive equipment such as computers, construction equipment and vehicles, and automobiles. Leasing allows firms to reduce capital outflow, acquire a seller's latest products, receive better services, and gain tax advantages.

The lessor, the firm providing the product, may be either the manufacturer or an independent firm. The benefits to the lessor include greater total revenue from leasing compared to selling and an opportunity to do business with customers who cannot afford to buy.

7-6k Primary Promotional Method

Business marketers tend to emphasize personal selling in their promotion efforts, especially for expensive items, custom-designed products, large-volume purchases, and situations requiring negotiations. The sale of many business products requires a great deal of personal contact. Personal selling is discussed in more detail in Chapter 17.

7-7 TYPES OF BUSINESS PRODUCTS

Business products generally fall into one of the following seven categories, depending on their use: major equipment, accessory equipment, raw materials, component parts, processed materials, supplies, and business services.

7-7a Major Equipment

Major equipment includes capital goods such as large or expensive machines, mainframe computers, blast furnaces, generators, airplanes, and buildings. (These items are also commonly called **installations**.) Major equipment is depreciated over time rather than charged as an expense in the year it is purchased. In addition, major equipment is often custom designed for each customer. Personal selling

In June 2013, Facebook started processing data through its brand-new, 300,000 square foot server farm, located on the edge of the Arctic Circle in Lulea, Sweden. The cutting-edge servers—and the facility itself—represent major equipment for Facebook.

is an important part of the marketing strategy for major equipment because distribution channels are almost always direct from the producer to the business user.

7-7b Accessory Equipment

Accessory equipment is generally less expensive and shorter-lived than major equipment. Examples include portable drills, power tools, microcomputers, and computer software. Accessory equipment is often charged as an expense in the year it is bought rather than depreciated over its useful life. In contrast to major equipment, accessories are more often standardized and are usually bought by more customers. These customers tend to be widely dispersed. For example, all types of businesses buy microcomputers.

Local industrial distributors (wholesalers) play an important role in the marketing of accessory equipment because business buyers often purchase accessories from them. Regardless of where accessories are bought, advertising is a more vital promotional tool for accessory equipment than for major equipment.

7-7c Raw Materials

Raw materials are unprocessed extractive or agricultural products—for example, mineral ore, timber, wheat, corn, fruits, vegetables, and fish. Raw materials become part of finished products. Extensive users, such as steel or lumber mills and food canners, generally buy huge quantities of raw materials. Because there is often a large number of relatively small sellers of raw materials, none can greatly influence price or supply. Thus, the market tends to set the price of raw materials, and individual producers have little pricing flexibility. Promotion is almost always via personal selling, and distribution channels are usually direct from producer to business user.

7-7d Component Parts

Component parts are either finished items ready for assembly or products that need very little processing before becoming part of some other product. Caterpillar diesel engines are component parts used in heavy-duty trucks. Other examples include spark plugs, tires, and electric motors for automobiles. A special feature of component parts is that they can retain their identity after becoming part of the final product. For example, automobile tires are clearly recognizable as part of a car. Moreover, because component parts often wear out, they may need to be replaced several times during the life of the final product. Thus, there are two important markets for many component parts: the OEM market and the replacement market.

The availability of component parts is often a key factor in OEMs meeting their production deadlines. When more than 2,000 workers rioted at a Foxconn factory in Taiyuan, China, the massive electronic parts manufacturer was forced to halt production and close the factory. Delays were forecasted for Acer, Apple, and several other large-name OEMs that rely on Foxconn's inexpensive, technologically advanced production. As China's largest private company, Foxconn employs 1.2 million people and supplies 40 percent of the world's electronics. A major disruption to its production would ripple across the entire electronics industry. Thankfully, the riot was quickly quelled, and Foxconn resumed operation without experiencing a significant impact on supply or delivery.[34]

accessory equipment goods, such as portable tools and office equipment, that are less expensive and shorter-lived than major equipment

raw materials unprocessed extractive or agricultural products, such as mineral ore, lumber, wheat, corn, fruits, vegetables, and fish

component parts either finished items ready for assembly or products that need very little processing before becoming part of some other product

The replacement market is composed of organizations and individuals buying component parts to replace worn-out parts. Because components often retain their identity in final products, users may choose to replace a component part with the same brand used by the manufacturer—for example, the same brand of automobile tires or battery. The replacement market operates differently from the OEM market, however. Whether replacement buyers are organizations or individuals, they tend to demonstrate the characteristics of consumer markets that were shown in Learning Outcome 7-6. Consider, for example, a replacement part for a piece of construction equipment such as a bulldozer or a crane. When a piece of equipment breaks down, it is usually important to acquire a replacement part and have it installed as soon as possible. Purchasers typically buy from local or regional dealers. Negotiations do not occur, and neither reciprocity nor leasing is usually an issue.

7-7e Processed Materials

Processed materials are products used directly in manufacturing other products. Unlike raw materials, they have had some processing. Examples include sheet metal, chemicals, specialty steel, treated lumber, corn syrup, and plastics. Unlike component parts, processed materials do not retain their identity in final products.

Timber, harvested from forests, is a raw material. Fluff pulp, a soft, white absorbent, is produced from loblolly pine timber by mills such as International Paper Co. The fluff pulp then becomes part of disposable diapers, bandages, and other sanitary products.[35]

Most processed materials are marketed to OEMs or to distributors servicing the OEM market. Processed materials are generally bought according to customer specifications or to some industry standard, as is the case with steel and plywood. Price and service are important factors in choosing a vendor.

7-7f Supplies

Supplies are consumable items that do not become part of the final product—for example, lubricants, detergents, paper towels, pencils, and paper. Supplies are normally standardized items that purchasing agents routinely buy. Supplies typically have relatively short lives and are inexpensive compared to other business goods. Because supplies generally fall into one of three categories—maintenance, repair, or operating supplies—this category is often referred to as MRO items. Competition in the MRO market is intense. Bic and Paper Mate, for example, battle for business purchases of inexpensive ball-point pens.

7-7g Business Services

Business services are expense items that do not become part of a final product. Businesses often retain outside providers to perform janitorial, advertising, legal, management consulting, marketing research, maintenance, and other services. Contracting an outside provider makes sense when it costs less than hiring or assigning an employee to perform the task, when an outside provider is needed for particular expertise, or when the need is infrequent.

7-8 BUSINESS BUYING BEHAVIOR

As you probably have already concluded, business buyers behave differently from consumers. Understanding how purchase decisions are made in organizations is a first step in developing a business selling strategy. Business buying behavior has five important

© iStockPhoto.com/james boulette

aspects: buying centers, evaluative criteria, buying situations, business ethics, and customer service.

7-8a Buying Centers

In many cases, more than one person is involved in a purchase decision. A salesperson must determine the buying situation and the information required from the buying organization's perspective to anticipate the size and composition of the buying center.[36]

A **buying center** includes all those people in an organization who become involved in the purchase decision. Membership and influence vary from company to company. For instance, in engineering-dominated firms like Bell Helicopter, the buying center may consist almost entirely of engineers. In marketing-oriented firms like Toyota and IBM, marketing and engineering have almost equal authority. In consumer goods firms like Clorox Corporation, product managers and other marketing decision makers may dominate the buying center. In a small manufacturing company, almost everyone may be a member.

The number of people involved in a buying center varies with the complexity and importance of a purchase decision. The average buying center includes more than one person and up to four per purchase.[37] The composition of the buying group will usually change from one purchase to another and sometimes even during various stages of the buying process. To make matters more complicated, buying centers do not appear on formal organization charts.

For example, even though a formal committee may have been set up to choose a new plant site, it is only part of the buying center. Other people, like the company president, often play informal yet powerful roles. In a lengthy decision-making process, such as finding a new plant location, some members may drop out of the buying center when they can no longer play a useful role. Others whose talents are needed then become part of the center. No formal announcement of "who is in" and "who is out" is ever made.

ROLES IN THE BUYING CENTER As in family purchasing decisions, several people may each play a role in the business purchase process:

▸ The *initiator* is the person who first suggests making a purchase.

▸ *Influencers/evaluators* are people who influence the buying decision. They often help define specifications and provide information for evaluating options.

Technical personnel are especially important as influencers.

▸ *Gatekeepers* are group members who regulate the flow of information. Frequently, the purchasing agent views the gatekeeping role as a source of his or her power. A secretary may also act as a gatekeeper by determining which vendors get an appointment with a buyer.

▸ The *decider* is the person who has the formal or informal power to choose or approve the selection of the supplier or brand. In complex situations, it is often difficult to determine who makes the final decision.

▸ The *purchaser* is the person who actually negotiates the purchase. It could be anyone from the president of the company to the purchasing agent, depending on the importance of the decision.

▸ *Users* are members of the organization who will actually use the product. Users often initiate the buying process and help define product specifications.

IMPLICATIONS OF BUYING CENTERS FOR THE MARKETING MANAGER Successful vendors realize the importance of identifying who is in the decision-making unit, each member's relative influence in the buying decision, and each member's evaluative criteria. Key influencers are frequently located outside of the purchasing department. Successful selling strategies often focus on determining the most important buying influences and tailoring sales presentations to the evaluative criteria most important to these buying center members. An example illustrating the basic buying center roles is shown in Exhibit 4.

Marketers are often frustrated by their inability to reach c-level (chief) executives who play important roles in many buying centers. Marketers who want to build executive-level contacts must become involved in the buying process early on. This is when 80 percent of executives get involved—when major purchase decisions are being made. Executives often ensconce themselves in the buying process because they want to understand current business issues, establish project objectives, and set the overall project strategy.[38] Senior executives are typically not involved in the middle phases of the buying process but often get involved again later in the process to monitor the deal's closing. Executives look for four characteristics in sales representatives:

▸ The ability to marshal resources

▸ An understanding of the buyer's business goals

▸ Responsiveness to requests

▸ Willingness to be held accountable

Exhibit 4
BUYING CENTER ROLES FOR COMPUTER PURCHASES

Role	Illustration
Initiator	Division general manager proposes to replace company's computer network.
Influencers/evaluators	Corporate controller's office and vice president of information services have an important say in which system and vendor the company will deal with.
Gatekeepers	Corporate departments for purchasing and information services analyze company's needs and recommend likely matches with potential vendors.
Decider	Vice president of administration, with advice from others, selects vendor the company will deal with and system it will buy.
Purchaser	Purchasing agent negotiates terms of sale.
Users	All division employees use the computers.

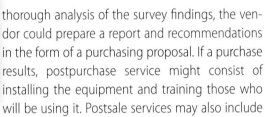

Some firms have developed strategies to reach executives throughout the buying process and during non-buying phases of the relationship. For example, FedEx Corp. has initiated a marketing effort called "access" aimed at c-level executives. It includes direct mail, e-mail, and a custom magazine prepared exclusively for c-level executives. It also hosts exclusive leadership events for these senior executives. Other firms have developed programs utilizing a combination of print, online, and events to reach the elusive c-level audience.[39]

7-8b Evaluative Criteria

Business buyers evaluate products and suppliers against three important criteria: quality, service, and price.

QUALITY In this case, *quality* refers to technical suitability. A superior tool can do a better job in the production process, and superior packaging can increase dealer and consumer acceptance of a brand. Evaluation of quality also applies to the salesperson and the salesperson's firm. Business buyers want to deal with reputable salespeople and companies that are financially responsible. Quality improvement should be part of every organization's marketing strategy.

SERVICE Almost as much as they want satisfactory products, business buyers want satisfactory service. A purchase offers several opportunities for service. Suppose a vendor is selling heavy equipment. Prepurchase service could include a survey of the buyer's needs. After thorough analysis of the survey findings, the vendor could prepare a report and recommendations in the form of a purchasing proposal. If a purchase results, postpurchase service might consist of installing the equipment and training those who will be using it. Postsale services may also include maintenance and repairs.

Another service that business buyers seek is dependability of supply. They must be able to count on delivery of what was ordered when it is scheduled to be delivered. Buyers also welcome services that help them sell their finished products. Services of this sort are especially appropriate when the seller's product is an identifiable part of the buyer's end product.

PRICE Business buyers want to buy at low prices—at the lowest prices, under most circumstances. However, a buyer who pressures a supplier to cut prices to a point at which the supplier loses money on the sale almost forces shortcuts on quality. The buyer also may, in effect, force the supplier to quit selling to him or her. Then a new source of supply will have to be found.

7-8c Buying Situations

Often, business firms, especially manufacturers, must decide whether to make something or buy it from an outside supplier. The decision is essentially one of economics. Can an item of similar quality be bought at a lower price elsewhere? If not, is manufacturing it in-house the best use of limited company resources? For example, Briggs & Stratton Corporation, a major manufacturer of four-cycle engines, might be able to save $150,000 annually on outside purchases by spending $500,000 on the equipment needed to produce gas throttles internally. Yet Briggs & Stratton could also use that $500,000 to upgrade its carburetor assembly line, which would save $225,000 annually. If a firm does decide to buy a product instead of making it, the purchase will be a new buy, a modified rebuy, or a straight rebuy.

NEW BUY A **new buy** is a situation requiring the purchase of a product for the first time. For example, suppose a manufacturing company needs a better way to page its managers while they are working on the shop floor. Currently, each of the several managers has a distinct ring—for example, two short and one long—that sounds over the plant intercom whenever he or she is being paged by anyone in the factory. The company decides to replace its buzzer system of paging with handheld wireless radio technology that will allow managers to communicate immediately with the department initiating the page. This situation represents the greatest opportunity for new vendors. No long-term relationship has been established for this product, specifications may be somewhat fluid, and buyers are generally more open to new vendors.

If the new item is a raw material or a critical component part, the buyer cannot afford to run out of supply. The seller must be able to convince the buyer that the seller's firm can consistently deliver a high-quality product on time.

MODIFIED REBUY A **modified rebuy** is normally less critical and less time-consuming than a new buy. In a modified rebuy situation, the purchaser wants some change in the original good or service. It may be a new color, greater tensile strength in a component part, more respondents in a marketing research study, or additional services in a janitorial contract.

Because the two parties are familiar with each other and credibility has been established, the buyer and seller can concentrate on the specifics of the modification. But in some cases, modified rebuys are open to outside bidders. The purchaser uses this strategy to ensure that the new terms are competitive. An example would be the manufacturing company buying radios with a vibrating feature for managers who have trouble hearing the ring over the factory noise. The firm may open the bidding to examine the price, quality, and service offerings of several suppliers.

STRAIGHT REBUY A **straight rebuy** is a situation vendors prefer. The purchaser is not looking for new information or other suppliers. An order is placed and the product is provided as in previous orders. Usually, a straight rebuy is routine because the terms of the purchase have been agreed to in earlier negotiations. An example would be the previously cited manufacturing company purchasing additional radios for new managers from the same supplier on a regular basis.

One common instrument used in straight rebuy situations is the purchasing contract. Purchasing contracts are used with products that are bought often and in high volume. In essence, the purchasing contract makes the buyer's decision making routine and promises the salesperson a sure sale. The advantage to the buyer is a quick, confident decision, and to the salesperson, reduced or eliminated competition. Nevertheless, suppliers must remember not to take straight rebuy relationships for granted. Retaining existing customers is much easier than attracting new ones.

7-8d Business Ethics

As we noted in Chapter 3, *ethics* refers to the moral principles or values that generally govern the conduct of an individual or a group. Ethics can also be viewed as the standard of behavior by which conduct is judged.

Although we have heard a lot about corporate misbehavior in recent years, most people, and most companies, follow ethical practices. To help achieve this, over half of all major corporations offer ethics training to employees. Many companies also have codes of ethics that help guide buyers and sellers. For example, Home Depot has a clearly written code of ethics available on its corporate Web site that acts as an ethical guide for all its employees.

7-8e Customer Service

Business marketers are increasingly recognizing the benefits of developing a formal system to monitor customer opinions and perceptions of the quality of customer service. Companies such as FedEx, IBM, and Oracle build their strategies not only around products but also around highly developed service skills.[40] These companies understand that keeping current customers satisfied is just as important as attracting new ones, if not more so. Leading-edge firms are obsessed not only with delivering high-quality customer service but also with measuring satisfaction, loyalty, relationship quality, and other indicators of nonfinancial performance. Delivering consistent, high-quality customer service is an important basis for establishing competitive advantage and differentiating one's company from competitors. Cisco Systems uses a Web-based survey to determine the pre- and post-sale satisfaction of customers.[41]

new buy a situation requiring the purchase of a product for the first time

modified rebuy a situation in which the purchaser wants some change in the original good or service

straight rebuy a situation in which the purchaser reorders the same goods or services without looking for new information or investigating other suppliers

Most firms find it necessary to develop measures unique to their own strategies, value propositions, and target markets. For example, Andersen Corporation assesses the loyalty of its trade customers by their willingness to continue carrying its windows and doors, recommend its products to colleagues and customers, increase their volume with the company, and put its products in their own homes. Basically, each firm's measures should not only ask "What are your expectations?" and "How are we doing?" but should also reflect what the firm wants its customers to do.

Some customers are more valuable than others. They may have greater value because they spend more, buy higher-margin products, have a well-known name, or have the potential of becoming a bigger customer in the future. Some companies selectively provide different levels of service to customers based on their value to the business. By giving the most valuable customers superior service, a firm is more likely to keep them happy, hopefully increasing retention of these high-value customers and maximizing the total business value they generate over time.

To achieve this goal, the firm must be able to divide customers into two or more groups based on their value. It must also create and apply policies that govern how service will be allocated among groups. Policies might establish which customers' phone calls get "fast tracked" and which customers are directed to use the Web and/or voice self-service, how specific e-mail questions are routed, and who is given access to online chat and who isn't.

Providing different customers with different levels of service is a very sensitive matter. It must be handled very carefully and very discreetly to avoid offending lesser-value, but still important, customers.

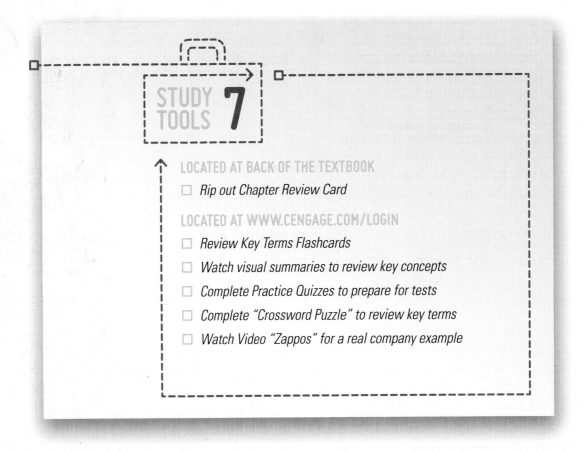

STUDY TOOLS 7

LOCATED AT BACK OF THE TEXTBOOK
☐ Rip out Chapter Review Card

LOCATED AT WWW.CENGAGE.COM/LOGIN
☐ Review Key Terms Flashcards
☐ Watch visual summaries to review key concepts
☐ Complete Practice Quizzes to prepare for tests
☐ Complete "Crossword Puzzle" to review key terms
☐ Watch Video "Zappos" for a real company example

THE IN-CROWD

Share your 4LTR Press story on Facebook at
www.facebook.com/4ltrpress for a chance to win.

To learn more about the In-Crowd opportunity 'like' us on Facebook.

8-1 MARKET SEGMENTATION

The term *market* means different things to different people. We are all familiar with the supermarket, stock market, labor market, fish market, and flea market. All these types of markets share several characteristics. First, they are composed of people (consumer markets) or organizations (business markets). Second, these people or organizations have wants and needs that can be satisfied by particular product categories. Third, they have the ability to buy the products they seek. Fourth, they are willing to exchange their resources, usually money or credit, for desired products. In sum, a **market** is (1) people or organizations with (2) needs or wants and with (3) the ability and (4) the willingness to buy. A group of people or an organization that lacks any one of these characteristics is not a market.

Market segmentation plays a key role in the marketing strategy of almost all successful organizations.

---

market people or organizations with needs or wants and the ability and willingness to buy

market segment a subgroup of people or organizations sharing one or more characteristics that cause them to have similar product needs

market segmentation the process of dividing a market into meaningful, relatively similar, and identifiable segments or groups

Within a market, a **market segment** is a subgroup of people or organizations sharing one or more characteristics that cause them to have similar product needs. At one extreme, we can define every person and every organization in the world as a market segment because each is unique. At the other extreme, we can define the entire consumer market as one large market segment and the business market as another large segment. All people have some similar characteristics and needs, as do all organizations.

From a marketing perspective, market segments can be described as somewhere between the two extremes. The process of dividing a market into meaningful, relatively similar, and identifiable segments, or groups, is called **market segmentation**. The purpose of market segmentation is to enable the marketer to tailor marketing mixes to meet the needs of one or more specific segments.

Chapter 8

Segmenting and Targeting Markets

Learning Outcomes

After you finish this chapter go to
p157 *for* **STUDY TOOLS**

8-2 THE IMPORTANCE OF MARKET SEGMENTATION

Until the 1960s, few firms practiced market segmentation. When they did, it was more likely a haphazard effort than a formal marketing strategy. Before 1960, for example, the Coca-Cola Company produced only one beverage and aimed it at the entire soft drink market. Today, Coca-Cola offers more than a dozen different products to market segments based on diverse consumer preferences for flavors and calorie and caffeine content. Coca-Cola offers traditional soft drinks, energy drinks (including POWERade), flavored teas, fruit drinks (Minute Maid), and water (Dasani).

Market segmentation plays a key role in the marketing strategy of almost all successful organizations and is a powerful marketing tool for several reasons. Most important, nearly all markets include groups of people or organizations with different product needs and preferences. Market segmentation helps marketers define customer needs and wants more precisely. Because market segments differ in size and potential, segmentation helps decision makers to more accurately define marketing objectives and better allocate resources. In turn, performance can be better evaluated when objectives are more precise.

To try and woo the emerging market of stay-at-home dads, many businesses have begun designing baby-related products that cater to men. Instead of frilly, flowery

On its Web site, Diaper Dude advises "fanny-pack phobes" that the company's camouflage-colored diaper bag can also be worn over the shoulder for a hipper look.

totes that make dads feel like mere stand-ins for moms, DadGear offers diaper bags and carriers in macho designs like granite and flaming skulls. Diaper Dude announced a new line of Major League Baseball-branded diaper bags, baby bottle holders, and pacifier pouches, while Jeep released a line of rugged "all-terrain strollers."[1]

8-3 CRITERIA FOR SUCCESSFUL SEGMENTATION

Marketers segment markets for three important reasons. First, segmentation enables marketers to identify groups of customers with similar needs and to analyze the characteristics and buying behavior of these groups. Second, segmentation provides marketers with information to help them design marketing mixes specifically matched with the characteristics and desires of one or more segments. Third, segmentation is consistent with the marketing concept of satisfying customer wants and needs while meeting the organization's objectives.

To be useful, a segmentation scheme must produce segments that meet four basic criteria:

1. **SUBSTANTIALITY:** A segment must be large enough to warrant developing and maintaining a special marketing mix. This criterion does not necessarily mean that a segment must have many potential customers. For example, marketers of custom-designed homes and business buildings, commercial airplanes, and large computer systems typically develop marketing programs tailored to each potential customer's needs. In most cases, however, a market segment needs many potential customers to make commercial sense. In the 1980s, home banking failed because not enough people owned personal computers. Today, a larger number of people own computers, and home banking is a thriving industry.

2. **IDENTIFIABILITY AND MEASURABILITY:** Segments must be identifiable and their size measurable. Data about the population within geographic boundaries, the number of people in various age categories, and other social and demographic characteristics are often easy to get, and they provide fairly concrete measures of segment size. Suppose that a social service agency wants to identify segments by their readiness to participate in a drug and alcohol program or in prenatal care. Unless the agency can measure how many people are willing, indifferent, or

unwilling to participate, it will have trouble gauging whether there are enough people to justify setting up the service.

3. **ACCESSIBILITY:** The firm must be able to reach members of targeted segments with customized marketing mixes. Some market segments are hard to reach—for example, senior citizens (especially those with reading or hearing disabilities), individuals who don't speak English, and the illiterate.

4. **RESPONSIVENESS:** Markets can be segmented using any criteria that seem logical. Unless one market segment responds to a marketing mix differently than other segments, however, that segment need not be treated separately. For instance, if all customers are equally price conscious about a product, there is no need to offer high-, medium-, and low-priced versions to different segments.

8-4 BASES FOR SEGMENTING CONSUMER MARKETS

Marketers use segmentation bases, or variables, which are characteristics of individuals, groups, or organizations, to divide a total market into segments. The choice of segmentation bases is crucial because an inappropriate segmentation strategy may lead to lost sales and missed profit opportunities. The key is to identify bases that will produce substantial, measurable, and accessible segments that exhibit different response patterns to marketing mixes.

Markets can be segmented using a single variable, such as age group, or several variables, such as age group, gender, and education. Although it is less precise, single-variable segmentation has the advantage of being simpler and easier to use than multiple-variable segmentation. The disadvantages of multiple-variable segmentation are that it is often harder to use than single-variable segmentation; usable secondary data are less likely to be available; and as the number of segmentation bases increases, the size of individual segments decreases. Nevertheless, the current trend is toward using more rather than fewer variables to segment most markets. Multiple-variable segmentation is clearly more precise than single-variable segmentation.

Consumer goods marketers commonly use one or more of the following characteristics to segment markets: geography, demographics, psychographics, benefits sought, and usage rate.

8-4a Geographic Segmentation

Geographic segmentation refers to segmenting markets by region of a country or the world, market size, market density, or climate. Market density means the number of people within a unit of land, such as a census tract. Climate is commonly used for geographic segmentation because of its dramatic impact on residents' needs and purchasing behavior. Snowblowers, water and snow skis, clothing, and air-conditioning and heating systems are products with varying appeal, depending on climate.

Consumer goods companies take a regional approach to marketing for four reasons. First, many firms need to find new ways to generate sales because of sluggish and intensely competitive markets. Second, computerized checkout stations with scanners give retailers an accurate assessment of which brands sell best in their region. Third, many packaged-goods manufacturers are introducing new regional brands intended to appeal to local preferences. Fourth, a more regional approach allows consumer goods companies to react more quickly to competition. At Target, local store managers pull school supply lists from all the nearby schools and stock extra of the items on those lists. If ten out of fifteen schools require composition notebooks instead of spiral notebooks, that Target will stock more composition notebooks in greater variety.[2]

8-4b Demographic Segmentation

Marketers often segment markets on the basis of demographic information because it is widely available and often related to consumers' buying and consuming behavior. Some common bases of **demographic segmentation** are age, gender, income, ethnic background, and family life cycle.

© Wuttichok Painichiwarapun/ShutterStock.com

segmentation bases (variables) characteristics of individuals, groups, or organizations

geographic segmentation segmenting markets by region of a country or the world, market size, market density, or climate

demographic segmentation segmenting markets by age, gender, income, ethnic background, and family life cycle

AGE SEGMENTATION Marketers use a variety of terms to refer to different age groups. Examples include newborns, infants, young children, tweens, Generation Y (also called Millennials), Generation X, baby boomers, and seniors. Age segmentation can be an important tool, as a brief exploration of the market potential of several age segments illustrates.

Many companies have long targeted parents of babies and young children with products such as disposable diapers, baby food, and toys. Recently, other companies that have not traditionally marketed to young children are developing products and services to attract this group. For example, Rosewood Hotels & Resorts began offering spa services for children, such as facials and manicures. Hyatt Hotels Corp. has introduced a children's menu, including a three-course meal developed by a renowned chef.[3]

Through allowances, earnings, and gifts, older children and teens account for and influence a great deal of consumption. Tweens (nine to twelve years old) desire to be kids but also want some of the fun of being a teenager. Many retailers serve this market with clothing that is similar in style to that worn by teenagers and young adults. Teen shoppers in the United States spend more than $208 billion of their own money and their parents' money each year on purchases for themselves and also have considerable influence over major family purchase decisions.[4]

The members of the Generation Y market were born between 1979 and 1994 and make up almost 30 percent of the adult population in the United States.[5] This group is the most educated, diverse, and technology-proficient generation ever. Most of their media consumption is online, including reading news and watching television shows. Millennials have formidable purchasing power, but they distrust advertising and are more likely to listen to their peers regarding product decisions. They like to buy experiences and technology, and want to have fun.[6] This group is also more civic-minded than other age cohorts. Seventy-four percent of millennials say they are more likely to pay attention to a company's overall message if the company has a deep commitment to a cause. The vast majority of Generation Y was hit hard by the recession. Many, having just started in career path jobs, have found their opportunities stalled, if they didn't lose their jobs. Companies that were relying on Gen Yers to make up for decreasing boomer interest, such as Disney and Sony Pictures, or Gap and Abercrombie & Fitch, have found themselves without a market as Gen Yers shut their wallets. Even typical life events, such as marriage and starting a family, have been postponed while the youngest generation struggles to find its footing on the treacherous economic ground. Many are living at home with their parents. Only companies able to offer very steep discounts have found purchase with the thrifty group. MGM Resorts International recently began offering rooms at $29 a night with $25 buckets of beer and $1 Jell-O shots to lure spring breakers. With success from its budget inns, the company steeply discounted rooms at its upscale Mandalay Bay and MGM Grand to $65 a night.[7]

Generation X is the group that was born after the baby boomers, between 1965 and 1978. This group is smaller than both Generation Y and baby boomers, making up only 16 percent of the total population.[8] Members of Generation X are at a life stage where they are often stuck between supporting their aging parents and young children (earning Gen X the nickname "the sandwich generation"). They have also grown up under a variety of influences—some traumatic—that make them a self-reliant and somewhat cynical generation. This group has a constant need for diversion and an ability to process a lot of information very quickly. Like Generation Y, they are tech savvy and highly connected, and spend time on social media sites like Facebook and LinkedIn. Gen X is the first generation to see a large increase in the number of women getting a college education and entering the work force. For many, this trend meant delaying or sidestepping marriage and having smaller families.[9] They tend to be disloyal to brands and skeptical of big business. Many of them are parents, and they make purchasing decisions with thought for and input from their families.

DINE OUT VANCOUVER GETS GEN X

Gen Xers desire an experience, not just a product. The desire to have an experience has led to an increase in offbeat events such as Vancouver, Canada's Dine Out Vancouver food festival. More than a series of tastings and tours, the seventeen-day festival features experiences such as a drag queen cabaret and dinner show inspired by the film *The Birdcage*, a private breakfast buffet at the Vancouver Art Gallery, and two secret underground speakeasy locations.[10]

© iStockphoto.com/walrusmail

People born between 1946 and 1964 are often called "baby boomers." Boomers make up 24.7 percent of the total population and they constitute almost one-third of the adult population. This cohort spends more annually than any other generation, and is just as likely as younger consumers to try new products and change brands.[11] Baby boomers are living longer, healthier, more active and connected lives, and will spend time and money doing whatever is necessary to maintain vitality as they age. They also are more interested in acquiring experiences (for example, travel) rather than more products.[12] Still, developing products for baby boomers is critical, as someone turns fifty every seven seconds. For-profit health care companies like Prismic Pharmaceuticals are working around the clock to develop new drugs for the aging and extremely health-conscious baby boomer generation. "Prismic is developing an extremely interesting portfolio," said board member Danilo Casadei Massari, "Our focus is on products that can cost-effectively address commonly occurring disorders in the aging 'baby boomer' population."[13]

Consumers age seventy and older are part of the war generation and the Great Depression generation. Together, this group is often called the silent generation for its ability to quietly persevere through great hardships.[14] The smallest generation of the last 100 years, members of this group tend to live modestly, save their money, and be civic minded.[15] Many in this group view retirement not as a passive time, but as an active time they use to explore new knowledge, travel, volunteer, and spend time with family and friends. However, as consumers age, they do require some modifications in the way they live and the products they purchase. According to gerontologist Stephen Golant, for example, aging individuals may need to install "well-placed handrails or grab bars, ramps, easy-access bathrooms, easy-access kitchens, stair lifts, widened doors or hallways, and modified sink faucets or cabinets" in their homes.[16]

GENDER SEGMENTATION In the United States, women make 85 percent of purchases of consumer goods each year.[17] They are an experienced purchasing group with the responsibility of purchasing the majority of household items. They also are increasingly part of what were once considered all-male markets, such as financial markets. Women tend to view money and

wealth differently than men do. They don't seek to accumulate money, but see it as a way to care for their families, improve their lives, and find security. Thus, financial advisors need to use different strategies to appeal to women.[18] Harley-Davidson, for many years a maker of large, macho-style motorcycles they called "big toys for big boys," is now trying to attract more women by pitching models with lower seats, designing smaller models, and advertising to women.[19] Marketers of products such as clothing, cosmetics, personal-care items, magazines, jewelry, and gifts still commonly segment markets by gender, and many of these marketers are going after the less-traditional male market. For example, Russell Simmons is developing a yoga line for men called Tantris, which will include clothes, mats, and even candles.[20] Even weight-loss programs, which currently have 90 percent female consumption, are starting to target men. Researchers have found that men are put off by female-oriented weight-loss commercials, so Weight Watchers, Jenny Craig, and Nutrisystem have begun producing advertisements targeted toward men. A new multimillion-dollar campaign reassures men that "Weight Watchers online is for men, too," and, "It's not all rainbows and lollipops" while male-oriented television spots feature popular sports figures, hyper-masculine imagery, and average men with whom consumers can relate. President of Weight Watchers David Burwick estimates that only 25 percent of men with weight problems actively seek to lose weight—a figure that Burwick intends to raise over the coming years.[21]

INCOME SEGMENTATION Income is a popular demographic variable for segmenting markets because income level influences consumers' wants and determines their buying power. Many markets are segmented

family life cycle (FLC) a series of stages determined by a combination of age, marital status, and the presence or absence of children

by income, including the markets for housing, clothing, automobiles, and food. Dollar stores, traditionally targeted at lower-income consumers, surged in growth as they began to target middle-income consumers during the Great Recession. In 2012, Dollar General announced that its fastest growing customer segment was shoppers who earned more than $70,000 a year.[22] Wholesale clubs Costco and Sam's Club appeal to many income segments. High-income customers looking for luxury want outstanding customer service. Because they spend large amounts of money, luxury consumers expect to be treated extraordinarily well and to feel a personal connection to a product or brand. Luxury product showrooms and retail locations must constantly evolve to accommodate these customers' needs and to provide an exceptional, high-tech in-store experience.[23] On the other hand, some companies have found success in marketing to the very poor. For multinational companies like Nestle and Unilever, people living in poverty in developing nations are steady customers for inexpensive basics.[24]

ETHNIC SEGMENTATION In the past, ethnic groups in the United States were expected to conform to a homogenized, Anglo-centric ideal. This was evident both in how mass-produced products were marketed as well as in the selective way that films, television, advertisements, and popular music portrayed America's diverse population. Until the 1970s, ethnic foods were rarely sold except in specialty stores. Increasing numbers of ethnic minorities and increased buying power have changed this. Hispanic Americans, African Americans, and Asian Americans are the three largest ethnic groups in the United States. In the American Southwest, Caucasian populations comprise less than half the population and have become the minority to other ethnic groups combined. To meet the needs and wants of expanding ethnic populations, some companies, such as McDonald's and Kmart, make products geared toward specific ethnic groups. For example, Kmart has teamed up with Selena Gomez and Sofia Vergara, both popular Hispanic actors, to develop clothing lines that appeal to Latina consumers.[25] The retailer also carries Fashion Fair Cosmetics, a line of beauty products created specifically for (and marketed toward) African American women.[26]

FAMILY LIFE CYCLE SEGMENTATION The demographic factors of gender, age, and income often do

not sufficiently explain why consumer buying behavior varies. Frequently, consumption patterns among people of the same age and gender differ because they are in different stages of the family life cycle. The **family life cycle (FLC)** is a series of stages determined by a combination of age, marital status, and the presence or absence of children.

The life cycle stage consisting of the married-couple household used to be considered the traditional family in the United States. Today, however, married couples make up less than half of households, down from nearly 80 percent in the 1950s. Single adults are increasingly in the majority. Already, unmarried Americans make up 42 percent of the workforce, 40 percent of home buyers, and one of the most potent consumer groups on record. Exhibit 1 illustrates numerous FLC patterns and shows how families' needs, incomes, resources, and expenditures differ at each stage. The horizontal flow shows the traditional FLC. The lower part of the exhibit gives some of the characteristics and purchase patterns of families in each stage of the traditional life cycle. The exhibit also acknowledges that about half of all first marriages end in divorce. If young marrieds move into the young divorced stage, their consumption patterns often revert to those of the young single stage of the cycle. About four out of five divorced persons remarry by middle age and reenter

Exhibit 1
FAMILY LIFE CYCLE

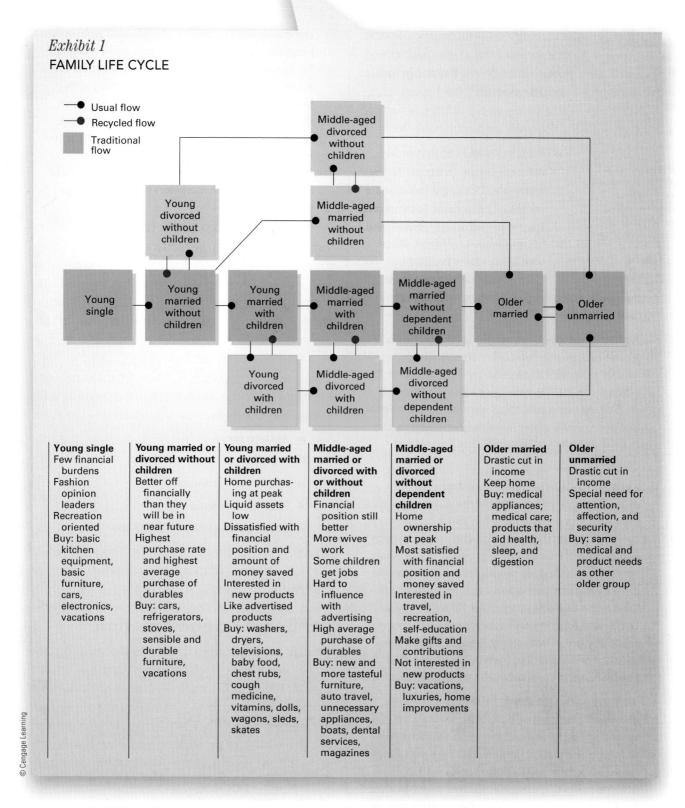

Young single	Young married or divorced without children	Young married or divorced with children	Middle-aged married or divorced with or without children	Middle-aged married or divorced without dependent children	Older married	Older unmarried
Few financial burdens Fashion opinion leaders Recreation oriented Buy: basic kitchen equipment, basic furniture, cars, electronics, vacations	Better off financially than they will be in near future Highest purchase rate and highest average purchase of durables Buy: cars, refrigerators, stoves, sensible and durable furniture, vacations	Home purchasing at peak Liquid assets low Dissatisfied with financial position and amount of money saved Interested in new products Like advertised products Buy: washers, dryers, televisions, baby food, chest rubs, cough medicine, vitamins, dolls, wagons, sleds, skates	Financial position still better More wives work Some children get jobs Hard to influence with advertising High average purchase of durables Buy: new and more tasteful furniture, auto travel, unnecessary appliances, boats, dental services, magazines	Home ownership at peak Most satisfied with financial position and money saved Interested in travel, recreation, self-education Make gifts and contributions Not interested in new products Buy: vacations, luxuries, home improvements	Drastic cut in income Keep home Buy: medical appliances; medical care; products that aid health, sleep, and digestion	Drastic cut in income Special need for attention, affection, and security Buy: same medical and product needs as other older group

© Cengage Learning

the traditional life cycle, as indicated by the "recycled flow" in the exhibit. Consumers are especially receptive to marketing efforts at certain points in the life cycle. For example, baby boomers have increased needs for health care services, while families with babies need diapers, toys, and baby clothes.

8-4c Psychographic Segmentation

Age, gender, income, ethnicity, FLC stage, and other demographic variables are usually helpful in developing segmentation strategies, but often, they don't paint the entire picture. Demographics provide the skeleton, but psychographics add meat to the bones. **Psychographic segmentation** is market segmentation on the basis of the following psychographic segmentation variables:

▸ **PERSONALITY: Personality reflects a person's traits, attitudes, and habits. Clothing is the ultimate personality descriptor. Fashionistas wear high-end, trendy clothes, and hipsters enjoy jeans and T-shirts with tennis shoes. People buy clothes that they feel represent their personalities and give others an idea of who they are.**

▸ **MOTIVES: Marketers of baby products and life insurance appeal to consumers' emotional motives—namely, to care for their loved ones. Using appeals to economy, reliability, and dependability, carmakers like Subaru and Suzuki target customers with rational motives. Carmakers like Mercedes-Benz, Jaguar, and Cadillac appeal to customers with status-related motives.**

▸ **LIFESTYLES: Lifestyle segmentation divides people into groups according to the way they spend their time, the importance of the things around them, their beliefs, and socioeconomic characteristics such as income and education. For example, record stores specializing in vinyl are targeting young people who are listening to independent labels and often pride themselves on being independent of big business. LEED-certified appliances appeal to environmentally conscious "green" consumers. PepsiCo is promoting its no-calorie, sugar-free flavored water, Aquafina FlavorSplash, to consumers who are health conscious.**

▸ **GEODEMOGRAPHICS: Geodemographic segmentation clusters potential customers into neighborhood lifestyle categories. It combines geographic, demographic, and lifestyle segmentations. Geodemographic segmentation helps marketers develop marketing programs tailored to prospective buyers who live in small geographic regions, such as neighborhoods, or who have very specific lifestyle and demographic characteristics. College students, for example, often share similar demographics and lifestyles and tend to cluster around campus. Knowing this, marketing teams for startups and tech**

companies like Foursquare often launch ambassador programs at insular college campuses. In exchange for free merchandise and résumé filler, ambassadors act as brand representatives. They covertly write brand names and company URLs on white boards, start Facebook fan pages, strike up conversations with fellow students about brands, and lobby school newspapers to plug the brands they represent. Through these programs, students are transformed into word-of-mouth marketers to their geodemographic peers.[27]

Psychographic variables can be used individually to segment markets or can be combined with other variables to provide more detailed descriptions of market segments. One approach is for marketers and advertisers to purchase information from a collector, such as eXelate Media, in order to reach the audience they want. eXelate, part of consumer research firm Nielsen, gathers information about Web-browsing habits through cookies placed on Web sites. Nielsen, using eXelate, organizes groups according to this information. One group, the "young digerati," includes twenty-five- to forty-five-year-olds who:

▸ **Are tech savvy**

▸ **Are affluent**

▸ **Live in trendy condos**

▸ **Read the *Economist***

▸ **Have an annual income of $88,000**

An automaker can purchase that list and the list of people who visit car blogs and then target ads to the young digerati interested in cars.[28]

8-4d Benefit Segmentation

Benefit segmentation is the process of grouping customers into market segments according to the benefits they seek from the product. Most types of market segmentation are based on the assumption that this variable and customers' needs are related. Benefit segmentation is different because it groups potential customers on the basis of their needs or wants rather than on some other characteristic, such as age or gender. The snack-food market, for example, can be divided into six benefit segments: nutritional snackers, weight watchers, guilty snackers, party snackers, indiscriminate snackers, and economical snackers.

Customer profiles can be developed by examining demographic information associated with people seeking

How does this advertisement appeal to the benefits a customer might seek?

percentages usually are not exact, the general idea often holds true. Multinational corporations require vast amounts of computer storage, but these giant enterprises make up just a small percentage of the data storage market. When storage manufacturer Actifio found that 80 percent of its customers were midsize enterprises that bought computer storage in relatively modest batches of 100 terabytes (about 100,000 gigabytes), it developed the Actifio 100T, a storage appliance that allowed midsize enterprises to scale up to two petabytes (about 2 million gigabytes) of capacity. In this way, Actifio's 80 percent of low-demand customers could transition over time toward its 20 percent of high-demand customers.[30]

Developing customers into heavy users is the goal behind many frequency/loyalty programs like the airlines' frequent flyer programs. Most supermarkets and other retailers have also designed loyalty programs that reward the heavy-user segment with deals available only to them, such as in-store coupon dispensing systems, loyalty card programs, and special price deals on selected merchandise.

certain benefits. This information can be used to match marketing strategies with selected markets. In 2012, Starbucks introduced Verismo, a brewing machine that can make single shots of espresso as well as lattes and other espresso-based drinks. Catering to customers who drink gourmet coffee, enjoy purchasing (and showing off) the latest kitchen gadgets, and have money to spend, Starbucks began selling the machines in high-end kitchenware stores such as Williams-Sonoma and Sur La Table. As Starbucks surmises, customers at these types of stores seek the types of benefits that Verismo provides.[29]

8-4e Usage-Rate Segmentation

Usage-rate segmentation divides a market by the amount of product bought or consumed. Categories vary with the product, but they are likely to include some combination of the following: former users, potential users, first-time users, light or irregular users, medium users, and heavy users. Segmenting by usage rate enables marketers to focus their efforts on heavy users or to develop multiple marketing mixes aimed at different segments. Because heavy users often account for a sizable portion of all product sales, some marketers focus on the heavy-user segment.

The **80/20 principle** holds that 20 percent of all customers generate 80 percent of the demand. Although the

8-5 BASES FOR SEGMENTING BUSINESS MARKETS

The business market consists of four broad segments: producers, resellers, government, and institutions. (For a detailed discussion of the characteristics of these segments, see Chapter 7.) Whether marketers focus on only one or on all four of these segments, they are likely to find diversity among potential

usage-rate segmentation
dividing a market by the amount of product bought or consumed

80/20 principle
a principle holding that 20 percent of all customers generate 80 percent of the demand

customers. Thus, further market segmentation offers just as many benefits to business marketers as it does to consumer product marketers.

8-5a Company Characteristics

Company characteristics, such as geographic location, type of company, company size, and product use, can be important segmentation variables. Some markets tend to be regional because buyers prefer to purchase from local suppliers, and distant suppliers may have difficulty competing in terms of price and service. Therefore, firms that sell to geographically concentrated industries benefit by locating close to their markets.

Segmenting by customer type allows business marketers to tailor their marketing mixes to the unique needs of particular types of organizations or industries. For example, Round Table Companies teamed with SmarterComics to produce fifty-page illustrated versions of the most popular business books such as *The Long Tail* by Chris Anderson and *How to Master the Art of Selling* by Tom Hopkins. Corey Michael Blake, founder of Round Table, wanted to make the most-read business books available to time-pressed businesspeople. By condensing and illustrating popular business texts, Blake found a new market for comic books and extended the business book market.[31]

Volume of purchase (heavy, moderate, light) is a commonly used basis for business segmentation. Another is the buying organization's size, which may affect its purchasing procedures, the types and quantities of products it needs, and its responses to different marketing mixes. Banks frequently offer different services, lines of credit, and overall attention to commercial customers based on their size. Many products, especially raw materials like steel, wood, and petroleum, have diverse applications. How customers use a product may influence the amount they buy, their buying criteria, and their selection of vendors. For example, a producer of springs may have customers who use the product in applications as diverse as making machine tools, bicycles, surgical devices, office equipment, telephones, and missile systems.

8-5b Buying Processes

Many business marketers find it helpful to segment customers and prospective customers on the basis of how they buy. For example, companies can segment some business markets by ranking key purchasing criteria, such as price, quality, technical support, and service. Atlas Overhead Door has developed a commanding position in the industrial door market by providing customized products in just four weeks, which is much faster than the industry average of twelve to fifteen weeks. Atlas's primary market is companies with an immediate need for customized doors.

The purchasing strategies of buyers may provide useful segments. Two purchasing profiles that have been identified are satisficers and optimizers. **Satisficers** contact familiar suppliers and place the order with the first one to satisfy product and delivery requirements. **Optimizers** consider numerous suppliers (both familiar and unfamiliar), solicit bids, and study all proposals carefully before selecting one.

The personal characteristics of the buyers themselves (their demographic characteristics, decision style, tolerance for risk, confidence level, job responsibilities, and so on) influence their buying behavior and thus offer a viable basis for segmenting some business markets.

8-6 STEPS IN SEGMENTING A MARKET

The purpose of market segmentation, in both consumer and business markets, is to identify marketing opportunities.

1. **SELECT A MARKET OR PRODUCT CATEGORY FOR STUDY:** Define the overall market or product category to be studied. It may be a market in which the firm already competes, a new but related market or product category, or a totally new market.

2. **CHOOSE A BASIS OR BASES FOR SEGMENTING THE MARKET:** This step requires managerial insight, creativity, and market knowledge. There are no scientific procedures for selecting segmentation variables. However, a successful segmentation scheme must produce segments that

meet the four basic criteria discussed earlier in this chapter.

3. **SELECT SEGMENTATION DESCRIPTORS:** After choosing one or more bases, the marketer must select the segmentation descriptors. Descriptors identify the specific segmentation variables to use. For example, if a company selects demographics as a basis of segmentation, it may use age, occupation, and income as descriptors. A company that selects usage-rate segmentation needs to decide whether to go after heavy users, nonusers, or light users.

4. **PROFILE AND ANALYZE SEGMENTS:** The profile should include the segments' size, expected growth, purchase frequency, current brand usage, brand loyalty, and long-term sales and profit potential. This information can then be used to rank potential market segments by profit opportunity, risk, consistency with organizational mission and objectives, and other factors important to the firm.

5. **SELECT MARKETS:** Selecting markets is not a part of but a natural outcome of the segmentation process. It is a major decision that influences and often directly determines the firm's marketing mix. This topic is examined in greater detail later in this chapter.

6. **DESIGN, IMPLEMENT, AND MAINTAIN APPROPRIATE MARKETING MIXES:** The marketing mix has been described as product, place (distribution), promotion, and pricing strategies intended to bring about a mutually satisfying exchange relationship with a market. These topics are explored in detail in Chapters 10 through 20.

Markets are dynamic, so it is important that companies proactively monitor their segmentation strategies over time. Often, once customers or prospects have been assigned to a segment, marketers think their task is done. Once customers are assigned to an age segment, for example, they stay there until they reach the next age bracket or category, which could be ten years in the future. Thus, the segmentation classifications are static, but the customers and prospects are changing. Dynamic segmentation approaches adjust to fit the changes that occur in customers' lives. For example, American Eagle mainly targets ten-year-old boys and girls with its 77kids stores. However, some segments have too many players, and choosing to enter those kinds of segments can be particularly challenging. For example, there are so many Web sites that use flash sales to drive traffic that the *New York Times* put together a list that they think are actually worth visiting.[32]

8-7 STRATEGIES FOR SELECTING TARGET MARKETS

So far, this chapter has focused on the market segmentation process, which is only the first step in deciding whom to approach about buying a product. The next task is to choose one or more target markets. A **target market** is a group of people or organizations for which an organization designs, implements, and maintains a marketing mix intended to meet the needs of that group, resulting in mutually satisfying exchanges. Because most markets will include customers with different characteristics, lifestyles, backgrounds, and income levels, it is unlikely that a single marketing mix will attract all segments of the market. Thus, if a marketer wishes to appeal to more than one segment of the market, it must develop different marketing mixes. The three general strategies for selecting target markets—undifferentiated, concentrated, and multisegment targeting—are illustrated in Exhibit 2, which also illustrates the advantages and disadvantages of each targeting strategy.

target market a group of people or organizations for which an organization designs, implements, and maintains a marketing mix intended to meet the needs of that group, resulting in mutually satisfying exchanges

The three major video game console manufacturers—Microsoft, Sony, and Nintendo—hope to court both casual and hardcore gamers alike. To target the hardcore set, a television advertisement might use rock music and an aggressive-sounding male voice actor to highlight the console's technical specs, the latest first-person shooter games, and a competitive multiplayer arena. An advertisement targeting casual gamers might instead use a female voice actor to highlight the console's ease of use, lighthearted family-based games, and socially connected multimedia apps.[33] Members of one market will not likely be persuaded to buy by a marketing mix targeted at the other.

Exhibit 2
ADVANTAGES AND DISADVANTAGES OF TARGET MARKETING STRATEGIES

Targeting Strategy	Advantages	Disadvantages
Undifferentiated Targeting	• Potential savings on production/marketing costs	• Unimaginative product offerings • Company more susceptible to competition
Concentrated Targeting	• Concentration of resources • Can better meet the needs of a narrowly defined segment • Allows some small firms to better compete with larger firms • Strong positioning	• Segments too small or changing • Large competitors may more effectively market to niche segment
Multisegment Targeting	• Greater financial success • Economies of scale in producing/marketing	• High costs • Cannibalization

© Cengage Learning

8-7a Undifferentiated Targeting

A firm using an **undifferentiated targeting strategy** essentially adopts a mass-market philosophy, viewing the market as one big market with no individual segments. The firm uses one marketing mix for the entire market. A firm that adopts an undifferentiated targeting strategy assumes that individual customers have similar needs that can be met with a common marketing mix.

The first firm in an industry sometimes uses an undifferentiated targeting strategy. With no competition, the firm may not need to tailor marketing mixes to the preferences of market segments. Henry Ford's famous comment about the Model T is a classic example of an undifferentiated targeting strategy: "They can have their car in any color they want, as long as it's black." At one time, Coca-Cola used this strategy with a single product and a single size of its familiar green bottle. Marketers of commodity products, such as flour and sugar, are also likely to use an undifferentiated targeting strategy.

One advantage of undifferentiated marketing is the potential for saving on production and marketing. Because only one item is produced, the firm should be able to achieve economies of mass production. Also, marketing costs may be lower when there is only one product to promote and a single channel of distribution. Too often, however, an undifferentiated strategy emerges by default rather than by design, reflecting a failure to consider the advantages of a segmented approach. The result is often sterile, unimaginative product offerings that have little appeal to anyone.

Another problem associated with undifferentiated targeting is that it makes the company more susceptible to competitive inroads. Hershey lost a big share of the candy market to Mars and other candy companies before it changed to a multisegment targeting strategy. Coca-Cola forfeited its position as the leading seller of cola drinks in supermarkets to PepsiCo in the late 1950s, when Pepsi began offering several sizes of containers.

You might think a firm producing a standard product such as toilet tissue would adopt an undifferentiated strategy. However, this market has industrial segments and consumer segments. Industrial buyers want an economical, single-ply product sold in boxes of a hundred rolls (or jumbo rolls a foot in diameter to use in public restrooms). The consumer market demands a more versatile product in smaller quantities. Within the consumer market, the product is differentiated with designer print or no print, as cushioned or noncushioned, and as economy priced or luxury priced. Undifferentiated marketing can succeed in certain situations, though. A small grocery store in a small, isolated town may define all of the people who live in the town as its target market. It may offer one marketing mix and generally satisfy everyone in town. This strategy is not likely to be as effective if there are three or four grocery stores in town.

undifferentiated targeting strategy a marketing approach that views the market as one big market with no individual segments and thus uses a single marketing mix

A bag of Intelligentsia coffee sits on a shelf before being shipped from the company's Chicago, Illinois, headquarters.

8-7b Concentrated Targeting

With a **concentrated targeting strategy**, a firm selects a market **niche** (one segment of a market) for targeting its marketing efforts. Because the firm is appealing to a single segment, it can concentrate on understanding the needs, motives, and satisfactions of that segment's members and on developing and maintaining a highly specialized marketing mix. Some firms find that concentrating resources and meeting the needs of a narrowly defined market segment is more profitable than spreading resources over several different segments.

Intelligentsia Coffee & Tea, a Chicago-based coffee roaster/retailer, targets serious coffee drinkers with hand-roasted, ground, and poured super-gourmet coffee or tea served by seriously educated baristas. The company also offers training classes for the at-home or out-of-town coffee aficionado. Starting price—$200 per class.

Small firms often adopt a concentrated targeting strategy to compete effectively with much larger firms. For example, Enterprise Rent-A-Car, number one in the car rental industry, started as a small company catering to people with cars in the shop. Some other firms use a concentrated strategy to establish a strong position in a desirable market segment. Porsche, for instance, targets an upscale automobile market through "class appeal, not mass appeal."

Concentrated targeting violates the old adage "Don't put all your eggs in one basket." If the chosen segment is too small or if it shrinks because of environmental changes, the firm may suffer negative consequences. For instance,

OshKosh B'gosh was highly successful selling children's wear in the 1980s. It was so successful, however, that the children's line came to define OshKosh's image to the extent that the company could not sell clothes to anyone else. Attempts at marketing older children's clothing, women's casual clothes, and maternity wear were all abandoned. Recognizing it was in the children's wear business, the company expanded into products such as kids' shoes, children's eyewear, and plush toys.

A concentrated strategy can also be disastrous for a firm that is not successful in its narrowly defined target market. Before Procter & Gamble (P&G) introduced Head & Shoulders shampoo, several small firms were already selling antidandruff shampoos. Head & Shoulders was introduced with a large promotional campaign, and the new brand captured over half the market immediately. Within a year, several of the firms that had been concentrating on this market segment went out of business.

8-7c Multisegment Targeting

A firm that chooses to serve two or more well-defined market segments and develops a distinct marketing mix for each has a **multisegment targeting strategy**. P&G offers eighteen different laundry detergents, each targeting a different segment of the market. For example, Tide is a tough, powerful cleaner, and Era is good for stain treatment and removal. Zipcar, a membership-based car sharing company that provides car rentals to its members billable by the hour or day, shifted its targeting strategy from urban centers, adding services for business and universities like the University of Minnesota, which has five Zipcar stations located around its campus. On campuses across the nation, Zipcar targeting is further subdivided into faculty/staff and student markets.[34]

Multisegment targeting offers many potential benefits to firms, including greater sales volume, higher profits, larger market share, and economies of scale in

concentrated targeting strategy a strategy used to select one segment of a market for targeting marketing efforts

niche one segment of a market

multisegment targeting strategy a strategy that chooses two or more well-defined market segments and develops a distinct marketing mix for each

cannibalization a situation that occurs when sales of a new product cut into sales of a firm's existing products

manufacturing and marketing. Yet it may also involve greater product design, production, promotion, inventory, marketing research, and management costs. Before deciding to use this strategy, firms should compare the benefits and costs of multisegment targeting to those of undifferentiated and concentrated targeting.

Another potential cost of multisegment targeting is **cannibalization**, which occurs when sales of a new product cut into sales of a firm's existing products. For example, as sales of Apple's iPad mini have risen, sales of the 9.7-inch iPad have fallen—so much so that Sharp Corp had to significantly cut back its production of the larger iPad's screens. Given that the tablet market continues to grow rapidly, this trend suggests that buyers may be choosing the less-expensive mini over the larger option—not opting for both, as Apple might hope. [35]

8-8 CRM AS A TARGETING TOOL

Recall from Chapter 1 that CRM entails tracking interactions with customers to optimize customer satisfaction and long-term company profits. Companies that successfully implement CRM tend to customize the goods and services offered to their customers based on data generated through interactions between carefully defined groups of customers and the company. CRM can also allow marketers to target customers with extremely relevant advertisements. In 2012, Facebook unveiled "Custom Audience" advertisements. Using this platform, businesses can enter lists of customer e-mail addresses, Facebook user IDs, or phone numbers into a Facebook database. They can then target ultra-specific Facebook ads directly to their customers based on personal and purchase information they collected through CRM. Hypothetically, if a woman named Chrissie spent her birthday at a hotel in the Bahamas, she might see the following Facebook ad from the hotel chain three weeks before her next birthday: "Hey Chrissie, if you liked your stay at our Bahamas location, spend this birthday in one of our Orlando suites—it's just a 136 mile drive from your home!"[36]

As many firms have discovered, a detailed and segmented understanding of customers can be advantageous. There are at least four trends that will lead to the continuing growth of CRM: personalization, time savings, loyalty, and technology.

▸▸ **PERSONALIZATION:** One-size-fits-all marketing is no longer relevant. Consumers want to be treated as the individuals they are, with their own unique sets of needs and wants. By its personalized nature, CRM can fulfill this desire.

▸▸ **TIME SAVINGS:** Direct and personal marketing efforts will continue to grow to meet the needs of consumers who no longer have the time to spend shopping and making purchase decisions. With the personal and targeted nature of CRM, consumers can spend less time making purchase decisions and more time doing the things that are important to them.

▸▸ **LOYALTY:** Consumers will be loyal only to those companies and brands that have earned their loyalty and reinforced it at every purchase occasion. CRM techniques focus on finding a firm's best customers, rewarding them for their loyalty, and thanking them for their business.

Zipcar representative Travis Reik explains the car-sharing process to University of Mississippi junior Abby Oliver shortly after Ole Miss announced a partnership with the company.

© ZUMA Press Inc./Alamy

▸ **TECHNOLOGY:** Mass-media approaches will decline in importance as advances in market research and database technology allow marketers to collect detailed information on their customers. New technology offers marketers a more cost-effective way to reach customers and enables businesses to personalize their messages. For example, My.Yahoo .com greets each user by name and offers information in which the user has expressed interest. Similarly, RedEnvelope.com helps customers keep track of special occasions and offers personalized gift recommendations. With the help of database technology, CRM can track a business's customers as individuals, even if they number in the millions.

CRM is a huge commitment and often requires a 180-degree turnaround for marketers who spent the last half of the twentieth century developing and implementing mass-marketing efforts. Although mass marketing will probably continue to be used, especially to create brand awareness or to remind consumers of a product, the advantages of CRM cannot be ignored.

8-9 POSITIONING

Marketers segment their markets and then choose which segment, or segments, to target with their marketing mix. Then, based on the target market(s), they can develop the product's **positioning**, a process that influences potential customers' overall perception of a brand, product line, or organization in general. **Position** is the place a product, brand, or group of products occupies in consumers' minds relative to competing offerings. Consumer goods marketers are particularly concerned with positioning. Coca-Cola has multiple cola brands, each positioned to target a different market. For example, Coca-Cola Zero is positioned on its bold taste and zero calories, Caffeine Free Coca-Cola is positioned as

a no-caffeine alternative, and Tab is positioned as a cola drink for dieters.[37]

Positioning assumes that consumers compare products on the basis of important features. Marketing efforts that emphasize irrelevant features are therefore likely to misfire. For example, Crystal Pepsi and a clear version of Coca-Cola's Tab failed because consumers perceived the "clear" positioning as more of a marketing gimmick than a benefit.

Effective positioning requires assessing the positions occupied by competing products, determining the important dimensions underlying these positions, and choosing a position in the market where the organization's marketing efforts will have the greatest impact. In 2013, NBC Universal partnered with *Esquire* magazine to rebrand and reposition ailing cable television channel G4 as the Esquire Network. Transitioning away from a focus on nerd culture, video games, and immature humor, the channel was repositioned to target men age eighteen to forty-nine who are upwardly mobile and highly educated—a demographic NBC Universal believes is underserved by current television offerings. While certain G4 programs like *American Ninja Warrior* were carried over to the new network, new programs focusing on cooking and travel were added to appeal to an older, more sophisticated demographic.[38] One positioning strategy that

positioning
developing a specific marketing mix to influence potential customers' overall perception of a brand, product line, or organization in general

position the place a product, brand, or group of products occupies in consumers' minds relative to competing offerings

Unique menu items help Kentucky Fried Chicken differentiate itself from other fast-food fried chicken restaurants.

AP Images/Wilfredo Lee

product differentiation a positioning strategy that some firms use to distinguish their products from those of competitors

perceptual mapping a means of displaying or graphing, in two or more dimensions, the location of products, brands, or groups of products in customers' minds

many firms use to distinguish their products from competitors is based on **product differentiation.** The distinctions between products can be either real or perceived. For example, Kentucky Fried Chicken differentiates itself from other fast-food fried chicken restaurants with its secret blend of eleven herbs and spices (perceived), as well as unique offerings like the Double Down, Famous Bowl, and Bucket & Bites Meal (real).[39] However, many everyday products, such as bleaches, aspirin, unleaded regular gasoline, and some soaps, are differentiated by such trivial means as brand names, packaging, color, smell, or "secret" additives. The marketer attempts to convince consumers that a particular brand is distinctive and that they should demand it.

Some firms, instead of using product differentiation, position their products as being similar to competing products or brands. Two examples of this positioning are artificial sweeteners advertised as tasting like sugar and margarine as tasting like butter.

8-9a Perceptual Mapping

Perceptual mapping is a means of displaying or graphing, in two or more dimensions, the location of products, brands, or groups of products in customers' minds. For example, Saks Incorporated, the department store chain, stumbled in sales when it tried to attract a younger core customer. To recover, Saks invested in research to determine its core customers in its fifty-four stores across the country. The perceptual map for the chocolate bar market (see Exhibit 3) shows that Divine Chocolate (a social enterprise) found that some consumers would pay a premium price for very high-quality chocolate made from fairtrade cocoa. Green & Black's exploited the opportunity to sell premium chocolate made from organic ingredients. Both these brands successfully moved into the high quality/high price quadrant before too many competitors beat them to it.

8-9b Positioning Bases

Firms use a variety of bases for positioning, including the following:

▸ **ATTRIBUTE:** A product is associated with an attribute, product feature, or customer benefit. In engineering its products, Seventh Generation focuses on removing common toxins and chemicals from household products to make them safe for everyone in the household.

▸ **PRICE AND QUALITY:** This positioning base may stress high price as a signal of quality or emphasize low price as an indication of value. Neiman Marcus uses the high-price strategy; Walmart has successfully followed the low-price and value strategy. The mass merchandiser Target has developed an interesting position based on price and quality. It is an "upscale discounter," sticking to low prices but offering higher quality and design than most discount chains.

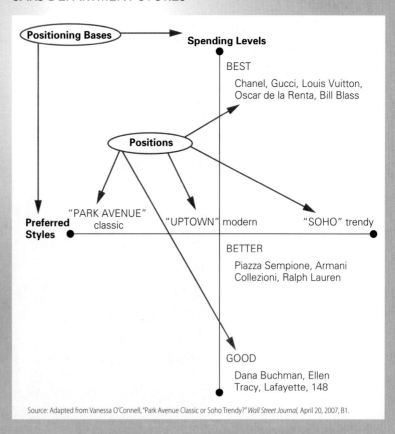

Exhibit 3
PERCEPTUAL MAP AND POSITIONING STRATEGY FOR SAKS DEPARTMENT STORES

Source: Adapted from Vanessa O'Connell, "Park Avenue Classic or Soho Trendy?" *Wall Street Journal,* April 20, 2007, B1.

▸ **USE OR APPLICATION:** Stressing uses or applications can be an effective means of positioning a product with buyers. Danone introduced its Kahlúa liqueur using advertising to point out 228 ways to consume the product.

▸ **PRODUCT USER:** This positioning base focuses on a personality or type of user. Gap Inc. has several different brands: Gap stores offer basic casual pieces, such as jeans and T-shirts, to middle-of-the-road consumers at mid-level prices; Old Navy offers low-priced, trendy casual wear geared to youth and college-age groups; and Banana Republic is a luxury brand offering fashionable, luxurious business and casual wear to twenty-five- to thirty-five-year-olds.[40]

▸ **PRODUCT CLASS:** The objective here is to position the product as being associated with a particular category of products—for example, positioning a margarine brand with butter. Alternatively, products can be disassociated with a category.

▸ **COMPETITOR:** Positioning against competitors is part of any positioning strategy. Apple positions the iPhone as cooler and more up to date than Windows-based smartphones, and Samsung positions the Galaxy series as cooler and more up to date than the iPhone.

▸ **EMOTION:** Positioning using emotion focuses on how the product makes customers feel. A number of companies use this approach. For example, Nike's "Just Do It" campaign didn't tell consumers what "it" is, but most got the emotional message of achievement and courage. Luxury smartphone manufacturer Vertu shifted from a high-price message to an emotional one, positioning the $10,880 Ti model as the phone that will make " nothing else ever feel the same."[41]

8-9c Repositioning

Sometimes products or companies are repositioned in order to sustain growth in slow markets or to correct positioning mistakes. **Repositioning** is changing consumers' perceptions of a brand in relation to competing brands. For example, Timex hired public relations company Brand at MHP to reposition its watches as fashion accessories in the United Kingdom. "We set out wanting to change the perception of Timex—perhaps a bit dusty and old-fashioned—amongst some of the most influential fashion bloggers in the UK," said Brand at MHP marketer Gemma Irvine. "In front of my very eyes, I saw these uber-glam and uber-lovely bloggers bewitched by the stylish Timex pieces."[42]

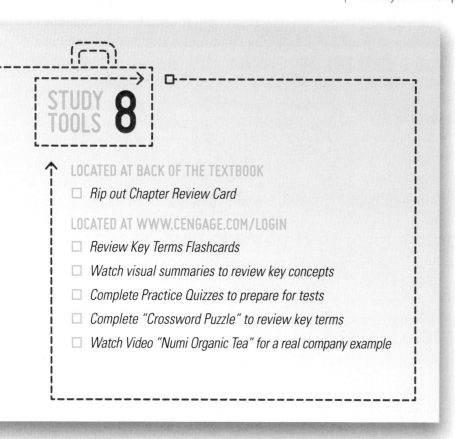

STUDY TOOLS **8**

LOCATED AT BACK OF THE TEXTBOOK
☐ *Rip out Chapter Review Card*

LOCATED AT WWW.CENGAGE.COM/LOGIN
☐ *Review Key Terms Flashcards*
☐ *Watch visual summaries to review key concepts*
☐ *Complete Practice Quizzes to prepare for tests*
☐ *Complete "Crossword Puzzle" to review key terms*
☐ *Watch Video "Numi Organic Tea" for a real company example*

THE ROLE OF MARKETING RESEARCH

Marketing research is the process of planning, collecting, and analyzing data relevant to a marketing decision. The results of this analysis are then communicated to management. Thus, marketing research is the function that links the consumer, customer, and public to the marketer through information. Marketing research plays a key role in the marketing system. It provides decision makers with data on the effectiveness of the current marketing mix and insights for necessary changes. Furthermore, marketing research is a main data source for management information systems. In other words, the findings of a marketing research project become data for management decision making.

Whether a research project costs $200 or $2 million, the same general process should be followed.

marketing research the process of planning, collecting, and analyzing data relevant to a marketing decision

Marketing research has three roles: descriptive, diagnostic, and predictive. Its *descriptive* role includes gathering and presenting factual statements. For example, what is the historic sales trend in the industry? What are consumers' attitudes toward a product and its advertising? Its *diagnostic* role includes explaining data, such as determining the impact on sales of a change in the design of the package. Its *predictive* function is to address "what if" questions. For example, how can the researcher use the descriptive and diagnostic research to predict the results of a planned marketing decision?

9-1a Management Uses of Marketing Research

Marketing research can help managers in several ways. First, it improves the quality of decision making, allowing marketers to explore the desirability of various alternatives before arriving at a path forward. Second, it helps managers trace problems. Was the initial decision incorrect? Did an unforeseen change in the external environment cause the plan to fail? How can the same mistake be avoided in the future? Questions like these can be answered through marketing research. Most importantly, sound marketing research can help managers serve their customers accurately and efficiently. When Home Depot marketing research revealed which brands of plumbing fixtures were traditionally used

Marketing Research

After you finish this chapter go to
p177 *for* **STUDY TOOLS**

throughout New York City, Brooklyn Home Depot store manager Rich Kantor was able to design his small pilot store to meet the exact needs of urban communities.

Marketing research also helps managers gauge the perceived value of their goods and services, as well as the level of customer satisfaction. A recent ForeSee Results survey of 6,200 mobile shoppers found that Amazon ranked first in smartphone-based shopping and service. Competing with twenty-four top m-commerce Web sites in categories such as merchandise selection, price, functionality, and content, Amazon topped the list with a score of 85 out of a possible 100 (beating Apple by just two points). This survey indicates that Amazon is on the right track in its mobile marketing strategy, while other companies have some catching up to do.[1]

9-1b Understanding the Ever-Changing Marketplace

Marketing research helps managers understand what is going on in the marketplace and take advantage of opportunities. Historically speaking, marketing research has been practiced for as long as marketing has existed. The early Phoenicians carried out market demand studies as they traded in the various ports of the Mediterranean Sea. Marco Polo's diary indicates he performed marketing research as he traveled to China. There is even evidence that the Spanish systematically conducted "market surveys" as they explored the New World, and there are examples of marketing research conducted during the Renaissance.

As the price of gasoline hit $4.00 plus per gallon, more and more manufacturers began looking at the hybrid and electric car market. However, before committing hundreds of millions of dollars to producing cars with these complex energy sources, they needed a better understanding of the market. Enter marketing research. When *Consumer Reports* asked consumers whether they would consider a hybrid or electric model for their next car purchase, roughly 75 percent indicated that they would. Ninety percent

cited gasoline costs as a reason they would consider an alternative energy vehicle, while 62 percent mentioned environmentalism and 56 percent indicated dependence on foreign oil as important factors. Women were disproportionally motivated by environmental factors, while owners of large sport utility vehicles were the most open to downsizing.[2] Although this material represents just a tiny piece of a nationwide study, you can see how the insights from such a study can be extremely valuable to car manufacturers.

9-2 STEPS IN A MARKETING RESEARCH PROJECT

Virtually all firms that have adopted the marketing concept engage in some marketing research because it offers decision makers many benefits. Some companies spend millions on marketing research; others, particularly smaller firms, conduct informal, limited-scale research studies.

Whether a research project costs $200 or $2 million, the same general process should be followed. The marketing research process is a scientific approach to decision making that maximizes the chance of getting accurate and meaningful results. Exhibit 1 traces the seven steps in the research process, which begins with the recognition of a marketing problem or opportunity. As changes occur in the firm's external environment, marketing managers are faced with the questions "Should we change the existing marketing mix?" and, if so, "How?" Marketing research may be used to evaluate product, promotion, distribution, or pricing alternatives.

Long struggling to reinvigorate sales of shampoo and conditioner line Pantene, Procter & Gamble (P&G) unveiled a new package design in 2010—the company's second high-profile repackaging effort in three years. However, P&G soon discovered that while the new package solved

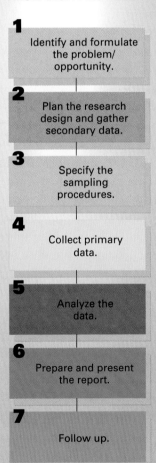

Exhibit 1

THE MARKETING RESEARCH PROCESS

1 Identify and formulate the problem/opportunity.

2 Plan the research design and gather secondary data.

3 Specify the sampling procedures.

4 Collect primary data.

5 Analyze the data.

6 Prepare and present the report.

7 Follow up.

© Cengage Learning

PANTENE'S MODIFIED PACKAGING BROUGHT BACK MORE FAMILIAR ELEMENTS, SUCH AS TELLING CUSTOMERS THAT PARTICULAR SHAMPOO IS DESIGNED TO MOISTURIZE HAIR.

certain marketing problems for the brand, it created a number of others. P&G marketing researchers found that the new packaging strayed too far from what customers wanted: hair care packaging that focused on solutions (more volume, shinier hair, smoother hair). Instead, Pantene alienated customers with its focus on hair type and by discontinuing long-standing favorites, such as two-in-one shampoo and conditioner. In 2011, P&G brought back the two-in-one conditioner and again changed packaging to be more readable and more in line with consumer expectations. The corrections have helped the Pantene line regain market share.[3]

The Pantene story illustrates an important point about problem/opportunity definition. The **marketing research problem** is information oriented. It involves determining what information is needed and how that information can be obtained efficiently and effectively. The **marketing research objective**, then, is to provide insightful decision-making information. This requires specific pieces of information needed to solve the marketing research problem. Managers must combine this information with their own experience and other information to make proper decisions. Initially, P&G's marketing research problem was to gather specific information about how a woman's hair affects her feelings and mood. The marketing research objectives were to reformulate Pantene to affect women's hair more positively and to reposition the brand as an antidote to bad hair days. When sales continued slipping after the 2010 launch, the marketing research problem became gathering information about what shampoo customers were buying and how the changes to Pantene's products affected former customers. The marketing research objectives were to reposition the brand as a value brand against salon brands through modified packaging and to bring popular products out of retirement to regain lost sales.

In contrast, the **management decision problem** is action oriented. Management problems tend to be much broader in scope and far more general than marketing research problems, which must be narrowly defined and specific if the research effort is to be successful. Sometimes several research studies must be conducted to solve a broad management problem. For Pantene, the management decision problem was deciding how to win sales back after the recession and several rebranding attempts.

9-2a Secondary Data

A valuable tool throughout the research process, particularly in the problem/opportunity identification stage, is **secondary data**—data previously collected for any purpose other than the one at hand. Secondary information originating within the company includes documents such as annual reports, reports to stockholders, product testing results perhaps made available to the news media, and house periodicals composed by the company's personnel for communication to employees, customers, or others. Often, this information is incorporated into a company's internal database.

Innumerable outside sources of secondary information also exist, principally in the forms of government departments and agencies (federal, state, and local) that compile and publish summaries of business data. Trade and industry associations also publish secondary data. Still more data are available in business periodicals and other news media that regularly publish studies and articles on the economy, specific industries, and even individual companies. The unpublished summarized secondary information from these sources corresponds to internal reports, memos, or special-purpose analyses with limited circulation. Economic considerations or priorities in the organization may preclude

marketing research problem determining what information is needed and how that information can be obtained efficiently and effectively

marketing research objective the specific information needed to solve a marketing research problem; the objective should be to provide insightful decision-making information

management decision problem a broad-based problem that uses marketing research in order for managers to take proper actions

secondary data data previously collected for any purpose other than the one at hand

publication of these summaries. Most of the sources listed above can be found on the Internet.

Secondary data save time and money if they help solve the researcher's problem. Even if the problem is not solved, secondary data have other advantages. They can aid in formulating the problem statement and suggest research methods and other types of data needed for solving the problem. In addition, secondary data can pinpoint the kinds of people to approach and their locations and serve as a basis of comparison for other data. The disadvantages of secondary data stem mainly from a mismatch between the researcher's unique problem and the purpose for which the secondary data were originally gathered, which are typically different. For example, a company wanted to determine the market potential for a fireplace log made of coal rather than compressed wood by-products. The researcher found plenty of secondary data about total wood consumed as fuel, quantities consumed in each state, and types of wood burned. Secondary data were also available about consumer attitudes and purchase patterns of wood by-product fireplace logs. The wealth of secondary data provided the researcher with many insights into the artificial log market. Yet nowhere was there any information that would tell the firm whether consumers would buy artificial logs made of coal.

The quality of secondary data may also pose a problem. Often, secondary data sources do not give detailed information that would enable a researcher to assess their quality or relevance. Whenever possible, a researcher needs to address these important questions: Who gathered the data? Why were the data obtained? What methodology was used? How were classifications (such as heavy users versus light users) developed and defined? When was the information gathered?

THE NEW AGE OF SECONDARY INFORMATION: THE INTERNET Although necessary in almost any research project, gathering secondary data has traditionally been a tedious and boring job. The researcher often had to write to government agencies, trade associations, or other secondary data providers and then wait days or weeks for a reply that might never come. Often, one or more trips to the library were required, and the researcher might have found that needed reports were checked out or missing. Now, however, the Internet has eliminated much of the drudgery associated with the collection of secondary data. The Internet has become a huge source of behavioral data based upon information collected from shopping sites such as Zappos and social networking sites like Facebook. We will examine this important trend in more detail later in the chapter.

9-2b Planning the Research Design and Gathering Primary Data

Good secondary data can help researchers conduct a thorough situation analysis. With that information, researchers can list their unanswered questions and rank them. Researchers must then decide the exact information required to answer the questions. The **research design** specifies which research questions must be answered, how and when the data will be gathered, and how the data will be analyzed. Typically, the project budget is finalized after the research design has been approved.

Sometimes research questions can be answered by gathering more secondary data; otherwise, primary data may be needed. **Primary data**, or information collected for the first time, are used for solving the particular problem under investigation. The main advantage of primary data is that they will answer a specific research question that secondary data cannot answer. When P&G was doing intensive research for Pantene, managers used a psychological questionnaire to determine how hair products affected women's daily attitudes. This primary data revealed that women using the new Pantene felt more excited, proud, interested, and attentive than the other group—positive emotions that the

© arek_malang/ShutterStock.com

Pantene research group could not have discovered through secondary research. Moreover, primary data are current, and researchers know the source. Sometimes researchers gather the data themselves rather than assign projects to outside companies. Researchers also specify the methodology of the research. Secrecy can be maintained because the information is proprietary. In contrast, much secondary data is available to all interested parties for relatively small fees or free.

Gathering primary data is expensive; costs can range from a few thousand dollars for a limited survey to several million for a nationwide study. For instance, a nationwide, fifteen-minute telephone interview with 1,000 adult males can cost $50,000 for everything, including a data analysis and report. Because primary data gathering is so expensive, firms may cut back on the number of in-person interviews to save money and use an Internet study instead. Larger companies that conduct many research projects use another cost-saving technique. They *piggyback studies*, or gather data on two different projects using one questionnaire. Nevertheless, the disadvantages of primary data gathering are usually offset by the advantages. It is often the only way of solving a research problem. And with a variety of techniques available

for research—including surveys, observations, and experiments—primary research can address almost any marketing question.

SURVEY RESEARCH The most popular technique for gathering primary data is **survey research**, in which a researcher interacts with people to obtain facts, opinions, and attitudes. Exhibit 2 summarizes the characteristics of traditional forms of survey research.

IN-HOME PERSONAL INTERVIEWS Although in-home personal interviews often provide high-quality information, they tend to be very expensive because of the interviewers' travel time and mileage costs. Therefore, they are rapidly disappearing from the American and European researchers' survey toolbox. They are, however, still popular in many countries around the globe.

MALL INTERCEPT INTERVIEWS The **mall intercept interview** is conducted in the common area of a shopping mall or in a market research office within the mall. To conduct this type of interview, the research firm rents office space in the mall or pays a significant daily

survey research the most popular technique for gathering primary data, in which a researcher interacts with people to obtain facts, opinions, and attitudes

mall intercept interview a survey research method that involves interviewing people in the common areas of shopping malls

Exhibit 2
CHARACTERISTICS OF TRADITIONAL FORMS OF SURVEY RESEARCH

Characteristic	In-Home Personal Interviews	Mall Intercept Interviews	Central-Location Telephone Interviews	Self-Administered and One-Time Mail Surveys	Mail Panel Surveys	Executive Interviews	Focus Groups
Cost	High	Moderate	Moderate	Low	Moderate	High	Low
Time span	Moderate	Moderate	Fast	Slow	Relatively slow	Moderate	Fast
Use of interviewer probes	Yes	Yes	Yes	No	Yes	Yes	Yes
Ability to show concepts to respondent	Yes (also taste tests)	Yes (also taste tests)	No	Yes	Yes	Yes	Yes
Management control over interviewer	Low	Moderate	High	N/A	N/A	Moderate	High
General data quality	High	Moderate	High to moderate	Moderate to low	Moderate	High	Moderate
Ability to collect large amounts of data	High	Moderate	Moderate to low	Low to moderate	Moderate	Moderate	Moderate
Ability to handle complex questionnaires	High	Moderate	High, if computer aided	Low	Low	High	N/A

© Cengage Learning

computer-assisted personal interviewing an interviewing method in which the interviewer reads questions from a computer screen and enters the respondent's data directly into the computer

computer-assisted self-interviewing an interviewing method in which a mall interviewer intercepts and directs willing respondents to nearby computers where each respondent reads questions off a computer screen and directly keys his or her answers into the computer

central-location telephone (CLT) facility a specially designed phone room used to conduct telephone interviewing

executive interview a type of survey that involves interviewing businesspeople at their offices concerning industrial products or services

focus group seven to ten people who participate in a group discussion led by a moderator

fee. One drawback is that it is hard to get a representative sample of the population. One advantage is the ability of the interviewer to probe when necessary—a technique used to clarify a person's response and ask for more detailed information.

Mall intercept interviews must be brief. Only the shortest ones are conducted while respondents are standing. Usually, researchers invite respondents into the office for interviews, which are still generally less than fifteen minutes long. The overall quality of mall intercept interviews is about the same as telephone interviews.

Marketing researchers are applying computer technology in mall interviewing. The first technique is **computer-assisted personal interviewing**. The researcher conducts in-person interviews, reads questions to the respondent off a computer screen, and directly keys the respondent's answers into the computer. A second approach is **computer-assisted self-interviewing**. A mall interviewer intercepts and directs willing respondents to nearby computers. Each respondent reads questions off a computer screen and directly keys his or her answers into the computer. The third use of technology is fully automated self-interviewing. Respondents are guided by interviewers or independently approach a centrally located computer station or kiosk, read questions off a screen, and directly key their answers into the station's computer.

TELEPHONE INTERVIEWS Telephone interviews cost less than personal interviews, but cost is rapidly increasing due to respondent refusals to participate. Most telephone interviewing is conducted from a specially designed phone room called a **central-location telephone (CLT) facility**. A CLT facility has many phone lines, individual interviewing stations, headsets, and sometimes monitoring equipment. The research firm typically will interview people nationwide from a single location. The federal "Do Not Call" law does not apply to survey research.

Most CLT facilities offer computer-assisted interviewing. The interviewer reads the questions from a computer screen and enters the respondent's data directly into the computer, saving time. Hallmark Cards found that an interviewer administered a printed questionnaire for its Shoebox greeting cards in twenty-eight minutes. The same questionnaire administered with computer assistance took only eighteen minutes. The researcher can stop the survey at any point and immediately print out the survey results, allowing the research design to be refined as necessary.

MAIL SURVEYS Mail surveys have several benefits: relatively low cost, elimination of interviewers and field supervisors, centralized control, and actual or promised anonymity for respondents (which may draw more candid responses). A disadvantage is that mail questionnaires usually produce low response rates because certain elements of the population tend to respond more than others. The resulting sample may therefore not represent the surveyed population. Another serious problem with mail surveys is that no one probes respondents to clarify or elaborate on their answers.

Mail panels offer an alternative to the one-shot mail survey. A mail panel consists of a sample of households recruited to participate by mail for a given period. Panel members often receive gifts in return for their participation. Essentially, the panel is a sample used several times. In contrast to one-time mail surveys, the response rates from mail panels are high. Rates of 70 percent (of those who agree to participate) are not uncommon.

EXECUTIVE INTERVIEWS An **executive interview** involves interviewing businesspeople at their offices concerning industrial products or services, a process that is very expensive. First, individuals involved in the purchase decision for the product in question must be identified and located, which can itself be expensive and time-consuming. Once a qualified person is located, the next step is to get that person to agree to be interviewed and to set a time for the interview.

Finally, an interviewer must go to the particular place at the appointed time. Long waits are frequently encountered; cancellations are not uncommon. This type of survey requires the very best interviewers because they are frequently interviewing on topics that they know very little about.

FOCUS GROUPS A **focus group** is a type of personal interviewing. Often recruited by random telephone screening, seven to ten people with certain desired characteristics form a focus group. These qualified consumers are usually offered an incentive (typically $30 to $50) to participate in a group discussion. The meeting place (sometimes resembling a living room, sometimes featuring a conference table) has audiotaping and perhaps videotaping equipment. It also likely has a viewing room with a one-way mirror so that clients (manufacturers or retailers) can watch the session. During the session, a moderator, hired by the research company, leads the group discussion. Focus groups can be used to gauge consumer response to a product or promotion and are occasionally used to brainstorm new-product ideas or to screen concepts for new products. Focus groups also represent an efficient way of learning how products are actually used in the home. Lewis Stone, former manager of Colgate-Palmolive's research and development division, says the following about focus groups:

> If it weren't for focus groups, Colgate-Palmolive Co. might never know that some women squeeze their bottles of dishwashing soap, others squeeeeeze them, and still others squeeeeeeeeeze out the desired amount. Then there are the ones who use the soap 'neat.' That is, they put the product directly on a sponge or washcloth and wash the dishes under running water until the suds run out. Then they apply more detergent.

Stone was explaining how body language, exhibited during focus groups, provides insights into a product that are not apparent from reading questionnaires on habits and practices. Panelists' descriptions of how they perform tasks highlight need gaps, which can improve an existing product or demonstrate how a new product might be received.

In 2011, there were approximately 263,000 focus groups conducted in the United States. Focus groups are increasingly conducted through the Web using Web cameras, the use of which increased 133 percent from 2010 to 2011.[4]

QUESTIONNAIRE DESIGN All forms of survey research require a questionnaire. Questionnaires ensure that all respondents will be asked the same series of questions. Questionnaires include three basic types of questions: open-ended, closed-ended, and scaled-response (see Exhibit 3). An **open-ended question** encourages an answer phrased in the respondent's own words. Researchers get a rich array of information based on the respondent's frame of reference (What do you think

about the new flavor?). In contrast, a **closed-ended question** asks the respondent to make a selection from a limited list of responses. Closed-ended questions can either be what marketing researchers call *dichotomous* (Do you like the new flavor? Yes or No.) or *multiple choice*. A **scaled-response question** is a closed-ended question designed to measure the intensity of a respondent's answer.

Closed-ended and scaled-response questions are easier to tabulate than open-ended questions because response choices are fixed. On the other hand, unless the researcher designs the closed-ended question very carefully, an important choice may be omitted. For example, suppose a food study asked this question: "Besides meat, which of the following items do you normally add to tacos that you prepare at home?"

Avocado	1	Olives (black/green)	6
Cheese (Monterey Jack/cheddar)	2	Onions (red/white)	7
Guacamole	3	Peppers (red/green)	8
Lettuce	4	Pimiento	9
Mexican hot sauce	5	Sour cream	0

The list seems complete, doesn't it? However, consider the following responses: "I usually add a green, avocado-tasting hot sauce," "I cut up a mixture of lettuce and spinach," "I'm a vegetarian—I don't use meat at all," and "My taco is filled only with guacamole." How would you code these replies? As you can see, the question needs an "other" category.

A good question must be clear and concise and avoid ambiguous language. The answer to the question "Do you live within ten minutes of here?" depends on the mode of transportation (maybe the person walks), driving speed, perceived time, and other factors. Language should also be clear. As such, jargon should be avoided, and wording should be geared to the target audience. A question such as "What is the level of efficacy of your preponderant dishwasher powder?" would probably be greeted by a lot of blank stares. It would be much simpler to say "Are you (1) very satisfied, (2) somewhat satisfied, or (3) not satisfied with your current brand of dishwasher powder?"

open-ended question an interview question that encourages an answer phrased in the respondent's own words

closed-ended question an interview question that asks the respondent to make a selection from a limited list of responses

scaled-response question a closed-ended question designed to measure the intensity of a respondent's answer

Exhibit 3

TYPES OF QUESTIONS FOUND ON QUESTIONAIRES FOR NATIONAL MARKET RESEARCH

Open-Ended Questions	Closed-Ended Questions	Scaled-Response Question

Open-Ended Questions

1. What advantages, if any, do you think ordering from a mail-order catalog offers compared to shopping at a local retail outlet? (*Probe*: What else?}

2. Why do you have one or more of your rugs or carpets professionally cleaned rather than cleaning them yourself or having someone else in the household clean them?

3. What is it about the color of the eye shadow that makes you like it the best?

Closed-Ended Questions

Dichotomous

1. Did you heat the pastry before serving It?
   Yes.. 1
   No.. 2

2. The federal government doesn't care what people like me think.
   Agree 1
   Disagree 2

Multiple Choice

1. I'd like you to think back to the last footwear of any kind that you bought. I'll read you a list of descriptions and would like for you to tell me which category they fall Into.
   (*Read list and circle proper category.*)
   Dress and/or formal.. 1
   Casual.. 2
   Canvas/trainer /gym shoes 3
   Specialized athletic shoes.................................... 4
   Boots 5

2. In the last three months, have you used Noxzema skin cream ...
   (*Circle all that apply.*)
   As a facial wash 1
   For moisturizing the skin..................................... 2
   For treating blemishes.. 3
   For cleansing the skin.. 4
   For treating dry skin 5
   For softening skin 6
   For sunburn... 7
   For making the facial skin smooth 8

Scaled-Response Question

Now that you have used the rug cleaner, would you say that you ... (*Circle one.*)
Would definitely buy it 1
Would probably buy it................. 2
Might or might not buy it.............. 3
Probably would not buy it............. 4
Definitely would not buy it 5

© Cengage Learning

Stating the survey's purpose at the beginning of the interview may improve clarity, but it may also increase the chances of receiving biased responses. Many times, respondents will try to provide answers that they believe are "correct" or that the interviewer wants to hear. To avoid bias at the question level, researchers should avoid leading questions and adjectives that cause respondents to think of the topic in a certain way.

Finally, to ensure clarity, the interviewer should avoid asking two questions in one—for example, "How did you like the taste and texture of the Pepperidge Farm coffee cake?" This should be divided into two questions, one concerning taste and the other texture.

OBSERVATION RESEARCH In contrast to survey research, **observation research** depends on watching what people do. Specifically, it can be defined as the systematic process of recording the behavioral patterns of people, objects, and occurrences without questioning them. A market researcher using the observation technique witnesses and records information as events occur or compiles evidence from records of past events. Carried a step further, observation may involve watching people or phenomena and may be conducted by human observers or machines. Examples of these various observational situations are shown in Exhibit 4.

Two common forms of people-watching-people research are one-way mirror observations and mystery shoppers. A one-way mirror allows the researchers to see the participants, but the participants cannot see the researchers.

MYSTERY SHOPPERS **Mystery shoppers** are researchers posing as customers who gather observational data about a store (e.g., are the shelves neatly stocked?) and collect data about customer/employee interactions.

observation research a research method that relies on four types of observation: people watching people, people watching an activity, machines watching people, and machines watching an activity

mystery shoppers researchers posing as customers who gather observational data about a store

Exhibit 4
OBSERVATIONAL SITUATIONS

Situation	Example
People watching people	Observers stationed in supermarkets watch consumers select frozen Mexican dinners; the purpose is to see how much comparison shopping people do at the point of purchase.
People watching an activity	An observer stationed at an intersection counts traffic moving in various directions.
Machines watching people	Movie or videotape cameras record behavior as in the people-watching-people example above.
Machines watching an activity	Traffic-counting machines monitor traffic flow.

© Cengage Learning

The interaction is not an interview, and communication occurs only so that the mystery shopper can observe the actions and comments of the employee. Mystery shopping is, therefore, classified as an observational marketing research method even though communication is often involved.

BEHAVIORAL TARGETING Behavioral targeting (BT) began as a simple process by placing cookies on users' browsers to track which Web sites they visited, how long they lingered, what they searched for, and what they bought. All of this information can be tracked anonymously—a "fly on the wall" perspective. While survey research is a great way to find out the "why" and the "how," behavioral targeting lets the researcher find out the "how much," the "how often," and the "where." Also, through **social media monitoring**, using automated tools to monitor online buzz, chatter, and conversations, a researcher can learn what is being said about the brand and the competition. For example, Accor Hotels tracks 4,000 of its hotels, along with 8,000 of its competitors' hotels (in eight languages). The hotel chain aggregates data from social media comments and evaluation sites such as Trip Advisor and Booking.com. This system allows Accor to identify underperforming hotels quickly and to act on individual negative comments.

Monitoring social media and tracking shopping behavior online are only two inputs into the new era of **big data**. Big data is the exponential growth in the volume, variety, and velocity of information and the development of complex, new tools to analyze and create meaning from such data. In the past, the flow of data was slow, steady, and predictable. Many firms collected sales numbers by store, by product line, and at most, perhaps by a few other measures. Today, data is constantly streaming in from social media, as well as other sources. Traditionally, all data was quantitative (countable), such as sales per store. Today, the variety of information includes e-mails, videos, scanner data, audio files, and other forms of information.

Today, more and more firms are using the latest technology to collect, analyze, and make strategic and tactical decisions. Adding big data to simple online tracking data makes the behavioral targeting of online advertising much more effective. With systems like IBM's Smarter Analytics, instead of learning which customers it has lost or might lose, a company can present timely offers or products to motivate them to stay. XO Communications used big data analysis to predict likely customer defections within ninety days. It used this information to reduce lost customers by 35 percent.[5]

THE SCOPE OF BIG DATA

Big data means big numbers. Here are some quantitative figures that demonstrate just how staggering the flow of big data is:

▸▸ **The Radio Frequency Identification used to track inventory provides up to 1,000 times the data of conventional bar code systems**

▸▸ **10,000 payment transactions are made every second around the world**

▸▸ **Walmart handles more than 1 million customer transactions an hour**

▸▸ **Over 4,000 tweets are sent each second**

▸▸ **Facebook has more than 900 million members generating social interaction data**

▸▸ **More than 5 billion people are calling, texting, tweeting, and browsing on mobile devices[6]**

© Cengage Learning / iStockPhoto.com/Axaulya

ethnographic research the study of human behavior in its natural context; involves observation of behavior and physical setting

experiment a method of gathering primary data in which the researcher alters one or more variables while observing the effects of those alterations on another variable

As mentioned in Chapter 8, Facebook advertisers armed with big data can target ads at users based upon their e-mail addresses and phone numbers.[7] Profile data stored on Facebook's servers enables advertisers to know where people live and work, what they like, and who they talk to. Other online databases provide data on shopping habits, income, and so forth. Clearly, big data affects everybody who interacts and shops online—as well as everybody who wants to market to them.

ETHNOGRAPHIC RESEARCH Ethnographic research comes to marketing from the field of anthropology. The technique is becoming increasingly popular in commercial marketing research. **Ethnographic research**, or the study of human behavior in its natural context, involves observation of behavior and physical setting. Ethnographers directly observe the population they are studying. As "participant observers," ethnographers can use their intimacy with the people they are studying to gain richer, deeper insights into culture and behavior—in short, what makes people do what they do.

The at-home consumption market is one that eludes much research. Anthropologists and other observational researchers can't sit in people's homes and monitor which electronic devices they are using and how they use them. Questionnaires rely on one-time truthful responses and the respondent's memory. However, some of the nation's biggest media companies got a look into people's homes by using iPhones to monitor media consumption. The Coalition for Innovative Media Measurement (CIMM), a collaboration between media and ad industries to determine how consumers view media and which devices they use, sponsored the study. The company gave 1,000 participants iPhones with a special app that they would log into every thirty minutes and answer questions about their media activities. Respondents gave frequent updates on what and how they consumed music and television, whether through streaming or downloading, on computers or television, or from subscription services or free sources. The results offered myriad breakdowns of information, but one key segment is mothers. CIMM compared three generations of mothers to determine when each group was most receptive to television, print, and digital advertising. This type of research may be the closest researchers have come to living with research participants and to understanding how Americans consume media. Knowing how and when Americans watch programs allows the media and ad industries to tailor delivery to the consumer and use the Internet to their advantage rather than be left behind with outdated business models.[8]

VIRTUAL SHOPPING Advances in computer technology have enabled researchers to simulate an actual retail store environment on a computer screen. Depending on the type of simulation, a shopper can "pick up" a package by touching its image on the monitor and rotate it to examine all sides. Like buying on most online retailers, the shopper touches the shopping cart to add an item to the basket. During the shopping process, the computer unobtrusively records the amount of time the consumer spends shopping in each product category, the time the consumer spends examining each side of a product, the quantity of the product the consumer purchases, and the order in which items are purchased.

Computer-simulated environments like this one offer a number of advantages over older research methods. First, the virtual store duplicates the distracting clutter of an actual market. Layouts can even be modified to reflect various types of retailers, such as drugstores or supermarkets, meaning that consumers can shop in an environment with a realistic level of complexity and variety. Second, researchers can set up and alter the tests very quickly. Data collection is also fast and error free because the information generated by the purchase is automatically tabulated and stored by the computer. Third, production costs are low because displays are created electronically. Once the hardware and software are in place, the cost of a test is largely a function of the number of respondents, who generally are given a small incentive to participate. Fourth, the simulation has a high degree of flexibility. It can be used to test entirely new marketing concepts or to fine-tune existing programs.[9]

Virtual shopping research is growing rapidly. According to the United States Department of Agriculture, each year, approximately 45,000 new consumer packaged goods are introduced to supermarkets alone.[10] All are vying for very limited retail shelf space. Any process, such as virtual shopping, that can speed product development time and lower costs is always welcomed by manufacturers. Some companies outside of retail have even begun experimenting with virtual shopping and other simulated environment tools—many telecom, financial, automotive, aviation, and fast-food companies are using such tools to better serve their customers.[11]

EXPERIMENTS An **experiment** is a method a researcher can use to gather primary data. The researcher

Here, virtual shopping is taken to the extreme—a virtual Woolworths supermarket located in Sydney, Australia's Town Hall Station allows commuters to browse a wall of virtual products, scan product barcodes using a smartphone app, and then pay for orders on the fly. Orders are then delivered directly to consumers' homes. Based on consumer data, Woolworths can automatically adjust its virtual layout and product mix to maximize sales.

Marianna Massey/Woolworths/Getty Images

alters one or more variables—price, package design, shelf space, advertising theme, advertising expenditures—while observing the effects of those alterations on another variable (usually sales). The best experiments are those in which all factors are held constant except the ones being manipulated. The researcher can then observe what changes in sales, for example, result from changes in the amount of money spent on advertising.

Holding all other factors constant in the external environment is a monumental and costly, if not impossible, task. Such factors as competitors' actions, weather, and economic conditions are beyond the researcher's control. Yet market researchers have ways to account for the ever-changing external environment. Mars, the candy company, was losing sales to other candy companies. Traditional surveys showed that the shrinking candy bar was not perceived as a good value. Mars wondered whether a bigger bar sold at the same price would increase sales enough to offset the higher ingredient costs. The company designed an experiment in which the marketing mix stayed the same in different markets but the size of the candy bar varied. The substantial increase in sales of the bigger bar quickly proved that the additional costs would be more than covered by the additional revenue. Mars increased the bar size—along with its market share and profits.

MOBILE RESEARCH Recall that iPhones were being used to gather viewing habits for part of an ethnographic study. Today, mobile devices and laptops are being used for all kinds of marketing research. Many respondents who agree to participate in a survey expect to be met on their own turf through their mobile devices. Already, about 26 percent of all surveys are conducted on a mobile device.[12] A few techniques that are now employed using mobile devices are:

▶▶ Location-based invitations to participate in a survey based upon the point of product evaluation, store entry, or purchase

▶▶ Product scanning during the shopping process use QR codes or bar codes

▶▶ Using cameras on mobile devices to upload digital images and videos[13]

In 2012, Disney had plans to develop a new national advertising campaign that featured Disney World and Disneyland. The company worked with Chatter Inc. to develop a suite of apps for focus groups. The groups began like traditional focus groups, then the moderators gave each participant an iPad and asked them to log in. The participants were told to review potential ideas and concepts for the new advertising campaign using a custom app. The app featured virtual green and red highlighters, and participants were asked to highlight what they liked in green and disliked in red. They could also type comments and use a sliding scale to rank each comment. The insights gained from the research helped Disney shape a multiyear advertising campaign.[14]

9-2c Specifying the Sampling Procedures

Once the researchers decide how they will collect primary data, their next step is to select the sampling procedures they will use. A firm can seldom take a census of all possible users of a new product, nor can they all be interviewed. Therefore, a firm must select a sample of the group to be interviewed. A **sample** is a subset from a larger population.

sample a subset from a larger population

universe the population from which a sample will be drawn

probability sample a sample in which every element in the population has a known statistical likelihood of being selected

random sample a sample arranged in such a way that every element of the population has an equal chance of being selected as part of the sample

nonprobability sample any sample in which little or no attempt is made to get a representative cross section of the population

convenience sample a form of nonprobability sample using respondents who are convenient or readily accessible to the researcher—for example, employees, friends, or relatives

measurement error an error that occurs when there is a difference between the information desired by the researcher and the information provided by the measurement process

sampling error an error that occurs when a sample somehow does not represent the target population

frame error an error that occurs when a sample drawn from a population differs from the target population

Several questions must be answered before a sampling plan is chosen. First, the population, or **universe**, of interest must be defined. This is the group from which the sample will be drawn. It should include all the people whose opinions, behavior, preferences, attitudes, and so on, are of interest to the marketer. For example, in a study whose purpose is to determine the market for a new canned dog food, the universe might be defined to include all current buyers of canned dog food.

After the universe has been defined, the next question is whether the sample must be representative of the population. If the answer is yes, a probability sample is needed. Otherwise, a nonprobability sample might be considered.

PROBABILITY SAMPLES A **probability sample** is a sample in which every element in the population has a known statistical likelihood of being selected. Its most desirable feature is that scientific rules can be used to ensure that the sample represents the population.

One type of probability sample is a **random sample**—a sample arranged in such a way that every element of the population has an equal chance of being selected as part of the sample. For example, suppose a university is interested in getting a cross section of student opinions on a proposed sports complex to be built using student activity fees. If the university can acquire an up-to-date list of all the enrolled students, it can draw a random sample by using random numbers from a table (found in most statistics books) to select students from the list. Common forms of probability and nonprobability samples are shown in Exhibit 5.

NONPROBABILITY SAMPLES Any sample in which little or no attempt is made to get a representative cross section of the population can be considered a **nonprobability sample**. Therefore, the probability of selection of each sampling unit is not known. A common form of a nonprobability sample is the **convenience sample**, which uses respondents who are convenient or readily accessible to the researcher—for instance, employees, friends, or relatives.

Nonprobability samples are acceptable as long as the researcher understands their nonrepresentative nature. Because of their lower cost, nonprobability samples are the basis of much marketing research.

TYPES OF ERRORS Whenever a sample is used in marketing research, two major types of errors may occur: measurement error and sampling error. **Measurement error** occurs when there is a difference between the information desired by the researcher and the information provided by the measurement process. For example, people may tell an interviewer that they purchase Crest toothpaste when they do not. Measurement error generally tends to be larger than sampling error.

Sampling error occurs when a sample somehow does not represent the target population. Sampling error can be one of several types. Nonresponse error occurs when the sample actually interviewed differs from the sample drawn. This error happens because the original people selected to be interviewed either refused to cooperate or were inaccessible.

Frame error, another type of sampling error, arises if the sample drawn from a population differs from the target population. For instance, suppose a telephone survey is conducted to find out Chicago beer drinkers' attitudes toward Coors. If a Chicago telephone directory is used as the *frame* (the device or

SAMPLE

UNIVERSE

list from which the respondents are selected), the survey will contain a frame error. Not all Chicago beer drinkers have phones, and many phone numbers are unlisted. An ideal sample (e.g., a sample with no frame error) matches all important characteristics of the target population to be surveyed. Could you find a perfect frame for Chicago beer drinkers?

Random error occurs when the selected sample is an imperfect representation of the overall population. Random error represents how accurately the chosen sample's true average (mean) value reflects the population's true average (mean) value. For example, we might take a random sample of beer drinkers in Chicago and find that 16 percent regularly drink Coors beer. The next day, we might repeat the same sampling procedure and discover that 14 percent regularly drink Coors beer. The difference is due to random error. Error is common to all surveys, yet it is often not reported or is underreported. Typically, the only error mentioned in a written report is sampling error.

9-2d Collecting the Data

Marketing research field service firms collect most primary data. A **field service firm** specializes in interviewing respondents on a subcontracted basis. Many have offices, often in malls, throughout the country. A typical marketing research study involves data collection in several cities, which requires the marketer to work with a comparable number of field service firms. Besides conducting interviews, field service firms provide focus group facilities, mall intercept locations, test product storage, and kitchen facilities to prepare test food products.

9-2e Analyzing the Data

After collecting the data, the marketing researcher proceeds to the next step in the research process: data analysis. The purpose of this analysis is to interpret and draw conclusions from the mass of collected data. The marketing researcher tries to organize and analyze those data by using one or more techniques common to marketing research: one-way frequency counts, cross-tabulations, and more sophisticated statistical analysis. Of these three techniques, one-way frequency counts are the simplest. One-way frequency tables simply record the responses to a question. For example, the answers to the question "What brand of microwave popcorn do you buy most often?" would provide a one-way frequency

Exhibit 5
TYPES OF SAMPLES

Probability Samples	
Simple Random Sample	Every member of the population has a known and equal chance of selection.
Stratified Sample	The population is divided into mutually exclusive groups (such as gender or age); then random samples are drawn from each group.
Cluster Sample	The population is divided into mutually exclusive groups (such as geographic areas); then a random sample of clusters is selected. The researcher then collects data from all the elements in the selected clusters or from a probability sample of elements within each selected cluster.
Systematic Sample	A list of the population is obtained—e.g., all persons with a checking account at XYZ Bank—and a skip interval is obtained by dividing the sample size by the population size. If the sample size is 100 and the bank has 1,000 customers, then the skip interval is 10. The beginning number is randomly chosen within the skip interval. If the beginning number is 8, then the skip pattern would be 8, 18, 28, and so on.
Nonprobability Samples	
Convenience Sample	The researcher selects the easiest population members from which to obtain information.
Judgment Sample	The researcher's selection criteria are based on personal judgment that the elements (persons) chosen will likely give accurate information.
Quota Sample	The researcher finds a prescribed number of people in several categories—e.g., owners of large dogs versus owners of small dogs. Respondents are not selected on probability sampling criteria.
Snowball Sample	Additional respondents are selected on the basis of referrals from the initial respondents. This method is used when a desired type of respondent is hard to find—e.g., persons who have taken round-the-world cruises in the last three years. This technique employs the old adage "Birds of a feather flock together."

© Cengage Learning

cross-tabulation a method of analyzing data that lets the analyst look at one question in relation to the responses to one or more other questions

distribution. One-way frequency tables are always done in data analysis, at least as a first step, because they provide the researcher with a general picture of the study's results. A **cross-tabulation** lets the analyst look at the responses to one question in relation to the responses to one or more other questions. For example, in Exhibit 6, what is the association between gender and the brand of microwave popcorn bought most frequently?

Researchers can use many other more powerful and sophisticated statistical techniques, such as hypothesis testing, measures of association, and regression analysis. A description of these techniques goes beyond the scope of this book but can be found in any good marketing research textbook. The use of sophisticated statistical techniques depends on the researchers' objectives and the nature of the data gathered.

9-2f Preparing and Presenting the Report

After data analysis has been completed, the researcher must prepare the report and communicate the conclusions and recommendations to management. This is a key step in the process. If the marketing researcher wants managers to carry out the recommendations, he or she must convince them that the results are credible and justified by the data collected.

Researchers are usually required to present both written and oral reports on the project. Today, the written report is no more than a copy of the PowerPoint slides used in the oral presentation. Both reports should be tailored to the audience. They should begin with a clear, concise statement of the research objectives, followed by a complete but brief and simple explanation of the research design or methodology employed. A summary of major findings should come next. The conclusion of the report should also present recommendations to management.

Most people who enter marketing will become research users rather than research suppliers. Thus, they must know what to notice in a report. As with many other items we purchase, quality is not always readily apparent. Nor does a high price guarantee superior quality. The basis for measuring the quality of a marketing research report is the research proposal. Did the report meet the objectives established in the proposal? Was the methodology outlined in the proposal followed? Are the conclusions based on logical deductions from the data analysis? Do the recommendations seem prudent, given the conclusions?

9-2g Following Up

The final step in the marketing research process is to follow up. The researcher should determine why management did or did not carry out the recommendations in the report. Was sufficient decision-making information included? What could have been done to make the report more useful to management? A good rapport between the product manager, or whoever authorized the project, and the market researcher is essential. Often, they must work together on many studies throughout the year.

Typically, the research process flows rather smoothly from one step to the next in the United States. However, conducting research in international markets can create a whole host of problems and challenges.

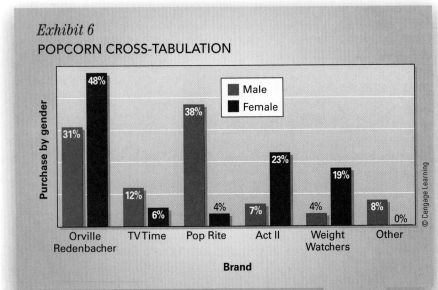

Exhibit 6
POPCORN CROSS-TABULATION

© Cengage Learning

9-3 THE PROFOUND IMPACT OF THE INTERNET ON MARKETING RESEARCH

Today, about one-third of the world's population is online.[15] In the United States, 245 million people— 78 percent of the population—are online, spanning every ethnic, socioeconomic, and educational divide.[16] Non-adopters of the Internet tend to be older, low-income consumers (age sixty-five and over with household income less than $30,000), who do not tend to be the target market for many goods and services.

More than 90 percent of U.S. marketing research companies conduct some form of online research. Online survey research has replaced computer-assisted telephone interviewing as the most popular mode of data collection, though there is no evidence of this or other traditional survey methods being completely replaced by online surveys.[17] Internet data collection is also rated as having the greatest potential for further growth.

9-3a Advantages of Internet Surveys

The huge growth in the popularity of Internet surveys is the result of the many advantages offered by the Internet. The specific advantages of Internet surveys, which are often sent to mobile devices, are many:

» **RAPID DEVELOPMENT, REAL-TIME REPORTING:** Internet surveys can be broadcast to thousands of potential respondents simultaneously. Respondents complete surveys simultaneously; then results are tabulated and posted for corporate clients to view as the returns arrive. The effect: survey results can be in a client's hands in significantly less time than would be required for traditional surveys.

» **DRAMATICALLY REDUCED COSTS:** The Internet can cut costs by 25 to 40 percent and provide results in half the time it takes to do traditional telephone surveys. Traditional survey methods are labor-intensive efforts incurring training, telecommunications, and management costs. Electronic methods eliminate these completely. While costs for traditional survey techniques rise proportionally with the number of interviews desired, electronic solicitations can grow in volume with little increase in project costs.

» **PERSONALIZED QUESTIONS AND DATA:** Internet surveys can be highly personalized for greater relevance to each respondent's own situation, thus speeding the response process.

» **IMPROVED RESPONDENT PARTICIPATION:** Internet surveys take half as much time to complete as phone interviews, can be accomplished at the respondent's convenience (for example, after work hours), and are much more stimulating and engaging. As a result, Internet surveys enjoy much higher response rates.

» **CONTACT WITH THE HARD-TO-REACH:** Certain groups—doctors, high-income professionals, top management in Global 2000 firms—are among the most surveyed on the planet and the most difficult to reach. Many of these groups are well represented online. Internet surveys provide convenient anytime/anywhere access that makes it easy for busy professionals to participate.

9-3b Uses of the Internet by Marketing Researchers

Marketing researchers use the Internet to administer surveys, conduct focus groups, and perform a variety of other types of marketing research.

METHODS OF CONDUCTING ONLINE SURVEYS There are several basic methods for conducting online surveys: Web survey systems, survey design and Web hosting sites, and online panel providers.

WEB SURVEY SYSTEMS Web survey systems are software systems specifically designed for Web questionnaire construction and delivery. They consist of an integrated questionnaire designer, Web server, database, and data delivery program designed for use by nonprogrammers. The Web server distributes the questionnaire and files responses in a database. The user can query the server at any time via the Web for completion statistics, descriptive statistics on responses, and graphical displays of data. Some popular online survey research software packages are Sawtooth CiW, Infopoll, SurveyMonkey, and SurveyPro.

SURVEY DESIGN AND WEB HOSTING SITES Several Web sites allow the researcher to design a survey online without loading design software. The survey is then administered on the design site's server. Some offer

© iStockphoto.com/bgblue

tabulation and analysis packages as well. One popular site that offers Web hosting services is Vovici.

ONLINE PANEL PROVIDERS Often, researchers use online panel providers for a ready-made sample population. Online panel providers such as Survey Sampling International and e-Rewards pre-recruit people who agree to participate in online market research surveys.

Some online panels are created for specific industries and may have a few thousand panel members, while the large commercial online panels have millions of people waiting to be surveyed. When people join online panels, they answer an extensive profiling questionnaire that enables the panel provider to target research efforts to panel members who meet specific criteria.

ONLINE FOCUS GROUPS A number of organizations are currently conducting focus groups online. The process is fairly simple. The research firm builds a database of respondents via a screening questionnaire on its Web site. When a client comes to a firm with a need for a particular focus group, the firm goes to its database and identifies individuals who appear to qualify. It sends an e-mail to these individuals, asking them to log on to a particular site at a particular time scheduled for the group. Many times, these groups are joined by respondents on mobile devices. The firm pays them an incentive for their participation.

The firm develops a discussion guide similar to the one used for a conventional focus group, and a moderator runs the group by typing in questions online for all to see. The group operates in an environment similar to that of a chat room so that all participants see all questions and all responses. The firm captures the complete text of the focus group and makes it available for review after the group has finished.

Online focus groups also allow respondents to view things such as a concept statement, a mockup of a print ad, or a short product demonstration video. The moderator simply provides a URL for the respondents to go to in another browser window.

More advanced virtual focus group software reserves a frame (section) of the screen for stimuli to be shown. Here, the moderator has control over what is shown in the stimulus area. One advantage of this approach is that the respondent does not have to do any work to see the stimuli. There are many other advantages of online groups:

- ▸ **BETTER PARTICIPATION RATES:** Typically, online focus groups can be conducted over the course of days; once participants are recruited, they are less likely to pull out due to time conflicts.

- ▸ **COST-EFFECTIVENESS:** Face-to-face focus groups incur costs for facility rental, airfare, hotel, and food. None of these costs is incurred with online focus groups.

- ▸ **BROAD GEOGRAPHIC SCOPE:** Time is flexible online; respondents can be gathered from all over the world.

- ▸ **ACCESSIBILITY:** Online focus groups allow access to individuals who otherwise might be difficult to recruit (e.g., business travelers, senior executives, mothers with infants).

- ▸ **HONESTY:** From behind their screen names, respondents are anonymous to other respondents and tend to talk more freely about issues that might create inhibitions in a face-to-face group.

WEB COMMUNITY RESEARCH A Web community is a carefully selected group of consumers who agree to participate in an ongoing dialogue with a particular corporation. All community interaction takes place on a custom-designed Web site. During the life of the community—which may last anywhere from six months to a year or more—community members respond to questions posed by the corporation on a regular basis. In addition to responding to the corporation's questions, community members talk to one another about topics that are of interest to them.

BENEFITS OF WEB COMMUNITY RESEARCH

The popularity and power of Web communities initially came from several key benefits:

- ▸ Engage customers in a space where they are comfortable, allowing clients to interact with them on a deeper level.

- ▸ Achieve customer-derived innovations.

- ▸ Establish brand advocates who are emotionally invested in a company's success.

- ▸ Offer real-time results, enabling clients to explore ideas that normal time constraints prohibit.

Additionally, Web communities help companies create a customer-focused organization by putting employees into direct contact with consumers from the comfort of their own desks, as well as providing cost-effective, flexible research.

9-3c The Role of Consumer-Generated Media in Marketing Research

Consumer-generated media (CGM) are media that consumers generate themselves and share among themselves. CGM comes from various sources, such as blogs, message boards, review sites, and podcasts. Because it is consumer based, CGM is trusted more than traditional forms of advertising and promotion.

CGM can be influenced but not controlled by marketers. Nielsen BuzzMetrics is the leading marketing research firm tracking CGM. BrandPulse is BuzzMetrics' most popular product. BrandPulse can tell a company how much "buzz" exists, where online discussion is taking place, the tone of the discussion, and which issues are most important. BrandPulse provides timely understanding of the opinions and trends affecting a company or brand. Depending on the information the customer needs, other BuzzMetrics products can go into further detail, such as detecting who would be a good candidate for relationship marketing programs.[21]

9-4 SCANNER-BASED RESEARCH

Scanner-based research is a system for gathering information from a single group of respondents by continuously monitoring the advertising, promotion, and pricing they are exposed to and the things they buy. The variables measured are advertising campaigns, coupons, displays, and product prices. The result is a huge database of marketing efforts and consumer behavior.

The two major scanner-based suppliers are SymphonyIRI Group Inc. and the Nielsen Company. Each has about half of the market. However, SymphonyIRI is the founder of scanner-based research. SymphonyIRI's first product is called **BehaviorScan**. A household panel (a group of 3,000 long-term participants in the research project) has been recruited and maintained in each BehaviorScan town. Each panel member shops with an ID card, which is presented at the checkout in scanner-equipped grocery stores and drugstores, allowing SymphonyIRI to track electronically each household's purchases, item by item, over time. It uses microcomputers to measure television viewing in each panel household and can send special commercials to panel member television sets. With such a measure of household purchasing, it is possible to manipulate marketing variables, such as television advertising or consumer promotions, or to introduce a new product and analyze real changes in consumer buying behavior.

SymphonyIRI's most successful product is **InfoScan**, a scanner-based sales-tracking service for the consumer packaged-goods industry. Retail sales, detailed consumer purchasing information (including measurement of store loyalty and total grocery basket expenditures), and promotional activity by manufacturers and retailers are monitored and evaluated for all bar-coded products. Data are collected weekly from more than 70,000 supermarkets, drugstores, and mass merchandisers.

Some companies have begun studying microscopic changes in

© scyther5/Shutterstock.com

skin moisture, heart rate, brain waves, and other biometrics to see how consumers react to things such as package designs and ads. This **neuromarketing** approach is a fresh attempt to better understand consumers' responses to promotion and purchase motivations.

9-5 WHEN SHOULD MARKETING RESEARCH BE CONDUCTED?

When managers have several possible solutions to a problem, they should not instinctively call for marketing research. In fact, the first decision to make is whether to conduct marketing research at all.

Some companies have been conducting research in certain markets for many years. Such firms understand the characteristics of target customers and their likes and dislikes about existing products. Under these circumstances, further research would be repetitive and waste money. P&G, for example, has extensive knowledge of the coffee market. After it conducted initial taste tests with Folgers Instant Coffee, P&G went into national distribution without further research. Sara Lee followed the same strategy with its frozen croissants, as did Quaker Oats with Chewy Granola Bars. This tactic, however, can backfire. Marketers may think they understand a particular market thoroughly and so bypass market research for a product, only to have the product fail and be withdrawn from the market.

If information were available and free, managers would rarely refuse more, but because marketing information can require a great deal of time and expense to accumulate, they might decide to forgo additional information. Ultimately, the willingness to acquire additional decision-making information depends on managers' perceptions of its quality, price, and timing. Research should be undertaken only when the expected value of the information is greater than the cost of obtaining it.

9-5a Customer Relationship Management

Recall from the beginning of the chapter that databases and big data play a key role in marketing decision making. A key subset of data management systems is a customer relationship management (CRM) system. CRM was introduced in Chapters 1 and 8. The key to managing relationships with customers is the CRM cycle (Exhibit 7).

To initiate the CRM cycle, a company must *identify customer relationships with the organization*. This may simply entail learning who the customers are or where they are located, or it may require more detailed information about the products and services they are using. Next, the company must *understand the interactions with current customers*. Companies accomplish this by collecting data on all types of communications a customer has with the company.

Using this knowledge of its customers and their interactions, the company then *captures relevant customer data on interactions*. Information technology is used not only to enhance the collection of

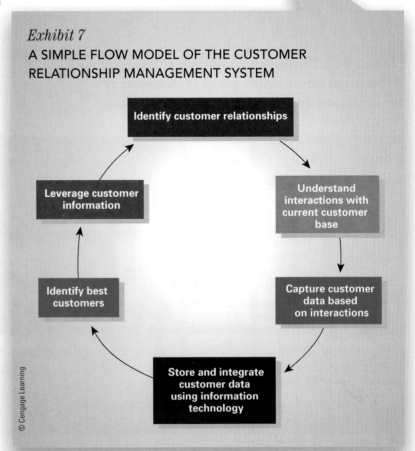

Exhibit 7

A SIMPLE FLOW MODEL OF THE CUSTOMER RELATIONSHIP MANAGEMENT SYSTEM

© Cengage Learning

customer data but also to *store and integrate customer data* throughout the company, and ultimately, to "get to know" customers on a more personal level. Customer data are the firsthand responses that are obtained from customers through investigation or by asking direct questions.

Every customer wants to be a company's main priority. Yet not all customers are equally important in the eyes of a business. Consequently, the company must *identify its profitable and unprofitable customers*. Data mining is an analytical process that compiles actionable data about the purchase habits of a firm's current and potential customers. Essentially, data mining transforms customer data into customer information a company can use to make managerial decisions. Data mining is examined in more detail in Chapter 14.

Once customer data are analyzed and transformed into usable information, the information must be *leveraged*. The CRM system sends the customer information to all areas of a business because the customer interacts with all aspects of the business. Essentially, the company is trying to enhance customer relationships by getting the right information to the right person in the right place at the right time.

9-6 COMPETITIVE INTELLIGENCE

Derived from military intelligence, competitive intelligence is an important tool for helping a firm overcome a competitor's advantage. Specifically, competitive intelligence can help identify the advantage and play a major role in determining how it was achieved. It also helps a firm identify areas where it can achieve its own competitive advantages.

Competitive intelligence (CI) helps managers assess their competitors and their vendors in order to become more efficient and effective competitors. Intelligence is analyzed information. It becomes decision-making intelligence when it has implications for the organization. For example, a primary competitor may have plans to introduce a product with performance standards equal to those of the company gathering the information but with a 15 percent cost advantage. The new product will reach the market in eight months. This intelligence has important decision-making and policy consequences for management. CI and environmental scanning (see Chapter 2) combine to create marketing intelligence.

The Internet is an important resource for gathering CI, but non-computer sources can be equally valuable. Some examples include company salespeople, industry experts, CI consultants, government agencies, Uniform Commercial Code filings, suppliers, periodicals, the Yellow Pages, and industry trade shows.

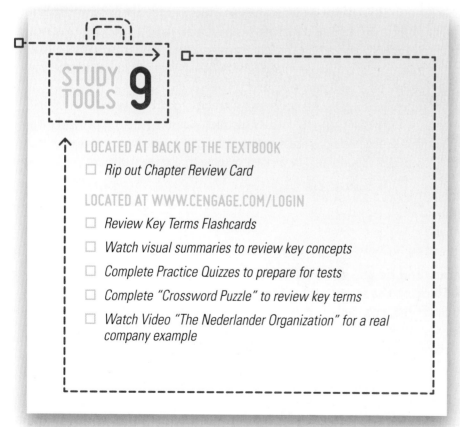

STUDY TOOLS 9

LOCATED AT BACK OF THE TEXTBOOK
☐ *Rip out Chapter Review Card*

LOCATED AT WWW.CENGAGE.COM/LOGIN
☐ *Review Key Terms Flashcards*
☐ *Watch visual summaries to review key concepts*
☐ *Complete Practice Quizzes to prepare for tests*
☐ *Complete "Crossword Puzzle" to review key terms*
☐ *Watch Video "The Nederlander Organization" for a real company example*

competitive intelligence (CI) an intelligence system that helps managers assess their competition and vendors in order to become more efficient and effective competitors

10-1 WHAT IS A PRODUCT?

The product offering, the heart of an organization's marketing program, is usually the starting point in creating a marketing mix. A marketing manager cannot determine a price, design a promotion strategy, or create a distribution channel until the firm has a product to sell. Moreover, an excellent distribution channel, a persuasive promotion campaign, and a fair price have no value when the product offering is poor or inadequate.

A marketing manager cannot determine a price, design a promotion strategy, or create a distribution channel until the firm has a product to sell.

product everything, both favorable and unfavorable, that a person receives in an exchange

business product (industrial product) a product used to manufacture other goods or services, to facilitate an organization's operations, or to resell to other customers

consumer product a product bought to satisfy an individual's personal wants or needs

A **product** may be defined as everything, both favorable and unfavorable, that a person receives in an exchange. A product may be a tangible good like a pair of shoes, a service like a haircut, an idea like "don't litter," or any combination of these three. Packaging, style, color, options, and size are some typical product features. Just as important are intangibles such as service, the seller's image, the manufacturer's reputation, and the way consumers believe others will view the product.

To most people, the term *product* means a tangible good. However, services and ideas are also products. (Chapter 12 focuses specifically on the unique aspects of marketing services.) The marketing process identified in Chapter 1 is the same whether the product marketed is a good, a service, an idea, or some combination of these.

10-2 TYPES OF CONSUMER PRODUCTS

Products can be classified as either business (industrial) or consumer, depending on the buyer's intentions. The key distinction between the two types of products is their intended use. If the intended use is a business purpose, the product is classified as a business or industrial product. As explained in Chapter 7, a **business product**, or **industrial product**, is used to manufacture other goods or services, to facilitate an organization's operations, or to resell to other customers. A **consumer product** is bought to satisfy an individual's personal wants or needs. Sometimes the same item can be classified as either a business or a consumer product, depending on its intended use.

Product Concepts

Learning Outcomes

After you finish this chapter go to
p192 *for* **STUDY TOOLS**

Examples include lightbulbs, pencils and paper, and computers.

We need to know about product classifications because business and consumer products are marketed differently. They are marketed to different target markets and tend to use different distribution, promotion, and pricing strategies.

Chapter 7 examined seven categories of business products: major equipment, accessory equipment, component parts, processed materials, raw materials, supplies, and services. This chapter examines an effective way of categorizing consumer products. Although there are several ways to classify them, the most popular approach includes these four types: convenience products, shopping products, specialty products, and unsought products. This approach classifies products according to how much effort is normally used to shop for them.

10-2a Convenience Products

A **convenience product** is a relatively inexpensive item that merits little shopping effort—that is, a consumer is unwilling to shop extensively for such an item. Candy, soft drinks, aspirin, small hardware items, dry cleaning, and car washes fall into the convenience product category.

Consumers perceive refrigerators as homogeneous, or basically similar.

© iStockphoto.com/97

Consumers buy convenience products regularly, usually without much planning. Nevertheless, consumers do know the brand names of popular convenience products, such as Coca-Cola, Bayer aspirin, and Old Spice deodorant. Convenience products normally require wide distribution in order to sell sufficient quantities to meet profit goals. For example, the gum brand Extra is available everywhere, including Walmart, Walgreens, gas stations, newsstands, and vending machines.

10-2b Shopping Products

A **shopping product** is usually more expensive than a convenience product and is found in fewer stores. Consumers usually buy a shopping product only after comparing several brands or stores on style, practicality, price, and lifestyle compatibility. They are willing to invest some effort into this process to get the desired benefits.

There are two types of shopping products: homogeneous and heterogeneous. Consumers perceive *homogeneous* shopping products as basically similar—for example, washers, dryers, refrigerators, and televisions. With homogeneous shopping products, consumers typically look for the lowest-priced brand that has the desired features. For example, they might compare Kenmore, Whirlpool, and General Electric refrigerators.

In contrast, consumers perceive *heterogeneous* shopping products as essentially different—for example, furniture, clothing, housing, and universities. Consumers often have trouble comparing heterogeneous shopping products because the prices, quality, and features vary so much. The benefit of comparing heterogeneous shopping products is "finding the best product or brand for me"; this decision is often highly individual. For example, it would be difficult to compare a small, private college with a large, public university, or IKEA with La-Z-Boy.

10-2c Specialty Products

When consumers search extensively for a particular item and are very reluctant to accept substitutes, that item is a **specialty product**. Omega watches, Rolls-Royce automobiles, Bose speakers, Ruth's Chris Steak House, and highly specialized forms of medical care are generally considered specialty products.

Marketers of specialty products often use selective, status-conscious advertising to maintain a product's exclusive image. Distribution is often limited to one or a very few outlets in a geographic area. Brand names and quality of service are often very important.

10-2d Unsought Products

A product unknown to the potential buyer or a known product that the buyer does not actively seek is referred to as an **unsought product**. New products fall into this category until advertising and distribution increase consumer awareness of them.

Some goods are always marketed as unsought items, especially needed products we do not like to think about or care to spend money on. Insurance, burial plots, and similar items require aggressive personal selling and highly persuasive advertising. Salespeople actively seek leads to potential buyers. Because consumers usually do not seek out this type of product, the company must go directly to them through a salesperson, direct mail, or direct response advertising.

10-3 PRODUCT ITEMS, LINES, AND MIXES

Rarely does a company sell a single product. More often, it sells a variety of things. A **product item** is a specific version of a product that can be designated as a distinct offering among an organization's products. Campbell's Cream of Chicken soup is an example of a product item (see Exhibit 1).

A group of closely related product items is called a **product line**. For example, the column in Exhibit 1 titled "Soups" represents one of Campbell's product lines. Different container sizes and shapes also distinguish items in a product line. Diet Coke, for example, is available in cans and various plastic containers. Each size and each container are separate product items.

An organization's **product mix** includes all the products it sells. All Campbell's products—soups, sauces, frozen entrées, beverages, and biscuits—constitute its product mix. Each product item in the product mix may require a separate marketing strategy. In some cases, however, product lines and even entire product mixes share some marketing strategy components. UPS promotes its various services by demonstrating its commitment to its line of work with the tagline "We [heart] Logistics." Organizations derive several benefits from organizing related items into product lines:

▸ **ADVERTISING ECONOMIES:** Product lines provide economies of scale in advertising. Several products can be advertised under the umbrella of the line. Campbell's can talk about its soup being "M'm, M'm, Good!" and promote the entire line.

unsought product a product unknown to the potential buyer or a known product that the buyer does not actively seek

product item a specific version of a product that can be designated as a distinct offering among an organization's products

product line a group of closely related product items

product mix all products that an organization sells

Exhibit 1
CAMPBELL'S PRODUCT LINES AND PRODUCT MIX

		Width of the Product Mix			
	Soups	**Sauces**	**Frozen Entrées**	**Beverages**	**Biscuits**
	Cream of Chicken	Cheddar Cheese	Macaroni and Cheese	Tomato Juice	Arnott's:
	Cream of Mushroom	Alfredo	Golden Chicken Fricassee	V-Fusion Juices	Water Cracker
	Vegetable Beef	Italian Tomato	Traditional Lasagna	V8 Splash	Butternut Snap
	Chicken Noodle	Hollandaise			Chocolate Ripple
	Tomato				Spicy Fruit Roll
	Bean with Bacon				Chocolate Wheaten
	Minestrone				
	Clam Chowder				
	French Onion				
	and more				

Depth of the Product Lines

Source: Campbell's Web site: www.campbellsoup.com.

▸ **PACKAGE UNIFORMITY:** A product line can benefit from package uniformity. All packages in the line may have a common look and still keep their individual identities. Again, Campbell's soup is a good example.

▸ **STANDARDIZED COMPONENTS:** Product lines allow firms to standardize components, thus reducing manufacturing and inventory costs. For example, General Motors uses the same parts on many automobile makes and models.

▸ **EFFICIENT SALES AND DISTRIBUTION:** A product line enables sales personnel for companies like Procter & Gamble to provide a full range of choices to customers. Distributors and retailers are often more inclined to stock the company's products if it offers a full line. Transportation and warehousing costs are likely to be lower for a product line than for a collection of individual items.

▸ **EQUIVALENT QUALITY:** Purchasers usually expect and believe that all products in a line are about equal in quality. Consumers expect that all Campbell's soups and all Gillette razors will be of similar quality.

Product mix width (or breadth) refers to the number of product lines an organization offers. In Exhibit 1, for example, the width of Campbell's product mix is five product lines. **Product line depth** is the number of product items in a product line. As shown in Exhibit 1, the sauces product line consists of four product items; the frozen entrée product line includes three product items.

Firms increase the *width* of their product mix to diversify risk. To generate sales and boost profits, firms spread risk across many product lines rather than depend on only one or two. Firms also widen their product mix to capitalize on established reputations. Patagonia, a popular outdoor clothing brand and retailer, recently launched a line of salmon jerky as the first products in its Patagonia Provisions line. Patagonia is hoping to provide food for climbers and other outdoor enthusiasts based on their reputation for high-quality, sustainable products.[1]

Firms increase the *depth* of their product lines to attract buyers with different preferences, to increase sales and profits by further segmenting the market, to capitalize on economies of scale in production and marketing, and to even out seasonal sales patterns.

10-3a Adjustments to Product Items, Lines, and Mixes

Over time, firms change product items, lines, and mixes to take advantage of new technical or product developments or to respond to changes in the environment. They may adjust by modifying products, repositioning products, or extending or contracting product lines.

PRODUCT MODIFICATION Marketing managers must decide if and when to modify existing products. **Product modification** changes one or more of a product's characteristics:

▸ **QUALITY MODIFICATION:** change in a product's dependability or durability. Reducing a product's quality may let the manufacturer lower the price and appeal to target markets unable to afford the original product. Conversely, increasing quality can help the firm compete with rival firms. For example, Barnes & Noble offers a color version of its Nook that runs Android apps, allowing it to compete with tablet and netbook makers, such as Dell and Asus. Increasing quality can also result in increased brand loyalty,

Women's swimsuits are known for coming in wide VARIETIES of styles, from functional to poolside lounging.

© Karkas/Shutterstock.com

greater ability to raise prices, or new opportunities for market segmentation.

▸ **FUNCTIONAL MODIFICATION: change in a product's versatility, effectiveness, convenience, or safety.** Men's swim trunks have been the target of recent makeovers as men are invited to office functions or weddings that involve water activities. For business professionals or men uncomfortable in oversized board shorts, companies like Lands' End are making swim trunks a little shorter and with narrower cuts, which cuts down on ballooning when entering the water and transitions more easily from water to lunch because they look more like normal shorts. These changes are not only for style but offer added convenience to men.[2]

▸ **STYLE MODIFICATION: aesthetic product change rather than a quality or functional change.** Clothing and auto manufacturers commonly use style modifications to motivate customers to replace products before they are worn out.

Planned obsolescence is a term commonly used to describe the practice of modifying products so that those that have already been sold become obsolete before they actually need replacement. For example, products such as printers and cell phones become obsolete because technology changes so quickly.

Some argue that planned obsolescence is wasteful; some claim it is unethical. Marketers respond that consumers favor style modifications because they like changes in the appearance of goods such as clothing and cars. Marketers also contend that consumers, not manufacturers and marketers, decide when styles are obsolete.

REPOSITIONING Repositioning, as Chapter 8 explained, involves changing consumers' perceptions of a brand. Long known for its adult magazine and television channels, Playboy Enterprises began a massive repositioning effort in 2009 when Scott Flanders assumed Hugh Hefner's role as CEO of the multimedia and lifestyle company. Hoping to diminish Playboy's association with pornographic images in favor of its role as an aspirational fashion and lifestyle brand, Flanders turned the company's focus toward licensing and partnerships with high-end manufacturers. In 2012, for example, the company launched a nudity-free iPhone app and sold off much of its risqué digital properties in favor of partnerships with art and fashion companies such as Dolce & Gabbana. The repositioning strategy appears to be working—the company's earnings rose more than 101 percent between 2009 and 2012.[3] Changing demographics, declining sales, or changes in the social environment often motivate firms to reposition established brands. For example, HTC, a smartphone maker that has lost significant market share to Apple and Samsung over the past year, has recently purchased majority shares in several music and gaming companies, including Beats Electronics, the popular headphone company. Realizing that making smartphones will be a losing battle for market share, HTC is hoping to expand its brand beyond gadgets and to become a technology icon that offers a suite of services to device owners, a more ubiquitous part of people's entertainment lives.[4]

PRODUCT LINE EXTENSIONS A **product line extension** occurs when a company's management decides to add products to an existing product line in order to compete more broadly in the industry. Greek yogurt—known for its creamy texture and tart taste—has skyrocketed in popularity recently. To meet growing demand, General Mills added a number of new Greek-themed products to its existing Yoplait yogurt product line in late 2012. The new Yoplait Greek offerings include six yogurts, six 100-calorie yogurts, three yogurt-and-granola packs, seven frozen yogurts, and two frozen smoothies. According to General Mills, sales of Greek-style yogurt is "significantly outpacing growth of the

planned obsolescence the practice of modifying products so those that have already been sold become obsolete before they actually need replacement

product line extension adding additional products to an existing product line in order to compete more broadly in the industry

WINGS FOR ALL TASTES.

In 2013, Red Bull extended its line of energy drinks with three new flavors—cranberry, lime, and blueberry.

Image Courtesy of the Advertising Archives

segment, and we've picked up nearly three points of market share."[5]

A company can add too many products, or demand can change for the type of products that were introduced over time. When this happens, a product line is overextended. Product lines can be overextended when:

»» **Some products in the line do not contribute to profits because of low sales or cannibalize sales of other items in the line.**

»» **Manufacturing or marketing resources are disproportionately allocated to slow-moving products.**

»» **Some items in the line are obsolete because of new-product entries in the line or new products offered by competitors.**

PRODUCT LINE CONTRACTION Sometimes marketers can get carried away with product extensions. (Does the world really need thirty-one varieties of Head & Shoulders shampoo?) Contracting product lines is a strategic way to deal with overextension. In March 2013, Internet pioneer Yahoo announced that it would be cutting seven products—the Yahoo BlackBerry app, Sports IQ, Yahoo Message Boards, Yahoo Avatars, Yahoo Clues, Yahoo App Search, and Yahoo Updates. "Ultimately, we're making these changes in an effort to sharpen our focus," said Jay Rossiter, Yahoo's executive vice president for platforms. "By continuing to hone in on our core products and experiences, we'll be able to make our existing products the very best they can be."[6]

Indeed, three major benefits are likely when a firm contracts an overextended product line. First, resources become concentrated on the most important products. Second, managers no longer waste resources trying to improve the sales and profits of poorly performing products. Third, new-product items have a greater chance of being successful because more financial and human resources are available to manage them.

10-4 BRANDING

The success of any business or consumer product depends in part on the target market's ability to distinguish one product from another.

Branding is the main tool marketers use to distinguish their products from those of the competition.

A **brand** is a name, term, symbol, design, or combination thereof that identifies a seller's products and differentiates them from competitors' products. A **brand name** is that part of a brand that can be spoken, including letters (GM, YMCA), words (Chevrolet), and numbers (WD-40, 7-Eleven). The elements of a brand that cannot be spoken are called the **brand mark**—for example, the well-known Mercedes-Benz and Delta Air Lines symbols.

10-4a Benefits of Branding

Branding has three main purposes: product identification, repeat sales, and new-product sales. The most important purpose is *product identification*. Branding allows marketers to distinguish their products from all others. Many brand names are familiar to consumers and indicate quality.

The term **brand equity** refers to the value of a company or brand name. A brand that has high awareness, perceived quality, and brand loyalty among customers has high brand equity—a valuable asset indeed. See Exhibit 2 for some classic examples of companies that leverage their brand equity to the fullest.

The term **global brand** refers to a brand that obtains at least one-third of its earnings from outside its home country, is recognizable outside its home base of customers, and

A ROTTING APPLE?

Starbucks, Lexus, and Apple are companies that have traditionally had high levels of brand equity. However, some reports indicate that Apple's brand equity may be slipping. In 2012, Apple's online customer satisfaction dropped to its lowest level in four years, brand loyalty dropped 5 percent, and competitors such as Samsung and Google began to usurp Apple's image as "cutting-edge cool." While Apple's brand equity remains among the strongest in the nation, Apple executives will certainly have these figures in mind as they position the company in coming years.[7]

© iStockPhoto.com/billnoll / © iStockPhoto.com/Gustavo Andrade

Exhibit 2

THE POWER OF BRAND EQUITY

Product Category	Dominant Brand Name
Children's Entertainment	Disney
Laundry Detergent	Tide
Tablet Computer	Apple
Toothpaste	Crest
Microprocessor	Intel
Soup	Campbell's
Bologna	Oscar Meyer
Ketchup	Heinz
Bleach	Clorox
Greeting Cards	Hallmark
Overnight Mail	FedEx
Copiers	Xerox
Gelatin	Jell-O
Hamburgers	McDonald's
Baby Lotion	Johnson & Johnson
Tissues	Kleenex
Acetaminophen	Tylenol
Coffee	Starbucks
Information Search	Google

Used with the permission of Chris Moorman. All Rights Reserved.

has publicly available marketing and financial data. Yum! Brands, which owns Pizza Hut, KFC, and Taco Bell, is a good example of a company that has developed strong global brands. Yum! believes that it must adapt its restaurants to local tastes and different cultural and political climates. In Japan, for instance, KFC sells tempura crispy strips. In northern England, KFC focuses on gravy and potatoes, and in Thailand, it offers rice with soy or sweet chili sauce.

The best generator of *repeat sales* is satisfied customers. Branding helps consumers identify products they wish to buy again and avoid those they do not. **Brand loyalty**, a consistent preference for one brand over all others, is quite high in some product categories. More than half the consumers in product categories such as cigarettes, mayonnaise, toothpaste, coffee, headache remedies, bath soap, and ketchup are loyal to one brand. Many students go to college and purchase the same brands they used at home rather than choosing by price. Brand identity is essential to developing brand loyalty.

The third main purpose of branding is to *facilitate new-product sales*. Having a well-known and respected company and brand name is extremely useful when introducing new products.

10-4b Branding Strategies

Firms face complex branding decisions. Firms may choose to follow a policy of using manufacturers' brands, private (distributor) brands, or both. In either case, they must then decide among a policy of individual branding (different brands for different products), family branding (common names for different products), or a combination of individual branding and family branding.

MANUFACTURERS' BRANDS VERSUS PRIVATE BRANDS The brand name of a manufacturer—such as Kodak, La-Z-Boy, and Fruit of the Loom—is called a **manufacturer's brand**. Sometimes "national brand" is used as a synonym for "manufacturer's brand." This term is not always accurate, however, because many manufacturers serve only regional markets. Using "manufacturer's brand" precisely defines the brand's owner.

A **private brand**, also known as a private label or store brand, is a brand name owned by a wholesaler or a retailer. Target's Archer Farms brand is a popular private label, for example. Private labels are increasing in popularity and price as customers develop loyalties to store brands such as Archer Farms. According to research conducted in the United Kingdom, 44 percent of shoppers believe that private label brands are simply repackaged national brands. Fifty-nine percent believe that national brands are more expensive only because more money is spent advertising them. Seventy percent believe that private label foods are just as good or better than national brands.[8] Today, private label products have a 29 percent market share of the food and beverage market—nearly ten points higher than ten years ago.[9]

Retailers love consumers' greater acceptance of private brands. Because overhead is low and there are no marketing costs, private label products bring 10 percent higher profit margins, on average, than manufacturers' brands. More than that, a trusted store brand can differentiate a chain from its competitors. Exhibit 3 illustrates key issues that wholesalers and retailers should consider in deciding whether to sell manufacturers' brands or private brands. Many firms offer a combination of both.

captive brand a brand manufactured by a third party for an exclusive retailer, without evidence of that retailer's affiliation

individual branding using different brand names for different products

family branding marketing several different products under the same brand name

co-branding placing two or more brand names on a product or its package

Instead of marketing private brands as cheaper and inferior to manufacturers' brands, many retailers are creating and promoting their own **captive brands**. These brands carry no evidence of the store's affiliation, are manufactured by a third party, and are sold exclusively at the chains. This strategy allows the retailer to ask a price similar or equal to manufacturers' brands, and the captive brands are typically displayed alongside mainstream products. For example, Simple Truth is Kroger's line of natural and organic products designed to meet consumer desire for upscale brands. It currently sells a half gallon of soy milk for twenty cents more than Silk, the popular manufacturer's brand.[10]

INDIVIDUAL BRANDS VERSUS FAMILY BRANDS
Many companies use different brand names for different products, a practice referred to as **individual branding**. Companies use individual brands when their products vary greatly in use or performance. For instance, it would not make sense to use the same brand name for a pair of dress socks and a baseball bat. Procter & Gamble targets different segments of the laundry detergent market with Bold, Cheer, Dash, Dreft, Era, Gain, and Tide.

In contrast, a company that markets several different products under the same brand name is practicing **family branding**. Jack Daniel's family brand includes whiskey, coffee, barbeque sauce, heat-and-serve meat products like brisket and pulled pork, mustard, playing cards, and clothing lines.

CO-BRANDING Co-branding entails placing two or more brand names on a product or its package. Three common types of co-branding are ingredient branding, cooperative branding, and complementary branding. *Ingredient branding* identifies the brand of a part that makes up the product. For example, Church & Dwight co-branded an entire line of Arm & Hammer laundry detergents with OxiClean, a popular household cleaner and stain remover. OxiClean is also co-branded with Kaboom shower cleaner and Xtra detergent.[11] *Cooperative branding* occurs when two brands receiving equal treatment (in the context of an advertisement) borrow from each other's brand equity. A promotional contest jointly sponsored by Ramada Inn, American Express, and United Airlines used cooperative branding. Guests at Ramada who paid with an American Express card were automatically entered in a contest and were eligible to win more than 100 getaways for two at any Ramada in the continental United States and round-trip airfare from United. Similarly, American Express and Walmart introduced a prepaid card targeting middle- and lower-income individuals who want to avoid fees charged by banks.[12] Finally, with *complementary branding*, products are advertised or marketed together to suggest

---

Exhibit 3
COMPARISON OF MANUFACTURERS' AND PRIVATE BRANDS FROM THE RESELLER'S PERSPECTIVE

Key Advantages of Carrying Manufacturers' Brands	Key Advantages of Carrying Private Brands
• Heavy advertising to the consumer by manufacturers such as Procter & Gamble helps develop strong consumer loyalties.	• A wholesaler or retailer can usually earn higher profits on its own brand. In addition, because the private brand is exclusive, there is less pressure to mark down the price to meet competition.
• Well-known manufacturers' brands, such as Fisher-Price, can attract new customers and enhance the dealer's (wholesaler's or retailer's) prestige.	• A manufacturer can decide to drop a brand or a reseller at any time or even become a direct competitor to its dealers.
• Many manufacturers offer rapid delivery, enabling the dealer to carry less inventory.	• A private brand ties the customer to the wholesaler or retailer. A person who wants a DieHard battery must go to Sears.
• If a dealer happens to sell a manufacturer's brand of poor quality, the customer may simply switch brands and remain loyal to the dealer.	• Wholesalers and retailers have no control over the intensity of distribution of manufacturers' brands. Walmart store managers don't have to worry about competing with other sellers of Sam's American Choice products or Ol' Roy dog food. They know that these brands are sold only in Walmart and Sam's Club stores.

© Cengage Learning

GET BETTER, FASTER.
GET FREE.

NIKE FREE'S ENGINEERED FLEXIBILITY HELPS IGNITE THE MUSCLES IN YOUR BODY FROM THE GROUND UP FOR IMPROVED STRENGTH, BALANCE AND FLEXIBILITY – SO YOU GET EVEN MORE FROM YOUR WORKOUT. AND WHEN COMBINED WITH ONE OF THE 60 CUSTOM BUILT WORKOUTS FROM THE NEW NIKE TRAINING CLUB APP, YOU CAN REACH YOUR GOALS WHATEVER THEY ARE. EVER WANTED A PERSONAL TRAINER IN YOUR POCKET? NOW YOU'VE GOT ONE.

NIKE FREE
NIKE.COM/FREE

This ad promotes Nike + iPod software that allows walkers and runners to keep track of the distance and pace of workouts.

Image courtesy of the Advertising Archives

usage, such as a spirits brand (Seagram's) and a compatible mixer (7Up).

Co-branding is a useful strategy when a combination of brand names enhances the prestige or perceived value of a product or when it benefits brand owners and users. Co-branding may also be used to increase a company's presence in markets where it has little room to differentiate itself or has limited market share. For example, the Asus-manufactured Nexus 7 tablet retails for $199.99—even though it costs approximately $200 to produce. Asus accepts selling the tablet at a slight loss because the Nexus 7 is co-branded as a Google product. By associating itself with a much larger and more recognizable company, Asus can build brand equity and position itself as a technological leader—a sensible long-term strategy for a manufacturer looking to build its brand.[13]

10-4c Trademarks

A **trademark** is the exclusive right to use a brand or part of a brand. Others are prohibited from using the brand without permission. A **service mark** performs the same function for services, such as H&R Block and Weight Watchers. Parts of a brand or other product identification may qualify for trademark protection. Some examples are:

▸▸ Sounds, such as the MGM lion's roar.

▸▸ Shapes, such as the Jeep front grille and the Coca-Cola bottle.

▸▸ Ornamental colors or designs, such as the decoration on Nike tennis shoes, the black-and-copper color combination of a Duracell battery, Levi's small tag on the left side of the rear pocket of its jeans, or the cutoff black cone on the top of Cross pens.

▸▸ Catchy phrases, such as Prudential's "Own a Piece of the Rock," Mountain Dew's "This Is How We Dew," and Nike's "Just Do It!"

▸▸ Abbreviations, such as Bud, Coke, or the Met.

It is important to understand that trademark rights come from use rather than registration. An intent-to-use application is filed with the U.S. Patent and Trademark Office, and a company must have a genuine intention to use the mark when it files and must actually use it within three years of the granting of the application. Trademark protection typically lasts for ten years.[14] To renew the trademark, the company must prove it is using the mark. Rights to a trademark last as long as the mark is used. Normally, if the firm does not use it for two years, the trademark is considered abandoned, and a new user can claim exclusive ownership of the mark.

The Digital Millennium Copyright Act (DMCA) explicitly applies trademark law to the digital world. This law includes financial penalties for those who violate trademarks or register an otherwise trademarked term as a domain name. The DMCA has come under some criticism for its more restrictive provisions. In 2013, controversy erupted over the reinstitution of a section prohibiting individuals from unlocking their smartphones—a consumer who disables her phone's restriction to a specific carrier may be subject to a prison term of up to five years and a $500,000 fine.[15]

Companies that fail to protect their trademarks face the possibility that their product names will become generic. A **generic product name** identifies a product by class or type and cannot be trademarked. Former brand names that were not sufficiently protected by their owners and were subsequently declared to be generic

trademark the exclusive right to use a brand or part of a brand

service mark a trademark for a service

generic product name identifies a product by class or type and cannot be trademarked

product names by U.S. courts include aspirin, cellophane, linoleum, thermos, kerosene, monopoly, cola, and shredded wheat.

Companies such as Rolls-Royce, Cross, Xerox, Levi Strauss, Frigidaire, and McDonald's aggressively enforce their trademarks. Rolls-Royce, Coca-Cola, and Xerox even run newspaper and magazine ads stating that their names are trademarks and should not be used as descriptive or generic terms. In 2013, athletic apparel company Under Armour filed a trademark infringement lawsuit against Nike over the company's use of advertising phrases "I Will" and "Protect this house." According to Under Armour, Nike's use of phrases such as "I will protect my home court" in online and social media outlets infringed upon an Under Armour marketing campaign that used similar phrases. Ten years earlier, Nike filed a suit against Under Armour over the use of the term "DRI-FIT."[16]

To try to stem the number of trademark infringements, violations carry steep penalties. But despite the

This is privately owned property.

So is **this,**

CAR-FRESHNER ®

Coconut

and **this,**

®

and **this,**

and **this...**

...no matter how you use it.

The LITTLE TREES® design is a registered trademark. This means it can only be used by the trademark owner (that's us) and those who have permission. In other words, it is illegal for you to use our trademark without our consent. To ask permission, e-mail legal@little-trees.com.
www.little-trees.com
The Tree design, LITTLE TREES and CAR-FRESHNER are trademarks. © 2011 by Julius Sämann Ltd.

Julius Sämann Ltd., which owns the rights to the famous LITTLE TREES air fresheners, and CAR-FRESHNER Corporation, its U.S. licensee, use ads like this one to discourage unauthorized copying of their intellectual property.

risk of incurring a penalty, infringement lawsuits are still common. Serious conflict can occur when brand names resemble one another too closely. In February 2012, high-fashion designer Christian Louboutin won a trademark ruling against Yves Saint Laurent for copying its signature red-soled shoes. Five months later, the Tokyo-based Bridgestone Corporation won a lawsuit against Chinese tire manufacturer Guangzhou Bolex Tyre over its use of the brand name Gemstone. The ruling in favor of Bridgestone (which manufactures tires under both the Bridgestone and Firestone brand names) was upheld by two Chinese courts, and Guangzhou Bolex Tyre was ordered to cease the production and sale of Gemstone tires.[17]

Companies must also contend with fake or unauthorized brands. Knockoffs of trademarked clothing lines are easy to find in cheap shops all over the world, and loose imitations are found in some reputable department stores as well. Today, whole stores are faked in China. Apple stores selling real iPhones and iPads in stores with sparse décor and bright lighting may seem authentic but are frequently imitating the real deal. Numerous fast-food restaurants have become victims of knockoff stores throughout China: Pizza Huh (Pizza Hut), Michael Alone (McDonald's), and Taco Bell Grande (Taco Bell) mimic the American chains' layouts and products. FBC, KFG, KLG, MFC, and OFC all lift Kentucky Fried Chicken's iconic logo, color scheme, and menu.[18]

In Europe, you can sue counterfeiters only if your brand, logo, or trademark is formally registered. Formal registration used to be required in each country in which a company sought protection. However, today a company can register its trademark in all European Union member countries with one application.

10-5 PACKAGING

Packages have always served a practical function—that is, they hold contents together and protect goods as they move through the distribution channel. Today, however, packaging is also a container for promoting the product and making it easier and safer to use.

10-5a Packaging Functions

The three most important functions of packaging are to contain and protect products; promote products; and facilitate the storage, use, and convenience of products. A fourth function of packaging that is becoming increasingly important is to facilitate recycling and reduce environmental damage.

CONTAINING AND PROTECTING PRODUCTS The most obvious function of packaging is to contain products that are liquid, granular, or otherwise divisible. Packaging also enables manufacturers, wholesalers, and retailers to market products in specific quantities, such as ounces.

Physical protection is another obvious function of packaging. Most products are handled several times between the time they are manufactured, harvested, or otherwise produced and the time they are consumed or used. Many products are also shipped, stored, and inspected several times between production and consumption. Some, like milk, need to be refrigerated. Others, like beer, are sensitive to light. Still others, like medicines and bandages, need to be kept sterile. Packages protect products from breakage, evaporation, spillage, spoilage, light, heat, cold, infestation, and many other conditions.

PROMOTING PRODUCTS Packaging does more than identify the brand, list the ingredients, specify features, and give directions. A package differentiates a product from competing products and may associate a new product with a family of other products from the same manufacturer. However, some products' packaging lacks useful information, like lightbulbs. GE is looking to remedy that by adding a lighting facts label to all their lighting packages. The label provides information about the bulb's brightness (lumens), energy cost, life span, light appearance, energy used, and mercury content. The label is one step in simplifying the lightbulb shopping process and will be used by all lighting companies in the future.[19]

Packages use designs, colors, shapes, and materials to try to influence consumers' perceptions and buying behavior. For example, marketing research shows that health-conscious consumers are likely to think that any food is probably good for them as long as it comes in green packaging. Packaging can also influence consumer perceptions of quality and/or prestige. England's Brothers Cider recently revamped its label and can designs in a move to

Brothers Cider's new packaging made use of tinted brown bottles and contemporary labels that employed a mix of classic and modern typefaces.

reposition Toffee Apple Cider, Festival Pear Cider, and other cider flavors as premium adult beverages. The company replaced bright green bottles with tinted brown ones, and swapped colorful graphic labels for designs that employ a mix of classic and modern typefaces. To bolster its new prestigious image, Brothers rolled out its package redesign alongside a $7.6 million countrywide marketing push.[20]

FACILITATING STORAGE, USE, AND CONVENIENCE Wholesalers and retailers prefer packages that are easy to ship, store, and stock on shelves. They also like packages that protect products, prevent spoilage or breakage, and extend the product's shelf life.

Consumers' requirements for storage, use, and convenience cover many dimensions. Consumers are constantly seeking items that are easy to handle, open, and reclose, although some consumers want packages that are tamperproof or childproof. Research indicates that hard-to-open packages are among consumers' top complaints—especially when it comes to clamshell electronics packaging. Indeed, Quora users voted clamshell packaging "the worst piece of design ever done." There is even a Wikipedia page devoted to "wrap rage," the

persuasive labeling a type of package labeling that focuses on a promotional theme or logo, and consumer information is secondary

informational labeling a type of package labeling designed to help consumers make proper product selections and lower their cognitive dissonance after the purchase

anger associated with trying to open clamshells and other poorly designed packages.[21] As oil prices force the cost of plastics used in packaging skyward, companies such as Amazon, Target, and Walmart are pushing suppliers to do away with excessive and infuriating packaging. Such packaging innovations as zipper tear strips, hinged lids, tab slots, screw-on tops, simple cardboard boxes, and pour spouts were introduced to solve these and other problems. Easy openings are especially important for kids and aging baby boomers.

Some firms use packaging to segment markets. For example, a C&H sugar carton with an easy-to-pour, reclosable top is targeted to consumers who don't do a lot of baking and are willing to pay at least twenty cents more for the package. Different-sized packages appeal to heavy, moderate, and light users. Campbell's soup is packaged in single-serving cans aimed at the elderly and singles market segments. Packaging convenience can increase a product's utility and, therefore, its market share and profits.

FACILITATING RECYCLING AND REDUCING ENVIRONMENTAL DAMAGE One of the most important packaging issues today is eco-consciousness, a trend that has recently been in and out of consumer and media attention. Studies conflict as to whether consumers will pay more

for eco-friendly packaging, though consumers repeatedly iterate the desire to purchase such products. A 2012 Ipsos poll found that 3 percent of consumers always buy eco-friendly products, while 6 percent never do, leaving a wide margin in between. Forty-six percent say they are more likely to buy a package if it is environmentally friendly, while 34 percent say it does not make a difference either way.[22]

10-5b Labeling

An integral part of any package is its label. Labeling generally takes one of two forms: persuasive or informational. **Persuasive labeling** focuses on a promotional theme or logo, and consumer information is secondary. Note that the standard promotional claims—such as "new," "improved," and "super"—are no longer very persuasive. Consumers have been saturated with "newness" and thus discount these claims.

Informational labeling, by contrast, is designed to help consumers make proper product selections and lower their cognitive dissonance after the purchase. Most major furniture manufacturers affix labels to their wares that explain the products' construction features, such as type of frame, number of coils, and fabric characteristics. The Nutritional Labeling and Education Act of 1990 mandated detailed nutritional information on most food packages and standards for health claims on food packaging. An important outcome of this legislation has been

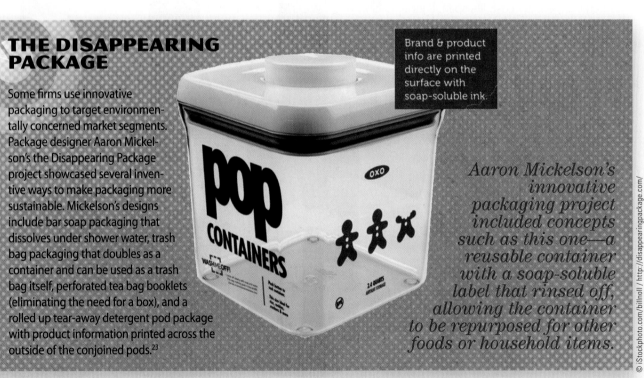

THE DISAPPEARING PACKAGE

Some firms use innovative packaging to target environmentally concerned market segments. Package designer Aaron Mickelson's the Disappearing Package project showcased several inventive ways to make packaging more sustainable. Mickelson's designs include bar soap packaging that dissolves under shower water, trash bag packaging that doubles as a container and can be used as a trash bag itself, perforated tea bag booklets (eliminating the need for a box), and a rolled up tear-away detergent pod package with product information printed across the outside of the conjoined pods.[23]

Brand & product info are printed directly on the surface with soap-soluble ink.

Aaron Mickelson's innovative packaging project included concepts such as this one—a reusable container with a soap-soluble label that rinsed off, allowing the container to be repurposed for other foods or household items.

guidelines from the Food and Drug Administration for using terms such as *low fat*, *light*, *reduced cholesterol*, *low sodium*, *low calorie*, *low carb*, and *fresh*. Getting the right information is very important to consumers, so some universities and corporations are working on new technologies to help consumers shop smart. For example, researchers at the Eindhoven University of Technology, the Universitá di Catania, CEA-Liten, and STMicroelectronics have developed a low-cost plastic converter that tests whether packaged foods are safe to eat. The converter then displays information about the food's freshness directly on its packaging, eliminating the need for "best before" dates that serve as cautious estimates at best. This not only reassures customers that they are buying fresh food; it prevents still-edible food from being thrown away once it is bought.[24]

GREENWASHING There are numerous products in every product category that use *greenwashing* to try and sell products. Greenwashing is when a product or company attempts to give the impression of environmental friendliness whether or not it is environmentally friendly.

As consumer demand for green products appeared to escalate, green certifications proliferated. Companies could create their own certifications and logos, resulting in more than 300 possible certification labels, ranging in price from free to thousands of dollars. Consumer distrust and confusion caused the Federal Trade Commission to issue new rules. Starting in late 2011, new regulations apply to labeling products with green-certification logos. If the same company that produced the product performed the certification, that relationship must be clearly marked. This benefits organizations such as Green Seal, which uses unbiased, third-party scientists and experts to verify claims about emissions or biodegradability, and hopes to increase consumer confidence in green products.[25]

10-5c Universal Product Codes

The **universal product codes (UPCs)** that appear on most items in supermarkets and other high-volume outlets were first introduced in 1974. Because the numerical codes appear as a series of thick and thin vertical lines, they are often called *bar codes*. The lines are read by computerized optical scanners that match codes with brand names, package sizes, and prices. They also print information on cash register tapes and help retailers rapidly and accurately prepare records of customer purchases, control inventories, and track sales. The UPC system and scanners are also used in scanner-based research (see Chapter 9).

universal product codes (UPCs) a series of thick and thin vertical lines (bar codes) readable by computerized optical scanners that represent numbers used to track products

10-6 GLOBAL ISSUES IN BRANDING AND PACKAGING

When planning to enter a foreign market with an existing product, a firm has three options for handling the brand name:

» **ONE BRAND NAME EVERYWHERE:** This strategy is useful when the company markets mainly one product and the brand name does not have negative connotations in any local market. The Coca-Cola Company uses a one-brand-name strategy in more than 195 countries around the world. The advantages of a one-brand-name strategy are greater identification of the product from market to market and ease of coordinating promotion from market to market.

» **ADAPTATIONS AND MODIFICATIONS:** A one-brand-name strategy is not possible when the name cannot be pronounced in the local language, when the brand name is owned by someone else, or when the brand name has a negative or vulgar connotation in the local language. The Iranian detergent Barf, for example, might encounter some problems in the U.S. market.

» **DIFFERENT BRAND NAMES IN DIFFERENT MARKETS:** Local brand names are often used when translation or pronunciation problems occur, when the marketer wants the brand to appear to be a local brand, or when regulations require localization. Unilever's Axe line of male grooming products is called Lynx in England, Ireland, Australia, and New Zealand. PepsiCo changed the name of its eponymous cola to Pecsi in Argentina to reflect the way the word is pronounced with an Argentinian accent.

In addition to global branding decisions, companies must consider global packaging needs. Three aspects of packaging that are especially important in international marketing are labeling, aesthetics, and climate considerations. The major *labeling* concern is properly translating ingredient, promotional, and instructional information on labels. Care must also be employed in meeting all local labeling requirements. Several years ago, an Italian judge ordered that all bottles of Coca-Cola be removed from retail shelves because the ingredients were not properly labeled. Labeling is also harder in countries like Belgium and Finland, which require packaging to be bilingual.

Package *aesthetics* may also require some attention. Even though simple visual elements of the brand, such as a symbol or logo, can be a standardizing element across products and countries, marketers must stay attuned to cultural traits in host countries. For example, colors may have different connotations. Red is associated with witchcraft in some countries, green may be a sign of danger, and white may be symbolic of death. Such cultural differences could necessitate a packaging change if colors are chosen for another country's interpretation. In the United States, green typically symbolizes an eco-friendly product, but that packaging could keep customers away in a country where green indicates danger. Aesthetics also influence package size. Soft drinks are not sold in six-packs in countries that lack refrigeration. In some countries, products such as detergent may be bought only in small quantities because of a lack of storage space. Other products, such as cigarettes, may be bought in small quantities, and even single units, because of the low purchasing power of buyers.

Extreme climates and long-distance shipping necessitate sturdier and more durable packages for goods sold overseas. Spillage, spoilage, and breakage are all more important concerns when products are shipped long distances or frequently handled during shipping and storage. Packages may also need to ensure a longer product life if the time between production and consumption lengthens significantly.

10-7 PRODUCT WARRANTIES

Just as a package is designed to protect the product, a warranty protects the buyer and gives essential information about the product. A warranty confirms the quality or performance of a good or service. An **express warranty** is a written guarantee. Express warranties range from simple statements—such as "100-percent cotton" (a guarantee of quality) and "complete satisfaction guaranteed" (a statement of performance)—to extensive documents written in technical language. In contrast, an **implied warranty** is an unwritten guarantee that the good or service is fit for the purpose for which it was sold. All sales have an implied warranty under the Uniform Commercial Code.

Congress passed the Magnuson-Moss Warranty–Federal Trade Commission Improvement Act in 1975 to help consumers understand warranties and get action from manufacturers and dealers. A manufacturer that promises a full warranty must meet certain minimum standards, including repair "within a reasonable time and without charge" of any defects and replacement of the merchandise or a full refund if the product does not work "after a reasonable number of attempts" at repair. Any warranty that does not live up to this tough prescription must be "conspicuously" promoted as a limited warranty.

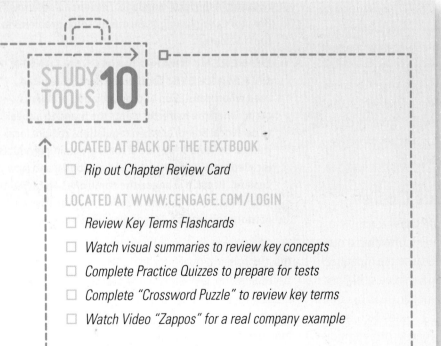

STUDY TOOLS 10

LOCATED AT BACK OF THE TEXTBOOK

☐ *Rip out Chapter Review Card*

LOCATED AT WWW.CENGAGE.COM/LOGIN

☐ *Review Key Terms Flashcards*

☐ *Watch visual summaries to review key concepts*

☐ *Complete Practice Quizzes to prepare for tests*

☐ *Complete "Crossword Puzzle" to review key terms*

☐ *Watch Video "Zappos" for a real company example*

USE THE TOOLS.

• Rip out the Review Cards in the back of your book to study.
Or Visit CourseMate to:
• Read, search, highlight, and take notes in the Interactive eBook
• Review Flashcards (Print or Online) to master key terms
• Test yourself with Auto-Graded Quizzes
• Bring concepts to life with Games, Videos,
  and Animations!

Go to CourseMate for **MKTG** to begin using these tools.
Access at **www.cengagebrain.com**

Complete the Speak Up
survey in CourseMate at
www.cengagebrain.com

Follow us at
www.facebook.com/4ltrpress

New products are important to sustain growth, increase revenues and profits, and replace obsolete items. Each year *Fast Company* rates and ranks its most innovative companies, based on the ability to buck tradition in the interest of reaching more people, building a better business, and spurring mass-market appeal for unusual or highly technical products or services. In 2012, the top four companies were Apple, Facebook, Google, and Amazon. It should come as little surprise that each of these companies is well known— their innovations have changed the way people communicate (Apple, Facebook, Google), and shop (Amazon).[1]

> The average fast-moving consumer goods company introduces seventy to eighty new products per year.

new product a product new to the world, the market, the producer, the seller, or some combination of these

11-1a Introduction of New Products

Some companies spend a considerable amount of money each year developing new products. For example, Procter & Gamble (P&G) has 8,000 employees, including 1,000 doctorate holders, working at its twenty-six innovation facilities around the world.[2] In fiscal year 2012, the company spent more than $2 billion on research and development.[3]

Sometimes it is difficult to decide when to replace a successful product. Gillette Co. has a history of introducing new shaving systems (razors and accompanying blades) before the previous generation of products begins experiencing a sales decline. In fact, Gillette *expects* to cannibalize the sales of older models with its newer introductions. In late 2012, Boeing Co. executives were trying to decide how and when to replace the successful 777 model aircraft (not to be confused with the 787 Dreamliner). Company executives agreed that the giant twin jet aircraft needed a makeover. However, the design of the replacement required complex decisions, tradeoffs, and risks.[4] Clearly, the introduction of a new product is a monumental undertaking with a lot of open-ended questions—even for an established, multi-billion dollar company.

11-1b Categories of New Products

The term **new product** is somewhat confusing because its meaning varies widely. Actually, the term has several "correct" definitions. A product can be new to the world, to the

Chapter 11

Developing and Managing Products

Learning Outcomes

After you finish this chapter go to
p210 *for* **STUDY TOOLS**

market, to the producer or seller, or some combination of these. There are six categories of new products:

‣ **NEW-TO-THE-WORLD PRODUCTS** (also called *discontinuous innovations*): These products create an entirely new market. For example, in early 2013, Taiwanese electronics company Polytron Technologies unveiled a completely transparent smartphone prototype. The device's new-to-the-world "Switchable Glass" technology employs liquid crystal molecules that display images only when electric current is run through them. Without power, the smartphone is completely see-through.[5] New-to-the-world products represent the smallest category of new products.

‣ **NEW PRODUCT LINES:** These products, which the firm has not previously offered, allow it to enter an established market. For example, Moleskine's first products were simple black-covered journals. Since then, the company has expanded into pens, travel bags, and even digital creative tools available on the iPhone and iPad.[6]

‣ **ADDITIONS TO EXISTING PRODUCT LINES:** This category includes new products that supplement a firm's established line. Fast-food restaurant chain Taco Bell and snack food manufacturer Frito-Lay have a longstanding partnership that has resulted in several product line additions. After the nacho cheese-flavored Doritos Locos taco proved to be the biggest launch in Taco Bell history, CEO Greg Creed announced that Cool Ranch- and Flamas-flavored versions of the Doritos Locos taco would soon be added to Taco Bell's product line. Indeed, in March 2013, the Cool Ranch Doritos Locos taco was added to Taco Bell menus across America.[7]

‣ **IMPROVEMENTS OR REVISIONS OF EXISTING PRODUCTS:** The "new and improved" product may be significantly or only slightly changed. In recent years, P&G's new product pipeline has focused more on reformulations than on new-to-the-world products. Examples include new scents of Tide laundry detergent and Secret deodorant.[8]

‣ **REPOSITIONED PRODUCTS:** These are existing products targeted at new markets or market segments, or ones repositioned to change the current market's perception of the product or company, which may be done to boost declining sales. Ford is repositioning its longtime favorite, the Mustang, to appeal to a younger group of buyers. Since 2005, the Mustang has had a retro style that appealed to baby boomer nostalgia. Now that boomers are exiting their sports car–buying years, Ford hopes to position the Mustang for Generation Y as they enter their strongest car buying years. To do so, the company will restyle the car to create a more modern, sleek look, though it will still have the signature shark-nose grille and round headlights that define the car.[9]

‣ **LOWER-PRICED PRODUCTS:** This category refers to products that provide performance similar to competing brands at a lower price. The HP LaserJet Color MFP is a scanner, copier, printer, and fax machine combined. This new product is priced lower than many conventional color copiers and much lower than the combined price of the four items purchased separately.

Attendees of the 2013 New York International Auto Show take turns sitting in a 2014 Ford Mustang GT coupe during a public preview. Ford hopes to position the 2014 Mustang for Generation Y as they enter their strongest car buying years.

STAN HONDA/AFP/Getty Images

11-2 THE NEW-PRODUCT DEVELOPMENT PROCESS

The management consulting firm Booz Allen Hamilton has studied the new-product development process for more than thirty years. Analyzing five major studies undertaken during this period, the firm has concluded that the companies most likely to succeed in developing and introducing new products are those that take the following actions:

» **Make the long-term commitment needed to support innovation and new-product development.**

» **Use a company-specific approach, driven by corporate objectives and strategies, with a well-defined new-product strategy at its core.**

» **Capitalize on experience to achieve and maintain competitive advantage.**

» **Establish an environment—a management style, organizational structure, and degree of top management support—conducive to achieving company-specific new-product and corporate objectives.**

Most companies follow a formal new-product development process, usually starting with a new-product strategy. Exhibit 1 traces the seven-step process, which is discussed in detail in this section. The exhibit is funnel-shaped to highlight the fact that each stage acts as a screen to filter out unworkable ideas.

11-2a New-Product Strategy

A **new-product strategy** links the new-product development process with the objectives of the marketing department, the business unit, and the corporation. A new-product strategy must be compatible with these objectives, and in turn, all three of the objectives must be consistent with one another.

A new-product strategy is part of the organization's overall marketing strategy. It sharpens the focus and provides general guidelines for generating, screening, and evaluating new-product ideas. The new-product strategy specifies the roles that new products must play in the organization's overall plan and describes the characteristics of products the organization wants to offer and the markets it wants to serve.

11-2b Idea Generation

New-product ideas come from many sources, including customers, employees, distributors, competitors, research and development (R&D), consultants, and other experts.

CUSTOMERS The marketing concept suggests that customers' wants and needs should be the springboard for developing new products. Companies can derive insight from listening to Internet chatter or reading blogs, which often indicate early trends or areas consumers are interested in seeing develop or change. Another approach for generating new-product ideas is using what some companies are calling "customer innovation centers." The idea is to provide a forum for meeting with customers and directly involving them in the innovation process.

EMPLOYEES Sometimes employees know a company's products and processes better than anyone else. Many firms have formal

new-product strategy a plan that links the new-product development process with the objectives of the marketing department, the business unit, and the corporation

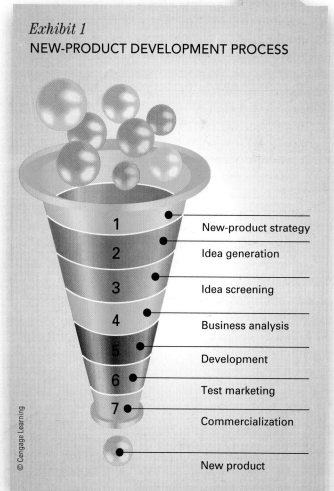

Exhibit 1
NEW-PRODUCT DEVELOPMENT PROCESS

1 New-product strategy
2 Idea generation
3 Idea screening
4 Business analysis
5 Development
6 Test marketing
7 Commercialization

New product

© Cengage Learning

and informal processes in place for employees to propose new product ideas. To encourage participation, some companies run contests, hold votes, and set up idea kiosks.[11]

PricewaterhouseCoopers uses a system called iPlace to encourage employee innovation. The system is so successful that 60 percent of employees participate in the idea-generation process; 140 of the 3,300 ideas have already been implemented.[12]

Some firms reward employees for coming up with creative new ideas. Many companies want to encourage risk-taking through new ideas and have begun implementing rewards for failing after taking a big risk. When senior Anchor Advisors consultant Brad Farris was just starting his career, his company was heading to a trade show without any new products to demonstrate. Wanting to have something—anything—on display at the show, Farris developed a new product that was rushed from concept to ready-to-show in just eight weeks. The new product was unveiled at the show—but customers absolutely hated it. Instead of firing or even scolding Farris, the company president commended him for his effort and thanked him for pulling the new product together so quickly. Looking back at the experience, Farris reflected on the importance of business leaders encouraging creativity: "It made a *huge* difference for me. Just that short discussion really energized me to keep trying new things and taking risks."[13]

DISTRIBUTORS A well-trained sales force routinely asks distributors about needs that are not being met. Because they are closer to end users, distributors are often more aware of customer needs than are manufacturers. The inspiration for Rubbermaid's Sidekick, a litter-free lunch box, came from a distributor who suggested that the company place some of its plastic containers inside a lunch box and sell the box as an alternative to plastic wrap and paper bags.

COMPETITORS No firms rely solely on internally generated ideas for new products. As discussed in Chapter 9, a big part of any organization's marketing intelligence system should be monitoring the performance of competitors' products. One purpose of competitive monitoring is to determine which, if any, of the competitors' products should be copied. There is plenty of information about competitors on the Internet. Fuld & Company is a preeminent research and consulting firm in the field of competitive intelligence. Its clients include more than half of the U.S. *Fortune* 500 list and numerous international firms.[14]

RESEARCH AND DEVELOPMENT R&D is carried out in four distinct ways. You learned about basic research and applied research in Chapter 4. The other two ways are product development and product modification. **Product development** goes beyond applied research by converting applications into marketable products. Product modification makes cosmetic or functional changes to existing products. Many new-product breakthroughs come from R&D activities. When Nike asked Olympic marathon competitors what

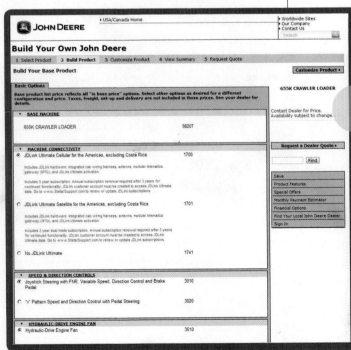

FOR JOHN DEERE CUSTOMERS, CUSTOMIZATION IS KEY

When John Deere asked customers what they wanted to see in the new 655K commercial bulldozer, they responded with an emphatic call for customization. Using their input, John Deere developed two transmission control systems (a V-pattern option and a joystick option) and two bucket types (a general-purpose bucket and a four-in-one multipurpose bucket) for customers to choose from.[10]

they wanted in a shoe, they said they wanted a sock. At Nike's Innovation Kitchen, engineers and designers went through numerous prototypes and developed entirely new machinery to mimic the snug, smooth fit of a sock while still maintaining the support and look of a tennis shoe. Four years of R&D resulted in the Nike Flyknit, a line of shoes knit like socks that won *Time* magazine's Best Inventions of 2012 list.[15] In an equally impressive example of R&D, Gillette Co. researchers observe about eighty men shaving every weekday morning at its shave-technology center in Reading, England to assess the performance and limitations of its current products and products not yet introduced.[16]

CONSULTANTS Outside consultants are always available to examine a business and recommend product ideas. Examples include the Weston Group, Booz Allen Hamilton, and Management Decisions Inc. Traditionally, consultants determine whether a company has a balanced portfolio of products and, if not, what new-product ideas are needed to offset the imbalance. For example, Continuum is an award-winning consultancy firm that designs new goods and services, works on brand makeovers, and conducts consumer research. Clients include PepsiCo, Moen, American Express, Samsung, Reebok, and Sprint.[17]

OTHER EXPERTS A technique that is being used increasingly to generate new product ideas is called "crowdsourcing." General information regarding ideas being sought is provided to a wide range of potential sources such as industry experts, independent researchers, and academics. These experts then develop ideas for the company. In addition to field experts, firms such as Quirky Inc. and General Electric Company have used crowdsourcing to generate ideas from the general public and freelance inventors. The Defense Advanced Research Projects Agency (DARPA), a branch of the Pentagon, is even using crowdsourcing to help design a new amphibious vehicle for the Marine Corps that will be used to storm beaches.[18] DARPA executives hope for a broad range of participants from small businesses to large

industry to academics.[19] For a more thorough discussion of crowdsourcing, see Chapter 18.

Creativity is the wellspring of new-product ideas, regardless of who comes up with them. A variety of approaches and techniques have been developed to stimulate creative thinking. The two considered most useful for generating new-product ideas are brainstorming and focus group exercises. The goal of **brainstorming** is to get a group to think of unlimited ways to vary a product or solve a problem. Group members avoid criticism of an idea, no matter how ridiculous it may seem. Objective evaluation is postponed. The sheer quantity of ideas is what matters. As noted in Chapter 9, an objective of focus group interviews is to stimulate insightful comments through group interaction. In the industrial market, machine tools, keyboard designs, aircraft interiors, and backhoe accessories have evolved from focus groups.

11-2c Idea Screening

After new ideas have been generated, they pass through the first filter in the product development process. This stage, called **screening**, eliminates ideas that are inconsistent with the organization's new-product strategy or are obviously inappropriate for some other reason. The new-product committee, the new-product department, or some other formally appointed group performs the screening review.

Concept tests are often used at the screening stage to rate concept (or product) alternatives. A **concept test** evaluates a new-product idea, usually before any prototype has been created. Typically, researchers get consumer reactions to descriptions and visual representations of a proposed product.

Concept tests are considered fairly good predictors of success for line extensions. They have also been relatively precise predictors of success for new products that are not copycat items, are not easily classified into existing product categories, and do not require major changes in consumer behavior—such as Betty Crocker Tuna Helper. However, concept tests are usually inaccurate in predicting the success of new products that create new consumption patterns and require major changes in consumer behavior—such as microwave ovens, digital music players, and computers.

brainstorming the process of getting a group to think of unlimited ways to vary a product or solve a problem

screening the first filter in the product development process, which eliminates ideas that are inconsistent with the organization's new-product strategy or are obviously inappropriate for some other reason

concept test a test to evaluate a new-product idea, usually before any prototype has been created

11-2d Business Analysis

New-product ideas that survive the initial screening process move to the **business analysis** stage, where preliminary figures for demand, cost, sales, and profitability are calculated. For the first time, costs and revenues are estimated and compared. Depending on the nature of the product and the company, this process may be simple or complex.

The newness of the product, the size of the market, and the nature of the competition all affect the accuracy of revenue projections. In an established market like soft drinks, industry estimates of total market size are available. Forecasting market share for a new entry in a new, fragmented, or relatively small niche is a bigger challenge.

Analyzing overall economic trends and their impact on estimated sales is especially important in product categories that are sensitive to fluctuations in the business cycle. If consumers view the economy as uncertain and risky, they will put off buying durable goods such as major home appliances, automobiles, and homes. Likewise, business buyers postpone major equipment purchases if they expect a recession. Understanding the market potential is important because costs increase dramatically once a product idea enters the development stage.

11-2e Development

In the early stage of **development**, the R&D or engineering department may develop a prototype of the product. A process called 3D printing, or additive manufacturing, is sometimes used to create three dimensional prototypes quickly and at a relatively low cost. During this stage, the firm should start sketching a marketing strategy. The marketing department should decide on the product's packaging, branding, labeling, and so forth. In addition, it should map out preliminary promotion, price, and distribution strategies. The feasibility of manufacturing the product at an acceptable cost should be thoroughly examined. The development stage can last a long time and thus be very expensive. It took ten years to develop Crest toothpaste, fifteen years to develop the Polaroid Colorpack camera and the Xerox copy machine, eighteen years to develop Minute Rice, and fifty-one years to develop the

COMMON QUESTIONS IN THE BUSINESS ANALYSIS STAGE

These questions are commonly asked during the business analysis stage:

▸▸ **What is the likely demand for the product?**

▸▸ **What impact would the new product probably have on total sales, profits, market share, and return on investment?**

▸▸ **How would the introduction of the product affect existing products? Would the new product cannibalize existing products?**

▸▸ **Would current customers benefit from the product?**

▸▸ **Would the product enhance the image of the company's overall product mix?**

▸▸ **Would the new product affect current employees in any way? Would it lead to increasing or reducing the size of the workforce?**

▸▸ **What new facilities, if any, would be needed?**

▸▸ **How might competitors respond?**

▸▸ **What is the risk of failure? Is the company willing to take the risk?**

television. Gillette developed three shaving systems over a twenty-seven-year period (Trac II, Atra, and Sensor) before introducing the Mach3 in 1998 and Fusion in 2006.[20] The time invested in development can often have tremendous payoff. Worldwide sales of razors and blades totaled about $13 billion in 2012. Sales of pre-shave products totaled about $2.77 billion, and after-shave sales totaled about 1.23 billion worldwide.[21]

The development process works best when all the involved areas (R&D, marketing, engineering, production, and even suppliers) work together rather than sequentially, a process called **simultaneous product development**. This approach allows firms to shorten the development process and reduce costs. With simultaneous product development, all relevant functional areas and outside suppliers participate in all stages of the development process. Rather than proceeding through highly structured stages, the cross-functional team operates in unison. Involving key suppliers early in the process capitalizes on their knowledge and enables them to develop critical component parts.

The Internet is a useful tool for implementing simultaneous product development. On the Web, multiple partners from a variety of locations can meet regularly to assess new-product ideas, analyze markets and demographics, and review cost information. Ideas judged to be feasible can quickly be converted into new products. The best-managed global firms leverage their global networks by sharing best practices, knowledge, and technology.[22] Without the Internet, it would be impossible to conduct simultaneous product development from different parts of the world. Some firms use online brain trusts to solve technical problems. InnoCentive Inc. is a network of 80,000 self-selected science problem solvers in 173 countries. Its clients include NASA, *Popular Science*, and *The Economist*. When one of InnoCentive's partners selects an idea for development, it no longer tries to develop the idea from the ground up with its own resources and time. Instead, it issues a brief to its network of thinkers, researchers, technology entrepreneurs, and inventors around the world, hoping to generate dialogue, suggestions, and solutions.

Innovative firms are also gathering a variety of R&D input from customers online. Threadless, a T-shirt company, and RYZ, an athletic shoe manufacturer, ask consumers to vote online for their favorite designs. The companies use these results to determine the products they sell over the Internet.[23]

Laboratory tests are often conducted on prototype models during the development stage. User safety is an important aspect of laboratory testing, which actually subjects products to much more severe treatment than is expected by end users. The Consumer Product Safety Act of 1972 requires manufacturers to conduct a "reasonable testing program" to ensure that their products conform to established safety standards.

Many products that test well in the laboratory are also tried out in homes or businesses. Examples of product categories well suited for such use tests include human and pet food products, household cleaning products, and industrial chemicals and supplies. These products are all relatively inexpensive, and their performance characteristics are apparent to users. For example, P&G tests a variety of personal and home-care products in the community around its Cincinnati, Ohio, headquarters.

11-2f Test Marketing

After products and marketing programs have been developed, they are usually tested in the marketplace. **Test marketing** is the limited introduction of a product and a marketing program to determine the reactions of potential customers in a market situation. Test marketing allows management to evaluate alternative strategies and to assess how well the various aspects of the marketing mix fit together. Even established products are test marketed to assess new marketing strategies.

The cities chosen as test sites should reflect market conditions in the new product's projected market area. Yet no "magic city" exists that can universally represent market conditions, and a product's success in one city doesn't

© Mike Flippo/Shutterstock.com

YOUR DESIGN HERE

guarantee that it will be a nationwide hit. When selecting test market cities, researchers should therefore find locations where the demographics and purchasing habits mirror the overall market. The company should also have good distribution in test cities. Wendy's uses Columbus, Ohio as a test market for new burgers. Because the city has a nearly perfect cross-section of America's demographic breakdown, it is the perfect testing ground for new products. Most recently, Wendy's has been testing the reception of its Black Label Hamburger.[24] Moreover, test locations should be isolated from the media. If the television stations in a particular market reach a very large area outside that market, the advertising used for the test product may pull in many consumers from outside the market. The product may then appear more successful than it really is.

THE HIGH COSTS OF TEST MARKETING Test marketing frequently takes one year or longer, and costs can exceed $1 million. Some products remain in test markets even longer. As cigarette sales have declined in recent years, cigarette companies have begun developing—and test marketing—alternative nicotine delivery devices.

In 2012, Altria Group, the parent company of cigarette manufacturer Philip Morris, test marketed a tobacco-free, chewable nicotine product called Verve in Virginia. Earlier in 2012, Altria test marketed a flavored wooden tobacco stick in Kansas. As of this printing, neither product has seen nationwide release.[25]

Despite the cost, many firms believe it is better to fail in a test market than in a national introduction. Because test marketing is so expensive, some companies do not test line extensions of well-known brands.

The high cost of test marketing is not just financial. One unavoidable problem is that test marketing exposes the new product and its marketing mix to competitors before its introduction. Thus, the element of surprise is lost. Competitors can also sabotage or "jam" a testing program by introducing their own sales promotion, pricing, or advertising campaign. The purpose is to hide or distort the normal conditions that the testing firm might expect in the market.

ALTERNATIVES TO TEST MARKETING Many firms are looking for cheaper, faster, safer alternatives to traditional test marketing. In the early 1980s, Information Resources Inc. pioneered one alternative: scanner-based research (discussed in Chapter 9). A typical supermarket scanner test costs about $300,000. Another alternative to traditional test marketing is **simulated (laboratory) market testing**. Advertising and other promotional materials for several products, including the test product, are shown to members of the product's target market. These people are then taken to shop at a mock or real store, where their purchases are recorded. Shopper behavior, including repeat purchasing, is monitored to assess the product's likely performance under true market conditions. Research firms offer simulated market tests for $25,000 to $100,000, compared to $1 million or more for full-scale test marketing.

The Internet offers a fast, cost-effective way to conduct test marketing. P&G uses the Internet to assess customer demand for potential new products. Many products that are not available in grocery stores or drugstores can be sampled from P&G's Web site devoted to samples and coupons, www.pgeveryday.com.[26]

Despite these alternatives, most firms still consider test marketing essential for most new

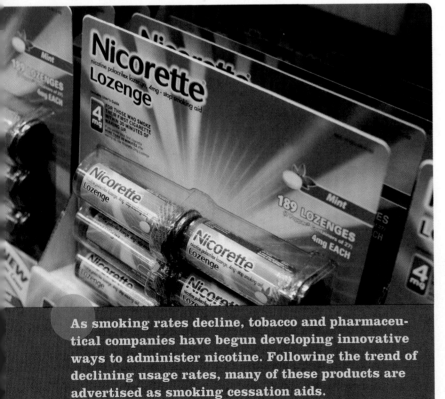

As smoking rates decline, tobacco and pharmaceutical companies have begun developing innovative ways to administer nicotine. Following the trend of declining usage rates, many of these products are advertised as smoking cessation aids.

© Kristoffer Tripplaar/Alamy

products. The high price of failure simply prohibits the widespread introduction of most new products without testing.

11-2g Commercialization

The final stage in the new-product development process is **commercialization**, the decision to market a product. The decision to commercialize the product sets several tasks in motion: ordering production materials and equipment, starting production, building inventories, shipping the product to field distribution points, training the sales force, announcing the new product to the trade, and advertising to potential customers.

The time from the initial commercialization decision to the product's actual introduction varies. It can range from a few weeks for simple products that use existing equipment to several years for technical products that require custom manufacturing equipment. And the total cost of development and initial introduction can be staggering.

cited factor in new-product failures is a poor match between product features and customer desires. For example, there are telephone systems on the market with more than 700 different functions, although the average user is happy with just 10 functions. Other reasons for failure include overestimation of market size, incorrect targeting or positioning, a price too high or too low, inadequate distribution, poor promotion, or simply an inferior product.

Estimates of the percentages of new products that fail vary. Many estimates range as high as 80 to 90 percent.[27] Failure can be a matter of degree, however. Absolute failure occurs when a company cannot recoup its development, marketing, and production costs—the product actually loses money for the company. A relative product failure results when the product returns a profit but fails to achieve sales, profit, or market share goals. Examples of product failures in 2012 include the Windows-based Nokia Lumia 900 smartphone, the Ultrabook notebook line from Intel, the Disney movie *John Carter*, and 3D TVs.[28]

High costs and other risks of developing and testing new products do not stop many companies, such as NewellRubbermaid, Colgate-Palmolive, Campbell Soup Company, and 3M, from aggressively developing and introducing new products. These companies depend on new products to increase revenues and profits. The most important factor in successful new-product introduction is a good match between the product and market needs—as

11-3 WHY SOME PRODUCTS SUCCEED AND OTHERS FAIL

Despite the amount of time and money spent on developing and testing new products, a large proportion of new product introductions fail. Products fail for a number of reasons. One common reason is that they simply do not offer any discernible benefit compared to existing products. Another commonly

Adam Gasson/PC Plus Magazine/Getty Images

SEVEN CHARACTERISTICS OF SUCCESSFUL PRODUCT INTRODUCTIONS

Firms that routinely experience success in new-product introductions tend to share the following seven characteristics:

▶▶ **A history of listening carefully to customers**

▶▶ **An obsession with producing the best product possible**

▶▶ **A vision of what the market will be like in the future**

▶▶ **Strong leadership**

▶▶ **A commitment to new-product development**

 ▶▶ **A project-based team approach to new-product development**

  ▶▶ **Getting every aspect of the product development process right**

© iStockphoto.com/bilinoll

the marketing concept would predict. Successful new products deliver a meaningful and perceivable benefit to a sizable number of people or organizations and are different in some meaningful way from their intended substitutes.

11-4 GLOBAL ISSUES IN NEW-PRODUCT DEVELOPMENT

Increasing globalization of markets and competition provides a reason for multinational firms to consider new-product development from a worldwide perspective. A firm that starts with a global strategy is better able to develop products that are marketable worldwide. In many multinational corporations, every product is developed for potential worldwide distribution, and unique market requirements are satisfied during development whenever possible.

Some global marketers design their products to meet regulations in their major markets and then, if necessary, meet smaller markets' requirements country by country. Nissan develops lead-country car models that, with minor changes, can be sold in most markets. With this approach, Nissan has been able to reduce the number of its basic models from forty-eight to eighteen. Some products, however, have little potential for global market penetration without modification. Succeeding in some countries (such as China) often requires companies to develop products that meet the unique needs of these populations.[29] In other cases, companies cannot sell their products at affordable prices and still make a profit in many countries.

11-5 THE SPREAD OF NEW PRODUCTS

Managers have a better chance of successfully marketing products if they understand how consumers learn about and adopt products.

11-5a Diffusion of Innovation

An **innovation** is a product perceived as new by a potential adopter. It really doesn't matter whether the product is "new to the world" or some other category of new product. If it is new to a potential adopter, it is an innovation in this context. **Diffusion** is the process by which the adoption of an innovation spreads. Five categories of adopters participate in the diffusion process.

INNOVATORS Innovators are the first 2.5 percent of all those who adopt the product. Innovators are eager to try new ideas and products, almost as an obsession. In addition to having higher incomes, they are more worldly and more active outside their community than noninnovators. They rely less on group norms and are more self-confident. Because they are well educated, they are more likely to get their information from scientific sources and experts. Innovators are characterized as being venturesome.

EARLY ADOPTERS Early adopters are the next 13.5 percent to adopt the product. Although early adopters are not the very first, they do adopt early in the product's life cycle. Compared to innovators, they rely much more on group norms and values. They are also more oriented to the local community, in contrast to the innovators' worldly outlook. Early adopters are more likely than innovators to be opinion leaders because of their closer affiliation with groups. Early adopters are a new product's best friends. Because viral, buzz, and word-of-mouth advertising is on the rise, marketers focus a lot of attention identifying the group that begins the viral marketing chain—the *influencers*. Part of the challenge is that this group of customers is distinguished not by demographics but by behavior. Influencers come from all age, gender, and income groups, and they do not use media any differently than other users who are considered followers. The characteristic influencers share is their desire to talk to others about their experiences with goods and services. A desire to earn the respect of others is a dominant characteristic among early adopters.

EARLY MAJORITY The next 34 percent to adopt are called the early majority. The early majority weighs the pros and cons before adopting a new product. They are likely to collect more information and evaluate more brands than early adopters, thereby extending the adoption process. They rely on the group for information but are unlikely to be opinion leaders themselves. Instead, they tend to be opinion leaders' friends and neighbors. Consumers trust positive word-of-mouth reviews from friends, family, and peers.[30] In fact, 92 percent of consumers around the world put their faith in word-of-mouth endorsements (including those obtained through social media) above all other forms of advertising—an increase of 18 percent since 2007.[31] Product discussions often drive teen conversations, so word-of-mouth marketing is particularly powerful among this demographic. According to Lauren Hutter, group planning director at BBDO New York, "It's their countercultural currency … It's how to break into the group, how you bring something into the mix."[32]

While word-of-mouth marketing is important to teens, actually getting them to discuss products concretely can be difficult. According to Eric Pakurar, executive director and head of strategy at G2 USA, "They kind of ping-pong back and forth. They do a little research, then talk to their friends, and then do a little more research and check back with their friends and family."[33] Other groups, such as adult men and women, also report word-of-mouth as the most important source of product information.[34] Many feel a responsibility to help friends and family make wise purchase decisions.

All word of mouth is not positive. Four out of five U.S. consumers report telling people around them about negative customer service experiences. Thirty-two percent of consumers share customer service experiences on social media, roughly half of which is negative.[35] The early majority is an important link in the process of diffusing new ideas because they are positioned between earlier and later adopters. A dominant characteristic of the early majority is deliberateness.

LATE MAJORITY The late majority is the next 34 percent to adopt. The late majority adopts a new product because most of their friends have already adopted it. Because they also rely on group norms, their adoption stems from pressure to conform. This group tends to be older and below average in income and education. They depend mainly on word-of-mouth communication rather than on the mass media. The dominant characteristic of the late majority is skepticism.

LAGGARDS The final 16 percent to adopt are called laggards. Like innovators, laggards do not rely on group norms. Their independence is rooted in their ties to tradition. Thus, the past heavily influences their decisions. By the time laggards adopt an innovation, it has probably been outmoded and replaced by something else. For example, they may have bought their first color television set after flat screen televisions were already widely diffused. Laggards have the longest adoption time and the lowest socioeconomic status. They tend to be suspicious of new products and alienated from a rapidly advancing society.

The dominant value of laggards is tradition. Marketers typically ignore laggards, who do not seem to be motivated by advertising or personal selling and are virtually impossible to reach online.

Note that some product categories may never be adopted by 100 percent of the population. The adopter categories refer to all of those who will eventually adopt a product, not the entire population.

11-5b Product Characteristics and the Rate of Adoption

Five product characteristics can be used to predict and explain the rate of acceptance and diffusion of a new product:

▸ **COMPLEXITY:** the degree of difficulty involved in understanding and using a new product. The more complex the product, the slower is its diffusion.

▸ **COMPATIBILITY:** the degree to which the new product is consistent with existing values and product knowledge, past experiences, and current needs. Incompatible products diffuse more slowly than compatible products.

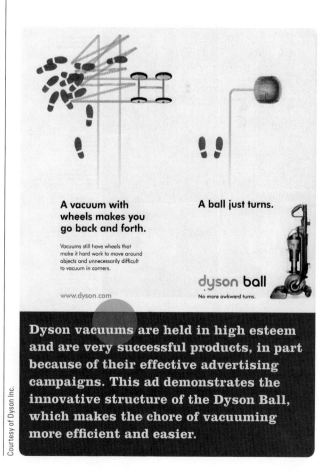

A vacuum with wheels makes you go back and forth.

Vacuums still have wheels that make it hard work to move around objects and unnecessarily difficult to vacuum in corners.

www.dyson.com

A ball just turns.

dyson ball
No more awkward turns.

Dyson vacuums are held in high esteem and are very successful products, in part because of their effective advertising campaigns. This ad demonstrates the innovative structure of the Dyson Ball, which makes the chore of vacuuming more efficient and easier.

▸ **RELATIVE ADVANTAGE:** the degree to which a product is perceived as superior to existing substitutes. Because it can store and play back thousands of songs, the iPod and its many variants have a clear relative advantage over the portable CD player.

▸ **OBSERVABILITY:** the degree to which the benefits or other results of using the product can be observed by others and communicated to target customers. For instance, fashion items and automobiles are highly visible and more observable than personal-care items.

▸ **"TRIALABILITY":** the degree to which a product can be tried on a limited basis. It is much easier to try a new toothpaste or breakfast cereal, for example, than a new personal computer.

11-5c Marketing Implications of the Adoption Process

Two types of communication aid the diffusion process: *word-of-mouth communication* among consumers and communication from marketers to consumers. Word-of-mouth communication, including social media and viral communication, within and across groups speeds diffusion. Opinion leaders discuss new products with their followers and with other opinion leaders. Marketers must therefore ensure that opinion leaders have the types of information desired in the media that they use. Suppliers of some products, such as professional and health care services, rely almost solely on word-of-mouth communication for new business.

The second type of communication aiding the diffusion process is *communication directly from the marketer to potential adopters*. Messages directed toward early adopters should normally use different appeals than messages directed toward the early majority, the late majority, or the laggards. Early adopters are more important than innovators because they make up a larger group, are more socially active, and are usually opinion leaders.

As the focus of a promotional campaign shifts from early adopters to the early majority and the late majority, marketers should study the dominant characteristics, buying behavior, and media characteristics of these target markets. Then they should revise messages and media strategy to fit. The diffusion model helps guide marketers in developing and implementing promotion strategy.

11-6 PRODUCT LIFE CYCLES

The product life cycle (PLC) is one of the most familiar concepts in marketing. Few other general concepts have been so widely discussed. Although some researchers and consultants have challenged the theoretical basis and managerial value of the PLC, many believe it is a useful marketing management diagnostic tool and a general guide for marketing planning in various life cycle stages.

The PLC is a biological metaphor that traces the stages of a product's acceptance, from its introduction (birth) to its decline (death). As Exhibit 2 shows, a product progresses through four major stages: introduction, growth, maturity, and decline.

The PLC concept can be used to analyze a brand, a product form, or a product category. The PLC for a

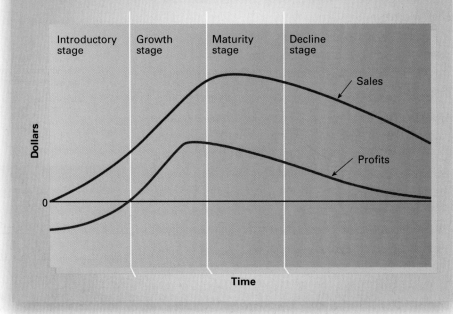

Exhibit 2
FOUR STAGES OF THE PRODUCT LIFE CYCLE

© Cengage Learning

product form is usually longer than the PLC for any one brand. The exception would be a brand that was the first and last competitor in a product form market. In that situation, the brand and product form life cycles would be equal in length. Product categories have the longest life cycles. A **product category** includes all brands that satisfy a particular type of need, such as shaving products, passenger automobiles, or soft drinks.

The time a product spends in any one stage of the life cycle may vary dramatically. Some products, such as fad items, move through the entire cycle in weeks. Fads are typically characterized by a sudden and unpredictable spike in sales followed by a rather abrupt decline. Examples of fad items are Silly Bandz, Beanie Babies, and Crocs. Other products, such as electric clothes washers and dryers, stay in the maturity stage for decades. Exhibit 2 illustrates the typical life cycle for a consumer durable good, such as a washer or dryer. In contrast, Exhibit 3 illustrates typical life cycles for styles (such as formal, business, or casual clothing), fashions (such as miniskirts or baggy jeans), and fads (such as leopard-print clothing). Changes in a product, its uses, its image, or its positioning can extend that product's life cycle.

The PLC concept does not tell managers the length of a product's life cycle or its duration in any stage. It does not dictate marketing strategy. It is simply a tool to help marketers forecast future events and suggest appropriate strategies.

11-6a Introductory Stage

The **introductory stage** of the PLC represents the full-scale launch of a new product into the marketplace.

Computer databases for personal use, room-deodorizing air-conditioning filters, and wind-powered home electric generators are all product categories that have recently entered the PLC. A high failure rate, little competition, frequent product modification, and limited distribution typify the introductory stage of the PLC.

Marketing costs in the introductory stage are normally high for several reasons. High dealer margins are often needed to obtain adequate distribution, and incentives are needed to get consumers to try the new product. Advertising expenses are high because of the need to educate consumers about the new product's benefits. Production costs are also often high in this stage, as product and manufacturing flaws are identified and corrected and efforts are undertaken to develop mass production economies.

Sales normally increase slowly during the introductory stage. Moreover, profits are usually negative because of R&D costs, factory tooling, and high introduction costs. The length of the introductory phase is largely determined by product characteristics, such as the product's advantages over substitute products, the educational effort required to make the product known, and management's commitment of resources to the new item. A short introductory period is usually preferred to help reduce the impact of negative earnings and cash flows. As soon as the product gets off the ground, the financial burden should begin to diminish. Also, a short introduction helps dispel some of the uncertainty as to whether the new product will be successful.

product category all brands that satisfy a particular type of need

introductory stage the full-scale launch of a new product into the marketplace

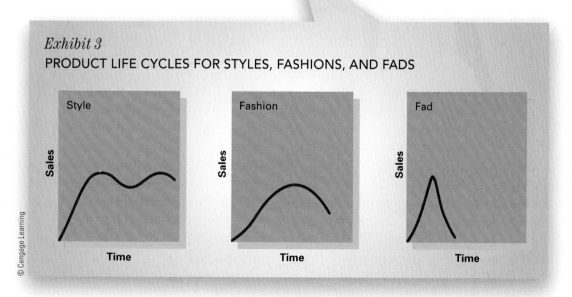

Exhibit 3
PRODUCT LIFE CYCLES FOR STYLES, FASHIONS, AND FADS

Style — Sales / Time

Fashion — Sales / Time

Fad — Sales / Time

© Cengage Learning

Promotion strategy in the introductory stage focuses on developing product awareness and informing consumers about the product category's potential benefits. At this stage, the communication challenge is to stimulate primary demand—demand for the product in general rather than for a specific brand. Intensive personal selling is often required to gain acceptance for the product among wholesalers and retailers. Promotion of convenience products often requires heavy consumer sampling and couponing. Shopping and specialty products demand educational advertising and personal selling to the final consumer.

11-6b Growth Stage

If a product category survives the introductory stage, it then advances to the **growth stage** of the life cycle. In this stage, sales typically grow at an increasing rate, many competitors enter the market, and large companies may start to acquire small pioneering firms. Profits rise rapidly in the growth stage, reach their peak, and begin declining as competition intensifies. Emphasis switches from primary demand promotion (e.g., promoting e-readers) to aggressive brand advertising and communication of the differences between brands (e.g., promoting Kindle versus Nook).

Distribution becomes a major key to success during the growth stage, as well as in later stages. Manufacturers scramble to sign up dealers and distributors and to build long-term relationships. Others are able to market direct to consumers using electronic media. Without adequate distribution, it is impossible to establish a strong market position.

Madewell, a workwear company founded in 1937, fell out of awareness until 2004, when the brand was purchased by Millard Drexler, who revamped its image into a casual, modern, and youthful collection. Drexler worked with J. Crew, leasing the Madewell brand name to the well-known company for $1 a year to develop the brand conscientiously, creating a solid foundation for growth in luxury denim. In 2011, the company approached $100 million in sales volume, generating profit for the first time. With such success, the plan to increase retail presence by 30 percent and add a

© fancy/Shutterstock.com

marketing campaign should only increase the company's growth.[36]

11-6c Maturity Stage

A period during which sales increase at a decreasing rate signals the beginning of the **maturity stage** of the life cycle. New users cannot be added indefinitely, and sooner or later the market approaches saturation. Normally, this is the longest stage of the PLC. Many major household appliances are in the maturity stage of their life cycles.

For shopping products such as durable goods and electronics, and many specialty products, annual models begin to appear during the maturity stage. Product lines are lengthened to appeal to additional market segments. Service and repair assume more important roles as manufacturers strive to distinguish their products from others. Product design changes tend to become stylistic (How can the product be made different?) rather than functional (How can the product be made better?).

As prices and profits continue to fall, marginal competitors start dropping out of the market. Dealer margins also shrink, resulting in less shelf space for mature items, lower dealer inventories, and a general reluctance to promote the product. Thus, promotion to dealers often intensifies during this stage in order to retain loyalty.

Heavy consumer promotion by the manufacturer is also required to maintain market share. Cutthroat competition during this stage can lead to price wars. Another characteristic of the maturity stage is the emergence of "niche marketers" that target narrow, well-defined, underserved segments of a market. Starbucks Coffee targets its gourmet line at new, young, affluent coffee drinkers, the only segment of the coffee market that is growing.

11-6d Decline Stage

A long-run drop in sales signals the beginning of the **decline stage**. The rate of decline is governed by how rapidly consumer tastes change or substitute products are adopted. Many convenience products and fad items lose their market overnight, leaving large inventories of unsold items, such as designer jeans. Others die more slowly. Landline telephone service is an example of a product in the decline stage of the product life cycle. Nearly 32 percent of American homes do not have a landline, which represents a continued steady increase since 2010—and a steady drop in the use of landlines.[37] People abandoning landlines to go wireless and households replacing landlines with Internet phones have both contributed to this long-term decline.

Some firms have developed successful strategies for marketing products in the decline stage of the PLC. They eliminate all nonessential marketing expenses and let sales decline as more and more customers discontinue purchasing the products. Eventually, the product is withdrawn from the market.

11-6e Implications for Marketing Management

The new-product development process, the diffusion process, and the PLC concept all have implications for marketing managers. The funnel shape of Exhibit 1 indicates that many new product ideas are necessary to produce one successful new product. The new-product development process is sometimes illustrated as a decay curve with roughly half of the ideas approved at one stage rejected at the next stage. While the actual numbers vary widely among firms and industries, the relationship between the stages can be generalized. This reinforces the notion that an organized effort to generate many ideas from various sources is important for any firm that wishes to produce a continuing flow of new products.

The major implication of the diffusion process to marketing managers is that the message may need to change over time. The targeted adopter and media may need to shift based on how various categories of adopters gather product information. A message developed for and targeted toward early adopters will not be perceived similarly by late majority adopters.

Exhibit 4 shows the relationship between the adopter categories and stages of the PLC. Note that the various categories of adopters buy products in different stages of the life cycle. Almost all sales in the maturity and decline stages represent repeat purchases.

Exhibit 4

RELATIONSHIP BETWEEN THE DIFFUSION PROCESS AND THE PRODUCT LIFE CYCLE

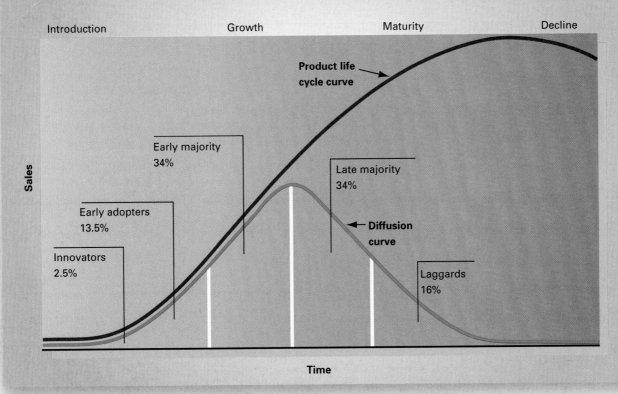

© Cengage Learning

ANATOMY OF A PRODUCT LIFE: VCR

VCR SALES DROPPED RAPIDLY IN THE FACE OF GROWING DVD COMPETITION.

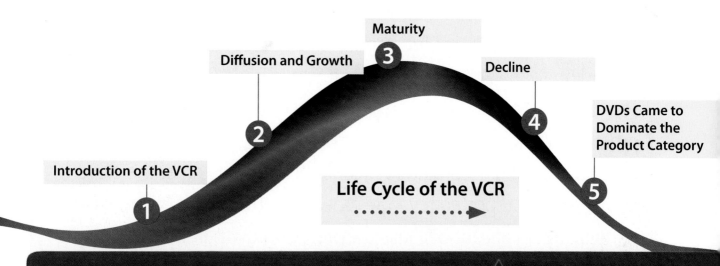

Maturity ③

Diffusion and Growth ②

Decline ④

DVDs Came to Dominate the Product Category ⑤

Introduction of the VCR ①

Life Cycle of the VCR
· · · · · · · · · · · · ·➤

Today, DVDs and even Blu-rays are under pressure from streaming video services like Netflix, Hulu, and Roku.

1977 VHS first sold in the United States

1992 100 millionth VCR sold

1997 First DVD titles released in the United States

2000 VCR sales peak at 23 million units

2001 DVD dollar sales surpass VHS sales

2006 More households own DVD players than VCRs

☐ 525/60   PCM 1, 2   ☐ STEREO   ☐ MONO
☐ 625/50   PCM 3, 4   ☐ STEREO   ☐ MONO

THE IMPORTANCE OF SERVICES

A service is the result of applying human or mechanical efforts to people or objects. Services involve a deed, a performance, or an effort that cannot be physically possessed. Today, the service sector substantially influences the U.S. economy. According to the Office of the United States Trade Representative, service industries accounted for 68 percent of U.S. gross domestic product (GDP) in 2012. These industries are responsible for four out of five U.S. jobs, and according to recent Census data, ten of the eleven service sectors reported revenue growth in 2011. These numbers are particularly significant because they reflect growth in the wake of the Great Recession. The largest gains came in the information services sector, particularly Internet publishing and broadcasting. The only sector to post a loss was the finance and insurance sector.[1]

In 2012, service industries accounted for 68 percent of U.S. GDP and four out of five U.S. jobs.

service the result of applying human or mechanical efforts to people or objects

The marketing process described in Chapter 1 is the same for all types of products, whether they are goods or services. In addition, although a comparison of goods and services marketing can be beneficial, in reality it is hard to distinguish clearly between manufacturing and service firms. Indeed, many manufacturing firms can point to service as a major factor in their success. For example, maintenance and repair services offered by the manufacturer are important to buyers of copy machines. Nevertheless, services have some unique characteristics that distinguish them from goods, and marketing strategies need to be adjusted for these characteristics.

Chapter **12**

Services and Nonprofit Organization Marketing

Learning Outcomes

After you finish this chapter go to
p227 *for* **STUDY TOOLS**

intangibility the inability of services to be touched, seen, tasted, heard, or felt in the same manner that goods can be sensed

search quality a characteristic that can be easily assessed before purchase

experience quality a characteristic that can be assessed only after use

credence quality a characteristic that consumers may have difficulty assessing even after purchase because they do not have the necessary knowledge or experience

inseparability the inability of the production and consumption of a service to be separated; consumers must be present during the production

heterogeneity the variability of the inputs and outputs of services, which causes services to tend to be less standardized and uniform than goods

12-2 HOW SERVICES DIFFER FROM GOODS

Services have four unique characteristics that distinguish them from goods. Services are intangible, inseparable, heterogeneous, and perishable.

12-2a Intangibility

The basic difference between services and goods is that services are intangible performances. Because of their **intangibility**, they cannot be touched, seen, tasted, heard, or felt in the same manner that goods can be sensed.

Evaluating the quality of services before or even after making a purchase is harder than evaluating the quality of goods because, compared to goods, services tend to exhibit fewer search qualities. A **search quality** is a characteristic that can be easily assessed before purchase—for instance, the color of an appliance or automobile. At the same time, services tend to exhibit more experience and credence qualities. An **experience quality** is a characteristic that can be assessed only after use, such as the quality of a meal in a restaurant. A **credence quality** is a characteristic that consumers may have difficulty assessing even after purchase because they do not have the necessary knowledge or experience. Medical and consulting services are examples of services that exhibit credence qualities.

These characteristics also make it harder for marketers to communicate the benefits of an intangible service than to communicate the benefits of tangible goods. Thus, marketers often rely on tangible cues to communicate a service's nature and quality. For example, Travelers Insurance

Company uses an umbrella symbol as a tangible reminder of the protection that insurance provides.

The facilities that customers visit, or from which services are delivered, are a critical tangible part of the total service offering. Messages about the organization are communicated to customers through such elements as the décor, the clutter or neatness of service areas, and the staff's manners and dress. Hotels know that guests form opinions quickly and are more willing to tweet them within the first fifteen minutes of their stay than ever before. Some hotels go to great lengths to make their guests feel at home right away. At the Ritz-Carlton, Toronto, the doormen radio guest names to the front desk and the bellhop so they can give them a personalized welcome.[2]

12-2b Inseparability

Goods are produced, sold, and then consumed. In contrast, services are often sold, produced, and consumed at the same time. In other words, their production and consumption are inseparable activities. This **inseparability** means that, because consumers must be present during the production of services like haircuts or surgery, they are actually involved in the production of the services they buy. That type of consumer involvement is rare in goods manufacturing.

Simultaneous production and consumption also means that services normally cannot be produced in a centralized location and consumed in decentralized locations, as goods typically are. Services are also inseparable from the perspective of the service provider. Thus, the quality of service that firms are able to deliver depends on the quality of their employees.

© James Steidl/Shutterstock.com

12-2c Heterogeneity

One great strength of McDonald's is consistency. Whether customers order a Big Mac in Chicago or Seattle, they know exactly what they are going to get. This is not the case with many service providers. Because services have greater **heterogeneity**, or variability of inputs and outputs, they tend to be less standardized and uniform than goods. For example, physicians in a group practice or barbers in a barbershop differ within each group in their technical and interpersonal skills. Because services tend to be labor intensive and production and consumption are inseparable, consistency and quality control can be hard to achieve.

Standardization and training help increase consistency and reliability. In the information technology sector, a number of certification programs are available to ensure that technicians are capable of working on (and within) complex enterprise software systems. Certifications such as the Cisco Certified Network Associate, CompTIA Security+, and Microsoft Certified Professional ensure a consistency of knowledge and ability among those who can pass these programs' rigorous exams.[3]

12-2d Perishability

Perishability is the fourth characteristic of services. **Perishability** refers to the inability of services to be stored, warehoused, or inventoried. An empty hotel room or airplane seat produces no revenue that day. The revenue is lost. Yet service organizations are often forced to turn away full-price customers during peak periods.

One of the most important challenges in many service industries is finding ways to synchronize supply and demand. The philosophy that some revenue is better than none has prompted many hotels to offer deep discounts on weekends and during the off-season.

12-3 SERVICE QUALITY

Because of the four unique characteristics of services, service quality is more difficult to define and measure than is the quality of tangible goods. Business executives rank the improvement of service quality as one of the most critical challenges facing them today.

Research has shown that customers evaluate service quality by the following five components:

▸▸ **Reliability:** the ability to perform the service dependably, accurately, and consistently. Reliability is performing the service right the first time. This component has been found to be the one most important to consumers.

▸▸ **Responsiveness:** the ability to provide prompt service. Examples of responsiveness include calling the customer back quickly, serving lunch fast to someone who is in a hurry, or mailing a transaction slip immediately. The ultimate in responsiveness is offering service twenty-four hours a day, seven days a week.

▸▸ **Assurance:** the knowledge and courtesy of employees and their ability to convey trust. Skilled employees who treat customers with respect and make customers feel that they can trust the firm exemplify assurance.

▸▸ **Empathy:** caring, individualized attention to customers. Firms whose employees recognize customers and learn their specific requirements are providing empathy.

▸▸ **Tangibles:** the physical evidence of the service. The tangible parts of a service include the physical facilities, tools, and equipment used to provide the service, as well as the appearance of personnel.[4]

Overall service quality is measured by combining customers' evaluations for all five components.

12-3a The Gap Model of Service Quality

A model of service quality called the **gap model** identifies five gaps that can cause problems in service delivery and influence customer evaluations of service quality.[5] These gaps are illustrated in Exhibit 1.

▸▸ **GAP 1:** the gap between what customers want and what management thinks customers want. This gap results from a lack of understanding or a misinterpretation of the customers' needs, wants, or desires. A firm that does little or no customer satisfaction research is likely to experience this gap. To close gap 1, firms must stay attuned to customer wishes by researching customer needs and satisfaction.

▸▸ **GAP 2:** the gap between what management thinks customers want and the quality specifications that management develops to provide the service. Essentially, this gap is the result of management's inability to translate customers' needs into delivery

---

perishability the inability of services to be stored, warehoused, or inventoried

reliability the ability to perform a service dependably, accurately, and consistently

responsiveness the ability to provide prompt service

assurance the knowledge and courtesy of employees and their ability to convey trust

empathy caring, individualized attention to customers

tangibles the physical evidence of a service, including the physical facilities, tools, and equipment used to provide the service

gap model a model identifying five gaps that can cause problems in service delivery and influence customer evaluations of service quality

Exhibit 1

GAP MODEL OF SERVICE QUALITY

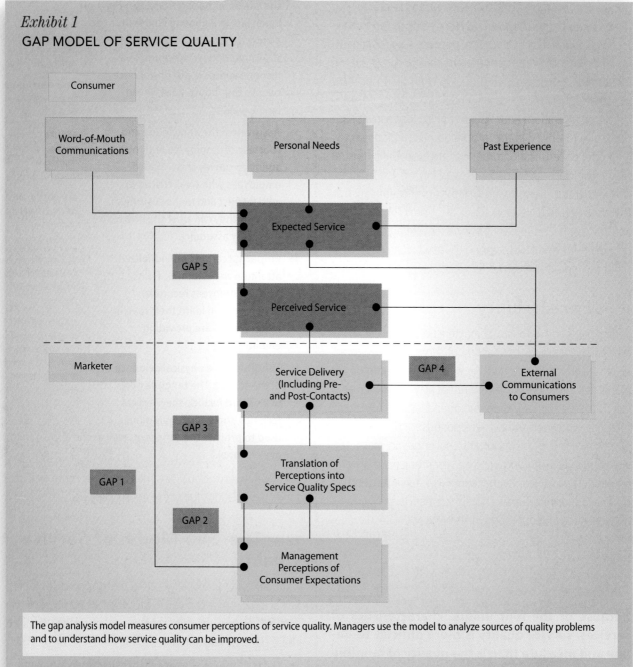

The gap analysis model measures consumer perceptions of service quality. Managers use the model to analyze sources of quality problems and to understand how service quality can be improved.

Source: From Valarie A. Zeithaml, Mary Jo Bitner, and Dwayne Gremler, *Services Marketing*, 6/e, © 2013 (New York: McGraw-Hill, 2012). Used by permission.

systems within the firm. For example, KFC used to rate its managers according to "chicken efficiency," or how much chicken they threw away at closing; customers who came in late would either have to wait for chicken to be cooked or settle for chicken several hours old.

▶▶ **GAP 3:** the gap between the service quality specifications and the service that is actually provided. If both gaps 1 and 2 have been closed, then gap 3 is due to the inability of management and employees to do

what should be done. Management needs to ensure that employees have the skills and the proper tools to perform their jobs. Other techniques that help to close gap 3 are training employees so they know what management expects and encouraging teamwork.

▶▶ **GAP 4:** the gap between what the company provides and what the customer is told it provides. This is clearly a communication gap. It may include misleading or deceptive advertising campaigns promising more than the firm can deliver or doing "whatever it takes" to get the business. To close this gap, companies need to create realistic customer expectations through honest, accurate communication about what the firms can provide.

▶▶ **GAP 5:** the gap between the service that customers receive and the service they want. This gap can be positive or negative. For example, if a patient expects to wait twenty minutes in the physician's office before seeing the physician but actually waits only ten minutes, the patient's evaluation of service quality will be high. However, a forty-minute wait would result in a lower evaluation.

When one or more of these gaps is large, service quality is perceived as low. As the gaps shrink, service quality

perception improves. In early 2013, Fifth Third Bank joined a growing number of financial institutions working quickly to close a persistent, gaping gap 1—customers' desire for full-featured mobile banking. To meet the needs of highly mobile, technologically tuned-in customers, Fifth Third launched a powerful mobile app whereby customers can view transactions, pay bills, transfer funds, or deposit checks simply by taking pictures of them with their smartphones. "The ways in which consumers interact with their bank are constantly evolving," said Larry McClanahan, vice president and director of Digital Delivery for Fifth Third Bank. "The enhancements we've made . . . reflect this shift in consumer preference and expectations."[7]

Several other companies consistently get their service quality right. According to MSN, the top five companies in terms of great customer service are:

1. **Amazon**
2. **Google**
3. **Apple**
4. **UPS**
5. **Hilton Worldwide**[8]

These companies have three core beliefs in common: good service starts at the top, service is seen as a continual challenge, and companies work best when people want to work for them.

HAS STARBUCKS FALLEN INTO GAP 3?

Starbucks used to stress the importance of "legendary service" during the company's extensive training program for new hires. However, a rash of labor cuts in recent years has both diminished the quality of Starbucks' barista training and forced employees to work longer hours with less help and resources—often resulting in a single stressed-out barista frantically working to serve a growing line of customers. The creeping incompetence, inaccuracy, and inattentiveness of Starbucks baristas was satirized in a *Saturday Night Live* skit in which even the automated Verismo espresso machine was neglectful and derisive toward its customers.[6]

© iStockphoto.com/billnoll / © B. O'Kane/Alamy

12-4 MARKETING MIXES FOR SERVICES

Services' unique characteristics—intangibility, inseparability of production and consumption, heterogeneity, and perishability—make marketing more challenging. Elements of the marketing mix (product, place, promotion, and pricing) need to be adjusted to meet the special needs created by these characteristics.

12-4a Product (Service) Strategy

A product, as defined in Chapter 10, is everything a person receives in an exchange. In the case of a service organization, the product offering is intangible and consists in large part of a process or a series of processes. Product strategies for service offerings include decisions on the type of process involved, core and supplementary services,

core service the most basic benefit the consumer is buying

supplementary services a group of services that support or enhance the core service

mass customization a strategy that uses technology to deliver customized services on a mass basis

standardization or customization of the service product, and the service mix.

SERVICE AS A PROCESS Two broad categories of things get processed in service organizations: people and objects. In some cases, the process is physical, or tangible, while in others the process is intangible. Based on these characteristics, service processes can be placed into one of four categories:

▸ **PEOPLE PROCESSING:** takes place when the service is directed at a customer. Examples are transportation services and health care.

▸ **POSSESSION PROCESSING:** occurs when the service is directed at customers' physical possessions. Examples are lawn care, dry cleaning, and veterinary services.

▸ **MENTAL STIMULUS PROCESSING:** refers to services directed at people's minds. Examples are theater performances and education.

▸ **INFORMATION PROCESSING:** describes services that use technology or brainpower directed at a customer's assets. Examples are insurance and consulting.[9]

Because customers' experiences and involvement differ for each of these types of services, marketing strategies may also differ. For example, people-processing services require customers to enter the *service factory*, which is a physical location, such as an aircraft, a physician's office, or a hair salon. In contrast, possession-processing services typically do not require the presence of the customer in the service factory. Marketing strategies for the former would therefore focus more on an attractive, comfortable physical environment and employee training on employee–customer interaction issues than would strategies for the latter.

CORE AND SUPPLEMENTARY SERVICE PRODUCTS The service offering can be viewed as a bundle of activities that includes the **core service**, which is the most basic benefit the customer is buying, and a group of **supplementary services** that support or enhance the core service. Exhibit 2 illustrates these concepts for a university. The core service

is education, which involves people processing. The supplementary services, some of which involve information processing, include food services, health care, parking, housing, and alumni services.

In many service industries, the core service becomes a commodity as competition increases. Thus, firms usually emphasize supplementary services to create a competitive advantage. On the other hand, some firms are positioning themselves in the marketplace by greatly reducing supplementary services.

CUSTOMIZATION/STANDARDIZATION An important issue in developing the service offering is whether to customize or standardize it. Customized services are more flexible and respond to individual customers' needs. They also usually command a higher price. Standardized services are more efficient and cost less.

Instead of choosing to either standardize or customize a service, a firm may incorporate elements of both by adopting an emerging strategy called **mass customization**. Mass customization uses technology to deliver customized services on a mass basis, which results in giving each customer whatever she or he asks for. For example, Swiss educational tech company Glubal (styled "glubal") recently launched an online service whereby prospective students can build their own academic programs based on course information provided by universities and other

Exhibit 2
CORE AND SUPPLEMENTARY SERVICES FOR A UNIVERSITY

Food Service
Financial Aid
Parking
Fitness
Community learning
Core Service
Janitorial Services
Education
Counseling (Career and Degree)
Entertainment
Alumni Services
Supplementary Services
Health Care
Housing

© Cengage Learning

Joleon Lescott and James Vaughan design customized Nike sneakers in Liverpool, England's NikeTown iD Studio. Nike iD is an example of mass customization, employing technology to deliver customized shoes, apparel, and bags on a mass basis.

educational facilities connected to the network. glubal offers students the opportunity to customize available offers to match their needs, locations, and life situations.[10]

THE SERVICE MIX Most service organizations market more than one service. For example, TruGreen offers lawn care, shrub care, carpet cleaning, and industrial lawn services. Each organization's service mix represents a set of opportunities, risks, and challenges. Each part of the service mix should make a different contribution to achieving the firm's goals. To succeed, each service may also need a different level of financial support. Designing a service strategy, therefore, means deciding what new services to introduce to which target market, what existing services to maintain, and what services to eliminate.

12-4b Place (Distribution) Strategy

Distribution strategies for service organizations must focus on such issues as convenience, number of outlets, direct versus indirect distribution, location, and scheduling. A key factor influencing the selection of a service provider is *convenience*. An interesting example of this is Kitchit. Hosting a large party is a huge undertaking, particularly if food is involved. Figuring out what to serve, how much to make, and where to get ingredients is a time-consuming process, particularly for those not in the food industry. Kitchit connects diners and party planners with high-profile chefs, providing chefs a new way to distribute their services. Event hosts choose from a variety of chefs in their area, then provide their chosen chef details about the event

such as location, number of guests, and how much they would like to spend. Once the chef agrees, he takes care of all the agreed-upon details, including shopping, cooking, and cleaning. Costs range from $40 a person for basic menus to more than $3,500 a guest for six course meals including wine and décor.[11]

An important distribution objective for many service firms is the number of outlets to use or the number of outlets to open during a certain time. Generally, the intensity of distribution should meet, but not exceed, the target market's needs and preferences. Having too few outlets may inconvenience customers; having too many outlets may boost costs unnecessarily. Intensity of distribution may also depend on the image desired. Having only a few outlets may make the service seem more exclusive or selective.

The next service distribution decision is whether to distribute services to end users *directly* or *indirectly* through other firms. Because of the intangible nature of services, many service firms have to use direct distribution or franchising. Examples include legal, medical, accounting, and personal-care services. The newest form of direct distribution is the Internet. Most major airlines are now using online services to sell tickets directly to consumers, which results in lower distribution costs for the airlines. Other firms with standardized service packages have developed indirect channels using independent intermediaries. For example, Bank of America offers teller and loan services to customers in small satellite facilities at Albertsons grocery stores in Texas.

The *location* of a service most clearly reveals the relationship between its target market strategy and distribution strategy. For time-dependent service providers such as airlines, physicians, and dentists, *scheduling* is often a more important factor.

12-4c Promotion Strategy

Consumers and business users have more trouble evaluating services than goods because services are less tangible. In turn, marketers have more trouble promoting intangible services than tangible goods. Here are four promotion strategies they can try:

▸ **STRESSING TANGIBLE CUES:** A tangible cue is a concrete symbol of the service offering. To make their intangible services more tangible, hotels turn down the bedcovers and put mints on the pillows. DoubleTree hotels offer their guests a warm chocolate chip cookie as they check in.

▸ **USING PERSONAL INFORMATION SOURCES:** A personal information source is someone consumers are familiar with (such as a celebrity) or someone they admire or can relate to personally. Service firms may seek to simulate positive word-of-mouth communication among present and prospective customers by using real customers in their ads.

▸ **CREATING A STRONG ORGANIZATIONAL IMAGE:** One way to create an image is to manage the evidence, including the physical environment of the service facility, the appearance of the service employees, and the tangible items associated with a service (such as stationery, bills, and business cards). For example, McDonald's golden arches are instantly recognizable. Another way to create an image is through branding.

▸ **ENGAGING IN POSTPURCHASE COMMUNICATION:** Postpurchase communication refers to the follow-up activities that a service firm might engage in after a customer transaction. Postcard surveys, telephone calls, and other types of follow-up show customers that their feedback matters.

PROFESSION: PILOT
CAREER: ACTOR

Celebrity endorsements can decrease perceived risk in choosing a service. For example, John Travolta endorses Breitling watches for their quality and endurance.

12-4d Price Strategy

Considerations in pricing a service are similar to the pricing considerations to be discussed in Chapters 19 and 20. However, the unique characteristics of services present two special pricing challenges.

First, in order to price a service, it is important to define the unit of service consumption. For example, should pricing be based on completing a specific service task (cutting a customer's hair), or should it be time based (how long it takes to cut a customer's hair)? Some services include the consumption of goods, such as food and beverages. Restaurants charge customers for food and drink rather than the use of a table and chairs.

Second, for services that are composed of multiple elements, the issue is whether pricing should be based on a "bundle" of elements or whether each element should be priced separately. A bundled price may be preferable when consumers dislike having to pay "extra" for every part of the service (e.g., paying extra for baggage or food on an airplane), and it is simpler for the firm to administer. Alternatively, customers may not want to pay for service elements they do not use. Many furniture stores now have "unbundled" delivery charges from the price of the furniture. Customers who wish to can pick up the furniture at the store, saving on the delivery fee.

Marketers should set performance objectives when pricing each service. Three categories of pricing objectives have been suggested:

▸▸ **REVENUE-ORIENTED PRICING** focuses on maximizing the surplus of income over costs. This is the same approach that many manufacturing companies use. A limitation of this approach is that determining costs can be difficult for many services.

▸▸ **OPERATIONS-ORIENTED PRICING** seeks to match supply and demand by varying prices. For example, matching hotel demand to the number of available rooms can be achieved by raising prices at peak times and decreasing them during slow times.

▸▸ **PATRONAGE-ORIENTED PRICING** tries to maximize the number of customers using the service. Thus, prices vary with different market segments' ability to pay, and methods of payment (such as credit) are offered that increase the likelihood of a purchase. Senior citizen and student discounts at movie theaters and restaurants are examples of patronage-oriented pricing.[12]

A firm may need to use more than one type of pricing objective. In fact, all three objectives probably need to be included to some degree in a pricing strategy, although the importance of each type may vary depending on the type of service provided, the prices that competitors are charging, the differing ability of various customer segments to pay, or the opportunity to negotiate price. For customized services (such as construction services), customers may also have the ability to negotiate a price.

12-5 RELATIONSHIP MARKETING IN SERVICES

Many services involve ongoing interaction between the service organization and the customer. Thus, they can benefit from relationship marketing, the strategy described in Chapter 1, as a means of attracting, developing, and retaining customer relationships. The idea is to develop strong loyalty by creating satisfied customers who will buy additional services from the firm and are unlikely to switch to a competitor. Satisfied customers are also likely to engage in positive word-of-mouth communication, thereby helping to bring in new customers.

Many businesses have found that it is more cost-effective to hang on to the customers they have than to focus only on attracting new ones. A bank executive, for example, found that increasing customer retention by 2 percent can have the same effect on profits as reducing costs by 10 percent.

Services that purchasers receive on a continuing basis (e.g., cable television, banking, insurance) can be considered membership services. This type of service naturally lends itself to relationship marketing. When services involve discrete transactions (e.g., in a movie theater, at a restaurant, or on public transportation), it may be more difficult to build membership-type relationships with customers. Nevertheless, services involving discrete transactions may be transformed into membership relationships using marketing tools. For example, the service could be sold in bulk (e.g., a theater series subscription or a commuter pass on public transportation). Or a service firm could offer special benefits to customers who choose to register with the firm (e.g., loyalty programs for hotels and airlines). The service firm that has a more formalized relationship with its customers has an advantage because it knows who its customers are and how and when they use the services offered.[13]

Relationship marketing can be practiced at three levels:

▸▸ **LEVEL 1:** The firm uses pricing incentives to encourage customers to continue doing business with it. Frequent-flyer programs are an example of level 1 relationship marketing. This level of relationship marketing is the least effective in the long term because its price-based advantage is easily imitated by other firms.

▸▸ **LEVEL 2:** This level of relationship marketing also uses pricing incentives but seeks to build social bonds with customers. The firm stays in touch with customers, learns about their needs, and designs services to meet those needs. Level 2 relationship marketing is often more effective than level 1 relationship marketing.

▸▸ **LEVEL 3:** At this level, the firm again uses financial and social bonds but adds structural bonds to the formula. Structural bonds are developed by offering value-added services that are not readily available from other firms.[14] Many high-end hotels leave treats in repeat-guests' hotel rooms when they celebrate special events, such as a cake for a couple celebrating their anniversary. They also leave treats in rooms where guests have children and boxes of chocolates for returning guests who send positive tweets about the hotel.[15]

© iStockphoto.com/Jan Tyler

12-6 INTERNAL MARKETING IN SERVICE FIRMS

Services are performances, so the quality of a firm's employees is an important part of building long-term relationships with customers. Employees who like their jobs and are satisfied with the firm they work for are more likely to deliver superior service to customers. In other words, a firm that makes its employees happy has a better chance of retaining customers. Thus, it is critical that service firms practice **internal marketing**, which means treating employees as customers and developing systems and benefits that satisfy their needs. While this strategy may also apply to goods manufacturers, it is even more critical in service firms. This is because in service industries, employees deliver the brand promise—their performance as a brand representative—directly to customers. To satisfy employees, companies have designed and instituted a wide variety of programs such as flextime, on-site day care, and concierge services. SAS Institute offers its employees unlimited sick time, free health care, intramural sports leagues, and the option of subsidized Montessori child care.[16]

12-7 NONPROFIT ORGANIZATION MARKETING

A nonprofit organization is an organization that exists to achieve some goal other than the usual business goals of profit, market share, or return on investment. Both nonprofit organizations and private-sector service firms market intangible products, and both often require the customer to be present during the production process. Both for-profit and nonprofit services vary greatly from producer to producer and from day to day, even from the same producer.

Few people realize that nonprofit organizations account for more than 20 percent of the economic activity in the United States. The cost of government (i.e., taxes), the predominant form of nonprofit organization, has become the biggest single item in the American family budget—more than housing, food, or health care. Together, federal, state, and local governments collect tax revenues that amount to more than one-third of the U.S. GDP. In addition to government entities, nonprofit organizations include hundreds of thousands of private museums, theaters, schools, and churches.

12-7a What Is Nonprofit Organization Marketing?

Nonprofit organization marketing is the effort by nonprofit organizations to bring about mutually satisfying exchanges with target markets. Although these organizations vary substantially in size and purpose and operate in different environments, most perform the following marketing activities:

- **Identify the customers they wish to serve or attract (although they usually use other terms, such as clients, patients, members, or sponsors)**
- **Explicitly or implicitly specify objectives**
- **Develop, manage, and eliminate programs and services**
- **Decide on prices to charge (although they use other terms, such as fees, donations, tuition, fares, fines, or rates)**
- **Schedule events or programs, and determine where they will be held or where services will be offered**
- **Communicate their availability through brochures, signs, public service announcements, or advertisements**

Often, the nonprofit organizations that carry out these functions do not realize they are engaged in marketing.

12-7b Unique Aspects of Nonprofit Organization Marketing Strategies

Like their counterparts in business organizations, nonprofit managers develop marketing strategies to bring about mutually satisfying exchanges with target markets. However, marketing in nonprofit organizations is unique in many ways—including the setting of marketing objectives, the selection of target markets, and the development of appropriate marketing mixes.

OBJECTIVES In the private sector, the profit motive is both an objective for guiding decisions and a criterion for evaluating results. Nonprofit organizations do

not seek to make a profit for redistribution to owners or shareholders. Rather, their focus is often on generating enough funds to cover expenses.

Most nonprofit organizations are expected to provide equitable, effective, and efficient services that respond to the wants and preferences of multiple constituencies. These include users, payers, donors, politicians, appointed officials, the media, and the general public. Nonprofit organizations cannot measure their success or failure in strictly financial terms.

The lack of a financial "bottom line" and the existence of multiple, diverse, intangible, and sometimes vague or conflicting objectives make prioritizing objectives, making decisions, and evaluating performance hard for nonprofit managers. They must often use approaches different from the ones commonly used in the private sector.

TARGET MARKETS Three issues relating to target markets are unique to nonprofit organizations:

- **APATHETIC OR STRONGLY OPPOSED TARGETS:** Private-sector organizations usually give priority to developing those market segments that are most likely to respond to particular offerings. In contrast, nonprofit organizations must often target

nonprofit organization marketing the effort by nonprofit organizations to bring about mutually satisfying exchanges with target markets

Russell Brand (left) and Mitch Winehouse speak on behalf of the Amy Winehouse Foundation at a 2013 press conference. The nonprofit foundation, established in memory of English singer-songwriter Amy Winehouse, leverages Brand's star power and other unique marketing strategies to provide support and education for troubled youths.

AP Images/Joel Ryan/Invision

those who are apathetic about or strongly opposed to receiving their services, such as vaccinations and psychological counseling.

» **PRESSURE TO ADOPT UNDIFFERENTI-ATED SEGMENTATION STRATEGIES:** Nonprofit organizations often adopt undifferentiated strategies (see Chapter 8) by default. Sometimes they fail to recognize the advantages of targeting, or an undifferentiated approach may appear to offer economies of scale and low per-capita costs. In other instances, nonprofit organizations are pressured or required to serve the maximum number of people by targeting the average user.

» **COMPLEMENTARY POSITIONING:** The main role of many nonprofit organizations is to provide services, with available resources, to those who are not adequately served by private-sector organizations. As a result, the nonprofit organization must often complement, rather than compete with, the efforts of others. The positioning task is to identify underserved market segments and to develop marketing programs that match their needs rather than target the niches that may be most profitable. For example, a university library may see itself as complementing the services of the public library rather than as competing with it.

PRODUCT DECISIONS There are three product-related distinctions between business and nonprofit organizations:

» **BENEFIT COMPLEXITY:** Nonprofit organizations often market complex behaviors or ideas. Examples include the need to exercise or eat right and the need to quit smoking. The benefits that a person receives are complex, long term, and intangible, and therefore are more difficult to communicate to consumers.

» **BENEFIT STRENGTH:** The benefit strength of many nonprofit offerings is quite weak or indirect. What are the direct, personal benefits to you of driving 55 miles per hour or donating blood? In contrast,

In August 2012, global nonprofit organization Avaaz unveiled this hard-hitting advertising campaign calling on South African President Jacob Zuma to ban the sale and trade of lion bones.

most private-sector service organizations can offer customers direct, personal benefits in an exchange relationship.

▸ **INVOLVEMENT:** Many nonprofit organizations market products that elicit very low involvement ("Prevent forest fires") or very high involvement ("Stop smoking"). The typical range for private-sector goods is much narrower. Traditional promotional tools may be inadequate to motivate adoption of either low- or high-involvement products.

PLACE (DISTRIBUTION) DECISIONS A nonprofit organization's capacity for distributing its service offerings to potential customer groups when and where they want them is typically a key variable in determining the success of those service offerings. For example, many large universities have one or more satellite campus locations to provide easier access for students in other areas. Some educational institutions also offer classes to students at off-campus locations through the use of interactive video technology or at home via the Internet.

The extent to which a service depends on fixed facilities has important implications for distribution decisions. Services like rail transit and lake fishing can be delivered only at specific points. Many nonprofit services, however, do not depend on special facilities.

PROMOTION DECISIONS Many nonprofit organizations are explicitly or implicitly prohibited from advertising, thus limiting their promotion options. Most federal agencies fall into this category. Other nonprofit organizations simply do not have the resources to retain advertising agencies, promotion consultants, or marketing staff. However, nonprofit organizations have a few special promotion resources to call on:

▸ **PROFESSIONAL VOLUNTEERS:** Nonprofit organizations often seek out marketing, sales, and advertising professionals to help them develop and implement promotion strategies. In some instances, an advertising agency donates its services in exchange for potential long-term benefits. Donated services create goodwill; personal contacts; and general

Courtesy of The American Academy of Orthopaedic Surgeons and the Orthopaedic Trauma Association (2010)

GET THE MESSAGE.
TEXTING WHILE DRIVING IS A DEADLY DISTRACTION.

AUTO ALLIANCE
DRIVING INNOVATION®

ORTHOPAEDIC
—TRAUMA—
ASSOCIATION

AAOS
AMERICAN ACADEMY OF
ORTHOPAEDIC SURGEONS

Join the conversation.
Visit DecideToDrive.org.

This is one example of a recent PSA. Others include increasing nutritional awareness to combat obesity and anti-tobacco ads.

awareness of the donor's organization, reputation, and competency.

▸▸ **SALES PROMOTION ACTIVITIES:** Sales promotion activities that use existing services or other resources are increasingly being used to draw attention to the offerings of nonprofit organizations. Sometimes nonprofit charities even team up with other companies for promotional activities.

▸▸ **PUBLIC SERVICE ADVERTISING:** A **public service advertisement (PSA)** is an announcement that promotes a program of a federal, state, or local government or of a nonprofit organization. Unlike a commercial advertiser, the sponsor of the PSA does not pay for the time or space. Instead, it is donated by the medium. PSAs are used, for example, to help educate students about the dangers of misusing and abusing prescription drugs, as well as where to seek treatment for substance abuse problems.

PRICING DECISIONS Five key characteristics distinguish the pricing decisions of nonprofit organizations from those of the profit sector:

▸▸ **PRICING OBJECTIVES:** The main pricing objective in the profit sector is revenue or, more specifically, profit maximization, sales maximization, or target return on sales or investment. Many nonprofit organizations must also be concerned about revenue. Often, however, nonprofit organizations seek to either partially or fully defray costs rather than to achieve a profit for distribution to stockholders. Nonprofit organizations also seek to redistribute income—for instance, through taxation and sliding-scale fees. Moreover, they strive to allocate resources

public service advertisement (PSA) an announcement that promotes a program of a federal, state, or local government or of a nonprofit organization

© iStockphoto.com/dem10

fairly among individuals or households or across geographic or political boundaries.

» **NONFINANCIAL PRICES:** In many nonprofit situations, consumers are not charged a monetary price but instead must absorb nonmonetary costs. The importance of those costs is illustrated by the large number of eligible citizens who do not take advantage of so-called "free" services for the poor. In many public assistance programs, about half the people who are eligible don't participate. Nonmonetary costs include time, embarrassment, and effort.

» **INDIRECT PAYMENT:** Indirect payment through taxes is common to marketers of "free" services, such as libraries, fire protection, and police protection. Indirect payment is not a common practice in the profit sector.

» **SEPARATION BETWEEN PAYERS AND USERS:** By design, the services of many charitable organizations are provided for those who are relatively poor and are largely paid for by those who are better off financially. Although examples of separation between payers and users can be found in the profit sector (such as insurance claims), the practice is much less prevalent.

» **BELOW-COST PRICING:** An example of below-cost pricing is university tuition. Virtually all private and public colleges and universities price their services below full cost.

12-8 GLOBAL ISSUES IN SERVICES MARKETING

The international marketing of services is a major part of global business, and the United States has become the world's largest exporter of services. Competition in international services is increasing rapidly, but many U.S. service industries have been able to enter the global marketplace because of their competitive advantages. U.S. banks, for example, have advantages in customer service and collections management.

For both for-profit and nonprofit service firms, the first step toward success in the global marketplace is determining the nature of the company's core products. Then, the marketing mix elements (additional services, place, promotion, pricing, and distribution) should be designed to take into account each country's cultural, technological, and political environment.

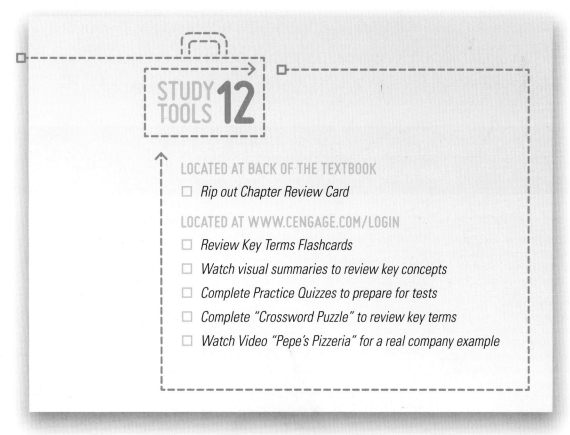

STUDY TOOLS 12

LOCATED AT BACK OF THE TEXTBOOK
☐ *Rip out Chapter Review Card*

LOCATED AT WWW.CENGAGE.COM/LOGIN
☐ *Review Key Terms Flashcards*
☐ *Watch visual summaries to review key concepts*
☐ *Complete Practice Quizzes to prepare for tests*
☐ *Complete "Crossword Puzzle" to review key terms*
☐ *Watch Video "Pepe's Pizzeria" for a real company example*

13-1 SUPPLY CHAINS AND SUPPLY CHAIN MANAGEMENT

Many modern companies are turning to supply chain management for competitive advantage. A company's **supply chain** includes all of the companies involved in all of the upstream and downstream flows of products, services, finances, and information, from initial suppliers (the point of origin) to the ultimate customer (the point of consumption). The goal of **supply chain management** is to coordinate and integrate all of the activities performed by supply chain members into a seamless process, from the source to the point of consumption, ultimately giving supply chain managers "total visibility" of the supply chain both inside and outside the firm. The philosophy behind supply chain management is that by visualizing the entire supply chain, supply chain managers can maximize strengths and efficiencies at each level to balance the supply and demand needs of each member in the supply chain. Understanding and integrating supply and demand information at every level will allow supply chain managers to optimize their decisions, reduce waste, and respond quickly to sudden changes in the supply chain.

In today's marketplace, products are being driven by customer demand and businesses' need to balance demand with supply.

supply chain the connected chain of all of the business entities, both internal and external to the company, that perform or support the logistics function

supply chain management a management system that coordinates and integrates all of the activities performed by supply chain members into a seamless process, from the source to the point of consumption, resulting in enhanced customer and economic value

Supply chain management reflects a completely customer-driven management philosophy. In the mass production era, manufacturers produced standardized products that were "pushed" down through marketing channels to consumers, who were convinced by salespeople to buy whatever was produced. In today's marketplace, however, customers who expect to receive product configurations and services matched to their unique needs are driving demand. The focus of businesses has shifted to determining how products and services are being "pulled" into the marketplace and partnering with members of the supply chain to enhance customer value. For example, when Ford launched the Focus Electric subcompact car in 2012, the company used a

Supply Chain Management

Learning Outcomes

After you finish this chapter go to
p245 *for* **STUDY TOOLS** - - - - - - →

"build-to-order" system, allowing every customer to customize his or her car and receive it within six weeks.[1]

This reversal of the flow of demand from "push" to "pull" has resulted in a radical reformulation of traditional marketing, production, and distribution functions toward a philosophy of **supply chain agility**. Agile companies synchronize their activities through the sharing of supply and demand information, spend more time than their competitors on activities that create direct customer benefits, partner closely with suppliers and service providers to reduce customer wait times for products, and constantly seek to reduce supply chain complexity through the evaluation and reduction of nonperforming stock-keeping units (SKUs), among other strategies. By managing the product pipeline in this way, companies are able to reduce supply chain costs while at the same time offering better service and therefore can deliver improved products at better prices to customers.

13-1a Benefits of Supply Chain Management

Supply chain management is a key means of differentiation for a firm and a critical component in marketing and corporate strategy. Companies that focus on supply chain management commonly report lower inventory, transportation, warehousing, and packaging costs; greater supply chain flexibility; improved customer service; and higher revenues. Research has shown a clear relationship between supply chain performance and profitability. Additionally, because well-managed supply chains are able to provide better value to customers with only marginal incremental expenditure on company assets, best-in-class supply chain companies such as Kimberly-Clark are becoming significantly more valuable investments for investors. Kimberly-Clark decided in 2004 to reorganize its supply chains by reducing distribution centers, increasing flexibility, and making its supply chain more "demand-driven." As a result, the company has decreased forecast errors by 15 to 35 percent each week, reduced fuel consumption by 2.4 million gallons per year, and reduced overall supply chain costs by millions of dollars per year.[2]

13-2 SUPPLY CHAIN INTEGRATION

A key principle of supply chain management is that multiple firms and their functional areas work together to perform tasks as a single, unified system rather than as several individual companies or business units acting in isolation. Companies in a world-class supply chain combine their resources, capabilities, and innovations across multiple business functions such that they are used for the best interest of the entire supply chain as a whole. The goal is that the overall performance of the supply chain will be greater than the sum of its parts. As firms become increasingly supply chain oriented, they develop management practices that are consistent with this system-oriented approach.

Management practices that reflect a highly coordinated effort between supply chain firms or across business functions within the same or different firms are said to be "integrated." In other words, **supply chain integration** occurs when multiple firms or their functional areas in a supply chain coordinate business processes so that they are seamlessly linked to one another. In a world-class supply chain, the customer may not know where the business activities of one firm or business unit end and where those of another begin—all the participating firms and business units appear to be reading from the same script.

In a supply chain, agility, which involves having a nimble quality recognized in many athletes, allows companies to adapt quickly to customer needs while reducing costs and increasing satisfaction.

© ostill/Shutterstock.com

In the modern supply chain, integration can be either internal or external to a focal firm or, in an ideal scenario, both. From an internal perspective, the very best companies develop a managerial orientation toward **demand-supply integration (DSI)**. Under the DSI philosophy, those functional areas in the company charged with creating customer demand (such as marketing, sales, or research/development) communicate frequently and are synchronized with the parts of the business charged with fulfilling the created demand (purchasing, manufacturing, and logistics). This type of alignment enhances customer satisfaction by ensuring that, for example, salespeople make promises to customers that can actually be delivered on or that raw materials being purchased actually meet customer specifications before they are placed into the process. Simultaneously, the company gains efficiencies from ordering and using only those materials that lead directly to sales. In short, companies operating under a DSI philosophy are better at their business because all of the different divisions within the company "play from the same sheet of music."[3]

Additionally, the practice of world-class supply chain management requires that different companies act as if a single mission and leadership connect them. To accomplish this task across companies that have different ownership and interests, five types of external integration are sought by firms interested in providing top-level service to customers:[4]

▸▸ **RELATIONSHIP INTEGRATION** is the ability of two or more companies to develop social connections that serve to guide their interactions when working together. More specifically, relationship integration is the capability to develop and maintain a shared mental framework across companies that describes how they will depend on one another when working together. This includes the ways in which they will collaborate on activities or projects so that the customer gains the maximum amount of total value possible from the supply chain.

▸▸ **MEASUREMENT INTEGRATION** reflects the idea that performance assessments should be transparent and measurable across the borders of different firms, and should also assess the performance of the supply chain as a whole while holding each individual firm or business unit accountable for meeting its own goals.

▸▸ **TECHNOLOGY AND PLANNING INTEGRATION** refers to the creation and maintenance of information technology systems that connect managers across the firms in the supply chain; it requires information hardware and software systems that can exchange information when needed between customers, suppliers, and internal operational areas of each of the supply chain partners.

▸▸ **MATERIAL AND SERVICE SUPPLIER INTEGRATION** requires firms to link seamlessly to those outsiders that provide goods and services to them so that they can streamline work processes and thereby provide smooth, high-quality customer experiences. Both sides need to have a common vision of the total value creation process and be willing to share the responsibility for satisfying customer requirements to make supplier integration successful.

▸▸ **CUSTOMER INTEGRATION** is a competency that enables firms to offer long-lasting, distinctive, value-added offerings to those customers who represent the greatest value to the firm or supply chain. Highly customer-integrated firms assess their own

demand-supply integration (DSI) a supply chain operational philosophy focused on integrating the supply-management and demand-generating functions of an organization

Relationally integrated supply chains have a set of rules, policies, and/or procedures that dictate how firms will work together and that specify how conflicts among supply chain partners will be resolved.

© Max Blain/Shutterstock.com

business processes bundles of interconnected activities that stretch across firms in the supply chain

customer relationship management (CRM) process allows companies to prioritize their marketing focus on different customer groups according to each group's long-term value to the company or supply chain

capabilities and then match them to customers whose desires they can meet and who offer large enough sales potential for the linkage to be profitable over the long term.

Organizational success in achieving both the internal and external types of integration is very important. Highly integrated supply chains (those that are successful in achieving many or all of these types of integration) have been shown to be better at satisfying customers, managing costs, delivering high-quality products, enhancing productivity, and utilizing company or business unit assets, all of which translate into greater profitability for the firms and their partners working together in the supply chain.

Integration involves a balance between barriers and enablers. Companies that work closely with their suppliers encounter problems such as corporate culture, information hoarding, and trust issues. For example, Häagen-Dazs and General Mills share information with their vanilla suppliers to increase yields and improve sustainability practices, but at the same time, giving supply chain partners this information enables those partners to share it with competitors. On the other hand, integration can be improved through long-term agreements, cross-organizational integrated product teams, and improved communication between partners. These factors all aid in integrating supply chain operations.[5]

13-3 THE KEY PROCESSES OF SUPPLY CHAIN MANAGEMENT

When firms practice good supply chain management, their functional departments or areas, such as marketing, research and development, and/or production, are integrated both within and across the linked firms. Integration, then, is "how" excellent supply chain management works. The business processes on which the linked firms work together represent the "what" of supply chain management—they are the objects of focus on which firms, departments, areas, and people work together when seeking to reduce supply chain costs or to generate additional revenues. **Business**

processes are composed of bundles of interconnected activities that stretch across firms in the supply chain; they represent key areas that some or all of the involved firms are constantly working on to reduce costs and/or generate revenues for everyone throughout supply chain management. There are eight critical business processes on which supply chain managers must focus:

1. **Customer relationship management**
2. **Customer service management**
3. **Demand management**
4. **Order fulfillment**
5. **Manufacturing flow management**
6. **Supplier relationship management**
7. **Product development and commercialization**
8. **Returns management**[6]

13-3a Customer Relationship Management

The **customer relationship management (CRM) process** allows companies to prioritize their marketing focus on different customer groups according to each group's long-term value to the company or supply chain. Once higher-value customers are identified, firms should focus more on providing customized products and better service to this group than to others. The CRM process includes customer segmentation by value and subsequent generation of customer loyalty for the most attractive segments. This process provides a set of comprehensive principles for the initiation and maintenance of customer relationships and is often carried out with the assistance of specialized CRM computer software. For example, C. H. Briggs, a specialty building materials distributor, integrated CRM software as part of an effort to serve its customers better. With this software, each company sales representative has access to every customer's purchasing history. With this information, representatives can shape the sales process to specific customers and uncover opportunities to improve service and decision-making throughout the company.[7]

13-3b Customer Service Management

Whereas the CRM process is designed to identify and build relationships with good customers, the customer service management process is designed to ensure that those customer relationships remain strong. The **customer service management process** presents a multi-company, unified response system to the customer whenever complaints, concerns, questions, or comments are voiced. When the process is well executed, it can have a strong positive impact on revenues, often as a result of quick positive response to negative customer feedback, and sometimes even in the form of additional sales gained through the additional customer contact. Customers expect service from the moment a product is purchased until it is disposed of, and the customer service management process allows for touch points between the buyer and seller throughout this life cycle. The use of customer care software enables companies to enhance their customer service management process. Dell's customer support software, Clear View, enables staff members at the tech company's customer service command centers to view information from Dell's internal systems (as well as that of its partners) in real time. This information is combined with a geographical system that allows Dell to match each customer's complaint with the proper service dispatch center, making its response both rapid and effective.[8]

13-3c Demand Management

The **demand management process** seeks to align supply and demand throughout the supply chain by anticipating customer requirements at each level and creating demand-related plans of action prior to actual customer purchasing behavior. At the same time, demand management seeks to minimize the costs of serving multiple types of customers who have variable wants and needs. In other words, the demand management process allows companies in the supply chain to satisfy customers in the most efficient and effective ways possible. The activities such as collecting customer data, forecasting future demand, and developing activities that serve to "smooth out" demand help bring available inventory into alignment with customer desires.

Though it is very difficult to predict exactly what items and quantities customers will buy prior to purchase, demand management can ease the pressure on the production process and allow companies to satisfy most of their customers through greater flexibility in manufacturing, marketing, and sales programs. Much of the uncertainty in demand planning can be mitigated, however, by conducting collaborative planning, forecasting, and replenishment (CPFR) activities with the company's customers and suppliers. Nissan's

Sunderland, United Kingdom, plant brings several different subassemblies together into one final assembly area using integrated machinery and a carefully monitored production process. The different subassemblies arrive just as the final assemblers are ready to work on them instead of keeping large amounts of inventory on hand. One of the most important features of this process is that the speed of the assembly line can be adjusted to match customer demand.[9]

One of the most fundamental processes in supply chain management is the order fulfillment process, which involves generating, filling, delivering, and providing on-the-spot service for customer orders. The **order fulfillment process** is a highly integrated

British Prime Minister David Cameron (center) talks to Production Supervisor Paul Kerry (left) and Executive Vice President of Nissan Andy Palmer as they view a battery used to power the electric Nissan Leaf hatchback during a visit to the Sunderland Nissan factory in March 2013.

© AFP/Getty Images

manufacturing flow management process concerned with ensuring that firms in the supply chain have the needed resources to manufacture with flexibility and to move products through a multi-stage production process

supplier relationship management process supports manufacturing flow by identifying and maintaining relationships with highly valued suppliers

process, often requiring persons from multiple companies and multiple functions to come together and coordinate to create customer satisfaction at a given place and time. The best order fulfillment processes reduce the time between order and customer receipt as much as possible while ensuring that the customer receives exactly what he or she wants. The shorter lead times are beneficial in that they allow firms to carry reduced inventory levels and free up cash that can be used on other projects. Overall, the order fulfillment process involves understanding both internal capabilities and external customer needs, and matching these together so that the supply chain maximizes profits while minimizing costs and waste. Amazon.com now uses Kiva robots to help workers pack three to four times as many orders per hour. The robots bring shelves to the packer based on what is in each customer's order, and the packer picks the correct item, packs it, and sends it off on another robot to be shipped, making the order fulfillment process in Amazon's warehouses go much faster.[10]

13-3e Manufacturing Flow Management

The **manufacturing flow management process** is concerned with ensuring that firms in the supply chain have the needed resources to manufacture with flexibility and to move products through a multi-stage production process. Firms with flexible manufacturing have the ability to create a wide variety of goods and/or services with minimized costs associated with changing production techniques. The manufacturing flow process includes much more than simple production of goods and services—it means creating flexible agreements with suppliers and shippers so that unexpected demand bursts can be accommodated.

The goals of the manufacturing flow management process are centered on leveraging the capabilities held by multiple members of the supply chain to improve overall manufacturing output in terms of quality, delivery speed, and flexibility, all of which tie to profitability. Depending on the product, supply chain managers may choose between a lean or agile supply chain strategy. In a lean supply chain, products are built before demand occurs, but

managers attempt to reduce as much waste as possible. Lean supply chains first appeared within the Toyota Production System (TPS) as early as the 1950s. Agile strategies lie on the other end of the continuum—they emphasize responsiveness as opposed to waste reduction. Instead of trying to forecast demand and reduce waste, agile supply chains wait for demand to occur and use communication and flexibility to fill that demand quickly.[11]

13-3f Supplier Relationship Management

The **supplier relationship management process** is closely related to the manufacturing flow management process and contains several characteristics that parallel the customer relationship management process. The manufacturing flow management process is highly dependent on supplier relationships for flexibility. Furthermore, in a way similar to that found in the customer relationship management process, supplier relationship management provides structural support for developing and maintaining relationships with suppliers. Thus, by integrating these two ideas, supplier relationship management supports manufacturing flow by identifying and maintaining relationships with highly valued suppliers.

REBUILDING A BROKEN RELATIONSHIP

During the Great Recession, many supplier relationships were strained—even broken. Because the entire supply chain relies on positive supplier relations, it is when things are hard that effective relationship management is most crucial. After a crisis passes, supplier relationships can be rebuilt through the following four steps:

1. **Acknowledge past mistakes**
2. **Find the real source of the problem**
3. **Identify and implement corrective actions**
4. **Monitor and maintain the relationship**[12]

© iStockPhoto.com/Felix Möckel / © iStockphoto.com/billnoll

Just as firms benefit from developing close-knit, integrated relationships with customers, close-knit, integrated relationships with suppliers provide a means through which performance advantages can be gained. For example, careful management of supplier relationships is a key step toward ensuring that firms' manufacturing resources are available. It is clear, then, that the supplier relationship management process has a direct impact on each supply chain member's bottom-line financial performance.

13-3g Product Development and Commercialization

The **product development and commercialization process** (discussed in detail in Chapter 11) includes the group of activities that facilitates the joint development and marketing of new offerings among a group of supply chain partner firms. In many cases, new products and services are not the sole responsibility of a single firm that serves as inventor, engineer, builder, marketer, and sales agent. Rather, they are often the product of a multicompany collaboration with multiple firms and business units playing unique roles in new-product development, testing, and launch activities, among others. The capability for developing and introducing new offerings quickly is key for competitive success versus rival firms, so it is often advantageous to involve many supply chain partners in the effort. The process requires the close cooperation of suppliers and customers who provide input throughout the process and serve as advisers and coproducer for the new offering(s).

Designing a new product with the help of suppliers and customers can allow a company to introduce features and cost cutting measures into final products. Customers provide information about what they want from the product, while suppliers can help to design for quality and manufacturability. If each supply chain partner shares responsibility for the design and manufacture of a new product, more obstacles can be identified early and opportunities for cost reduction are made possible.[13]

13-3h Returns Management

The final supply chain management process deals with situations in which customers choose to return a product to the retailer or supplier, thereby creating a reversed flow of goods within the supply chain. The **returns management process** enables firms to manage volumes of returned product efficiently while minimizing returns-related costs and maximizing the value of the returned assets to the firms in the supply chain. Returns have the potential to affect a firm's financial position in a major and negative way if mishandled. In certain industries, such as apparel e-retailing, returns can amount to as much as 40 percent of sales volume.

In addition to the value of managing returns from a pure asset-recovery perspective, many firms are discovering that returns management also creates additional marketing and customer service touch points that can be leveraged for added customer value above and beyond normal sales and promotion-driven encounters. Handling returns gives the company an additional opportunity to please the customer, and customers who have positive experiences with the returns management process can become very confident buyers who are willing to reorder, since they know any problems they encounter with purchases will be quickly and fairly rectified. In addition, the returns management

product development and commercialization process includes the group of activities that facilitates the joint development and marketing of new offerings among a group of supply chain partner firms

returns management process enables firms to manage volumes of returned product efficiently while minimizing returns-related costs and maximizing the value of the returned assets to the firms in the supply chain

Titus Green assembles a recycled iPhone at a Green Citizen recycling facility in Burlingame, California. Green Citizen collects and disposes old electronics in the San Francisco Bay area, tracking each device to ensure that it is either recycled back into raw material or refurbished and resold.

process allows the firm to recognize weaknesses in product design and/or areas for potential improvement through the direct customer feedback that initiates the process.

The mobile phone industry has been able to use returns management to its advantage. In 2010, about 96 million mobile phones were returned to the manufacturer. With a return of between 35 and 75 percent of their original value in the secondary market, reselling 250,000 out of the 96 million returned phones would result in more than $20 million in additional revenue. Returns management also allows mobile phone companies to reclaim rare materials such as gold, silver, and palladium. In 2011, reclaimed metals from 1 million returned mobile phones brought in more than $2.8 million.[14]

13-4 HOW SUPPLY CHAIN FUNCTIONS IMPACT COMPANY SUCCESS

Critical to the success of any supply chain is orchestrating the means by which products move physically through it. This is accomplished via the execution of three interdependent groups of supply chain functions that exist within a business organization. These intertwined functions are often described as a sequence of "source, make, and deliver," in reference to the firm's supply management, production, and logistics areas. As mentioned earlier, supply chain management coordinates and integrates all of the activities performed by supply chain members into a seamless process. In a world-class supply chain organization, these three groups of functions are supported by a well-developed supply chain information system and are coordinated by a supply chain team. The **supply chain team**, in concert with the supply chain information system, orchestrates the movement of goods, services, and information from the source to the consumer. Supply chain teams typically cut across organizational boundaries, embracing all parties who participate in moving the product to market. The best supply chain teams also move beyond the organization to include the external participants in the chain, such as suppliers, transportation carriers, and third-party logistics

suppliers. Members of the supply chain communicate, coordinate, and cooperate extensively.

13-4a Supply Management

Beginning with the "source" category, one of the most important links in the supply chain is that between the manufacturer and the supplier. Supply management professionals are on the front lines of the organization, facing the supply base. Supply managers plan strategies, develop specifications, select suppliers, and negotiate price and service levels. The supply management function's ability to foster supply chain relationships, share knowledge across different functions, and contribute to strategic plans not only increases the company's ability to innovate and be flexible in responding to customer requests but can also directly affect the company's bottom line through cost reduction and quality improvement.

The goal of most supply management activities is to reduce the costs of raw materials and supplies. Purchasing professionals within the supply management group have traditionally relied on tough negotiations to get the lowest price possible from suppliers of raw materials, supplies, and components. Perhaps the biggest contribution purchasing can make to supply chain management, however, is in the area of vendor relations. Smart companies manage suppliers strategically in order to reduce the total cost of materials and services while assuring supplier success as well. Through good supplier relations, cooperative relationships develop. These relationships reduce costs and improve efficiency with the aim of lowering prices and enhancing profits. By integrating suppliers into their companies' businesses, supply managers have become better able to streamline purchasing processes, manage inventory levels, and reduce overall costs of the sourcing and procurement operations.

13-4b Inventory Control

The organization's **inventory control system** develops and maintains an adequate assortment of materials or products to meet a manufacturer's or a customer's demands. Inventory decisions, for both raw materials and finished goods, have a big impact on supply chain costs and the level of service provided. If too many products are kept in inventory, costs increase—as do risks of obsolescence, theft, and damage. If too few products are kept on hand, then the company risks product shortages and angry customers, and ultimately lost sales. The goal of inventory management, therefore, is to keep inventory levels as low as possible while maintaining an adequate supply of goods to meet customer demand.

If a company knew each day how many goods or services it would sell, it could ideally hold no inventory in stock—it would buy or produce exactly the amount of finished goods it needed each day to satisfy customer demands, and would begin and end the day with no inventory on hand. However, because customer orders are somewhat unpredictable by nature, most companies choose to carry inventory as a sort of insurance policy against customer **stockouts**. Inventory is held in many forms by modern business organizations. **Cycle stocks** of inventory include those items that are expected to be sold as finished goods (or the materials that go into making finished goods) in a given demand period. In effect, cycle stock is the inventory that supports what the business expects to sell during the period. However, other types of inventory are also important for a company to consider. **Safety stocks**, also called **buffer stocks**, are extra allotments of inventory that companies sometimes choose to hold in the event that demand spikes or if forecasts regarding the amount of demand are too low. At any given time, companies may also have **in-transit inventory** moving into the business from a supplier or out on the way to a customer. **Work-in-process inventory** reflects inventory that is being assembled or manufactured from its raw state into finished goods for sale. Additionally, during certain times of the year when sales are traditionally higher, the company may hold some **seasonal inventory** to augment the demand in excess of cycle stock that is expected to occur. For example, in North America and many other world regions, retailers and manufacturers acquire extra inventory to accommodate the back-to-school and Christmas/Hanukkah holiday seasons.

Managing inventory from the supplier to the manufacturer is called **materials requirement planning (MRP)**, or **materials management**. This system also encompasses the sourcing and procurement operations, signaling when raw materials, supplies, or components will need to be replenished for the production of more goods. The system that manages the finished goods inventory from manufacturer to end user is commonly referred to as **distribution resource planning (DRP)**. Both inventory systems use various inputs, such as sales forecasts, available inventory, outstanding orders, lead times, and mode of transportation to be used, to determine what needs to be done to replenish goods at all points in the supply chain. Marketers identify demand at each level in the supply chain, from the retailer back up the chain to the manufacturer, and use electronic data interchange to transmit important information throughout the channel.

Some inventory replenishment systems use little or no forecasting. These **automatic replenishment programs** trigger shipments only when a good is sold to the end user and use an electronic link connected with bar-code scanners so that the supplier can view inventory in real time. When stock at the customer's location drops below predetermined levels, the supplier takes responsibility for restocking the shelves or the warehouse. This process often results in lower inventory levels.

13-4c Order Processing

Let's now turn to the "make" group of business logistics functions. The manufacturing process begins with a customer order. An **order processing system** processes the requirements of the customer and sends the information into the supply chain via the logistics information system. The order goes to the manufacturer's warehouse. If the product is in stock, the order is filled, and arrangements are made to ship it. If the product is not in stock, the order triggers a replenishment request that finds its way to the factory floor.

Proper order processing is critical to good service. As an order enters the system, management must monitor two flows: the flow of goods and the flow of information. Good communication among sales representatives,

stockout a situation where a customer demand for an inventory item goes unfulfilled because the requested item is unavailable at the needed time and place

cycle stock inventory held temporarily for the purpose of fulfilling predicted demand in a period

safety (buffer) stock extra inventory held in addition to cycle stock as insurance against unexpected demand increases

in-transit inventory inventory that is currently moving within a transportation network to or from the company's facilities (plant, warehouse, or sales location)

work-in-process inventory materials inventory that is currently in the process of being converted into finished goods

seasonal inventory an extra inventory buffer that is held in response to predictable demand increases that occur annually

materials requirement planning (MRP or materials management) an inventory control system that manages the replenishment of raw materials, supplies, and components from the supplier to the manufacturer

distribution resource planning (DRP) an inventory control system that manages the replenishment of goods from the manufacturer to the final consumer

automatic replenishment program a real-time inventory system that triggers shipments only when a good is sold to the end user

order processing system a system whereby orders are entered into the supply chain and filled

electronic data interchange (EDI) information technology that replaces the paper documents that usually accompany business transactions, such as purchase orders and invoices, with electronic transmission of the needed information to reduce inventory levels, improve cash flow, streamline operations, and increase the speed and accuracy of information transmission

smart RFID (radio-frequency identification) an inventory handling and tracking system that employs radio-frequency electromagnetic fields to transfer and read product data via an electronic tag

build-to-stock a production method whereby products are made in advance of demand based on forecasts and are stored until customer orders arrive

office personnel, and warehouse and shipping personnel is essential to correct order processing. Shipping incorrect merchandise or partially filled orders can create just as much dissatisfaction as stockouts or slow deliveries. The flow of goods and information must be continually monitored so that mistakes can be corrected before an invoice is prepared and the merchandise shipped.

Order processing is becoming more automated through the use of computer technology known as **electronic data interchange (EDI)**. The basic idea of EDI

GOOD COMMUNICATION AMONG SALES REPRESENTATIVES, OFFICE PERSONNEL, AND WAREHOUSE AND SHIPPING PERSONNEL IS ESSENTIAL TO CORRECT ORDER PROCESSING.

is to replace the paper documents that usually accompany business transactions, such as purchase orders and invoices, with electronic transmission of the needed information. One example of EDI is the use of radio-frequency identification. **Smart RFID (radio-frequency identification)**, an inventory handling and tracking system that employs radio-frequency electromagnetic fields to transfer and read product data via an electronic tag, is another type of advanced computer technology that is helping companies manage their supply chains. JCPenney began rolling out RFID technology in their stores in 2012 and plans to use RFID technology for every item in every retail location. This not only reduces risks related to shoplifting but also increases store efficiency. Future plans for JCPenney include removing the cash system and using RFID technology to allow customers to check out from anywhere in the store. This move will cut out point-of-sale stations, which currently account for about 10 percent of each retail store's labor costs.[15] American Apparel tested similar technology and saw individual store sales rise as much as 14.3 percent over stores without the smart RFID tags. When theft is reduced, merchandise that shoplifters tend to target remains available for sale, increasing a store's likelihood of having better sales figures.[16]

13-4d Production

Under traditional mass-market **build-to-stock** manufacturing, production begins when forecasts call for additional products to be made or when inventory control systems signal low inventory levels. The firm then makes a product and transports the finished goods to its own warehouses or those of intermediaries, where the goods wait to be ordered by retailers or customers. For example, many types of convenience goods, such as toothpaste, deodorant, and detergent, are manufactured based on past sales and demand and then sent to retailers to resell. Build-to-stock production scheduling, based on forecasts and push selling, obviously has its disadvantages, the most notable being that companies risk making products that may become obsolete or that consumers don't want in the first place.

In the modern "pull" manufacturing environment, production of goods or services is not scheduled until

© Goodluz/Shutterstock.com

the customer (specifying a desired configuration) places an order. This process, known as **mass customization**, or **build-to-order**, uniquely tailors mass-market goods and services to the needs of the individuals who buy them. Several companies are using mass customization to give themselves an edge over competition. Mars allows customers to create their own personalized bags of M&Ms with their choice of colors, packaging, and illustrations. Similarly, Levi Strauss now offers customized jeans based on detailed measurements rather than on traditional clothing sizes.[17] Companies as diverse as Mars, Levi Strauss, BMW, Dell, and Mattel—as well as a host of Web-based businesses—are adopting mass customization to maintain or obtain a competitive edge.

A hybrid strategy that minimizes the risks and maximizes the benefits of both the build-to-stock and build-to-order strategies is **postponement**. With postponement, the product is partially produced based on generic forecasts of aggregate demand and is shipped to distribution locations near where demand is forecasted to occur. Then, once customers place an order, the production process is completed to the customers' specifications. This strategy allows companies to maximize customer satisfaction (by giving them exactly what they want) while at the same time controlling costs (by minimizing the number of basic units needed to do so).

The emergence of these different approaches to production has lead to the development of parallel operational philosophies known as lean, agile, and leagile supply chain management. Based on the Toyota Production System, the lean system emphasizes reduction of waste and maximization of efficiency in a build-to-stock system. Alternatively, an agile system employs a more expensive but more effective "wait-and-see" approach that includes the use of flexible production and quick reaction to customer demand changes. The hybrid leagile system allows for the use of build-to-stock strategies for high volume, stable demand products, and build-to-order strategies for everything else. This strategy was popularly employed for the production of Toyota's Scion brand of cars, with the base model produced in a Japanese factory and a number of customer options added at a small plant near the Port of Long Beach, California.[18]

13-4e Warehousing and Materials Handling

Finally, we consider the functional areas that together make up the "deliver," or distribution, functions of the supply chain. Although some manufacturing processes may eliminate the need to warehouse many raw materials, manufacturers may keep some safety stock on hand in the event of an emergency, such as a strike at a supplier's plant or a catastrophic event that temporarily stops the flow of raw materials to the production line. Likewise, the final user may not need or want the goods at the same time the manufacturer produces and wants to sell them. Products such as grain and corn are produced seasonally, but consumers demand them year-round. Other products, such as Christmas ornaments and frozen turkeys, are produced year-round, but consumers do not want them until autumn or winter. Therefore, management must have a storage system to hold these products until they are shipped.

Storage helps manufacturers manage supply and demand, or production and consumption. It provides time utility to buyers and sellers, which means that the seller stores the product until the buyer wants or needs it. But storing additional product does have disadvantages, including the costs of insurance on the stored product, taxes, obsolescence or spoilage, theft, and warehouse operating costs. Another drawback is opportunity costs—that is, the opportunities lost because money is tied up in stored product instead of being used for something else.

Because businesses are focusing on cutting supply chain costs, the warehousing industry is investing in services using sophisticated tracking technology such as materials-handling systems. An effective **materials-handling system** moves inventory into, within, and out of a warehouse quickly with minimal handling. With a manual, non-automated materials-handling system, a product may be handled more than a dozen times. Each time it is handled, the cost and risk of damage increase; each lifting of a product stresses its packaging. Consequently, most manufacturers today have moved to automated systems. Scanners quickly identify goods entering and leaving a warehouse through bar codes affixed to the packaging. Automatic storage and retrieval systems store and pick goods in the warehouse or distribution center. Automated materials-handling systems decrease product handling, ensure accurate placement of product, and improve the accuracy of order picking and the

mass customization (build-to-order) a production method whereby products are not made until an order is placed by the customer; products are made according to customer specifications

postponement a hybrid production method whereby basic units of a finished good are manufactured in advance of actual demand and held in strategic form or location until demand occurs, when final customization takes place

materials-handling system a method of moving inventory into, within, and out of a warehouse

PepsiCo Chairman and CEO Indra Nooyi addresses the audience at PepsiCo's Annual Shareholders' Meeting in Plano, Texas.

AP Images/PRNewsFoto/PepsiCo

rates of on-time shipment. When discussing PepsiCo's plans for increasing revenue in 2013, Chairman and CEO Indra Nooyi stressed the importance of "increasing automation across the value chain from raw materials handling through to the route truck, to implementing new processing technologies that enable us to both increase asset utilization and reduce input cost."[19] Some companies choose to use third-party logistics providers for their warehousing and distribution needs—you will learn more about these specialized service providers shortly.

13-4f Transportation

Transportation has traditionally accounted for 5 to 10 percent of the price of goods, though steadily rising fuel costs have recently elevated this proportion to as much as 17 percent. Shortages of petroleum and risks in oil markets have created new supply chain costs for narrow margin businesses like Dollar Tree.[20] Supply chain logisticians must decide which mode of transportation to use to move products from supplier to producer and from producer to buyer. These decisions are, of course, related to all other logistics decisions. The five major modes of transportation are railroads, motor carriers, pipelines, water transportation, and airways. Maersk, a global container shipping line, drastically reduced the cost of shipping overseas by manufacturing the Triple E, a container ship that can carry 18,000 containers (each one twenty feet long) at once. These quarter-mile-long ships are the largest seafaring vessels ever built. Larger ships have a greater economy of scale (meaning that they can transport so many more items that the price per

item decreases drastically), enabling companies to ship a greater variety of items, from wheat and trucks to tablets and powdered milk. In fact, environmental and port capacity concerns prompted the British Broadcasting Company to question whether the Triple E was *too* big.[21] In general, supply chain managers choose a mode of transportation on the basis of several criteria:

▸▸ **RELATIVE COST:** The total amount a specific carrier charges to move the product from the point of origin to the destination.

▸▸ **TRANSIT TIME:** The total time a carrier has possession of goods, including the time required for pickup and delivery, handling, and movement between the point of origin and the destination.

▸▸ **RELIABILITY:** The consistency with which the carrier delivers goods on time and in acceptable condition.

▸▸ **CAPABILITY:** The ability of the carrier to provide the appropriate equipment and conditions for moving specific kinds of goods, such as those that must be transported in a controlled environment (e.g., under refrigeration).

▸▸ **ACCESSIBILITY:** A carrier's ability to move goods over a specific route or network.

▸▸ **TRACEABILITY:** The relative ease with which a shipment can be located and transferred.

The mode of transportation used depends on the needs of the shipper as they relate to these six criteria. Exhibit 1 compares the basic modes of transportation based on these criteria.

Exhibit 1
CRITERIA FOR RANKING MODES OF TRANSPORTATION

	Highest				Lowest
Relative Cost	Air	Truck	Rail	Pipe	Water
Transit Time	Water	Rail	Pipe	Truck	Air
Reliability	Pipe	Truck	Rail	Air	Water
Capability	Water	Rail	Truck	Air	Pipe
Accessibility	Truck	Rail	Air	Water	Pipe
Traceability	Air	Truck	Rail	Water	Pipe

© Cengage Learning

In many cases, especially in a build-to-order environment, the transportation network replaces the warehouse or eliminates the expense of storing inventories, as goods are timed to arrive the moment they're needed on the assembly line or for shipment to customers.

13-4g Supply Chain Technologies

Finally, it is important to note that all of the source, make, and deliver functions must be supported by adequate information systems architecture. The most prominent of these elements, the **logistics information system**, serves as the link connecting all of the operational components of the supply chain. The components of the system include, for example, software for materials acquisition and handling, warehouse-management and enterprise-wide solutions, data storage and integration in data warehouses, mobile communications, EDI, RFID chips, and the Internet. Working together, the components of the logistics information system are the fundamental enablers of successful supply chain management.

In addition to the logistics information system, several other technological advances and business trends are affecting the job of the supply chain manager today. Advanced computer technology has boosted the efficiency of logistics dramatically with tools such as automatic identification systems (auto ID) using bar coding and radio frequency technology, communications technology, and supply chain software systems that help synchronize the flow of goods and information with customer demand. Looking again at Amazon.com's state-of-the-art fulfillment centers, warehouse management system technology is used to maximize efficiency. Incoming product is immediately sent to the first available empty shelf space. That means a shipment of golf balls could end up next to snow tires. As online orders come in, Kiva robot pods pull moveable shelves and take them to the employees who pull the order items (indicated with a laser pointer), scan them, pack them, and place them on another Kiva pod to go to shipping.

13-5 SUSTAINABLE SUPPLY CHAIN MANAGEMENT

In response to the need for firms to both reduce costs and act as leaders in protecting the natural environment, many are adopting sustainable supply chain management principles as a key part of their supply chain strategies. Sustainable supply chain management involves the integration and balancing of environmental, social, and economic thinking into all phases of the supply chain management process. In doing so, the organization both better addresses current business needs and develops long-term initiatives that allow it to mitigate risks and avail itself of future opportunities in ways that preserve resources for future generations and ensure long-term viability. Such activities include environmentally friendly materials sourcing; the design of products with consideration given to their social and environmental impact; and end-of-life product management that includes easy recycling and/or clean disposal. By enacting sustainable supply chain management principles, companies can simultaneously generate cost savings, protect the earth's natural resources, and ensure that socially responsible business practices are enacted.

UPS works continuously to develop a more sustainable supply chain. By integrating new transportation technology into its fulfillment networks, UPS mechanics and employees are able to facilitate package delivery in ways that are more fuel- and emissions-efficient—the proof lies in the 3.3 percent reduction in fuel use per package from 2009 to 2010. UPS has logged 200 million miles on alternative fuel vehicles and offers carbon-neutral delivery in thirty-six countries.[22] In addition to environmental sustainability, modern businesses are also balancing economic success with social sustainability practices like human rights, labor rights, employee diversity initiatives, and quality of life concerns. A common misconception surrounding both environmental and social sustainability is that their practice increases supply chain costs disproportionately and therefore should be enacted only when business leaders are willing to act altruistically or for the purposes of good public relations. However, recent research on these subjects has demonstrated a strong business case for supporting many sustainability initiatives. As examples, the recycling of used pallets is both an environmentally sustainable practice and cheaper than purchasing new ones, and the employment of disabled workers in distribution operations ensures both social sustainability (via opportunities for economically disadvantaged people)

logistics information system the link that connects all the logistics functions of the supply chain

sustainable supply chain management a supply chain management philosophy that embraces the need for optimizing social and environmental costs in addition to financial costs

outsourcing (contract logistics) a manufacturer's or supplier's use of an independent third party to manage an entire function of the logistics system, such as transportation, warehousing, or order processing

third-party logistics company (3PL) a firm that provides functional logistics services to others

fourth-party logistics company (4PL or logistics integrator) a consulting-based organization that assesses another's entire logistical service needs and provides integrated solutions, often drawing on multiple 3PLs for actual service

and better overall performance for the employer. Nowhere has the latter been better demonstrated than by Lowe's home improvement stores, where the hiring and training of disabled workers increased productivity in the host facilities by up to 20 percent from 2010 to 2012. The company found that disabled workers were far less likely to miss work and were often as effective at performing job tasks as their abled counterparts, while frequently exceeding them in terms of execution of process and safety standards.[23]

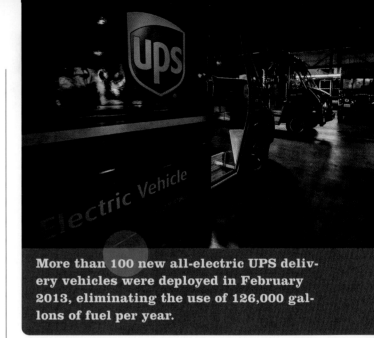

More than 100 new all-electric UPS delivery vehicles were deployed in February 2013, eliminating the use of 126,000 gallons of fuel per year.

13-6 TRENDS IN SUPPLY CHAIN MANAGEMENT

Several technological advances and business trends are affecting the job of the supply chain manager today. Some of the business trends that are affecting supply chain management include outsourcing logistics, maintaining a secure supply chain and minimizing supply chain risk, and maintaining a sustainable supply chain. While these trends exert pressure on managers to change the way their supply chains function, electronic distribution is being used and changed frequently to help make supply chain management more integrated and easier to track.

13-6a Outsourcing Logistics Functions

Partnering organizations are becoming increasingly efficient at dividing responsibility for supply chain management. **Outsourcing**, or **contract logistics**, is a rapidly growing initiative in which a manufacturer or supplier turns over an entire logistical function (often buying and managing transportation, warehousing, and/or light postponed manufacturing) to an independent **third-party logistics company (3PL)**. These service providers sell logistics solutions instead of physical products. Common 3PL products include warehouse space, transportation solutions, information sharing, manufacturing postponement, and enhanced technological innovations. When a firm's order fulfillment process is managed diligently, the

amount of time between order placement and receipt of the customer's payment following order shipment (known as the *order-to-cash cycle*) is minimized as much as possible. Since many firms do not view order fulfillment as a core competency (versus, for example, product development or marketing), they often outsource this function to a 3PL that specializes in the order fulfillment process. The 3PL becomes a semi-permanent part of the firm's supply chain and is assigned to manage one or more specialized functions.[24] Other, more comprehensive partners, often known as **fourth-party logistics companies (4PLs)** or **logistics integrators**, create and manage entire solutions for getting products where they need to be, when they need to be there. Many times, 3PLs and 4PLs provide a firm's only interaction with the customer, so they need to represent the needs and interests of the entire firm and supply chain. Developing and training these firms' employees to be empowered and to respond to the customer's needs in the best interest of the supply chain is becoming increasingly important.

Outsourcing enables companies to cut inventories, locate stock at fewer plants and distribution centers, and still provide the same level of service or even better. The companies then can refocus investment on their core business. In the hospitality industry, Avendra negotiates with suppliers to obtain virtually everything a hotel might need, from food and beverages to golf course maintenance. For example, by relying on Avendra to manage many aspects of the supply chain, companies like Fairmont Hotels & Resorts and InterContinental Hotels Group can concentrate on their core function—providing hospitality. The most progressive companies are engaging in vested outsourcing relationships, whereby both parties collaborate deeply to find mutually beneficial arrangements that allow both parties to "win" by reducing overall costs while achieving better performance.[25]

Because a logistics service provider is focused on logistical functions only, clients receive better service in a timely, efficient manner, thereby increasing their customers' satisfaction and boosting the perception of added value to a company's offerings. In many recent instances, North American companies have been **offshoring**, or outsourcing logistics to service providers located in countries with lower labor costs, such as China or India. However, as fuel costs have risen and security issues become more prominent, many companies have begun to relocate outsourced operations closer to home. **Nearshoring** to locations such as Mexico or the Caribbean nations ensures low costs while reducing supply chain risk. Nearshoring not only allows a company to manufacture its products more closely to major demand centers, it also gives the supplier a chance to make its presence known at a local level. Mexican-based IT firm Rural Sourcing Inc. has long worked with customers in Mexico, but an influx of American partners has led the company to grow an average of 150 percent annually over the last four years.[26]

13-6b Supply Chain Risk, Security, and Resiliency

Throughout history, it has been important for organizations to protect their supplies and assets from unexpected disruptions, delays, and damage. It was not until the 9/11 tragedy in the United States, however, that the management of **supply chain risk** became a critical business focus. Modern companies undertake contingency and crisis planning to mitigate the effects of disruptions such as terrorist attacks, disastrous weather events or other acts of God, systems failures such power grid failure or widespread computer viruses, and volatile changes in supply or demand. The potential for such events leads to supply chain inefficiencies for a variety of reasons. For example, as many companies have begun to outsource services and manufacturing globally, supply chains have become longer and more vulnerable to theft, piracy, or contamination. At the same time, shortened product life cycles and rapid technological advances have increased the likelihood of inventory becoming obsolete while sitting in the warehouse or retail store. These and similar issues are costly to address, and can increase the prices of commonly demanded products and services by up to 10 percent or more. As supply chains become leaner due to cost reduction initiatives, they also become more vulnerable when something goes wrong. When a fire destroyed an electronics plant that supplied both Nokia and Ericsson in 2000, Nokia's supply chain was able to react quickly to secure supply. Ericsson, left without supply, suffered losses estimated at $390 million and was unable to sustain its market share advantage.

Leading supply chain companies are enacting two sets of countermeasures to deal with supply chain risks.

In October 2012, Hurricane Sandy ravaged the American Atlantic seaboard, causing widespread flooding and power outages. The storm disrupted both national and international supply chains, forcing countless New York and New Jersey companies to shut down for days (or even weeks) after the storm dissipated. Here, a fleet of taxis sits idle in a flooded lot in Hoboken, New Jersey.

Michael Bocchieri/Getty Images

Proactive **supply chain security** measures seek to protect key inventory and assets from damage, theft, or destruction, while reactive **supply chain resiliency** measures ensure that the supply chain is back up and running as soon as possible in the event that a disruption occurs. Security measures are enacted when the probability of a disruptive event occurring is high or the impact of the event on the supply chain would be disastrous. Companies focus on resiliency when the probability and impact of a disruptive event are deemed less significant. Yet, many firms are enacting both types of these countermeasures simultaneously. To improve its resilience following the North Pacific earthquake and tsunami of 2012, Toyota asked its Japanese-based suppliers to spread its production capacity across a broader geographic area in the event another earthquake were to hit the island. Additionally, the company is using multiple distribution centers such that any single disruption would leave it with sufficient finished goods inventory to continue selling cars.[27]

13-6c Electronic Distribution

Electronic distribution is the most recent development in the logistics arena. Broadly defined, **electronic distribution** includes any kind of product or service that can be distributed electronically, whether over traditional forms such as fiber-optic cable or through satellite transmission of electronic signals. Companies like E*TRADE, Apple (iTunes), and Movies.com have built their business models around electronic distribution.

In the near future, however, electronic distribution will not be limited only to products and services that are mostly composed of information that can therefore be easily digitized. Experiments with **three-dimensional printing (3DP)** have been successful in industries such as auto parts, biomedical, and even fast food. Using 3DP technology, objects are built to precise specifications using raw materials at or near the location where they will be consumed. Charge Bikes prints customized titanium bicycle parts based on customer specifications, thus reducing

the need to transport complete frames around the world before they can be assembled and sold.[28] Shipping raw materials such as powdered titanium is cheaper than shipping finished bicycles because it can be packaged in a perfectly cubic container, making transportation much more efficient and cost effective. Powdered titanium is used only as it is needed, so virtually no waste is produced during printing.[29]

13-6d Global Logistics and Supply Chain Management

Global markets present their own sets of challenges for supply chain managers. Strategically, there are many reasons why a company might wish to globalize its supply chain. The allure of foreign markets is strong, due to increasing demand for imported products worldwide. Cheap labor advantages and trade barriers/tariffs have encouraged firms to expand their global manufacturing operations. At the same time, globalization has brought about great uncertainty for modern companies, and specifically, their supply chains. Moving operations offshore exposes companies to risks associated with geopolitical conflict, foreign nationalization of assets and knowledge diffusion, and highly variable quality standards. Foreign suppliers are often less reliable, and due to the lengthening of the supply

AP Images/GlobeNewswire

In 2013, consumer-grade 3DP company MakerBot and smartphone manufacturer Nokia joined forces to create a free downloadable file that allows MakerBot owners to print phone cases for the latest Nokia Lumia smartphones at home in about an hour.

chain, variability in transportation service can lead to service failures. It is important to consider how sourcing and logistics will be impacted by supply chain globalization.

From a supply management standpoint, it often makes sense to procure goods and services from offshore suppliers. From an economic perspective, lower labor rates, government subsidies, and low materials costs are attractive, but are sometimes outweighed by the costs of quality variation and loss of intellectual property. Still, moving offshore also exposes the company to new technologies, introduces competition to domestic suppliers who have become lackadaisical, and build brand equity. Companies moving offshore must carefully consider the pros and cons, and build supply management systems that can manage very diverse tasks.

Logistically, it is critical for importers of any size to understand and cope with the legalities of trade in other countries. Shippers and distributors must be aware of the permits, licenses, and registrations they may need to acquire and, depending on the type of product they are importing, the tariffs, quotas, and other regulations that apply in each country. Sometimes, the complexities of handling overseas logistics are too great to overcome. Transportation can be a major issue for companies dealing with global supply chains. Uncertainty regarding shipping usually tops the list of reasons companies, especially smaller ones, resist international markets. In some instances, poor infrastructure makes transportation dangerous and unreliable. And the process of moving goods across the borders of even the most industrialized nations can still be complicated by government regulations. In many cases, companies will want to hire freight forwarders, export management companies, or trading companies to handle overseas logistical needs. These agents can ensure that deals struck there are economically viable and yield the expected benefits.

As the world continues to globalize, supply chain management will undoubtedly continue to take on a globalized flavor. Worldwide, the resources needed to manufacture and sell increasingly demanded goods are becoming more scarce, and market boundaries are melting together. Free trade is expanding, and consumers in nations where demand has been traditionally low are viewing goods and placing orders via the Internet. Efforts to achieve world-class global supply chain management mean that the balancing of supply and demand—and the satisfaction of more and more customers worldwide—are becoming a reality for many companies.

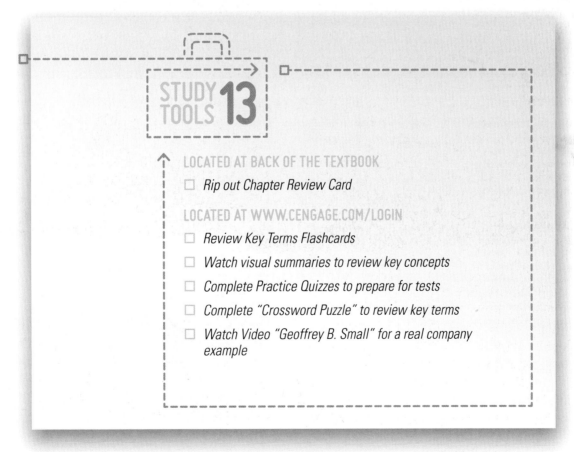

STUDY TOOLS 13

↑ LOCATED AT BACK OF THE TEXTBOOK
- ☐ *Rip out Chapter Review Card*

LOCATED AT WWW.CENGAGE.COM/LOGIN
- ☐ *Review Key Terms Flashcards*
- ☐ *Watch visual summaries to review key concepts*
- ☐ *Complete Practice Quizzes to prepare for tests*
- ☐ *Complete "Crossword Puzzle" to review key terms*
- ☐ *Watch Video "Geoffrey B. Small" for a real company example*

14-1 MARKETING CHANNELS AND CHANNEL INTERMEDIARIES

A marketing channel can be viewed as a canal or pipeline through which products, their ownership, communication, financing and payment, and accompanying risk flow to the consumer. A **marketing channel** (also called a **channel of distribution**) is a business structure of interdependent organizations that reaches from the point of production to the consumer and facilitates the downstream physical movement of goods through the supply chain. Channels represent the "place" or "distribution" element of the marketing mix (product, price, promotion, and place).

Retailers link the consumer and the supply chain, and are charged with facilitating the eventual purchase of goods manufactured upstream in the channel.

marketing channel (channel of distribution) a set of interdependent organizations that eases the transfer of ownership as products move from producer to business user or consumer

channel members all parties in the marketing channel who negotiate with one another, buy and sell products, and facilitate the change of ownership between buyer and seller in the course of moving the product from the manufacturer into the hands of the final consumer

Many different types of organizations participate in marketing channels. **Channel members** (also called *intermediaries*, *resellers*, and *middlemen*) negotiate with one another, buy and sell products, and facilitate the change of ownership between buyer and seller in the course of moving the product from the manufacturer into the hands of the final consumer. As products move to the final consumer, channel members facilitate the distribution process by providing specialization and division of labor, overcoming discrepancies, and providing contact efficiency.

14-1a How Marketing Channels Work

According to the concept of *specialization and division of labor*, breaking down a complex task into smaller, simpler ones and allocating them to specialists will create greater efficiency and lower average production costs via economies of scale. Marketing channels attain economies of scale through specialization and division of labor by aiding upstream producers (who often lack motivation, financing, or expertise) to market to end users or consumers. In some cases, such as for consumer goods like soft drinks, the

Chapter 14

Marketing Channels and Retailing

Learning Outcomes

After you finish this chapter go to
p269 *for* **STUDY TOOLS**

cost of marketing directly to millions of consumers—taking and shipping individual orders—is prohibitive. For this reason, producers engage other channel members such as wholesalers and retailers to do what the producers are not well suited to do. Some channel members can accomplish certain tasks more efficiently than others because they have built strategic relationships with key suppliers or customers or have unique capabilities. Their specialized expertise enhances the overall performance of the channel.

Because customers, like businesses, are specialized, they rely on other entities for the fulfillment of most of their needs. Imagine what your life would be like if you had to grow your own food, make your own clothes, produce your own television shows, and assemble your own automobile! Luckily, members of marketing channels are available to undertake these tasks for us. However, not all goods and services produced by channel members exist in exactly the ways we'd like, at least at first. Marketing channels are valuable because they aid producers in creating time, place, form, and exchange utility for customers, such that products become aligned with their needs. Channel members provide **form utility** when they transform oats grown on a distant farm into the Cheerios that we like to eat for breakfast. **Time utility** and **place utility** are created when a transport company hired by the producer physically moves boxes of cereal to a store near our homes in time for our next scheduled shopping trip. And a retailer, who is willing to swap the desired product for some amount of money we are reasonably willing to give, creates **exchange utility** in doing so.

14-1b Contact Efficiency—The Special Retailer Role

Retailers are those firms in the channel that sell directly to consumers as their primary function. A critical role fulfilled by retailers within the marketing channel is that they provide contact efficiency for consumers. Suppose you had to buy your milk at a dairy, your meat at a stockyard, and so forth. You would spend a great deal of time, money, and energy just shopping for a few groceries. Retailers

simplify distribution by cutting the number of transactions required by consumers, making an assortment of goods available in one location. Consider the example illustrated in Exhibit 1. Four consumers each want to buy a tablet computer. Without a retail intermediary like Best Buy, tablet manufacturers Samsung, Asus, Microsoft, Apple, and Lenovo would each have to make four contacts to reach the four consumers who are in the target market, for a total of twenty transactions. However, when Best Buy acts as an intermediary between the producer and consumers, each producer needs to make only one contact, reducing the number to nine transactions. This benefit to customers accrues whether the retailer operates in a physical store location or online format.

14-1c Functions and Activities of Intermediaries

Intermediaries in a channel negotiate with one another, facilitate the change of ownership between buyers and sellers, and physically move products from the manufacturer to the final consumer. The most prominent difference separating intermediaries is whether they take title to the product. *Taking title* means they own the merchandise and control the terms of the sale—for example, price and delivery date. Retailers and merchant wholesalers are examples

As a retailer, Home Depot creates exchange utility when a customer purchases finished lumber. Here, Val Cijunelis selects wood for a home project at a Home Depot location in Algonquin, Illinois.

of intermediaries that take title to products in the marketing channel and resell them. **Merchant wholesalers** are organizations that facilitate the movement of products and services from the manufacturer to producers, resellers, governments, institutions, and retailers. All merchant wholesalers take title to the goods they sell, and most of them operate one or more warehouses where they receive goods, store them, and later reship them to retailers, manufacturers, and institutional clients. Since wholesalers do not typically alter the form of a good or sell it directly to the consumer, their value hinges on their providing time and place utility and contact efficiency to retailers.

Other intermediaries do not take title to goods and services they market but do facilitate the exchange of ownership between sellers and buyers. **Agents and brokers** simply facilitate the sale of a product from producer to end user by representing retailers, wholesalers, or manufacturers. Unlike wholesalers, agents or brokers only facilitate sales and generally have little input into the terms of the sale. They do, however, get a fee or commission based on sales volume. For example, when selling a home, the owner usually hires a real estate agent who then brings potential buyers to see the house. The agent facilitates the sale by bringing the buyer and owner together but never actually takes ownership of the home.

Variations in channel structures are due in large part to variations in the numbers and types of wholesaling intermediaries. Generally, product characteristics, buyer considerations, and market conditions determine the types and number of intermediaries the manufacturer should use:

▸▸ **Standardized, customized, or highly complex products such as insurance are usually sold through an agent or broker who may represent one or multiple companies. In contrast, a standardized product such as soda is sold through a merchant wholesaler and retailer channel.**

merchant wholesaler an institution that buys goods from manufacturers and resells them to businesses, government agencies, and other wholesalers or retailers and that receives and takes title to goods, stores them in its own warehouses, and later ships them

agents and brokers wholesaling intermediaries who do not take title to a product but facilitate its sale from producer to end user by representing retailers, wholesalers, or manufacturers

Exhibit 1

HOW MARKETING CHANNELS REDUCE THE NUMBER OF REQUIRED TRANSACTIONS

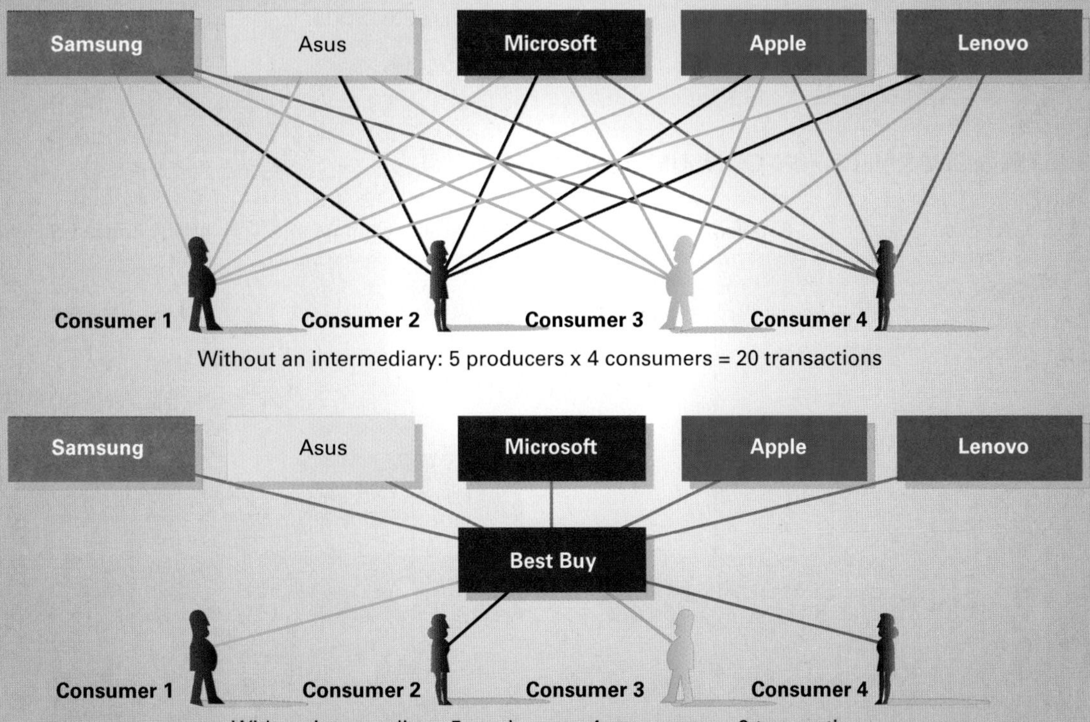

Without an intermediary: 5 producers x 4 consumers = 20 transactions

With an intermediary: 5 producers + 4 consumers = 9 transactions

© Cengage Learning

- ▶▶ Buyer considerations such as purchase frequency or customer wait time influence channel choice. When there is no time pressure, customers may save money on books by ordering online and taking direct distribution from a wholesaler. However, if a book is needed immediately, it will have to be purchased at retail—at the school bookstore—and will include a markup.

- ▶▶ Market characteristics such as how many buyers are in the market and whether they are concentrated in a general location also influence channel design. In a home sale, the buyer and seller are localized in one area, which facilitates the use of a simple agent/broker relationship, whereas mass-manufactured goods such as automobiles may require parts from all over the world and therefore many intermediaries.

14-1d Channel Functions Performed by Intermediaries

Retailing and wholesaling intermediaries in marketing channels perform essential functions that enable goods to flow between producer and consumer. *Transactional* functions involve contacting and communicating with prospective buyers to make them aware of existing products and to explain their features, advantages, and benefits. Intermediaries in the channel also provide *logistical* functions. Logistics functions typically include transportation and storage of assets, as well as their sorting, accumulation, consolidation, and/or allocation for the

purpose of conforming to customer requirements. These issues are described in detail in Chapter 13. The third basic channel function, *facilitating*, includes research and financing. Research provides information about channel members and consumers by getting answers to key questions: Who are the buyers? Where are they located? Why do they buy? Financing ensures that channel members have the money to keep products moving through the channel to the ultimate consumer. Although individual members can be added to or deleted from a channel, someone must still perform these essential functions. Producers, end users, or consumers can perform them, as can channel intermediaries such as wholesalers and retailers, and sometimes nonmember channel participants such as service providers.

14-2 CHANNEL STRUCTURES

A product can take many routes to reach its final consumer. Marketers and consumers each search for the most efficient channel from many available alternatives. Marketing a consumer convenience good such as candy differs from marketing a specialty good like a Prada handbag. Exhibit 2 illustrates the four ways manufacturers can route products to consumers.

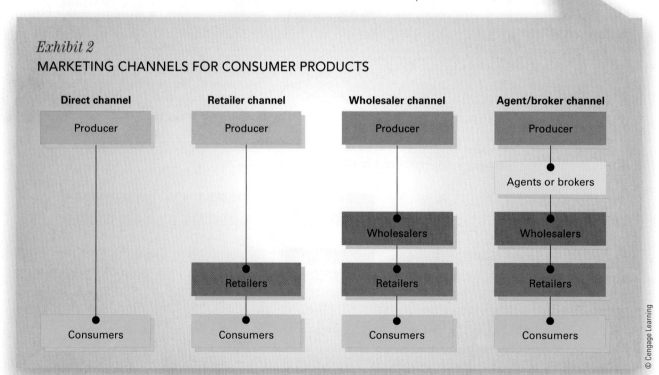

Exhibit 2
MARKETING CHANNELS FOR CONSUMER PRODUCTS

Direct channel	Retailer channel	Wholesaler channel	Agent/broker channel
Producer	Producer	Producer	Producer
			Agents or brokers
		Wholesalers	Wholesalers
	Retailers	Retailers	Retailers
Consumers	Consumers	Consumers	Consumers

© Cengage Learning

When possible, producers use the **direct channel** to sell directly to consumers. Direct marketing activities—including telemarketing, mail order and catalog shopping, and forms of electronic retailing such as online shopping and shop-at-home television networks—are good examples of this type of channel structure. There are no intermediaries. Producer-owned stores and factory outlet stores—like Sherwin-Williams, Polo Ralph Lauren, Oneida, and WestPoint Home—are examples of direct channels.

By contrast, when one or more channel members are small companies lacking in marketing power, an *agent/ broker channel* may be the best solution. Agents or brokers bring manufacturers and wholesalers together for negotiations, but they do not take title to merchandise. Ownership passes directly to one or more wholesalers and then to retailers, who sell to the ultimate consumer.

Most consumer products are sold through distribution channels similar to the other two alternatives: the retailer channel and the wholesaler channel. A *retailer channel* is most common when the retailer is large and can buy in large quantities directly from the manufacturer. Walmart, Sears, and car dealers are examples of retailers that often bypass a wholesaler. A *wholesaler channel* is commonly used for low-cost items that are frequently purchased, such as candy, cigarettes, and magazines.

14-2a Channels for Business and Industrial Products

As Exhibit 3 illustrates, five channel structures are common in business and industrial markets. First, *direct channels* are typical in business and industrial markets. For example, manufacturers buy large quantities of raw materials, major equipment, processed materials, and supplies directly from other manufacturers. Manufacturers that require suppliers to meet detailed technical specifications often prefer direct channels. Apple uses a direct channel to purchase high-resolution retina displays for its innovative third-generation iPad. To ensure supply for iPad construction, Apple takes direct shipments of screens from Sharp, LG, and Samsung.[1]

Alternatively, companies selling standardized items of moderate or low value often rely on *industrial distributors*. In many ways, an industrial distributor is like a supermarket for organizations. Industrial distributors are wholesalers and channel members that buy and take title to products. Moreover, they usually keep inventories of their products and sell and service them. Often small manufacturers cannot afford to employ their own sales force. Instead, they rely on manufacturers' representatives or selling agents to sell

direct channel a distribution channel in which producers sell directly to consumers

Exhibit 3
CHANNELS FOR BUSINESS AND INDUSTRIAL PRODUCTS

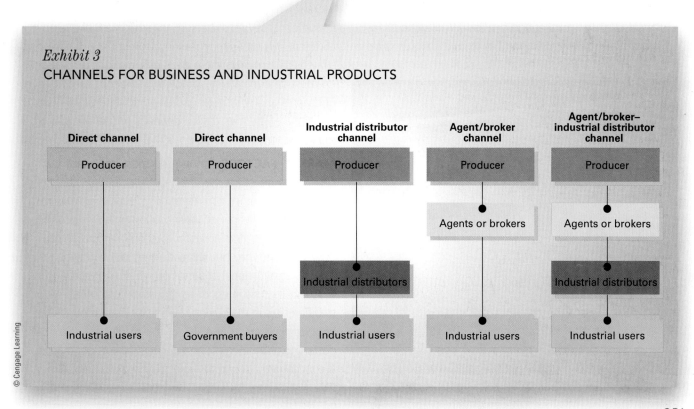

© Cengage Learning

to either industrial distributors or users. Additionally, the Internet has enabled virtual distributors to emerge and has forced traditional industrial distributors to expand their business model. Many manufacturers and consumers are bypassing distributors and going direct, often via the Internet.

14-2b Alternative Channel Arrangements

Rarely does a producer use just one type of channel to move its product. It usually employs several different or alternative channels, which include multiple channels, nontraditional channels, and strategic channel alliances. When a producer selects two or more channels to distribute the same product to target markets, this arrangement is called **dual distribution** (or **multiple distribution**). Dual distribution systems differ from single channel systems, and managers should recognize those differences. Multiple channels must be organized and managed as a group—managers must try to make the whole system work well. As more people embrace online shopping, an increasing number of retailers are using multiple distribution channels. This distribution arrangement allows retailers to reach a wider customer base, but may also lead to competition between distribution channels through cannibalization (that is, one channel takes

Some customers browse in a store and then buy online at a lower price. This is especially true at luxury brand locations such as Jimmy Choo and Michael Kors.

sales away from another). Two separate channels may complement each other. For example, some customers use "showrooming," or browsing in the store and then buying online at a lower price. Additionally, **nontraditional channels** may help differentiate a firm's product from the competition. Nontraditional channels include the Internet, mail-order channels, or infomercials. Although nontraditional channels may limit a brand's coverage, they can give a producer serving a niche market a way to gain market access and customer attention without having to establish channel intermediaries and can also provide another avenue of sales for larger firms. Furthermore, companies often form **strategic channel alliances** that enable them to use another manufacturer's already-established channel. Alliances are used most often when the creation of marketing channel relationships may be too expensive and time consuming. Whirlpool signed a deal with Chinese retailer Suning Appliance Company to have access to its 1,700 stores in China. This helps Whirlpool reach growing markets in smaller cities and broadens its small market in China.[2]

14-2c Factors Affecting Channel Choice

Managers must answer many questions before choosing a marketing channel. Managers must decide what role distribution will play in the overall marketing strategy. In addition, they must be sure that the channel strategy chosen is consistent with product, promotion, and pricing strategies. In making these decisions, marketing managers must determine what factors will influence the choice of channel and what level of distribution intensity will be appropriate. The final choice depends on the analysis of market factors, product factors, and producer factors.

MARKET FACTORS Among the most important market factors affecting the choice of distribution channel are target customer considerations. Specifically, managers should answer the following questions: Who are the potential customers? What do they buy? Where do they buy? When do they buy? How do they buy? Additionally, the choice of channel depends on whether the producer is selling to consumers or to industrial customers—due to differences in the buying routines of these groups. The geographic location and size of the market are also important to channel selection. As a rule, if the target market is concentrated in one or more specific areas, then direct

© iStockPhoto.com/Ian Hamilton

selling through a sales force is appropriate, whereas intermediaries would be less expensive in broader markets.

PRODUCT FACTORS Complex, customized, and expensive products tend to benefit from shorter and more direct marketing channels. These types of products sell better through a direct sales force. Examples include pharmaceuticals, scientific instruments, airplanes, and mainframe computer systems. On the other hand, the more standardized a product is, the longer its distribution channel can be and the greater the number of intermediaries that can be involved. For example, with the exception of flavor and shape, the formula for chewing gum is about the same from producer to producer. As a result, the distribution channel for gum tends to involve many wholesalers and retailers.

The product's life cycle is also an important factor in choosing a marketing channel. In fact, the choice of channel may change over the life of the product. As products become more common and less intimidating to potential users, producers tend to look for alternative channels. Similarly, perishable products such as vegetables and milk have a relatively short life span, and fragile products like china and crystal require a minimum amount of handling. Therefore, both require fairly short marketing channels. Online retailers such as eBay facilitate the sale of unusual or difficult-to-find products that benefit from a direct channel.

PRODUCER FACTORS Several factors pertaining to the producer itself are important to the selection of a marketing channel. In general, producers with large financial, managerial, and marketing resources are better able to use more direct channels. These producers have the ability to hire and train their own sales forces, warehouse their own goods, and extend credit to their customers. Smaller or weaker firms, on the other hand, must rely on intermediaries to provide these services for them. Compared to producers with only one or two product lines, producers that sell several products in a related area are able to choose channels that are more direct. Sales expenses then can be spread over more products.

A producer's desire to control pricing, positioning, brand image, and customer support also tends to influence channel selection. For instance, firms that sell products with exclusive brand images, such as designer perfumes and clothing, usually avoid channels in which discount retailers are present. Manufacturers of upscale products, such as Gucci (handbags) and Godiva (chocolates), may sell their wares only in expensive stores in order to maintain an image of exclusivity. Many producers have opted to risk their image, however, and test sales in discount channels. For example, Levi Strauss expanded its distribution to include JCPenney, Sears, and Walmart.

14-2d Levels of Distribution Intensity

Organizations have three options for intensity of distribution: intensive distribution, selective distribution, or exclusive distribution. **Intensive distribution** is a form of distribution aimed at maximum market coverage. Here, the manufacturer tries to have the product available in every outlet where potential customers might want to buy it. If buyers are unwilling to search for a product, it must be made very accessible to buyers. The next level of distribution, **selective distribution**, is achieved by screening dealers and retailers

intensive distribution a form of distribution aimed at having a product available in every outlet where target customers might want to buy it

selective distribution a form of distribution achieved by screening dealers to eliminate all but a few in any single area

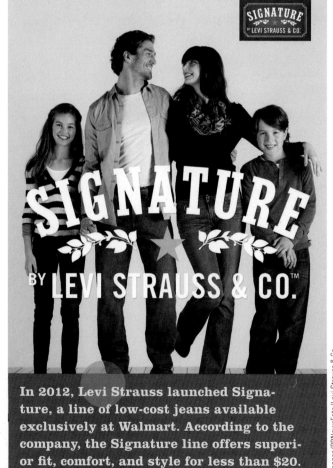

In 2012, Levi Strauss launched Signature, a line of low-cost jeans available exclusively at Walmart. According to the company, the Signature line offers superior fit, comfort, and style for less than $20.

AP Images/PRNewsFoto/Levi Strauss & Co.

Source: https://www.spotify.com/us/, http://store.steampowered.com, https://play.google.com/store/movies, http://www.gilt.com, http://shoedazzle.com

exclusive distribution a form of distribution that establishes one or a few dealers within a given area

to eliminate all but a few in any single area. Because only a few are chosen, the consumer must seek out the product. For example, HBO selectively distributes its popular television shows through a series of its own subscription-based channels (HBO, HBO on Demand, and HBO Go for mobile devices) and sells subscriptions or single episodes through Apple, Amazon.com, and Sony's online stores but does not stream them through Netflix or Hulu Plus. The most restrictive form of market coverage is **exclusive distribution**, which entails only one or a few dealers within a given area. Because buyers may have to search or travel extensively to buy the product, exclusive distribution is usually confined to consumer specialty goods, a few shopping goods, and major industrial equipment. Products such as Rolls-Royce automobiles, Chris-Craft powerboats, and Pettibone tower cranes are distributed under exclusive arrangements.

EMERGING DISTRIBUTION STRUCTURES In recent years, rapid changes in technology and communication have led to the emergence of new, experimental distribution methods and channel structures. For example, fashion flash sale sites like Gilt, JackThreads, and RueLaLa have recently boomed in popularity. On these sites, new designer clothing items are made available every day—often at a discount of 15 to 80 percent and always for an extremely limited time. The average fashion flash sale shopper is between twenty-five and forty years of age and makes $100,000 a year—an ideal demographic for many marketers.

Another emerging channel structure involves renting items that are usually only sold to end consumers. For example, some Web sites allow customers to rent and return high fashion products (renttherunway.com), handbags and accessories (lovemeandleaveme.com), and even furniture (fashionfurniture.com). Rental versus retail channels open up an entirely new customer base for certain products that were once reserved for a much smaller group.

As early as the 1920s, subscription services such as book-of-the-month clubs have provided customers products periodically. Recently, subscription services have expanded far beyond books and magazines to include clothing (bombfell.com), shoes (shoedazzle.com), and beauty (birchbox.com). Many Web sites require subscriptions to view premium content, and streaming media services like Spotify, Netflix, and OnLive offer a wholly new type of subscription service.

Digital marketplaces like Steam and the Google Play Store constitute another recent trend in marketing channels. Digital licensing adds an interesting facet to customer sales; instead of selling a tangible product, digital marketplaces sell the *rights* to songs, movies, and television shows through their Web sites and applications. Instead of leaving home to purchase a physical album, game, or movie, consumers can select specific media and download them directly to their computers or mobile devices.

14-3 TYPES OF CHANNEL RELATIONSHIPS

A marketing channel is more than a set of institutions linked by economic ties. Social relationships play an important role in building unity among channel members. Marketing managers should carefully consider the types of relationships they choose to foster between their company and other companies and in doing so pay close attention to the benefits and hazards associated with each relationship type. Relationships among channel members range from "loose" to "tight," taking the form of a continuum stretching from single transactions to complex interdependent relationships such as partnerships or alliances. The choice of relationship type is important for channel management because each relationship type carries with it different levels of time, financial, and resource investment. There are three basic types of relationships, organized here by degree of closeness:

- **Arm's-length relationships** are considered by channel members to be temporary or one-time-only and often arise from a sudden or unique need. These relationships are characterized by the companies' unwillingness or lack of ability to develop a closer type of relationship. Both parties typically retain their independence and pursue only their own interests while attempting to benefit from the goods or services provided by the other. A major weakness of arm's-length relationships is the potential for opportunism. Opportunistic behavior may occur when the members do not have a common goal; when members have not formed a formal relationship; when one company is more dependent on the other than vice versa; or when there is uncertainty within the relationship and the market. Arm's-length relationships include real estate purchases. New retail locations are often considered one-at-a-time, and so both the purchasing organization and the selling organization may be suspicious of opportunistic behavior from the other party involved.

The fashion industry works diligently to protect its designers by running ads such as this one to deter people from buying knockoffs on the street.

- **Cooperative relationships,** generally administered using some kind of formal contract, are used when a company wants less ambiguity but doesn't want the long-term and/or capital investment necessary in an integrated relationship. Cooperative relationships tend to be more flexible than integrated relationships but are more structured than arm's-length relationships, and they include non-equity agreements such as franchising and licensing as well as joint ventures and strategic alliances. For example, Coca-Cola entered into a cooperative relationship with McDonald's to increase sales. The two companies work closely and have a clearly defined relationship, but remain two separate entities.

- **Integrated relationships** are closely bonded relationships characterized by formal arrangements that explicitly define the relationships of the channel members. These relationships may take two forms. With *vertical integration,* all the related channel members are owned by a single legal entity, whereas in a *supply chain,* several companies act as one. American Apparel takes pride in its vertical integration approach. The company manufactures all of the clothing sold in its stores, allowing the company greater control over its operations. On the other hand, companies like Samsung work with select suppliers to manufacture their products. The companies remain separate but work as one, viewing success as a group outcome.

- **Co-opetition** mixes elements of cooperation and competition between two partners. Two companies work together on some initiatives while still competing in other areas. Microsoft and Apple cooperate by allowing their competitors to use their software, such as Microsoft Word and Apple iTunes. The two firms compete with one another in an effort to get consumers to purchase their products, but once the product is purchased, cooperation allows software to be used on either platform.

arm's-length relationship a relationship between companies that is loose, characterized by low relational investment and trust, and usually taking the form of a series of discrete transactions with no or low expectation of future interaction or service

cooperative relationship a relationship between companies that takes the form of informal partnership with moderate levels of trust and information sharing as needed to further each company's goals

integrated relationship a relationship between companies that is tightly connected, with linked processes across and between firm boundaries and high levels of trust and interfirm commitment

co-opetition a relationship that mixes elements of cooperation and competition between two partners

channel power the capacity of a particular marketing channel member to control or influence the behavior of other channel members

channel control a situation that occurs when one marketing channel member intentionally affects another member's behavior

channel captain a member of a marketing channel that exercises authority and power over the activities of other channel members

channel conflict a clash of goals and methods between distribution channel members

horizontal conflict a channel conflict that occurs among channel members on the same level

vertical conflict a channel conflict that occurs between different levels in a marketing channel, most typically between the manufacturer and wholesaler or between the manufacturer and retailer

The term *supply chain* is misleading. Distribution channels consist of multiple suppliers and customers working together. Companies may work with several different suppliers and customers, and so viewing the channel as a chain (with one company connected between two others) paints an incomplete picture. Instead, a distribution channel is more like a network than a chain. Several companies work with each other and multiple connections occur at each level of the channel.

14-3a Global Channel Relationships

Some countries enact economic policies that directly or indirectly regulate channel choices. For example, due to the size of India's market, many companies are interested in operating there. India does not explicitly prohibit foreign retailers from entering its market, but it protects its businesses by levying heavy taxes on foreign retailers. To address this issue, many companies have entered joint ventures with local Indian companies. Swedish furniture maker IKEA and fashion chain H&M are two of the most recent companies to apply for joint ventures in India. Through joint ventures, foreign companies are able to compete effectively in India's available distribution channels.[3]

Marketers must also be aware that many countries have "gray" marketing channels in which products are distributed through unauthorized channel intermediaries. It is estimated that sales of counterfeit luxury items like Prada handbags and Big Bertha golf clubs have reached almost $2 billion a year. The Internet has also proved to be a way for pirates to circumvent authorized distribution channels, especially in the case of popular prescription drugs.

14-3b Social Influences in Channels

In addition to considering the multiple different types of channel relationships and their costs and benefits, managers must also be aware of the social dimensions that are constantly affecting their relationships. The basic social dimensions of channels are power, control, leadership, conflict, and partnering. **Channel power** is a channel member's ability to control or influence the behavior of other channel members. For example, Amazon's size and buying power have allowed it to pressure its suppliers into selling to Amazon at the lowest possible prices—even to the detriment of those suppliers. According to supply chain analyst Bob Ferrari, "Every company and its associated supply chain arm needs to have a strategy regarding Amazon . . . We may well view more corporate casualties in the coming months as a result of the 'Amazon effect.'"[4] **Channel control** occurs when one channel member's power affects another member's behavior. To achieve control, a channel member assumes channel leadership and exercises authority and power. This member is termed the **channel captain**. In one marketing channel, a manufacturer may be the captain because it controls new-product designs and product availability, while in another, a retailer may be a follower because it lacks relative power and control over the retail price, inventory levels, and postsale service.

Inequitable channel relationships often lead to **channel conflict**, which is a clash of goals and methods among the members of a distribution channel. In a broad context, conflict may not be bad. Often it arises because staid, traditional channel members refuse to keep pace with the times. Removing an outdated intermediary may result in reduced costs for the entire channel. The Internet has forced many intermediaries to offer services such as merchandise tracking and inventory availability online. Conflict within a channel can be either horizontal or vertical. **Horizontal conflict** occurs among channel members on the same level, such as two or more different wholesalers or two or more different retailers that handle the same manufacturer's brands. This type of channel conflict is found most often when manufacturers practice dual or multiple distribution strategies. When Apple changed its distribution strategy and began opening its own stores, it angered its traditional retail partners, some of whom ultimately filed lawsuits against the company. However, much more serious is **vertical conflict**, which occurs between different levels in a marketing channel, most typically between the manufacturer and wholesaler or the manufacturer and retailer. Producer-versus-wholesaler conflict occurs when the producer chooses to bypass the wholesaler and deals directly with the consumer or retailer.

Regardless of who holds power or what conflicts arise, channel members rely heavily on one another. **Channel partnering** is the joint effort of all channel members to create a channel that serves customers and creates a competitive advantage. Channel partnering is vital if each member is to gain something needed from other members.

14-4 THE ROLE OF RETAILING

Retailing represents all the activities directly related to the sale of goods and services to the ultimate consumer for personal, nonbusiness use, and has enhanced the quality of our daily lives. When we shop for groceries, hair styling, clothes, books, and many other products and services, we patronize retailers. The U.S. economy depends heavily on the retail sector: approximately two-thirds of the U.S. gross domestic product came from retail activity in 2012.[5]

Retailing affects all people directly or indirectly. The retailing industry is one of the largest employers in the United States, with more than 1.5 million U.S. retailers employing more than 15 million people—about one in five American workers. And the industry is expected to grow to more than 16 million by 2018.[6] In addition, retail trade accounts for 10.8 percent of all U.S. employment,

and almost 10 percent of all businesses in 2012 were classified as retailers.[7] Yet, retailing is still largely a mom-and-pop business. Almost nine out of ten retail companies employ fewer than twenty employees, and according to the National Retail Federation, over 95 percent of all retailers operate just one store.[8] Though most retailers are quite small, a few giant organizations such as Walmart dominate the industry; Walmart's annual U.S. sales are greater than the sales of the four next largest U.S. retailers combined. As the retail environment changes, so too do retailers. Current innovations in retail include the use of social media, new business models, shopper marketing, and new store formats.

14-5 CLASSES OF RETAIL OPERATIONS

Retail establishments can be classified according to ownership, level of service, product assortment, and price, and retailers use the latter three variables to position themselves in the competitive marketplace. These variables can be combined in several ways to create distinctly different retail operations. Exhibit 4 depicts the major types of retail stores and classifies

channel partnering the joint effort of all channel members to create a channel that serves customers and creates a competitive advantage

retailing all the activities directly related to the sale of goods and services to the ultimate consumer for personal, nonbusiness use

Exhibit 4
TYPES OF STORES AND THEIR CHARACTERISTICS

Type of Retailer	Level of Service	Product Assortment	Price	Gross Margin
Department store	Moderately high to high	Broad	Moderate to high	Moderately high
Specialty store	High	Narrow	Moderate to high	High
Supermarket	Low	Broad	Moderate	Low
Drugstore	Low to moderate	Medium	Moderate	Low
Convenience store	Low	Medium to narrow	Moderately high	Moderately high
Full-line discount store	Moderate to low	Medium to broad	Moderately low	Moderately low
Specialty discount store	Moderate to low	Medium to broad	Moderately low to low	Moderately low
Warehouse club	Low	Broad	Low to very low	Low
Off-price retailer	Low	Medium to narrow	Low	Low
Restaurant	Low to high	Narrow	Low to high	Low to high

© Cengage Learning

them by level of service, product assortment, price, and gross margin.

14-5a Ownership Arrangement

Depending on the type of ownership arrangement, a retailer can also gain advantages from broad brand identity or freedom to take risks and innovate. Retail ownership takes one of three forms: independent, part of a chain, or a franchise outlet. An **independent retailer** is a retailer owned by a single person or group and is not operated as part of a larger network. Around the world, most retailers are independent, operating singular stores within a local community. Local florists and ethnic food markets typically fit this classification. Alternatively, a **chain store** is part of a group of the same stores owned and operated by a single organization. Under this form of ownership, a home office for the entire chain handles many administrative tasks. The home office also buys most of the merchandise sold in the stores. Gap and Starbucks are retail chains. A **franchise** is a business where the operator is granted a license to operate and sell a product under a larger supporting organization, such as Subway and Quiznos. Franchising is covered in greater detail later in this chapter.

14-5b Level of Service

The level of service that retailers provide can be classified along a continuum, from full-service to self-service. Some retailers, such as exclusive clothing stores, offer high levels of service. They provide alterations, credit, delivery, consulting, liberal return policies, layaway, gift-wrapping, and personal shopping. By contrast, retailers such as factory outlets and warehouse clubs offer virtually no services.

14-5c Product Assortment

The third basis for positioning or classifying retailers is by the width and depth of their product line. Specialty stores such as Best Buy, Toys"R"Us, and GameStop have the most concentrated product assortments, usually carrying single or narrow product lines but with considerable depth. For example, a specialty pet store like PetSmart may carry as many as twenty brands of dog food in a large variety of

flavors, shapes, and sizes. On the other end of the spectrum, full-line discounters typically carry broad assortments of merchandise with limited depth. Other retailers, such as Nike factory outlet stores, may carry only part of a single line.

Stores often modify their product assortments in order to accommodate environmental factors. In the wake of the 2012 shooting at Sandy Hook Elementary School, demand for semiautomatic rifles and handguns surged. Many specialized weapons retailers like South Dakota's Rapid Fire Firearms responded to the environmental shift by increasing their stocks of weapons and ammunition while adding armor-plated backpacks and other child-protection products to their product lines. Conversely, big-box retailers Dick's Sporting Goods and Walmart temporarily ceased online and in-store rifle sales in respect of the mourning families. These stores' broad product assortments allowed them to respond to the post-tragedy climate in a different manner without taking a devastating financial hit.[9]

14-5d Price

Price is the fourth way to position retail stores. Traditional department stores and specialty stores typically charge the full "suggested retail price." In contrast, discounters, factory outlets, and off-price retailers use low prices

This December 2012 photo shows a wall that typically displays about twenty-five military-style rifles. Like many gun stores across America, Casper, Wyoming's Rocky Mountain Discount Sports sold out of firearms after the Sandy Hook Elementary School shootings in Newtown, Connecticut sparked concern over the possibility of anti-gun legislation.

AP Images/Casper Star-Tribune, Alan Rogers

to lure shoppers. The last column in Exhibit 4 shows the typical **gross margin**—how much the retailer makes as a percentage of sales after the cost of the goods sold is subtracted. (Margins will be covered in more detail in Chapter 19.)

14-5e Types of Retail Operations

Traditionally, there have been several distinct types of retail stores, each offering a different product assortment, type of service, and price level according to its customers' shopping preferences. Recently, however, retailers are experimenting with alternative formats that make it harder to classify them. For instance, supermarkets are expanding their nonfood items and services, discounters are adding groceries, drugstores are becoming more like convenience stores, and department stores are experimenting with smaller stores. Nevertheless, many stores still fall into the basic types.

DEPARTMENT STORES A **department store** carries a wide variety of shopping and specialty goods, including apparel, cosmetics, housewares, electronics, and sometimes furniture. Each department is treated as a separate buying center, and central management sets broad policies about the types of merchandise carried and prices. Macy's, JCPenney, Sears, Dillard's, and Nordstrom are some of the large U.S. department store chains.

SPECIALTY STORES A **specialty store** is not only a type of store but also a method of retail operations—namely, specializing in a given type of merchandise. A typical specialty store carries a deeper but narrower assortment of specialty merchandise, and their knowledgeable salesclerks offer more attentive customer service. The Children's Place, Williams-Sonoma, and Foot Locker are examples of successful chain specialty retailers. Consumers usually consider price to be secondary in specialty outlets.

SUPERMARKETS Supermarkets are large, departmentalized, self-service retailers that specialize in food and some nonfood items. Some conventional supermarkets are being replaced by bigger *superstores*, which are often twice their size. Superstores meet the needs of today's customers for convenience, variety, and service by offering one-stop shopping for many food and nonfood needs, as well as many services—including pharmacies, flower shops, salad bars, photo processing, banking, etc. Their tendency to offer a wide variety of nontraditional goods and services under one roof is called **scrambled merchandising**.

DRUGSTORES Drugstores stock pharmacy-related products and services as their main draw, but they also carry an extensive selection of cosmetics, health and beauty aids, seasonal merchandise, greeting cards, toys, and some non-refrigerated convenience foods. As competition has increased from mass merchandisers and supermarkets with their own pharmacies, as well as from direct mail prescription services, drugstores have added services such as twenty-four-hour drive-through pharmacies and low-cost health clinics staffed by nurse practitioners.

CONVENIENCE STORES A **convenience store** can be defined as a miniature supermarket, carrying only a limited line of high-turnover convenience goods. These self-service stores are typically located near residential areas and are often open twenty-four hours a day, seven days a week. Convenience stores offer exactly what their name implies: convenient location, long hours, and fast service. The customer pays a surcharge for convenience, so prices are almost always higher at a convenience store than at a supermarket.

DISCOUNT STORES The **discount store** is a retailer that competes on the basis of low prices, high turnover, and high volume. Discounters can be classified into several major categories:

▸ *Full-line discount stores* offer consumers very limited service and carry a much broader assortment of well-known, nationally branded "hard goods," including housewares, toys, automotive parts, hardware, sporting goods, garden items, and clothing. As with department stores, national chains dominate the discounters; Walmart is the largest full-line discount store in terms of sales.

▸ *Supercenters* combine a full line of groceries and general merchandise with a wide range of services, including pharmacy, dry cleaning, portrait studios, photo finishing, hair salons, optical shops, and restaurants—all in one location. For supercenter operators such as

Target, food is a customer magnet that sharply increases the store's overall volume while taking customers away from traditional supermarkets.

▸▸ **Single-line specialty discount stores are another type of discount store—for example, stores selling sporting goods, electronics, auto parts, office supplies, housewares, or toys. These stores offer a nearly complete selection of single-line merchandise and use self-service, discount prices, high volume, and high turnover to their advantage. A *category killer* is a specialty discount store that heavily dominates its narrow merchandise segment. Examples include Best Buy for electronics, Staples and Office Depot for office supplies, and IKEA for home furnishings.**

▸▸ **A *warehouse membership club* is a limited-service merchant wholesaler that sells a limited selection of brand name appliances, household items, and groceries. These are usually sold in bulk from warehouse outlets on a cash-and-carry basis to members only. Currently, the leading stores in this category are Sam's Club, Costco, and BJ's Wholesale Club.**

OFF-PRICE RETAILERS An **off-price retailer** sells at prices 25 percent or more below traditional department store prices because it pays cash for its stock and usually doesn't ask for return privileges. Off-price retailers buy manufacturers' overruns at cost or even less. They also absorb goods from bankrupt stores, irregular merchandise, and unsold end-of-season output. Today, there are hundreds of off-price retailers; among the best known are TJMaxx, Ross Stores, Marshalls, and Tuesday Morning. Factory outlets are an interesting variation on the off-price concept. A **factory outlet** is an off-price retailer that is owned and operated by a manufacturer. Thus, it carries one line of merchandise—its own. With factory outlets, manufacturers can regulate where their surplus is sold, and they can realize higher profit margins than they would by disposing of the goods through independent wholesalers and retailers.

USED GOODS RETAILERS Used goods retailers turn customers into suppliers: items purchased from one of the other types of retailers can be resold to a different customer. Used goods retailers can be either brick-and-mortar locations (such as Goodwill stores) or electronic marketplaces. Internet sites like eBay allow customers to sell their previously purchased products without needing a physical selling location.

RESTAURANTS Restaurants straddle the line between retailing establishments and service establishments. Restaurants do sell tangible products—food and drink—but they also provide a valuable service for consumers in the form of food preparation and food service. Most restaurants could even fall into the definition of a specialty retailer given that most concentrate their menu offerings on a distinctive type of cuisine—for example, Olive Garden Italian restaurants and Starbucks coffeehouses.

14-5f Non-store Retailing

The retailing formats discussed so far have been in-store methods, in which customers must physically shop at stores. In contrast, **non-store retailing** is shopping without visiting a store. Because consumers demand convenience, non-store retailing is currently growing faster than in-store retailing. The major forms of non-store retailing are automatic vending, direct retailing, direct marketing, and electronic retailing.

AUTOMATIC VENDING **Automatic vending** implies the use of machines to offer goods for sale—for example, the soft drink, candy, or snack vending machines found in college cafeterias and office buildings. Vending is the most pervasive retail business in the United States, and retailers are constantly seeking new opportunities to sell via vending. Many vending machines today sell nontraditional kinds of merchandise such as DVDs, digital cameras, perfumes, and even ice cream. Self-service technologies (SST) represent another form of automatic vending. Automatic teller machines, pay-at-the-pump gas stations, and ticket kiosks at movie theaters allow customers to purchase products that once required assistance from a company employee.

DIRECT RETAILING In **direct retailing**, representatives sell products door-to-door, office-to-office, or at home sales parties. Companies like Avon, Mary Kay, and The Pampered Chef have used this approach for years. Man Cave, a new home sales party developed for men, is "like Mary Kay on steroids." Affiliates of this system invite male friends and

Tupperware has long used direct marketing as its primary method of driving sales.

direct marketing (direct response marketing) techniques used to get consumers to make a purchase from their home, office, or other nonretail setting

telemarketing the use of the telephone to sell directly to consumers

shop-at-home television network a specialized form of direct response marketing whereby television shows display merchandise, with the retail price, to home viewers

online retailing (e-tailing) a type of shopping available to consumers with personal computers and access to the Internet

family over for a testosterone-fueled party, at which they use Man Cave products and serve Man Cave foods. Affiliates are then commissioned on the sale of beer mugs, grilling tools, frozen steaks, and other Man Cave products.[10]

DIRECT MARKETING Direct marketing, sometimes called **direct response marketing**, refers to the techniques used to get consumers to make a purchase from their home, office, or other nonretail setting. Those techniques include telemarketing, direct mail, catalogs and mail order, and online retailing. Shoppers using these methods are less bound by traditional shopping situations. Time-strapped consumers and those who live in rural or suburban areas are most likely to be direct response shoppers because they value the convenience and flexibility that direct marketing provides.

TELEMARKETING Telemarketing is the use of the telephone to sell directly to consumers. It consists of outbound sales calls, usually unsolicited, and inbound calls—that is, orders through toll-free 800 numbers or fee-based 900 numbers. The use of telemarketing is not at all insignificant in modern marketing; recent estimates indicate that 5,000 U.S. companies will spend more than $15 billion on inbound and outbound calls by 2015.[11]

DIRECT MAIL Direct mail can be the most efficient or the least efficient retailing method, depending on the quality of the mailing list and the effectiveness of the mailing piece. With direct mail, marketers can precisely target their customers according to demographics, geographics, and even psychographics. Direct mailers are becoming more

sophisticated in targeting the "right" customers. Using statistical methods to analyze census data, lifestyle and financial information, and past purchase and credit history, direct mailers can pick out those most likely to buy their products. According to the Direct Marketing Association, every year U.S companies spend more than $163 billion on direct marketing, representing 52.1 percent of their advertising expenditures and generating almost $2 trillion in sales.[12]

SHOP-AT-HOME TELEVISION NETWORKS Shop-at-home television networks are specialized forms of direct response marketing. Their shows display merchandise, with the retail price, to home viewers. Viewers can phone in their orders directly on a toll-free line and shop with a credit card. The shop-at-home industry has quickly grown into a multi-billion-dollar business with a loyal customer following. Shop-at-home networks can reach nearly every home with a television set. The best-known shop-at-home networks are HSN (formerly the Home Shopping Network) and the QVC (Quality, Value, Convenience) Network.

ONLINE RETAILING Online retailing, or **e-tailing**, allows customers to shop over the Internet. Online shopping accounted for more than $200 billion in sales in 2012. Sales from this increasingly popular segment are expected to grow to at least $327 billion by 2016.[13] Consumers have found this type of shopping convenient and, in many instances, less costly. Consumers can shop without leaving home, choose from a wide selection of merchants, use shopping comparison services to search the Web for the best price, and then have the items delivered to their doorsteps. Technological advances like interactive shopping tools and live chats offer a substitute for the in-store experience of physically examining products and speaking to salespeople face-to-face. Shoppers can look at a much wider variety of products online because they are not limited to the available space in the retail store. Further, they can take their time deciding what to buy and from whom to buy.

14-5g Franchising

As you read at the beginning of this section, a *franchise* is a continuing relationship in which a franchisor grants to a franchisee the business rights to operate or sell a product. The **franchisor** originates the trade name, product, methods of operation, and so on. The **franchisee**, in return, pays the franchisor for the right to use its name, product, or business methods. A franchise agreement between the two parties usually lasts for ten to twenty years, at which time the agreement can be renewed if both parties are agreeable.

To be granted the rights to a franchise, a franchisee usually pays an initial, one-time franchise fee. The amount of this fee depends solely on the individual franchisor, but it generally ranges from $50,000 to $250,000 or higher. In addition to this initial franchise fee, the franchisee is expected to pay royalty fees, usually in the range of 3 to 7 percent of gross revenues but occasionally as high as 12 percent or more. The franchisee may also be expected to pay advertising fees, which usually cover the cost of promotional materials and, if the franchise organization is large enough, regional or national advertising.

Two basic forms of franchises are used today: product and trade name franchising and business format franchising. In *product and trade name franchising*, a dealer agrees to sell certain products provided by a manufacturer or a wholesaler. This approach has been used most widely in the auto and truck, soft drink bottling, tire, and gasoline service industries. For example, a local tire retailer may hold a franchise to sell Michelin tires. *Business format franchising* is an ongoing business relationship between a franchisor and a franchisee. Typically, a franchisor "sells" a franchisee the rights to use the franchisor's format or approach to doing business. This form of franchising has rapidly expanded through retailing, restaurant, food service, hotel and motel, printing, and real estate franchises.

THE TOP TEN NEW FRANCHISES OF 2013

According to *Entrepreneur*, the top ten new franchises for 2013 were:

1. Kona Ice
2. Menchie's
3. Orange Leaf Frozen Yogurt
4. ShelfGenie
5. Bricks 4 Kidz
6. Smashburger
7. GameTruck
8. Paul Davis Emergency Services
9. Signal 88 Security
10. Mac Tools[14]

14-6 RETAIL MARKETING STRATEGY

Retailers must develop marketing strategies based on their periodic goals and overall strategic plans. Periodic retailing goals might include more traffic, higher sales of a specific item, developing a more upscale image, or creating heightened public awareness of the retail operation. The strategies that retailers use to obtain their goals might include a sale, updated décor, or a new advertisement. The key tasks in strategic retailing are defining and selecting a target market and developing the retailing mix to successfully meet the needs of the chosen target market.

14-6a Defining a Target Market

The first and foremost task in developing a retail strategy is to define the target market. This process begins with market segmentation, the topic of Chapter 8. Successful retailing has always been based on knowing the customer. Sometimes retailing chains flounder when management loses sight of the customers the stores should be serving.

Target markets in retailing are often defined by demographics, geographics, and psychographics. For example, movie studios and theatres have begun targeting baby boomers with films about aging, such as the Dustin Hoffman-directed *Quartet* and Austrian film *Amour*. Even the 2012 James Bond action film *Skyfall* dealt with themes of aging in a rapidly changing world. Baby boomers have not been a prime target market for movies since their college days in the mid-1970s, but now that they are empty nesters with time and money to spare, vast numbers of baby boomers are going out to the movies.[15] Determining a target market is a prerequisite to creating the retailing mix. For example, Target's merchandising approach for sporting goods is to match its product assortment to the demographics of the local store and region.

14-6b Choosing the Retailing Mix

Retailers combine the elements of the retailing mix to come up with a single retailing method to attract the target market. The **retailing mix** consists of six Ps: the four Ps of the marketing mix (product, place, promotion, and price) plus presentation and personnel (see Exhibit 5). The combination of the six Ps projects a store's image, which influences consumers' perceptions. Using these impressions of stores, shoppers position one store against another. A retail manager must make sure that the store's positioning is aligned with target customers' expectations.

PRODUCT The first element in the retailing mix is the *product offering*, also called the *product assortment* or *merchandise mix*. Developing a product offering is essentially a question of the width and depth of the product assortment. *Width* refers to the assortment of products offered; *depth* refers to the number of different brands offered within each assortment. Price, store design, displays, and service are important to consumers in determining where to shop, but the most critical factor is merchandise selection. This reasoning also holds true for online retailers. Amazon.com, for instance, offers considerable width in its product assortment with millions of different items, including books, music, toys, videos, tools and hardware, health and beauty aids, electronics, and

software. Conversely, online specialty retailers, such as 1-800-Flowers.com and Polo.com, focus on a single category of merchandise, hoping to attract loyal customers with a larger depth of products at lower prices and excellent customer service. Many online retailers purposely focus on single product line niches that could never garner enough foot traffic to support a traditional brick-and-mortar store. For instance, Web sites such as bugbitingplants.com and petflytrap.com sell and ship live carnivorous plants in the United States. After determining what products will satisfy target customers' desires, retailers must find sources of supply and evaluate the products. When the right products are found, the retail buyer negotiates a purchase contract.

PROMOTION Retail promotion strategy includes advertising, public relations and publicity, and sales promotion. The goal is to help position the store in consumers' minds. Retailers design intriguing ads, stage special events, and develop promotions aimed at their target markets. Today's grand openings are a carefully orchestrated blend of advertising, merchandising, goodwill, and glitter. All the elements of an opening—press coverage,

retailing mix a combination of the six Ps—product, place, promotion, price, presentation, and personnel—to sell goods and services to the ultimate consumer

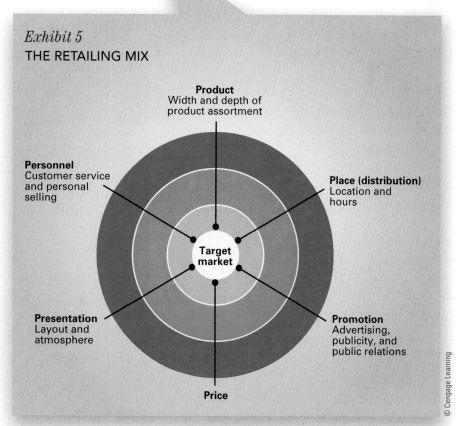

Exhibit 5
THE RETAILING MIX

Product Width and depth of product assortment

Place (distribution) Location and hours

Promotion Advertising, publicity, and public relations

Price

Presentation Layout and atmosphere

Personnel Customer service and personal selling

Target market

© Cengage Learning

special events, media advertising, and store displays—are carefully planned.

Retailers' advertising is carried out mostly at the local level. Local advertising by retailers usually provides specific information about their stores, such as location, merchandise, hours, prices, and special sales. In contrast, national retail advertising generally focuses on image. For example, Target uses advertisements similar to designer fashion advertisements to depict high-quality goods. Paired with the ubiquitous red target and tag line "Expect more. Pay less," Target is demonstrating that it sells products that consumers normally aspire to own at prices they can afford.

Target's advertising campaign also takes advantage of cooperative advertising, another popular retail advertising practice. Traditionally, marketers would pay retailers to feature their products in store mailers, or a marketer would develop a television campaign for the product and simply tack on several retailers' names at the end. But Target's advertising uses a more collaborative trend by integrating products such as Tide laundry detergent or Coca-Cola into the actual campaign. Another common form of cooperative advertising involves promotion of exclusive products. For example, Target hires famous trendy designers for temporary partnerships, during which they develop reasonably priced

Heidi Klum and other Victoria's Secret models celebrate at an opening ceremony for a New York store. The women are part of the Victoria's Secret promotion strategy.

© ny1/ny1/ZUMA Press/Newscom

product lines available exclusively at Target stores. Recently, Target teamed up with Neiman Marcus to offer a collection of holiday luxury items. These items were sold both at Target and Neiman Marcus stores, as well as on both stores' online outlet stores.

PLACE The retailing axiom "location, location, location" has long emphasized the importance of place to the retail mix. The *location* decision is important first because the retailer is making a large, semi-permanent commitment of resources that can reduce its future flexibility. Second, the location will affect the store's future growth and profitability.

Site location begins by choosing a community. Important factors to consider are the area's economic growth potential, the amount of competition, and geography. For instance, retailers like TJMaxx and Walmart often build stores in new communities that are still under development. Fast-food restaurants tend to place a priority on locations with other fast-food restaurants because being located in clusters helps to draw customers for each restaurant. However, even after careful research, the perfect position can be elusive in the face of changing markets. Food trucks circumvent this problem by being able to relocate at will. By moving from spot to spot over the course of a day and parking outside events and heavily trafficked areas, food trucks can maximize their exposure and adapt to changing markets.[16]

After settling on a geographic region or community, retailers must choose a specific site. In addition to growth potential, the important factors to consider are neighborhood socioeconomic characteristics, traffic flows, land costs, zoning regulations, and public transportation. A particular site's visibility, parking, entrance and exit locations, accessibility, and safety and security issues are also important considerations.

Additionally, a retailer should consider how its store will fit into the surrounding environment. Retail decision makers probably would not locate a Dollar General store next door to a Neiman Marcus department store. Furthermore, retailers face decisions related to whether to have a freestanding unit or to become a tenant in a shopping center or mall. Large retailers like Target and sellers of shopping goods like furniture and cars can use an isolated, freestanding location because they are "destination stores." A **destination store** is a store consumers seek out and purposely plan to visit. An isolated store location may have the advantages of low site cost or rent and no nearby competitors. On the other

atmosphere the overall impression conveyed by a store's physical layout, décor, and surroundings

hand, it may be hard to attract customers to a freestanding location, and no other retailers are around to share costs.

Freestanding units are increasing in popularity as retailers strive to make their stores more convenient to access, more enticing to shop, and more profitable. Freestanding sites now account for more than half of all retail construction starts in the United States as more and more retailers are deciding not to locate in pedestrian malls. Perhaps the greatest reason for developing a freestanding site is greater visibility. Retailers often feel they get lost in huge centers and malls, but freestanding units can help stores develop an identity with shoppers. Also, an aggressive expansion plan may not allow time to wait for shopping centers to be built. Drugstore chains like Walgreens have been purposefully relocating their existing shopping center stores to freestanding sites, especially street corner sites for drive-through accessibility.

Shopping centers first appeared in the 1950s when the U.S. population started migrating to the suburbs. The first shopping centers were *strip centers*, typically located along busy streets. They usually included a supermarket, a variety store, and perhaps a few specialty stores. Then *community shopping centers* emerged, with one or two small department stores, more specialty stores, a couple restaurants, and several apparel stores. These community shopping centers provided off-street parking and a broader variety of merchandise. *Regional malls* offering a much wider variety of merchandise started appearing in the mid-1970s. Regional malls are either entirely enclosed or roofed to allow shopping in any weather. Most are landscaped with trees, fountains, sculptures, and the like to enhance the shopping environment. They have acres of free parking. The *anchor stores* or *generator stores* (often major department stores) are usually located at opposite ends of the mall to create heavy foot traffic.

According to shopping center developers, *lifestyle centers* are emerging as the newest generation of shopping centers. Lifestyle centers typically combine outdoor shopping areas composed of upscale retailers and restaurants, with plazas, fountains, and pedestrian streets. They appeal to retail developers looking for an alternative to the traditional shopping mall, a concept rapidly losing favor among shoppers. Though shopping malls bring multiple retail locations together, location is often not the most important motivator for a customer to choose a specific store. Instead, most shoppers look for stores that guarantee product availability, more service employees, and time-saving opportunities.

Many smaller specialty lines are opening shops inside larger stores to expand their retail opportunities without risking investment in a separate store. Toys"R"Us worked with Macy's to open a store-within-a-store at twenty-four Macy's locations during the 2012 holiday season. The 1,500-square-foot toy sections offered dolls, puzzles, and other potential stocking stuffers.[17] The Toys"R"Us modules reflect a popular trend of pop-up shops—tiny, temporary stores that stay in one location only for a few months. Pop-up shops help retailers reach a wide market while avoiding high rent at retail locations. They have become the marketing tool du jour for large companies.

PRICE Another important element in the retailing mix is price. Retailing's ultimate goal is to sell products to consumers, and the right price is critical to ensure sales. Because retail prices are usually based on the cost of the merchandise, an essential part of pricing is efficient and timely buying. Another pricing strategy is "value-based pricing," which focuses on the value of the product to the customer more than the cost of the product to the supplier. Price is also a key element in a retail store's positioning strategy. Higher prices often indicate a level of quality and help reinforce the prestigious image of retailers, as they do for Lord & Taylor and Neiman Marcus. On the other hand, discounters and off-price retailers, such as Target and TJMaxx, offer a good value for the money.

PRESENTATION The presentation of a retail store helps determine the store's image and positions the retail store in consumers' minds. For instance, a retailer that wants to position itself as an upscale store would use a lavish or sophisticated presentation. The main element of a store's presentation is its **atmosphere**, the overall impression conveyed by a store's physical layout, décor, and surroundings. The atmosphere might create a relaxed or busy feeling, a sense of luxury or efficiency, a friendly or cold attitude, a sense of organization or clutter, or a fun or serious mood. Urban Outfitters stores, targeted to Generation Y consumers, use raw concrete, original brick, rusted steel, and unfinished wood to convey an urban feel. These are the most influential factors in creating a store's atmosphere:

▸ **EMPLOYEE TYPE AND DENSITY:** Employee type refers to an employee's general characteristics— for instance, neat, friendly, knowledgeable, or service oriented. Density is the number of employees per 1,000 square feet of selling space. Whereas low employee density creates a "do-it-yourself," casual atmosphere, high employee density denotes readiness to serve the customer's every whim.

▸ **MERCHANDISE TYPE AND DENSITY:** A prestigious retailer like Nordstrom or Neiman Marcus carries the best brand names and displays them in a neat, uncluttered arrangement. Discounters and off-price retailers often carry seconds or out-of-season goods crowded into small spaces and hung on long racks by category—tops, pants, skirts, etc.—creating the impression that "We've got so much stuff, we're practically giving it away."

▸ **FIXTURE TYPE AND DENSITY:** Fixtures can be elegant (rich woods) or trendy (chrome and smoked glass); they can even consist of old, beat-up tables, as in an antiques store. The fixtures should be consistent with the general atmosphere the store is trying to create.

▸ **SOUND:** Sound can be pleasant or unpleasant for a customer. Music can entice customers to stay in the store longer and buy more or to eat quickly and leave a table for others. It can also control the pace of the store traffic, create an image, and attract or direct the shopper's attention.

▸ **ODORS:** Smell can either stimulate or detract from sales. Research suggests that people evaluate merchandise more positively, spend more time shopping, and are generally in a better mood when an agreeable odor is present. Retailers use fragrances as an extension of their retail strategy.

▸ **VISUAL FACTORS:** Colors can create a mood or focus attention and therefore are an important factor in atmosphere. Red, yellow, and orange are considered warm colors and are used when a feeling of warmth and closeness is desired. Cool colors like blue, green, and violet are used to open up closed-in

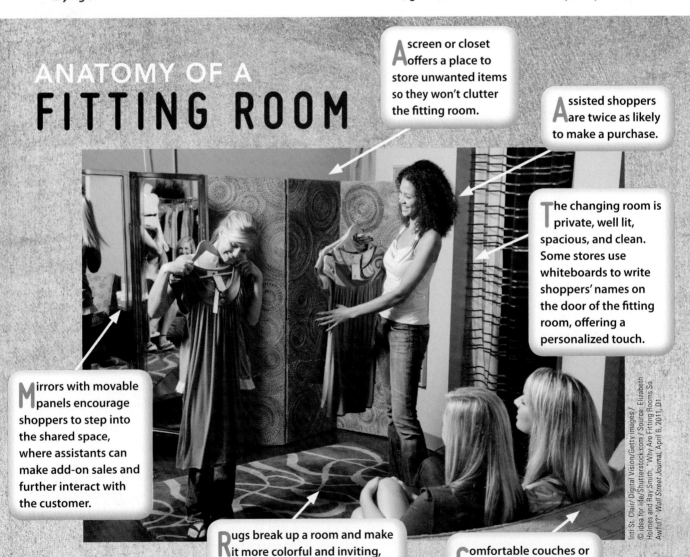

ANATOMY OF A
FITTING ROOM

A screen or closet offers a place to store unwanted items so they won't clutter the fitting room.

Assisted shoppers are twice as likely to make a purchase.

The changing room is private, well lit, spacious, and clean. Some stores use whiteboards to write shoppers' names on the door of the fitting room, offering a personalized touch.

Mirrors with movable panels encourage shoppers to step into the shared space, where assistants can make add-on sales and further interact with the customer.

Rugs break up a room and make it more colorful and inviting, which encourages customers to stay longer in the store.

Comfortable couches or chairs offer shoppers a place to rest.

Int'l St. Clair/Digital Vision/Getty images / © idea for life/Shutterstock.com / Source: Elizabeth Holmes and Ray Smith, "Why Are Fitting Rooms So Awful?" *Wall Street Journal*, April 6, 2011, D1.

places and create an air of elegance and cleanliness. Many retailers have found that natural lighting, either from windows or skylights, can lead to increased sales. Outdoor lighting can also affect consumer patronage.

The **layout** of retail stores is also a key factor in their success. The goal is to use all of the store's space effectively, including aisles, fixtures, merchandise displays, and non-selling areas. In addition to making shopping easy and convenient for the customer, an effective layout has a powerful influence on traffic patterns and purchasing behavior. Layout also includes where products are placed in the store. Many technologically advanced retailers are using a technique called *market-basket analysis* to sift through the data collected by their point-of-purchase scanning equipment. The analysis looks for products that are commonly purchased together to help retailers find ideal locations for each product. Walmart uses market-basket analysis to determine where in the store to stock products for customer convenience. Kleenex tissues, for example, are in the paper-goods aisle and beside the cold medicines.

PERSONNEL People are a unique aspect of retailing. Most retail sales involve a customer–salesperson relationship, if only briefly. Sales personnel provide their customers with the amount of service prescribed by the retail strategy of the store.

Retail salespeople serve another important selling function: they persuade shoppers to buy. They must therefore be able to persuade customers that what they are selling is what the customer needs. Salespeople are trained in two common selling techniques: trading up and suggestion selling. *Trading up* means persuading customers to buy a higher-priced item than they originally intended to purchase. To avoid selling customers something they do not need or want, however, salespeople should take care when practicing trading-up techniques. *Suggestion selling*, a common practice among most retailers, seeks to broaden customers' original purchases with related items. For example, if you buy a new printer at Office Depot, the sales representative will ask if you would like to purchase paper, a USB cable, and/or extra ink cartridges. Suggestion selling by sales or service associates should always help shoppers recognize true needs rather than sell them unwanted merchandise.

Providing great customer service is one of the most challenging elements in the retail mix because customer expectations for service vary greatly. What customers expect in a department store is very different from what they expect in a discount store. Customer expectations also change. Ten years ago, shoppers wanted personal one-on-one attention. Today, most customers are happy to help themselves as long as they can easily find what they need.

14-6c Channels and Retailing Decisions for Services

The fastest-growing part of our economy is the service sector. Although distribution in the service sector is difficult to visualize, the same skills, techniques, and strategies used to manage inventory can also be used to manage service inventory, such as hospital beds, bank accounts, or airline seats. The quality of the planning and execution of distribution can have a major impact on costs and customer satisfaction.

Because service industries are so customer oriented, customer service is a priority. To manage customer relationships, many service providers, such as insurance carriers, physicians, hair salons, and financial services, use technology to schedule appointments, manage accounts, and disburse information. Service distribution focuses on four main areas:

▸▸ **MINIMIZING WAIT TIMES:** Minimizing the amount of time customers wait in line is a key factor in maintaining the quality of service.

▸▸ **MANAGING SERVICE CAPACITY:** If service firms don't have the capacity to meet demand, they must either turn down some prospective customers, let service levels slip, or expand capacity.

▸▸ **IMPROVING SERVICE DELIVERY:** Service firms are now experimenting with different distribution channels for their services. Choosing the right distribution channel can increase the times that services are available or add to customer convenience.

▸▸ **ESTABLISHING CHANNEL-WIDE NETWORK COHERENCE:** Because services are to some degree intangible, service firms also find it necessary to standardize their service quality across different geographic regions to maintain their brand image.

14-6d Shopper Marketing

Shopper marketing is about first understanding how a brand's target consumers behave as shoppers in different channels and formats, and then using this information in business-based strategies and initiatives that are carefully designed to deliver balanced benefits to all stakeholders—brands, retailers, and shoppers. It may sound simple,

data mining the process of discovering patterns in large data sets for the purposes of extracting knowledge and understanding human behavior

but it is anything but. Whereas brand manufacturers used to advertise widely and tried to ensure that their products were available wherever consumers shopped, now they are placing far more emphasis on partnering with specific retailers. Brand manufacturers work with retailers on everything from in-store initiatives to customized retailer-specific products. Shopper marketing brings brand managers and account managers together to connect with consumers along the entire path to purchase, whether it be at home, on the go, or in the store. Both manufacturers and retailers now think about consumers specifically while they are in shopping mode. They are digging deeply into differences in shopping attitudes, perceptions, emotions, and behaviors—and how the shopping experience shapes these differences. More and more companies are conducting or participating in large-scale research projects to better understand both how shoppers think when they shop and what factors affect this thought process.

Shopper marketing is becoming increasingly popular as businesses see the implications of this new method of customer research. One implication is the strategic alignment of customer segments. Brands' core target consumers are compared to retailers' most loyal shoppers in an effort to find intersecting areas where brands and retailers can pool their resources. The ideal outcome is a more focused marketing effort and a three-way win for brands, retailers, *and* shoppers.

Shopper marketing also has significant supply chain implications. As in-store initiatives become more unique and short-term and products become more customized,

QUALITY OF SERVICE IS DIRECTLY TIED TO HOW LONG PEOPLE HAVE TO WAIT IN LINE.

© fStop/Alamy

supply chains must react more quickly to customer demand changes. Thus, shopper marketing has increased the need for sophisticated analytics and metrics. As with many modern business efforts, shopper marketing is forcing managers to coordinate better, measure more, think more creatively, and move faster.

14-7 THE RELATIONSHIP BETWEEN RETAILER DECISION MAKING AND CUSTOMER DATA

Retailers decide what to sell on the basis of what their target market wants to buy. They can base their decision on market research, past sales, fashion trends, customer requests, and other sources. **Data mining** uses complex mathematical models to help retailers make better product mix decisions. Dillard's, Target, and Walmart use data mining to determine which products to stock at what price, how to manage markdowns, and how to advertise to draw target customers. The data they collect and store allows manufacturers and retailers to gain better insight into who is buying their products. Instead of simply unloading products into the distribution channel and leaving marketing and relationship building to dealers, auto manufacturers today are using Web sites to keep in touch with customers and prospects, learn about their lifestyles and hobbies, understand their vehicle needs, and develop relationships in the hope that these consumers will reward them with brand loyalty in the future. BMW and other vehicle manufacturers have databases with names of millions of consumers who have expressed an interest in their products.

14-8 NEW DEVELOPMENTS IN RETAIL AND CHANNEL MANAGEMENT

With online shopping increasing but customers not always able to be home to sign for packages, there have been new developments in package delivery. Amazon has developed a new delivery option for its customers. In large cities, Amazon Lockers sit in banks at some drugstores, department stores, and office supply stores like Staples. Customers can have small packages dropped at a nearby set of lockers, enter their information, and retrieve the package at their convenience.[18]

With technology changing rapidly, there are always new trends developing in both retail and in channel management. Mobile commerce is continuing to be the avenue with the largest growth in both retail and channel decision making, in part because of its more than $5 billion in yearly revenue. For example, eBay added to its virtual auction empire during the 2012 holiday season by opening up pop-up shops where shoppers scanned QR codes (quick response codes that act like a customer barcode for a programmed URL) on each item. The QR code directed shoppers to eBay's payment screen. The auction giant also handed out shopping guides with QR codes next to popular gifts to encourage customers to shop with eBay.[19]

M-commerce (mobile e-commerce) enables consumers using wireless mobile devices to connect to the Internet and shop. Essentially, m-commerce goes beyond text message advertisements to allow consumers to purchase goods and services using wireless mobile devices, such as mobile telephones, smartphones, and tablet computers. M-commerce users adopt the new technology because it saves time and offers more convenience in a greater number of locations.

Many major companies, ranging from Polo Ralph Lauren to Sears, already offer shopping on mobile phones, and the growth potential is huge. In 2012, 34 percent of North American mobile phone users made online purchases via their phones (versus only 19 percent in 2011).[20] In the United States, 87 percent of adults own a cell phone, 45 percent own a smartphone, 31 percent own a tablet, and 26 percent own an e-reader.[21] Fifty-five percent of adults use the Internet on their mobile devices, and 31 percent report that they go online with their mobile device more than they do with a desktop or laptop computer.[22] The gap between the number of smartphones owned and smartphones used for purchases is closing rapidly. During the 2012 holiday season, 27 percent of smartphone owners checked prices using some kind of price comparison app, 28 percent read reviews online while inside a store, and 46 percent used their smartphones to call a friend or family member for purchase advice.[23] All told, more than 58 percent of the thousands surveyed used their mobile devices for one or more of these reasons.[24]

Along with smartphone technology, companies are starting to look into new ways to connect with their customers. Social shopping allows multiple retailers to sell products to customers through social media sites. Aaramshop brings hundreds of neighborhood grocery stores to customers through Facebook; customers make their purchases online and their specific neighborhood stores take care of delivering the items directly to customers' homes.[25] Home delivery extends beyond groceries in many heavily populated areas. In China and India, McDonald's has started delivering directly to its customers instead of making consumers come to them.

On the demand management side, facial recognition technology allows market researchers to record consumers' nonverbal reactions to products and advertisements, giving them more information about customer preferences. Some retailers are also using facial recognition technology to display specific advertisements and recommendations to customers by determining the gender and age group to which each customer belongs.

STUDY TOOLS 14

LOCATED AT BACK OF THE TEXTBOOK

☐ *Rip out Chapter Review Card*

LOCATED AT WWW.CENGAGE.COM/LOGIN

☐ *Review Key Terms Flashcards*

☐ *Watch visual summaries to review key concepts*

☐ *Complete Practice Quizzes to prepare for tests*

☐ *Complete "Crossword Puzzle" to review key terms*

☐ *Watch Video "New Balance Hubway" for a real company example*

15-1 THE ROLE OF PROMOTION IN THE MARKETING MIX

Few goods or services, no matter how well developed, priced, or distributed, can survive in the marketplace without effective promotion—communication by marketers that informs, persuades, and reminds potential buyers of a product in order to influence an opinion or elicit a response.

Few goods or services can survive in the marketplace without effective promotion.

promotion communication by marketers that informs, persuades, and reminds potential buyers of a product in order to influence an opinion or elicit a response

promotional strategy a plan for the optimal use of the elements of promotion: advertising, public relations, personal selling, sales promotion, and social media

competitive advantage one or more unique aspects of an organization that cause target consumers to patronize that firm rather than competitors

Promotional strategy is a plan for the optimal use of the elements of promotion: advertising, public relations, personal selling, sales promotion, and social media. Promotion is a vital part of the marketing mix, informing consumers of a product's benefits and thereby positioning the product in the marketplace. As Exhibit 1 shows, the marketing manager determines the goals of the company's promotional strategy in light of the firm's overall goals for the marketing mix—product, place (distribution), promotion, and price. Using these overall goals, marketers combine the elements of the promotional strategy (the promotional mix) into a coordinated plan. The promotion plan then becomes an integral part of the marketing strategy for reaching the target market.

The main function of a marketer's promotional strategy is to convince target customers that the goods and services offered provide a competitive advantage over the competition. A **competitive advantage** is the set of unique features of a company and its products that are perceived by the target market as significant and superior to those of the competition. Such features can include high product quality, rapid delivery, low prices, excellent service, or a feature not offered by the competition. From its humble beginnings in 2005, real estate search engine and database Web site Zillow has become one of the most-used tools for house hunters. Zillow's intuitive design and innovative tools (such as its comprehensive real estate listings, home value tracker, and mortgage estimator) are clear competitive advantages over competitors' cluttered, confusing, and inaccurate offerings. According to CEO Spencer Rascoff, Zillow's success can be attributed to another less obvious competitive advantage—its transparent, fun, and meritocratic company culture. Zillow's employee-forward culture drives innovation and encourages employees to provide the best service possible.[1]

Marketing Communications

After you finish this chapter go to **p289** for STUDY TOOLS

© iStockPhoto.com/Vladimir Volkov

Exhibit 1

ROLE OF PROMOTION IN THE MARKETING MIX

Overall marketing objectives

Marketing mix
- Product
- Place (distribution)
- Promotion
- Price

Promotional mix
- Advertising
- Public relations
- Sales promotion
- Personal selling
- Social media

Promotion plan

Target market

© Cengage Learning

15-2 MARKETING COMMUNICATION

Promotional strategy is closely related to the process of communication. As humans, we assign meaning to feelings, ideas, facts, attitudes, and emotions. **Communication** is the process by which meanings are exchanged or shared through a common set of symbols. When a company develops a new product, changes an old one, or simply tries to increase sales of an existing good or service, it must communicate its selling message to potential customers. Marketers communicate information about the firm and its products to the target market and various publics through its promotion programs.

When Nestlé's Buitoni Beef Ravioli and Beef Tortellini were found to be contaminated with horse DNA, the Swiss food company quickly issued an apology to its customers in a press release: "Our tests have found traces of horse DNA in two products. The mislabeling of products means they fail to meet the very high standards consumers expect from us...actions being taken to deal with this

issue will result in higher standards and enhanced traceability." Nestlé was one of many companies that had to apologize after traces of horse meat were found in supermarkets and manufactured food goods across Europe in early 2013. While business communication is often used to promote products and services, it must also be used, at times, to acknowledge mistakes and propose new paths forward.[2]

Communication can be divided into two major categories: interpersonal communication and mass communication. **Interpersonal communication** is direct, face-to-face communication between two or more people. When communicating face-to-face, people see the other person's reaction and can respond almost immediately. A salesperson speaking directly with a client is an example of an interpersonal marketing communication.

Mass communication involves communicating a concept or message to large audiences. A great deal of marketing communication is directed to consumers as a whole, usually through a mass medium such as television or newspapers. When a company advertises, it generally does not personally know the people with whom it is trying to communicate. Furthermore, the company often cannot respond immediately to consumers' reactions to its messages (unless they are using social media or other Internet-based marketing tools). Instead, the marketing manager must wait to see whether people are reacting

© AFP/Getty Images

It is essential for businesses of all stripes to communicate information to current and potential customers. Here, Fédération Internationale de Football Association (FIFA) executive committee member Theo Zwanziger answers questions during a press conference following a 2013 meeting of the FIFA executive comittee in Zurich, Switzerland.

communication
the process by which we exchange or share meaning through a common set of symbols

interpersonal communication
direct, face-to-face communication between two or more people

mass communication
the communication of a concept or message to large audiences

positively or negatively to the mass-communicated promotion. Any clutter from competitors' messages or other distractions in the environment can reduce the effectiveness of the mass-communication effort.

15-2a The Communication Process

Marketers are both senders and receivers of messages. As *senders*, marketers attempt to inform, persuade, and remind the target market to adopt courses of action compatible with the need to promote the purchase of goods and services. As *receivers*, marketers attune themselves to the target market in order to develop the appropriate messages, adapt existing messages, and spot new communication opportunities. In this way, most marketing communication is a two-way, rather than one-way, process. The two-way nature of the communication process is shown in Exhibit 2.

THE SENDER AND ENCODING The **sender** is the originator of the message in the communication process. In an interpersonal conversation, the sender may be a parent, a friend, or a salesperson. For an advertisement, press release, or social media campaign,

the sender is the company or organization itself. It can sometimes be difficult to tell who the sender of a promotional message is, especially in the case of bold, avant-garde advertisements. Sometimes, senders intentionally obfuscate their identities in order to build buzz around an advertisement. In 2013, a video titled "Elevator Murder Experiment" was uploaded to YouTube. In the video, the reactions of unsuspecting bystanders are secretly filmed as they witness a staged strangulation in a public New York City elevator. After the video went viral, it was revealed to be an advertisement for the Colin Farrell film *Dead Man Down*, which features a similar scenario.[3]

Encoding is the conversion of the sender's ideas and thoughts into a message, usually in the form of words or signs. A basic principle of encoding is that what matters is not what the source says but what the receiver hears. One way of conveying a message that the receiver will hear properly is to use concrete words and pictures.

Continuing the above example, *Dead Man Down*'s grim themes, extreme violence, and gritty settings were encoded into the elevator prank video. The video even incorporates

sender the originator of the message in the communication process

encoding the conversion of a sender's ideas and thoughts into a message, usually in the form of words or signs

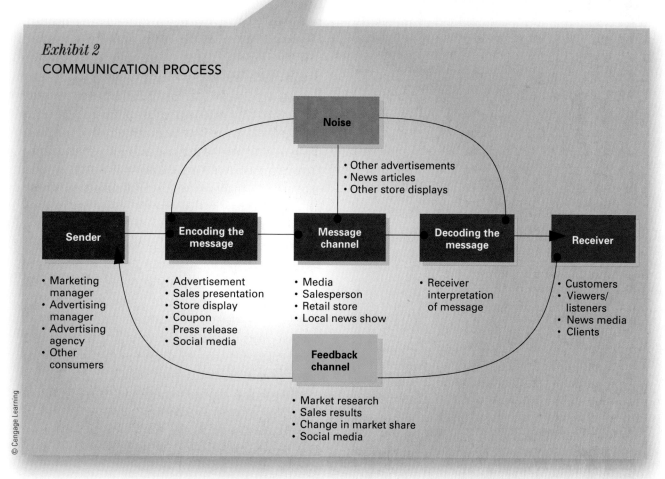

Exhibit 2
COMMUNICATION PROCESS

Noise
- Other advertisements
- News articles
- Other store displays

Sender
- Marketing manager
- Advertising manager
- Advertising agency
- Other consumers

Encoding the message
- Advertisement
- Sales presentation
- Store display
- Coupon
- Press release
- Social media

Message channel
- Media
- Salesperson
- Retail store
- Local news show

Decoding the message
- Receiver interpretation of message

Receiver
- Customers
- Viewers/ listeners
- News media
- Clients

Feedback channel
- Market research
- Sales results
- Change in market share
- Social media

© Cengage Learning

one of the film's plot points—murder in an elevator. Less overtly, the video encodes sentiments such as "you won't know what to expect" and "difficult ethical choices will need to be made"—provocative selling points for a gruesome action thriller.

MESSAGE TRANSMISSION Transmission of a message requires a **channel**—a voice, radio, newspaper, computer, smartphone, or other communication medium. A facial expression or gesture can also serve as a channel. *Dead Man Down's* marketing team used social media as the primary channel on which it distributed the advertisement. After marketers posted the video to YouTube, individuals fascinated by the social experiment ran with it. They shared the video with their friends in person, posted it to Facebook and Twitter, and shared it through several other unorthodox channels. Eventually, local and national media outlets published print articles and ran television segments about the video, creating new channels for the campaign as they did so.[4]

Reception occurs when the message is detected by the receiver and enters his or her frame of reference. In a two-way conversation such as a sales pitch given by a sales representative to a potential client, reception is normally high. Similarly, when the message is a recommendation from a friend, the reception is high as well. By contrast, the desired receivers may or may not detect the message when it is mass communicated because most media are cluttered by **noise**—anything that interferes with, distorts, or slows down the transmission of information. In some media overcrowded with advertisers, such as newspapers and television, the noise level is high and the reception level is low.

THE RECEIVER AND DECODING Marketers communicate their message through a channel to customers, or **receivers**, who will decode the message. It is important to note that there can be multiple receivers as consumers share their experiences and their recommendations online through social networks and other types of social media (as happened with the "Elevator Murder Experiment" video). Online conversations are becoming an increasingly influential way to promote products and services. Indeed, this new empowerment of the receiver has transformed marketing and advertising. Receivers can easily share new information with their friends and followers on social media, and those new receivers can then share that information as well. This leads to a more diverse interrelationship between senders and receivers of social media messages. **Decoding** is the interpretation of the language and symbols sent by the source through a channel. Common understanding between two communicators, or a common frame of reference, is required for effective communication. Therefore, marketing managers must ensure a proper match between the message to be conveyed and the target market's attitudes and ideas.

Even though a message has been received, it may not necessarily be properly decoded because of selective exposure, distortion, and retention. When people receive a message, they tend to manipulate it to reflect their own biases,

lemonade's **new sweetie**

new frozen **strawberry** lemonade

If this ad for frozen lemonade is on a downtown billboard in the summer, it will be seen by the target audience—thirsty, hot people. But the same location in the winter is going to have a negative effect—cold, hurried commuters aren't going to be interested in a frosty beverage.

© Terri Miller/E-Visual Communications, Inc.

needs, experiences, and knowledge. Therefore, differences in age, social class, education, culture, and ethnicity can lead to miscommunication. Further, because people don't always listen or read carefully, they can easily misinterpret what is said or written. In fact, researchers have found that consumers misunderstand a large proportion of both printed and televised communications. YouTubers who watched "Elevator Murder Experiment" and simply clicked away without absorbing that it was a viral advertisement for *Dead Man Down* received the message but could not decode it because they did not have adequate information. Bright colors and bold graphics have been shown to increase consumers' comprehension of marketing communication. Even these techniques are not foolproof, however.

Marketers targeting consumers in foreign countries must also worry about the translation and possible miscommunication of their promotional messages by other cultures. Global marketers must decide whether to standardize or customize the message for each global market in which they sell.

FEEDBACK In interpersonal communication, the receiver's response to a message is direct **feedback** to the source. Feedback may be verbal, as in saying "I agree," or nonverbal, as in nodding, smiling, frowning, or gesturing. Mass communicators are often cut off from direct feedback, so they must rely on market research, social media, or analysis of viewer responses for indirect feedback. They might use such measurements as the percentage of television viewers who recognized, recalled, or stated that they were exposed to the company's messages. Indirect feedback enables mass communicators to decide whether to continue, modify, or drop a message.

Some receivers found the "Elevator Murder Experiment" advertising stunt tasteless and macabre, while others praised it as an ingenious use of social media. YouTube users provided direct feedback by commenting on the video's page and clicking either the "Like" or "Dislike" button (the video garnered nearly 10,000 likes, versus approximately 700 dislikes). Regardless

of receivers' feedback, the video was effective, garnering more than 2.6 million views in just three days.[5]

With the increase in online advertising, marketers are able to get more feedback than before the Internet became such a driving social force. Using analytics, marketers can see how long consumers stay on a Web site and which pages they view. Moreover, social media enable companies such as JCPenney and Comcast to provide instant feedback by responding to consumers' posts on Facebook and to complaints posted on Twitter.

Clearly, the Internet and social media have had an impact on the communication model. That model shows the feedback channel as primarily impersonal and numbers driven. In the traditional communication process, marketers can see the results of consumer behavior (e.g., a drop or rise in sales) but are able to explain those changes only by using their judgment. When marketers launch a social media campaign, they create an unfiltered feedback channel. Social media campaigns enable marketers to personalize the feedback channel by opening the door for direct conversation with consumers. However, because social media conversations occur in real time and are public, any negative posts or complaints are highly visible. Thus, many companies have a crisis communication strategy to deal with negative information.

Dead Man Down's "Elevator Murder Experiment" campaign proved to be successful, though some consumers felt that the grisly video crossed the line into bad taste.

Source: http://www.youtube.com

15-3 THE GOALS OF PROMOTION

People communicate with one another for many reasons. They seek amusement, ask for help, give assistance or instructions, provide information, and express ideas and thoughts. Promotion, on the other hand, seeks to modify behavior and thoughts in some way. For example, promoters may try to persuade consumers to eat at Burger King rather than at McDonald's. Promotion also strives to reinforce existing behavior—for instance, getting consumers to continue dining at Burger King once they have switched. The source (the seller) hopes to project a favorable image or to motivate purchase of the company's goods and services.

Promotion can perform one or more of four tasks: *inform* the target audience, *persuade* the target audience, *remind* the target audience, or *connect* with the audience. The ability to *connect* to consumers is one task that can be facilitated through social media. Often a marketer will try to accomplish two or more of these tasks at the same time.

15-3a Informing

Informative promotion seeks to convert an existing need into a want or to stimulate interest in a new product. It is generally more prevalent during the early stages of the product life cycle. People typically will not buy a product or service or support a nonprofit organization until they know its purpose and its benefits to them. Informative messages are important for promoting complex and technical products such as automobiles, computers, and investment services. For example, shortly after Google unveiled the Google Glass wearable computer and display, it released a series of commercials showing various practical uses for the device. A commercial titled "How It Feels" demonstrated point-of-view video and photo capture, messaging, video chatting, search, weather, mapping, and more. Even though it did not overtly explain the device's functions, the ad informed viewers how the device could record once-in-a-lifetime moments and provide the perfect solutions for life's little problems.[6] Informative promotion is also important for a "new" brand being introduced into an "old" product class. When the upstart video game console Ouya began its Kickstarter campaign, it used a video to inform backers about its unique benefits (such as its low cost, open development, free-to-play games, and Web-based game market).[7] When it launched in June 2013,

Ouya again used informative promotion to distinguish itself from seasoned competitors. New products cannot establish themselves against more mature products unless potential buyers are aware of them, value their benefits, and understand their positioning in the marketplace.

15-3b Persuading

Persuasive promotion is designed to stimulate a purchase or an action. Persuasion normally becomes the main promotion goal when the product enters the growth stage of its life cycle. By this time, the target market should have general product awareness and some knowledge of how the product can fulfill its wants. Therefore, the promotional task switches from informing consumers about the product category to persuading them to buy the company's brand rather than that of the competitor. At this time, the promotional message emphasizes the product's real and perceived competitive advantages, often appealing to emotional needs such as love, belonging, self-esteem, and ego satisfaction. For example, advertisers of Android-based smartphones try to persuade users to purchase their companies' devices instead of an iPhone (or even instead of another brand of Android phone). Advertising messages, therefore, highlight the unique technological benefits of Android phones such as a faster processors and larger screens.

Persuasion can also be an important goal for very competitive mature product categories such as household items and soft drinks. In a marketplace characterized by many competitors, the promotional message often encourages brand switching and aims to convert some buyers into loyal users. Critics believe that some promotional messages and techniques can be too persuasive, causing consumers to buy products and services they don't really need.

15-3c Reminding

Reminder promotion is used to keep the product and brand name in the public's mind. This type of promotion prevails during the maturity stage of the life cycle. It assumes that the target market has already been persuaded of the merits of the good or service. Its purpose is simply to trigger a memory. Colgate toothpaste and other consumer products often use reminder promotion.

15-3d Connecting

The idea behind social media is to form relationships with customers and potential customers through technological ties such as Facebook, Twitter, YouTube, or other social media platforms. Indeed, some companies, such as Starbucks, have their own social networks that allow customers to share ideas, information, and feedback. By facilitating this exchange of information through a transparent process, brands are increasingly connecting with their customers in hopes they become brand advocates that promote the brand through their own social networks. Tools for connection include social networks, social games, social publishing tools, as well as social commerce.

15-4 THE PROMOTIONAL MIX

Most promotional strategies use several ingredients—which may include advertising, public relations, sales promotion, personal selling, and social media—to reach a target market. That combination is called the **promotional mix**. The proper promotional mix is the one that management believes will meet the needs of the target market and fulfill the organization's overall goals. The more funds allocated to each promotional ingredient and the more managerial emphasis placed on each technique, the more important that element is thought to be in the overall mix.

15-4a Advertising

Almost all companies selling a good or a service use advertising, whether in the form of a multi-million-dollar campaign or a simple classified ad in a newspaper. **Advertising** is any form of impersonal paid communication in which the sponsor or company is identified. Traditional media—such as television, radio, newspapers, magazines, pay-per-click online advertising, banner advertising, direct mail, billboards, and transit advertising (such as on buses and taxis and at bus stops)—are most commonly used to transmit advertisements to consumers. With the increasing fragmentation of traditional media choices, marketers are using new methods, such as Web sites, e-mail, blogs, and interactive video kiosks to send their advertisements to consumers. However, as the Internet becomes a more vital component of many companies' promotion and marketing mixes, consumers and lawmakers are increasingly concerned about possible violations of consumers' privacy. Social networking sites like Facebook are having to re-examine their privacy policies.

One of the primary benefits of advertising is its ability to communicate to a large number of people at one time. Cost per contact, therefore, is typically very low. Advertising has the advantage of being able to reach the masses (e.g., through national television networks), but it can also be microtargeted to small groups of potential customers, such as television ads on a targeted cable network. Although the *cost per contact* in advertising is very low, the *total cost* to advertise is typically very high. This hurdle tends to restrict advertising on a national basis. Chapter 16 examines advertising in greater detail.

This ad for Colgate is designed to remind customers of the brand, not inform them of how to use it

15-4b Public Relations

Concerned about how they are perceived by their target markets, organizations often spend large sums to build a positive public image. **Public relations** is the marketing function that evaluates public attitudes, identifies areas within the organization the public may be interested in, and executes a program of action to earn public understanding and acceptance. Public relations helps an organization communicate with its customers, suppliers, stockholders, government officials, employees, and the community in which it operates. Marketers use

promotional mix the combination of promotional tools—including advertising, public relations, personal selling, sales promotion, and social media—used to reach the target market and fulfill the organization's overall goals

advertising impersonal, one-way mass communication about a product or organization that is paid for by a marketer

public relations the marketing function that evaluates public attitudes, identifies areas within the organization the public may be interested in, and executes a program of action to earn public understanding and acceptance

publicity public information about a company, product, service, or issue appearing in the mass media as a news item

sales promotion marketing activities—other than personal selling, advertising, and public relations—that stimulate consumer buying and dealer effectiveness

public relations not only to maintain a positive image but also to educate the public about the company's goals and objectives, introduce new products, and help support the sales effort.

A public relations program can generate favorable **publicity**—public information about a company, product, service, or issue appearing in the mass media as a news item. Social media sites like Twitter can provide large amounts of publicity quickly. Organizations generally do not pay for the publicity and are not identified as the source of the information, but they can benefit tremendously from it. However, although organizations do not directly pay for publicity, it should not be viewed as free. Preparing news releases, staging special events, and persuading media personnel to broadcast or print publicity messages costs money. Public relations and publicity are examined further in Chapter 16.

15-4c Sales Promotion

Sales promotion consists of all marketing activities—other than personal selling, advertising, and public relations—that stimulate consumer purchasing and dealer effectiveness. Sales promotion is generally a short-run tool used to stimulate immediate increases in demand. Sales promotion can be aimed at end consumers, trade customers, or a company's employees. Sales promotions include free samples, contests, premiums, trade shows, vacation giveaways, and coupons. Increasingly, companies such as LivingSocial and Groupon have combined social networks and sales promotions. Facebook is a growing platform through which companies run sweepstakes. For example, JPMorgan Chase ran a sweepstakes where Facebook users entered a drawing for a $1,000 grocery store gift card by "liking" the Chase Freedom Facebook page. In the past, Chase Freedom has run other Facebook sweepstakes where players could "like" the page to win $1 million. In addition to being entered into the large drawing, players were entered for a chance to win $500 every hour. The company runs this type of sweepstakes to educate potential customers about its cash-back rewards program available through the Chase Freedom credit card.[8]

Marketers often use sales promotion to improve the effectiveness of other ingredients in the promotional mix, especially advertising and personal selling. Research

Many companies are using Facebook as a platform to run sweepstakes or contests. For sweepstakes such as those run by JPMorgan Chase for its Chase Freedom credit card, consumers can enter to win by "liking" the Facebook page and filling out a brief form.

shows that sales promotion complements advertising by yielding faster sales responses.

15-4d Personal Selling

Personal selling is a purchase situation involving a personal, paid-for communication between two people in an attempt to influence each other. In this dyad, both the buyer and the seller have specific objectives they wish to accomplish. The buyer may need to minimize cost or assure a quality product, for instance, while the salesperson may need to maximize revenue and profits.

Traditional methods of personal selling include a planned presentation to one or more prospective buyers for the purpose of making a sale. Whether it takes place face-to-face or over the phone, personal selling attempts to persuade the buyer to accept a point of view. For example, a car salesperson may try to persuade a car buyer that a particular model is superior to a competing model in certain features, such as gas mileage. Once the buyer is somewhat convinced, the salesperson may attempt to elicit some action from the buyer, such as a test-drive or a purchase. Frequently, in this traditional view of personal selling, the objectives of the salesperson are at the expense of the buyer, creating a win-lose outcome.

More current notions on personal selling emphasize the relationship that develops between a salesperson and a buyer. Initially, this concept was more typical in business-to-business selling situations, involving the sale of products like heavy machinery or computer systems. More recently, both business-to-business and business-to-consumer selling focus on building long-term relationships rather than on making a one-time sale.

Relationship selling emphasizes a win-win outcome and the accomplishment of mutual objectives that benefit both buyer and salesperson in the long term. Rather than focusing on a quick sale, relationship selling attempts to create a long-term, committed relationship based on trust, increased customer loyalty, and a continuation of the relationship between the salesperson and the customer. Personal selling, like other promotional mix elements, is increasingly dependent on the Internet. Most companies use their Web sites to attract potential buyers seeking information on products and services and to drive customers to their physical locations where personal selling can close the sale. Personal selling is discussed further in Chapter 17.

15-4e Social Media

Social media are promotion tools used to facilitate conversations among people online. When used by marketers, these tools facilitate consumer empowerment. For the first time, consumers are able to speak directly to other consumers, the company, and Web communities. Social media include blogs (online journals), microblogs (Twitter), podcasting (online audio shows), vodcasts (online videos and newscasts, especially on YouTube), and social networks such as Facebook and LinkedIn. Initially, these tools were used primarily by individuals for self-expression. For example, a lawyer might develop a blog to talk about politics because that is her hobby. Or a college freshman might develop a profile on Facebook to stay in touch with his high school friends. But soon, businesses saw that these tools could be used to engage with consumers as well. Indeed, social media have become a "layer" in promotional strategy. Social media are ubiquitous—it just depends on how deep that layer goes for each brand. The rise of blogging, for example, has created a completely new way for marketers to manage their image, connect with consumers, and generate interest in and desire for their companies' products. Now marketers are using social media as integral aspects of their campaigns and as a way to extend the benefits of their traditional media. Social media are discussed in more detail in Chapter 18.

THE COST OF NOT HARNESSING SOCIAL MEDIA Avon has long been one of the top direct sales companies. Its salespeople go door to door supplying their friends and family with all of their makeup needs. However, in recent years, as customers have become more and more pressed for time, Avon and its representatives have seen sales drop. Customers are shopping online for their makeup, and Avon hasn't made the transition. Its current system requires shoppers to select their representative from a drop-down list, and if they get the name wrong, the sale gets credited elsewhere. This is not only frustrating for the representatives but also for the consumer, who can easily shop at other large beauty retail Web sites. Avon's Mark brand has an app that allows representatives to show products and videos, but it is limited to the Mark brand. Mary Kay, one of Avon's main competitors, gives each rep her own site and is

personal selling a purchase situation involving a personal, paid-for communication between two people in an attempt to influence each other

developing tracking tools and training to facilitate smart use of the site. If Avon doesn't get into the social media and mobile marketing game, its $1.7 billion in U.S. sales won't be growing and is likely to drop as customers seek more savvy brands.[9]

15-4f The Communication Process and the Promotional Mix

The Internet has changed how businesses promote their brands. Traditionally, marketing managers have been in charge of defining the essence of the brand. This included complete brand control and mostly one-way communication between the brand and customers. All of the content and messages were focused on defining and communicating the brand value. The focus for many campaigns was pure entertainment, and the brand created all of the content for campaigns—from the Web site to television spots to print ads.

That approach has now changed. The consumer has much more control (which makes some brands quite nervous!). The communication space is increasingly controlled by the consumer, as is the brand message. Perception is

paid media a category of promotional tactic based on the traditional advertising model, whereby a brand pays for media space

earned media a category of promotional tactic based on a public relations or publicity model that gets customers talking about products or services

reality as consumers have more control to adapt the brand message to fit their ideas. Instead of repetition, social media rely on the idea of customization and adaption of the message. Information is positioned as more valuable as opposed to being strictly entertaining. Probably the most important aspect is the idea of consumer-generated content, whereby consumers are able to both take existing content and modify it or to create completely new content for a brand. For example, Doritos has the "Crash the Super Bowl" promotion, where ordinary people are invited to create television commercials for Doritos that are then uploaded to www.crashthesuperbowl.com and voted on by millions of Doritos fans. The winning spots then run during the Super Bowl.

As a result of the impact of social media as well as the proliferation of new platforms, tools, and ideas, promotional tactics can also be categorized according to media type—paid, earned, or owned, as shown in Exhibit 3. **Paid media** is based on the traditional advertising model, whereby a brand pays for media space. Traditionally, paid media has included television, magazine, outdoor, radio, or newspaper advertising. Increasingly, paid media comes in the form of display advertising on Web sites or pay-per-click advertising on search engines such as Google. Paid media is quite important, especially as it migrates to the Web. **Earned media** is based on a public relations or publicity model. The idea is to get people talking about the brand—whether through media coverage (as in traditional public relations) or through word of mouth (through sharing on social media sites). Search engine optimization (SEO), where companies

Exhibit 3
DIGITAL MEDIA TYPES

Social media are concentrated here, between owned and earned media, with some (but not much) paid media depending on the strategy.

Owned Media
• Web sites
• Blogs
• Social media presence

Paid Media
• Banner ads
• Sponsored posts

Earned Media
• Media coverage
• SEO
• Publicity activities

Source: Adapted from Dave Fleet, "Why Paying Bloggers for Posts Changes the Game," *DaveFleet.com*, December 12, 2010, http://davefleet.com/2010/12/bloggers-money-posts-game (Accessed May 22, 2012).

embed key words into content to increase their positioning on search engine results pages (SERPs), can also be considered earned media. **Owned media** is a new form of promotional tactic where brands are becoming publishers of their own content in order to maximize the brand's value to customers as well as increase their search rank in Google. Owned media includes the company's Web sites as well as its official presence on Facebook, Twitter, YouTube channels, blogs, and other platforms. This media is controlled by the brand but continuously keeps the customer and his or her needs in mind as it creates videos, blog posts, contests, photos, and other pieces of content.

The elements of the promotional mix differ in their ability to affect the target audience. For instance, promotional mix elements may communicate with the consumer directly or indirectly. The message may flow one way or two ways. Feedback may be fast or slow, a little or a lot. Likewise, the communicator may have varying degrees of control over message delivery, content, and flexibility. Exhibit 4 outlines characteristics among the promotional mix elements with respect to mode of communication, marketer's control over the communication process, amount and speed of feedback, direction of message flow, marketer's control over the message, identification of the sender, speed in reaching large audiences, and message flexibility.

From Exhibit 4, you can see that most elements of the promotional mix are indirect and impersonal when used to communicate with a target market, providing only one direction of message flow. For example, advertising, public relations, and sales promotion are generally impersonal, one-way means of mass communication. Because they provide no opportunity for direct feedback, it is more difficult to adapt these promotional elements to changing consumer preferences, individual differences, and personal goals.

Personal selling, on the other hand, entails direct two-way communication. The salesperson receives immediate feedback from the consumer and can adjust the message in response. Unlike other promotional tools, personal selling is very slow in dispersing the marketer's message to large audiences. Because a salesperson can communicate to only one person or a small group of persons at one time, it is a poor choice if the marketer wants to send a message to many potential buyers. Social media are also considered two-way communication, though not quite as immediate as personal selling. Social media can disperse messages to a wide audience and allow for engagement and feedback from customers through Twitter, Facebook, and blog posts.

owned media a new category of promotional tactic based on brands becoming publishers of their own content in order to maximize the brands' value to customers

Exhibit 4
CHARACTERISTICS OF THE ELEMENTS IN THE PROMOTIONAL MIX

	Advertising	Public Relations	Sales Promotion	Personal Selling	Social Media
Mode of Communication	Indirect and impersonal	Usually indirect and impersonal	Usually indirect and impersonal	Direct and face-to-face	Indirect but instant
Communicator Control over Situation	Low	Moderate to low	Moderate to low	High	Moderate
Amount of Feedback	Little	Little	Little to moderate	Much	Much
Speed of Feedback	Delayed	Delayed	Varies	Immediate	Intermediate
Direction of Message	One-way	One-way	Mostly one-way	Two-way	Two-way, multiple ways
Control over Message Content	Yes	No	Yes	Yes	Varies, generally no
Identification of Sponsor	Yes	No	Yes	Yes	Yes
Speed in Reaching Large Audience	Fast	Usually fast	Fast	Slow	Fast
Message Flexibility	Same message to all audiences	Usually no direct control over message audiences	Same message to varied targets	Tailored to prospective buyer	Some of the most targeted opportunities

© Cengage Learning

15-5 PROMOTIONAL GOALS AND THE AIDA CONCEPT

The ultimate goal of any promotion is to get someone to buy a good or service or, in the case of nonprofit organizations, to take some action (e.g., donate blood). A classic model for reaching promotional goals is called the **AIDA concept**.[10] The acronym AIDA stands for *attention*, *interest*, *desire*, and *action*—the stages of consumer involvement with a promotional message.

This model proposes that consumers respond to marketing messages in a cognitive (thinking), affective (feeling), and conative (doing) sequence. First, a promotion manager may focus on attracting a consumer's *attention* by training a salesperson to use a friendly greeting and approach or by using loud volume, bold headlines, movement, bright colors, and the like in an advertisement. Next, a good sales presentation, demonstration, or advertisement creates *interest* in the product and then, by illustrating how the product's features will satisfy the consumer's needs, arouses *desire*. Finally, a special offer or a strong closing sales pitch may be used to obtain purchase *action*.

The AIDA concept assumes that promotion propels consumers along the following four steps in the purchase-decision process:

1. **ATTENTION:** The advertiser must first gain the attention of the target market. A firm cannot sell something if the market does not know that the good or service exists. When Apple introduced the iPad, it quickly became one of the largest electronics product launches in history. To create awareness and gain attention for its revolutionary tablet computer, Apple not only used traditional media advertising but also contacted influential bloggers and journalists so that they would write about the product in blogs, newspapers, and magazines. Because the iPad was a brand extension of the Apple computer, it required less effort than an entirely new brand would have. At the same time, because the iPad was an innovative new product line, the promotion had to get customers' attention and create awareness of a new idea from an established company.

AIDA concept a model that outlines the process for achieving promotional goals in terms of stages of consumer involvement with the message; the acronym stands for attention, interest, desire, and action

2. **INTEREST:** Simple awareness of a brand seldom leads to a sale. The next step is to create interest in the product. A print ad cannot tell potential customers all the features of the iPad. Therefore, Apple had to arrange iPad demonstrations and target messages to innovators and early adopters to create interest in the new tablet computer. To do this, Apple used both online videos on YouTube and personal demonstrations in Apple Stores. The iPad also received extensive media coverage from both online and traditional media outlets.

3. **DESIRE:** Potential customers for the Apple iPad may like the concept of a portable tablet computer, but they may not necessarily think that it is better than a laptop or smartphone. Therefore, Apple had to create brand preference with the iTunes Music Store, apps, multiple functionality, power, light weight, and other features of the iPad. Specifically, Apple had to convince potential customers that the iPad was the best solution to their desire for a combination tablet computer and smartphone.

4. **ACTION:** Some potential target market customers may have been persuaded to buy an iPad but had yet to make the actual purchase. To motivate them to take action, Apple continued advertising to communicate the features and benefits more effectively. And the strategy worked. According to the Pew Research Center, 11.4 percent of Americans—nearly 3.6 million people—own an iPad.[11]

The four steps of the AIDA process describe how consumers make purchases. These steps are:

1. ATTENTION: First, Apple uses a number of media outlets to gain the attention of the target market.

2. INTEREST: Next, it arranges iPad demonstrations and develops target messages to create interest among innovators and early adopters.

3. DESIRE: Then, Apple creates brand preference and convinces potential customers that they want the new iPad.

4. ACTION: Finally, having been attracted to the new iPad and convinced that they need it, customers purchase the iPad.

© iStockPhoto.com/Hocus Focus Studio

Most buyers involved in high-involvement purchase situations pass through the four stages of the AIDA model on the way to making a purchase. The promoter's task is to determine where on the purchase ladder most of the target consumers are located and design a promotion plan to meet their needs. For example, if Apple learned from its market research that many potential customers were in the desire stage but had not yet bought an iPad for some reason, then Apple could place advertising on Google and perhaps in video games to target younger individuals, who are the primary target market, with messages to motivate them to buy an iPad.

The AIDA concept does not explain how all promotions influence purchase decisions. The model suggests that promotional effectiveness can be measured in terms of consumers progressing from one stage to the next. However, the order of stages in the model, as well as whether consumers go through all steps, has been much debated. A purchase can occur without interest or desire, perhaps when a low-involvement product is bought on impulse. Regardless of the order of the stages or consumers' progression through these stages, the AIDA concept helps marketers by suggesting which promotional strategy will be most effective.[12]

15-5a AIDA and the Promotional Mix

Exhibit 5 depicts the relationship between the promotional mix and the AIDA model. It shows that although advertising does have an impact in the later stages, it is most useful in gaining attention for goods or services. By contrast, personal selling reaches fewer people at first. Salespeople are more effective at creating customer interest for merchandise or a service and at creating desire. For example, advertising may help a potential computer purchaser gain knowledge about competing brands, but the salesperson may be the one who actually encourages the buyer to decide a particular brand is the best choice. The salesperson also has the advantage of having the computer physically there to demonstrate its capabilities to the buyer.

Public relations has its greatest impact in gaining attention for a company, good, or service. Many companies can attract attention and build goodwill by sponsoring community events that benefit a worthy cause such as antidrug and antigang programs. Such sponsorships project a positive image of the firm and its products into the minds of consumers and potential consumers. Book publishers push to get their titles on the best-seller lists of major publications, such as *Publishers Weekly* or the *New York Times*. Book authors like *The Hunger Games'* Suzanne Collins also make appearances on talk shows and at bookstores to personally sign books and speak to fans.

Sales promotion's greatest strength is in creating strong desire and purchase intent. Coupons and other price-off promotions are techniques used to persuade customers to buy new products. Frequent-buyer sales promotion programs, popular among retailers, allow consumers to accumulate points or dollars that can be redeemed for goods. Frequent buyer programs tend to increase purchase intent and loyalty and encourage repeat purchases.

Social media are a strong way to gain attention and interest in a brand, particularly if content goes viral. It can then reach a massive audience. Social media are also effective at engaging with customers and enabling companies to maintain interest in the brand if properly managed.

Exhibit 5
THE PROMOTIONAL MIX AND AIDA

	Attention	Interest	Desire	Action
Advertising	●	●	○	●
Public Relations	●	●	○	●
Sales Promotion	○	○	●	○
Personal Selling	○	●	●	●
Social Media	●	●	○	○

● Very effective   ○ Somewhat effective   ● Not effective

© Cengage Learning

15-6 INTEGRATED MARKETING COMMUNICATIONS

Ideally, marketing communications from each promotional mix element (personal selling, advertising, sales promotion, social media, and public relations) should be integrated. That is, the message reaching the consumer should be the same regardless of whether it is from an advertisement, a salesperson in the field, a magazine article, a Facebook fan page, or a coupon in a newspaper insert.

From the consumer's standpoint, a company's communications are already integrated. Consumers do not think in terms of the five elements of promotion: personal selling, advertising, sales promotion, public relations, and social media. Instead, everything is an "ad." The only people who recognize the distinctions among these communications elements are the marketers themselves. Unfortunately, many marketers neglect this fact when planning promotional messages and fail to integrate their communication efforts from one element to the next. The most common rift typically occurs between personal selling and the other elements of the promotional mix.

This unintegrated, disjointed approach to promotion has propelled many companies to adopt the concept of **integrated marketing communications (IMC)**. IMC is the careful coordination of all promotional messages—traditional advertising, direct marketing, social media, interactive, public relations, sales promotion, personal selling, event marketing, and other communications—for a product or service to assure the consistency of messages at every contact point where a company meets the consumer. Following the concept of IMC, marketing managers carefully work out the roles that various promotional elements will play in the marketing mix. Timing of promotional activities is coordinated, and the results of each campaign are carefully monitored to improve future use of the promotional mix tools. Typically, a marketing communications director is appointed who has overall responsibility for integrating the company's marketing communications.

The IMC concept has been growing in popularity for several reasons. First, the proliferation of thousands of media choices beyond traditional television has made promotion a more complicated task. Instead of promoting a product just through mass-media options, like television and magazines, promotional messages today can appear in many varied sources. Further, the mass market has also fragmented—more selectively segmented markets and

TEVA'S NEW INTEGRATED MARKETING CAMPAIGN UNFOLLOWS THE CROWD

In 2013, footwear company Teva launched "Unfollow," parent brand Deckers' largest integrated marketing campaign to date. This global marketing effort coincided with the debut of TevaSphere, a line of footwear that features a first-of-its-kind sole. Beginning with a one-minute online video, the Unfollow campaign was communicated across a wide variety of digital and physical channels. Notable components included print advertisements in outlets such as *Outside* and *Men's Journal*; a contest spanning Instagram, Twitter, and Facebook that asked entrants to submit photos capturing what it meant to unfollow; a Twitter trending topic (#unfollow); promotional partnerships whereby each customer received a free one-month membership to an outdoor fitness class with a TevaSphere purchase; and a series of YouTube videos chronicling the design and production of TevaSphere shoes. Spanning seventeen countries across the world, Unfollow was communicated more like a life philosophy than a coordinated marketing campaign. According to a Deckers press release, "Unfollow is best understood as a choice to pursue an approach that differs from the norm, in search of a better, more compelling experience."[13]

an increase in niche marketing have replaced the traditional broad market groups that marketers promoted to in years past. Finally, marketers have slashed their advertising spending in favor of promotional techniques that generate immediate sales responses and those that are more easily measured, such as direct marketing. Online advertising has earned a bigger share of the budget as well due to its measurability. Thus, the interest in IMC is largely a reaction to the scrutiny that marketing communications has come under and, particularly, to suggestions that uncoordinated promotional activity leads to a strategy that is wasteful and inefficient.

15-7 FACTORS AFFECTING THE PROMOTIONAL MIX

Promotional mixes vary a great deal from one product and one industry to the next. Normally, advertising and personal selling are used to promote goods and services. These primary tools are often supported and supplemented by sales promotion. Public relations helps develop a positive image for the organization and the product line. Social media have been used more for consumer goods, but business-to-business marketers are increasingly using these media. A firm may choose not to use all five promotional elements in its promotional mix, or it may choose to use them in varying degrees. The particular promotional mix chosen by a firm for a product or service depends on several factors: the nature of the product, the stage in the product life cycle, target market characteristics, the type of buying decision, funds available for promotion, and whether a push or a pull strategy will be used.

15-7a Nature of the Product

Characteristics of the product itself can influence the promotional mix. For instance, a product can be classified as either a business product or a consumer product. (Refer to Chapters 7 and 10.) As business products are often custom-tailored to the buyer's exact specifications, they are often not well suited to mass promotion. Therefore, producers of most business goods rely more heavily on personal selling than on advertising, but advertising still serves a purpose in the promotional mix. Advertising in trade media can also help locate potential customers for the sales force. For example, print media advertising often includes coupons soliciting the potential customer to "fill this out for more detailed information."

By contrast, because consumer products generally are not custom-made, they do not require the selling efforts of a company representative who can tailor them to the user's needs. Thus, consumer goods are promoted mainly through advertising or social media to create brand familiarity. Television and radio advertising, consumer-oriented magazines, and increasingly the Internet and other highly targeted media are used to promote consumer goods, especially nondurables. Sales promotion, the brand name, and the product's packaging are about twice as important for consumer goods as for business products. Persuasive personal selling is important at the retail level for goods such as automobiles and appliances.

The costs and risks associated with a product also influence the promotional mix. As a general rule, when the costs or risks of buying and using a product increase, personal selling becomes more important. Inexpensive items cannot support the cost of a salesperson's time and effort unless the potential volume is high. On the other hand, expensive and complex machinery, cars, and new homes represent a considerable investment. A salesperson must assure buyers that they are spending their money wisely and not taking an undue financial risk.

Social risk is an issue as well. Many consumer goods are not products of great social importance because they do not reflect social position. People do not experience much social risk in buying a loaf of bread. However, buying many specialty products such as jewelry and clothing involves a social risk. Many consumers depend on sales personnel for guidance in making the "proper" choice.

15-7b Stages in the Product Life Cycle

The product's stage in its life cycle is a big factor in designing a promotional mix (see Exhibit 6). During the *introduction stage*, the basic goal of promotion is to inform the target audience that the product is available. Initially, the emphasis is on the general product class—for example, smartphones. This emphasis gradually changes to gaining attention for a particular brand, such as Apple, Nokia, Samsung, Sony Ericsson, or Motorola. Typically, both extensive advertising and public relations inform the target audience of the product class or brand and heighten awareness levels. Sales promotion encourages early trial of the product, and personal selling gets retailers to carry the product.

When the product reaches the *growth stage* of the life cycle, the promotion blend may shift. Often a change is necessary because different types of potential buyers are targeted. Although advertising and public relations continue to be major elements of the promotional mix, sales promotion can be reduced because consumers need fewer incentives to purchase. The promotional strategy is to emphasize the product's differential advantage over the competition. Persuasive promotion is used to build and maintain brand loyalty during the growth stage. By this stage, personal selling has usually succeeded in getting adequate distribution for the product.

As the product reaches the *maturity stage* of its life cycle, competition becomes fiercer, and thus persuasive and reminder advertising are more strongly emphasized. Sales promotion comes back into focus as product sellers try to increase their market share.

All promotion, especially advertising, is reduced as the product enters the *decline stage*. Nevertheless, personal selling and sales promotion efforts may be maintained, particularly at the retail level.

15-7c Target Market Characteristics

A target market characterized by widely scattered potential customers, highly informed buyers, and brand-loyal repeat purchasers generally requires a promotional mix with more advertising and sales promotion and less personal selling. Sometimes, however, personal selling is required even when buyers are well informed and geographically dispersed. Although industrial installations may be sold to well-educated people with extensive work experience, salespeople must be present to explain the product and work out the details of the purchase agreement.

Often firms sell goods and services in markets where potential customers are hard to locate. Print advertising can be used to find them. The reader is invited to go online, call, or mail in a reply card for more information. As the online queries, calls, or cards are received, salespeople are sent to visit the potential customers.

15-7d Type of Buying Decision

The promotional mix also depends on the type of buying decision—for example, a routine decision or a complex

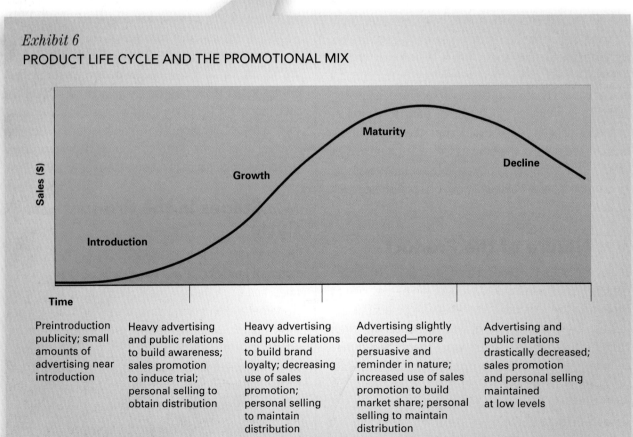

Exhibit 6
PRODUCT LIFE CYCLE AND THE PROMOTIONAL MIX

© Cengage Learning

decision. For routine consumer decisions like buying toothpaste, the most effective promotion calls attention to the brand or reminds the consumer about the brand. Advertising, and especially sales promotion, are the most productive promotion tools to use for routine decisions.

If the decision is neither routine nor complex, advertising and public relations help establish awareness for the good or service. Suppose a man is looking for a bottle of wine to serve to his dinner guests. As a beer drinker, he is not familiar with wines, yet he has read an article in a popular magazine about the Robert Mondavi Winery and has seen an advertisement for the wine. He may be more likely to buy this brand because he is already aware of it. Online reviews are often important in this type of buying decision as well because the consumer has any number of other consumers' reviews easily accessible.

By contrast, consumers making complex buying decisions are more extensively involved. They rely on large amounts of information to help them reach a purchase decision. Personal selling is most effective in helping these consumers decide. For example, consumers thinking about buying a car typically research the car online using corporate and third-party Web sites. However, few people buy a car without visiting the dealership. They depend on a salesperson to provide the information they need to reach a decision. In addition to online resources, print advertising may also be used for high-involvement purchase decisions because it can often provide a large amount of information to the consumer.

15-7e Available Funds

Money, or the lack of it, may easily be the most important factor in determining the promotional mix. A small, undercapitalized manufacturer may rely heavily on free publicity if its product is unique. If the situation warrants a sales force, a financially strained firm may turn to manufacturers' agents, who work on a commission basis with no advances or expense accounts. Even well-capitalized organizations may not be able to afford the advertising rates of publications like *Time*, *Sports Illustrated*, and the *Wall Street Journal*, or the cost of running television commercials during *Modern Family*, *The Voice*, or the Super Bowl. The price of a high-profile advertisement in these media could support several salespeople for an entire year.

When funds are available to permit a mix of promotional elements, a firm will generally try to optimize its return on promotion dollars while minimizing the *cost per contact*, or the cost of reaching one member of the target market. In general, the cost per contact is very high for personal selling, public relations, and sales promotions like sampling and demonstrations. On the other hand, given the number of people national advertising and social media reach, they have a very low cost per contact. Usually, there is a trade-off among the funds available, the number of people in the target market, the quality of communication needed, and the relative costs of the promotional elements. There are plenty of low-cost options available to companies without a huge budget. Many of these include online strategies and public relations efforts, in which the company relies on free publicity.

Despite myriad car advertisements, such as this one for an Infiniti, most people rely on sales personnel for guidance when purchasing a car.

15-7f Push and Pull Strategies

The last factor that affects the promotional mix is whether a push or a pull promotional strategy will be used. Manufacturers may use aggressive personal selling and trade advertising to convince a wholesaler or a retailer to carry and sell their merchandise. This approach is known as a **push strategy** (see Exhibit 7). The wholesaler, in turn, must often push the merchandise forward by persuading the retailer to handle the goods. The retailer then uses advertising, displays, and other forms of promotion to convince the consumer to buy the "pushed" products. Walmart uses aggressive discounts to push products out of its stores. In 2013, First Lady Michelle Obama praised the retailer for using drastically reduced prices to push fresh meat, produce, and other healthy options to consumers in low-income areas. The move proved a win-win strategy; fresh foods generated 70 percent of Walmart's sales growth in recent years, and since 2011, customers have saved more than $2.3 billion on fresh fruits and vegetables by shopping at Walmart.[14] This concept also applies to services.

At the other extreme is a **pull strategy**, which stimulates consumer demand to obtain product distribution. Rather than trying to sell to the wholesaler, the manufacturer using a pull strategy focuses its promotional efforts on end consumers or opinion leaders. Social media and content marketing (e.g., ensuring there is valuable, quality content on Web sites and social media) are the most recent (and best) example of pull strategy. The idea is that social media content does not interrupt a consumer's experience with media (like a commercial interrupts your favorite television program). Instead, the content invites customers to experience it on social media or a Web site. Teva's Unfollow campaign (discussed in the box "Teva's New Integrated Marketing Campaign Unfollows the Crowd") is a good example of enticing consumers to the content. Consumer demand

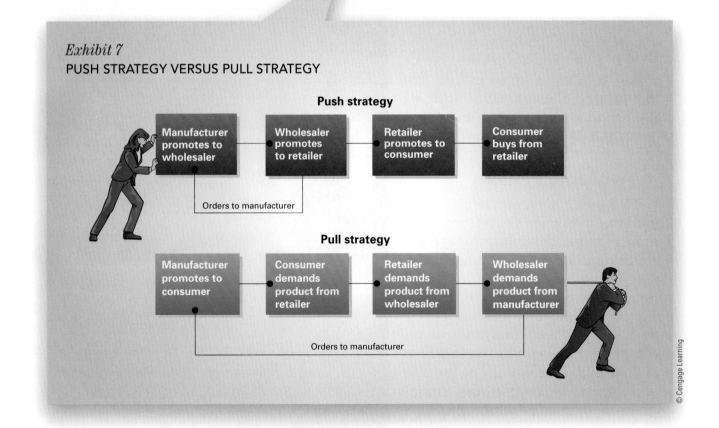

Exhibit 7
PUSH STRATEGY VERSUS PULL STRATEGY

© Cengage Learning

pulls the product through the channel of distribution (see Exhibit 7). Heavy sampling, introductory consumer advertising, cents-off campaigns, and couponing are part of a pull strategy.

Rarely does a company use a pull or a push strategy exclusively. Instead, the mix will emphasize one of these strategies. For example, pharmaceutical companies generally use a push strategy (personal selling and trade advertising) to promote their drugs and therapies to physicians. Sales presentations and advertisements in medical journals give physicians the detailed information they need to prescribe medication to their patients. Most pharmaceutical companies supplement this push promotional strategy with a pull strategy targeted directly to potential patients through advertisements in consumer magazines and on television.

Lay's calls attention to its commitment to natural ingredients as a distinguishing attribute in order to help customers make a routine buying decision—purchasing Lay's snack food.

STUDY TOOLS 15

LOCATED AT BACK OF THE TEXTBOOK
☐ *Rip out Chapter Review Card*

LOCATED AT WWW.CENGAGE.COM/LOGIN
☐ *Review Key Terms Flashcards*
☐ *Watch visual summaries to review key concepts*
☐ *Complete Practice Quizzes to prepare for tests*
☐ *Complete "Crossword Puzzle" to review key terms*
☐ *Watch Video "Pepe's Pizzeria" for a real company example*

THE EFFECTS OF ADVERTISING

Advertising was defined in Chapter 15 as impersonal, one-way mass communication about a product or organization that is paid for by a marketer. It is a popular form of promotion, especially for consumer packaged goods and services. Advertising expenditures typically increase annually. Advertising expenditures by the top 100 U.S. advertisers grew almost 5 percent in 2011, following a whopping 8.8 percent growth in 2010. Google increased expenditures 61 percent to $1 billion, while Amazon increased expenditures 60 percent to $778 million. Leading the growth in the sharply rebounding banking and automotive industries were Citigroup, which increased its advertising by 40 percent in 2011 to $707 million, and Fiat's Chrysler Group, which increased spending by 48 percent to a formidable $1.8 billion.

The top 100 global marketers spend more than $131.3 billion on measured media.

In 2012, advertising expenditures rose another 3 percent. Much of this growth can be attributed to the Summer Olympic Games and the 2012 U.S. presidential election. Large advertisers also played an important role in this growth: Comcast, Toyota, and Berkshire Hathaway all increased their ad spending by double digits in 2012. Kantar Media forecasts a 5.3 percent global spending increase for 2013 and a 6.1 percent increase for 2014. Sixty percent of this growth is forecasted to come from developing countries.[1] With the economic recovery, firms are spending staggeringly large amounts of money to convince people to spend their own money.

Advertising and marketing services, agencies, and other firms that provide marketing and communications services employ millions of people across America. Just as the producers of goods and services need marketers to build awareness of their products,

Chapter 16

Advertising, Public Relations, and Sales Promotion

After you finish this chapter go to **p311** *for* **STUDY TOOLS**

© iStockPhoto.com/OSTILL

media outlets such as magazines and Web sites need marketing teams to coordinate with producers and transmit those messages to consumers. The longer one thinks about the business of marketing, the more unique positions within the industry become apparent. One particular area that has continued to see rapid growth is the data side of marketing. Companies are collecting huge amounts of information and need skilled, creative, Web-savvy people to interpret the data coming in from Web, mobile, and other digital ad campaigns. One Microsoft study estimates that 90 percent of enterprise companies have a dedicated budget for addressing big data. Forty-nine percent of the demand for big data is driven by sales and marketing departments. According to IDC program vice president Dan Vesset, "A lot of the ultimate potential is in the ability to discover potential connections, and to predict potential outcomes in a way that wasn't really possible before. Before, you only looked at these things in hindsight."[2]

16-1a Advertising and Market Share

The five most profitable U.S. brands in 2012 were Exxon Mobil, Chevron, Apple, Microsoft, and Ford.[3] These brands were built over many years by heavy advertising and marketing investments long ago. Today's advertising dollars for successful consumer brands are spent on maintaining brand awareness and market share.

New brands with a small market share tend to spend proportionately more for advertising and sales promotion than those with a large market share, typically for two reasons. First, beyond a certain level of spending for advertising and sales promotion, diminishing returns set in. That is, sales and market share improvements slow down and eventually decrease no matter how much is spent on advertising and sales promotion. This phenomenon is called the **advertising response function**. Understanding the advertising response function helps marketers use budgets wisely. A market leader like Johnson & Johnson's Neutrogena typically spends proportionately less on advertising than a newer line such as Unilever's Vaseline Spray & Go brand. Neutrogena has already captured the attention of the majority of its target market. It only needs to remind customers of its product.

The second reason new brands tend to require higher spending for advertising and sales promotion is that a certain minimum level of exposure is needed to measurably affect purchase habits. If Vaseline advertised its Spray & Go moisturizers in only one or two publications and bought only one or two television spots, it would not achieve the exposure needed to penetrate consumers' perceptual defenses and affect purchase intentions.

16-1b The Effects of Advertising on Consumers

Advertising affects consumers' daily lives, informing them about products and services and influencing their attitudes, beliefs, and ultimately their purchases. Advertising affects the television programs people watch, the content of the newspapers they read, the politicians they elect, the medicines they take, and the toys their children play with. Consequently, the influence of advertising on the U.S. socioeconomic system has been the subject of extensive debate in nearly all corners of society.

Though advertising cannot change consumers' deeply rooted values and attitudes, advertising may succeed in transforming a person's negative attitude toward a product into a positive one. For instance, serious or dramatic advertisements are more effective at changing consumers' negative attitudes. Humorous ads, on the other hand, have been shown to be more effective at shaping attitudes when consumers already have a positive image of an advertised brand. In 2013, the well-regarded Hilton Hotels & Resorts teamed up with satirical Web site and newspaper *The Onion* to develop a humorous new marketing campaign. The resulting interactive Web site, Hilton Urgent Vacation Care, provided diagnoses for people suffering from "vacationitis," a chronic illness with symptoms such as "straight to voicemailaria," "yellow Post-It fever," and "commuteritis." After listing their symptoms, users were prescribed Hilton vacations of different types and durations depending on the severity of their affliction—doctor's orders.[4]

Advertising also reinforces positive attitudes toward brands. A brand with a distinct personality is more likely to have a larger base of loyal customers and market share. The more consistent a brand's personality, the more likely a customer will build a relationship with that brand over his or her lifetime. Consider Disney, for example—for nearly 100 years, Disney has built and nurtured a consistent brand personality, sustaining countless lifelong customer relationships along the way.[5] This is why market leaders spend billions of dollars annually to reinforce and remind their loyal customers about the benefits of their products.

Advertising can also affect the way consumers rank a brand's attributes. In years past, car ads emphasized such brand attributes as roominess, speed, and low maintenance. Today, however, car marketers have added safety, versatility, customization, and fuel efficiency to the list.

16-2 MAJOR TYPES OF ADVERTISING

A firm's promotional objectives determine the type of advertising it uses. If the goal of the promotion plan is to improve the image of the company or the industry, **institutional advertising** may be used. In contrast, if the advertiser wants to enhance the sales of a specific good or service, **product advertising** should be used.

16-2a Institutional Advertising

Historically, advertising in the United States has been product oriented. Today, however, companies market multiple products and need a different type of advertising. Institutional advertising, or corporate advertising, is designed to establish, change, or promote the corporation's identity as a whole. It usually does not ask the audience to do anything but maintain a favorable attitude toward the advertiser and its goods or services.

A form of institutional advertising called **advocacy advertising** is typically used to safeguard against negative consumer attitudes and to enhance the company's credibility among consumers who already favor its position. Corporations often use advocacy advertising to express their views on controversial issues. For example, in

celebration of the one-year anniversary of New York's Marriage Equality Act, Nabisco's Oreo posted a gay pride-themed image (an Oreo cookie with six rainbow-colored layers of cream filling) on its Facebook page. Accompanying the image were the phrases "Pride" and "Proudly support love!" Responses to the images were mixed: "I'm never eating Oreos again. This is just disgusting," wrote one commenter, while another replied, "I didn't think it was possible for me to love Oreo's more than I already did!!" Though controversial, the post drew a considerable amount of support from fans, generating approximately 15,000 shares and 87,000 likes.[7] Alternatively, a firm's advocacy campaign might react to criticism or blame, or to ward

Old Spice uses irreverence and humor to appeal to customers. Such personality has won the company a huge fan base.

BECOME ONE OF THE FRESHEST SMELLING PLACES ON EARTH.

Old Spice

Image courtesy of The Advertising Archives

institutional advertising a form of advertising designed to enhance a company's image rather than promote a particular product

product advertising a form of advertising that touts the benefits of a specific good or service

advocacy advertising a form of advertising in which an organization expresses its views on controversial issues or responds to media attacks

off increases in regulation, damaging legislation, or the unfavorable outcome of a lawsuit.

16-2b Product Advertising

Unlike institutional advertising, product advertising promotes the benefits of a specific good or service. The product's stage in its life cycle often determines which type of product advertising is used: pioneering advertising, competitive advertising, or comparative advertising.

PIONEERING ADVERTISING Pioneering advertising is intended to stimulate primary demand for a new product or product category. Heavily used during the introductory stage of the product life cycle, pioneering advertising offers consumers in-depth information about the benefits of the product class. Pioneering advertising also

Make the RIGHT Choice! Baked or Fried

Always baked. Never fried.

What form of advertising is the Kellogg Company using in this Pop-Tarts advertisement? What does that say about the Pop-Tarts brand?

seeks to create interest. For example, Samsung recently released a line of televisions that not only have Internet access and connect to DIRECTV without a set-top box, but also include face recognition, voice control, and gesture control. To increase demand for these premium features, Samsung released several ads that show every member of the family—even a toddler—using the voice recognition and gesture control on the television.[8]

COMPETITIVE ADVERTISING Firms use competitive or brand advertising when a product enters the growth phase of the product life cycle and other companies begin to enter the marketplace. Instead of building demand for the product category, the goal of **competitive advertising** is to influence demand for a specific brand. Often, promotion becomes less informative and appeals more to emotions during this phase. Generally, this is where an emphasis on branding begins. Advertisements focus on showing subtle differences between brands, building recall of a brand name, and creating a favorable attitude toward the brand. GEICO uses competitive advertising that discusses the attributes of the brand, how little time it takes to get a quote, how much customers can save, and the ease of submitting a claim. All of its campaigns use humor to promote the brand above others in the industry but without actively comparing GEICO with other insurance companies.

COMPARATIVE ADVERTISING Comparative advertising directly or indirectly compares two or more competing brands on one or more specific attributes. Some advertisers even use comparative advertising against their own brands. Products experiencing slow growth or those entering the marketplace against strong competitors are more likely to employ comparative claims in their advertising. In contrast to GEICO's "Fifteen minutes can save you 15 percent or more on car insurance" tagline that doesn't explicitly mention any other insurance company, 21st Century Insurance takes on its major competitors directly in its "Shopping Carts" television ad campaign. The ad features two cars, one labeled GEICO, the other 21st Century. As shopping carts pour down on the cars like rain, a voiceover explains that since both cars are covered, both get the same repairs.[9] Then the commercial goes on to explain that 21st Century Insurance customers who switch from GEICO save an average of $508 a year.[10] 21st Century is explicitly comparing its insurance rates with those of its main competitors and capitalizing on customers' desire for great coverage at the lowest prices.

Before the 1970s, comparative advertising was allowed only if the competing brand was veiled and unidentified. In 1971, however, the Federal Trade Commission (FTC) fostered the growth of comparative advertising by saying that the advertising provided information to the customer and that advertisers were more skillful than the government in communicating this information. Federal rulings prohibit advertisers from falsely describing competitors' products and allow competitors to sue if ads show their products or mention their brand names in an incorrect or false manner. FTC rules also apply to advertisers making false claims about their own products.

16-3 CREATIVE DECISIONS IN ADVERTISING

Advertising strategies are typically organized around an advertising campaign. An **advertising campaign** is a series of related advertisements focusing on a common theme, slogan, and set of advertising appeals. It is a specific advertising effort for a particular product that extends for a defined period of time.

Before any creative work can begin on an advertising campaign, it is important to determine what goals or objectives the advertising should achieve. An **advertising objective** identifies the specific communication task that a campaign should accomplish for a specified target audience during a specified period. The objectives of a specific advertising campaign often depend on the overall corporate objectives and the product being advertised.

The DAGMAR approach (Defining Advertising Goals for Measured Advertising Results) is one method of setting objectives. According to this method, all advertising objectives should precisely define the target audience, the desired percentage change in some specified measure of effectiveness, and the time frame in which that change is to occur.

Once objectives are defined, creative work can begin on the advertising campaign. Advertising campaigns often follow the AIDA model, which was discussed in Chapter 15. Depending on where consumers are in the AIDA process, the creative development of an advertising campaign might focus on creating attention, arousing interest, stimulating desire, or ultimately leading to the action of buying the product. Specifically, creative decisions include identifying product benefits, developing and evaluating advertising appeals, executing the message, and evaluating the effectiveness of the campaign.

16-3a Identifying Product Benefits

A well-known rule of thumb in the advertising industry is "Sell the sizzle, not the steak"—that is, in advertising, the goal is to sell the benefits of the product, not its attributes. Consumers don't buy attributes, they buy benefits. An attribute is simply a feature of the product such as its easy-open package, special formulation, or new lower price. A benefit is what consumers will receive or achieve by using the product, such as convenience or ease of use. A benefit should answer the consumer's question "What's in it for me?" Benefits might be such things as pleasure, improved health, savings, or relief. A quick test to determine whether you are offering attributes or benefits in your advertising is to ask "So?" Consider this example:

- ▸ **ATTRIBUTE:** "DogsBestFriend is an all-natural skin care lotion for dogs that combines traditional medicines and Nigella sativa seed oils with the newest extraction technology." "So . . . ?"

- ▸ **BENEFIT:** "So . . . DogsBestFriend acts as a natural replacement for hydrocortisone, antihistamines, and topical antibiotics that is powerful enough to combat inflammation, itching, and pain, yet safe enough to use on dogs of all ages."[11]

16-3b Developing and Evaluating Advertising Appeals

An **advertising appeal** identifies a reason for a person to buy a product. Developing advertising appeals, a challenging task, is typically the responsibility of the creative team (e.g., art directors and copywriters) in the advertising agency. Advertising appeals typically play off consumers' emotions or address some need or want consumers have.

Advertising campaigns can focus on one or more advertising appeals. Often the appeals are quite general, thus allowing the firm to develop a number of subthemes or mini campaigns using both advertising and sales promotion. Several possible advertising appeals are listed in Exhibit 1.

Choosing the best appeal from those developed usually requires market research. Criteria for evaluation

advertising campaign a series of related advertisements focusing on a common theme, slogan, and set of advertising appeals

advertising objective a specific communication task that a campaign should accomplish for a specified target audience during a specified period

advertising appeal a reason for a person to buy a product

include desirability, exclusiveness, and believability. The appeal first must make a positive impression on and be desirable to the target market. It must also be exclusive or unique. Consumers must be able to distinguish the advertiser's message from competitors' messages. Most important, the appeal should be believable. An appeal that makes extravagant claims not only wastes promotional dollars but also creates ill will for the advertiser.

The advertising appeal selected for the campaign becomes what advertisers call its **unique selling proposition**. The unique selling proposition often becomes all or part of the campaign's slogan. High-end leather goods manufacturer Saddleback Leather uses its Web site to build brand personality and convey the company's unique selling proposition: its products are extremely tough and rugged—just like the consumers who buy them. First-person narratives recount trips to Mexican bullfighting rings, shark diving in Bora Bora, backpacking along the red sand dunes of Texas, and other adventures in exotic, often perilous locations. Of course, Saddleback Leather's messenger bags and luggage are up to the task, accompanying their sojourning owner everywhere he goes—even into the ocean.[12]

Saddleback Leather's slogan drives home its products' unique selling proposition: "They'll fight over it when you're dead."[13]

16-3c Executing the Message

Message execution is the way an advertisement portrays its information. In general, the AIDA plan (see Chapter 15) is a good blueprint for executing an advertising message. Any ad should immediately draw the reader's, viewer's, or listener's attention. The advertiser must then use the message to hold interest, create desire for the good or service, and ultimately motivate a purchase.

The style in which the message is executed is one of the most creative elements of an advertisement. Exhibit 2 lists some examples of executional styles used by advertisers. Executional styles often dictate what type of media is to be employed to convey the message. For example, scientific executional styles lend themselves well to print advertising, where more information can be conveyed. Testimonials by athletes are one of the more popular executional styles.

Injecting humor into an advertisement is a popular and effective executional style. Humorous executional styles are more often used in radio and television advertising than in print or magazine advertising, where humor is less easily communicated. Recall that humorous ads are typically used for lower-risk, low-involvement, routine purchases such as candy, cigarettes, and casual jeans than for higher-risk purchases or those that are expensive, durable, or flamboyant.[14]

Sometimes an executional style must be modified to make a marketing campaign more effective. Nowhere is this more evident than in the political realm, where advertisements for issues and candidates must account for ever-changing poll numbers and public sentiments. Six months before the 2012 U.S. presidential election, campaign advertisements taking aim at President Barack Obama shifted in tone from sharply combative and accusatory to concerned—even mournful—about the state of the economy. According to Republican pollster Frank Luntz, focus group research indicated that "ads that attack Obama too personally turn people off in ways that will keep them turned

Exhibit 1
COMMON ADVERTISING APPEALS

Appeal	Goal
Profit	Lets consumers know whether the product will save them money, make them money, or keep them from losing money.
Health	Appeals to those who are body conscious or who want to be healthy; love or romance is used often in selling cosmetics and perfumes.
Fear	Can center around social embarrassment, growing old, or losing one's health; because of its power, requires advertiser to exercise care in execution.
Admiration	Frequently highlights celebrity spokespeople.
Convenience	Is often used for fast-food restaurants and microwave foods.
Fun and Pleasure	Are the keys to advertising vacations, beer, amusement parks, and more.
Vanity and Egotism	Are used most often for expensive or conspicuous items such as cars and clothing.
Environmental Consciousness	Centers around protecting the environment and being considerate of others in the community.

Exhibit 2
TEN COMMON EXECUTIONAL STYLES FOR ADVERTISING

Executional Style	Description
Slice-of-Life	Depicts people in normal settings, such as at the dinner table or in their car. McDonald's often uses slice-of-life styles showing youngsters munching on french fries from Happy Meals on family outings.
Lifestyle	Shows how well the product will fit in with the consumer's lifestyle. As his Volkswagen Jetta moves through the streets of the French Quarter, a Gen X driver inserts a techno music CD and marvels at how the rhythms of the world mimic the ambient vibe inside his vehicle.
Spokesperson/ Testimonial	Can feature a celebrity, company official, or typical consumer making a testimonial or endorsing a product. Sheryl Crow represented Revlon's Colorist hair coloring, while Beyoncé Knowles was named the new face of American Express. Dell Inc. founder Michael Dell touts his vision of the customer experience via Dell in television ads.
Fantasy	Creates a fantasy for the viewer built around use of the product. Carmakers often use this style to let viewers fantasize about how they would feel speeding around tight corners or down long country roads in their cars.
Humorous	Advertisers often use humor in their ads, such as Snickers' "You're not you when you're hungry" campaign featuring popular comedic actors like Betty White and Robin Williams.
Real/Animated Product Symbols	Creates a character that represents the product in advertisements, such as the Energizer Bunny or Starkist's Charlie the Tuna. GEICO's suave gecko and disgruntled cavemen became cult classics for the insurance company.
Mood or Image	Builds a mood or image around the product, such as peace, love, or beauty. De Beers ads depicting shadowy silhouettes wearing diamond engagement rings and diamond necklaces portrayed passion and intimacy while extolling that "a diamond is forever."
Demonstration	Shows consumers the expected benefit. Many consumer products use this technique. Laundry detergent spots are famous for demonstrating how their product will clean clothes whiter and brighter. Fort James Corporation demonstrated in television commercials how its Dixie Rinse & ReUse disposable stoneware product line can stand up to the heat of a blowtorch and survive a cycle in a clothes washer.
Musical	Conveys the message of the advertisement through song. For example, Nike ads depicted a marathoner's tortured feet and a surfer's thigh scarred by a shark attack while strains of Joe Cocker's "You Are So Beautiful" could be heard in the background.
Scientific	Uses research or scientific evidence to give a brand superiority over competitors. Pain relievers like Advil, Bayer, and Excedrin use scientific evidence in their ads.

off." The Republican campaign shifted its executional style, opting for advertisements that appealed to citizens' worries and frustrations. In one ad, a forlorn-looking woman declares, "I supported President Obama because he spoke so beautifully. But since then, things have gone from bad to much worse."[15]

16-3d Post-Campaign Evaluation

Evaluating an advertising campaign can be the most demanding task facing advertisers. How can an advertiser assess if the campaign led to an increase in sales or market share or elevated awareness of the product? Many advertising campaigns aim to create an image for the good or service instead of asking for action, so their real effect is unknown. So many variables shape the effectiveness of an ad that advertisers often must guess whether their money has been well spent. Nonetheless, marketers spend considerable time studying advertising effectiveness and its probable impact on sales, market share, or awareness.

Testing ad effectiveness can be done before and/or after the campaign. Before a campaign is released, marketing managers use pretests to determine the best advertising appeal, layout, and media vehicle. After advertisers implement a campaign, they use several monitoring techniques to determine whether the campaign has met its original goals. Even if a campaign has been highly successful, advertisers still typically do a post-campaign analysis to identify how the campaign might have been more efficient and what factors contributed to its success.

16-4 MEDIA DECISIONS IN ADVERTISING

A major decision for advertisers is the choice of medium— the channel used to convey a message to a target market.

medium the channel used to convey a message to a target market

media planning the series of decisions advertisers make regarding the selection and use of media, allowing the marketer to optimally and cost-effectively communicate the message to the target audience

cooperative advertising an arrangement in which the manufacturer and the retailer split the costs of advertising the manufacturer's brand

Media planning, therefore, is the series of decisions advertisers make regarding the selection and use of media, enabling the marketer to optimally and cost-effectively communicate the message to the target audience. Specifically, advertisers must determine which types of media will best communicate the benefits of their product or service to the target audience and when and for how long the advertisement will run.

Promotional objectives and the appeal and executional style of the advertising strongly affect the selection of media. Both creative and media decisions are made at the same time: creative work cannot be completed without knowing which medium will be used to convey the message to the target market. In many cases, the advertising objectives dictate the medium and the creative approach to be used. For example, if the objective is to demonstrate how fast a product operates, a television commercial that shows this action may be the best choice.

U.S. advertisers spend roughly $300 billion annually on media monitored by national reporting services—newspapers, magazines, radio, television, the Internet, and outdoor. The remainder is spent on unmonitored media, such as direct mail, trade exhibits, cooperative advertising, brochures, coupons, catalogs, and special events. About 48 percent of every media dollar goes toward television ads (cable, syndicated, spot, and network), 19 percent to magazines, 2.7 percent to outdoor advertising, and about 16.5 percent to newspaper ads.[16] But these traditional mass-market media are declining in usage as more targeted media are growing. Between 2011 and 2012, spending on magazine advertising declined 3.8 percent, and Internet advertising rose 12.2 percent in the United States [17]

16-4a Media Types

Advertising media are channels that advertisers use in mass communication. The six major advertising media are newspapers, magazines, radio, television, the Internet, and outdoor media.

Exhibit 3 summarizes the advantages and disadvantages of some of these major channels. In recent years, however, alternative media channels have emerged that give advertisers innovative ways to reach their target audience and avoid advertising clutter.

NEWSPAPERS Newspapers are one of the oldest forms of media. The advantages of newspaper advertising include geographic flexibility and timeliness. Although there has been a decline in circulation as well as in the number of newspapers, nationally, there are still several major newspapers including the *Wall Street Journal*, *USA Today*, the *New York Times*, the *Los Angeles Times*, and the *Washington Post*. But most newspapers are local. Because newspapers are generally a mass-market medium, however, they may not be the best vehicle for marketers trying to reach a very narrow market. Newspaper advertising also encounters distractions from competing ads and news stories. Therefore, one company's ad may not be particularly visible.

The main sources of newspaper ad revenue are local retailers, classified ads, and cooperative advertising. In **cooperative advertising**, the manufacturer and the retailer split the costs of advertising the manufacturer's brand. For example, Estée Lauder may split the cost of an advertisement with Macy's department store provided that the ad focuses on Estée Lauder's products. One reason manufacturers use cooperative advertising is the

Jennifer Lopez drives a Fiat for a commercial, which is part music video, and uses her celebrity to sell the car more than the car itself.

Icono, PacificCoastNews/Newscom

Exhibit 3

ADVANTAGES AND DISADVANTAGES OF MAJOR ADVERTISING MEDIA

Medium	Advantages	Disadvantages
Newspapers	Geographic selectivity and flexibility; short-term advertiser commitments; news value and immediacy; year-round readership; high individual market coverage; co-op and local tie-in availability; short lead time	Little demographic selectivity; limited color capabilities; low pass-along rate; may be expensive
Magazines	Good reproduction, especially for color; demographic selectivity; regional selectivity; local market selectivity; relatively long advertising life; high pass-along rate	Long-term advertiser commitments; slow audience buildup; limited demonstration capabilities; lack of urgency; long lead time
Radio	Low cost; immediacy of message; can be scheduled on short notice; relatively no seasonal change in audience; highly portable; short-term advertiser commitments; entertainment carryover	No visual treatment; short advertising life of message; high frequency required to generate comprehension and retention; distractions from background sound; commercial clutter
Television	Ability to reach a wide, diverse audience; low cost per thousand; creative opportunities for demonstration; immediacy of messages; entertainment carryover; demographic selectivity with cable stations	Short life of message; some consumer skepticism about claims; high campaign cost; little demographic selectivity with network stations; long-term advertiser commitments; long lead times required for production; commercial clutter
Internet	Fastest-growing medium; ability to reach a narrow target audience; relatively short lead time required to create Web-based advertising; moderate cost; ability to measure ad effectiveness; ability to engage consumers through search engine marketing, social media, display advertising, and mobile marketing	Most ad exposure relies on "click-through" from display ads; measurement for social media needs much improvement; not all consumers have access to the Internet, and many consumers are not using social media
Outdoor Media	Repetition; moderate cost; flexibility; geographic selectivity	Short message; lack of demographic selectivity; high "noise" level distracting audience

impracticality of listing all their dealers in national advertising. Also, cooperative advertising encourages retailers to devote more effort to the manufacturer's lines.

MAGAZINES Magazines are another traditional medium that has been successful. Some of the top magazines according to circulation include *AARP*, *Better Homes and Gardens*, *Reader's Digest*, *National Geographic*, and *Good Housekeeping*. However, compared to the cost of other media, the cost per contact in magazine advertising is usually high. The cost per potential customer may be much lower, however, because magazines are often targeted to specialized audiences and thus reach more potential customers.

RADIO Radio has several strengths as an advertising medium: selectivity and audience segmentation, a large out-of-home audience, low unit and production costs, timeliness, and geographic flexibility. Local advertisers are the most frequent users of radio advertising, contributing over 75 percent of all radio ad revenue. Like newspapers, radio also lends itself well to cooperative advertising.

TELEVISION Television broadcasters include network television, independent stations, cable television, and direct broadcast satellite television. Network television reaches a wide and diverse market, and cable television and direct broadcast satellite systems, such as DIRECTV and DISH Network, broadcast a multitude of channels devoted to highly segmented markets. Because of its targeted channels, cable television is often characterized as "narrowcasting" by media buyers.

Advertising time on television can be very expensive, especially for network and popular cable channels. Special events and first-run prime-time shows for top-ranked television programs command the highest rates for a typical commercial. For example, running a thirty-second spot during sitcom *Two and a Half Men* costs $247,261, while running one during NFL Sunday Football costs $545,142. A thirty-second spot during the Super Bowl costs approximately $3.8 million. Why pay so much for such a short commercial? Doritos estimates that its 2013 Super Bowl ad generated about $90 million worth of free publicity from media outlets discussing the ad.[18] An alternative

infomercial a thirty-minute or longer advertisement that looks more like a television talk show than a sales pitch

advergaming placing advertising messages in Web-based, mobile, console, or handheld video games to advertise or promote a product, service, organization, or issue

to a commercial spot is the **infomercial**, a thirty-minute or longer advertisement, which is relatively inexpensive to produce and air. Advertisers say the infomercial is an ideal way to present complicated information to potential customers, which other advertising vehicles typically don't allow time to do. Beachbody's P90X and Insanity exercise DVDs are advertised through infomercials.

Probably the most significant trend to affect television advertising is the rise in popularity of digital video recorders (DVRs). For every hour of television programming, an average of fifteen minutes is dedicated to nonprogram material (ads, public service announcements, and network promotions), so the popularity of DVRs among ad-weary viewers is hardly surprising. Like marketers and advertisers, networks are also highly concerned about ad skipping. If consumers are not watching advertisements, then marketers will spend a greater proportion of their advertising budgets on alternative media, and a critical revenue stream for networks will disappear.

THE INTERNET With global annual ad revenues of almost $120 billion in 2013, the Internet has become a versatile advertising medium able to target specific groups. Spending on online advertising is expected to be more than $163 billion by 2016 and represent 25.9 percent of all advertising expenditures.[19] Online advertising includes search engine marketing (e.g., pay-per-click ads like Google AdWords), display advertising (e.g., banner ads, video ads), social media advertising (e.g., Facebook ads), e-mail marketing, and mobile marketing (including mobile advertising and SMS). Some online channels like Google offer the ability to *audience buy* (whereby advertisers can purchase ad space targeted to a highly specific group), but others, such as Turner Digital's FunnyOrDie.com, believe that the complex cookie-based strategy poses too many risks.[20]

Popular Internet sites and search engines generally sell advertising space to marketers to promote their goods and services. Internet surfers click on these ads to be linked to more information about the advertised product or service. Both leading advertisers and companies whose ad budgets are not as large have become big Internet advertisers. Because of the relative low cost and high targetability, search engines generate nearly half of all Internet ad revenue. Display and banner ads are the next largest source of Internet revenue, followed by classifieds and digital video.[21]

Another popular Internet advertising format is **advergaming**, whereby companies put ad messages in Web-based, mobile, console, or handheld video games to advertise or promote a product, service, organization, or issue. Indeed, the issue of gamification is fast becoming one that is important for marketers, whether in video games or social media. *Gamification* is the process of using game thinking and mechanics to engage an audience and solve problems. Thus, rewards, incentives, and competition are all important aspects in social media games like *FarmVille 2* and *Candy Crush Saga.*[22] Sometimes the entire game amounts to a virtual commercial; other times advertisers sponsor games or buy ad space for a product placement in them. Many of these are social games, played on Facebook or similar sites, where players can interact with one another. Social gaming has a huge audience—according to Facebook CEO Mark Zuckerberg, 235 million people play social games on Facebook every month. Social casino games alone generated $1.6 billion in 2012 and are projected to generate $2.4 billion in 2015.[23]

More than three-fourths of Americans have mobile phones, and over one-third of those are smartphones. Fifty-five percent of mobile phone owners access the Web on their phones, making mobile Web sites and apps more important.[24] Mobile advertising has substantial upside potential given that there are more than 4 billion cell phone users in the world, and an increasing number of those users have smartphones or tablets with Internet access. As devices such as the iPad continue to grow in popularity, mobile advertising spending will continue to grow worldwide.

OUTDOOR MEDIA Outdoor or out-of-home advertising is a flexible, low-cost medium that may take a variety of forms. Examples include billboards, skywriting, giant inflatables, mini billboards in malls and on bus stop shelters, signs in sports arenas, and lighted moving signs in bus terminals and airports, as well as ads painted on cars, trucks, buses, water towers, manhole covers, drinking glass coasters, and even people, called "living advertising." The plywood scaffolding surrounding downtown construction sites often holds ads, which in places like Manhattan's Times Square, can reach over a million viewers a day.

Outdoor advertising reaches a broad and diverse market and is therefore ideal for promoting convenience products and services as well as directing consumers to local businesses. One of outdoor advertising's main advantages over other media is that its exposure frequency is very high, yet the amount of clutter from competing ads is very low. Outdoor advertising also can be customized to local marketing needs, which is why local businesses are the leading outdoor advertisers in any given region.

ALTERNATIVE MEDIA To cut through the clutter of traditional advertising media, advertisers are developing new media vehicles, like shopping carts in grocery stores, computer screen savers, DVDs, CDs, interactive kiosks in department stores, advertisements run before movies at the cinema, posters on bathroom stalls, and "advertainments"—mini movies that promote a product and are shown via the Internet.

Marketers are looking for more innovative ways to reach captive and often bored commuters. For instance, subway systems are now showing ads via lighted boxes installed along tunnel walls. Other advertisers seek consumers at home. Some marketers have begun replacing

hold music on customer service lines with advertisements and movie trailers. This strategy generates revenue for the company being called and catches undistracted consumers for advertisers. The trick is to amuse and interest this captive audience without annoying them during their ten- to fifteen-minute wait. After Yahoo! CEO Marissa Mayer called her company's on-hold message "garbage," audio production startup Jingle Punks hired Canadian rapper Snow (known for his 1992 hit "Informer") to write a humorous on-hold jingle for Yahoo! (you can hear the jingle at www.youtube.com/watch?v=vRmVDADlnOU). Yahoo! has yet to implement the jingle, however.[25]

© CB2/ZOB/WENN/Newscom

Outdoor advertising is very diverse. This clever ad for Mondo Pasta is strategically placed on the side of a boat to make it look like the rope is pasta!

16-4b Media Selection Considerations

An important element in any advertising campaign is the **media mix**, the combination of media to be used. Media mix decisions are typically based on several factors: cost per contact, cost per click, reach, frequency, target audience considerations, flexibility of the medium, noise level, and the life span of the medium.

Cost per contact, also referred to as **cost per thousand (CPM)**, is the cost of reaching one member of the target market. Naturally, as the size of the audience increases, so does the total cost. Cost per contact enables an advertiser to compare the relative costs of specific media vehicles (such as television versus radio or magazine versus newspaper), or more specifically, within a media category (such as *People* versus *US Weekly*). Thus, an advertiser debating whether to spend local advertising dollars for television spots or radio spots could consider the cost per contact of each. Alternatively, if the question is which magazine to advertise in, she might choose the one with the greater reach. In either case, the advertiser can pick the vehicle with the lowest cost per contact to maximize advertising punch for the money spent. **Cost per click** is the cost associated with a consumer clicking on a display or banner ad. Although there are several variations, this option enables the marketer to pay only for "engaged" consumers—those who opted to click on an ad.

Reach is the number of target customers who are exposed to a commercial at least once during a specific period, usually four weeks. Media plans for product introductions and attempts at increasing brand awareness usually emphasize reach. For example, an advertiser might try to reach 70 percent of the target audience during the first three months of the campaign. Reach is related to a medium's ratings, generally referred to in the industry as *gross ratings points*, or *GRP*. A television program with a higher GRP means that more people are tuning in to the show and the reach is higher. Accordingly, as GRP increases for a particular medium, so does cost per contact.

Because the typical ad is short-lived and because often only a small portion of an ad may be perceived at one time, advertisers repeat their ads so that potential customers will remember the message. **Frequency** is the number of times an individual is exposed to a given message during a specific period. Advertisers use average frequency to measure the intensity of a specific medium's coverage. For example, Coca-Cola might want an average exposure frequency of five for its Powerade television ads. That means that each of the television viewers who saw the ad saw it an average of five times.

Media selection is also a matter of matching the advertising medium with the product's target market. If marketers are trying to reach teenage females, they might select *Teen Vogue* magazine. A medium's ability to reach a precisely defined market is its **audience selectivity**. Some media vehicles, like general newspapers and network television, appeal to a wide cross section of the population. Others—such as *Brides*, *Popular Mechanics*, *Architectural Digest*, *Lucky*, MTV, ESPN, and Christian radio stations—appeal to very specific groups.

The *flexibility* of a medium can be extremely important to an advertiser. For example, because of layouts and design, the lead time for magazine advertising is considerably longer than for other media types and so is less

flexible. By contrast, radio and Internet advertising provide maximum flexibility. If necessary, an advertiser can change a radio ad on the day it is aired.

Noise level is the level of distraction experienced by the target audience in a medium. Noise can be created by competing ads, as when a street is lined with billboards or when a television program is cluttered with competing ads. Whereas newspapers and magazines have a high noise level, direct mail is a private medium with a low noise level. Typically, no other advertising media or news stories compete for direct mail readers' attention.

Media have either a short or a long *life span*, which means that messages can either quickly fade or persist as tangible copy to be carefully studied. A radio commercial may last less than a minute, but advertisers can overcome this short life span by repeating radio ads often. In contrast, a magazine has a relatively long life span, which is further increased by a high pass-along rate.

Media planners have traditionally relied on the above factors in selecting an effective media mix, with reach, frequency, and cost often the overriding criteria.

WITH SO MANY WAYS TO AVOID COMMERCIALS (SUCH AS USING A DVR), COMPANIES ARE USING SEVERAL DIFFERENT MEDIA TO REACH CONSUMERS ACROSS MULTIPLE PLATFORMS.

© Artpose Adam Borkowski/Shutterstock.com

Well-established brands with familiar messages, however, probably need fewer exposures to be effective, while newer or unfamiliar brands likely need more exposures to become familiar. In addition, today's media planners have more media options than ever before. (Today, there are over 1,600 television networks across the country, whereas forty years ago there were only three.)

The proliferation of media channels is causing *media fragmentation* and forcing media planners to pay as much attention to where they place their advertising as to how often the advertisement is repeated. That is, marketers should evaluate reach *and* frequency in assessing the effectiveness of advertising. In certain situations, it may be important to reach potential consumers through as many media vehicles as possible. When this approach is considered, however, the budget must be large enough to achieve sufficient levels of frequency to have an impact. In evaluating reach versus frequency, therefore, the media planner ultimately must select an approach that is most likely to result in the ad being understood and remembered when a purchase decision is being made.

Advertisers also evaluate the qualitative factors involved in media selection. These include such things as attention to the commercial and the program, involvement, program liking, lack of distractions, and other audience behaviors that affect the likelihood that a commercial message is being seen and, hopefully, absorbed. While advertisers can advertise their product in as many media as possible and repeat the ad as many times as they like, the ad still may not be effective if the audience is not paying attention. Additional research highlights the benefits of cross-media advertising campaigns. Viewers who encounter ads both on television and online are most likely to remember and respond to them. Listerine ran a recent campaign on the ABC television network and ABC.com and found that its mouthwash sales increased 33 percent more among viewers who saw the ad in both places.[26]

16-4c Media Scheduling

After choosing the media for the advertising campaign, advertisers must schedule the ads. A **media schedule** designates the medium or media to be used (such as magazines, television, or radio), the specific vehicles (such as *People* magazine, the show *Mad Men* on television, or Rush Limbaugh's national radio program), and the insertion dates of the advertising.

There are four basic types of media schedules:

▸ **A continuous media schedule allows the advertising to run steadily throughout the advertising period. Examples include Ivory soap and Charmin toilet tissue, which may have an ad in the newspaper every Sunday and a television commercial on NBC every Wednesday at 7:30 p.m. over a three-month time period. Products in the later stages of the product life cycle, which are advertised on a reminder basis, often use a continuous media schedule.**

▸ **With a flighted media schedule, the advertiser may schedule the ads heavily every other month or every two weeks to achieve a greater impact with an increased frequency and reach at those times. Movie studios might schedule television advertising on Wednesday and Thursday nights, when moviegoers are deciding which films to see that weekend.**

▸ **A pulsing media schedule combines continuous scheduling with flighting. Continuous advertising is simply heavier during the best sale periods. A retail department store may advertise on a year-round basis but place more advertising during certain sale periods such as Thanksgiving, Christmas, and back-to-school. For example, beer may be advertised more heavily during the summer months and football season given the higher consumption levels at those times.**

▸ **Certain times of the year call for a seasonal media schedule. Products like Sudafed cold tablets and Coppertone sunscreen, which are used more during certain times of the year, tend to follow a seasonal strategy.**

New research comparing continuous media schedules and flighted ones has found that continuous schedules are more effective than are flighted ones at driving sales through television advertisements. This research suggests that it may be important to reach a potential customer as close as possible to the time at which he makes a purchase.

media schedule designation of the media, the specific publications or programs, and the insertion dates of advertising

continuous media schedule a media scheduling strategy in which advertising is run steadily throughout the advertising period; used for products in the later stages of the product life cycle

flighted media schedule a media scheduling strategy in which ads are run heavily every other month or every two weeks to achieve a greater impact with an increased frequency and reach at those times

pulsing media schedule a media scheduling strategy that uses continuous scheduling throughout the year coupled with a flighted schedule during the best sales periods

seasonal media schedule a media scheduling strategy that runs advertising only during times of the year when the product is most likely to be used

Therefore, the advertiser should maintain a continuous schedule over as long a period of time as possible. Often called *recency planning*, this theory of scheduling is now commonly used for scheduling television advertising for frequently purchased products such as Coca-Cola and Tide detergent. Recency planning's main premise is that advertising works by influencing the brand choice of people who are ready to buy. Mobile advertising may be one of the most promising tactics for contacting consumers when they are thinking about a specific product. For example, a GPS-enabled mobile phone can get text messages for area restaurants around lunchtime to advertise specials to professionals working in a big city.

16-5 PUBLIC RELATIONS

Public relations is the element in the promotional mix that evaluates public attitudes, identifies issues that may elicit public concern, and executes programs to gain public understanding and acceptance. Public relations is a vital link in a forward-thinking company's marketing communication mix. Marketing managers plan solid public relations campaigns that fit into overall marketing plans and focus on targeted audiences. These campaigns strive to maintain a positive image of the corporation in the eyes of the public. As such, they should capitalize on the factors that enhance the firm's image and minimize the factors that could generate a negative image. The concept of earned media is based on public relations and publicity.

Publicity is the effort to capture media attention—for example, through articles or editorials in publications or through human-interest stories on radio or television programs. Corporations usually initiate publicity through press releases that further their public relations plans. A company about to introduce a new product or open a new store may send press releases to the media in the hope that the story will be published or broadcast. Savvy publicity can often create overnight sensations or build up a reserve of goodwill with consumers. Corporate donations and sponsorships can also create favorable publicity.

16-5a Major Public Relations Tools

Public relations professionals commonly use several tools, many of which require an active role on the part of the public relations professional, such as writing press releases and engaging in proactive media relations. Sometimes, however, these techniques create their own publicity.

NEW-PRODUCT PUBLICITY Publicity is instrumental in introducing new products and services. Publicity can help advertisers explain what's different about their new product by prompting free news stories or positive word of mouth about it. During the introductory period, an especially innovative new product often needs more exposure than conventional, paid advertising affords. Public relations professionals write press releases or develop videos in an effort to generate news about their new product. They also jockey for exposure of their product or service at major events, on popular television and news shows, or in the hands of influential people. Consider the publicity Apple generated

American actor Robert Downey Jr. visited Beijing, China in April 2013 to build publicity for *Iron Man 3*, a highly-anticipated film in which he starred.

AP Images/Wei ni bj

THE MANY DUTIES OF PUBLIC RELATIONS DEPARTMENTS

Public relations departments may perform any or all of the following functions:

▸ **PRESS RELATIONS:** Placing positive, news-worthy information in the news media or in the hands of influential bloggers to attract attention to a product, a service, or a person associated with the firm or institution

▸ **PRODUCT PUBLICITY:** Publicizing specific products or services through a variety of traditional and online channels

▸ **CORPORATE COMMUNICATION:** Creating internal and external messages to promote a positive image of the firm or institution

▸ **PUBLIC AFFAIRS:** Building and maintaining local, national, or global community relations

▸ **LOBBYING:** Influencing legislators and government officials to promote or defeat legislation and regulation

▸ **EMPLOYEE AND INVESTOR RELATIONS:** Maintaining positive relationships with employees, shareholders, and others in the financial community

▸ **CRISIS MANAGEMENT:** Responding to unfavorable publicity or a negative event

for the release of the iPad, which included press coverage in traditional media as well as online blogs and forums. That was a small aspect of the entire marketing campaign.

PRODUCT PLACEMENT Marketers are increasingly using product placement to reinforce brand awareness and create favorable attitudes. **Product placement** is a strategy that involves getting one's product, service, or name to appear in a movie, television show, radio program, magazine, newspaper, video game, video or audio clip, book, or commercial for another product; on the Internet; or at special events. Indeed, a product mention on the recently ended *Oprah Winfrey Show* was linked to increased sales for many products, especially books. Including an actual product, such as a can of Pepsi, adds a sense of realism to

a movie, television show, video game, book, or similar vehicle that cannot be created by a can simply marked "soda." Product placements are arranged through barter (trade of product for placement), through paid placements, or at no charge when the product is viewed as enhancing the vehicle it is placed in.

Global product placement expenditures total about $7.4 billion annually ($4.3 billion in the United States alone).[27] More than two-thirds of product placements are in movies and television shows, but placements in other alternative media are growing, particularly on the Internet and in video games. Digital technology now enables companies to "virtually" place their products in any audio or video production. Virtual placement not only reduces the cost of product placement for new productions but also enables companies to place their products in previously produced programs, such as reruns of television shows. Overall, companies obtain valuable product exposure, brand reinforcement, and increased sales through product placement, often at a much lower cost than in mass media like television ads.

CONSUMER EDUCATION Some major firms believe that educated consumers are more loyal customers. Financial planning firms often sponsor free educational seminars on money management, retirement planning, and investing in the hope that the seminar participants will choose the sponsoring organization for their future financial needs.

SPONSORSHIP Sponsorships are increasing both in number and as a proportion of companies' marketing budgets, with U.S. spending projected to reach almost $20 billion in 2013.[28] Probably the biggest reason for the increasing use of sponsorships is the difficulty of reaching audiences and differentiating a product from competing brands through the mass media.

With **sponsorship**, a company spends money to support an issue, cause, or event that is consistent with corporate objectives, such as improving brand awareness or enhancing corporate image. The biggest category is sports, which accounts for almost 70 percent of spending in sponsorships and has seen steady growth despite the recession.[29] Nonsports categories include entertainment

product placement a public relations strategy that involves getting a product, service, or company name to appear in a movie, television show, radio program, magazine, newspaper, video game, video or audio clip, book, or commercial for another product; on the Internet; or at special events

sponsorship a public relations strategy in which a company spends money to support an issue, cause, or event that is consistent with corporate objectives, such as improving brand awareness or enhancing corporate image

crisis management a coordinated effort to handle all the effects of unfavorable publicity or another unexpected unfavorable event

tours and attractions, causes, arts, festivals, fairs and annual events, and association and membership organizations.

Although the most popular sponsorship events are still those involving sports, music, or the arts, companies have recently been turning to more specialized events such as tie-ins with schools, charities, and other community service organizations. Marketers sometimes even create their own events tied around their products. In late 2012, energy drink manufacturer Red Bull hosted Stratos, a multimillion-dollar event where Austrian Felix Baumgartner skydived from the edge of space—nearly 24 miles above Earth's surface. Baumgartner became the first human to break the sound barrier in free fall, reaching 833.9 miles per hour before touching down safely in New Mexico. A major marketing victory for Red Bull, Stratos set its own record as the most-watched YouTube live stream of all time—more than 8 million viewers tuned in to the event.[30]

Corporations sponsor issues as well as events. Sponsorship issues are quite diverse, but the three most popular are education, health care, and social programs. Firms often donate a percentage of sales or profits to a worthy cause favored by their target market.

COMPANY WEB SITES Companies increasingly are using the Internet in their public relations strategies. Company Web sites are used to introduce new products; provide information to the media including social media news releases; promote existing products; obtain consumer feedback; communicate legislative and regulatory information; showcase upcoming events; provide links to related sites (including corporate and non-corporate blogs, Facebook, and Twitter); release financial information; interact with customers and potential customers; and perform many more marketing activities. In addition, social media are playing a larger role in how companies interact with customers online, particularly through sites like Facebook, Yelp, or Twitter. Indeed, online reviews (good and bad) from opinion leaders and other consumers help marketers sway purchasing decisions in their favor.

16-5b Managing Unfavorable Publicity

Although marketers try to avoid unpleasant situations, crises do happen. In our free-press environment, publicity is not easily controlled, especially in a crisis. **Crisis management** is the coordinated effort to handle the effects of unfavorable publicity, ensuring fast and accurate communication in times of emergency.

When the Villa Fresh Italian Kitchen ran "Dub the Dew," an online contest to name a green apple–flavored variety of Mountain Dew exclusive to the restaurant, it wasn't long before Internet trolls descended. These digital pranksters submitted absurd and offensive names (such as "diabeetus," "gushing granny," and "Hitler did nothing wrong"), then voted their submissions to the top of the contest leaderboard en masse. The contest's Web site was quickly taken offline, and Mountain Dew tweeted that the contest "lost to the internet." In an attempt to manage the crisis, the Villa Fresh Italian Kitchen issued an apologetic statement: "'Dub the Dew,' a local market promotional campaign that was created by one of our customers—not Mountain

Felix Baumgartner jumps out of a capsule—nearly 24 miles above Earth's surface—during the Red Bull Stratos event.

AP Images/zu dapd

Dew – was compromised. We are working diligently with our customer's team to remove all offensive content that was posted and putting measures in place to ensure this doesn't happen again."[31]

16-6 SALES PROMOTION

In addition to using advertising and public relations, marketing managers can use sales promotion to increase the effectiveness of their promotional efforts. Sales promotion consists of marketing communication activities other than advertising, personal selling, and public relations, in which a short-term incentive motivates consumers or members of the distribution channel to purchase a good or service immediately, either by lowering the price or by adding value.

Sales promotion is usually cheaper than advertising and easier to measure. A major national television advertising campaign often costs $5 million or more to create, produce, and place. In contrast, promotional campaigns using the Internet or direct marketing methods can cost less than half that amount. It is also very difficult to determine how many people buy a product or service as a result of radio or television ads. With sales promotion, marketers know the precise number of coupons redeemed or the number of contest entries received.

Sales promotion usually has more effect on behavior than on attitudes. Giving the consumer an incentive to make an immediate purchase is the goal of sales promotion, regardless of the form it takes. Sales promotion is usually targeted toward either of two distinctly different markets. **Trade sales promotion** is directed to members of the marketing channel, such as wholesalers and retailers. **Consumer sales promotion** is targeted to the ultimate consumer market. The objectives of a promotion depend on the general behavior of targeted customers (see Exhibit 4). For example, marketers who are targeting loyal users of their product need to reinforce existing behavior or increase product usage. An effective tool for strengthening brand loyalty is the *frequent buyer program*, which rewards consumers for repeat purchases. Other types of promotions are more effective with customers who are prone to brand switching or with those who are loyal to a competitor's product. A cents-off coupon, free sample, or eye-catching display in a store will often entice shoppers to try a different brand.

sales promotion
marketing communication activities other than advertising, personal selling, and public relations, in which a short-term incentive motivates consumers or members of the distribution channel to purchase a good or service immediately, either by lowering the price or by adding value

trade sales promotion
promotion activities directed to members of the marketing channel, such as wholesalers and retailers

consumer sales promotion
promotion activities targeted to the ultimate consumer market

---

Exhibit 4
TYPES OF CONSUMERS AND SALES PROMOTION GOALS

Type of Buyer	Desired Results	Sales Promotion Examples
Loyal customers People who buy your product most or all of the time	Reinforce behavior, increase consumption, change purchase timing	• Loyalty marketing programs, such as frequent buyer cards or frequent shopper clubs • Bonus packs that give loyal consumers an incentive to stock up or premiums offered in return for proofs of purchase
Competitor's customers People who buy a competitor's product most or all of the time	Break loyalty, persuade to switch to your brand	• Sampling to introduce your product's superior qualities compared to their brand • Sweepstakes, contests, or premiums that create interest in the product
Brand switchers People who buy a variety of products in the category	Persuade to buy your brand more often	• Any promotion that lowers the price of the product, such as coupons, price-off packages, and bonus packs • Trade deals that help make the product more readily available than competing products
Price buyers People who consistently buy the least expensive brand	Appeal with low prices or supply added value that makes price less important	• Coupons, price-off packages, refunds, or trade deals that reduce the price of the brand to match that of the brand that would have been purchased

Source: From *Sales Promotion Essentials*, 2nd ed., by Don E. Schultz, William A. Robinson, and Lisa A. Petrison. Reprinted by permission of McGraw-Hill Education.

Once marketers understand the dynamics occurring within their product category and determine the particular customers and behaviors they want to influence, they can then go about selecting promotional tools to achieve these goals.

16-6a Tools for Trade Sales Promotion

As we'll discuss in section 16-6b, consumer promotions pull a product through the channel by creating demand. However, trade promotions *push* a product through the distribution channel (see Chapter 13). When selling to members of the distribution channel, manufacturers use many of the same sales promotion tools used in consumer promotions, such as sales contests premiums and point-of-purchase displays. Several tools, however, are unique to manufacturers and intermediaries:

▸ **TRADE ALLOWANCES:** A **trade allowance** is a price reduction offered by manufacturers to intermediaries such as wholesalers and retailers. The price reduction or rebate is given in exchange for doing something specific, such as allocating space for a new product or buying something during special periods. For example, a local Best Buy outlet could receive a special discount for running its own promotion on Sony surround sound systems.

▸ **PUSH MONEY:** Intermediaries receive **push money** as a bonus for pushing the manufacturer's brand through the distribution channel. Often the push money is directed toward a retailer's salespeople. LinoColor, the leading high-end scanner company, produces a Picture Perfect Rewards catalog filled with merchandise retailers can purchase with points accrued for every LinoColor scanner they sell.

▸ **TRAINING:** Sometimes a manufacturer will train an intermediary's personnel if the product is rather complex—as frequently occurs in the computer and telecommunications industries. For example, representatives of a speaker manufacturer like Bang & Olufsen may train salespeople in how to demonstrate the new features of the latest models of sound systems to consumers.

▸ **FREE MERCHANDISE:** Often a manufacturer offers retailers free merchandise in lieu of quantity discounts. Occasionally, free merchandise is used as payment for trade allowances normally provided through other sales promotions. Instead of giving a retailer a price reduction for buying a certain quantity of merchandise, the manufacturer may throw in extra merchandise "free" (i.e., at a cost that would equal the price reduction).

▸ **STORE DEMONSTRATIONS:** Manufacturers can also arrange with retailers to perform an in-store demonstration. Food manufacturers often send representatives to grocery stores and supermarkets to let customers sample a product while shopping.

▸ **BUSINESS MEETINGS, CONVENTIONS, AND TRADE SHOWS:** Trade association meetings, conferences, and conventions are an important aspect of sales promotion and a growing, multi-billion-dollar market. At these shows, manufacturers, distributors, and other vendors have the chance to display their goods or describe their services to potential customers. Companies participate in trade shows to attract and identify new prospects, serve current customers, introduce new products, enhance corporate image, test the market response to new products, enhance corporate morale, and gather competitive product information.

Trade promotions are popular among manufacturers for many reasons. Trade sales promotion tools help manufacturers gain new distributors for their products, obtain wholesaler and retailer support for consumer sales promotions, build or reduce dealer inventories, and improve trade relations. Car manufacturers annually sponsor dozens of auto shows for consumers. The shows attract millions of consumers, providing dealers with increased store traffic as well as good leads.

16-6b Tools for Consumer Sales Promotion

Marketing managers must decide which consumer sales promotion devices to use in a specific campaign. The methods chosen must suit the objectives to ensure success of the overall promotion plan. The popular tools for consumer sales promotion discussed in the following pages have also been easily transferred to online versions to entice Internet users to visit sites, purchase products, or use services on the Web.

COUPONS AND REBATES A **coupon** is a certificate that entitles consumers to an immediate price reduction when the product is purchased. Coupons are a particularly good way to encourage product trial and repurchase. They are also likely to increase the amount of a product bought. Coupons can be distributed in stores as instant coupons on packaging, on shelf displays with pull-off coupon dispensers, and at cash registers, printed based on what the customer purchased; through freestanding inserts (FSIs); and through various Internet daily deal sites.

FSIs, the promotional coupons inserts found in newspapers, are the traditional way of circulating printed coupons. FSIs are used to distribute almost 90 percent of coupons. Such traditional types of coupon distribution, which also include direct mail and magazines, have been declining for several years, as consumers used fewer coupons. In 2012, consumers redeemed 2.9 billion coupons, a 17 percent decrease from 2011.[32]

The Internet is changing the face of coupons. In addition to Internet coupon sites such as Valpak.com and Coolsavings.com, and social coupon sites such as Groupon and LivingSocial, there are also deal sites like DealSurf.com that aggregate offers from different sites for convenience. While daily deal sites have been quite popular with consumers, sites like Groupon and LivingSocial are coming under some fire as many small businesses claim they lose money or drown under the flood of coupon redemptions. American Express is using Twitter hashtags to drive card use. Customers first sync their credit cards to their Twitter accounts and then send a tweet using an approved hashtag. The cardholder receives automatic discounts from partner businesses when she makes a purchase with her American Express Card.[33]

A **rebate** is similar to a coupon in that a rebate offers the purchaser a price reduction; however, because the purchaser must mail in a rebate form and usually some proof of purchase, the reward is not as immediate. Manufacturers prefer rebates for several reasons. Rebates allow manufacturers to offer price cuts to consumers directly. Manufacturers have more control over rebate promotions because they can be rolled out and shut off quickly. Further, because buyers must fill out forms with their names, addresses, and other data, manufacturers use rebate programs to build customer databases. Perhaps the best reason of all to offer rebates is that although rebates are particularly good at enticing purchase, most consumers never bother to redeem them—only 40 percent of consumers eligible for rebates collect them.[34]

PREMIUMS A **premium** is an extra item offered to the consumer, usually in exchange for some proof that the promoted product has been purchased. Premiums reinforce the consumer's purchase decision, increase consumption, and persuade nonusers to switch brands. The best example of the use of premiums is the McDonald's Happy Meal, which rewards children with a small toy. Premiums can also include more product for the regular price, such as two-for-the-price-of-one bonus packs or packages that include more of the product. Some companies attach a premium to the product's package, such as a small sample of a complementary hair product attached to a shampoo bottle.

LOYALTY MARKETING PROGRAMS A **loyalty marketing program** builds long-term, mutually beneficial relationships between a company and its key customers. One of the most popular types of loyalty programs, the **frequent buyer program**, rewards loyal consumers for making multiple purchases. The objective of loyalty marketing programs is to build long-term, mutually beneficial relationships between a company and its key customers.

There are more than 2.1 billion loyalty program memberships in the United States;

American Express is experimenting with Twitter to offer cardholders *great deals* at participating businesses.

rebate a cash refund given for the purchase of a product during a specific period

premium an extra item offered to the consumer, usually in exchange for some proof of purchase of the promoted product

loyalty marketing program a promotional program designed to build long-term, mutually beneficial relationships between a company and its key customers

frequent buyer program a loyalty program in which loyal consumers are rewarded for making multiple purchases of a particular good or service

sampling a promotional program that allows the consumer the opportunity to try a product or service for free

the average household has signed up for 18 programs.[35] Popularized by the airline industry through frequent-flyer programs, loyalty marketing enables companies to strategically invest sales promotion dollars in activities designed to capture greater profits from customers already loyal to the product or company. Co-branded credit cards are an increasingly popular loyalty marketing tool. Most department stores only offer loyalty programs if a customer opens their branded credit card. However, high-end chain Bloomingdales recently changed its rewards program to include anyone who will sign up. Members of the new Loyalist program receive one point for each dollar they spend and receive a $25 gift card after earning 5,000 points. While Bloomingdale's credit card holders receive more points per dollar spent, the company is hoping to monitor a greater number of its shoppers' spending habits by enabling non-cardholders to join Loyalist.[36]

Through loyalty programs, shoppers receive discounts, alerts on new products, and other types of enticing offers. In exchange, retailers are able to build customer databases that help them better understand customer preferences.

CONTESTS AND SWEEPSTAKES Contests and sweepstakes are generally designed to create interest in a good or service, often to encourage brand switching. *Contests* are promotions in which participants use some skill or ability to compete for prizes. A consumer contest usually requires entrants to answer questions, complete sentences, or write a paragraph about the product and submit proof of purchase. Winning a *sweepstakes*, on the other hand, depends on chance, and participation is free. Sweepstakes usually draw about ten times more entries than contests do.

While contests and sweepstakes may draw considerable interest and publicity, generally they are not effective tools for generating long-term sales. To increase their effectiveness, sales promotion managers must make certain the award will appeal to the target market. Offering several smaller prizes to many winners instead of one huge prize to just one person often will increase the effectiveness of the promotion, but there's no denying the attractiveness of a jackpot-type prize.

SAMPLING Sampling allows the customer to try a product risk-free. In a recent study, in-store sampling proved to be the most successful promotional tactic when researchers introduced a new dairy product to grocery stores. In-store sampling events increased sales 116 percent, outperforming end cap displays (70 percent), ad circulars (63 percent), and temporary price reductions (48 percent).[37]

Samples can be directly mailed to the customer, delivered door-to-door, packaged with another product, or demonstrated or distributed at a retail store or service outlet. Sampling at special events is a popular, effective, and high-profile distribution method that permits marketers to piggyback onto fun-based consumer activities—including sporting events, college fests, fairs and festivals, beach events, and chili cook-offs. Distributing samples to specific location types, such as health clubs, churches, or doctors' offices, is also one of the most efficient methods of sampling. Online sampling is catching up in popularity, however, with the growth of social media. Brands not only run contests through Facebook but also connect with fans, show commercials, and offer samples of new products in exchange for "liking" the brand.

AP Images/Diane Bondareff/Invision for The J.M. Smucker Company

Nine-year-old Jacob C. poses with his mole chicken torta after being named the grand prize winner of the 11th Annual Jif Most Creative Sandwich Contest in March 2013. Jacob was presented with a $25,000 college fund for his winning recipe.

POINT-OF-PURCHASE PROMOTION A **point-of-purchase (P-O-P) display** includes any promotional display set up at the retailer's location to build traffic, advertise the product, or induce impulse buying. P-O-P displays include shelf "talkers" (signs attached to store shelves), shelf extenders (attachments that extend shelves so products stand out), ads on grocery carts and bags, end-aisle and floor-stand displays, television monitors at supermarket checkout counters, in-store audio messages, and audiovisual displays. One big advantage of the P-O-P display is that it offers manufacturers a captive audience in retail stores. Approximately 76 percent of all retail purchase decisions are made in-store, and 57 percent of shoppers buy more than they anticipated once in the store, so P-O-P displays can be very effective.[38] Other strategies to increase sales include adding cards to the tops of displays, changing messages on signs on the sides or bottoms of displays, adding inflatable or mobile displays, and using signs that advertise the brand's sports, movie, or charity tie-in.

16-6c Trends in Sales Promotion

The biggest trend in sales promotion on both the trade and consumer side has been the increased use of the Internet. Social media–, e-mail-, and Web site–based promotions have expanded dramatically in recent years. Marketers are now spending billions of dollars annually on such promotions. Sales promotions online have proved effective and cost-efficient, generating response rates three to five times higher than off-line promotions. The most effective types of online sales promotions are free merchandise, sweepstakes, free shipping with purchases, and coupons. One major goal of retailers is to add potential customers to their databases and expand marketing touch points.

Marketers have discovered that online coupon distribution provides another vehicle for promoting their products. The redemption rate of online coupons—7.72 percent—is much higher than the redemption rate of traditional coupons—0.51 percent.[39] Online coupons can help marketers lure new customers, and with the speed of online feedback, marketers can track the success of a coupon in real time and adjust it based on changing market conditions.[40]

Online versions of loyalty programs are also popping up, and although many types of companies have these programs, the most successful are those run by hotel and airline companies.

> **point of purchase (P-O-P) display** a promotional display set up at the retailer's location to build traffic, advertise the product, or induce impulse buying

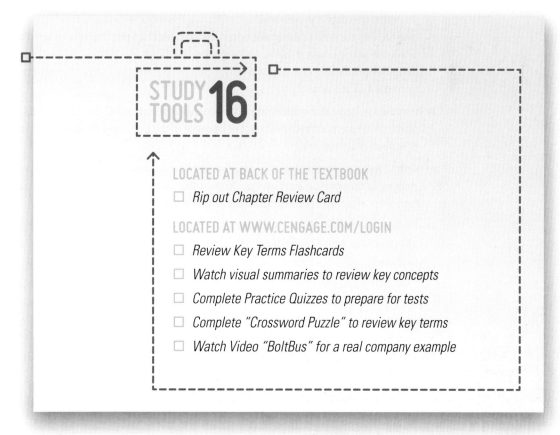

STUDY TOOLS **16**

LOCATED AT BACK OF THE TEXTBOOK
- ☐ *Rip out Chapter Review Card*

LOCATED AT WWW.CENGAGE.COM/LOGIN
- ☐ *Review Key Terms Flashcards*
- ☐ *Watch visual summaries to review key concepts*
- ☐ *Complete Practice Quizzes to prepare for tests*
- ☐ *Complete "Crossword Puzzle" to review key terms*
- ☐ *Watch Video "BoltBus" for a real company example*

17-1 PERSONAL SELLING

As mentioned in Chapter 15, *personal selling* is a purchase situation involving a personal, paid-for communication between two people in an attempt to influence each other. In a sense, all businesspeople are salespeople. An individual may become a plant manager, a chemist, an engineer, or a member of any profession and yet still have to sell. During a job search, applicants must "sell" themselves to prospective employers in an interview.

> Advertising offers the consumer a reason to buy; sales promotion offers an incentive to buy.

Personal selling offers several advantages over other forms of promotion:

▸▸ Personal selling provides a detailed explanation or demonstration of the product. This capability is especially needed for complex or new goods and services.

▸▸ The sales message can be varied according to the motivations and interests of each prospective customer. Moreover, when the prospect has questions or raises objections, the salesperson is there to provide explanations. By contrast, advertising and sales promotion can respond only to the objections the copywriter thinks are important to customers.

▸▸ Personal selling can be directed only to qualified prospects. Other forms of promotion include some unavoidable waste because many people in the audience are not prospective customers.

▸▸ Costs can be controlled by adjusting the size of the sales force (and resulting expenses) in one-person increments. On the other hand, advertising and sales promotion must often be purchased in fairly large amounts.

▸▸ Perhaps the most important advantage is that personal selling is considerably more effective than other forms of promotion in obtaining a sale and gaining a satisfied customer.

Personal selling may also work better than other forms of promotion given certain customer and product characteristics. Generally speaking, personal selling becomes more important as the number of potential customers decreases, as the complexity of the product increases, and as the value of the product grows (see Exhibit 1). For highly complex goods such as business jets and private communication systems, a salesperson is needed to determine the prospective customer's needs, explain the product's basic advantages, and propose the exact features and accessories that will

Personal Selling and Sales Management

After you finish this chapter go to
p330 *for* **STUDY TOOLS**

relationship selling (consultative selling) a sales practice that involves building, maintaining, and enhancing interactions with customers in order to develop long-term satisfaction through mutually beneficial partnerships

meet the client's needs. Many upscale clothing retailers offer free personal shopping, whereby consultants pull designer clothing they believe will fit the customer's style and specified need. This free service encourages customers to continue using personal shoppers and develop a relationship with the store. Even some low-end retailers have begun offering free personal shopper programs. At Minnesota's Arc Value Village Thrift Store, customers can arrange free seventy-five-minute meetings with personal shoppers and "thrift stylists"—a service that's much beloved by young adults and other individuals just entering (or reentering) the workforce.[1] Technology now plays an important role in personal selling through the use of social media like LinkedIn and Facebook, as well as through the use of blogs and Twitter to establish expertise within a field.

17-2 RELATIONSHIP SELLING

Until recently, marketing theory and practice concerning personal selling focused almost entirely on a planned presentation to prospective customers for the sole purpose of making the sale. Marketers were most concerned with making a one-time sale and then moving on to the next prospect. Traditional personal selling methods attempted to persuade the buyer to accept a point of view or convince the buyer to take some action. Frequently, the objectives of the salesperson were at the expense of the buyer, creating a win–lose outcome. Although this type of sales approach has not disappeared entirely, it is being used less and less often by professional salespeople.

In contrast, modern views of personal selling emphasize the relationship that develops between a salesperson and a buyer. **Relationship selling**, or **consultative selling**, is a multistage process that emphasizes personalization and empathy as key ingredients in identifying prospects and developing them as long-term, satisfied customers. With relationship selling, the objective is to build long-term branded relationships with consumers and buyers. The focus, therefore, is on building mutual trust between the buyer and seller through the delivery of long-term, value-added benefits that are anticipated by the buyer.

Relationship or consultative salespeople, therefore, become consultants, partners, and problem solvers for their customers. They strive to build long-term relationships with key accounts by developing trust over time. The emphasis shifts from a one-time sale to a long-term relationship in which the salesperson works with the customer to develop solutions for enhancing the customer's bottom line. Research has shown that positive customer–salesperson relationships contribute to trust, increased customer loyalty, and the intent to continue the relationship with the salesperson.[2] Thus, relationship selling provides a win–win situation for both buyer and seller.

The end result of relationship selling tends to be loyal customers who purchase from the company time after time. A relationship selling strategy focused on retaining customers costs a company less than constantly prospecting and selling to new customers.

Relationship selling is more typically used in selling situations for industrial-type goods, such as heavy machinery and computer systems, and services, such as airlines and insurance, than in those for consumer goods. Exhibit 2 lists the key differences between traditional personal selling and relationship or consultative selling. These differences will become more apparent as we explore the personal selling process later in the chapter.

Exhibit 1

COMPARISON OF PERSONAL SELLING AND ADVERTISING/SALES PROMOTION

Personal selling is more important if . . .	Advertising and sales promotion are more important if . . .
The product has a high value.	The product has a low value.
It is a custom-made product.	It is a standardized product.
There are few customers.	There are many customers.
The product is technically complex.	The product is easy to understand.
Customers are concentrated.	Customers are geographically dispersed.
Examples: Insurance policies, custom windows, airplane engines	**Examples:** Soap, magazine subscriptions, cotton T-shirts

© Cengage Learning

17-2a Selling in the Technology Age

Personal selling has taken a technological turn in the last decade. Younger shoppers tend to research styles and prices before setting foot in a store. Some even browse other stores' Web sites while trying on clothes in competitors' stores. This type of shopper pushes salespeople away, but stores that embrace this love of technology and independence can gain loyal customers. For example, stores carrying Bobbi Brown cosmetics provide touch-screen televisions that allow customers to see how to apply a smoky eye—even without talking to a makeup artist. At Unknwn, a shoe store owned by LeBron James, there are fifty iPads available throughout the store to tell customers about the merchandise. Some stores even have touchpads

© Tyler Olson/Shutterstock.com

to customize lighting and music in dressing rooms. Even grocery stores with self-checkout registers appeal to this group. By allowing customers to minimize sales contact when they want to while still having a dedicated sales team ready, these stores give customers what they want and build their loyalty.[3]

17-3 CUSTOMER RELATIONSHIP MANAGEMENT AND PERSONAL SELLING

As we have discussed throughout the text, customer relationship management (CRM) is the ultimate goal of a new trend in marketing that focuses on understanding customers as individuals instead of as part of a group. To do so, marketers are making their communications more customer specific using the CRM cycle, covered in Chapter 9, and by developing relationships with their customers through touch points and data mining. CRM was initially popularized as one-to-one marketing. But CRM is a much broader approach to understanding and serving customer needs than is one-to-one marketing.

Throughout the text, our discussion of a CRM system has assumed two key points. First, customers take center stage in any organization. Second, the business must

Exhibit 2

KEY DIFFERENCES BETWEEN TRADITIONAL SELLING AND RELATIONSHIP SELLING

Traditional Personal Selling	Relationship or Consultative Selling
Sell products (goods and services)	Sell advice, assistance, and counsel
Focus on closing sales	Focus on improving the customer's bottom line
Limited sales planning	Consider sales planning as top priority
Spend most contact time telling customers about product	Spend most contact time attempting to build a problem-solving environment with the customer
Conduct product-specific needs assessment	Conduct discovery in the full scope of the customer's operations
Lone wolf approach to the account	Team approach to the account
Proposals and presentations based on pricing and product features	Proposals and presentations based on profit impact and strategic benefits to the customer
Sales follow-up is short term, focused on product delivery	Sales follow-up is long term, focused on long-term relationship enhancement

Source: Robert M. Peterson, Patrick Schul, and George H. Lucas Jr., "Consultative Selling: Walking the Walk in the New Selling Environment," *National Conference on Sales Management Proceedings*, March 1996.

manage the customer relationship across all points of customer contact throughout the entire organization. By identifying customer relationships, understanding the customer base, and capturing customer data, marketers and salespeople can leverage the information not only to develop deeper relationships but also to close more sales with loyal customers.

17-3a Identify Customer Relationships

Companies that have CRM systems follow a customer-centric focus or model. **Customer-centric** is an internal management philosophy similar to the marketing concept discussed in Chapter 1. Under this philosophy, the company customizes its product and service offering based on data generated through interactions between the customer and the company. This philosophy transcends all functional areas of the business, producing an internal system where all of the company's decisions and actions are a direct result of customer information.

Customer-centric companies continually learn ways to enhance their product and service offerings. **Learning** in a CRM environment involves collecting customer information through comments and feedback on product and service performance.

Each unit of a business typically has its own way of recording what it learns, and perhaps even has its own customer information system. The departments' different interests make it difficult to pull all of the customer information together in one place using a common format. To overcome this problem, companies using CRM rely on knowledge management. **Knowledge management** is a process by which customer information is centralized and shared in order to enhance the relationship between customers and the organization. Information collected includes experiential observations, comments, customer actions, and qualitative facts about the customer.

As Chapter 1 explained, *empowerment* involves delegating authority to solve customers' problems. Usually, organizational representatives are able to make changes

during interactions with customers through phone, fax, e-mail, social media, or face-to-face.

An **interaction** occurs when a customer and a company representative exchange information and develop learning relationships. With CRM, the customer—not the organization—defines the terms of the interaction, often by stating his or her preferences. The organization responds by designing products and services around customers' desired experiences. Social media have created numerous new ways for companies to interact with customers. For example, CNN uses Facebook to have conversations with its viewers and track sentiments about popular news stories. For major news events, CNN uses the data collected through viewer interaction to develop interactive Web pages about leading stories, thereby creating a second platform for interaction. For example, the Facebook + CNN Elections Insight page, which tracked and segmented opinion trends during the 2012 U.S. presidential election, garnered 1.4 million visits and 43,000 shares—likely leading to even more interactions for CNN. [4]

The success of CRM—building lasting and profitable relationships—can be directly measured by the effectiveness of the interaction between the customer and the organization. In fact, what further differentiates CRM from other strategic initiatives is the organization's ability to establish and manage interactions with its current customer base. The more latitude (empowerment) a company gives its representatives, the more likely the interaction will conclude in a way that satisfies the customer.

17-3b Understand Interactions of the Current Customer Base

The interaction between the customer and the organization is the foundation on which a CRM system is built. Only through effective interactions can organizations learn about the expectations of their customers, generate and manage knowledge about them, negotiate mutually satisfying commitments, and build long-term relationships.

Exhibit 3 illustrates the customer-centric approach for managing customer interactions. Following a customer-centric approach, an interaction can occur through a formal or direct communication channel, such as a phone, the Internet, or a salesperson. Any activity or touch point a customer has with an organization, either directly or indirectly, constitutes an interaction.

Companies that effectively manage customer interactions recognize that data provided by customers affect a

Exhibit 3

CUSTOMER-CENTRIC APPROACH FOR MANAGING CUSTOMER INTERACTIONS

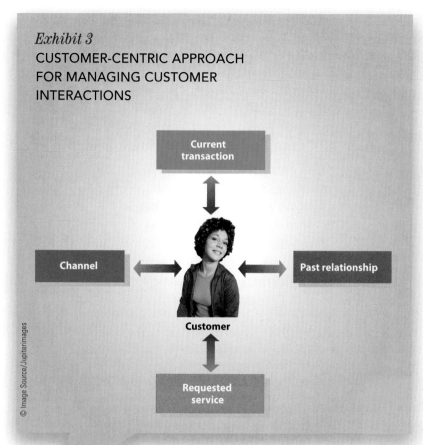

© Image Source/Jupiterimages

marketing efforts, develop new products, and deliver a degree of individual customization to improve customer relationships.

As social media have become more popular, many companies have begun to use these media for "social" CRM. In March 2013, ZDNet journalist Paul Greenberg named Attensity, Gigya, Jive Software, Get Satisfaction, Lithium, and Nimble as companies to watch in the field of social CRM.[5] Essentially, social CRM takes the most successful aspects of traditional CRM, such as behavioral targeting, and expands them to include ways to engage customers through social media. This new paradigm includes a new customer recommendation value called the *net promoter score*. The net promoter score measures how much a customer influences the behavior of other customers through recommendations on social media. Social CRM also enables marketers to focus more on the relationship aspect of CRM. For example, REI empowers customers to "carve your own adventure" through its YouTube channel. JetBlue uses Facebook and Twitter to provide advice and updates to travelers. To use social CRM effectively, companies must understand which sites customers use, whether they post opinions, and the major influencers in the category.

Another touch point is through **point-of-sale interactions** in stores or at information kiosks. Many point-of-sale software programs enable customers to easily provide information about themselves without feeling violated. The information is then used for marketing and merchandising activities and to accurately identify the store's best customers and the types of products they buy. Data collected at point-of-sale interactions are also used to increase customer satisfaction through the development of in-store services and customer recognition promotions.

wide variety of **touch points**. In a CRM system, touch points are all areas of a business where customers have contact with the company and data might be gathered. Touch points might include a customer registering for a particular service; a customer communicating with customer service for product information; a customer completing and returning the warranty information card for a product; or a customer talking with salespeople, delivery personnel, and product installers. Data gathered at these touch points, once interpreted, provide information that affects touch points inside the company. Interpreted information may be redirected to marketing research to develop profiles of extended warranty purchasers, to production to analyze recurring problems and repair components, and to accounting to establish cost-control models for repair service calls.

Web-based interactions are an increasingly popular touch point for customers to communicate with companies on their own terms. Web users can evaluate and purchase products, make reservations, input preferential data, and provide customer feedback on services and products. Data from these Web-based interactions are then captured, compiled, and used to segment customers, refine

17-3c Capture Customer Data

Vast amounts of data can be obtained from the interactions between an organization and its customers. Therefore, in a CRM system, the issue is not how much data can be obtained, but rather what types of data should be acquired and how the data can effectively be used for relationship enhancement.

The traditional approach for acquiring data from customers is through channel interactions. Channel interactions include store visits, conversations with salespeople, interactions via the Web, traditional phone conversations, and wireless communications. In a CRM system, channel interactions are viewed as prime information sources based on the channel selected to initiate the interaction rather than on the data acquired. In some cases, companies use online chat to answer questions customers have about products they are looking for. For example, 24 Hour Fitness has an online chat window that opens when a potential customer begins to review the Web site. If the visitor remains on the site, the online chat window asks if he or she needs help finding something specific.

Interactions between the company and the customer facilitate the collection of large amounts of data. Companies can obtain not only simple contact information (name, address, phone number) but also data pertaining to the customer's current relationship with the organization—past purchase history, quantity and frequency of purchases, average amount spent on purchases, sensitivity to promotional activities, and so forth.

In this manner, a lot of information can be captured from one individual customer across several touch points. Multiply this by the thousands of customers across all of the touch points within an organization, and the volume of data can rapidly become unmanageable for company personnel. The large volume of data resulting from a CRM initiative can be managed effectively only through technology. Once customer data are collected, the question of who owns those data becomes extremely salient. In its privacy statement, Toysmart.com declared that it would never sell information registered at its Web site, including children's names and birth dates, to a third party. When the company filed for bankruptcy protection, it said the information collected constituted a company asset that needed to be sold off to pay creditors. Despite the outrage at this announcement, many dot-coms closing their doors found they had little in the way of assets and followed Toysmart's lead.

17-3d Leverage Customer Information

Data mining identifies the most profitable customers and prospects. Managers can then design tailored marketing strategies to best appeal to the identified segments. In CRM, this is commonly referred to as leveraging customer information to facilitate enhanced relationships with customers. Exhibit 4 shows some common CRM marketing database applications.

CAMPAIGN MANAGEMENT Through campaign management, all areas of the company participate in the development of programs targeted to customers. **Campaign management** involves monitoring and leveraging customer interactions to sell a company's products and to increase customer service. Campaigns are based directly on data obtained from customers through various interactions. Campaign management includes monitoring the success

This advertisement for L'Oréal directs a highly-segmented group of customers to its Facebook page, where the company will continue to engage them though social CRM.

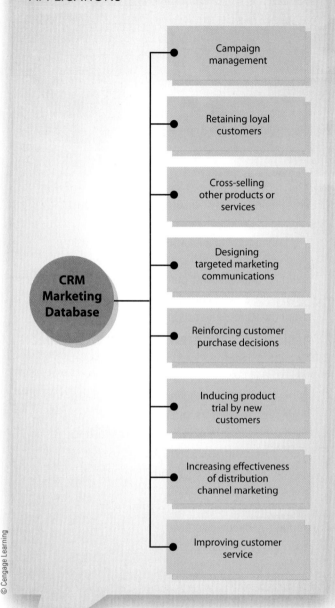

Exhibit 4

COMMON CRM MARKETING DATABASE APPLICATIONS

CRM Marketing Database

- Campaign management
- Retaining loyal customers
- Cross-selling other products or services
- Designing targeted marketing communications
- Reinforcing customer purchase decisions
- Inducing product trial by new customers
- Increasing effectiveness of distribution channel marketing
- Improving customer service

© Cengage Learning

HAPPY BIRTHDAY!

Sending customers a birthday e-mail with a special offer or promotion code is a popular reward program among businesses of all scopes and sizes. According to one study, 16 percent of companies with e-mail programs send birthday e-mail greetings. Personal touches like this give companies an edge over their competitors, increase sales, and strengthen customer loyalty.

▸▸ **Some companies offer coupon codes that require minimum purchases. Urban Outfitters offers customers 20 percent off an order of $50 or more, Fabric.com offers 15 percent off an order of $40, and Delta Air Lines offers $100 or more off trips costing at least $599.**

▸▸ **Some companies are more lenient, offering codes without restrictions. Art.com offers $10 off, the NBA store offers 15 percent off, and Founders Club offers 40 percent off—all without required minimum purchase amounts.**

▸▸ **Other companies offer free goods or services. Dairy Queen offers customers a free Blizzard ice cream treat on their birthday, while Giorgio's Italian Food & Pizzeria offers a free entrée. Each offer, however, requires a purchase of equal or greater value.**

▸▸ **Finally, some companies go the extra mile and offer complete birthday packages. Kimpton Hotels & Restaurants, for example, offers 20 percent off any hotel stay, two glasses of champagne and dessert, and a "surprise gift."[8]**

© iStockphoto.com/walrusmail

of the communications based on customer reactions through sales, orders, callbacks to the company, and so on. If a campaign appears unsuccessful, it is evaluated and changed to better achieve the company's desired objective.

Campaign management involves developing customized product and service offerings for the appropriate customer segment, pricing these offerings attractively, and communicating these offers in a manner that enhances customer relationships. Customizing product and service offerings requires managing multiple interactions with customers, as well as giving priority to those products and services that are viewed as most desirable for a specifically designated customer. Even within a highly defined market segment, individual customer differences will emerge. Therefore, interactions among customers must focus on individual experiences, expectations, and desires.

RETAINING LOYAL CUSTOMERS If a company has identified its best customers, then it should make every effort to maintain and increase their loyalty. When a company retains an additional 5 percent of its customers each

sales process (sales cycle) the set of steps a salesperson goes through in a particular organization to sell a particular product or service

A small company, such as this Gorilla Cheese food truck, may use the services of Belly to reward customers for their loyalty.

year, profits will increase by as much as 25 percent. What's more, improving customer retention by a mere 2 percent can decrease costs by as much as 10 percent.[6]

Loyalty programs reward loyal customers for making multiple purchases. The objective is to build long-term mutually beneficial relationships between a company and its key customers. Small- and medium-sized businesses can team up with reward management firm Belly to develop very individual rewards programs, such as getting to throw eggs at a food truck after a specified number of purchases or having the owner of your favorite bagel store sing to you after buying 100 bagels. The unique rewards reflect each business's personality and (ideally) those of its customers, making the rewards programs highly motivating.[7] In addition to rewarding good customers, loyalty programs provide businesses with a wealth of information about their customers and shopping trends, which can be used to make future business decisions.

CROSS-SELLING OTHER PRODUCTS AND SERVICES
CRM provides many opportunities to cross-sell related products. Marketers can use the database to match product profiles and consumer profiles so that they can cross-sell customers products that match their demographic, lifestyle, or behavioral characteristics. As it moved out of the Great Recession era, Discover stimulated growth by branching out beyond credit cards, developing several new banking and finance products. With a wealth of information about credit card customers in hand, Discover used aggressive cross-selling to establish a base for new products such as private student and home loans, checking accounts, direct payroll deposits, CDs, and IRAs. "Our loyal customer base is the foundation both for growing credit card market share and for cross-selling additional direct banking products," said Discover President of U.S. Cards Harit Talwar, "A large part of

the sales in the new consumer banking products are cross-sells to our loyal card members."[9]

Internet companies use product and customer profiling to reveal cross-selling opportunities while a customer is surfing their site. Past purchases on a particular Web site and the site a surfer comes from give online marketers clues about the surfer's interests and what items to cross-sell.

DESIGNING TARGETED MARKETING COMMUNICATIONS
Using transaction and purchase data, a database allows marketers to track customers' relationships to the company's products and services and modify the marketing message accordingly.

Customers can also be segmented into infrequent users, moderate users, and heavy users. A segmented communications strategy can then be developed based on which group the customer falls into. Communications to infrequent users might encourage repeat purchases through a direct incentive such as a limited-time price discount for ordering again. Online marketers for retailers like GNC and Newegg send out periodic e-mails with discounts to customers who made previous purchases. Communications to moderate users may use fewer incentives and more reinforcement of past purchase decisions. Communications to heavy users would be designed around loyalty and reinforcement of the purchase rather than around price promotions.

17-4 STEPS IN THE SELLING PROCESS

Completing a sale requires several steps. The **sales process**, or **sales cycle**, is simply the set of steps a salesperson goes through to sell a particular product or service. The sales process or cycle can be unique for each product or service, depending on the features of the product or service, characteristics of customer segments, and internal processes in place within the firm such as how leads are gathered.

Some sales take only a few minutes to complete, but others may take much longer. Sales of technical products like a Boeing or Airbus airplane and customized goods and services typically take many months, perhaps even years, to complete. On the other end of the spectrum, sales of less technical products like stationery are generally more routine and may take only a few days. Whether a salesperson spends a few minutes or a few years on a sale, there are seven basic steps in the personal selling process:

1. **Generating leads**

2. **Qualifying leads**

3. **Approaching the customer and probing needs**

4. **Developing and proposing solutions**

5. **Handling objections**

6. **Closing the sale**

7. **Following up**

Like other forms of promotion, these steps of selling follow the AIDA concept discussed in Chapter 15. Once a salesperson has located a prospect with the authority to buy, he or she tries to get the prospect's attention. A thorough needs assessment turned into an effective sales proposal and presentation should generate interest. After developing the customer's initial desire (preferably during the presentation of the sales proposal), the salesperson seeks action in the close by trying to get an agreement to buy. Follow-up after the sale, the final step in the selling process, not only lowers cognitive dissonance (refer to Chapter 6) but also may open up opportunities to discuss future sales. Effective follow-up will also lead to repeat business in which the process may start all over again at the needs assessment step.

Traditional selling and relationship selling follow the same basic steps. They differ in the relative importance placed on key steps in the process. Traditional selling efforts are transaction oriented, focusing on generating as many leads as possible, making as many presentations as possible, and closing as many sales as possible. Minimal effort is placed on asking questions to identify customer needs and wants or matching these needs and wants to

the benefits of the product or service. In contrast, salespeople practicing relationship selling emphasize an upfront investment in the time and effort needed to uncover each customer's specific needs and wants and meet them with the product or service offering. By doing their homework up front, salespeople create the conditions necessary for a relatively straightforward close. Look at each step of the selling process individually.

17-4a Step 1: Generating Leads

Initial groundwork must precede communication between the potential buyer and the salesperson. **Lead generation**, or **prospecting**, is the identification of those firms and people most likely to buy the seller's offerings. These firms or people become "sales leads" or "prospects."

Sales leads can be obtained in several different ways, most notably through advertising, trade shows and conventions, social media, webinars, or direct mail and telemarketing programs. Favorable publicity also helps to create leads. Company records of past client purchases are another excellent source of leads. Many sales professionals are also securing valuable leads from their firm's Web site.

Another way to gather a lead is through a **referral**—a recommendation from a customer or business associate. The advantages of referrals over other forms of prospecting include highly qualified leads, higher closing rates, larger initial transactions, and shorter sales cycles. Referrals are typically as much as ten times more productive in generating sales than are cold calls. Unfortunately, although most clients are willing to give referrals, many salespeople do not ask for them. Effective sales training can help to overcome this reluctance to ask for referrals. To increase the number of referrals, some companies even pay or send small gifts to customers or suppliers that provide referrals. Generating referrals is one area that social media and technology can usually make much more efficient.

Networking is using friends, business contacts, coworkers, acquaintances, and fellow members in professional and civic organizations to identify potential clients. Indeed, a number of national networking clubs have been started for the sole purpose of generating leads and providing valuable business advice. Increasingly, sales professionals are also using online networking sites like LinkedIn

lead generation (prospecting) identification of those firms and people most likely to buy the seller's offerings

referral a recommendation to a salesperson from a customer or business associate

networking a process of finding out about potential clients from friends, business contacts, coworkers, acquaintances, and fellow members in professional and civic organizations

cold calling a form of lead generation in which the salesperson approaches potential buyers without any prior knowledge of the prospects' needs or financial status

lead qualification determination of a sales prospect's (1) recognized need, (2) buying power, and (3) receptivity and accessibility

to connect with targeted leads and clients around the world, twenty-four hours a day. Some of LinkedIn's estimated 200 million users have reported response rates between 20 and 30 percent—Google reports a 70 percent response rate using LinkedIn's InMail service—versus 4.4 percent from direct marketing efforts.[10]

Before the advent of more sophisticated methods of lead generation, such as direct mail and telemarketing, most prospecting was done through **cold calling**—a form of lead generation in which the salesperson approaches potential buyers without any prior knowledge of the prospects' needs or financial status. Although cold calling is still used in generating leads, many sales managers have realized the inefficiencies of having their top salespeople use their valuable selling time searching for the proverbial "needle in a haystack." Passing the job of cold calling to a lower-cost employee, typically an internal sales support person, allows salespeople to spend more time and use their relationship-building skills on prospects who have already been identified.

17-4b Step 2: Qualifying Leads

When a prospect shows interest in learning more about a product, the salesperson has the opportunity to follow up, or qualify, the lead. Personally visiting unqualified prospects wastes valuable salesperson time and company resources. Many leads often go unanswered because salespeople are given no indication as to how qualified the leads are in terms of interest and ability to purchase. Unqualified prospects give vague or incomplete answers to a salesperson's specific questions, try to evade questions on budgets, and request changes in standard procedures like prices or terms of sale. In contrast, qualified leads are real prospects who answer questions, value your time, and are realistic about money and when they are prepared to buy. Salespeople who are given accurate information on qualified leads are more than twice as likely to follow up.[11]

> NETWORKING SITES SUCH AS LINKEDIN CAN PROVIDED MORE QUALITY LEADS THAN COLD CALLING, BUT COLD CALLING IS STILL USED BY SOME ORGANIZATIONS.

Lead qualification involves determining whether the prospect has three things:

1. **A RECOGNIZED NEED:** The most basic criterion for determining whether someone is a prospect for a product is a need that is not being satisfied. The salesperson should first consider prospects who are aware of a need but should not disregard prospects who have not yet recognized that they have one. With a little more information about the product, they may decide they do have a need for it. Preliminary interviews and questioning can often provide the salesperson with enough information to determine whether there is a need.

2. **BUYING POWER:** Buying power involves both authority to make the purchase decision and access to funds to pay for it. To avoid wasting time and money, the salesperson needs to identify the purchasing authority and his or her ability to pay before making a presentation. Organizational charts and information about a firm's credit standing can provide valuable clues.

3. **RECEPTIVITY AND ACCESSIBILITY:** The prospect must be willing to see the salesperson and be accessible to the salesperson. Some prospects simply refuse to see salespeople. Others, because of their stature in their organization, will see only a salesperson or sales manager with similar stature.

Often the task of lead qualification is handled by a telemarketing group or a sales support person who *prequalifies* the lead for the salesperson. Prequalification systems free sales representatives from the time-consuming task of following up on leads to determine need, buying power, and receptiveness. Prequalification systems may even set up initial appointments with the prospect for the salesperson. The result is more time for the sales force to spend in front of interested customers.

Companies are increasingly using their Web sites and other software to qualify leads. When qualifying leads

© iStockphoto.com/Hocus Focus Studio

online, companies want visitors to register, indicate the products and services they are interested in, and provide information on their time frames and resources. Leads from the Internet can then be prioritized (those indicating short time frames, for instance, are given a higher priority) and then transferred to salespeople. Enticing visitors to register also enables companies to customize future electronic interactions.

17-4c Step 3: Approaching the Customer and Probing Needs

Before approaching customers, the salesperson should learn as much as possible about the prospect's organization and its buyers. This process, called the **preapproach**, describes the "homework" that must be done by the salesperson before contacting the prospect. This may include visiting company Web sites, consulting standard reference sources such as Moody's, Standard & Poor's, or Dun & Bradstreet, or contacting acquaintances or others who may have information about the prospect. Reading the prospect's social media sites (following the company's Twitter feed and reading its Facebook page, for example) is a great way to get to know the company culture, become acquainted with customer needs, and learn more about daily activities.[12] Another preapproach task is to determine whether the actual approach should be a personal visit, a phone call, a letter, or some other form of communication.

During the sales approach, the salesperson either talks to the prospect or secures an appointment for a future time in which to probe the prospect further as to his or her needs. Relationship selling theorists suggest that salespeople should begin developing mutual trust with their prospect during the approach. Salespeople must sell themselves before they can sell the product. Small talk that projects sincerity and some suggestion of friendship is encouraged to build rapport with the prospect, but remarks that could be construed as insincere should be avoided.

The salesperson's ultimate goal during the approach is to conduct a **needs assessment** to find out as much as possible about the prospect's situation. The salesperson should be determining how to maximize the fit between what he or she can offer and what the prospective customer wants. As part of the needs assessment, the consultative salesperson must know everything there is to know about the following:

preapproach a process that describes the "homework" that must be done by a salesperson before he or she contacts a prospect

needs assessment a determination of the customer's specific needs and wants and the range of options the customer has for satisfying them

▸ **THE PRODUCT OR SERVICE:** Product knowledge is the cornerstone for conducting a successful needs analysis. The consultative salesperson must be an expert on his or her product or service, including technical specifications, features and benefits, pricing and billing procedures, warranty and service support, performance comparisons with the competition, other customers' experiences with the product, and current advertising and promotional campaign messages. For example, a salesperson who is attempting to sell a Xerox copier to a doctor's office should be very knowledgeable about Xerox's selection of copiers, their attributes, capabilities, technological specifications, and postpurchase servicing.

▸ **CUSTOMERS AND THEIR NEEDS:** The salesperson should know more about customers than he knows about himself. That's the secret to relationship and consultative selling, where the salesperson acts not only as a supplier of products and services but also as a trusted consultant and adviser. The professional salesperson brings each client business-building ideas and solutions to problems. For example,

© Goodluz/Shutterstock.com

if the Xerox salesperson is asking the "right" questions, then he or she should be able to identify copy-related areas where the doctor's office is losing or wasting money. Rather than just selling a copier, the Xerox salesperson can act as a consultant on how the doctor's office can save money and time.

▸ **THE COMPETITION:** The salesperson must know as much about the competitor's company and products as he or she knows about his or her own company. Competitive intelligence includes many factors: who the competitors are and what is known about them, how their products and services compare, advantages and disadvantages, and strengths and weaknesses. For example, if the Canon copy machine is less expensive than the Xerox copier, the doctor's office may be leaning toward purchasing the Canon. But if the Xerox salesperson can point out that the cost of long-term maintenance and toner cartridges is lower for the Xerox copier, offsetting its higher initial cost, the salesperson may be able to persuade the doctor's office to purchase the Xerox copier.

▸ **THE INDUSTRY:** Knowing the industry requires active research by the salesperson. This means attending industry and trade association meetings, reading articles published in industry and trade journals, keeping track of legislation and regulation that affect the industry, being aware of product alternatives and innovations from domestic and foreign competition, and having a feel for economic and financial conditions that may affect the industry. It is also important to be aware of economic downturns, as businesses may be looking for less expensive financing options.

Creating a *customer profile* during the approach helps salespeople optimize their time and resources. This profile is then used to help develop an intelligent analysis of the prospect's needs in preparation for the next step, developing and proposing solutions. Customer profile information is typically stored and manipulated using sales force automation software packages designed for use on laptop computers. Sales force automation software provides sales reps with a computerized and efficient method of collecting customer information for use during the entire sales process. Further, customer and sales data stored in a computer database can be easily shared among sales team members. The information can also be appended with industry statistics, sales or meeting notes, billing data, and other information that may be pertinent to the prospect or the prospect's company. The more salespeople know about their prospects, the better they can meet their needs.

A salesperson should wrap up the sales approach and need-probing mission by summarizing the prospect's need, problem, and interest. The salesperson should also get a commitment from the customer to some kind of action, whether it's reading promotional material or agreeing to a demonstration. This commitment helps to qualify the prospect further and justify additional time invested by the salesperson. When doing so, however, the salesperson should take care not to be too pushy or overbearing—a good salesperson will read a customer's social cues. The salesperson should reiterate the action he or she promises to take, such as sending information or calling back to provide answers to questions. The date and time of the next call should be set at the conclusion of the sales approach as well as an agenda for the next call in terms of what the salesperson hopes to accomplish, such as providing a demonstration or presenting a solution.

17-4d Step 4: Developing and Proposing Solutions

Once the salesperson has gathered the appropriate information about the client's needs and wants, the next step is to determine whether her company's products or services match the needs of the prospective customer. The salesperson then develops a solution, or possibly several solutions, in which the salesperson's product or service solves the client's problems or meets a specific need.

These solutions are typically presented to the client in the form of a sales proposal presented at a sales presentation. A **sales proposal** is a written document or professional presentation that outlines how the company's product or service will meet or exceed the client's needs. The **sales presentation** is the formal meeting in which the salesperson has the opportunity to present the sales proposal. The presentation should be explicitly tied to the prospect's expressed needs. Further, the prospect should be involved in the presentation by being encouraged to participate in demonstrations or by exposure to computer exercises, slides, video or audio, flip charts, photographs, and the like. Technology has become an important part of presenting solutions for many salespeople.

Because the salesperson often has only one opportunity to present solutions, the quality of both the sales proposal and the presentation can make or break the sale. Salespeople must be able to present the proposal and handle any customer objections confidently and professionally. For a powerful presentation, salespeople must be well prepared, use direct eye contact, ask open-ended questions, be poised, use hand gestures and voice inflection, focus on the customer's needs, incorporate visual elements that impart valuable information, know how to operate the audio/visual or computer equipment being used for the presentation, and make sure the equipment works. Nothing dies faster than a boring presentation. Often customers are more likely to remember how salespeople present themselves than what they say.

17-4e Step 5: Handling Objections

Rarely does a prospect say "I'll buy it" right after a presentation. Instead, the prospect often raises objections or asks questions about the proposal and the product. The potential buyer may insist that the price is too high or that the good or service will not satisfy the present need.

One of the first lessons every salesperson learns is that objections to the product should not be taken personally as confrontations or insults. A good salesperson considers objections a legitimate part of the purchase decision. To handle objections effectively, the salesperson should anticipate specific objections such as concerns about price, fully investigate the objection with the customer, be aware of what the competition is offering, and, above all, stay calm.

Often salespeople can use objections to close the sale. If the customer tries to pit suppliers against each other to drive down the price, the salesperson should be prepared to point out weaknesses in the competitor's offer and stand by the quality in his or her own proposal.

17-4f Step 6: Closing the Sale

At the end of the presentation, the salesperson should ask the customer how he or she would like to proceed. If the customer exhibits signs that he or she is ready to purchase, all questions have been answered, and objections have been met, then the salesperson can try to close the sale. Customers often give signals during or after

the presentation that they are ready to buy or are not interested. Examples include changes in facial expressions, gestures, and questions asked. The salesperson should look for these signals and respond appropriately.

Closing requires courage and skill. A salesperson should keep an open mind when asking for the sale and be prepared for both a yes and a no. The typical salesperson makes several hundred sales calls a year, many of which are repeat calls to the same client in an attempt to make a sale. Building a good relationship with the customer is very important. Often, if the salesperson has developed a strong relationship with the customer, only minimal efforts are needed to close a sale.

Negotiation often plays a key role in the closing of the sale. **Negotiation** is the process during which both the salesperson and the prospect offer special concessions in an attempt to arrive at a sales agreement. For example, the salesperson may offer a price cut, free installation, or a trial order. Effective negotiators, however, avoid using price as a negotiation tool. Because companies spend millions on advertising and product development to create value, when salespeople give in to price negotiations too quickly, it decreases the value of the product. Instead, effective salespeople should emphasize value to the customer, rendering price a nonissue. Salespeople should also be prepared to ask for trade-offs and try to avoid giving unilateral concessions. Moreover, if the customer asks for a 5 percent discount, the salesperson should ask for something

negotiation the process during which both the salesperson and the prospect offer special concessions in an attempt to arrive at a sales agreement

© iStockphoto.com/Okea

follow-up the final step of the selling process, in which the salesperson ensures delivery schedules are met, goods or services perform as promised, and the buyers' employees are properly trained to use the products

in return, such as higher volume or more flexibility in delivery schedules.

More and more U.S. companies are expanding their marketing and selling efforts into global markets. Salespeople selling in foreign markets should tailor their presentation and closing styles to each market. Different personalities and skills will be successful in some countries and absolute failures in others. For instance, if a salesperson is an excellent closer and always focuses on the next sale, doing business in Latin America might be difficult because people there want to take a long time building a personal relationship with their suppliers.

17-4g Step 7: Following Up

Salespeople's responsibilities do not end with making the sales and placing the orders. One of the most important aspects of their jobs is **follow-up**—the final step in the selling process, in which they must ensure delivery schedules are met, goods or services perform as promised, and buyers' employees are properly trained to use the products.

In the traditional sales approach, follow-up with the customer is generally limited to successful product delivery and performance. A basic goal of relationship selling is to motivate customers to come back again and again by developing and nurturing long-term relationships. Exhibit 5 depicts the time involved in the sales process and how those elements relate to the traditional and relationship selling approaches.

Most businesses depend on repeat sales, and repeat sales depend on thorough and continued follow-up by the salesperson. When customers feel abandoned, cognitive dissonance arises and repeat sales decline. Today, this issue is more pertinent than ever because customers are far less loyal to brands and vendors. Buyers are more inclined to look for the best deal, especially when they experience poor postsale follow-up. Automated e-mail follow-up marketing—a combination of sales automation and Internet technology—is enhancing customer satisfaction as well as bringing in more business for some marketers. After the initial contact with a prospect, a software program automatically sends a series of personalized e-mail messages over a period of time.

17-5 SALES MANAGEMENT

There is an old adage in business that nothing happens until a sale is made. Without sales, there is no need for accountants, production workers, or even a company president. Sales provide the fuel that keeps the corporate engines humming. Companies such as Cisco Systems, International Paper, Johnson Controls, and several thousand other manufacturers would cease to exist without successful salespeople. Even companies such as Procter & Gamble and Kraft Foods, which mainly sell consumer goods and use extensive advertising campaigns, still rely on salespeople to move products through the channel of distribution. Thus, sales management is

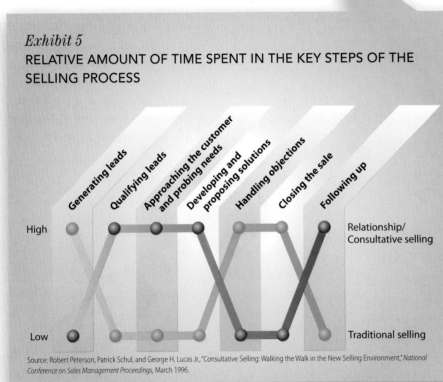

Exhibit 5
RELATIVE AMOUNT OF TIME SPENT IN THE KEY STEPS OF THE SELLING PROCESS

Source: Robert Peterson, Patrick Schul, and George H. Lucas Jr., "Consultative Selling: Walking the Walk in the New Selling Environment," *National Conference on Sales Management Proceedings*, March 1996.

one of marketing's most critical specialties. Effective sales management stems from a success-oriented sales force that accomplishes its mission economically and efficiently. Poor sales management can lead to unmet sales and profit objectives or even to the downfall of the corporation.

Just as selling is a personal relationship, so is sales management. Although the sales manager's basic job is to maximize sales at a reasonable cost while also maximizing profits, he or she also has many other important responsibilities and decisions:

1. **Defining sales goals and the sales process**

2. **Determining the sales force structure**

3. **Recruiting and training the sales force**

4. **Compensating and motivating the sales force**

5. **Evaluating the sales force**

17-5a Defining Sales Goals and the Sales Process

Effective sales management begins with a determination of sales goals. Without goals to achieve, salesperson performance would be mediocre at best, and the company would likely fail. Like any marketing objective, sales goals should be stated in clear, precise, and measurable terms

PART OF SALES MANAGEMENT IS DEFINING SALES GOALS FOR THE SALES FORCE.

© iStockPhoto.com/Hocus Focus Studio

and should always specify a time frame for their completion. Overall sales force goals are usually stated in terms of desired dollar sales volume, market share, or profit level. For example, a life insurance company may have a goal to sell $50 million in life insurance policies annually, to attain a 12 percent market share, or to achieve $1 million in profits. Individual salespeople are also assigned goals in the form of quotas. A **quota** is a statement of the salesperson's sales goals, usually based on sales volume alone but sometimes including key accounts (those with greatest potential), new accounts, repeat sales, and specific products.

17-5b Determining the Sales Force Structure

Because personal selling is so costly, no sales department can afford to be disorganized. Proper design helps the sales manager organize and delegate sales duties and provides direction for salespeople. Sales departments are most commonly organized by geographic regions, by product line, by marketing function performed (such as account development or account maintenance), by market or industry, or by individual client or account. The sales force for Hewlett-Packard (HP) could be organized into sales territories covering New England, the Midwest, the South, and the West Coast or into distinct groups selling different product lines. HP salespeople might also be assigned to a specific industry or market, for example, the telecommunications industry, or to key clients such as AT&T, Virgin Mobile, and Verizon.

Market- or industry-based structures and key account structures are gaining popularity in today's competitive selling environment, especially with the emphasis on relationship selling. Being familiar with one industry or market allows sales reps to become experts in their fields and thereby offer better solutions and service. Further, by organizing the sales force around specific customers, many companies hope to improve customer service, encourage collaboration with other arms of the company, and unite salespeople in customer-focused sales teams.

17-5c Recruiting and Training the Sales Force

Sales force recruitment should be based on an accurate, detailed description of the sales task as defined by the sales manager. For example, General Electric (GE) uses its Web site to provide prospective salespeople with explanations of different career entry paths and video accounts of what it is like to have a career at GE. Aside from the usual characteristics such as level of experience or education, what traits should sales managers look for in applicants?

- **EGO STRENGTH: Great salespeople should have a strong, healthy self-esteem and the ability to bounce back from rejection.**
- **SENSE OF URGENCY AND COMPETITIVENESS: These traits push their sales to completion as well as help them persuade people.**
- **ASSERTIVENESS: Effective salespeople have the ability to be firm in one-to-one negotiations, to lead the sales process, and to get their point across confidently without being overbearing or aggressive.**
- **SOCIABLE: Wanting to interact with others is a necessary trait for great salespeople.**
- **RISK TAKERS: Great salespeople are willing to put themselves in less-than-assured situations, and in doing so, often are able to close unlikely sales.**
- **CAPABLE OF UNDERSTANDING COMPLEX CONCEPTS AND IDEAS: Quick thinking and comprehension allow salespeople to quickly grasp and sell new products or enter new sales areas.**
- **CREATIVITY: Great salespeople develop client solutions in creative ways.**
- **EMPATHETIC: Empathy—the ability to place oneself in someone else's shoes—enables salespeople to understand the client.**

In addition to these traits, almost all successful salespeople say their sales style is relationship oriented rather than transaction oriented.[14] After the sales recruit has been hired and given a brief orientation, training begins. A new salesperson generally receives instruction in company policies and practices, selling techniques, product knowledge, industry and customer characteristics, and nonselling duties such as filling out sales and market information reports or using a sales automation computer program.

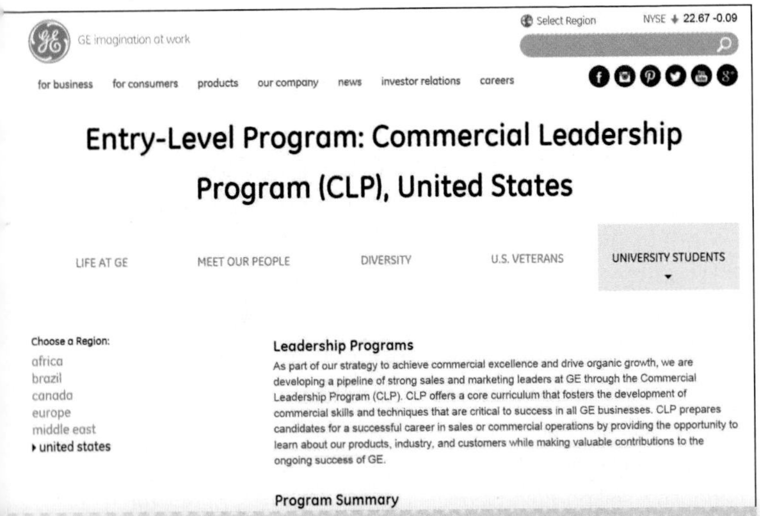

GE imagination at work
Select Region
NYSE 22.67 -0.09
for business
for consumers
products
our company
news
investor relations
careers
Entry-Level Program: Commercial Leadership Program (CLP), United States
LIFE AT GE
MEET OUR PEOPLE
DIVERSITY
U.S. VETERANS
UNIVERSITY STUDENTS
Choose a Region:
africa
brazil
canada
europe
middle east
united states
Leadership Programs
As part of our strategy to achieve commercial excellence and drive organic growth, we are developing a pipeline of strong sales and marketing leaders at GE through the Commercial Leadership Program (CLP). CLP offers a core curriculum that fosters the development of commercial skills and techniques that are critical to success in all GE businesses. CLP prepares candidates for a successful career in sales or commercial operations by providing the opportunity to learn about our products, industry, and customers while making valuable contributions to the ongoing success of GE.
Program Summary

THE REAL DEAL

Firms that sell complex products generally offer the most extensive training programs. Once applicants are hired at **General Electric**, they enter one of the many "rotational" training programs depending on their interest and major. For example, the Sales and Marketing Commercial Leadership Program (CLP) is geared toward developing skills needed for a successful career at GE. The program ranges from one to two years, depending on which GE business area the employee selects, and includes several rotations between business headquarters and the field. On completing the program, the new employees are better prepared to sell GE products because of their high level of product knowledge and on-the-job experience interacting with customers.[13]

© iStockphoto.com/billnoll / Source: www.ge.com/careers/students/clp/index.html

17-5d Compensating and Motivating the Sales Force

Compensation planning is one of the sales manager's toughest jobs. Only good planning will ensure that compensation attracts, motivates, and retains good salespeople. Generally, companies and industries with lower levels of compensation suffer higher turnover rates, which increase costs and decrease effectiveness. Therefore, compensation needs to be competitive enough to attract and motivate the best salespeople. Firms sometimes take profit into account when developing their compensation plans. Instead of paying salespeople on overall volume, they pay according to the profitability achieved from selling each product. Still other companies tie a part of the salesperson's total compensation to customer satisfaction assessed through periodic customer surveys.

As the emphasis on relationship selling increases, many sales managers believe that tying a portion of a salesperson's compensation to a client's satisfaction with the salesperson and the company encourages relationship building. To determine this, sales managers can survey clients on a salesperson's ability to create realistic expectations and his or her responsiveness to customer needs. At PeopleSoft, which was once one of the world's largest applications software companies, structure, culture, and strategies were built around customer satisfaction. Sales force compensation was tied to both sales quotas and a satisfaction metric that allows clients to voice their opinions on the service provided.[15]

Although the compensation plan motivates a salesperson to sell, sometimes it is not enough to produce the volume of sales or the profit margin required by sales management. Sales managers, therefore, often offer rewards or incentives, such as recognition at ceremonies, plaques, vacations, merchandise, and pay raises or cash bonuses. Cash awards are the most popular sales incentive and are used by virtually all companies. Another possibility is to reward salespeople with a Visa gift card, available from Visa in any amount between $25 and $600. The gift card, which functions like a credit card, can be personalized with a message about the salesperson's performance. It can then be reloaded at the employer's discretion. To recognize and further motivate employees, GE uses various rewards, including stock options, recognition programs unique to each department, tuition assistance, and product discounts.[16] Rewards may help increase overall sales volume, add new accounts, improve morale and goodwill, move slow items, and bolster slow sales. They can also be used to achieve long-term or short-term objectives, such as unloading overstocked inventory and meeting a monthly or quarterly sales goal. In motivating their sales force, sales managers must be careful not to encourage unethical behavior.

17-5e Evaluating the Sales Force

The final task of sales managers is evaluating the effectiveness and performance of the sales force. To evaluate the sales force, the sales manager needs feedback—that is, regular information from salespeople. Typical performance measures include sales volume, contribution to profit, calls per order, sales or profits per call, or percentage of calls achieving specific goals such as sales of products that the firm is heavily promoting.

Performance information helps the sales manager monitor a salesperson's progress through the sales cycle and pinpoint where breakdowns might be occurring. For example, by learning the number of prospects an individual salesperson has in each step of the sales cycle process and determining where prospects are falling out of the sales cycle, a manager can determine how effective a salesperson might be at lead generation, needs assessment, proposal generation, presenting, closing, and follow-up stages. This information can then tell a manager which sales skills might need to be reassessed or retrained. For example, if a sales manager notices that a sales rep seems to be letting too many prospects slip away after presenting proposals, it might mean he or she needs help with developing proposals, handling objections, or closing sales.

17-5f The Impact of Technology on Personal Selling and Sales Management

Will the increasingly sophisticated technology now available at marketers' fingertips eliminate the need for salespeople? Experts agree that a relationship between the salesperson and customer will always be necessary. Technology, however, can certainly help to improve that relationship. Cell phones, laptops, pagers, e-mail, and electronic organizers allow salespeople to be more accessible

The Internet has had a significant impact on personal selling—even among the least-seasoned salespeople. Here, Christine MacLeod of Eastern Massachusetts Girl Scout Troop 71911 (left) swipes a credit card using a ROAMpay scanner while selling cookies in Cambridge, Massachusetts. Devices like ROAMpay transform smartphones into mobile credit card readers, using their wireless network connections to transfer information securely and instantaneously.

to both clients and the company. Moreover, the Internet provides salespeople with vast resources of information on clients, competitors, and the industry.

E-business—buying, selling, marketing, collaborating with partners, and servicing customers electronically using the Internet—has had a significant impact on personal selling. Virtually all large companies and most medium and small companies are involved in e-commerce and consider it to be necessary to compete in today's marketplace. For customers, the Web has become a powerful tool, providing accurate and up-to-date information on products, pricing, and order status. The Internet also facilitates cost-effective processing of orders and service requests. Although on the surface the Internet might appear to be a threat to the job security of salespeople, the Web is actually freeing sales reps from tedious administrative tasks like shipping catalogs, placing routine orders, or tracking orders. This leaves them more time to focus on the needs of their clients.

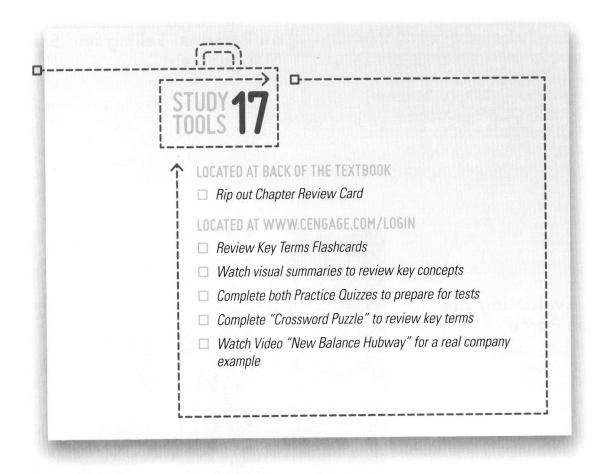

STUDY TOOLS 17

LOCATED AT BACK OF THE TEXTBOOK
☐ *Rip out Chapter Review Card*

LOCATED AT WWW.CENGAGE.COM/LOGIN
☐ *Review Key Terms Flashcards*
☐ *Watch visual summaries to review key concepts*
☐ *Complete both Practice Quizzes to prepare for tests*
☐ *Complete "Crossword Puzzle" to review key terms*
☐ *Watch Video "New Balance Hubway" for a real company example*

ONE APPROACH.
70 UNIQUE SOLUTIONS.

WHAT ARE SOCIAL MEDIA?

The most exciting thing to happen to marketing and promotion is the increasing use of online technology to promote brands, particularly using social media. Social media have changed the way that marketers can communicate with their brands—from mass messages to intimate conversations. As marketing moves into social media, marketers must remember that for most people, social media are meant to be a social experience, not a marketing experience. In fact, the term *social media* means different things to different people, though most people think it refers to digital technology. The American Bar Association uses a definition developed by social media expert Brian Solis. According to Solis, **social media** is "any tool or service that uses the Internet to facilitate conversations."[1] However, social media can also be defined relative to traditional advertising like television and magazines: whereas traditional marketing media offer a mass-media method of interacting with consumers, social media offer more one-to-one ways to meet consumers.

"Interaction and engagement [on social media] is something that you don't necessarily see in traditional media. That's why we [at Ford] continue to accelerate our digital advertising investment to more than 25% of our media dollars." Jim Farley, Ford Global Sales and Marketing Vice President[2]

social media any tool or service that uses the Internet to facilitate conversations

Social media have several implications for marketers and the ways that they interact with their customers. First, marketers must realize that they often do not control the content on social media sites. Consumers are sharing their thoughts, wishes, and experiences about brands with the world through social media. Because of this level of visibility and discussion,

Social Media and Marketing

Learning Outcomes

After you finish this chapter go to
p350 *for* **STUDY TOOLS**

marketers must realize that having a great ad campaign is not enough—the product or service must be great, too.

Second, the ability to share experiences quickly and with such large numbers of people amplifies the impact of word of mouth in a way that can eventually affect a company's bottom line. Many companies are developing mascots to drive their marketing message on social media. For example, Progressive auto insurance's perky saleswoman Flo has more than 3.5 million Facebook fans that read her posts about Progressive products. According to the company, since Flo began appearing in ads, the company has seen yearly gains in the number of policies taken out. Kraft is hoping to catch similar success with Mel the MilkBite granola bar. His conflicted personality has drawn more than 270,000 likes and much sympathy for the part milk, part granola bar mascot.[3]

Third, social media allow marketers to listen. Domino's Pizza listened to what was being posted about its products (much of which was not nice) and decided to use that information to change its product. Social media, along with traditional marketing research, allowed Domino's to gain the insight needed to completely reinvent its pizza. And Domino's then used the simple act of transparency to launch an award-winning promotional campaign. Dell and Gatorade have taken social media monitoring to a whole new level as they literally put social media at the center of their marketing efforts.

Fourth, social media provide more sophisticated methods of measuring how marketers meet and interact with consumers than traditional advertising does. Currently, social media include tools and platforms like social networks, blogs, microblogs, and media sharing sites, which can be accessed through a growing number of devices including smartphones, e-readers, televisions, tablets, video game consoles, and netbooks. This technology changes daily, offering consumers new ways to experience social media platforms. As such, social media must constantly innovate to keep up with consumer demands.

Finally, social media allow marketers to have much more direct and meaningful conversations with customers. Social media offer a form of relationship building that will ultimately bring the customer and brand closer. Indeed, the culture of *participation* that social media foster may well prove to be a fifth "P" for marketing.

At the basic level, consumers of social media want to exchange information, collaborate with others, and have conversations. Social media are designed for people to socialize with each other. They have changed how and where conversations take place, even globalizing human interaction through rapidly evolving technology. Google+ Hangouts, a popular facet of the fledgling Google+ social network, allows individuals around the world to video chat in real time. Competing with products such as Apple's FaceTime and Microsoft's Skype, Hangouts offers unique innovations such as live streaming and recording. Various companies have used Hangouts to conduct team meetings and webinars, offer consulting services, and host live press conferences. Taylor Swift, for example, used Hangouts to announce the release of her 2012 album *Red*. During the live chat, Swift took questions from thousands of fans around the world and debuted the album's first single (which quickly shot to the top of Apple's iTunes charts).[4] Clearly, conversations are happening online; it is up to the marketer to decide if engaging in those conversations will be profitable and to find the most effective method of entering the conversation.

Marketers are interested in online communication because it is wildly popular: brands, companies, individuals, and celebrities promote their messages online. In fact, some social media are becoming so important that celebrities, sports stars, and even hotels are hiring coaches to help them strike the correct tone. One such coach, Cassie Petrey, helps Britney Spears, Carly Rae Jepsen, Will.I.Am, and other clients navigate the perilous landscape of Twitter. Having worked as a social media consultant since 2007, Petrey instructs her clients on best practices and advises them how to leverage their personal brands in online spaces. She also monitors their Twitter feeds in real time, acting as editor, security guard, and advisor all at once. Petrey believes that social media coaches are underutilized among the entertainment elite, even suggesting that celebrities should have social media advisors accompany them to galas and award shows. "It can get really busy if you're doing interviews on the red carpet," she says, "and it's just nice to have someone with you who can say, 'Hey, you should take a picture with your other-famous-person friend right now. Here you go, now you should tweet it.'"[5] Some companies go so far as to require Facebook and Twitter training for high-profile employees. The UFC, for example, puts its fighters through social media training every year. Fighters who take the training to heart and attract fans or produce creative content receive money from the $240,000 bonus pool reserved for social media excellence.[6]

18-1a How Consumers Use Social Media

Before beginning to understand how to leverage social media for brand building, it is important to understand which consumers are using and how they are using it. It is safe to assume that many of your customers are active on Facebook. Recall from Chapter 4 that if it were a country, Facebook would be the third largest in the world. Other social networks, like hi5 and Bebo, offer an alternative for more segmented demographics. hi5 offers a wide variety of social games (covered later in this chapter), adding two or three each week. Bebo is popular with tweens and teens, though that age group is increasingly moving to Facebook.

Videos are another of the most popular tools by which marketers reach consumers, and YouTube is by far the largest online video repository—it has more content than any major television network. Flickr, Twitter, and blogs—all of which will be discussed in more detail later on—are some of the other most popular social media destinations among consumers. Every day:

▸▸ **2 million blog posts are written**

▸▸ **4.7 billion minutes are spent on Facebook**

▸▸ **Half a million tweets are posted**

▸▸ **More than 860,000 hours of video are uploaded to YouTube[7]**

The bottom line, according to Universal McCann's Comparative Study on Social Media Trends, is that "if you are online, you are using social media."[8]

Increased usage of alternative platforms like smartphones and tablet computers has further contributed to the proliferation of social media usage. In the United States, 87 percent of American adults own a cell phone, while 45 percent own a smartphone. These numbers jump to 93 percent and 63 percent for adults age eighteen to twenty-nine. Among all adults, 55 percent access the Internet on a mobile phone, and 40 percent have accessed a social media Web site.[9] Tablet usage has hit critical mass among mobile surfers—one in four smartphone users owns a tablet as

well.[10] According to Mark Donovan, senior vice president of mobile at ComScore, "Tablets are one of the most rapidly adopted consumer technologies in history and are poised to fundamentally disrupt the way people engage with the digital world both on-the-go and perhaps most notably, in the home."[11] The overall impact of tablet computing on social media (and thus the discipline of marketing) is yet to be seen, but given the incredible impact that the smartphone has had in its short life span, tablets could indeed prove to be game changing.

SOCIAL COMMERCE A new area of growth in social media is **social commerce**, which combines social media with the basics of e-commerce. Social commerce is a subset of e-commerce that involves the interaction and user contribution aspects of social online media to assist online buying and selling of products and services.[12] Basically, social commerce relies on user-generated content on Web sites to assist consumers with purchases. The current social commerce darling is Pinterest (recall Uniqlo's inventive Pinterest campaign from Chapter 5). Pinterest lets users collect ideas and products from all over the Web and "pin" favorite items to individually curated pinboards. Other users browse boards by theme, keyword, or product; click on what they like; and either visit the originating sites or re-pin the items on their own pinboards. Social commerce sites often include ratings and recommendations (as Amazon.com does) and social shopping tools (as Groupon does). In general, social commerce sites are designed to help consumers make more informed decisions on purchases and services.

Social commerce is expected to generate $30 billion each year by 2015, with half of all online sales coming through social media sites.[13] As companies move into social commerce sites such as Pinterest, consumer interactions across the sites may change. One way that companies are leveraging social commerce traffic is by running promotions. For example, in 2011, Lands' End ran a promotion called "Lands' End Canvas Pin It to Win It" whereby fans who pinned certain items to designated Lands' End Canvas pinboards were eligible to win those items. Several companies have followed

social commerce a subset of e-commerce that involves the interaction and user contribution aspects of social online media to assist online buying and selling of products and services

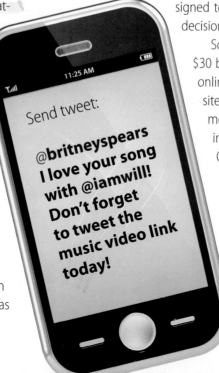

© Jojje/Shutterstock.com

11:25 AM

Send tweet:

@britneyspears I love your song with @iamwill! Don't forget to tweet the music video link today!

crowdsourcing
using consumers to develop
and market products

Lands' End's lead, orchestrating their own "pin it to win it" contests. Some companies riff on the idea in their own unique ways, while others, offering prizes unrelated to the pinned items or the companies themselves, simply use the contest format as a sort of marketing channel to advertise their brands. In 2013, for example, Favorite Family Recipes offered two iPad Minis as prizes for users who followed and pinned the logos of thirteen associated Pinterest boards.[14] This type of promotion can undermine the authenticity that many consumers rely on when using social commerce sites. However, some companies hope to cultivate authentic relationships by staying away from promotions. Whole Foods pins items that relate to the company's values but are not promotional or linked back to the Whole Foods site. Customers have built a relationship with Whole Foods based on upcycled products and recipes, rather than free products.[15]

18-1b Social Media and Integrated Marketing Communications

While marketers typically employ a social media strategy alongside traditional channels like print and broadcast, many budget pendulums are swinging toward social media. Forrester Research predicts that mobile marketing, social media, e-mail marketing, display advertising, and search marketing will grow from 19 percent of advertising spending in 2011 to more than 35 percent of spending by 2016, equaling television spending today. The bulk of this budget will still go to search marketing and display

advertising (the latter almost tripling by 2016), but substantial investments will also be made in mobile marketing and social media.[16]

A unique consequence of social media is the widespread shift from one-to-many communication to many-to-many communication. Instead of simply putting a brand advertisement on television with no means for feedback, marketers can use social media to have conversations with consumers, forge deeper relationships, and build brand loyalty. Social media also allow consumers to connect with each other, share opinions, and collaborate on new ideas according to their interests.

With social media, the audience is often in control of the message, the medium, the response, or all three. This distribution of control is often difficult for companies to adjust to, but the focus of social marketing is unavoidably on the audience, and the brand must adapt to succeed. The interaction between producer and consumer becomes less about entertaining and more about listening, influencing, and engaging.

Using consumers to develop and market products is called **crowdsourcing**. Crowdsourcing describes how the input of many people can be leveraged to make decisions that used to be based on the input of only a few people.[17] Companies get feedback on marketing campaigns, new-product ideas, and other marketing decisions by asking customers to weigh in. One company called Talenthouse is offering up the crowd to help musicians fulfill all sorts of needs—for example, someone to design album art or sew a dress for a lead singer. Talenthouse has users submit work to be voted on by Facebook and Twitter peers. The winner gets the job (though the musician has the final say in who wins). Some musicians see Talenthouse as a way to gain publicity or to help aspiring artists. In 2013, English singer-songwriter Ellie Goulding set up a contest for Talenthouse competitors to submit a photograph that showed people connecting with music at a concert or festival. The winner received £1,000 (about $1,500), a new laptop, special promotion, and a job as the official photographer for an Ellie Goulding concert.[18] Crowdsourcing offers a way for companies to engage heavy users of a brand and receive input, which in turn increases

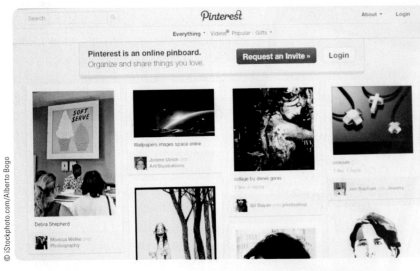

© iStockphoto.com/Alberto Bogo

those users' brand advocacy and lessens the likelihood that a change will be disliked enough to drive away loyal customers.

18-2 CREATING AND LEVERAGING A SOCIAL MEDIA CAMPAIGN

Social media is an exciting new field, and its potential for expanding a brand's impact is enormous. Because the costs are often minimal and the learning curve is relatively low, some organizations are tempted to dive headfirst into social media. However, as with any marketing campaign, it is always important to start with a strategy. For most organizations, this means starting with a marketing or communications plan, as covered in Chapter 2. Important evaluative areas such as situation analysis, objectives, and evaluation are still essential. It is important to link communication objectives (for example, improving customer service) to the most effective social media tools (for example, Twitter) and to be able to measure the results to determine if the objectives were met. It is also important to understand the various types of media involved.

The new communication paradigm created by a shift to social media marketing raises questions about categorization. In light of the convergence of traditional and digital media, researchers have explored different ways that interactive marketers can categorize media types. One such researcher, Sean Corcoran of Forrester Research, devised the distinction among owned, earned, and paid media (recall these concepts from Chapter 15). The purpose of owned media is to develop deeper relationships with customers. A brand's Facebook presence, YouTube channel, Twitter presence, Pinterest presence, and presence on other social platforms constitute owned media. Additional content such as videos, webinars, recommendations, ratings, and blog posts are also considered owned media since they are sharable on social media platforms. In an interactive space, media are *earned* through word of mouth or online buzz about something the brand is doing. Earned media include viral videos, retweets, comments on blogs, and other forms of customer feedback resulting from a

social media presence. When consumers pass along brand information in the form of retweets, blog comments, or ratings and recommendations, this is an example of earned media. In other words, the word of mouth is spread online rather than face-to-face. Paid media are similar to marketing efforts that utilize traditional media, like newspaper, magazine, and television advertisements. In an interactive space, paid media include display advertising, paid search words, and other types of direct online advertising.[19] Ads purchased on Facebook, for example, are considered paid media since the brand is paying for the text-based or visual ad that shows up on the right-hand side of Facebook profiles.

As a result, social media can really be thought of as an additional "layer" that many brands decide to develop. Some layers are quite deep—Doritos, Old Spice, and Nike can be said to have deeper layers of social media since these are brands that people talk about. Other brands, for example, many B-to-B brands, may have a more shallow social media layer and provide access on only one or two social media platforms. At the end of the day, it really depends on the type of product being sold and the customer's propensity to participate in social media.

To leverage all three types of media, marketers must follow a few key guidelines. First, they must maximize owned media by reaching out beyond their existing Web sites to create portfolios of digital touch points. This is especially true for brands with tight budgets, as the organization may not be able to afford much paid media. Second, marketers must recognize that aptitude at public and media relations

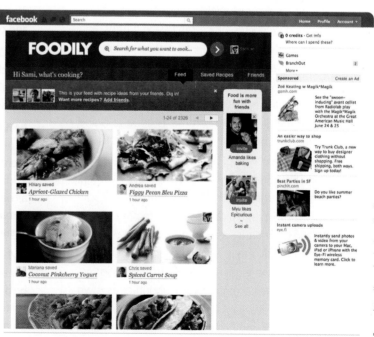

Source: https://www.facebook.com/foodily

no longer translates into earned media. Instead, marketers must learn how to listen and respond to stakeholders. This will stimulate word of mouth. Finally, marketers must understand that paid media must serve as a catalyst to drive customer engagement and expand into emerging channels.[20] If balanced correctly, all three types of media can be powerful tools for interactive marketers.

18-2a The Listening System

The first action a marketing team should take when initiating a social media campaign is simple—it should just listen. Customers are on social media and assume that the brand is there as well. They expect a new level of engagement with brands. Developing an effective listening system is necessary to both understanding and engaging an online audience. Marketers must not only hear what is being said about the brand, the industry, the competition, and the customer, but they must also pay attention to who is saying what and act upon that information. The specific ways that customers and noncustomers rate, rank, critique, praise, deride, recommend, snub, and generally discuss brands are all important. Thus, social media have created a new method of market research: customers telling marketers what they want and need (and don't want and don't need).

Once a company has started listening, it typically wants to develop a more formalized approach. **Social media monitoring** is the process of identifying and assessing what is being said about a company, individual, product, or brand. It can involve *text mining* specific key words on social networking Web sites, blogs, discussion forums, and other social media. Negative comments and complaints are of particular importance, both because they can illuminate unknown brand flaws and because they are the comments that tend to go viral. Listening is important because consumers believe that if negative comments about a brand go unanswered, that brand is insincere, and consumers will take their business elsewhere. Online tools such as Google Alerts, Google Blog Search, Twitter Search, Social Mention, and Socialcast are extremely helpful in monitoring social media. Larger companies typically use an enterprise system such as Radian6 to monitor social media.

In Exhibit 1, social media strategist Jeremiah Owyang and Jim Sterne outline eight stages of effective listening. Listening to customers communicate about one's own brand can be very revealing, but social media are also a great way to monitor competitors' online presences, fans, and followers. Paying attention to the ways that competing brands attract and engage with their customers can be particularly enlightening for both small businesses and global brands.

18-2b Social Media Objectives

After establishing a listening platform, the organization should develop a list of objectives for its social media team to accomplish. These objectives must be developed with a clear understanding of how social media change the communication dynamic with and for customers. Remember—attempting to reach a mass audience with a static message will never be as successful as influencing people through conversation. Marketing managers must set objectives that reflect this reality. Here are some practical ideas that marketing managers should consider when setting social media objectives:

▸ **LISTEN AND LEARN:** Monitor what is being said about the brand and competitors, and glean insights about audiences. Use online tools and do research to implement the best social media practices. If you have established a listening strategy, this objective should already be accomplished.

▸ **BUILD RELATIONSHIPS AND AWARENESS:** Open dialogues with stakeholders by giving them compelling content across a variety of media. Engage in conversations, and answer customers' questions candidly. This will both increase Web traffic and boost your search engine ranking. This is where crowdsourcing can be useful for product development and communication campaign feedback.

▸ **PROMOTE PRODUCTS AND SERVICES:** The clearest path to increasing the bottom line using social media is to get customers talking about products and services, which ultimately translates into sales.

▸ **MANAGE YOUR REPUTATION:** Develop and improve the brand's reputation by responding to comments and criticism that appear on blogs and forums. Additionally, organizations can position themselves as helpful and benevolent by participating in other forums and discussions. Social media make it much easier to establish and communicate expertise.

▸ **IMPROVE CUSTOMER SERVICE:** Customer comments about products and services will not always be positive. Use social media to search out displeased customers and engage them directly in order to solve their service issues.

Exhibit 1
EIGHT STAGES OF EFFECTIVE LISTENING

Stage	Description	Resources Required	Purpose
Stage 1: Without objective	The organization has established a listening system but has no goals.	Social media notification tools (Google Alerts)	Keep up with brand and competitor information.
Stage 2: Tracking brand mentions	The organization tracks mentions in social space but has no guidance on next steps.	A listening platform with key word report capabilities (Radian6)	Track discussions, understand sentiment, and identify influencers to improve overall marketing strategy.
Stage 3: Identifying market risks and opportunities	The organization seeks discussions online that may result in identification of problems and opportunities.	A listening platform with a large staff dedicated to the client (Converseon)	Staff seeks out discussions and reports to other teams, like product development and sales. These teams then engage the customers directly or conduct further research.
Stage 4: Improving campaign efficiency	The organization uses tools to get real-time data on marketing efficiency.	Web analytics software (Google Analytics)	See a wealth of information about consumers' behavior on their Web sites (and social media).
Stage 5: Measuring customer satisfaction	The organization collects information about satisfaction, including measures of sentiment.	Insight platforms that offer online focus-group solutions	Measure impact of satisfaction or frustration during interaction.
Stage 6: Responding to customer inquiry	The organization identifies customers where they are (e.g., Twitter).	A customer service team is allowed to make real-time responses.	Generate a high sense of satisfaction for customer but generates public complaints.
Stage 7: Better understanding of customers	The organization adds social information to demographics and psychographics to gain a better profile.	Social customer relationship management (CRM) systems to sync data	Social CRM marries database and social media to create a powerful analytical tool. (See Chapters 9 and 17 for more on CRM.)
Stage 8: Being proactive and anticipating customer demands	The organization examines previous patterns of data and social behavior to anticipate needs.	Advanced customer database with predictive application (yet to be created)	Modify social media strategy to preempt consumer behavior modifications based on trends.

Sources: Jeremiah Owyang, "Web Strategy Matrix: The Eight Stages of Listening," *Web Strategy*, November 10, 2009, www.web-strategist.com/blog/2009/11/10/evolution-the-eight-stages-of-listening/; Jim Sterne, *Social Media Metrics* (Hoboken, NJ: John Wiley & Sons, 2010).

18-3 EVALUATION AND MEASUREMENT OF SOCIAL MEDIA

Social media have the potential to revolutionize the way organizations communicate with stakeholders. Given the relative ease and efficiency with which organizations can use social media, a positive return on investment (ROI) is likely for many—if not most—organizations. A Forrester Research report found that 95 percent of marketers planned to increase or maintain their investments in social media. However, though they understand that it is a worthwhile investment, most marketers have not been able to figure out how to measure the benefits of social media.

As with traditional advertising, marketers lack hard evidence as to the relative effectiveness of these tools. Some marketers accept this unknown variable and focus on the fact that social media are less about ROI than about deepening relationships with customers; others work tirelessly to better understand the measurement of social media's effectiveness. A recent Ragan/NASDAQ OMX Corporate Solutions survey found that 40 percent of marketers are unsure of what evaluative tools to use, and 69 percent are only "somewhat satisfied" or "not satisfied at all" with how their companies measure social media. "I'm not sure what to measure or how," said one survey participant. "I know it's important, but I can't show my boss how many retweets a post received and expect him to care."[21]

While literally hundreds of metrics have been developed to measure social media's value, these metrics are meaningless unless they are tied to key performance indicators.[22] For example, a local coffee shop manager may measure the success of her social media presence by the raw number of friends on Facebook and followers on Twitter she has accumulated. But these numbers depend entirely on context. The rate of accumulation, investment per fan and follower, and comparison to similarly sized coffee shops are all important variables to consider. Without context, measurements are meaningless. This is a hot topic, and several marketing blogs cover the areas of social media measurement. Jim Sterne's book *Social Media Metrics* is one of the best sources information on monitoring and using social media metrics.

18-4 SOCIAL BEHAVIOR OF CONSUMERS

Social media have changed the way that people interact in their everyday lives. Some say that social media have made people smarter by giving people (especially children) access to so much information and interactivity. Social media allow people to stay in touch in ways never before experienced. Social media have also re-invented politics and civic engagement (the Occupy Wall Street movement grew worldwide through social media like Twitter). Social media have drastically changed the advertising business from an industry based on mass-media models (e.g., television) to an industry based on relationships and conversations. This all has implications for how consumers use social media and the purposes for which they use those media.[23]

Once objectives have been determined and measurement tools have been implemented, it is important to identify the consumer the marketer is trying to reach. Who is using social media? What types of social media do they use? How do they use social media? Are they just reading content, or do they actually create it? Does Facebook attract younger users? Do Twitter users retweet viral videos? These types of questions must be considered because they determine not only which tools will be most effective but also, more importantly, whether launching a social media campaign even makes sense for a particular organization.

Understanding an audience necessitates understanding how that audience uses social media. In Groundswell, Charlene Li and Josh Bernoff of Forrester Research identify six categories of social media users:

1. **CREATORS:** Those who produce and share online content like blogs, Web sites, articles, and videos

WHICH METRICS ARE MOST EFFECTIVE?

Many social media marketers will simply need to start with good measurable objectives, determine what needs to be measured, and figure it out. Still, some social media metrics to consider include:

➤ **BUZZ:** volume of consumer-created buzz for a brand based on posts and impressions, by social channel, by stage in the purchase channel, by season, and by time of day.

➤ **INTEREST:** number of "likes," fans, followers, and friends; growth rates; rate of virality or pass along; and change in pass along over time.

➤ **PARTICIPATION:** number of comments, ratings, social bookmarks, subscriptions, page views, uploads, downloads, embeds, retweets, Facebook posts, pins, and time spent with social media platform.

➤ **SEARCH ENGINE RANKS AND RESULTS:** increases and decreases on searches and changes in key words.

➤ **INFLUENCE:** media mentions, influences of bloggers reached, influences of customers reached, and second-degree reach based on social graphs.

➤ **SENTIMENT ANALYSIS:** positive, neutral, and negative sentiment; trends of sentiment; and volume of sentiment.

➤ **WEB SITE METRICS:** clicks, click-through rates, and percentage of traffic.

2. **CRITICS:** Those who post comments, ratings, and reviews of products and services on blogs and forums

3. **COLLECTORS:** Those who use RSS feeds to collect information and vote for Web sites online

4. **JOINERS:** Those who maintain a social networking profile and visit other sites

5. **SPECTATORS:** Those who read blogs, listen to podcasts, watch videos, and generally consume media

6. **INACTIVES:** Those who do none of these things[24]

A Forrester Research study determined that 24 percent of social media users function as creators, 36 percent function as critics, 23 percent function as collectors, 68 percent function as joiners, 73 percent function as spectators, and 14 percent function—or rather, don't function—as inactives.[25] Participation in most categories has slowed slightly, prompting analysts to recommend that marketers re-examine how they are engaging with their customers online.

Despite the apparent slowdown, research also shows that more social networking "rookies" are classified as joiners. Another bright spot is a new category, "conversationalists," or people who post status updates on social networking sites and microblogging services such as Twitter. Conversationalists represent 36 percent of users.[26] This type of classification gives marketers a general idea of who is using social media and how to engage them. It is similar to any type of market segmentation—especially the 80/20 rule. Those who are creating content and active on social media could be those consumers most likely to actively engage with a brand as well as actively post negative comments on social media. The critics and collectors make up most of this group. However, it is important not to miss the joiners and spectators, because they are eager to follow and act on the comments of their fellow customers.

18-5 SOCIAL MEDIA TOOLS: CONSUMER- AND CORPORATE-GENERATED CONTENT

Given that it is important for marketers to engage with customers on social media for the reasons mentioned earlier, there are a number of tools and platforms that can be employed as part of an organization's social media strategy. Blogs, microblogs, social networks, media creation and sharing sites, social news sites, location-based social networking sites, review sites, and virtual worlds and online gaming all have their place in a company's social marketing plan. These are all tools in a marketing manager's toolbox, available when applicable to the marketing plan but not necessarily to be used all at once. Because of the breakneck pace at which technology changes, this list of resources will surely look markedly different five years from now. More tools emerge every day, and branding strategies must keep up with the ever-changing world of technology. For now, the resources highlighted in this section remain a marketer's strongest set of platforms for conversing and strengthening relationships with customers.

18-5a Blogs

Blogs have become staples in many social media strategies and are often a brand's social media centerpiece. A **blog** is a publicly accessible Web page that functions as an interactive journal, whereby readers can post comments on the author's entries. Some experts believe that every company should have a blog that speaks to current and potential customers, not as consumers, but as people.[27] Blogs allow marketers to create content in the form of posts,

JOINER   CREATOR   CONVERSATIONALIST

corporate blogs blogs that are sponsored by a company or one of its brands and maintained by one or more of the company's employees

noncorporate blogs independent blogs that are not associated with the marketing efforts of any particular company or brand

microblogs blogs with strict post length limits

which ideally build trust and a sense of authenticity in customers. Once posts are made, audience members can provide feedback through comments. Because it opens a dialogue and gives customers a voice, the comments section of a blog post is one of the most important avenues of conversation between brands and consumers.

Blogs can be divided into two broad categories: corporate and professional blogs, and noncorporate blogs such as personal blogs. **Corporate blogs** are sponsored by a company or one of its brands and are maintained by one or more of the company's employees. They disseminate marketing-controlled information and are effective platforms for developing thought leadership, fostering better relationships with stakeholders, maximizing search engine optimization, attracting new customers, endearing the organization with anecdotes and stories about brands, and providing an active forum for testing new ideas. Many companies, however, have moved away from corporate blogs, replacing the in-depth writing and comment monitoring that come with blog maintenance with the quick, easy, and more social Facebook, Twitter, or Tumblr. In 2010, 50 percent of companies used corporate blogs. In 2011, only 37 percent of companies maintained a blog. Bank of America stopped using its corporate blog in order to focus solely on Facebook and Twitter, where its customers are.[28]

On the other hand, **noncorporate blogs** are independent and not associated with the marketing efforts of any particular company or brand. Because these blogs contain information not controlled by marketers, they are perceived to be more authentic than corporate blogs. Mommy bloggers, women who review children's products and discuss family-related topics on their personal blogs, use noncorporate blogs. The goal of mommy blogs is to share parenting tips and experiences and become part of a community. Food blogs are especially popular, particularly those posting restaurant reviews, diet and exercise tips, and recipes.

Because of the popularity of these and other types of blogs, many bloggers receive products and/or money from companies in exchange for a review. Many bloggers disclose where they received the product or if they were paid, but an affiliation is not always clear. Because of this, bloggers must disclose any financial relationship with a

company per Federal Trade Commission rules. Marketing managers need to understand the rules behind offering complimentary products to bloggers before using them as a way to capitalize on the high potential for social buzz; four out of five noncorporate bloggers post brand or product reviews. Even if a company does not have a formal social media strategy, chances are the brand is still out in the blogosphere, whether or not a marketing manager approached a blogger.

18-5b Microblogs

Microblogs are blogs that entail shorter posts than traditional blogs. Twitter, the most popular microblogging platform, requires that posts be no more than 140 characters in length. However, there are several other platforms, including Tumblr, Plurk, and, of course, Facebook's status updates. Unlike Twitter, these platforms allow users to post longer pieces of text, videos, images, and links. While some microblogs (such as Tumblr) do not have text length limits, their multimedia-based cultures discourage traditional blog-length text posts. The content posted on microblogs ranges from five-paragraph news stories to photos of sandwiches with the ingredients as captions (scanwiches .com). While Tumblr is growing rapidly, Twitter, originally designed as a short messaging system used for internal communication, is wildly popular and is used as a communication and research tool by individuals and brands around the world. Twitter is effective for disseminating breaking news, promoting longer blog posts and campaigns, sharing links, announcing events, and promoting sales. By following, retweeting, responding to potential customers' tweets, and tweeting content that inspires customers to engage the brand, corporate Twitter users can lay a foundation for meaningful two-way conversation quickly and effectively. Celebrities also flock to Twitter to interact with fans, discuss tour dates, and efficiently promote themselves directly to fans. Research has found that when operated correctly, corporate Twitter accounts are well respected and well received. Twitter can be used to build communities, aid in customer service, gain prospects, increase awareness, and, in the case of nonprofits, raise funds.

The ways a business can use microblogs to successfully engage with customers are almost limitless. A wide variety of companies find Tumblr's easy and customizable format a great way to promote an individual brand. Mashable uses its Tumblr to give a glimpse inside the offices and share the company's sense of humor. Ace Hotel, located in New York, Portland, Seattle, and Palm Springs, shows off its properties and local art exhibits on a spare, gallery-like Tumblr. Lure Fishbar shows off its delectable food on its Tumblr.[29]

18-5c Social Networks

Social networking sites allow individuals to connect—or network—with friends, peers, and business associates. Connections may be made around shared interests, shared environments, or personal relationships. Depending on the site, connected individuals may be able to send each other messages, track each other's activity, see each other's personal information, share multimedia, comment on each other's blog and microblog posts—or do all of these things. Depending on a marketing team's goals, several social networks might be engaged as part of a social media strategy: Facebook is the largest and fastest-growing network; hi5 caters to younger audiences; LinkedIn is geared toward professionals and businesses who use it to recruit employees; and niche networks like Bebo, Last.fm, We Are Teachers, BlackPlanet, and Match.com cater to specialized markets. There is a niche social network for just about every demographic and interest. Beyond those already established, an organization may decide to develop a brand-specific social network or community. Although each social networking site is different, some marketing goals can be accomplished on any such site. Given the right strategy, increasing awareness, targeting audiences, promoting products, forging relationships, highlighting expertise and leadership, attracting event participants, performing research, and generating new business are attainable marketing goals on any social network.

FACEBOOK Facebook originated as a community for college students that opened to the general public as its popularity grew. It now has hundreds of millions of users, making it the most popular social networking site by far. Growth in new profiles is highest among baby boomers, who use Facebook as a way to connect with old friends and keep up with family. Facebook is popular not only with individuals, but also with groups and companies. How an individual uses Facebook differs from the way a group or company uses Facebook, as you can see in Exhibit 2. Individual Facebook users create profiles, while brands, organizations, and nonprofit causes operate as pages. As opposed to individual profiles, all pages are public and are thus subject to search engine indexing.

By maintaining a popular Facebook page, a brand not only increases its social media presence, it also helps to optimize search engine results. Pages often include photo and video albums, brand information, and links to external sites. The most useful page feature, however, is the Timeline. The Timeline allows a brand to communicate directly with fans via status updates, which enables marketers to build databases of interested stakeholders. When an individual becomes a fan of your organization or posts on your Timeline, that information is shared with the individual's friends, creating a mini viral marketing campaign. Other Facebook marketing tools include groups, applications, and ads. Facebook is an extremely important platform for social marketers.

Facebook has proved to be fertile ground for new marketing ideas and campaigns. Many companies use Facebook as a way to share photos of the business they are doing, whether that is images of the plant where the product is made or finished construction on a new project. Offering guides relevant to a company's product as a way to educate interested customers has worked well for Kitchen Cabinet Kings, which found that educated customers make more purchases. Modify Watches allows fans

social networking sites Web sites that allow individuals to connect—or network—with friends, peers, and business associates

Exhibit 2
FACEBOOK LINGO

Non-Individual (Usually Corporate)	Individual
Page	Profile
Fan of a page, tells fan's friends that the user is a fan, creates mini viral campaign	Friend a person, send private messages, write on the Timeline, see friend-only content
Public, searchable	Privacy options, not searchable unless user enabled

© Cengage Learning

to vote on new designs and alerts them to limited stock sales and other promotions, rewarding its followers.[30]

LINKEDIN LinkedIn is used primarily by professionals who wish to build their personal brands online and businesses that are recruiting employees and freelancers. LinkedIn features many of the same services as Facebook (profiles, status updates, private messages, company pages, and groups) but is oriented around business and professional connections—it is designed to be information-rich rather than multimedia-rich. LinkedIn serves as a virtual rolodex, providing recruiters and job seekers alike a network to connect and conduct business. LinkedIn's question-and-answer forum, endorsement system, job classifieds platform, and recent acquisition of presentation-hosting Web site SlideShare set it apart from Facebook as a truly business-oriented space.[31]

18-5d Media Sharing Sites

Media sharing sites allow users to upload and distribute multimedia content like videos and photos. YouTube, Flickr, and Pinterest are particularly useful to brands' social marketing strategies because they add a vibrant interactive channel on which to disseminate content. Instagram, Vine, and Snapchat are newer (but hugely popular) media sharing platforms that will likely prove useful to marketers as well. Suffice to say, the distribution of user-generated content has changed markedly over the past few years. Today, organizations can tell compelling brand stories through videos, photos, and audio.

Photo sharing sites allow users to archive and share photos. Flickr, Picasa, Twitpic, Photobucket, Facebook, and Imgur all offer free photo hosting services that can be utilized by individuals and businesses alike.

Video creation and distribution have also gained popularity among marketers because of video's rich ability to tell stories. YouTube, the highest-trafficked video-based Web site and the third-highest-trafficked site overall, allows users to upload and stream their videos to an enthusiastic and active community.[32] YouTube is not only large (in terms of visitors), but it also attracts a diverse base of users: age and gender demographics are remarkably balanced.

Many entertainment companies and movie marketers have used YouTube as a showcase for new products, specials, and movie trailers. For example, Lionsgate purchased ad space on the YouTube home page in fifteen countries to promote the *Avatar* movie trailer. Some teen clothing brands like Forever 21 and JCPenney build followings on YouTube by posting hauls—videos made by teens that focus on fashion. Clearly, user-generated content can be a powerful tool for brands that can use it effectively.

A podcast, another type of user-generated media, is a digital audio or video file that is distributed serially for other people to listen to or watch. Podcasts can be streamed online, played on a computer, uploaded to a portable media player (like an iPod), or downloaded onto a smartphone. Podcasts are like radio shows that are distributed through various

In April 2013, Facebook launched Home, a mobile software application that replaces the stock user interface on Android smartphones. According to CEO Mark Zuckerberg, the driving idea behind Home was to bring content directly to the user without requiring him or her to open a separate app.

AP Images/Marcio Jose Sanchez

means and not linked to a scheduled time slot. While they have not experienced the exponential growth rates of other digital platforms, podcasts have amassed a steadily growing number of loyal devotees. For example, Etsy, an online marketplace for handmade and vintage wares, offers a podcast series introducing favorite craftspeople to the world—driving business for those individuals.

18-5e Social News Sites

Social news sites allow users to decide which content is promoted on a given Web site by voting that content up or down. Users post news stories and multimedia on crowdsourced sites such as Reddit and Digg for the community to vote on. The more interest from readers, the higher the story or video is ranked. Marketers have found that these sites are useful for promoting campaigns, creating conversations around related issues, and building Web site traffic.

If marketing content posted to a crowdsourced site is voted up, discussed, and shared enough to be listed among the most popular topics of the day, it can go viral across other sites, and eventually, the entire Web. Social bookmarking sites such as Delicious and StumbleUpon are similar to social news sites but the objective of their users is to collect, save, and share interesting and valuable links. On these sites, users categorize links with short, descriptive tags. Users can search the site's database of links by specific tags or can add their own tags to others' links. In this way, tags serve as the foundation for information gathering and sharing on social bookmarking sites.[33]

18-5f Location-Based Social Networking Sites

Considered by many to be the next big thing in social marketing, location sites like Foursquare and Loopt

should be on every marketer's radar. Essentially, **location-based social networking sites** combine the fun of social networking with the utility of location-based GPS technology. Foursquare, one of the most popular location sites, treats location-based micronetworking as a game: Users earn badges and special statuses based on their number of visits to particular locations. Users can write and read short reviews and tips about businesses, organize meet-ups, and see which Foursquare-using friends are nearby. Foursquare updates can also be posted to linked Twitter and Facebook accounts for followers and friends to see. Location sites such as Foursquare are particularly useful social marketing tools for local businesses, especially when combined with sales promotions like coupons, special offers, contests, and events. Location sites can be harnessed to forge lasting relationships with and deeply engrained loyalty in customers.[35] For example, a local restaurant can allow consumers to check in on Foursquare using their smartphones and receive coupons for that day's purchases. Since the location site technology is relatively new, many brands are still figuring out how best to utilize Foursquare. Facebook added Places to capitalize on this location-based technology, which allows people to "check in" and share their location with their online friends. It will be interesting to see how use of this technology grows over time.

18-5g Review Sites

Individuals tend to trust other people's opinions when it comes to purchasing. According to Nielsen Media Research, more than 70 percent of consumers said that they trusted online consumer opinions. This percentage is much higher than that of consumers who trust traditional advertising. Based on the early work of Amazon.com and eBay to integrate user opinions into product and seller pages, countless Web sites allowing users to voice their opinions have sprung up across every segment of the Internet market. **Review sites** allow consumers to post, read, rate, and comment on opinions regarding all kinds of products and services. For example, Yelp, the most active local review directory on the Web, combines customer

social news sites Web sites that allow users to decide which content is promoted on a given Web site by voting that content up or down

location-based social networking sites Web sites that combine the fun of social networking with the utility of location-based GPS technology

review sites Web sites that allow consumers to post, read, rate, and comment on opinions regarding all kinds of products and services

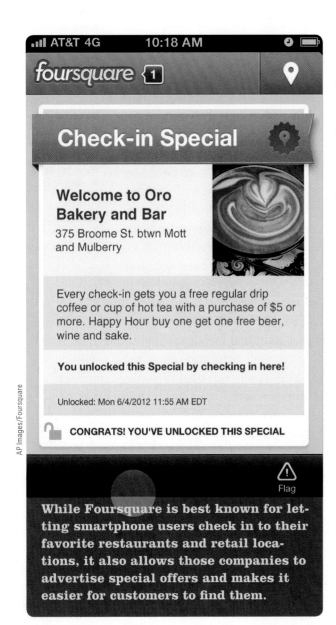

While Foursquare is best known for letting smartphone users check in to their favorite restaurants and retail locations, it also allows those companies to advertise special offers and makes it easier for customers to find them.

critiques of local businesses with business information and elements of social networking to create an engaging, informative experience. On Yelp, users scrutinize local restaurants, fitness centers, tattoo parlors, and other businesses, each of which has a detailed profile page. Business owners and representatives can edit their organizations' pages and respond to Yelp reviews both privately and publicly. Yelp even rewards its most popular (and prolific) reviewers with Elite status. Businesses like Worthington, Ohio's Pies & Pints will throw Elite-only parties to allow these esteemed Yelpers to try out their restaurant, hoping to receive a favorable review. Pies & Pints' February 2013 party for Yelp Elites garnered nineteen reviews averaging four-and-a-half stars out of five.[36] By giving marketers the opportunity to respond to their customers directly and put

their businesses in a positive light, review sites certainly serve as useful tools for local and national businesses.

18-5h Virtual Worlds and Online Gaming

Virtual worlds and online gaming present additional opportunities for marketers to engage with consumers. These include massive multiplayer online games (MMOGs) such as *EverQuest Next* and *The Elder Scrolls Online* as well as online communities (or virtual worlds) such as *Second Life*, *Poptropica*, and *Habbo Hotel*. Consultancy firm KZero Worldwide reported that almost 800 million people participate in some sort of virtual world experience, and the sector's annual revenue approaches $1 billion. Some of the most popular and profitable games, including *Diamond Dash* and *FarmVille 2*, are built on the Facebook platform. Much of these games' revenue comes from in-game advertising—virtual world environments are often fertile grounds for branded content. Organizations such as IBM and the American Cancer Society have developed profitable trade presences in *Second Life*, but others have abandoned the persistent online community as its user base has declined—the average number of users logged into *Second Life* dropped almost 25 percent between 2009 and 2013.[37] Although virtual worlds are unfamiliar to and even intimidating for many traditional marketers, the field is an important, viable, and growing consideration for social media marketing.

One area of growth is social gaming. Nearly 25 percent of people play games like *Words with Friends* and *Draw Something*, either within social networking sites like Facebook or on mobile devices. Interestingly, the typical player is a forty-five-year-old woman with a full-time job and college education (while users who play on mobile devices tend to be younger). Women are most likely to play with real-world friends or relatives as opposed to strangers. Most play multiple times per week, and more than 30 percent play daily. Facebook is by far the largest social network for gaming, though hi5 is hoping to win over more users with its large variety of games. The top five games on Facebook are *FarmVille 2*, *Texas HoldEm Poker*, *Candy Crush Saga*, *CoasterVille*, and *Diamond Dash*. Rovio's *Angry Birds* nets 200 million users per month, while Social Point's *Dragon City* entices more than 10 million users a day. These games are attractive because they can be played in just five minutes, perhaps while waiting for the train.[38] A growing trend among mobile games is to use mobile ads to generate revenue for the game-makers. As long as the ads are not overly intrusive, most users opt to play the free game with ads over the paid version that doesn't have ads. This strategy has proven quite fruitful—the *Angry Birds* franchise earned Rovio nearly $100 million in 2011, with much of that revenue coming from the free version of the game.[39]

Another popular type of online gaming targets a different group—MMOGs tend to draw eighteen- to thirty-four-year-old males. In MMOG environments, thousands of people play simultaneously, and the games have revenues of more than $400 billion annually. Regardless of the type of experience, brands must be creative in how they integrate into games. Social and real-world-like titles are the most appropriate for marketing and advertising (as opposed to fantasy games), and promotions typically include special events, competitions, and sweepstakes. In some games (like *The Sims*), having ads increases the authenticity. For example, Nike offers shoes in *The Sims Online* that allow the player to run faster.

ROVIO HAS LEVERAGED THE ANGRY BIRDS BRAND INTO AN EXTREMELY SUCCESSFUL MERCHANDISING AND LICENSING BUSINESS!

© iStockphoto.com/Ziva_K

18-6 SOCIAL MEDIA AND MOBILE TECHNOLOGY

While much of the excitement in social media has been based on Web sites and new technology uses, much of the growth lies in new platforms. These platforms include the multitude of smartphones like Android and BlackBerry devices as well as iPads and other tablets. The major implication of this development is that consumers now can access popular Web sites like Facebook, Mashable, Twitter, and Foursquare from all their various platforms.

18-6a Mobile and Smartphone Technology

Worldwide, there are almost 6 billion mobile phones in use, 17 percent of which are smartphones.[40] It is no surprise, then, that the mobile platform is such an effective marketing tool—especially when targeting a younger audience. Smartphones up the ante by allowing individuals to do nearly everything they can do with a computer—from anywhere. With a smartphone in hand, reading a blog, writing an e-mail, scheduling a meeting, posting to Facebook, playing a multiplayer game, watching a video, taking a picture, using GPS, and surfing the Internet might all occur during one ten-minute bus ride. Smartphone technology, often considered the crowning achievement in digital convergence and social media integration, has opened the door to modern mobile advertising as a viable marketing strategy.

U.S. mobile advertising reached $17 billion in 2012, representing a 14 percent increase over 2011.[41] There are several reasons for the recent popularity of mobile marketing. First, an effort to standardize mobile platforms has resulted in a low barrier to entry. Second, especially given mobile marketing's younger audiences, there are more consumers than ever acclimating to once-worrisome privacy and pricing policies. Third, because most consumers carry their smartphones with them at all times, mobile marketing is uniquely effective at garnering consumer attention in real time. Fourth, mobile marketing is measurable: metrics and usage statistics make it an effective tool for gaining insight into consumer behavior. Finally, mobile marketing's response rate is higher than that of traditional media types like print and broadcast advertisement. Some common mobile marketing tools include:

- **SMS (SHORT MESSAGE SERVICE):** 160-character text messages sent to and from cell phones. SMS is typically integrated with other tools.

- **MMS (MULTIMEDIA MESSAGING SERVICE):** Similar to SMS but allows the attachment of images, videos, ringtones, and other multimedia to text messages.

- **MOBILE WEB SITES (MOBI AND WAP WEB SITES):** Web sites designed specifically for viewing and navigation on mobile devices.

- **MOBILE ADS:** Visual advertisements integrated into text messages, applications, and mobile Web sites. Mobile ads are often sold on a cost-per-click basis.

- **BLUETOOTH MARKETING:** A signal is sent to Bluetooth-enabled devices, which allows marketers to send targeted messages to users based on their geographic locations.

- **SMARTPHONE APPLICATIONS (APPS):** Software designed specifically for mobile and tablet devices. These apps include software to turn phones into scanners for various types of barcodes.

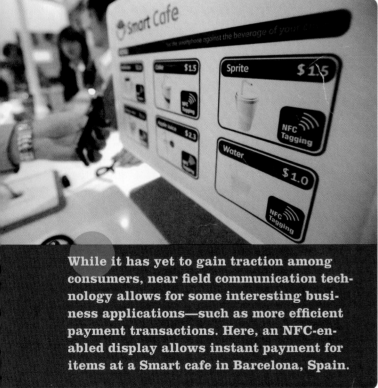

While it has yet to gain traction among consumers, near field communication technology allows for some interesting business applications—such as more efficient payment transactions. Here, an NFC-enabled display allows instant payment for items at a Smart cafe in Barcelona, Spain.

Chris Ratcliffe/Bloomberg/Getty Images

A popular use for barcode scanning apps is the reading and processing of Quick Response (QR) codes. When scanned by a smartphone's QR reader app, a QR code takes the user to a specific site with content about or a discount for products or services. Uses range from donating to a charity by scanning the code to simply checking out the company's Web site for more information. For example, Modify Watches offers a watch face with no hands. Instead it has a QR code that, when scanned, shows the correct time.[42]

Another smartphone trend is called "near field communication" (NFC), which uses small chips hidden in or behind products that, when touched by compatible devices, will transfer the information on the chip to the device. Barnes & Noble is hoping to work with publishers to ship hardcover books containing NFC chips to Barnes & Noble stores. The chips will be embedded with editorial reviews about that book from Barnes & Noble's Web site. When a NOOK user touches the hardcover with her NOOK, the book reviews will display on her tablet, helping her make a purchase decision.[43] In March 2013, Samsung unveiled the Galaxy S4 smartphone, which can track users' eye movements and shift screen content depending on where they are looking. While a relatively new technology, eye tracking has interesting implications for mobile marketing in the near future.[44]

Finally, mobile marketing is particularly powerful when combined with geo-location platforms such as Foursquare, whereby people can "check in" to places and receive benefits and special offers. These platforms allow retailers and other businesses to incentivize multiple visits, visits at certain times of the day, and positive customer reviews.

18-6b Applications and Widgets

Given the widespread adoption of Apple's iPhone, RIM's BlackBerry line, Android-based phones, and other smartphones, it's no surprise that millions of applications have been developed for the mobile market. Dozens of new and unique apps that harness mobile technology are added to mobile marketplaces every day. While many apps perform platform-specific tasks, others convert existing content into a mobile-ready format. Whether offering new or existing content, when an app is well branded and integrated into a company's overall marketing strategy, it can create buzz and generate customer engagement.

Web widgets, also known as gadgets and badges, are software applications that run entirely within existing online platforms. Essentially, a Web widget allows a developer to embed a simple application such as a weather forecast, horoscope, or stock market ticker into a Web site, even if the developer did not write (or does not understand) the application's source code. From a marketing perspective, widgets allow customers to display company information (such as current promotions, coupons, or news) on their own Web sites or smartphone home screens. Widgets are often cheaper than apps to develop, can extend an organization's reach beyond existing platforms, will broaden the listening system, and can make an organization easier to find.[45]

18-7 THE SOCIAL MEDIA PLAN

To effectively use the tools in the social media toolbox it is important to have a clearly outlined social media plan. The social media plan is linked to larger plans such as a promotional plan or marketing plan and should fit appropriately into the objectives and steps in those plans (for more information, review Chapters 2 and 16). It is important to research throughout the development of the social media plan to keep abreast of the rapidly changing social media world. There are six stages involved in creating an effective social media plan:

1. **LISTEN TO CUSTOMERS:** This is covered in more detail in section 18-2a.

2. **SET SOCIAL MEDIA OBJECTIVES:** Set objectives that can be specifically accomplished through social media, with special attention to how to measure the results. Numerous metrics are available, some of which are mentioned throughout the chapter.

3. **DEFINE STRATEGIES:** This includes examining trends and best practices in the industry.

4. **IDENTIFY THE TARGET AUDIENCE:** This should line up with the target market defined in the marketing plan, but in the social media plan, pay special attention to how that audience participates and behaves online.

5. **SELECT THE TOOLS AND PLATFORMS:** Based on the result of step 4, choose the social media tools and platforms that will be most relevant. These choices are based on the knowledge of where the target audience participates on social media.

6. **IMPLEMENT AND MONITOR THE STRATEGY:** Social media campaigns can be fluid, so it is important to keep a close eye on what is successful and what isn't. Based on the observations, make changes as needed. It becomes important, therefore, to go back to the listening stage to interpret how consumers are perceiving the social media campaign.

Listening to customers and industry trends, as well as continually revising the social media plan to meet the needs of the changing social media market, are keys to successful social media marketing. There are numerous industry leaders sharing some of their best practices, and sources such as *Fast Company* and the *Wall Street Journal* report regularly on how large and small companies are successfully using social media to gain market share and sales. A good example of using social media strategies is HubSpot, a company that practices what it preaches. HubSpot advocates the benefits of building valuable content online and then using social media to pull customers to its Web site. Social engine profiles have increased HubSpot's Web site traffic, which has made its lead generation program much more effective.

18-7a The Changing World of Social Media

As you read through the chapter, some of the trends that are noted may already seem ancient to you. The rate of change in social media is astounding—usage statistics change daily for sites like Facebook and Twitter. Some things that are in the rumor mill as we write this may have exploded in popularity; others may have fizzled out without even appearing on your radar. In Exhibit 3, we've listed some of the items that seem to be on the brink of exploding on to the social

TO WIDGET OR NOT TO WIDGET

Allowing customers to promote up-to-date marketing material on their own blogs and Web sites is very appealing, but before investing in a marketing-oriented widget, a number of questions should be considered:

▸▸ Does my organization regularly publish compelling content, such as news, daily specials, or coupons, on its Web site or blog?

▸▸ Does my content engage individuals or appeal to their needs as customers?

▸▸ Is my content likely to inspire conversations with the company or with other customers? Will customers want to share my content with others?

If you can answer yes to these questions, a widget may be an effective tool for your organization.

Exhibit 3
SOCIAL MEDIA TRENDS

Trend	Change	Where Is It Now?
Facebook	Bigger, unified News Feed	
Google+	Animated GIF support	
Twitter	Broader support for Cards feature	
Bing	Rewards program offers prizes for using Bing Search	
Spotify	The ability to follow friends and musicians	
Google Wallet, Bitcoin, and NFC-enabled payment options	Replace credit cards with various forms of digital payment	
Gilt, JackThreads, and other social shopping sites	Integration with Facebook	
Groupon, LivingSocial, and other deal-a-day Web sites	The mainstreaming of social couponing	
HTML5	Flash and other proprietary platforms giving way to Web-based media and apps	

media scene. Take a moment to fill in the current state of each in the third column. Have you heard of it? Has it come and gone? Maybe it is still rumored, or maybe it has petered out. This exercise highlights not only the speed with which social media change but also the importance of keeping tabs on rumors. Doing so may give you a competitive advantage by being able to understand and invest in the next big social media site.

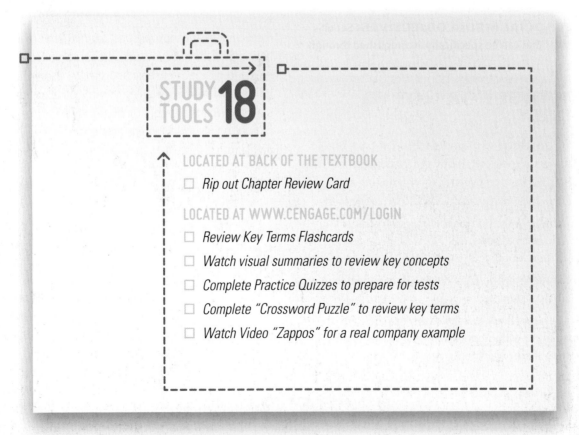

STUDY TOOLS **18**

LOCATED AT BACK OF THE TEXTBOOK
- ☐ *Rip out Chapter Review Card*

LOCATED AT WWW.CENGAGE.COM/LOGIN
- ☐ *Review Key Terms Flashcards*
- ☐ *Watch visual summaries to review key concepts*
- ☐ *Complete Practice Quizzes to prepare for tests*
- ☐ *Complete "Crossword Puzzle" to review key terms*
- ☐ *Watch Video "Zappos" for a real company example*

INDEX

A

Aaramshop, 269
AARP, 299
ABB, 83
ABC (network), 58, 303
Abercrombie & Fitch, 144
Academic Partnerships, 66
Accelerator principle (multiplier effect), 130
Accenture, 40
Accessibility, 143, 240, 322
Accessory equipment, 133
Accor Hotels, 87, 88, 167
Ace Hotel, 343
Actifio, 149
Adaptation, product and promotion, 85
Adidas, 43
Adjacent innovation, 17
Adopters, early, 204, 206, 210
Adoption process, marketing implications, 205–206
Advantage, relative, 206
Advergaming, 300
Advertainments, 301
Advertising, 2, 12, 28, 62, 92, 270, 277, 281, 283–286, 290–304
  advocacy, 293
  comparative, 294, 295
  comparison to personal selling, 314
  competitive, 294
  cooperative, 298
  corporate, 293
  decisions in, 295–297
  display, 337
  economies, 181
  effectiveness, 297
  effects on consumers, 292–293
  e-mail, 65
  executional styles, 297
  global, 84
  in-game, 346
  mass media, 94
  media decisions, 297–304
  medium, 302
  mobile, 304
  online, 124, 275, 300, 337
  pioneering, 294
  prices, minimum (MAPs), 369
  product, 293, 294–295
  public service (PSA), 226
  social media, 300
  trade, 288
  types of, 293–295, 297–299, 301
Advertising appeal, 295–296
Advertising campaign, 295
Advertising objective, 295
Advertising response function, 292
Advocacy advertising, 293
AEG, 126

Aerospace Corporation, 40
Aetna, 8, 9
Afghanistan, 74
Africa, 81, 84
African Americans, 57, 58, 146
After-sales support, 8
Age, 80, 143, 146
  and family life cycle stage, 110
Age segmentation, 144
Agents and brokers, 249, 251
Agile supply chain management, 234, 239
Agreement, bilateral and trade, 76
Agriculture, 77
AIDA concept, 282–283, 295, 296, 321
  steps, 282
AIG, 41
Airbus, 321
AirTran Airways, 39
Albania, 78
Alberto Culver, 58
Alibaba.com, 123
Alliances, strategic, 81
Allocative effect, 370
Allowances, 379–381
Alternative media, 301
Alternatives,
  evaluation, 90, 92, 95–96
  strategic, 16
Altria Group, 202
Amae, 127
Amazon, 16, 23, 25, 160, 190, 194, 217, 256, 269, 290, 362, 367, 377
  Amazon.com, 234, 241, 254, 263, 335, 345
  AmazonFresh, 380
Amedisys Home Health, 10
American Airlines, 53, 378
American Apparel, 128, 254
American Association of Advertising Agencies (AAAA), 32
American Bar Association, 332
American Cancer Society, 107, 346
American Eagle, 151
American Express, 6, 50, 115, 186, 199, 309
American Girl, 54, 55
American Heart Association, 107
American International Group (AIG), 36
American Marketing Association, 2, 6
American Values Survey, 51
Ampacet, 112
Amy Winehouse Foundation, 223
Anchor Advisors, 198
Anchor stores, 165
Anchoring, 375
Andersen Corporation, 138
Anderson, Chris, 150

Android, 347
Angola, 74
Angry Birds, 346, 347
Anheuser Busch InBev, 293
Anschutz Entertainment Group (AEG), 125
Ansoff's strategic opportunity matrix, 16–18
Antidumping rules, 87
Apple, 5, 6, 18, 19, 51, 55, 62, 97, 120, 123, 154, 157, 160, 183, 184, 185, 188, 194, 217, 244, 248, 251, 254, 256, 282, 283, 285, 292, 304, 348, 359, 360, 367, 377
  Facetime, 334
Applied research, 61
Appreciates, 86
Apps, 65, 348, 349
APV, 71
Arby's, 46
Arc Value Village Thrift Store, 314
Argentina, 76, 80
Ariba, Inc., 83
Aristotle, 36
Arm & Hammer 186
Arm's-length relationship, 255
Art.com, 319
Ashley, 4
Asia, 84
Asian Americans, 57, 58, 146
Aspirational reference group, 106
Assertiveness, 328
Assets, 26
Association of Hispanic Advertising Agencies (AHAA), 57
Association of Public and Land-Grant Universities, 66
Assurance, 215
Asus, 187, 248
Atag Holdings NV, 79
Atlas Overhead Door, 150
Atmosphere, 265
Attensity, 317
Attention, 282
Attitude, 101, 106, 116, 118
Attribute, 156, 295
Auctions, 368
Audience, target, 349
Audience selectivity, 302
Audit, marketing, 30
Australia, 76, 80
Austria, 78
Automatic identification systems (auto ID), 241
Automatic replenishment program, 237
Automatic vending, 260
Avaaz, 224
Avator, 344
Aveda, 38
Avendra, 242
Average fixed cost, (AFC), 362

Average total cost, (ATC), 362
Average variable cost (AVC), 362
Aviation Security Act of 2001, 64
Avon, 260, 279, 280
Awareness, 125

B

Babelfish.com, 74
Baby boomers, 53, 56–57, 144, 145, 263, 343
Bad, 36
Bad Ad Program, 64
Badges, 348
Bait pricing, 384
Banana Republic, 157
Bancorp Inc., 103
Bang & Olufsen, 308
Bank of America, 36, 220, 342
Bankrate.com, 382
Banks, Doug, 58
Bar codes, 191, 269
Barclays, 123
Barf, 191
Barnes & Noble, 50, 109, 182, 348
Barneys New York, 7
Barriers, trade, 78, 79
Barter, 4, 87, 354
Base price, 378–387
Basic research, 61
Basing-point pricing, 381
Baumgartner, Felix, 306
Baydin, 29
Bayer, 116, 180
BBDO New York, 205
Beachbody, 300
Bean, Leon Leonwood, 7
Beanie Babies, 207
Beats Electronics, 20, 183
Bebo, 335, 343
Behavioral targeting (BT), 65, 167
BehaviorScan, 175
Belgium, 78, 80, 192
Belief(s), 116–117
Bell Helicopter, 135
Bellucci, Monica, 84
Belly, 320
Below-cost pricing, 227
Ben & Jerry's, 22, 44, 45
Benchmark, 27
Benefit, 295
Benefit complexity, of nonprofit organizations, 224
Benefit segmentation, 148–149
Benefit strength, of nonprofit organizations, 224
Berkshire Hathaway, 290
Bernoff, Josh, 340
Best Buy, 23, 55, 248, 258, 260
Best Inventions of 2012 list, 199
BET, 58
Better Homes and Gardens, 299
Betty Crocker, 199

Plan, marketing, *see* Marketing plan
Planned obsolescence, 183
Planning, 21
  distribution resource (DRP), 237
  materials requirement (MRP), 237
  strategic, 14–31
Plato, 36
Playboy Enterprises, 183
PLC, *see* Product life cycle
Plurk, 342
Podcast, 279, 344, 345
Point of maximization, 365
Point of purchase (P-O-P) display, 311
Point-of-sale interactions, 317
Poison Prevention Labeling Act of 1970, 64
Poland, 78
Political and legal factors of marketing, 62–66
Political structure and actions, 75–80
Pollution, 44
Polo Ralph Lauren, 251, 263, 269
Polytron Technologies, 196
Poptropico, 346
Popular Science, 201
Population, 53–55, 80
Pop-up shops, 265
Porsche, 153
Portfolio matrix, 18
Portugal, 74, 78
Position, 155
Positioning, 155–157
Possession processing, 218
Post, 14
Postaudit tasks, 30
Post-campaign evaluation, 297
Postconventional morality, 37
Postponement, 239
Postpurchase behavior, 90, 92, 97
Postpurchase communication, 220
Pottery Barn, 54
Power, buying, 322
Prada, 256
Preapproach, 323
Preconventional morality, 37
Predatory pricing, 378
Premium, 278, 309
Prequalified leads, 322
Presentation, 265
  sales, 324
Press relations, 305
Press releases, 304
Prestige pricing, 370
Previous experience, 99
Price, 21, 29, 48, 83, 113, 136, 156, 258–259, 265, 352–355
  base, 378
  buyers, 307
  cost determinant of, 362–365
  demand determinant of, 357
  discrimination, 377–378
  information effect of, 354
  relationship to quality, 369–371
  sacrifice effect of, 354
  setting the right, 372–390
  steps in setting the right, 372
Price bundling, 384
Price equilibrium, 359

Price fixing, 376–377
Price shading, 388
Price skimming, 374, 375
Price strategy, 221, 374
  choosing, 374–376
  legality of, 376–378
Priceline, 8
PricewaterhouseCoopers, 198
Pricing, 8, 29, 62, 86–87, 352–371
  bait, 384
  basing-point, 381
  below-cost, 227
  break-even, 365
  decisions, of nonprofit organizations, 226
  delayed-quotation, 387
  demand-oriented, 388
  during difficult economic times, 387–390
  dynamic, 361–362
  escalator, 388
  flexible (variable pricing), 382
  FOB (free on board) origin, 381
  freight absorption, 381
  geographic, 381–382
  goals, establishing, 372–374
  leader (loss-leader pricing), 383
  markup, 364
  odd–even pricing (psychological pricing), 384
  operations-oriented, 221
  patronage-oriented, 221
  pay what you want, 386
  penetration, 375
  predatory, 378
  prestige, 370
  product line, 387
  professional services, 382–383
  profit maximization, 364
  revenue-oriented, 221
  single-price tactic, 382
  status quo, 357, 376
  tactics, other, 382–386
  two-part, 386
  uniform delivered, 381
  value-based, 379–381, 389
  zone, 381
Pricing lining, 383
Pricing objectives, 355–357
  profit-oriented, 355
  sales-oriented, 356
Primary data, 162–169
Primary goal, 12
Primary membership group, 105
Primary promotional method, 132
Printing, three dimensional (EDP), 244
Prismic Pharmaceuticals, 145
Privacy, 62
  consumer, 65
  policies, 65
Private brand, 185, 186
Private Education Tax Credit, 126
Private label, 185
Probability sample, 170, 171
Problem child (question mark), 19
Processed materials, 134
Processing,
  information, 218
  mental stimulus, 218
  people, 218
  possession, 218

Procter & Gamble (P&G), 6, 19, 20, 22, 43, 50, 56, 60, 61, 78, 79, 84, 103, 111, 120, 128, 153, 160, 161, 162, 176, 182, 186, 194, 196, 201, 202, 293, 326, 356
Producers, 127–128
  versus-wholesaler conflict, 256
Product(s), 21, 28, 48, 83, 178–192, 205–206, 217, 263, 285
  adaptation, 85
  and trade name franchising, 262
  assortment, 258, 263
  benefits, identifying, 295
  consumer, 178
  convenience, 180
  customer involvement, 100
  design, 24
  developing and managing, 194–211
  durability, 361
  experience, 94
  identification, 184
  improvements/revisions of existing, 196
  introductions, successful, 203
  invention, 85
  knowledge, 323
  lower priced, 196
  low-involvement, 97
  new, *see* New products
  new-to-the-world, 196
  offering, 263
  promoting, 189
  repositioned, 196
  shopping, 180
  specialty, 180
  strategies, 28
  unsought, 181
  user, 157
  warranties, 192
  why they succeed or fail, 203–204
Product advertising, 293–295
Product category, 207
Product decisions, 84–85
  of nonprofit organizations, 224
Product development, 17, 198
  simultaneous, 200
Product development and commercialization process, 235
Product differentiation, 115, 116, 156
Product item, 181
  lines, and mixes, 181–184
Product life cycle (PLC), 206–211, 253
  and diffusion process, 210
  and promotional mix, 286
  for styles, fashions, and fads, 207
  stages, 206, 285–286, 365–367
  VCR, 211
Product line, 181
  additions to existing, 196
  contraction, 184
  overextended, 184
Product line depth, 182
Product line extension, 183
Product line pricing, 387
  McDonald's, 390

Product management, end-of-life, 241
Product mix, 181
Product mix width, 182
Product modification, 182, 198
Product placement, 305
  global, 305
  virtual, 305
Product/service differentiation competitive advantage, 25
Product (service) strategy, 217–219
Production, 238–239
  innovations, 24
Production orientation, 4–5
Professional services pricing, 382–383
Profit(s), 42, 223, 296, 352, 354
  estimating, 374
  profit-oriented pricing objectives, 355
  satisfactory, 355
Profit maximization, 355, 364
Profit organizations, 226
Progressive, 334
Project Runway, 19
Pro-Line, 58
Promotion, 12, 21, 28, 48, 62, 83, 94, 263, 270
  adaptation, 85
  decisions, of nonprofit organizations, 225
  goals, 276–277
  in the marketing mix, 270–272
  informative, 276
  persuasive, 276
  reminder, 276
  sales, 92, 278, 281, 307–311
  strategies, 28–29, 220, 369
Promotional allowance (trade allowance), 379
Promotional goals, and AIDA concept, 282–283
Promotional method, primary, 132
Promotional mix, 277–281
  and AIDA, 283
  and product life cycle, 286
  and the communication process, 280–281
  factors affecting, 285–289
Promotional strategy, 270
Proposal, sales, 324
Prospects, unqualified, 322
Protectionism, 77
Protectionist movement, 79
Prototype, 200
Prudential, 187
PSA, 225
Psychographics, 111
Psychographic segmentation, 147–149
Psychological factors, 118
Public Health Cigarette Smoking Act of 1971, 64
Public Health Smoking Act of 1970, 64
Public relations, 270, 277–278, 281, 283, 284, 304–307
  departments, duties of, 305
  tools, 304–306
Public service advertisement (PSA), 226
  of nonprofit organizations, 226
Public sources of information, 93

THE IMPORTANCE OF PRICE

Price means one thing to the consumer and something else to the seller. To the consumer, it is the cost of something. To the seller, price is revenue—the primary source of profits. In the broadest sense, price allocates resources in a free-market economy. Marketing managers are frequently challenged by the task of price setting. Yet over the past two decades, managers have learned that meeting the challenge of setting the right price can have a significant impact on the firm's bottom line. Large organizations that successfully manage prices do so by creating a pricing infrastructure within the company. This means defining pricing goals, searching for ways to create greater customer value, assigning authority and responsibility for pricing decisions, and creating tools and systems to continually improve pricing decisions.

> Trying to set the right price is one of the most stressful and pressure-filled tasks of the marketing manager.

price that which is given up in an exchange to acquire a good or service

Achieving pricing excellence is a very worthwhile activity, though it does not always follow an expected path. For years, the Humane Society charged $40 for a person to adopt a dog and $25 for a person to adopt a cat. While many dogs and cats were adopted, a staggering 85 percent were also returned.

The California Veterinary Medical Association conducted a survey on animal return rates, finding that the lower the adoption price, the greater the likelihood that the pet would be returned. In response to this study, the Humane Society raised the cost of adoption for both cats and dogs to $110, and sure enough, the rate of return dropped to just 1 percent. Because of the Humane Society's strategic price management, the company arrived at a price that better served itself, its customers, and its rescues.[1]

19-1a What Is Price?

Price is that which is given up in an exchange to acquire a good or service. Price plays two roles in the evaluation of product alternatives: as a measure of sacrifice and as an information

Pricing Concepts

Learning Outcomes

After you finish this chapter go to
p371 *for* **STUDY TOOLS** - - - - - →

cue. To some degree, these are two opposing effects.[2]

THE SACRIFICE EFFECT OF PRICE Price is, again, "that which is given up," which means what is sacrificed to get a good or service. In the United States, the sacrifice is usually money, but it can be other things as well. It may also be time lost while waiting to acquire the good or service. Price might also include "lost dignity" for individuals who lose their jobs and must rely on charity.

THE INFORMATION EFFECT OF PRICE Consumers do not always choose the lowest-priced product in a category, such as shoes, cars, or wine, even when the products are otherwise similar. One explanation of this behavior, based upon research, is that we infer quality information from price.[3] That is, higher quality equals higher price. The information effect of price may also extend to favorable price perceptions by others because higher prices can convey the prominence and status of the purchaser to other people. Thus, both a Swatch and a Rolex can tell time accurately, but they convey different meanings. The price–quality relationship will be discussed later in the chapter.

VALUE IS BASED UPON PERCEIVED SATISFACTION Consumers are interested in obtaining a "reasonable price." "Reasonable price" really means "perceived reasonable value" at the time of the transaction. When high-end housewares retailer Williams-Sonoma launched a $279 bread maker, the company garnered only mediocre returns. Undeterred, Williams-Sonoma released a second, slightly larger bread maker with similar features for $429. The more expensive model flopped, but when it was released, sales of the smaller, less expensive model skyrocketed. Though nothing changed about the smaller model's features or marketing mix, the $429 model affected people's perceptions, making the $279 model look like a much better value.[4]

Price can relate to anything with perceived value, not just money. When goods and services are exchanged, the trade is called *barter*. During the early

A BARGAIN AT JUST $279!

years of Harvard University, tuition could be bartered for with livestock, lumber, or construction stones. Today, more than $12 billion of goods and services are traded in the United States without any currency changing hands.[5]

19-1b The Importance of Price to Marketing Managers

As noted in the chapter introduction, prices are the key to revenues, which in turn are the key to profits for an organization. **Revenue** is the price charged to customers multiplied by the number of units sold. Revenue is what pays for every activity of the company: production, finance, sales, distribution, and so on. What's left over (if anything) is **profit**. Managers usually strive to charge a price that will earn a fair profit.

Price × Units = Revenue

To earn a profit, managers must choose a price that is not too high or too low—a price that equals the perceived value to target consumers. If, in consumers' minds, a price is set too high, the perceived value will be less than the cost, and sale opportunities will be lost. Many mainstream purchasers of cars, sporting goods, Blu-rays, tools, wedding gowns, and computers are buying used (or *pre-owned*) items to get a better deal. Pricing a new product too high gives some shoppers an incentive to go to a pre-owned or consignment retailer.[6] Lost sales mean lost revenue. Conversely, if a price is too low, the consumer might perceive it as a great value, but the firm loses revenue it could have earned.

Trying to set the right price is one of the most stressful and pressure-filled tasks of the marketing manager, as trends in the consumer market attest:

▸▸ **Confronting a flood of new products, potential buyers carefully evaluate the price of each one against the value of existing products.**

▸▸ **The increased availability of bargain-priced private and generic brands has put downward pressure on overall prices.**

▸▸ **Many firms are trying to maintain or regain their market share by cutting prices.**

▸▸ **The Internet has made comparison shopping easier.**

▸▸ **The United States was in a recession from late 2007 until 2009 and was still recovering very slowly in 2013.**

In the business market, buyers are also becoming more price sensitive and better informed. Computerized information systems enable organizational buyers to compare price and performance with great ease and accuracy. Improved

© iStockPhoto.com/Lev Kropotov

communication and the increased use of direct marketing and computer-aided selling have also opened up many markets to new competitors. Finally, competition in general is increasing, so some installations, accessories, and component parts are being marketed like indistinguishable commodities.

19-2 PRICING OBJECTIVES

To survive in today's highly competitive marketplace, companies need pricing objectives that are specific, attainable, and measurable. Realistic pricing goals then require periodic monitoring to determine the effectiveness of the company's strategy. For convenience, pricing objectives can be divided into three categories: profit oriented, sales oriented, and status quo.

19-2a Profit-Oriented Pricing Objectives

Profit-oriented pricing objectives include profit maximization, satisfactory profits, and target return on investment.

PROFIT MAXIMIZATION *Profit maximization* means setting prices so that total revenue is as large as possible relative to total costs. Profit maximization does not always signify unreasonably high prices, however. Both price and profits depend on the type of competitive environment a firm faces, such as whether it is in a monopoly position (being the only seller) or in a much more competitive situation. Also, remember that a firm cannot charge a price higher than the product's perceived value. Many firms do not have the accounting data they need for maximizing profits.

Sometimes managers say that their company is trying to maximize profits—in other words, trying to make as much money as possible. Although this goal may sound impressive to stockholders, it is not good enough for planning.

In attempting to maximize profits, managers can try to expand revenue by increasing customer satisfaction, or they can attempt to reduce costs by operating more efficiently. A third possibility is to attempt to do both. Some companies may focus too much on cost reduction at the expense of the customer or rely so heavily on customer satisfaction to increase revenue that costs creep up unnecessarily. However, a company can maintain or slightly cut costs while increasing customer loyalty through customer service initiatives, loyalty programs, and customer relationship management programs and allocating fewer resources to programs that are designed to improve efficiency and reduce costs. Both types of programs, of course, are critical to the success of the firm.

return on investment (ROI) net profit after taxes divided by total assets

SATISFACTORY PROFITS Satisfactory profits are a reasonable level of profits. Rather than maximizing profits, many organizations strive for profits that are satisfactory to the stockholders and management—in other words, a level of profits consistent with the level of risk an organization faces. In a risky industry, a satisfactory profit may be 35 percent. In a low-risk industry, it might be 7 percent.

TARGET RETURN ON INVESTMENT The most common profit objective is a target **return on investment (ROI)**, sometimes called the firm's return on total assets. ROI measures management's overall effectiveness in generating profits with the available assets. The higher the firm's ROI, the better off the firm is. Many companies use a target ROI as their main pricing goal. In summary, ROI is a percentage that puts a firm's profits into perspective by showing profits relative to investment.

Return on investment is calculated as follows:

$$\text{Return on investment} = \frac{\text{Net profits after taxes}}{\text{Total assets}}$$

Assume that in 2013 Johnson Controls had assets of $4.5 million, net profits of $550,000, and a target ROI of 10 percent. This was the actual ROI:

$$\text{ROI} = \frac{\$550,000}{\$4,500,000} = 12.2 \text{ percent}$$

As you can see, the ROI for Johnson Controls exceeded its target, which indicates that the company prospered in 2013.

Comparing the 12.2 percent ROI with the industry average provides a more meaningful picture, however. Any ROI needs to be evaluated in terms of the competitive environment, risks in the industry, and economic conditions. Generally speaking, firms seek ROIs in the 10 to 30 percent range. In some industries, such as the grocery industry, however, a return of under 5 percent is common and acceptable.

A company with a target ROI can predetermine its desired level of profitability. The marketing manager can use the standard, such as 10 percent ROI, to determine whether a particular price and marketing mix are feasible. In addition, however, the manager must weigh the risk of a given strategy even if the return is in the acceptable range.

19-2b Sales-Oriented Pricing Objectives

Sales-oriented pricing objectives are based either on market share or on dollar or unit sales.

MARKET SHARE **Market share** is a company's product sales as a percentage of total sales for that industry. Sales can be reported in dollars or in units of product. It is very important to know whether market share is expressed in revenue or units because the results may be different. Consider four companies competing in an industry with 2,000 total unit sales and total industry revenue of $4,000 (see Exhibit 1). Company A has the largest unit market share at 50 percent, but it has only 25 percent of the revenue market share. In contrast, company D has only a 15 percent unit share but the largest revenue share: 30 percent. Usually, market share is expressed in terms of revenue and not units.

Many companies believe that maintaining or increasing market share is an indicator of the effectiveness of their marketing mix. Larger market shares have indeed often meant higher profits, thanks to greater economies of scale, market power, and ability to compensate top-quality management. Conventional wisdom also says that market share and ROI are strongly related. For the most part they are; however, many companies with low market share survive and even prosper. To succeed with a low market share, companies need to compete in industries with slow growth and few product changes—for instance, industrial supplies. Otherwise, they must vie in an industry that makes frequently bought items, such as consumer convenience goods.

The conventional wisdom about market share and profitability isn't always reliable, however. Because of extreme competition in some industries, many market share leaders either do not reach their target ROI or actually lose money. Procter & Gamble switched from market share to ROI objectives after realizing that profits don't automatically follow from a large market share.

Still, the struggle for market share can be all-consuming in certain industries. For example,

Exhibit 1
TWO WAYS TO MEASURE MARKET SHARE (UNITS AND REVENUE)

Company	Units Sold	Unit Price	Total Revenue	Unit Market Share (%)	Revenue Market Share (%)
A	1,000	$1.00	$1,000	50	25
B	200	4.00	800	10	20
C	500	2.00	1,000	25	25
D	300	4.00	1,200	15	30
Total	2,000		$4,000		

© Cengage Learning

Samsung's success with the 5.3-inch-screen Galaxy Note *phablet* (smartphone-tablet hybrid) led to a groundswell of competition in the hybrid market as Sony, HTC, Lenovo, and other technology companies introduced their own phablets in 2013. This intense competition for recognition in a small, unproven market meant that companies had to offer the latest technology for the absolute lowest prices possible, resulting in razor-thin profit margins.[7] On the other hand, the steadily growing smartphone and tablet markets allow companies to operate with less pressure on their profit margins, making them more reliable markets to enter.

SALES MAXIMIZATION Rather than strive for market share, sometimes companies try to maximize sales. A firm with the objective of maximizing sales ignores profits, competition, and the marketing environment as long as sales are rising.

If a company is strapped for funds or faces an uncertain future, it may try to generate a maximum amount of cash in the short run. Management's task when using this objective is to calculate which price–quantity relationship generates the greatest cash revenue. Sales maximization can also be effectively used on a temporary basis to sell off excess inventory.

Maximization of cash should never be a long-run objective because cash maximization may mean little or no profitability.

Samsung's success with the Galaxy Note phablet led to a groundswell of competition in the hybrid market. The LG Optimus G Pro, for example, boasts a 5.5-inch screen and twice as much memory as the Note.

19-2c Status Quo Pricing Objectives

Status quo pricing seeks to maintain existing prices or to meet the competition's prices. This third category of pricing objectives has the major advantage of requiring little planning. It is essentially a passive policy.

Often, firms competing in an industry with an established price leader simply meet the competition's prices. These industries typically have fewer price wars than those with direct price competition. In other cases, managers regularly shop competitors' stores to ensure that their prices are comparable.

Status quo pricing often leads to suboptimal pricing. This occurs because the strategy ignores customers' perceived value of both the firm's goods or services and those offered by its competitors. Status quo pricing also ignores demand and costs. Although the policy is simple to implement, it can lead to a pricing disaster.

19-3 THE DEMAND DETERMINANT OF PRICE

After marketing managers establish pricing goals, they must set specific prices to reach those goals. The price they set for each product depends mostly on two factors: the demand for the good or service and the cost to the seller for that good or service. When pricing goals are mainly sales oriented, demand considerations usually dominate. Other factors, such as distribution and promotion strategies, perceived quality, needs of large customers, the Internet, and the stage of the product life cycle, can also influence price.

19-3a The Nature of Demand

Demand is the quantity of a product that will be sold in the market at various prices for a specified period. The quantity of a product that people will buy depends on its price. The higher the price, the fewer goods or services consumers will demand. Conversely, the lower the price, the more goods or services they will demand.

This trend is illustrated in the graph in Exhibit 2a, which shows the demand per week for gourmet cookies at a local retailer at various prices. This graph is called a *demand curve*. The vertical axis of the graph shows different prices of gourmet cookies, measured in dollars per package. The horizontal axis measures the quantity of gourmet cookies that will be demanded per week at each price. For example, at a price of $2.50, 50 packages will

status quo pricing a pricing objective that maintains existing prices or meets the competition's prices

demand the quantity of a product that will be sold in the market at various prices for a specified period

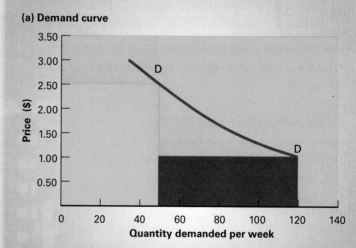

Exhibit 2

DEMAND CURVE AND DEMAND SCHEDULE FOR GOURMET COOKIES

(a) Demand curve

(b) Demand schedule

Price per package of gourmet cookies ($)	Packages of gourmet cookies demanded per week
3.00	35
2.50	50
2.00	65
1.50	85
1.00	120

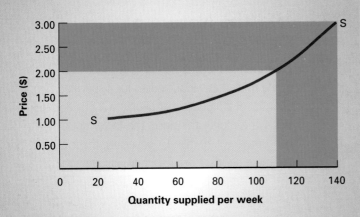

Exhibit 3

SUPPLY CURVE AND SUPPLY SCHEDULE FOR GOURMET COOKIES

(a) Supply curve

(b) Supply schedule

Price per package of gourmet cookies ($)	Packages of gourmet cookies supplied per week
3.00	140
2.50	130
2.00	110
1.50	85
1.00	25

cookie manufacturers will obtain more resources (flour, eggs, chocolate) and produce more gourmet cookies. If the price consumers are willing to pay for gourmet cookies increases, producers can afford to buy more ingredients.

Output tends to increase at higher prices because manufacturers can sell more cookies and earn greater profits. The *supply schedule* in Exhibit 3b shows that at $2, suppliers are willing to place 110 packages of gourmet cookies on the market, but they will offer 140 packages at a price of $3.

19-3b How Demand and Supply Establish Prices

At this point, combine the concepts of demand and supply to see how competitive market prices are determined. So far, the premise is that if the price is X, then consumers will purchase Y amount of gourmet cookies. The demand curve cannot predict consumption, nor can the supply curve alone forecast production. Instead, we need to look at what happens when supply and demand interact—as shown in Exhibit 4.

At a price of $3, the public would demand only 35 packages of gourmet cookies. However, suppliers stand ready to place 140 packages on the market at this price (data from the demand and supply schedules). If they do, they would create a surplus of 105 packages of

be sold per week; at $1.00, consumers will demand 120 packages—as the *demand schedule* (Exhibit 2b) shows.

Notice how the demand curve slopes downward and to the right, which indicates that more gourmet cookies are demanded as the price is lowered. In other words, if cookie manufacturers put a greater quantity on the market, then their hope of selling all of it will be realized only by selling it at a lower price. One reason more is sold at lower prices than at higher prices is that lower prices bring in new buyers. With each reduction in price, existing customers may also buy more.

Supply is the quantity of a product that will be offered to the market by a supplier or suppliers at various prices for a specified period. The graph in Exhibit 3a illustrates the resulting *supply curve* for gourmet cookies. Unlike the falling demand curve, the supply curve for gourmet cookies slopes upward and to the right. At higher prices, gourmet

supply the quantity of a product that will be offered to the market by a supplier at various prices for a specified period

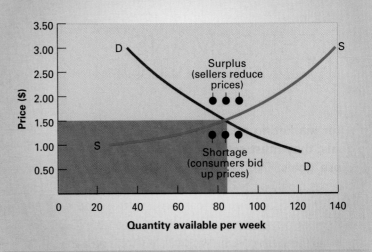

Exhibit 4
EQUILIBRIUM PRICE FOR GOURMET COOKIES

358   PART SIX: Pricing Decisions

gourmet cookies. How does a merchant eliminate a surplus? She lowers the price.

At a price of $1.00, 120 packages would be demanded, but only 25 would be placed on the market. A shortage of 95 units would be created. If a product is in short supply and consumers want it, how do they entice the dealer to part with one unit? They offer more money—that is, pay a higher price.

Now let's examine a price of $1.50. At this price, 85 packages are demanded and 85 are supplied. When demand and supply are equal, a state called **price equilibrium** is achieved. A temporary price below equilibrium—say, $1.00—results in a shortage because at that price the demand for gourmet cookies is greater than the available supply. Shortages put upward pressure on price. As long as demand and supply remain the same, however, temporary price increases or decreases tend to return to equilibrium. At equilibrium, there is no inclination for prices to rise or fall.

Prices may fluctuate during a trial-and-error period as the market for a good or service moves toward equilibrium. Sooner or later, however, demand and supply will settle into proper balance.

19-3c Elasticity of Demand

To appreciate demand analysis, you should understand the concept of elasticity. **Elasticity of demand** refers to consumers' responsiveness or sensitivity to changes in price. **Elastic demand** is a situation in which consumer demand is sensitive to price changes. Conversely, **inelastic demand** means that an increase or a decrease in price will not significantly affect demand for the product.

Elasticity over the range of a demand curve can be measured by using this formula:

$$\text{Elasticity } (E) = \frac{\text{Percentage change in quantity demanded of good A}}{\text{Percentage change in price of good A}}$$

If E is greater than 1, demand is elastic.

If E is less than 1, demand is inelastic.

If E is equal to 1, demand is unitary.

Unitary elasticity means that an increase in sales exactly offsets a decrease in prices, so total revenue remains the same.

Exhibit 5a shows a very elastic demand curve. Decreasing the price of Apple iPhones from $300 to $200 increases sales from 18,000 units to 59,000 units.

Revenue increases from $5.4 million ($300 × 18,000) to $11.8 million ($200 × 59,000). The price decrease results in a large increase in sales and revenue.

Exhibit 5b shows a completely inelastic demand curve. The state of Nevada dropped its used-car vehicle inspection fee from $20 to $10. The state continued to inspect about 400,000 used cars annually. Decreasing the price (inspection fee) 50 percent did not cause people to buy more used cars. Demand is completely inelastic for inspection fees, which are required by law. Thus, it also follows that Nevada could double the original fee to $40 and double the state's inspection revenues.

© iStockPhoto.com/Patrick Herrera

Elasticity can be measured by observing these changes in total revenue:

➤ **If price goes down and revenue goes up, demand is elastic.**

➤ **If price goes down and revenue goes down, demand is inelastic.**

➤ **If price goes up and revenue goes up, demand is inelastic.**

➤ **If price goes up and revenue goes down, demand is elastic.**

➤ **If price goes up or down and revenue stays the same, elasticity is unitary.**

Exhibit 5
ELASTICITY OF DEMAND FOR APPLE IPHONES AND AUTO INSPECTION STICKERS

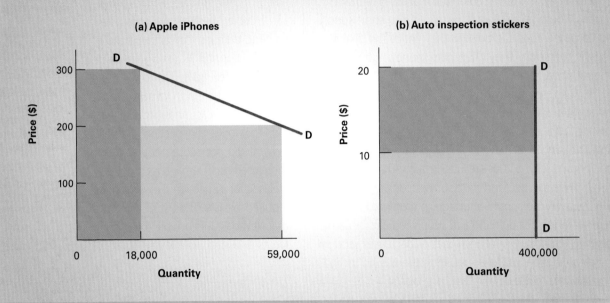

People won't stop buying used cars if the inspection fee increases—within a reasonable range.

Exhibit 6 presents the demand curve and demand schedule for three-ounce bottles of Spring Break suntan lotion. Let's follow the demand curve from the highest price to the lowest and examine what happens to elasticity as the price decreases.

INELASTIC DEMAND The initial decrease in the price of Spring Break suntan lotion from $5.00 to $2.25 results in a decrease in total revenue of $969 ($5,075 – $4,106). When price and total revenue fall, demand is inelastic. The decrease in price is much greater than the increase in suntan lotion sales (810 bottles). Demand is therefore not very flexible in the price range $5.00 to $2.25.

When demand is inelastic, sellers can raise prices and increase total revenue. Often items that are relatively inexpensive but convenient tend to have inelastic demand.

ELASTIC DEMAND In the example of Spring Break suntan lotion, shown in Exhibit 6, when the price is dropped from $2.25 to $1.00, total revenue increases by $679 ($4,785 – $4,106). An increase in total revenue when price falls indicates that demand is elastic. Let's measure Spring Break's elasticity of demand when the price drops from $2.25 to $1.00 by applying the formula presented earlier:

$$E = \frac{\text{Change in quantity/(Sum of quantities/2)}}{\text{Change in price/(Sum of prices/2)}}$$

$$= \frac{(4{,}785 - 1{,}825)/[(1{,}825 + 4{,}785)/2]}{(2.25 - 1.00)/[(2.25 + 1.00)/2]}$$

$$= \frac{2{,}960/3{,}305}{1.25/1.63}$$

$$= \frac{0.896}{0.769} = 51.17$$

Because *E* is greater than 1, demand is elastic.

FACTORS THAT AFFECT ELASTICITY Several factors affect elasticity of demand, including the following:

▸ **AVAILABILITY OF SUBSTITUTES:** When many substitute products are available, the consumer can easily switch from one product to another, making demand elastic. The same is true in reverse: A person with complete renal failure will pay whatever is charged for a kidney transplant because there is no substitute.

▸ **PRICE RELATIVE TO PURCHASING POWER:** If a price is so low that it is an inconsequential part of an individual's budget, demand will be inelastic.

dynamic pricing a strategy whereby prices are adjusted over time to maximize a company's revenues

Exhibit 6
DEMAND FOR THREE-OUNCE BOTTLES OF SPRING BREAK SUNTAN LOTION

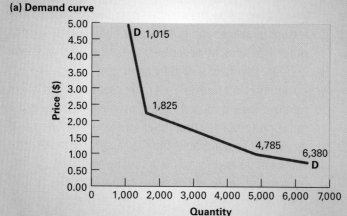

(a) Demand curve

(b) Demand schedule

Price ($)	Quantity demanded	Total revenue (price × quantity)	Elasticity
5.00	1,015	$5,075	Inelastic
2.25	1,825	4,106	
1.00	4,785	4,785	Elastic
0.75	6,380	4,785	Unitary

© Cengage Learning

▸▸ **PRODUCT DURABILITY:** Consumers often have the option of repairing durable products rather than replacing them, thus prolonging their useful life. In other words, people are sensitive to the price increase, and demand is elastic.

▸▸ **A PRODUCT'S OTHER USES:** The greater the number of different uses for a product, the more elastic demand tends to be. If a product has only one use, as may be true of a new medicine, the quantity purchased probably will not vary as price varies. A person will consume only the prescribed quantity, regardless of price. On the other hand, a product like steel has many possible applications. As its price falls, steel becomes more economically feasible in a wider variety of applications, thereby making demand relatively elastic.

▸▸ **RATE OF INFLATION:** Recent research has found that when a country's inflation rate (the rate at which the price level is rising) is high, demand becomes more elastic. In other words, rising price levels make consumers more price sensitive. During inflationary periods, consumers base their timing (when to buy) and quantity decisions on price promotions. This suggests that a brand gains additional sales or market share if the product is effectively promoted or if the marketing manager keeps the brand's price increases low relative to the inflation rate.[8]

Examples of both elastic and inelastic demand abound in everyday life. The slow recovery of the housing market following the Great Recession is in part a function of elasticity of demand. Once a house is bought, however, a resident must have the utilities turned on—a cost that represents inelastic demand. In 2012, concert tickets sales dropped as prices rose—another example of elasticity.[9] On the other hand, demand for some tickets was highly inelastic. The Rolling Stones are still selling out concerts with tickets priced at up to $400.

19-4 THE POWER OF DYNAMIC PRICING AND YIELD MANAGEMENT SYSTEMS

When competitive pressures are high, a company must know when it can raise prices to maximize its revenues. More and more companies are turning to **dynamic pricing** to help adjust prices. Dynamic pricing is most useful when two product or service characteristics

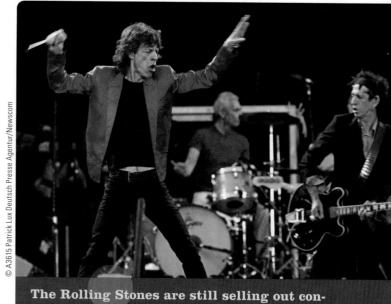

© A3615 Patrick Lux Deutsch Presse Agentur/Newscom

The Rolling Stones are still selling out concerts with tickets priced at up to $400.

© iStockphoto.com/walrusmail

yield management systems (YMS) a technique for adjusting prices that uses complex mathematical software to profitably fill unused capacity by discounting early purchases, limiting early sales at these discounted prices, and overbooking capacity

variable cost a cost that varies with changes in the level of output

fixed cost a cost that does not change as output is increased or decreased

average variable cost (AVC) total variable costs divided by quantity of output

average total cost (ATC) total costs divided by quantity of output

average fixed cost (AFC) total fixed costs divided by quantity of output

co-exist. First, the product/service expires at a given point in time. Airline flights and vacant hotel rooms eventually lose their ability to make money, as do products with "sell before" dates such as meat and dairy items. Second, capacity is fixed well in advance and can only be increased at a high cost. For example, Delta has eight flights a day to Chicago. To increase that number to twelve flights would probably be very expensive. A Hyatt hotel in Denver has 120 rooms available for February twenty-sixth. To increase the number to 160 would involve huge construction costs.

Developed in the airline industry, **yield management systems (YMS)** use complex mathematical software to profitably fill unused capacity. The software employs techniques such as discounting early purchases, limiting early sales at these discounted prices, and overbooking capacity. One of the key inputs in airlines' yield management systems is what has been the historical pattern of demand for a specific flight. Other service industries are now using YMS as well. Several Major League Baseball teams, such as the Cincinnati Reds, Kansas City Royals, and Los Angeles

Angels, adopted dynamic ticket pricing in advance of the 2013 season. In the new system, single-game ticket prices fluctuate depending on factors like fan interest, a team's record, weather, and remaining inventory.[11]

Now dynamic pricing and YMS are spreading beyond service industries as their popularity increases. The lessons of airlines and hotels aren't entirely applicable to other industries, however, because plane seats and hotel beds are perishable—if they go empty, the revenue opportunity is lost forever. So it makes sense to slash prices to move toward capacity if it's possible to do so without reducing the prices that other customers pay. Cars and steel aren't so perishable, but the capacity to make them is. An underused factory is a lost revenue opportunity. So it makes sense to cut prices to use up capacity if it's possible to do so while getting other customers to pay full price.

19-5 THE COST DETERMINANT OF PRICE

Sometimes companies minimize or ignore the importance of demand and decide to price their products largely or solely on the basis of costs. Prices determined strictly on the basis of costs may be too high for the target market, thereby reducing or eliminating sales. On the other hand, cost-based prices may be too low, causing the firm to earn a lower return than it should. Nevertheless, costs should generally be part of any price determination, if only as a floor below which a good or service must not be priced in the long run.

The idea of cost may seem simple, but it is actually a multifaceted concept, especially for producers of goods and services. A **variable cost** is a cost that varies with changes in the level of output; an example of a variable cost is the cost of materials. In contrast, a **fixed cost** does not change as output is increased or decreased. Examples include rent and executives' salaries.

To compare the cost of production to the selling price of a product, it is helpful to calculate costs per unit, or average costs. **Average variable cost (AVC)** equals total variable costs divided by quantity of output. **Average total cost (ATC)** equals total costs divided by quantity of output. As the graph in Exhibit 7a shows, AVC and ATC are basically U-shaped curves. In contrast, **average fixed cost (AFC)**, total fixed costs divided by quantity of output,

DYNAMIC PRICING TO THE EXTREME

Pioneered by Amazon but adopted by countless online retailers, database- and cookie-based dynamic pricing uses a customer's purchase history, location, Internet history, and usage statistics to arrive at a final sale price.[10] For example, consider that you live in Oklahoma and you are using Mozilla's Firefox browser to shop for a new showerhead. You have reviewed prices across several online stores and have searched for online coupon codes. You don't plan to buy anything besides the showerhead at this time. You have bought from Home Depot's online store before, and you have looked at the particular showerhead's product page several times. Hypothetically, Home Depot could take all of these factors into account before calculating a final price for you.

declines continually as output increases because total fixed costs are constant.

Marginal cost (MC) is the change in total costs associated with a one-unit change in output. Exhibit 7b shows that when output rises from seven to eight units, the change in total cost is from $640 to $750; therefore, MC is $110.

All the curves illustrated in Exhibit 7a have definite relationships:

▸▸ AVC plus AFC equals ATC.

▸▸ MC falls for a while and then turns upward, in this case with the fourth unit. At that point, diminishing returns set in, meaning that less output is produced for every additional dollar spent on variable input.

▸▸ MC intersects both AVC and ATC at their lowest possible points.

marginal cost (MC) the change in total costs associated with a one-unit change in output

Exhibit 7

HYPOTHETICAL SET OF COST CURVES AND A COST SCHEDULE

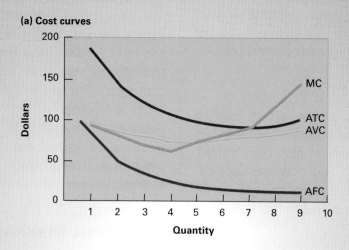

(a) Cost curves

(b) Cost schedule

	Total-cost data, per week				Average-cost data, per week			
(1) Total product (Q)	(2) Total fixed cost (TFC)	(3) Total variable cost (TVC)	(4) Total cost (TC)	(5) Average fixed cost (AFC)	(6) Average variable cost (AVC)	(7) Average total cost (ATC)	(8) Marginal cost (MC)
			$TC = TFC + TVC$	$AFC = \dfrac{TFC}{Q}$	$AVC = \dfrac{TVC}{Q}$	$ATC = \dfrac{TC}{Q}$	$MC = \dfrac{\text{change in TC}}{\text{change in Q}}$
0	$100	$ 0	$ 100	—	—	—	—
1	100	90	190	$100.00	$90.00	$190.00	$ 90
2	100	170	270	50.00	85.00	135.00	80
3	100	240	340	33.33	80.00	113.33	70
4	100	300	400	25.00	75.00	100.00	60
5	100	370	470	20.00	74.00	94.00	70
6	100	450	550	16.67	75.00	91.67	80
7	100	540	640	14.29	77.14	91.43	90
8	100	650	750	12.50	81.25	93.75	110
9	100	780	880	11.11	86.67	97.78	130
10	100	930	1,030	10.00	93.00	103.00	150

markup pricing
the cost of buying the product from the producer, plus amounts for profit and for expenses not otherwise accounted for

keystoning the practice of marking up prices by 100 percent, or doubling the cost

profit maximization a method of setting prices that occurs when marginal revenue equals marginal cost

marginal revenue (MR) the extra revenue associated with selling an extra unit of output or the change in total revenue with a one-unit change in output

▸ **When MC is less than AVC or ATC, the incremental cost will continue to pull the averages down. Conversely, when MC is greater than AVC or ATC, it pulls the averages up, and ATC and AVC begin to rise.**

▸ **The minimum point on the ATC curve is the lowest cost point for a fixed-capacity firm, although it is not necessarily the most profitable point.**

Costs can be used to set prices in a variety of ways. Markup pricing is relatively simple. Profit maximization pricing and break-even pricing use the more complicated concepts of cost.

19-5a Markup Pricing

Markup pricing, the most popular method used by wholesalers and retailers to establish a selling price, does not directly analyze the costs of production. Instead, **markup pricing** uses the cost of buying the product from the producer, plus amounts for profit and for expenses not otherwise accounted for. The total determines the selling price.

A retailer, for example, adds a certain percentage to the cost of the merchandise received to arrive at the retail price. An item that costs the retailer $1.80 and is sold for $2.20 carries a markup of 40 cents, which is a markup of 22 percent of the cost ($0.40 ÷ $1.80). Retailers tend to discuss markup in terms of its percentage of the retail price—in this example, 18 percent ($0.40 ÷ $2.20). The difference between the retailer's cost and the selling price (40 cents) is the gross margin.

The formula for calculating the retail price given a certain desired markup is as follows:

$$\text{Retail price} = \frac{\text{Cost}}{1 - \text{Desired return on sales}}$$

$$= \frac{\$1.80}{1.00 - 0.18}$$

$$= \$2.20$$

If the retailer wants a 30 percent return, then:

$$\text{Retail price} = \frac{\$1.80}{1.00 - 0.30}$$

$$= \$2.57$$

The reason that retailers and others speak of markups on selling price is that many important figures in financial reports, such as gross sales and revenues, are sales figures, not cost figures.

To use markup based on cost or selling price effectively, the marketing manager must calculate an adequate gross margin—the amount added to cost to determine price. The margin must ultimately provide adequate funds to cover selling expenses and profit. Once an appropriate margin has been determined, the markup technique has the major advantage of being easy to employ.

Markups are often based on experience. For example, many small retailers mark up merchandise 100 percent over cost. (In other words, they double the cost.) This tactic is called **keystoning**. Some other factors that influence markups are the merchandise's appeal to customers, past response to the markup (an implicit demand consideration), the item's promotional value, the seasonality of the good, its fashion appeal, the product's traditional selling price, and competition. Most retailers avoid any set markup because of such considerations as promotional value and seasonality.

19-5b Profit Maximization Pricing

Producers tend to use more complicated methods of setting prices than distributors use. One is **profit maximization**, which occurs when marginal revenue equals MC. You learned earlier that MC is the change in total costs associated with a one-unit change in output. Similarly, **marginal revenue (MR)** is the extra revenue associated with selling an extra unit of output. As long as the revenue of the last unit produced and sold is greater than the cost of the last unit produced and sold, the firm should continue manufacturing and selling the product.

Exhibit 8 shows the MRs and MCs for a hypothetical firm, using the cost data from Exhibit 7b. The profit-maximizing quantity, where MR = MC, is six units. You might say, "If profit is zero, why produce the sixth unit? Why not stop at five?" In fact, you would be right. The firm, however, would not know that the fifth unit would produce zero profits until it determined that profits were no longer increasing. Economists suggest producing up to the point where MR = MC. If MR is just one penny greater than MC, it will still increase total profits.

19-5c Break-Even Pricing

Now let's take a closer look at the relationship between sales and cost. **Break-even analysis** determines what sales volume must be reached before the company breaks even (its total costs equal total revenue) and no profits are earned.

The typical break-even model assumes a given fixed cost and a constant AVC. Suppose that Universal Sportswear, a hypothetical firm, has fixed costs of $2,000 and that the cost of labor and materials for each unit produced is 50 cents. Assume that it can sell up to 6,000 units of its product at $1 without having to lower its price.

Exhibit 9a illustrates Universal Sportswear's break-even point. As Exhibit 9b indicates, Universal Sportswear's total variable costs increase by 50 cents every time a new unit is produced, and total fixed costs remain constant at $2,000 regardless of the level of output. Therefore, for 4,000 units of output, Universal Sportswear has $2,000 in fixed costs and $2,000 in total variable costs (4,000 units x $0.50), or $4,000 in total costs.

Revenue is also $4,000 (4,000 units x $1), giving a net profit of $0 at the break-even point of 4,000 units. Notice that once the firm gets past the break-even point, the gap between total revenue and total costs gets wider and wider because both functions are assumed to be linear.

The formula for calculating break-even quantities is simple:

$$\text{Break-even quantity} = \frac{\text{Total fixed costs}}{\text{Fixed cost contribution}}$$

Fixed cost contribution is the price minus the AVC. Therefore, for Universal Sportswear,

$$\text{Break-even quantity} = \frac{\$2,000}{(\$1.00 - \$0.50)} = 4,000 \text{ units}$$

The advantage of break-even analysis is that it provides a quick estimate of how much the firm must sell to break even and how much profit can be earned if a higher sales volume is obtained. If a firm is operating close to the break-even point, it may want to see what can be done to reduce costs or increase sales. Moreover, in a simple break-even analysis, it is not necessary to compute MCs and MRs because price and average cost per unit are assumed to be constant. Also, because accounting data for marginal cost and revenue are frequently unavailable, it is convenient not to have to depend on that information.

Break-even analysis is not without several important limitations. Sometimes it is hard to know whether a cost is fixed or variable. If labor wins a tough guaranteed-employment contract, are the resulting expenses a fixed cost? More important than cost determination is the fact that simple break-even analysis ignores demand. How does Universal Sportswear know it can sell 4,000 units at $1? Could it sell the same 4,000 units at $2 or even $5?

19-6 OTHER DETERMINANTS OF PRICE

Other factors besides demand and costs can influence price. For example, the stages in the product life cycle, the competition, the product distribution strategy, the promotion strategy, guaranteed price matching, demands of large customers, and the perceived quality can all affect pricing.

19-6a Stages in the Product Life Cycle

As a product moves through its life cycle (see Chapter 11), the demand for the product and the competitive conditions tend to change:

break-even analysis a method of determining what sales volume must be reached before total revenue equals total costs

---

Exhibit 8
POINT OF MAXIMIZATION

Quantity	Marginal Revenue (MR)	Marginal Cost (MC)	Cumulative Total Profit
0	—	—	—
1	$140	$ 90	$ 50
2	130	80	100
3	105	70	135
4	95	60	170
5	85	70	185
6*	80	80	185
7	75	90	170
8	60	110	120
9	50	130	40
10	40	150	(70)

*Break-even point

Exhibit 9
COSTS, REVENUES, AND BREAK-EVEN POINT FOR UNIVERSAL SPORTSWEAR

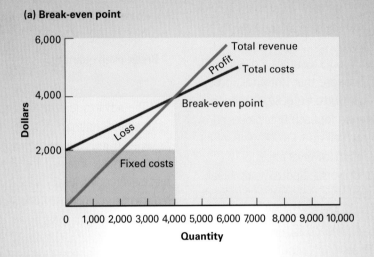

(a) Break-even point

(b) Costs and revenues

Output	Total fixed costs	Average variable costs	Total variable costs	Average total costs	Average revenue (price)	Total revenue	Total costs	Profit or loss
500	$2,000	$0.50	$ 250	$4.50	$1.00	$ 500	$2,250	($1,750)
1,000	2,000	0.50	500	2.50	1.00	1,000	2,500	(1,500)
1,500	2,000	0.50	750	1.83	1.00	1,500	2,750	(1,250)
2,000	2,000	0.50	1,000	1.50	1.00	2,000	3,000	(1,000)
2,500	2,000	0.50	1,250	1.30	1.00	2,500	3,250	(750)
3,000	2,000	0.50	1,500	1.17	1.00	3,000	3,500	(500)
3,500	2,000	0.50	1,750	1.07	1.00	3,500	3,750	(250)
4,000*	2,000	0.50	2,000	1.00	1.00	4,000	4,000	0
4,500	2,000	0.50	2,250	0.94	1.00	4,500	4,250	250
5,000	2,000	0.50	2,500	0.90	1.00	5,000	4,500	500
5,500	2,000	0.50	2,750	0.86	1.00	5,500	4,750	750
6,000	2,000	0.50	3,000	0.83	1.00	6,000	5,000	1,000

*Break-even point

▸▸ **INTRODUCTORY STAGE:** Management usually sets prices high during the introductory stage. One reason is that it hopes to recover its development costs quickly. In addition, demand originates in the core of the market (the customers whose needs ideally match the product's attributes) and thus is relatively inelastic. On the other hand, if the target market is highly price sensitive, management often finds it better to price the product at the market level or lower. When companies introduce highly innovative products such as consumer electronics, medical devices, and pharmaceuticals, they must properly estimate the elasticity or demand for those products. This is particularly true today, when some life cycles are measured in months, not years.

▸▸ **GROWTH STAGE:** As the product enters the growth stage, prices generally begin to stabilize for several reasons. First, competitors have entered the market, increasing the available supply. Second, the product has begun to appeal to a broader market, often lower-income groups. Finally, economies of scale are lowering costs, and the savings can be passed on to the consumer in the form of lower prices.

▸▸ **MATURITY STAGE:** Maturity usually brings further price decreases as competition increases and inefficient, high-cost firms are eliminated. Distribution channels become a significant cost factor, however, because of the need to offer wide product lines for highly segmented markets, extensive service requirements, and the sheer number of dealers necessary to absorb high-volume production. The manufacturers that remain in the market toward the end of the maturity stage typically offer similar prices. At this stage, price increases are usually cost initiated, not demand initiated. Nor do price reductions in the late phase of maturity stimulate much demand. Because demand is limited and producers have similar cost structures, the remaining competitors will probably match price reductions.

▸▸ **DECLINE STAGE:** The final stage of the life cycle may see further price decreases as the few remaining competitors try to salvage the last vestiges of demand. When only one firm is left in the market, prices begin to stabilize. In fact, prices may eventually rise dramatically if the product survives and moves into the specialty goods category, as horse-drawn carriages and vinyl records have.

19-6b The Competition

Competition varies during the product life cycle, of course, and so at times it may strongly affect pricing decisions. Although a firm may not have any competition at first, the high prices it charges may eventually induce another firm to enter the market.

Often, in hotly competitive markets, price wars break out. In early 2013, a price war erupted between adjacent Chevron and Maverik gas stations in West Valley City, Utah. Rates at the competing companies ticked down, cent by cent, until bottoming out at $2.67 a gallon—nearly 70 cents cheaper per gallon than the local average. As cars lined up around the block at both stations, Maverik station owner Namairr Khan offered his take: "We don't want to be lower than them, we don't want to be higher than them so we are just competing. Just fun competition."[12]

Wars over e-book pricing caused Apple and the big six publishers to move to an agency model. In that model, the retailer receives 30 percent of the e-book selling price, and the publisher receives 70 percent of the sale. The major ramification of this model means that discounting books

New releases on *vinyl* can cost from $11 to $30, but rare or collectable records can cost hundreds of dollars!

without a publisher's approval loses the retailer money, because it must still pay the originally agreed upon price. It also means that Amazon loses money on its aggressively discounted books.[13]

19-6c Distribution Strategy

An effective distribution network can often overcome other minor flaws in the marketing mix.[14] For example, although consumers may perceive a price as being slightly higher than normal, they may buy the product anyway if it is being sold at a convenient retail outlet.

Adequate distribution for a new product can often be attained by offering a larger-than-usual profit margin to distributors. A variation on this strategy is to give dealers a large trade allowance to help offset the costs of promotion and further stimulate demand at the retail level.

Manufacturers have gradually been losing control within the distribution channel to wholesalers and retailers, which often adopt pricing strategies that serve their own purposes. For instance, some distributors are **selling against the brand**: They place well-known brands on the shelves at high prices while offering

selling against the brand stocking well-known branded items at high prices in order to sell store brands at discounted prices

other brands—typically, their private label brands, such as Kroger canned pears—at lower prices. Of course, sales of the higher-priced brands decline.

Wholesalers and retailers may also go outside traditional distribution channels to buy gray-market goods, as discussed in Chapter 14. Distributors obtain the goods through unauthorized channels for less than they would normally pay, so they can sell the goods with a bigger-than-normal markup or at a reduced price. Imports seem to be particularly susceptible to gray marketing. Although consumers might pay less for gray-market goods, they often find that the manufacturer won't honor the warranty.

Manufacturers can regain some control over price by using an exclusive distribution system, by franchising, or by avoiding doing business with price-cutting discounters. Manufacturers can also package merchandise with the selling price marked on it or place goods on consignment. The best way for manufacturers to control prices, however, is to develop brand loyalty in consumers by delivering quality and value.

19-6d The Impact of the Internet and Extranets

The Internet, **extranets** (private electronic networks), and wireless setups are linking people, machines, and companies around the globe—and connecting sellers and buyers as never before. These links are enabling buyers to quickly and easily compare products and prices, putting them in a better bargaining position. At the same time, the technology allows sellers to collect detailed data about customers' buying habits, preferences, and even spending limits so that sellers can tailor their products and prices.

USING SHOPPING BOTS A shopping bot is a program that searches the Web for the best price for a particular item that you wish to purchase. *Bot* is short for *robot*. Shopping bots theoretically give pricing power to the consumer. The more information that the shopper has, the more efficient his or her purchase decision will be.

There are two general types of shopping bots. The first is the broad-based type that searches a wide range

of product categories such as Google Shopping, Nextag, and PriceGrabber. These sites operate using a Yellow Pages type of model in that they list every retailer they can find. The second is the niche-oriented type that searches for prices for only one type of product such as consumer electronics (CNET), event tickets (SeatGeek), or travel-related services (Kayak).[15]

Shopping bots have been around for quite some time, and security protocols have been developed to limit bot trawls. Still, shopping bots remain a powerful and impactful marketing tool to this day. In fact, the 2012 holiday shopping season marked one of the largest spikes in bot traffic history.[16]

INTERNET AUCTIONS The Internet auction business is huge. Among the most popular consumer auction sites are the following:

» **WWW.UBID.COM:** Offers a large range of product categories. "My page" consolidates all of the user's activity in one place.

» **WWW.EBAY.COM:** The most popular auction site.

» **WWW.BIDZ.COM:** Buys closeout deals in very large lots and offers them online in its no-reserve auctions.

Even though consumers are spending billions on Internet auctions, business-to-business auctions are likely to be the dominant form in the future. Recently, Whirlpool began holding online auctions. Participants bid on the price of the items that they would supply to Whirlpool but with a twist: they had to include the date when Whirlpool would have to pay for the items. The company wanted to see which suppliers would offer the longest grace period before requiring payment. Five auctions held over five months helped Whirlpool uncover savings of close to $2 million and more than doubled the grace period.

Whirlpool's success is a sign that the business-to-business auction world is shifting from haggling over prices to niggling over parameters of the deal. Warranties, delivery dates, transportation methods, customer support, financing options, and quality have all become bargaining chips.

© iStockphoto.com/mark wragg

19-6e Promotion Strategy

Price is often used as a promotional tool to increase consumer interest. During the 2013 Super Bowl, fast-food chain Subway aired a commercial featuring various athletes and actors mispronouncing the name of its price-based "FebruANY" promotion. During this month-long promotion, Subway's footlong sandwiches were marked down to $5 for basic sandwiches and $6 for special sandwiches.[17] As another example, the weekly flyers sent out by grocery stores in the Sunday newspaper advertise many products with special low prices.

Pricing can be a tool for trade promotions as well. The outdoor sporting industry has long used a full-price model, whereby vendors set minimum advertised prices (MAPs) that specialty retailers cannot sell below. This maintains brand prestige and profit margins but makes it difficult for smaller retailers to drive purchases with special sales and promotions. In advance of the 2012 winter season, however, a handful of vendors relaxed their MAP guidelines amidst a series of disappointing holiday sales periods dominated by online and big-box sporting goods retailers. Burton Snowboards, for example, allowed specialty retailers to advertise equipment for up to 15 percent off and outerwear for up to 20 percent off. "I grew up in a world where we never broke price," said Burton U.S. Director of Sales Mark Wakeling. "But unprecedented conditions call for unprecedented actions. The hope was to allow dealers the flexibility to sell product at a small discount now, rather than much larger discounts in April."[18]

19-6f Demands of Large Customers

Manufacturers find that their large customers such as department stores often make specific pricing demands that the suppliers must agree to. Department stores are making greater-than-ever demands on their suppliers to cover the heavy discounts and markdowns on their own selling floors. They want suppliers to guarantee their stores' profit margins, and they insist on cash rebates if the guarantee isn't met. They are also exacting fines for violations of ticketing, packing, and shipping rules. Cumulatively, the demands are nearly wiping out profits for all but the very biggest suppliers, according to fashion designers and garment makers.

Walmart is one of the largest retailers in the world, and the company uses that size to encourage companies to meet its needs. When Walmart decided that its grocery department needed to have everyday low prices instead of periodic rollbacks, it talked to its major suppliers, such as ConAgra, General Mills, and McCormick & Co., to discuss the possibility of offering a consistently lower price to drive business. Some companies, like ConAgra, are struggling to lower costs while grain and other ingredients are steadily increasing in price. Other companies, like Kraft, have been steadily lowering costs and are having an easier time meeting Walmart's demands. The risk of not working with Walmart? Either your product is important enough to drive traffic that Walmart doesn't raise the product price (as happened to Clorox Bleach) or it raises prices and market share drops quickly.[19]

19-6g The Relationship of Price to Quality

As mentioned at the beginning of the chapter, when a purchase decision involves great uncertainty, consumers tend to rely on a high price as a predictor of good quality. Reliance on price as an indicator of quality seems to occur for all products, but it reveals itself more strongly for some items than for others.[20] Among the products that benefit from this phenomenon are coffee, aspirin, shampoo, clothing, furniture, whiskey, education, and many services. In the absence of other information, people typically assume that prices are higher because the products contain better materials, because they are made more carefully, or, in the case of professional services, because the provider has more expertise.

A consumer's psychological state at the time of purchase has a significant impact on his perception of price and quality. If a person has recently been worrying about debt and spending, he is more likely to focus on value than quality when making a purchase. Thus, he might perceive a low price as an indicator of value and opt for a product with a lower price tag. If he has spent the morning troubleshooting a failing product, he is more likely to perceive a low price as an indicator of low quality. He will likely opt for a product with a higher price tag, based on the belief that higher price equates to better craftsmanship.[21]

In general, when perceived higher- and lower-quality products are offered in settings where consumers have difficulty making comparisons, then price promotions have an equal effect on sales. Comparisons are more difficult in end-of-aisle displays, feature advertising, and the like.

Knowledgeable merchants take these consumer attitudes into account when devising their pricing strategies. **Prestige pricing** is charging a high price to help promote a high-quality image. A successful prestige pricing strategy requires a retail price that is reasonably consistent with consumers' expectations. No one goes shopping at Gucci in New York and expects to pay $9.95 for a pair of loafers. In fact, demand would fall drastically at such a low price. In addition to prestige pricing, research has found two other basic effects associated with the price-quality relationship: *hedonistic* and *allocative effects*.[22] High purchase prices may create feelings of pleasure and excitement associated with consuming higher-priced products. This is the hedonistic effect. Hedonistic consumption refers to pursuing emotional responses associated with using a product, such as pleasure, excitement, arousal, good feelings, and fun.

The allocative effect refers to the notion that consumers must allocate their budgets across alternative goods and services. The more you spend on one product, the less you have to spend on all others. Consumers sensitive to the allocative effects likely prefer low prices. However, managers must be aware that setting low prices or lowering prices with a discount may lower perceptions of product quality, prestige value, and hedonistic value. This is because of the negative cues associated with lower selling prices.[23]

Marketers are often hesitant to alter the quality or price of an established brand—and with good reason. Customers grow accustomed to their favorite brands' characteristics. A change in quality or price may disrupt a product's hedonistic and allocative effects, affecting consumers' desire to purchase that product. In 2013, growing global demand created a shortage of supply for bourbon producer Maker's Mark. Instead of raising prices to reduce demand, Maker's Mark announced that it would dilute its whiskey, reducing the alcohol content from 45 percent to 42 percent. A public outcry erupted, and retailers, bartenders, and loyal fans alike took to social media to express their disappointment with the company. Maker's Mark eventually reversed the decision to dilute its whiskey, announcing, "We're humbled by your overwhelming response and passion for Maker's Mark. While we thought we were doing what's right, this is your brand—and you told us in large numbers to change our decision."[24]

Some of the latest research on price–quality relationships has focused on consumer durable goods. The researchers first conducted a study to ascertain the dimensions of quality. These are (1) ease of use, (2) versatility (the ability of a product to perform more functions, or be more flexible), (3) durability, (4) serviceability (ease of

© iStockphoto.com/Chris Gramly

obtaining quality repairs), (5) performance, and (6) prestige. The researchers found that when consumers focused on prestige and/or durability to assess quality, price was a strong indicator of perceived overall quality. Price was less important as an indicator of quality if the consumer was focusing on one of the other four dimensions of quality.[25]

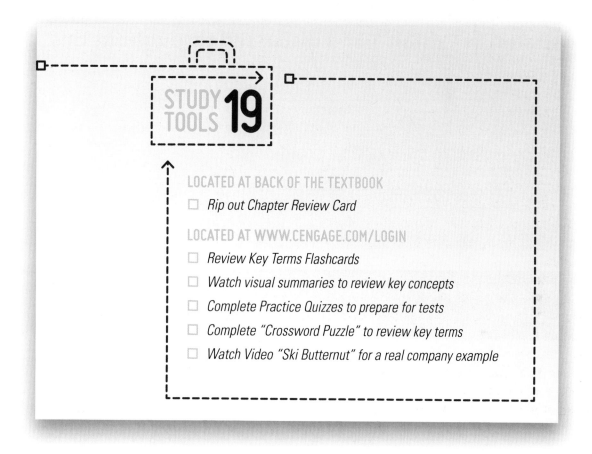

STUDY TOOLS 19

LOCATED AT BACK OF THE TEXTBOOK
☐ *Rip out Chapter Review Card*

LOCATED AT WWW.CENGAGE.COM/LOGIN
☐ *Review Key Terms Flashcards*
☐ *Watch visual summaries to review key concepts*
☐ *Complete Practice Quizzes to prepare for tests*
☐ *Complete "Crossword Puzzle" to review key terms*
☐ *Watch Video "Ski Butternut" for a real company example*

Setting the right price on a product is a four-step process, illustrated in Exhibit 1 and discussed throughout this chapter:

1. Establish pricing goals.

2. Estimate demand, costs, and profits.

3. Choose a price strategy to help determine a base price.

4. Fine-tune the base price with pricing tactics.

All pricing objectives have trade-offs that managers must weigh.

20-1a Establish Pricing Goals

The first step in setting the right price is to establish pricing goals. Recall from Chapter 19 that pricing objectives fall into three categories: profit oriented, sales oriented, and status quo. These goals are derived from the firm's overall objectives. A good understanding of the marketplace and of the consumer can sometimes tell a manager very quickly whether a goal is realistic.

All pricing objectives have trade-offs that managers must weigh. A profit maximization objective may require a bigger initial investment than the firm can commit to or wants to commit to. Reaching the desired market share often means sacrificing short-term profit because without careful management, long-term profit goals may not be met. Meeting the competition is the easiest pricing goal to implement. But can managers really afford to ignore demand and costs, the life cycle stage, and other considerations? When creating pricing objectives,

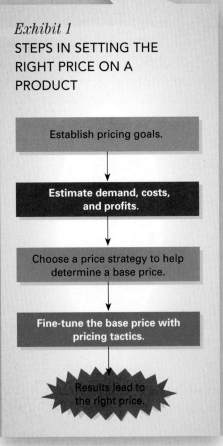

Exhibit 1

STEPS IN SETTING THE RIGHT PRICE ON A PRODUCT

Establish pricing goals.

Estimate demand, costs, and profits.

Choose a price strategy to help determine a base price.

Fine-tune the base price with pricing tactics.

Results lead to the right price.

© Cengage Learning

Chapter **20**

Setting the Right Price

Learning Outcomes

20-1 *Describe the procedure for setting the right price* 372–376

20-2 *Identify the legal constraints on pricing decisions* 376–378

20-3 *Explain how discounts, geographic pricing, and other pricing tactics can be used to fine-tune the base price* 378–387

20-4 *Discuss product line pricing* 387

20-5 *Describe the role of pricing during periods of inflation and recession* 387–389

After you finish this chapter go to
p389 *for* **STUDY TOOLS**

© iStockPhoto.com/Sven Hoppe

price strategy a basic, long-term pricing framework that establishes the initial price for a product and the intended direction for price movements over the product life cycle

price skimming a pricing policy whereby a firm charges a high introductory price, often coupled with heavy promotion

managers must consider these trade-offs in light of the target customer, the environment, and the company's overall objectives.

20-1b Estimate Demand, Costs, and Profits

Chapter 19 explained that total revenue is a function of price and quantity demanded and that quantity demanded depends on elasticity. Elasticity is a function of the perceived value to the buyer relative to the price. The types of questions managers consider when conducting marketing research on demand and elasticity are key. Some questions for market research on demand and elasticity are:

▸▸ **What price is so low that consumers would question the product's quality?**

▸▸ **What is the highest price at which the product would still be a bargain?**

▸▸ **What is the price at which the product is starting to get expensive?**

▸▸ **What is the price at which the product becomes too expensive to consider buying?**

After establishing pricing goals, managers should estimate total revenue at a variety of prices. Next, they should determine corresponding costs for each price. They are then ready to estimate how much profit, if any, and how much market share can be earned at each possible price. Managers can study the options in light of revenues, costs, and profits. In turn, this information can help determine which price can best meet the firm's pricing goals.

20-1c Choose a Price Strategy

The basic, long-term pricing framework for a good or service should be a logical extension of the pricing objectives. The marketing manager's chosen **price strategy** defines the initial price and gives direction for price movements over the product life cycle.

The price strategy sets a competitive price in a specific market segment based on a well-defined positioning strategy. Changing a price level from premium to super premium may require a change in the product itself, the target customers served, the promotional strategy, or the distribution channels.

A company's freedom in pricing a new product and devising a price strategy depends on the market conditions and the other elements of the marketing mix. If a firm launches a new item resembling several others already on the market, its pricing freedom will be restricted. To succeed, the company will probably have to charge a price close to the average market price. In contrast, a firm that introduces a totally new product with no close substitutes will have considerable pricing freedom.

Despite its strategic value, pricing research is an underused tool. McKinsey & Company's Pricing Benchmark Survey estimates that fewer than 15 percent of *Fortune* 500 companies do systematic pricing research.[1]

Strategic pricing decisions tend to be made without an understanding of the likely buyer or the competitive response. Managers often make tactical pricing decisions without reviewing how they may fit into the firm's overall pricing or marketing strategy. Fewer than 5 percent of Fortune 500 companies have full-time functions dedicated to pricing, so many companies make pricing decisions and changes without an existing process for managing the pricing activity. As a result, many of them do not have a serious pricing strategy and do not conduct pricing research to develop their strategy.[2]

The conventional wisdom is that store brands such as Target's Archer Farms and Kroger's Simple Truth should be priced lower than manufacturer's national brands. In fact, private label products are priced an average of 29 percent less than their national brand counterparts.[3] However, savvy retailers doing pricing strategy research have found that store brands don't necessarily have to be cheap. When store brands are positioned as gourmet or specialty items, consumers will even pay more for them than for gourmet national brands. A few examples of high-priced store brands are Safeway's Open Nature Greek Yogurt, Archer Farms Roasted Almonds, and Sam's Club Simply Right Premium diapers.[4]

Companies that do serious planning for creating a price strategy can select from three basic approaches: price skimming, penetration pricing, and status quo pricing.

PRICE SKIMMING Price skimming is sometimes called a "market-plus" approach to pricing because it denotes a high price relative to the prices of competing products. The term *price skimming* is derived from the phrase "skimming the cream off the top." Companies often use this strategy for new products when the product is perceived by the target market as having unique advantages.

Often companies will use skimming and then lower prices over time. This is called "sliding down the demand curve." Hardcover book publishers, such as HarperCollins, lower the price when the books are rereleased in paperback. Other manufacturers maintain skimming prices throughout a product's life cycle. A manager of the factory that produces Chanel purses (retailing for over $2,000 each) told one of your authors that it takes back unsold inventory and destroys it rather than selling it at a discount.

Price skimming works best when the market is willing to buy the product even though it carries an above-average price. Airlines tend to use a variation of price skimming surrounding popular travel times or destinations. During the 2012 Olympic Games in London, for instance, prices for travel to Europe rose more than 10 percent.[5] Firms can also effectively use price skimming when a product is well protected legally, when it represents a technological breakthrough, or when it has in some other way blocked the entry of competitors. Managers may follow a skimming strategy when production cannot be expanded rapidly because of technological difficulties, shortages, or constraints imposed by the skill and time required to produce a product. As long as demand is greater than supply, skimming is an attainable strategy.

A successful skimming strategy enables management to recover its product development costs quickly. Even if the market perceives an introductory price as too high, managers can lower the price. Firms often believe it is better to test the market at a high price and then lower the price if sales are too slow. Successful skimming strategies are not limited to products. Well-known athletes, lawyers, and hairstylists are experts at price skimming. Naturally, a skimming strategy will encourage competitors to enter the market.

A variation of skimming called *anchoring* can come into play in pricing a product line. The strategy typically is used by luxury retailers. An anchor is a high-priced product that may never sell but makes everything else look cheap by comparison (recall the $429 Williams-Sonoma bread maker from Chapter 19). Thus, Ford's $60,445 Mustang Shelby GT500 Convertible makes the $21,995 Mustang V6 seem inexpensive by comparison.[6]

© Nicemonkey/Shutterstock.com

PENETRATION PRICING Penetration pricing is at the opposite end of the spectrum from skimming. **Penetration pricing** means charging a relatively low price for a product as a way to reach the mass market. The low price is designed to capture a large share of a substantial market, resulting in lower production costs. If a marketing manager has made obtaining a large market share the firm's pricing objective, penetration pricing is a logical choice.

Penetration pricing does mean lower profit per unit, however. Therefore, to reach the break-even point, it requires a higher volume of sales than would a skimming policy. The recovery of product development costs may be slow. As you might expect, penetration pricing tends to discourage competition.

A penetration strategy tends to be effective in a price-sensitive market. Price should decline more rapidly when demand is elastic because the market can be expanded through a lower price. Also, price sensitivity and greater competitive pressure should lead to a lower initial price and a relatively slow decline in the price later to a stable low price. The ultra-low-cost airline Spirit is now the most profitable U.S. airline.[7] Its cut-rate fares include little more than a seat—nearly everything else is sold à la carte. The only complimentary item in the cabin is ice. If you want water with your ice, it costs $3.00.

Although Walmart is typically associated with penetration pricing, other chains have done an excellent job of following this strategy as well. Fast-food restaurants use value menus and low-priced foods to entice customers to visit one chain over another. Longtime king of fast-food McDonald's built its brand on simple fare offered at rock-bottom prices that competitors simply cannot match. However, McDonald's has lost ground recently—posting its first monthly sales decline in nine years—as it has moved away from a penetration pricing strategy and toward a fast-casual model. Hoping to compete with higher-quality chains like Panera Bread and Chipotle Mexican Grill, McDonald's has deemphasized its popular Dollar Menu and introduced pricier espresso drinks and premium burgers like the Angus Deluxe. McDonald's has acknowledged

penetration pricing a pricing policy whereby a firm charges a relatively low price for a product initially as a way to reach the mass market

status quo pricing charging a price identical to or very close to the competition's price

unfair trade practice acts laws that prohibit wholesalers and retailers from selling below cost

price fixing an agreement between two or more firms on the price they will charge for a product

the error of moving away from penetration pricing, however, and CEO Don Thompson has promised more aggressive pricing in the months to come.[8]

If a firm has a low fixed cost structure and each sale provides a large contribution to those fixed costs, penetration pricing can boost sales and provide large increases in profits—but only if the market size grows or if competitors choose not to respond. Low prices can attract additional buyers to the market. The increased sales can justify production expansion or the adoption of new technologies, both of which can reduce costs. And, if firms have excess capacity, even low-priced business can provide incremental dollars toward fixed costs.

Penetration pricing can also be effective if an experience curve will cause costs per unit to drop significantly. The experience curve proposes that per-unit costs will go down as a firm's production experience increases. Manufacturers that fail to take advantage of these effects will find themselves at a competitive cost disadvantage relative to others that are further along the curve.

The big advantage of penetration pricing is that it typically discourages or blocks competition from entering a market. The disadvantage is that penetration means gearing up for mass production to sell a large volume at a low price. If the volume fails to materialize, the company will face huge losses from building or converting a factory to produce the failed product.

Sometimes, multinational firms will follow a skimming strategy in developed countries and a penetration strategy in developing countries. Nokia, for example, views low-income consumers in developing countries as crucial to its long-run growth strategy. The company known for its cutting-edge Windows-based smartphones in developed countries has created the 1,087 rupee ($20) Nokia 105 for the India market. By contrast, Nokia's Lumia 920 smartphone retails for almost $600 off contract. In developing markets, Nokia prices its products by determining what the consumer can afford and adjusting features and manufacturing processes to meet the target price. While it does not have an eight-megapixel camera or the latest quad-core processor, the sturdy Nokia 105 offers standard cellphone service to residents living in remote areas and comes with a flashlight, an FM radio, and a battery that can last thirty-five days without a charge. Nokia hopes that, as

the Indian economy grows, customers will trade up to more expensive products.[9]

STATUS QUO PRICING The third basic price strategy a firm may choose is **status quo pricing**, also called meeting the competition or going rate pricing (see also Chapter 19). It means charging a price identical to or very close to the competition's price.

Although status quo pricing has the advantage of simplicity, its disadvantage is that the strategy may ignore demand or cost or both. If the firm is comparatively small, however, meeting the competition may be the safest route to long-term survival.

20-2 THE LEGALITY OF PRICE STRATEGY

As we mentioned in Chapter 4, some pricing decisions are subject to government regulation. Among the issues that fall into this category are unfair trade practices, price fixing, price discrimination, and predatory pricing.

20-2a Unfair Trade Practices

In over half the states, **unfair trade practice acts** put a floor under wholesale and retail prices. Selling below cost in these states is illegal. Wholesalers and retailers must usually take a certain minimum percentage markup on their combined merchandise cost and transportation cost. The most common markup figures are 6 percent at the retail level and 2 percent at the wholesale level. If a specific wholesaler or retailer can provide "conclusive proof" that operating costs are lower than the minimum required figure, lower prices may be allowed.

The intent of unfair trade practice acts is to protect small local firms from giants like Walmart, which operates very efficiently on razor-thin profit margins. State enforcement of unfair trade practice laws has generally been lax, however, partly because low prices benefit local consumers.

20-2b Price Fixing

Price fixing is an agreement between two or more firms on the price they will charge for a product. Suppose two or more executives from competing firms meet to decide how much to charge for a product or to decide which of them will submit the lowest bid on a certain contract. Such practices are illegal under the Sherman Act and the Federal Trade Commission Act. Offenders have received fines and sometimes prison terms. Price fixing is one area where the law is quite clear, and the U.S. Justice Department's enforcement is vigorous.

In 2012, the U.S. Department of Justice sued Apple and five large publishers for price fixing. The suit claims that the companies agreed to raise best-seller e-book prices, setting the price point between $12.99 and $14.99. The new business model was then allegedly forced on Amazon to prevent the company from continuing to sell e-books for $9.99. Hachette Book Group, Simon & Schuster Inc., and HarperCollins quickly settled out of court and now allow all retailers, including Amazon, to discount their books. But Apple, Macmillan, and Penguin maintain that the charges are false and have not agreed to a settlement.[10]

Price fixing occurs in B-to-B sales as well. In 2013, General Electric (GE) sued rival appliance manufacturer Whirlpool and two European parts suppliers, claiming that the companies colluded to set prices at "supra-competitive levels." According to GE, the Danish, Italian, and American companies acted as a price-fixing cartel, forcing GE to overpay on refrigerator compressors, and resulting in decreased manufacturing capacity and limited product availability. This lawsuit followed a 2010 price-fixing case filed against Whirlpool and Panasonic, which were found guilty and forced to pay $140.9 million in criminal fines.[11]

Most price-fixing cases focus on high prices charged to customers. A reverse form of price fixing occurs when powerful buyers force their suppliers' prices down. Recently, Maine blueberry growers alleged that four big processors conspired to push down the price they would pay for fresh wild berries. A state court jury agreed and awarded millions in damages.[12] Some price-fixing accusations are less clear-cut. For instance, Leegin Creative Leather Products sought to control its brand image by insisting that retailers charge a certain minimum price for its products. Leegin sued a boutique, Kay's Kloset, for offering its products at a lower price. The suit was decided in favor of Kay's, but appeals are ongoing and may influence the pricing and retail strategies of luxury goods companies trying to control their brand image.[13]

20-2c Price Discrimination

The Robinson-Patman Act of 1936 prohibits any firm from selling to two or more different buyers, within a reasonably short time, commodities (not services) of like grade and quality at different prices where the result would be to substantially lessen competition. The act also makes it illegal for a seller to offer two buyers different supplementary services and for buyers to use their purchasing power to force sellers into granting discriminatory prices or services. For a firm to violate the Robinson-Patman Act, it must meet the following six criteria:

1. There must be price discrimination—that is, the seller must charge different prices to different customers for the same product.

2. The transaction must occur in interstate commerce.

3. The seller must discriminate by price among two or more purchasers—that is, the seller must make two or more actual sales within a reasonably short time.

4. The products sold must be commodities or other tangible goods.

5. The products sold must be of like grade and quality, not necessarily identical. If the goods are truly

In March 2013, Judge Denise Cote granted the Justice Department's request to make Apple CEO Tim Cook testify in the ongoing e-book price fixing case. Apple attempted to block Cook's deposition, citing that eleven other Apple executives had already testified. Cote ruled, however, that Cook's private conversations with former CEO Steve Jobs may have produced unique information about Apple's involvement in the scandal.

interchangeable and substitutable, then they are of like grade and quality.

6. **There must be significant competitive injury.**

The Robinson-Patman Act provides three defenses for a seller charged with price discrimination (in each case the burden is on the seller to prove the defense):

▸ **COST:** A firm can charge different prices to different customers if the prices represent manufacturing or quantity discount savings.

▸ **MARKET CONDITIONS:** Price variations are justified if designed to meet fluid product or market conditions. Examples include the deterioration of perishable goods, the obsolescence of seasonal products, a distress sale under court order, and a legitimate going-out-of-business sale.

▸ **COMPETITION:** A reduction in price may be necessary to stay even with the competition. Specifically, if a competitor undercuts the price quoted by a seller to a buyer, the law authorizes the seller to lower the price charged to the buyer for the product in question.

In recent years, plaintiffs (mostly small companies) won just 4 percent of their Robinson-Patman suits.[14] A pair of landmark cases have raised the burden of proof for small companies that bring suits. In the first case, a cigarette manufacturer alleged that a larger rival was effectively selling its products at a loss in an effort to stifle competition. The Supreme Court ruled against the plaintiff because it hadn't proved a crucial point—that the larger company intended to hike prices later on to make back the money it had lost through deep discounts.

In the second case, a truck dealer alleged that a manufacturer hurt its business by offering other dealers better prices. The Supreme Court ruled against the dealer in a 2006 decision. The court's reasoning, according to the majority opinion written by Justice Ruth Bader Ginsburg, was that the dealer did not demonstrate that the different pricing made it more difficult to compete with rivals for the same customers at the same time.[15]

20-2d Predatory Pricing

Predatory pricing is the practice of charging a very low price for a product with the intent of driving competitors out of business or out of a market. Once competitors have been driven out, the firm raises its prices. This practice is illegal under the Sherman Act and the Federal Trade Commission Act. To prove predatory pricing, the Justice Department must show that the predator—the destructive company—explicitly tried to ruin a competitor and that the predatory price was below the predator's average variable cost.

Prosecutions for predatory pricing suffered a major setback when a federal judge threw out a predatory pricing suit filed by the Justice Department against American Airlines. The Justice Department argued that the definition should be updated and that the test should be whether there was any business justification, other than driving away competitors, for American's aggressive pricing. Under that definition, the Justice Department attorneys thought they had a great case. Whenever a fledgling airline tried to get a toehold in the Dallas market, American would meet its fares and add flights. As soon as the rival retreated, American would jack its fares back up.

Under the average variable cost definition, however, the case would have been almost impossible to win. The reason is that, like a high-tech industry, the airline industry has high fixed costs and low marginal costs. Once a flight is scheduled, the marginal cost of providing a seat for an additional passenger is almost zero. Thus, it is very difficult to prove that an airline is pricing below its average variable cost. The judge was not impressed by the Justice Department's argument, however, and kept the average variable cost definition of predatory pricing.

20-3 TACTICS FOR FINE-TUNING THE BASE PRICE

After managers understand both the legal and the marketing consequences of price strategies, they should set a base price—the general price level at which the company expects to sell the good or service. The general price level is correlated with the pricing policy: above the market (price skimming), at the market (status quo pricing), or below the market (penetration pricing). The final step, then, is to fine-tune the base price.

Fine-tuning techniques are short-run approaches that do not change the general price level. They do, however, result in changes within a general price level. These pricing tactics allow the firm to adjust for competition in certain

predatory pricing the practice of charging a very low price for a product with the intent of driving competitors out of business or out of a market

base price the general price level at which the company expects to sell the good or service

markets, meet ever-changing government regulations, take advantage of unique demand situations, and meet promotional and positioning goals. Fine-tuning pricing tactics include various sorts of discounts, geographic pricing, and other pricing strategies.

20-3a Discounts, Allowances, Rebates, and Value-Based Pricing

A base price can be lowered through the use of discounts and the related tactics of allowances, rebates, low or zero percent financing, and value-based pricing. Managers use the various forms of discounts to encourage customers to do what they would not ordinarily do, such as paying cash rather than using credit, taking delivery out of season, or performing certain functions within a distribution channel.[16] The following are the most common tactics:

▸ **QUANTITY DISCOUNTS: When buyers get a lower price for buying in multiple units or above a specified dollar amount, they are receiving a quantity discount. A cumulative quantity discount is a deduction from list price that applies to the buyer's total purchases made during a specific period; it is intended to encourage customer loyalty. In contrast, a noncumulative quantity discount is a deduction from list price that applies to a single order rather than to the total volume of orders placed during a certain period. It is intended to encourage orders in large quantities.**

▸ **CASH DISCOUNTS: A cash discount is a price reduction offered to a consumer, an industrial user, or a marketing intermediary in return for prompt payment of a bill. Prompt payment saves the seller carrying charges and billing expenses and allows the seller to avoid bad debt.**

▸ **FUNCTIONAL DISCOUNTS: When distribution channel intermediaries, such as wholesalers or retailers, perform a service or function for the manufacturer, they must be compensated. This compensation, typically a percentage discount from the base price, is called a functional discount (or trade discount). Functional discounts vary greatly from channel to channel, depending on the tasks performed by the intermediary.**

▸ **SEASONAL DISCOUNTS: A seasonal discount is a price reduction for buying merchandise out of season. It shifts the storage function to the**

purchaser. **Seasonal discounts also enable manufacturers to maintain a steady production schedule year-round.**

▸ **PROMOTIONAL ALLOWANCES: A promotional allowance (also known as a trade allowance) is a payment to a dealer for promoting the manufacturer's products. It is both a pricing tool and a promotional device. As a pricing tool, a promotional allowance is like a functional discount. If, for example, a retailer runs an ad for a manufacturer's product, the manufacturer may pay half the cost.**

▸ **REBATES: A rebate is a cash refund given for the purchase of a product during a specific period. The advantage of a rebate over a simple price reduction for stimulating demand is that a rebate is a temporary inducement that can be taken away without altering the basic price structure. A manufacturer that uses a simple price reduction for a short time may meet resistance when trying to restore the price to its original, higher level.**

▸ **ZERO PERCENT FINANCING: During the mid- and late-2000s, new-car sales receded. To get people back into the automobile showrooms, manufacturers offered zero percent financing, which enabled purchasers to borrow money to pay for new cars with no interest charge. The tactic created a huge increase in sales but not without cost to the manufacturers. A five-year interest-free car loan represented a cost of over $3,000 on a typical vehicle sold during a zero percent promotion.**

VALUE-BASED PRICING Value-based pricing, also called *value pricing*, is a pricing strategy that has grown out of the quality movement. It became very popular during the recent recession. Instead of figuring prices based on costs or

quantity discount a price reduction offered to buyers buying in multiple units or above a specified dollar amount

cumulative quantity discount a deduction from list price that applies to the buyer's total purchases made during a specific period

noncumulative quantity discount a deduction from list price that applies to a single order rather than to the total volume of orders placed during a certain period

cash discount a price reduction offered to a consumer, an industrial user, or a marketing intermediary in return for prompt payment of a bill

functional discount (trade discount) a discount to wholesalers and retailers for performing channel functions

seasonal discount a price reduction for buying merchandise out of season

promotional allowance (trade allowance) a payment to a dealer for promoting the manufacturer's products

rebate a cash refund given for the purchase of a product during a specific period

value-based pricing setting the price at a level that seems to the customer to be a good price compared to the prices of other options

competitors' prices, it starts with the customer, considers the competition, and then determines the appropriate price. The basic assumption is that the firm is customer driven, seeking to understand the attributes customers want in the goods and services they buy and the value of that bundle of attributes to customers. Because very few firms operate in a pure monopoly, however, a marketer using value-based pricing must also determine the value of competitive offerings to customers. Customers determine the value of a product (not just its price) relative to the value of alternatives. In value-based pricing, therefore, the price of the product is set at a level that seems to the customer to be a good price compared with the prices of other options.

Shoppers in competitive markets are seeing prices fall as Walmart pushes rivals to match its value prices. The firm continued to up the ante in 2012 by offering consistently lower prices in its grocery and health and beauty departments.[17] Such reduced prices have conditioned consumers to expect inexpensive goods every day. Walmart's success with this evolving market—and traditional grocers' lack thereof—has prompted other retailers with considerable amounts of buyer-side pressure to enter the grocery business. For example, since launching the AmazonFresh grocery delivery service in 2007, Amazon has led the pack of online grocery services and expanded its share of the grocery market tremendously. While the future of online grocery shopping remains unknown, Amazon has used its sizable power to claim a stake in this tightening market.[18]

PRICING PRODUCTS TOO LOW Sometimes managers price their products too low, thereby reducing company profits. This seems to happen for two reasons. First, managers attempt to buy market share through aggressive pricing. Usually, however, these price cuts are quickly met by competitors. Thus, any gain in market share is short-lived, and overall industry profits end up falling. Second, managers have a natural tendency to want to make decisions that can be justified objectively.

The problem is that companies often lack hard data on the complex determinants of profitability, such as the relationship between price changes and sales volumes, the link between demand levels and costs, and the likely responses of competitors to price changes. In contrast, companies usually have rich, unambiguous information on costs, sales, market share, and competitors' prices. As a result, managers tend to make pricing decisions based on current costs, projected short-term share gains, or current competitor prices rather than on long-term profitability.

The problem of "underpricing" can be solved by linking information about price, cost, and demand within the same decision support system. The demand data can be developed via marketing research. This will enable managers to get the hard data they need to calculate the effects of pricing decisions on profitability. In 2012, satellite television provider DIRECTV unveiled a new state-of-the-art DVR box, lowered the cost of its NFL Sunday Ticket football package, added new channels to its lineup, launched the DIRECTV Everywhere mobile service, and went through a

NEW LOWER PRICE

KARLSTAD two chaises + sofa

$997

10 YEAR
IKEA

Have a seat. Or two. Or three.

With the KARLSTAD series, you have the flexibility to create the perfect seating combination. Combine the different KARLSTAD pieces to create a solution that sits right with your home. Sink into an extra soft loveseat. Or pair it with an armchair or a free-standing chaise — whatever works best for you. You can even choose from a variety of legs and washable covers. So go ahead, find your comfort combination.

IKEA

IKEA-USA.com/KARLSTAD

KARLSTAD seating has a 10-year limited warranty. See **IKEA** store or **IKEA**-USA.com

In this advertisement, IKEA is using value-based pricing to bring customers into the store and to encourage shoppers to buy as much seating as they need.

public and costly negotiation with media conglomerate Viacom over programming costs. It came as little surprise, then, that DIRECTV announced in February 2013 that it would need to raise subscriber rates by an average of 4.5 percent. Realizing its services were underpriced, DIRECTV weighed the benefit of additional revenue against the costs of bad publicity and decreased demand, arriving at a new pricing structure that maximized customer approval while supporting the company's growing expenditures.[19]

20-3b Geographic Pricing

Because many sellers ship their wares to a nationwide or even a worldwide market, the cost of freight can greatly affect the total cost of a product. Sellers may use several different geographic pricing tactics to moderate the impact of freight costs on distant customers. The following methods of geographic pricing are the most common:

▸▸ **FOB ORIGIN PRICING:** FOB origin pricing, also called FOB factory or FOB shipping point, is a price tactic that requires the buyer to absorb the freight costs from the shipping point ("free on board"). The farther buyers are from sellers, the more they pay, because transportation costs generally increase with the distance merchandise is shipped.

▸▸ **UNIFORM DELIVERED PRICING:** If the marketing manager wants total costs, including freight, to be equal for all purchasers of identical products, the firm will adopt uniform delivered pricing, or "postage stamp" pricing. With uniform delivered pricing, the seller pays the actual freight charges and bills every purchaser an identical, flat freight charge.

▸▸ **ZONE PRICING:** A marketing manager who wants to equalize total costs among buyers within large geographic areas—but not necessarily all of the seller's market area—may modify the base price with a zone-pricing tactic. Zone pricing is a modification of uniform delivered pricing. Rather than using a uniform freight rate for the entire United States (or its total market), the firm divides it into segments or zones and charges a flat freight rate to all customers in a given zone. The U.S. Postal Service's parcel post rate structure is probably the best-known zone-pricing system in the country.

▸▸ **FREIGHT ABSORPTION PRICING:** In freight absorption pricing, the seller pays all or part of the actual freight charges and does not pass them on to the buyer. The manager may use this tactic in intensely competitive areas or as a way to break into new market areas.

▸▸ **BASING-POINT PRICING:** With basing-point pricing, the seller designates a location as a basing point and charges all buyers the freight cost from that point, regardless of the city from which the goods are shipped. Thanks to

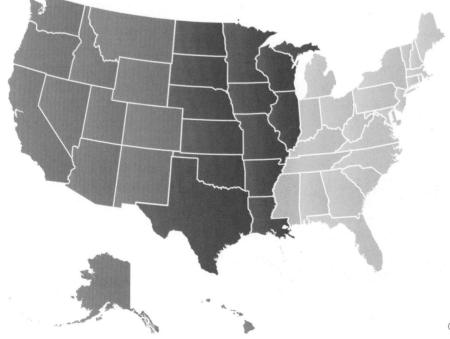

Charging customers shipping fees based on the zone in which they are located is a popular GEOGRAPHIC PRICING *tactic.*

several adverse court rulings, basing-point pricing has waned in popularity. Freight fees charged when none were actually incurred, called phantom freight, have been declared illegal.

20-3c Other Pricing Tactics

Unlike geographic pricing, other pricing tactics are unique and defy neat categorization. Managers use these tactics for various reasons—for example, to stimulate demand for specific products, to increase store patronage, and to offer a wider variety of merchandise at a specific price point. Such pricing tactics include a single-price tactic, flexible pricing, professional services pricing, price lining, leader pricing, bait pricing, odd–even pricing, price bundling, and two-part pricing.

SINGLE-PRICE TACTIC A merchant using a **single-price tactic** offers all goods and services at the same price (or perhaps two or three prices). A new startup company called MATTER specializes in high-quality, in-depth reporting on science and technology. It publishes one story a month (and will be moving to weekly stories as subscriptions increase) in a long-form narrative style over a wide variety of digital platforms. Each story costs 99 cents, or MATTER lovers can purchase a monthly subscription.[20] This type of single-price selling removes price comparisons from the buyer's decision-making process. The retailer enjoys the benefits of a simplified pricing system and minimal clerical errors.

While the single-price tactic is alluring to retailers and customers alike, the strategy does have certain pitfalls. For one, continually rising material and infrastructure costs can prove a headache for retailers following this strategy. In times of inflation, they must frequently raise the selling price. What's more, a single-pricing strategy eliminates the possibility of maximizing the profitability of leading products. For example, Walt Disney World charges $89 per adult ticket no matter the time of year, no matter the day of the week, and no matter which theme park a customer visits. If Disney adopted a tiered pricing structure—or even a dynamic pricing system—it could better balance supply and demand, maximizing sales on peak and slow days alike.[21] Similarly, if MATTER's customers overwhelmingly purchased one story in particular, MATTER might be able to charge a premium price for that story and improve the company's profitability.

FLEXIBLE PRICING Flexible pricing (or **variable pricing**) means that different customers pay different prices for essentially the same merchandise bought in equal quantities. This tactic is often found in the sale of shopping goods, specialty merchandise, and most industrial goods except supply items. Car dealers and many appliance retailers commonly follow the practice. It allows the seller to adjust for competition by meeting another seller's price. Thus, a marketing manager with a status quo pricing objective might readily adopt the tactic. Flexible pricing also enables the seller to close a sale with price-conscious consumers.

The obvious disadvantages of flexible pricing are the lack of consistent profit margins, the potential ill will of high-paying purchasers, the tendency for salespeople to automatically lower the price to make a sale, and the possibility of a price war among sellers.

TRADE-INS Flexible pricing and trade-ins often go hand in hand. A shortage of used cars has caused trade-in values to skyrocket in recent years. The average value of one- to three-year-old vehicles jumped from $15,000 in 2008 to more than $23,000 in 2011, and it continued to rise through 2012.[22] Trade-ins occur for other products as well, such as musical instruments, sporting goods, jewelry, and some appliances. If a trade-in is involved, the consumer must negotiate two prices, one for the new product and one for the existing product. The existence of a trade-in raises several questions for the purchaser. For example, will the new product's price differ depending on whether there is a trade-in? Are consumers better off trading in their used product toward the purchase of the new one from the same retailer, or should they keep the two transactions separate by dealing with different retailers? Several financial management guides, such as Bankrate.com, advise consumers to keep the two transactions separate.[23]

Recent research found that trade-in customers tend to care more about the trade-in value they receive than the price they pay for the new product. Thus, these buyers tend to pay more than purchasers without a trade-in. Analysis of data from the automobile market found that, on average, trade-in customers end up paying $452 more than customers who simply buy a new car from a dealer.[24]

PROFESSIONAL SERVICES PRICING Professional services pricing is used by people with lengthy experience, training, and often certification by a licensing board—for example, lawyers, physicians, and family counselors.

Professionals sometimes charge customers at an hourly rate, but sometimes fees are based on the solution of a problem or performance of an act (such as an eye examination) rather than on the actual time involved.

Those who use professional pricing have an ethical responsibility not to overcharge a customer. Because demand is sometimes highly inelastic, such as when a person requires heart surgery to survive, there may be a temptation to charge "all the traffic will bear."

PRICE LINING When a seller establishes a series of prices for a type of merchandise, it creates a price line. **Price lining** is the practice of offering a product line with several items at specific price points. Wireless providers use price lining for cell phones that are purchased with a two-year contract. The top tier is usually priced at $299 (the highest the market will pay), and subsequent tiers are $249, $199, $149, $99, and $49.

Price lining reduces confusion for both the salesperson and the consumer. The buyer may be offered a wider variety of merchandise at each established price. Price lines may also enable a seller to reach several market segments. For buyers, the question of price may be quite simple: all they have to do is find a suitable product at the predetermined price. Moreover, price lining is a valuable tactic for the marketing manager, because the firm may be able to carry a smaller total inventory than it could without price lines. The results may include fewer markdowns, simplified purchasing, and lower inventory carrying charges.

Price lines also present drawbacks, especially if costs are continually rising. Sellers can offset rising costs in three ways. First, they can begin stocking lower-quality merchandise at each price point. Second, sellers can change the prices, although frequent price line changes confuse buyers. Third, sellers can accept lower profit margins and hold quality and prices constant. This third alternative has short-run benefits, but its long-run handicaps may drive sellers out of business.

LEADER PRICING **Leader pricing** (or **loss-leader pricing**) is an attempt by the marketing manager to attract customers by selling a product near or even below cost in the hope that shoppers will buy other items once they are in the store. This type of pricing appears weekly in the newspaper advertising of supermarkets. Leader pricing is normally used on well-known items that consumers can easily recognize as bargains. The trend of geo-social loss leader campaigns is growing in popularity as companies see how successful leader pricing is at enticing people to buy. Daily deal sites Groupon and LivingSocial are two of the biggest leader pricing sources, but some companies are turning to local deal providers to cut down on the cost of the promotion and to avoid deal hunters. For example, Urban Escape Day Spa in Colorado used SaveLocal to send out a coupon for $25 off a $75 massage. While he sold fewer vouchers than he would have through Groupon, the owner retained more revenue from the SaveLocal vouchers and captured more repeat customers.[26]

price lining the practice of offering a product line with several items at specific price points

leader pricing (loss-leader pricing) a price tactic in which a product is sold near or even below cost in the hope that shoppers will buy other items once they are in the store

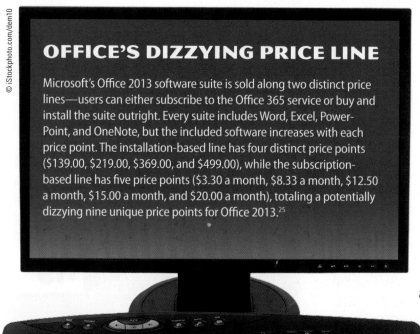

© iStockphoto.com/dem10

OFFICE'S DIZZYING PRICE LINE

Microsoft's Office 2013 software suite is sold along two distinct price lines—users can either subscribe to the Office 365 service or buy and install the suite outright. Every suite includes Word, Excel, PowerPoint, and OneNote, but the included software increases with each price point. The installation-based line has four distinct price points ($139.00, $219.00, $369.00, and $499.00), while the subscription-based line has five price points ($3.30 a month, $8.33 a month, $12.50 a month, $15.00 a month, and $20.00 a month), totaling a potentially dizzying nine unique price points for Office 2013.[25]

Leader pricing is not limited to products. Health clubs offer a one-month free trial as a loss leader.

BAIT PRICING In contrast to leader pricing, which is a genuine attempt to give the consumer a reduced price, bait pricing is deceptive. **Bait pricing** tries to get consumers into a store through false or misleading price advertising and then uses high-pressure selling to persuade them to buy more expensive merchandise. You may have seen this ad or a similar one:

> REPOSSESSED . . . Singer slant-needle sewing machine . . . take over 8 payments of $5.10 per month . . . ABC Sewing Center.

This is bait. When a customer goes in to see the machine, a salesperson says that it has just been sold or else shows the prospective buyer a piece of junk. Then the salesperson says, "But I've got a really good deal on this fine new model." This is the switch that may cause a susceptible consumer to walk out with a $400 machine. The Federal Trade Commission considers bait pricing a deceptive act and has banned its use in interstate commerce. Most states also ban bait pricing, but sometimes enforcement is lax.

ODD–EVEN PRICING Odd–even pricing (or **psychological pricing**) means pricing at odd-numbered prices to connote a bargain and pricing at even-numbered prices to imply quality. For years, many retailers have priced their products in odd numbers—for example, $99.95—to make consumers feel they are paying a lower price for the product. In addition, Robert Schindler, a professor at Rutgers Business School, conducted a study that revealed the difference between pricing a product at .99 and .00 resulted in the .99 item far outselling the .00 item![27] Even-numbered pricing is often used for "prestige" items, such as a fine perfume at $100 a bottle or a good watch at $500. The demand curve for such items would also be saw-toothed, except that the outside edges would represent even-numbered prices and, therefore, elastic demand.

A study at the University of Chicago revealed that a person's two cents is worth a lot. When the price of margarine dropped 18 cents, from 89 cents to 71 cents, sales improved 65 percent. But when the price fell again, this time from 71 cents to 69 cents, sales grew by 222 percent![28]

PRICE BUNDLING **Price bundling** is marketing two or more products in a single package for a special price. For example, Microsoft offers "suites" of software that bundle spreadsheets, word processing, graphics, e-mail, Internet access, and groupware for networks of microcomputers. Price bundling can stimulate demand for the bundled items if the target market perceives the price as a good value.

Services like hotels and airlines sell a perishable commodity (hotel rooms and airline seats) with relatively constant fixed costs. Bundling can be an important income stream for these businesses because the variable cost tends to be low—for instance, the cost of cleaning a hotel room. Therefore, most of the revenue can help cover fixed costs and generate profits.

Bundling has also been used in the telecommunications industry. Companies offer local service, long distance, DSL Internet service, wireless, and even cable television in various menus of bundling. Telecom companies use bundling as a way to protect their market share and fight off competition by locking customers into a group of services. For consumers, comparison shopping

Pizza Hut's Big Dinner Box bundles several of the fast-food pizza chain's most popular menu items.

may be difficult since they may not be able to determine how much they are really paying for each component of the bundle.

The Internet has turned the economics of print publishing upside down—and then upside down again. Magazine publishers have experimented with using bundling to maintain (or salvage) their revenue streams, but some have found it difficult to set prices for bundled goods. In 2011, Time Inc. launched an "All Access" *Sports Illustrated* subscription that included the magazine in print, online, on Android smartphones, and on Android tablets for $48 a year. Two years later, the magazine decreased that price to $39. "That price, we found, was higher than the market commanded," explained Time Inc.'s Steve Sachs. Hearst, parent company of *Cosmopolitan* and *Esquire*, has experimented with bundling but now offers many digital editions to subscribers free of charge. Condé Nast has taken a different approach, charging *New Yorker* subscribers more to renew if they have activated digital access. While upcharged bundling was once seen as the perfect solution for print's transition into the digital world, its future in the industry is uncertain—now more than ever.[29]

Unbundling entails reducing the bundle of services that comes with the basic product. To help hold the line on costs, some stores require customers to pay for gift wrapping. Airlines charge for selecting a good seat, food, and checked baggage, all services that used to be bundled into the price of the ticket.

Clearly, price bundling can influence consumers' purchase behavior. But what about the decision to consume a particular bundled product or service? Some research has focused on how people consume certain bundled products or services. According to this research, the key to consumption behavior is how closely consumers can link the costs and benefits of the exchange.[30] In complex transactions like a holiday package, it may be unclear which costs are paying for which benefits. In such cases, consumers tend to mentally downplay their up-front costs for the bundled product, so they may be more likely to forgo a benefit that's part of the bundle, like a free dinner.

Similarly, when people buy season tickets to a concert series, sporting event, or other activity, the sunk costs (price of the bundle) and the pending benefit (going to see an event) become decoupled. This reduces the likelihood of consumption of the event over time.

Theatergoers who purchase tickets to a single play are almost certain to use those tickets. This is consistent with the idea that in a one-to-one transaction (i.e., one payment, one benefit), the costs and benefits of that transaction are tightly coupled, resulting in strong sunk cost pressure to consume the pending benefit.

A theater manager might expect a no-show rate of 20 percent when the percentage of season ticket holders is high but a no-show rate of only 5 percent when the percentage of season ticket holders is low. With a high number of season ticket holders, a manager could oversell performances and maximize the revenue for the theater.

The physical format of the transaction also figures in. A ski lift pass in the form of a booklet of tickets strengthens the cost–benefit link for consumers, whereas a single pass for multiple ski lifts weakens that link.

Though price bundling of services can result in a lower rate of total consumption of that service, the same is not necessarily true for products. Consider the purchase of an expensive bottle of wine. When the wine is purchased as a single unit, its cost and eventual benefit are tightly coupled. As a result, the cost of the wine will be important, and a person will likely reserve that wine for a special occasion. When purchased as part of a bundle (e.g., as part of a case of wine), however, the cost and benefit of that

© Kzenon/Shutterstock.com

Many gyms include the price of classes, use of racquetball courts, and other amenities. However, by using two-part pricing, some health clubs have dramatically increased revenue.

individual bottle of wine will likely become decoupled, reducing the impact of the cost on eventual consumption. Thus, in contrast to the price bundling of services, the price bundling of physical goods could lead to an increase in product consumption.

TWO-PART PRICING Two-part pricing means establishing two separate charges to consume a single good or service. Airlines have moved to a two-part pricing system, charging the base ticket price, then offering passengers additional perks such as meals, extra leg room, in-flight movies, and trip insurance for additional costs. In 2012, these fees resulted in approximately $152 million in profit for the airline industry.[31]

Consumers sometimes prefer two-part pricing because they are uncertain about the number and the types of activities they might use at places like an amusement park. Also, the people who use a service most often pay a higher total price. Two-part pricing can increase a seller's revenue by attracting consumers who would not pay a high fee even for unlimited use. For example, a health club might be able to sell only 100 memberships at $700 annually with unlimited use of facilities, for a total revenue of $70,000. However, it could sell 900 memberships at $200 with a guarantee of using the racquetball courts ten times a month. Every use over ten would require the member to pay a $5 fee. Thus, membership revenue would provide a base of $180,000, with some additional usage fees throughout the year.

Research has shown that when consumers are thinking of buying a good or service with two-part pricing, they may mentally process the base price, such as a membership fee, more thoroughly than the extra fee or surcharge (playing a game of tennis). Thus, they can underestimate the total price compared with when prices are not partitioned.[32] The researchers also found that low-perceived benefit components should be priced relatively low and vice versa. Consumers find a higher total price more acceptable when the high-benefit component is priced high than when the low-benefit component is priced high. For example, assume John joins a health club and swims at the club four times a month. John really enjoys working out and views being a member of the club as part of a healthy lifestyle (high value). He also swims after a workout once a week to unwind and relax. For John, swimming is not that important but is enjoyable (low

A "PAY WHAT YOU WANT" SUCCESS STORY

Since 2010, more than two dozen short-term Humble Bundle sales have allowed online shoppers to pay what they want for digital collections of e-books, apps, music albums, and most notably, independent computer games. When they purchase a bundle, customers can decide how much of the price they want to go to Humble Bundle organizers, how much they want to go to the media's creators, and how much they want to go to charity organizations such as the Electronic Frontier Foundation. Customers who pay more than the going average receive one or more bonus items, driving up the average and increasing profitability. Humble Indie Bundle 7, which ran from December 19, 2012, through January 2, 2013, raised more than $2.65 million, with the average customer paying $6.69 for the bundle of nine games and one movie.[33]

value). If the club charges $60 a month dues and $5 per swim, John perceives this as acceptable. According to the research, John would find it less attractive if the monthly dues were $40 and each swim was $10. Yet the total cost is the same!

PAY WHAT YOU WANT To many people, paying what you want or what you think something is worth is a very risky tactic. Obviously, it wouldn't work for expensive durables like automobiles. Imagine someone paying $1 for a new BMW! Yet this model has worked in varying degrees in restaurants and other service businesses. One of your authors has patronized a restaurant close to campus that asks diners to "pay what you think it is worth." After several years, the restaurant is still in business. The owner says that the average lunch donation is around $8. Social pressures can come into play in a "pay what you want" environment because an individual doesn't want to appear poor or cheap to his or her peers.

20-3d Consumer Penalties

More and more businesses are adopting **consumer penalties**—extra fees paid by consumers for violating the terms of a purchase agreement. Businesses impose consumer penalties for two reasons: they will allegedly (1) suffer an irrevocable revenue loss and/or (2) incur significant additional transaction costs should customers be unable or unwilling to complete their purchase obligations. For the company, these customer payments are part of doing business in a highly competitive marketplace.

With profit margins in many companies increasingly coming under pressure, organizations are looking to stem losses resulting from customers not meeting their obligations. However, the perceived unfairness of a penalty may affect some consumers' willingness to patronize a business in the future.

20-4 PRODUCT LINE PRICING

Product line pricing is setting prices for an entire line of products. Compared to setting the right price on a single product, product line pricing encompasses broader concerns. In product line pricing, the marketing manager tries to achieve maximum profits or other goals for the entire line rather than for a single component of the line.

20-4a Relationships among Products

The manager must first determine the type of relationship that exists among the various products in a line:

» **If items are complementary, an increase in the sale of one good causes an increase in demand for the complementary product, and vice versa. For example, the sale of ski poles depends on the demand for skis, making these two items complementary.**

» **Two products in a line can also be substitutes for each other. If buyers buy one item in the line, they are less likely to buy a second item in the line.**

» **A neutral relationship can also exist between two products. In other words, demand for one of the products is unrelated to demand for the other.**

20-4b Joint Costs

Joint costs are costs that are shared in the manufacturing and marketing of several products in a product line. These costs pose a unique problem in product pricing (e.g., the production of televisions that combine televisions and Blu-ray players).

Any assignment of joint costs must be somewhat subjective because costs are actually shared. Suppose a company produces two products, X and Y, in a common production process, with joint costs allocated on a weight basis. Product X weighs 1,000 pounds, and product Y weighs 500 pounds. Thus, costs are allocated on the basis of $2 for X for every $1 for Y. Gross margins (sales less the cost of goods sold) might then be as follows:

	Product X	Product Y	Total
Sales	$20,000	$6,000	$26,000
Less cost of goods sold	15,000	7,500	22,500
Gross margin	$ 5,000	($1,500)	$ 3,500

This statement reveals a loss of $1,500 on product Y. However, the firm must realize that overall it earned a $3,500 profit on the two items in the line. Also, weight may not be the right way to allocate the joint costs. Instead, the firm might use other bases, including market value or quantity sold.

20-5 PRICING DURING DIFFICULT ECONOMIC TIMES

Pricing is always an important aspect of marketing, but it is especially crucial in times of inflation and recession. The firm that does not adjust to economic trends may lose ground that it can never make up.

20-5a Inflation

When the economy is characterized by high inflation, special pricing tactics are often necessary. They can be subdivided into cost-oriented and demand-oriented tactics.

COST-ORIENTED TACTICS One popular cost-oriented tactic is *culling products with a low profit margin* from the product line. However, this tactic may backfire for three reasons:

» **A high volume of sales on an item with a low profit margin may still make the item highly profitable.**

» **Eliminating a product from a product line may reduce economies of scale, thereby lowering the margins on other items.**

» **Eliminating the product may affect the price-quality image of the entire line.**

Another popular cost-oriented tactic is **delayed-quotation pricing**, which is used for industrial installations and many accessory items. The price of the product is not set until the item is either finished or delivered. Long

product line pricing setting prices for an entire line of products

joint costs costs that are shared in the manufacturing and marketing of several products in a product line

delayed-quotation pricing a price tactic used for industrial installations and many accessory items in which a firm price is not set until the item is either finished or delivered

escalator pricing a price tactic in which the final selling price reflects cost increases incurred between the time the order is placed and the time delivery is made

price shading the use of discounts by salespeople to increase demand for one or more products in a line

production lead times force many firms to adopt this policy during periods of inflation. Builders of nuclear power plants, ships, airports, and office towers sometimes use delayed-quotation tactics.

Escalator pricing is similar to delayed-quotation pricing in that the final selling price reflects cost increases incurred between the time an order is placed and the time delivery is made. An escalator clause allows for price increases (usually across the board) based on the cost-of-living index or some other formula. As with any price increase, management's ability to implement such a policy is based on inelastic demand for the product. Often it is used only for extremely complex products that take a long time to produce or with new customers. Another tactic growing in popularity is to hold prices constant but add new fees.

Any cost-oriented pricing policy that tries to maintain a fixed gross margin under all conditions can lead to a vicious circle. For example, a price increase will result in decreased demand, which in turn increases production costs (because of lost economies of scale). Increased production costs require a further price increase, leading to further diminished demand, and so on.

DEMAND-ORIENTED TACTICS Demand-oriented pricing tactics use price to reflect changing patterns of demand caused by inflation or high interest rates. Cost changes are considered, of course, but mostly in the context of how increased prices will affect demand.

Price shading is the use of discounts by salespeople to increase demand for one or more products in a line. Often, shading becomes habitual and is done routinely without much forethought. To make the demand for a good or service more inelastic and to create buyer dependency, a company can use several strategies:

▸▸ **CULTIVATE SELECTED DEMAND:** Marketing managers can target prosperous customers who will pay extra for convenience or service. In cultivating close relationships with affluent organizational customers, marketing managers should avoid putting themselves at the mercy of a dominant firm. They can more easily raise prices when an account is readily replaceable. Finally, in companies where engineers exert more influence than purchasing departments do, performance is favored over price. Often a preferred vendor's pricing range expands if other suppliers prove technically unsatisfactory.

© Dragana Gerasimoski/Shutterstock.com

▸▸ **CREATE UNIQUE OFFERINGS:** Marketing managers should study buyers' needs. If the seller can design distinctive goods or services uniquely fitting buyers' activities, equipment, and procedures, a mutually beneficial relationship will evolve. By satisfying targeted buyers in a superior way, marketing managers can make them dependent. Cereal manufacturers have been able to pass along costs by marketing unique value-added or multi-ingredient cereals.

▸▸ **CHANGE THE PACKAGE DESIGN:** Another way companies pass on higher costs is to shrink product sizes but keep prices the same. By the same token, however, some packaging designs help companies keep prices low. General Mills developed a new, smaller Cheerios box that allows for more cereal and less air. The new box cuts costs and keeps prices down.

▸▸ **HEIGHTEN BUYER DEPENDENCE:** Owens Corning Fiberglass supplies an integrated insulation service that includes commercial and scientific training for distributors and seminars for end users. This practice freezes out competition and supports higher prices.

20-5b Recession

As discussed in Chapter 4, a recession is a period of reduced economic activity, such as occurred in the United States in 2007–2009. Reduced demand for goods and services, along with higher rates of unemployment, is a common trait of a recession. Yet astute marketers can often find opportunity during recessions. A recession is an excellent time to build market share because competitors are struggling to make ends meet.

According to pricing strategy consultants Paul Hunt and Greg Thomas, using pricing research to adjust prices during a recession or difficult economic conditions can result in a profit improvement of 20 percent, sometimes more.[34]

Two effective pricing tactics to hold or build market share during a recession are value-based pricing and bundling. *Value-based pricing*, discussed earlier in the chapter, stresses to customers that they are getting a good value for their money.

Researchers have found that relaxed shoppers are willing to pay up to 15 percent more than less-relaxed ones.[35] This helps explain why more high-end hotels and luxury boutiques provide relaxing environments. Doug Wood, president and chief operating officer of casual clothing retailer Tommy Bahama, says he realized that the locations with the best holiday sales were those greeting shoppers with trays of complimentary mimosas and snacks from their attached restaurants. In 2010, all thirteen restaurant-attached Tommy Bahamas offered food during the last two weeks of December. The following year, they offered it every day starting in mid-November. "Our shoppers come in more stressed than we'd like," he says, adding that snacks in stores boost traffic to Tommy Bahama restaurants as well.[36]

Bundling or *unbundling* can also stimulate demand during a recession. If features are added to a bundle, consumers may perceive the offering as having greater value. Conversely, companies can unbundle offerings and lower base prices to stimulate demand.

Recessions are a good time for marketing managers to study the demand for individual items in a product line and the revenue they produce. Pruning unprofitable items can save resources to be better used elsewhere.

Prices often fall during a recession as competitors try desperately to maintain demand for their wares. Even if demand remains constant, falling prices mean lower profits or no profits. Falling prices, therefore, are a natural incentive to lower costs. During the past recession, companies implemented new technology to improve efficiency and then slashed payrolls. They also discovered that suppliers were an excellent source of cost savings; the cost of purchased materials accounts for slightly more than half of most U.S. manufacturers' expenses. Specific strategies that companies use with suppliers include the following:

▸▸ **RENEGOTIATING CONTRACTS:** Sending suppliers letters demanding price cuts of 5 percent or more; putting out for rebid the contracts of those that refuse to cut costs.

▸▸ **OFFERING HELP:** Dispatching teams of experts to suppliers' plants to help reorganize and suggest other productivity-boosting changes; working with suppliers to make parts simpler and cheaper to produce.

▸▸ **KEEPING THE PRESSURE ON:** To make sure that improvements continue, setting annual, across-the-board cost reduction targets, often of 5 percent or more a year.

▸▸ **PARING DOWN SUPPLIERS:** To improve economies of scale, slashing the overall number of suppliers, sometimes by up to 80 percent, and boosting purchases from those that remain.

STUDY TOOLS **20**

LOCATED AT BACK OF THE TEXTBOOK

☐ *Rip out Chapter Review Card*

LOCATED AT WWW.CENGAGE.COM/LOGIN

☐ *Review Key Terms Flashcards*

☐ *Watch visual summaries to review key concepts*

☐ *Complete Practice Quizzes to prepare for tests*

☐ *Complete "Crossword Puzzle" to review key terms*

☐ *Watch Video "BoltBus" for a real company example*

ANATOMY OF PRODUCT LINE PRICING: McDONALD'S

There would probably be little demand for a menu item that was out of the price/value range established by other items in McDonald's product line. For example, a $10 burger would be well out of the price range that McDonald's customers expect for that product class.

1 ... offers several related products.

2 ... sells related products individually and in combinations.

WHAT WOULD YOU PAY FOR A FAST-FOOD BURGER?
$1 $2 $3 $10

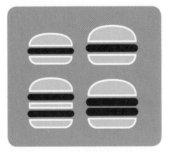

3 ... offers a line of products of various sizes, qualities, and prices.

4 ... presents a limited number of prices for all its product offerings.

© iStockphoto.com/Petek ARICI / © 2007-2008 McDonald's

ENDNOTES

1

1. Announcement to the AMA Academic Council from Patricia K. Goodrich, Senior Director, Professional Development, American Marketing Association, October 25, 2007.
2. Lydia Dishman, "Secrets of America's Happiest Companies," *Fast Company*, January 10, 2013, www.fastcompany.com/3004595 /secrets-americas-happiest-companies (Accessed January 11, 2013).
3. "The 100 Best Companies to Work For," *Fortune*, February 6, 2012, 117–127.
4. Philip Kotler and Kevin Lane Keller, *A Framework for Marketing Management*, 5th ed. (Upper Saddle River, NJ: Prentice Hall, 2011), 4–5.
5. Josh Lowensohn, "Apple's Thunderbolt Cable Gets a Price Drop, Shorter Version," *CNET*, January 9, 2013, http://news.CNET .com/8301-13579_3-57563157-37/apples -thunderbolt-cable-gets-a-price-drop-shorter -version (Accessed January 11, 2013).
6. Inc. Staff, "10 Ways to Support Your Best Customers," *Inc.*, August 3, 2010, www.inc .com/guides/2010/07/10-ways-to-support -your-best-customers.html (Accessed January 11, 2013).
7. "Beyond Satisfaction: J.D. Power 2012 Customer Service Champions," *J.D. Power and Associates*, March 13, 2012, www .jdpower.com/content/press-release/VvdlTdu /beyond-satisfaction-j-d-power-2012 -customer-service-champions-press-release .htm (Accessed January 11, 2013).
8. Ian Paul, "RIM at CES: 5 Things to Know about BlackBerry 10," *PC World*, January 10, 2013, www.pcworld.com /article/2024740/rim-at-ces-5-things-to -know-about-blackberry-10.html (Accessed January 11, 2013).
9. "The 'Green' Gap between Environmental Concerns and the Cash Register," *Nielsen Wire*, August 31, 2011, http://blog.nielsen .com/nielsenwire/global/the-green-gap -between-environmental-concerns-and-the -cash-register (Accessed January 11, 2013).
10. A.G. Laffey and Ron Charon, cited in George S. Day and Christine Moorman, *Strategy from the Outside In: Profiting from Customer Value*, (New York City, NY: McGraw-Hill, 2010), 235.
11. Day and Moorman, 261–262.
12. "The Customer Is Not an Interruption in Our Work; He Is the Purpose of It," *Quote Investigator*, August 2, 2012, http:// quoteinvestigator.com/2012/08/02/gandhi -customer (Accessed April 2, 2013).
13. Day and Moorman, 4.
14. Ibid.
15. Daniel Lyons, "The Customer Is Always Right," *Newsweek*, January 4, 2010, 85–86.

16. "2010 Post-Recession Consumer Study," Ogilvy & Mather, March 15, 2010, www .ogilvy.com/News/Press-Releases/March -2010-Eyes-Wide-Open.aspx (Accessed April 16, 2012).
17. Eric Wilson, "Social Shopping: Everybody Wants In," *New York Times*, March 25, 2012, www.nytimes.com/imagepages /2012/03/25/fashion/25SOCIALSHOP _GRAPHIC.html?scp=1&sq=social%20 shopping&st=cse (Accessed April 16, 2012).
18. "Coastal.com Receives STELLAService Elite Seal for Outstanding Customer Service," *Fort Mill Times*, January 2, 2013, www.fortmilltimes.com/2013/01/02 /2412135/coastalcom-receives-stellaservice .html (Accessed January 11, 2013).
19. Inc. Staff, "10 Ways to Support Your Best Customers," *Inc.*, August 3, 2010, www .inc.com/guides/2010/07/10-ways-to -support-your-best-customers.html (Accessed April 16, 2012).
20. Matt Granite, "Who Has the Best Customer Service," *WGRZ*, January 11, 2013, www .wgrz.com/news/article/195940/37/Who -Has-The-Best-Customer-Service (Accessed January 11, 2013).
21. Karen Aho, "2012 Customer Service Hall of Shame," *MSN*, July 9, 2012, http://money .msn.com/investing/2012-customer-service -hall-of-shame-1 (Accessed January 11, 2013).
22. Harley Manning, "How The 'Most Improved' Companies Raised Their Customer Experience Game Last Year," *Harley Manning's Blog*, April 25, 2011, http://blogs .forrester.com/harley_manning/11-04 -25-how_the_most_improved_companies _raised_their_customer_experience_game _last_year (Accessed April 16, 2012).
23. "Manzama Announces Record Quarter, 100% Retention Rate among Existing Clients," *PRNewswire*, January 7, 2013, www .prnewswire.com/news-releases/manzama -announces-record-quarter-100-retention -rate-among-existing-clients-185902892 .html (Accessed January 14, 2013).
24. Karen Aho, "The 2012 Customer Service Hall of Fame," *MSN*, July 10, 2012, http:// money.msn.com/investing/2012-customer -service-hall-of-fame-1 (Accessed August 2, 2012).
25. Robin William, "Getting Employees to Act on Your Brand Promise," *Gallup*, December 19, 2012, http://businessjournal.gallup .com/content/159425/getting-employees -act-brand-promise.aspx (Accessed January 14, 2013).
26. Nicole Singleton, "'We're in the Business of Making People Better,'" *The Blount Countian*, January 2, 2013, www.blountcountian .com/news/2013-01-02/News/Were_in_the

_business_of_making_people_better.html (Accessed January 14, 2013).
27. Shalini Ramachandran and Jeffrey A. Trachtenberg, "End of Era for Britannica," *Wall Street Journal*, March 14, 2012, B1.
28. Katherine Barrett and Richard Greene, "Dashboard Confessionals, Eliminating Duplicative Services, and Henry Ford on Innovation," *Governing*, February 17, 2011, www.governing.com/topics/mgmt /Dashboard-Confessionals-Eliminating -Duplicative-Services-and-Henry-Ford-on -Innovation.html (Accessed April 16, 2012).
29. "Yaris – It's a Car!" *Toyota*, www.toyota .com/itsacar (Accessed January 14, 2013).
30. U.S. Census Bureau, "U.S. & World Population Clocks," May 31, 2012, www.census .gov/main/www/popclock.html (Accessed August 3, 2012).
31. Nina Golgowski, "Average American Consumes One Ton of Food a Year While Equating a Gallon of Soda a Week," *Daily Mail*, January 1, 2012, www.dailymail.co.uk /news/article-2080940/Average-American -consumes-ton-food-year-equating-gallon -soda-week.html (Accessed June 28, 2012).

2

1. Keith Stuart, "Project Shield: Nvidia Enters the Portable Console Battle," *Guardian*, January 7, 2013, www.guardian.co.uk /technology/gamesblog/2013/jan/07/nvidia -announces-shield-games-console (Accessed January 14, 2013).
2. Christopher Palmeri, "Disney Takes Aim at SpongeBob and Dora." *Bloomberg Businessweek*, March 26–April 1, 2012, 21–22.
3. Thomas Lee, "Canada: Target's Next Bull's-eye," *Star Tribune*, January 13, 2013, www .startribune.com/business/186633251.html (Accessed January 14, 2013).
4. Charles Blakeman, "Stop Looking at Your Numbers," *BusinessBlogsHub*, www .businessblogshub.com/2012/09/stop -looking-at-your-numbers (Accessed September 22, 2012).
5. Troy L. Smith, "Frontier Inks Partnership to Provide Green Electricity," *Rochester Business Journal*, December 18, 2012, www .rbj.net/article.asp?aID=193463 (Accessed January 10, 2013).
6. Ian Paul, "Nintendo Wii U On Sale Nov. 18; What You Need to Know," *PC World*, November 16, 2012, www.pcworld.com /article/2014304/nintendo-wii-u-on-sale-nov -18-what-you-need-to-know.html (Accessed January 10, 2013).
7. David Lipke, "Ugg Goes Upscale with Men's Collection Line," *Women's Wear Daily*, March 28, 2012, www.wwd.com/menswear -news/clothing-furnishings/ugg-goes-upscale

-with-mens-collection-line-5833195 (Accessed April 16, 2012).

8. "GoPro Hero 3 HD Camera Picked as Top Device in 2013 according to iTrustNews," *PRWeb*, January 5, 2013, www.prweb.com /releases/prwebgopro-hero-3/gopro-hero-hd /prweb10293699.htmp (Accessed January 15, 2013).

9. Jon Gambrell, "Troubled BlackBerry Maker Sees Africa Potential," *Bloomberg Businessweek,* www.businessweek.com /ap/2012-09-25/troubled-blackberry-maker -sees-africa-potential (Accessed September 25, 2012).

10. Tatiana Boncompagni, "Social Media Breathes Life into Shelved Products," www .nytimes.com/2012/05/03/fashion/social -media-breathes-new-life (Accessed September 25, 2012).

11. Peter Burrows and Jim Aley, "Why the iPad's Success May Spell the End of the Computer Industry as We Know It," *Bloomberg Businessweek*, March 26–April 1, 2012, 4–5.

12. Samantha Critchell, "Posen Filling Kors' 'Project Runway' Hot Seat," *Bloomberg Businessweek*, December 18, 2012, www .businessweek.com/ap/2012-12-18/posen -filling-kors-project-runway-hot-seat (Accessed January 14, 2013).

13. Trefis Team, "P&G Walls away from Foods, Sells Pringles for $2.3 Billion," www.trefis .com/stock/pg/articles/47714 (Accessed September 25, 2012).

14. Matthew Garrahan, "Dr Dre Beats New Paths in Music," *Financial Times*, January 11, 2013, www.ft.com/intl /cms/s/2/70a003d4-5bd7-11e2-bf31 -00144feab49a.html (Accessed January 15, 2013); Todd Martens, "Beats Aligns with TopSpin, Picks Daisy Subscription Service Chief," January 10, 2013, www.latimes .com/entertainment/envelope/cotown /la-et-ct-beats-partners-with-topspin-daisy -subscription-service-20130110,0,305852 .story (Accessed January 15, 2013).

15. "Ben & Jerry's Ice Cream - Ben & Jerry's Mission Statement," Ben & Jerry's, www .benjerry.com/activism/mission-statement (Accessed April 16, 2012).

16. Damon Poeter, "Report: Dell 'In Talks' to Go Private," *PC Magazine*, January 14, 2013, www.pcmag.com/article2 /0,2817,2414282,00.asp (Accessed January 15, 2013).

17. Ann Zimmerman, "Can Electronics Stores Survive?" *Wall Street Journal*, August 31, 2012, B1, B2.

18. Meg Handley, "Should the U.S. Export Natural Gas?," *U.S. News & World Report*, January 10, 2013, www.usnews.com/news /articles/2013/01/10/should-the-us-export -natural-gas (Accessed January 15, 2013).

19. Eloise Lee and Robert Johnson, "The Chinese Navy is Betting Big on its New Submarine Hunting Drones," articles .businessinsider.com/2012-04-12/news /31328668 (Accessed September 25, 2012).

20. Lindsay Peyton, "CrossFit Gyms Multiply in Memorial, West Houston," *Houston Chronicle*, January 8, 2013, www.chron .com/memorial/news/article/CrossFit-gyms -multiply-in-Memorial-West-Houston -4175562.php (Accessed January 15, 2013).

21. "Blue Bell History," www.bluebell.com/the _little_creamery/our_history.html (Accessed January 15, 2013).

22. "Our Story," The Chef's Garden, www .chefs-garden.com/our-story (Accessed April 16, 2012); "Research and Development," The Chef's Garden, www.chefs-garden.com /research-and-development (Accessed April 16, 2012).

23. Claire Atlinson, "Redbox Instant to Allow Subscribers to Stream Movies Straight to TVs," *New York Post*, January 10, 2013, www.nypost.com/p/news/business/up _stream_swim_SbrwwvfABL6e2EDfPJ7n2H (Accessed January 15, 2013).

24. "How to Play the Email Game," *The Email Game*, http://emailgame.baydin.com/index .html (Accessed February 20, 2013).

25. James O'Toole, "J.C. Penney CEO Ron Johnson Out after Troubled Tenure," *CNN*, April 8, 2013, http://money.cnn .com/2013/04/08/investing/ron-johnson-jc -penney/index.html (Accessed April 9, 2013); Jennifer Reingold, "Retail's New Radical," *Fortune*, March 19, 2012, 125–131.

3

1. Adapted from Edwin M. Epstein, "The Good Company: Rhetoric or Reality? Corporate Social Responsibility and Business Ethics Redux," *American Business Law Journal*, July 2, 2007, 207.

2. Natasha Singer, "Web Sites Accused of Collecting Data on Children," *New York Times*, August 22, 2012, www.nytimes .com/2012/08/22/business/media/web-sites -accussed-of-collecting-data-on-children .html (Accessed January 16, 2013).

3. Alan Duke, "Immigration Fight Changes Arizona, Groups Say," *CNN*, June 26, 2012, www.cnn.com/2012/06/25/us/arizona -immigration-impact/index.html (Accessed January 16, 2013).

4. Catherine Rainbow, "Descriptions of Ethical Theories and Principles," www.bio.davidson .edu/people/kabernd/Indep/carainbow /Theories.htm (Accessed January 16, 2013). Reprinted with permission.

5. "Internet Encyclopedia of Philosophy: Moral Relativism," *The University of Tennessee at Martin*, May 30, 2012, www.iep.utm.edu /moral-re/ (Accessed January 16, 2013).

6. "Internet Encyclopedia of Philosophy: Virtue Ethics," *The University of Tennessee at Martin*, July 7, 2010, www.iep.utm.edu/virtue/ (Accessed January 16, 2013).

7. Jonathan Stempel, "U.S. Sues Bank of America over 'Hustle' Mortgage Fraud," *Reuters*, October 24, 2013, www.reuters .com/article/2012/10/24/us-bankofamerica -fraud-lawsuit-idUSBRE89N171201 21024 (Accessed January 16, 2013); Jonathan Stempel, "AIG Sues NY Fed over Right to Sue Bank of America, Others," *Reuters*, January 11, 2013, www.reuters.com/article/2013/01/12/us -aig-newyorkfed-bankofamerica-maidenla -idUSBRE90B02420130112 (Accessed January 16, 2013).

8. T. M. McDevitt and J. E. Ormrod, "Kohlberg's Three Levels and Six Stages of Moral Reasoning," *Education.com*, February 17, 2012, www.education.com/reference/article /kohlbergs-moral-reasoning/ (Accessed January 16, 2012).

9. Anusorn Singhapakdi, Scott Vitell, and Kenneth Kraft, "Moral Intensity and Ethical Decision Making of Marketing Professionals," *Journal of Business Research*, 36, no. 3, (1996): 245–255; Ishmael Akaah and Edward Riordan, "Judgments of Marketing Professionals about Ethical Issues in Marketing Research: A Replication and Extension," *Journal of Marketing Research*, 26, no. 1, (1989): 112–120; see also Shelby Hunt, Lawrence Chonko, and James Wilcox, "Ethical Problems of Marketing Researchers," *Journal of Marketing Research*, 21, no. 3, (1984): 309–324; Kenneth Andrews, "Ethics in Practice," *Harvard Business Review*, September 1989, 99–104; Thomas Dunfee, Craig Smith, and William T. Ross, Jr., "Social Contracts and Marketing Ethics," *Journal of Marketing*, 63, no. 3, (1999): 14–32; Jay Handelman and Stephen Arnold, "The Role of Marketing Actions with a Social Dimension: Appeals to the Institutional Environment," *Journal of Marketing*, 63, no. 3 (1999): 33–48; and David Turnipseed, "Are Good Soldiers Good? Exploring the Link between Organizational Citizenship Behavior and Personal Ethics," *Journal of Business Research*, 55, no. 1, (2002): 1–15.

10. "A Strong Ethical Culture Is Key to Cutting Misconduct on the Job," Ethics Resource Center, June 23, 2010, http://ethics.org /news/strong-ethical-culture-key-cutting -misconduct-job (Accessed April 16, 2012).

11. Ibid.

12. John Lyons, "Skin-Deep Gains for Amazon Tribe," *Wall Street Journal*, May 5, 2011, A1, A14.

13. "Origins of a Movement: Officer," *Bentley University*, http://cbe.bentley.edu/origins-eoA (Accessed January 16, 2013).

14. "PepsiCo Global Code of Conduct," *PepsiCo*, www.pepsico.com/download /codeofconduct/English_Global_Code_Of _Conduct_EN.pdf (Accessed January 16, 2012).

15. Terry Mann, "Ethics Training for the Workplace," eHow.com, April 12, 2012, www .ehow.com/facts_5957733_ethics-training -workplace.html (Accessed January 16, 2013).

16. David McGrath Schwartz, "Lobbyists Sit through Ethics Training in Carson City," *Las Vegas Sun*, January 13, 2013, www .lasvegassun.com/news/2013/jan/13 /lobbyists-sit-through-ethics-training-carson -city/ (Accessed January 17, 2013).

17. "National Business Ethics Survey 2011," Ethics Resource Center, www.ethics.org /nbes/findings.html (Accessed April 16, 2012).

18. Ibid; also see Kelly Martin, Jean Johnson, and Joseph French, "Institutional Pressures and Marketing Ethics Initiatives: The Focal Role of Organizational Identity," *Journal of the Academy of Marketing Science*, January 2012, 574–591.

19. Adam J. Wiederman, "How 'Everyday Low Prices' Are Costing Americans Their Jobs," *DailyFinance*, August 10, 2012, www .dailyfinance.com/2012/08/10/how

-everyday-low-prices-are-costing-americans -their-jobs/ (Accessed January 17, 2013).

20. "American International Group," *Google*, April 12, 2013, https://www.google.com /finance?q=NYSE:AIG (Accessed April 12, 2013).

21. Patrick Byrne and Robert Enslow, "Being Milton Friedman," *Chicago Tribune,* July 31, 2012, http://articles.chicagotribune .com/2012-07-31/news/ct-oped-0731 -friedman-20120731_1_free-market -economic-theory-school-choice-milton -friedman (Accessed August 2, 2012).

22. Wendy Koch, "Starbucks Reveals $1 Reusable Cup to Curb Trash," *USA Today*, January 2, 2013, www.usatoday.com/story /news/nation/2013/01/02/starbucks-reusable -cup-trash/1804095/ (Accessed January 17, 2013).

23. This section is adapted from Archie B. Carroll, "The Pyramid of Corporate Social Responsibility: Toward the Moral Management of Organizational Stakeholders," *Business Horizons*, 34, no. 4, (1991): 39–48; see also Kirk Davidson, "Marketers Must Accept Greater Responsibilities," *Marketing News*, February 2, 1998, 6.

24. Joe Light, "Sustainability Jobs Get Green Light at Large Firms," *Wall Street Journal*, July 11, 2011, http://online.wsj.com/article /SB10001424052702304793504576434430 1780569100.html (Accessed April 16, 2012).

25. "The Global 100: World Leaders in Clean Capitalism," *Corporate Knights,"* www .global100.org/ (Accessed January 17, 2013).

26. John Garrett, "Benefits of Corporate Social Responsibility," *Facilities Management Advisors*, March 10, 2012, http://facilities managementadvisors.com/2012/03/10 /benefits-of-corporate-social-responsibility/ (Accessed January 16, 2013).

27. "Annual Review of Business Policies & Actions to Advance Sustainability," *The United National Global Compact*, June 2012, www.unglobalcompact.org/docs /news_events/8.1/2011_Global_Compact _Implementation_Survey.pdf (Accessed January 17, 2013).

28. Ibid.

29. "Marketing Power - American Marketing Association," *American Marketing Association*, www.marketingpower.com (Accessed January 17, 2013).

30. James Temple, "Projecting Warming's Impact on Bay Area," January 5, 2013, www.sfgate .com/technology/article/Projecting-warming -s-impact-on-Bay-Area-4170481.php (Accessed January 17, 2013).

31. Sharon Hill, "Tires Recycled into Rubber Mulch," *Windsor Star*, January 16, 2013, http://blogs.windsorstar.com/2013 /01/16/tires-recycled-into-rubber-mulch (Accessed January 17, 2013).

32. "Consumers Don't Trust Green Product Claims, Survey Says," *Environmental Leader*, March 28, 2012, www.environmentalleader .com/2012/03/consumers-dont-trust-green -product-claims-survey-says/ (Accessed January 17, 2013).

33. "Ben & Jerry's Mission Statement," *Ben & Jerry's*, www.benjerry.com/activism/mission -statement (Accessed January 17, 2013).

34. "One for One," *TOMS Shoes*, www.toms .com/our-movement (Accessed January 17, 2013).

35. Xueming Luo and C.B. Bhattacharya, "The Debate over Doing Good: Corporate Social Performance, Strategic Marketing Levers, and Firm-Idiosyncratic Risk," *Journal of Marketing*, 73, no.6, (2009): 198–213; also see: Stefanie Rosen Robinson, Caglar Irmak, and Satish Jayachandran, "Choice a Cause in Cause-Related Marketing," *Journal of Marketing,* July 2012, 126–139; and Ty Henderson and Neeraj Arora, "Promoting Brands across Categories with a Social Cause: Implementing Effective Embedded Premium Programs," *Journal of Marketing,* November 2012, 41–60.

36. "Shelf Awareness for Wednesday, February 29, 2012," *Shelf Awareness*, February 29, 2012, www.shelf-awareness.com/issue .html?issue=1677#m15192 (Accessed April 16, 2012).

4

1. "Walmart's Makeover," *Fortune*, December 26, 2011, 50–55.

2. "Can I Help You?" *Fortune*, April 30, 2012, 63–68; "AmEx in Action," *Fortune,* April 30, 2012, 64.

3. "Shelf Awareness for Friday, January 18, 2013," *Shelf Awareness*, January 18, 2013, www.shelf-awareness.com/issue .html?issue=1909#m18698 (Accessed January 18, 2013).

4. "Is Proctor & Gamble Losing Its Edge? As Challenges Mount, Critics Wonder if Doubling Down on Digital is Best Bet for Fending Off Competition," *Advertising Age*, March 25, 2012, http://adage.com /print/233705 (Accessed January 21, 2013); "Procter & Gamble Tops Estimates, Raises Outlook," *CNBC*, January 25, 2013, www .cnbc.com/id/100405906/Procter_amp _Gamble_Tops_Estimates_Raises_Outlook (Accessed April 11, 2013).

5. "2012 American Values Survey," *Pew Research Center*, June 4, 2012, www.people -press.org/2012/06/04/partisan-polarization -surges-in-bush-obama-years (Accessed January 21, 2013).

6. "Social Media Report 2012," *The Nielsen Company*, http://blog.nielsen.com /nielsenwire/social/2012 (Accessed January 21, 2013).

7. Delia Paunescu, "The Follower's Future: Where Social Media Is Headed In 2012," *VisionMonday*, January 23, 2012, www .visionmonday.com/ViewContent/tabid/211 /content_id/31991/catId/183/Default.aspx (Accessed April 17, 2012).

8. Quirk's Staff, "Research Shows Social Networking Site Users More Socially Connected," *Quirk's Marketing Research Review*, August 2011, 8.

9. "The Making of a Billion," *Bloomberg Businessweek,* October 8, 2012, 66.

10. "The Importance of Being Liked," *Marketing News,* March 15, 2012, 5.

11. Mark Hardy and Keith Phillips, "A Close Friend, but Not a Trusted One?" *Quirk's Marketing Research Review*, August 2011, 46.

12. Josh Bernoff, "Living in Facebook's Bizarro World," *Marketing News*, March 31, 2012, 11.

13. "Demystifying Social Media," *McKinsey Quarterly,* April 2012, www.mckinsey quarterly.com/article_print.aspx?L2 =16&L3=16&ar=2958 (Accessed January 21, 2013).

14. Ibid.

15. "World Development Indicators and Global Development Finance," *Google*, October 31, 2013, www.google.com/publicdata /explore?ds=d5bncppjof8f9 (Accessed January 21, 2013).

16. "Population Leaves Heartland Behind," *Wall Street Journal*, April 11, 2011, A6.

17. Ibid.

18. Patrick Danner, "A 'Home within a Home,'" *San Antonio Express-News*, January 18, 2013, www.mysanantonio.com/life /home_and_garden/article/A-home-within -a-home-4206742.php (Accessed January 21, 2013).

19. Laura Wood, "Research and Markets: Tween Sensibility, Spending and Influence 2013 – How Do Marketers Reach Tweens?" *Business Wire*, November 26, 2013, www .businesswire.com/news/home /20121126005915/en/Research-Markets -Tween-Sensibility-Spending-Influence-2013 (Accessed January 21, 2013).

20. Kathy Grannis, "Back-to-School Spending Grows as Parents Restock, Replenish Children's Needs," *National Retail Foundation*, July 19, 2012, www.nrf.com/modules .php?name=News&op=viewlive&sp _id=1405 (Accessed January 21, 2013).

21. Anjali Athavaley, "Make Room for Junior Decorators," *Wall Street Journal*, December 1, 2010, online.wsj.com/article/SB1000142 4052748704679204575646671354210974 .html (Accessed April 17, 2012).

22. "Blame the Kardashians," *Quirk's Marketing Research Review*, April 2012, 12.

23. "Tweens' Secret Lives Online," *Wall Street Journal,* May 2, 2012, D1–D2.

24. "American Girl Stores," *American Girl*, www.americangirl.com/stores/ (Accessed January 21, 2013).

25. Melony Roy, "Tumblr, Snap-Chat More Popular with Teens, Young Adults than Facebook," *CNBC*, January 20, 2013, http:// philadelphia.cbslocal.com/2013/01/20 /tumblr-snap-chat-more-popular-with-teens -young-adults-than-facebook (Accessed April 11, 2013); "Teens 2012: Truth, Trends, and Myths about Teen Online Behavior," *Pew Research Center*, July 11, 2012, http:// pewinternet.com/Presentations/2012/July /Teens-2012-Truth-Trends-and-Myths -About-Teen-Online-Behavior.aspx (Accessed January 21, 2013).

26. Quentin Fottrell, "Why Teens Snub Online Retail," *Smart Money*, July 26, 2012, http:// blogs.smartmoney.com/advice/2012/07/26 /why-teens-snub-online-retail/ (Accessed January 21, 2013).

27. John Zaremba, "Teen Marketing Techniques," *eHow*, www.ehow.com/way _6167462_teen-marketing-techniques.html (Accessed January 21, 2013); Brian Theriot, "Teen Marketing Tips," *suite101*, April 22, 2010, www.suite101.com/content/teen -marketing-tips-a228866.

28. "Teenage Consumer Spending Statistics," *Statistic Brain*, September 8, 2012, www.statisticbrain.com/teenage-consumer-spending-statistics/ (Accessed January 21, 2013).

29. "A Star Customer Falls Back to Earth," *Bloomberg Businessweek*, March 26, 2012, 19–20.

30. "Talk to Me, Not at Me," *Quirk's Marketing Research Review*, February 2012, 10–11.

31. Dune Lawrence and Nora Zimmett, "Generation X Stymied by Boomers," *Bloomberg*, September 15, 2013, www.bloomberg.com/news/2011-09-15/generation-x-stymied-by-baby-boomers-refusing-to-give-up-jobs.html (Accessed January 21, 2013).

32. "What Is the Place of Generation X in Our Economy?" *Minnesota Public Radio*, December 20, 2012, http://minnesota.publicradio.org/display/web/2012/12/19/daily-circuit-gen-x-economy (Accessed January 21, 2013).

33. "Segmentation By Generation," *Marketing News*, May 15, 2011, 20–23.

34. Ibid.

35. Halah Touryalai, "Baby Boomer Spending Habits: Here's What's Really Hurting Their Retirement," *Forbes*, October 15, 2012, www.*Forbes*.com/sites/halahtouryalai/2012/10/15/baby-boomer-spending-habits-heres-whats-really-hurting-their-retirement (Accessed January 21, 2013).

36. Steve Olenski, "Marketers and Advertisers, Are You Keeping an Eye on the Baby Boomers?," *Forbes*, June 25, 2012, www.*Forbes*.com/sites/marketshare/2012/06/25/marketers-advertisers-are-you-keeping-eye-baby-boomers/ (Accessed January 21, 2013).

37. "Segmentation By Generation," *Marketing News*.

38. Ibid.

39. Ursula Pari, "Baby Boomers Targeted with Older Models," *KSAT*, November 13, 2012, www.ksat.com/news/Baby-Boomers-targeted-with-older-models/-/478452/17394394/-/628ibj/-/index.html (Accessed January 21, 2013).

40. "How to Market to an Aging Boomer: Flattery, Subterfuge, and Euphemism," *Wall Street Journal*, February 5–6, 2011, A1, A12.

41. Matt Waldman, "Hispanic Consumer Market in the U.S. Is Larger than the Entire Economies of All but 13 Countries in the World, according to Annual UGA Selig Center Multicultural Economic Study," Terry College of Business, May 1, 2012, www.terry.uga.edu/news/releases/2012/buying-power.html (Accessed January 22, 2013).

42. "The Start of Majority-Minority," *Adweek*, May 21, 2012, www.adweek.com/sa-article/start-majority-minority-140665 (Accessed January 22, 2013).

43. Ibid.

44. "The 2012 Statistical Abstract: Population," *United States Census Bureau*, June 27, 2012, www.census.gov/compendia/statab/cats/population.html (Accessed January 22, 2013).

45. "Hispanic Fast Facts," *AHAA*, January 2013, http://ahaa.org/default.asp?contentID=161 (Accessed January 22, 2013).

46. Greg Allen, "Media Outlets Adapt to Growing Hispanic Audience," *NPR*, April 3, 2012, www.npr.org/2012/04/03/149845056/media-outlets-adapt-to-growing-hispanic-audience (Accessed January 22, 2013).

47. "Artistic Expression," *Marketing News*, May 15, 2011, 10.

48. "The 2012 Statistical Abstract: Population: Households, Families, Group Quarters," *United States Census Bureau*, June 27, 2012, www.census.gov/compendia/statab/cats/population/households_families_group_quarters.html (Accessed January 22, 2013).

49. Luke Rosiak, "Fathers Disappear from Households across America," *Washington Times*, December 25, 2012, www.washingtontimes.com/news/2012/dec/25/fathers-disappear-from-households-across-america/?page=all (Accessed January 22, 2013).

50. Authors' projections based upon U.S. Census.

51. "Asians Top Immigration Class," *Wall Street Journal*, June 19, 2012, A3; "America's New Tiger Immigrants," *Wall Street Journal*, June 30–July 1, 2012, C3.

52. Ibid.

53. "State of the Asian American Consumer: Growing Market, Growing Impact Report," *Nielsen*, www.nielsen.com/asians(Accessed January 22, 2013).

54. "Families' Financial Strain Detailed," *Beaufort Gazette*, June 12, 2012, 8A.

55. "Incomes Fell or Stagnated in Most States Last Year," *Wall Street Journal*, September 20, 2012, A6.

56. Tami Luhby, "The Low-Wage Jobs Explosion," *CNN*, August 31, 2012, http://money.cnn.com/2012/08/31/news/economy/low-wage-jobs/index.html (Accessed January 22, 2013).

57. "Fast Facts: Income of Young Adults," *Institute of Education Sciences*, http://nces.ed.gov/fastfacts/display.asp?id=77 (Accessed January 22, 2013).

58. "Incomes Fell…" *Wall Street Journal*.

59. "Marketing in 2012: The end of the Middle," *Marketing News*, January 31, 2012, 22–23.

60. Marilyn Geewax, "Did the Great Recession Bring Back the 1930s?," *NPR*, July 11, 2012, www.npr.org/2012/07/11/155991507/did-the-great-recession-bring-back-the-1930s (Accessed January 22, 2013).

61. Blair Speedy, "Retailers Take Private Labels Upmarket," *The Australian*, January 19, 2013, www.theaustralian.com.au/business/companies/retailers-take-private-labels-upmarket/story-fn91v9q3-1226557047523 (Accessed January 23, 2013).

62. Jeff Edelstein, "Generation X Will Not Go into Debt over Fiscal Cliff," *Trentonian*, January 7, 2013, www.trentonian.com/article/20130106/OPINION03/130109864/generation-x-will-not-got-into-debt-over-fiscal-cliff (Accessed January 22, 2013).

63. "At P&G, the Innovation Well Runs Dry," *Business Week*, September 10, 2012, 24–25.

64. Howard Baldwin, "Time Off to Innovate: Good Idea or a Waste of Tech Talent?," *Computer World*, July 24, 2012, www.computerworld.com/s/article/9229373/Time_off_to_innovate_Good_idea_or_a_waste_of_tech_talent_ (Accessed January 23, 2013).

65. Kent Gardiner and William Sauers, "Protecting the Crown Jewels: How to Deal with International Trade Secrets Theft," *Inside Counsel,* August 24, 2012, www.insidecounsel.com/2012/08/24/protecting-the-crown-jewels-how-to-deal-with-inter (Accessed January 23, 2012).

66. "Myths of the Big R&D Budget," *Wall Street Journal*, June 15, 2012, B1–B2.

67. "Health Care TV Spot – Ana Maria," *YouTube*, January 10, 2013, www.youtube.com/watch?v=6w-zoseqxUw (Accessed January 23, 2013).

68. "FTC Bureau of Competition," FTC, April 9, 2012, www.ftc.gov/bc (Accessed April 17, 2012).

69. "Pretexting," FTC, www.ftc.gov/bsp/edu/microsites/idtheft/consumers/pretexting.html (Accessed April 17, 2012).

70. "Digital-Privacy Rules Taking Shape," *Wall Street Journal*, March 27, 2012, B1.

71. Ibid.

72. "The Selling of You," *Wall Street Journal*, April 7–8, 2012, C1–C2.

73. Ibid.

74. "Ad Networks Bypass iPhone Privacy Rules," *Wall Street Journal*, June 5, 2012, B4.

75. Ibid.

76. "Online Tracking Ramps Up," *Wall Street Journal*, June 18, 2012, B1–B2.

77. Tamar Lewin, "Public Universities to Offer Free Online Classes for Credit," *New York Times*, January 23, 2013, www.nytimes.com/2013/01/23/education/public-universities-to-offer-free-online-classes-for-credit.html (Accessed January 23, 2013).

5

1. "International Trade Statistics 2012," *World Trade Organization*, www.wto.org/english/res_e/statis_e/its2012_e/its12_toc_e.htm (Accessed January 28, 2013).

2. "Caterpillar Reports Record Sales and Profit," January 26, 2012, http://online.barrons.com/article/PR-CO-20120126-906557.html.

3. "SBA Export Express—A Fact Sheet for Small Businesses," http://sba.gov/content/sba-export-express-fact-sheet-small-businesse (Accessed January 28, 2013).

4. "Exports of Goods and Services (% of GDP)," The World Bank, http://data.worldbank.org/indicator/NE.EXP.GNFS.ZS (Accessed January 28, 2013).

5. "Exports of Goods and Services (% of GDP) in the United States," *Trading Economics*, www.tradingeconomics.com/united-states/exports-of-goods-and-services-percent-of-gdp-wb-data.html (Accessed January 28, 2013).

6. Arash Massoudi, "Exports Play Vital Role in Supporting U.S. Employment," *International Trade Administration*, http://trade.gov/publications/ita-newsletter/0510/exports-play-vital-role-in-supporting-us-employment-0510.asp (Accessed January 28, 2013).

7. Kenneth Rapoza, "For American Exporters, Mexico Is the China Next Door," *Forbes*, January 25, 2013, www.*Forbes*.com/sites/kenrapoza/2013/01/25/for-american

-exporters-mexico-is-the-china-door/ (Accessed January 28, 2013).

8. Francisco Sanchez, "The National Export Initiative: Making Progress and Striving for More," March 6, 2012, http://blog.trade.gov/2012/03/06/the-national-export-initiative-making-progress-and-striving-for-more/ (Accessed January 29, 2013).

9. "Program Announcement No. OIT-STEP-2012-01," U.S. Small Business Administration, March 27, 2012, www.sba.gov/sites/default/files/files/STEP%202012%20PROGRAM%20ANNOUNCEMENT%20MARCH%2027%202012.pdf (Accessed January 29, 2013).

10. Martin Neil Baily, Matthew Slaughter, and Laura Tyson, "The Global Jobs Competition Heats Up," Wall Street Journal, July 1, 2010, A19.

11. Ibid.

12. "Profits On An Overseas Holiday," Bloomberg Businessweek, March 21, 2011, 63–69.

13. Ibid.

14. Theodore Levitt, "The Globalization of Markets," Harvard Business Review, May 1983, 92–100.

15. "Coca-Cola Launches Global Ads for London 2012 Olympic Games Starring Mark Ronson," Coca-Cola, February 15, 2012, www.coca-colacompany.com/media-center/press-releases/coca-cola-launches-global-ads-for-london-2012-olympic-games-starring-mark-ronson (Accessed January 28, 2013).

16. Leslie Kwoh, "Cinnabon Finds Sweet Success in Russia, Mideast," Wall Street Journal, December 26, 2012, B5.

17. "GNI per Capita, Atlas Method (current US$)," The World Bank, http://data.worldbank.org/indicator/NY.GNP.PCAP.CD/countries?order=wbapi_data_value_2011+wbapi_data_value+wbapi_data_value-last (Accessed January 28, 2013).

18. Ibid.

19. Barbara Jones, "Hamburgers Cost £32 and a One-bed Flats Go for £7,500 a Month… this Boy Lives in the Most Expensive City in the World (Sadly for Him, He's on the Wrong Side of the Tracks)," Daily Mail, August 4, 2013, www.dailymail.co.uk/news/article-2183616/Luanda-The-capital-Angola-expensive-city-world.html (Accessed January 28, 2013).

20. Hibah Yousuf, "Slowdown in China? Not for Luxury Brands," CNN, April 26, 2012, http://money.cnn.com/2012/04/24/markets/china-luxury-brands/index.htm (Accessed January 29, 2013).

21. "What the Chinese Want," Wall Street Journal, May 19-20, 2012, C1–C2.

22. "Chasing China's Shoppers," Wall Street Journal, June 15, 2012, B1, B4.

23. "After Controversial Ruling, Walmart Eyes India Stores," Wall Street Journal, September 22–23, 2012, A9.

24. Kenneth Rapoza, "China Imports of U.S. Goods a Record-breaker," Forbes, March 28, 2012, www.Forbes.com/sites/kenrapoza/2012/03/28/china-imports-of-u-s-goods-a-record-breaker/ (Accessed January 29, 2013).

25. Victoria McGrane, "World Bank Report: Less Complex Regulation Is Best for Developing Nations," Wall Street Journal, September 13, 2012, http://blogs.wsj.com/economics/2012/09/13/world-bank-report-less-complex-regulation-is-best-for-developing-nations/ (Accessed January 28, 2013).

26. Malavika Sharma, "IKEA India Plans Give Scant Reassurance to Foreigners," Bloomberg, January 9, 2013, www.bloomberg.com/news/2013-01-09/ikea-india-plans-give-scant-reassurance-to-foreigners.html (Accessed January 29, 2013).

27. "Three Decades of U.S. Tariffs on Imported Ethanol Ends," AgriMarketing, December 27, 2011, www.agrimarketing.com/s/71905 (Accessed January 29, 2013).

28. "International Trade Statistics 2011," World Trade Organization, www.wto.org/english/res_e/statis_e/its2011_e/its11_toc_e.html (Accessed January 29, 2013).

29. "Lamy Reports to General Council on Doha Round and Urges Negotiators to 'Change Gears,'" July 25, 2012, www.wto.org/english/news_e/news12_e/gc_rpt_25jul12_e.htm (Accessed January 29, 2013).

30. Siobhan Gorman and Juro Osawa, "Huawei Fires Back at the U.S.," Wall Street Journal, October 8, 2012, http://online.wsj.com/article/SB10000872396390443982904578044190738613734.html (Accessed January 29, 2013).

31. Robert Brown, "NAFTA Links 450 Million Persons in a $17 Trillion Market," Borderzine, February 16, 2012, http://borderzine.com/2012/02/nafta-links-450-million-persons-in-a-17-trillion-market/ (Accessed January 29, 2013).

32. "2011(1-7)ROC-NORTH AMERICA TRADE STATISTICS," The Bureau of Foreign Trade, MOEA, www.trade.gov.tw/english/Pages/Detail.aspx?nodeID=670&pid=328426 (Accessed January 29, 2013).

33. "North American Free Trade Agreement Fast Facts," North America Free Trade Agreement, April 4, 2012, www.naftanow.org/facts (Accessed January 28, 2012).

34. "U.S. Trade with the CAFTA-DR Countries," Office of the United States Trade Representative, www.ustr.gov/about-us/press-office/fact-sheets/2011/may/us-trade-cafta-dr-countries (Accessed January 28, 2013).

35. "Countries," European Union, http://europa.eu/about-eu/countries/index_en.htm (Accessed January 28, 2013).

36. Victor Mallet and Peter Spiegel, "Spain and EU Reject Talk of Bailout," Financial Times, April 10, 2012, www.ft.com/intl/cms/s/0/2a3f04fc-832a-11e1-9f9a-00144feab49a.html (Accessed April 18, 2012).

37. Paul Sonne, "EU Fines Unilever, P&G Over Pricing," Wall Street Journal, April 14, 2011, http://online.wsj.com/article/SB10001424052748703551304576260350721684500.html (Accessed January 28, 2013).

38. Kimberly Amadeo, "World's Largest Economy," About.com, http://useconomy.about.com/od/grossdomesticproduct/p/largest_economy.htm (Accessed January 29, 2012).

39. "Countries and Regions: United States," European Commission, January 9, 2013, http://ec.europa.eu/trade/creating-opportunities/bilateral-relations/countries/united-states/ (Accessed January 29, 2013).

40. Harry Papachristou, "Factbox: Greek Austerity and Reform Measures," Reuters, February 19, 2012, www.reuters.com/article/2012/02/19/us-greece-austerity-idUSTRE81I05T20120219 (Accessed April 18, 2012).

41. Dominic Sacco, "Tetris Jenga and Bop It Ready to Drop," Licensing.biz, January 29, 2013, www.licensing.biz/news/10649/Tetris-Jenga-and-Bop-It-ready-to-drop (Accessed January 29, 2013).

42. "Frequently Asked Questions about Franchising," International Franchise Association, www.franchise.org/industrysecondary.aspx?id=10008 (Accessed January 28, 2013).

43. Dan Kislenko, "Wine & Spirits: California Winemakers Mark Centennial of Robert Mondavi's Birth," The Record, January 11, 2013, www.therecord.com/living/article/868341--wines-spirits-california-winemakers-mark-centennial-of-robert-mondavi-s-birth (Accessed January 29, 2013).

44. "October 2012," U.S. Department of Commerce Bureau of Economic Analysis, www.bea.gov/scb/account_articles/international/iidguide.htm#page3%20Y6 (Accessed January 29, 2013).

45. James K. Jackson, "Foreign Direct Investment in the United States: An Economic Analysis," October 26, 2012, www.fas.org/sgp/crs/misc/RS21857.pdf (Accessed January 29, 2013).

46. "Foreign Investment Surges," Wall Street Journal, June 15, 2012, A1, A2.

47. "Domino's Sticks to Its Ways Abroad," Wall Street Journal, April 17, 2012, B10.

48. "Top 30 Strangest Pringles Flavors from Around the World," TechEBlog, April 13, 2012, www.techeblog.com/index.php/tech-gadget/top-30-strangest-pringles-flavors-from-around-the-world (Accessed January 29, 2013).

49. "Want Some Milk With Your Green Tea Oreos?" Bloomberg Businessweek, May 7, 2012, 25–26.

50. Nadeen El Ajou, "McDonald's UAE Showcases Talent of Regional Artists in Advertising Campaign for Big Mac," AME Info, January 22, 2013, www.ameinfo.com/mcdonalds-uae-showcases-talent-regional-artists-326667 (Accessed January 28, 2013).

51. Nidhi Dutt, "Mobile Tech Brings Big Retail Brands to Rural India," BBC News, March 27, 2011, www.bbc.co.uk/news/business-12841993 (Accessed April 18, 2012).

52. "A Continent Goes Shopping," The Economist, August 18, 2013, www.economist.com/node/21560582 (Accessed January 29, 2013).

53. Brian Wingfield, "U.S. Sets Anti-Dumping Duties on China Solar Imports," Bloomberg, October 10, 2012, www.bloomberg.com/news/print/2012-10-10/u-s-sets-anti-dumping-duties-on-china-solar-imports.html (Accessed January 29, 2013).

54. "Suggested Reading about Countertrade," Exporter-Sources.com, http://exporter-sources.com/suggested-reading-about-countertrade (Accessed January 29, 2013).

55. "TrustYou Selected by Global Hotel Leader Accor as Social Media Solution," *PR Newswire*, London, March 7, 2012.
56. Sheila Shayon, "Uniqlo Mesmerizes Pinterest Users with Mass Pinning," *Brandchannel*, June 26, 2012, www.brandchannel.com/home/post/Uniqlo-Dry-Mesh-Project-Pinterest-062612.aspx (Accessed January 29, 2013).
57. Ibid.

6

1. Jock Busuttil, "Why Sales Needs to Align with Product Management to Win More Business," *Business 2 Community*, October 29, 2012, www.business2community.com/product-management/why-sales-needs-to-align-with-product-management-to-win-more-business-0312500 (Accessed January 30, 2013).
2. Adi Robertson, "LG France Says Nexus 4 Production Ramping Up after Google Underestimated Demand," *The Verge*, January 21, 2013, www.theverge.com/2013/1/21/3899550/lg-france-says-nexus-4-production-ramping-up (Accessed January 30, 2013).
3. Thad Rueter, "Most Shoppers Go Online to Research Products before Buying in Stores," *Internet Retailer*, March 30, 2012, www.internetretailer.com/2012/03/30/most-shoppers-go-online-research-products (Accessed January 30, 2013).
4. "Google Annual Search Statistics," *Statistics Brain*, July 14, 2012, www.statisticbrain.com/google-searches/ (Accessed January 30, 2013).
5. Hui Chen, "The Impact of Comments and Recommendation System on Online Shopper Buying Behavior," *Journal of Networks*, 7, no. 2, (February 2012): 345.
6. Joshua Condon, "Consumer Reports Drops Prius C from 'Recommended' List," *MSN*, May 31, 2012, http://editorial.autos.msn.com/blogs/autosblogpost.aspx?post=fc2cb903-20bb-49ce-b424-89f4665aa953 (Accessed January 30, 2012).
7. Wendy Moe and Michael Trusov, "The Value of Social Dynamics in Online Ratings Forums," *Journal of Marketing Research*, 48, no. 3 (2011): 444–456.
8. "Long Island Launches UFC Gym," *UFC*, October 22, 2012, www.ufc.com/news/ufc-gym-long-island-press-release (Accessed January 31, 2013).
9. "AMG Strategic Advisors Releases Findings from Study Analyzing Trade Promotion Effectiveness," *CNBC*, January 22, 2013, www.cnbc.com/id/100397604/AMG_Strategic_Advisors_Releases_Findings_from_Study_Analyzing_Trade_Promotion_Effectiveness (Accessed January 31, 2013).
10. Ibid.
11. Matt Townsend, "Replacing the Extinct Impulse Buyer," *Bloomberg Businessweek*, November 14–20, 2012, 28–29.
12. The material on "types of involvement" was adapted from Barry Babin and Eric Harris, *CB²* (Mason, OH: South-Western Cengage Learning, 2011), 88–89.

13. Adam Nason, "Elevation Prostator, the 2012 Pints for Prostates Beer, Up Next in Rare Beer Club," *BeerPulse*, August 29, 2012, http://beerpulse.com/2012/08/elevation-prostator-the-2012-pints-for-prostates-beer-up-next-in-rare-beer-club/ (Accessed January 31, 2013).
14. Christina Constantini, "10 Brands Capitalizing on the Latino Immigrant Market," *ABC News Univision*, November 16, 2012, http://abcnews.go.com/ABC_Univision/10-brands-capitalizing-latino-immigrant-market/story?id=17739431 (Accessed January 31, 2013).
15. "10 Expensive Luxury Smartphones that You'll Probably Never Own," *Phone Arena*, June 14, 2012, www.phonearena.com/news/10-expensive-luxury-smartphones-that-youll-probably-never-own_id31248#3-Tag-Heuer-Link (Accessed February 1, 2013).
16. "How to Apply: WIC Income Eligibility Guidelines 2012-2013," *USDA Food & Nutrition Service*, www.fns.usda.gov/wic/howtoapply/incomeguidelines12-13.htm (Accessed February 5, 2013).
17. "Global Luxury Goods Industry to Generate Additional US$74 Billion in New Sales by 2017," *MarketWatch*, September 13, 2012, www.marketwatch.com/story/global-luxury-goods-industry-to-generate-additional-us74-billion-in-new-sales-by-2017-2012-09-13-417315 (Accessed February 1, 2013).
18. "One of the World's Largest Clothing Retailers Is Warning about Cotton Price Inflation," *Business Insider*, March 29, 2012, www.businessinsider.com/hm-cotton-price-inflation-2012-3 (Accessed February 1, 2013).
19. "Reference Groups and Family," *McGraw-Hill Answers*, http://answers.mheducation.com/marketing/consumer-behavior/reference-groups-and-family#reference-group-influence (Accessed February 4, 2013).
20. Ibid.
21. Ulrich Orth and Lynn Kahle, "Intrapersonal Variation in Consumer Susceptibility to Normative Influence: Toward a Better Understanding of Brand Choice Decisions," *Journal of Social Psychology*, 148, no. 4, (2008): 429.
22. "Opinion Leaders: The Circle of Influence," *Washington Post*, www.washingtonpost.com/wp-adv/media_kit/wp/pdf/OpinionLeaderBook_MediaKit.pdf (Accessed February 4, 2013).
23. Joann Pan, "Parents to Online Advertisers: Stop Tracking Our Kids," *Mashable*, December 6, 2012, http://mashable.com/2012/12/06/tracking-children-online-coppa/ (Accessed February 4, 2013).
24. Rob Heidrick, "The Couple that Buys Together Decides Together," *Texas Enterprise*, May 3, 2012, www.texasenterprise.utexas.edu/article/couple-buys-together-decides-together (Accessed February 4, 2013).
25. Christian Kurz, "Consumer Insights: Nickelodeon's 'International GPS: Kids' Influence,'" *Viacom*, August 20, 2012, http://blog.viacom.com/2012/08/consumer-insights-nickelodeons-international-gps-kids-influence (Accessed February 4, 2013).
26. Ibid.

27. "Kids Increasingly Influencing Parents' Buying Decisions: Study," *The Indian Express*, December 6, 2013, www.indianexpress.com/news/kids-increasingly-influencing-parents-buying-decisions-study/1040940 (Accessed February 4, 2013).
28. Will Palley, "Gen Z: Digital in their DNA," *J. Walter Thompson Company*, www.jwtintelligence.com/wp-content/uploads/2012/04/F_INTERNAL_Gen_Z_0418122.pdf (Accessed February 4, 2013).
29. Karen Robinson-Jacobs, "Dr Pepper Expands Line of 10-Calorie Sodas," *The Dallas Morning News*, December 20, 2012, http://bizbeatblog.dallasnews.com/2012/12/dr-pepper-parent-expands-line-of-10-calorie-sodas.html/ (Accessed February 4, 2013).
30. Tricia Duryee, "Look, Men Shop Online, Too!" *All Things D*, May 2, 2012, http://allthingsd.com/20120502/look-men-shop-online-too/ (Accessed February 5, 2013).
31. Jessica Dickler, "Stay-at-home Dads: More Men Choosing Kids over Career," *CNN*, April 30, 2012, http://money.cnn.com/2012/04/30/pf/stay-at-home-dad/index.htm (Accessed February 5, 2013).
32. Courtney Reagan, "Why Men Are Outshopping Women Online," *USA Today*, May 5, 2012, http://usatoday30.usatoday.com/money/industries/retail/story/2012-05-05/cnbc-men-outshop-women-online/54778076/1 (Accessed February 5, 2013).
33. "B&N's Tablet Customer: Marketing to 'Julie,'" *Shelf Awareness*, March 20, 2012, www.shelf-awareness.com/issue.html?issue=1695 (Accessed April 18, 2012).
34. Abby Ellin, "Million Moms Rips JCPenney on Gay 'Culture War,'" *ABC*, May 3, 2012, http://abcnews.go.com/blogs/business/2012/05/million-moms-rips-jcpenney-on-gay-culture-war/ (Accessed February 5, 2013).
35. "Ampacet - Managing the Elements of Success," *Ampacet*, www.ampacet.com (Accessed April 18, 2012).
36. Sanjay Gupta, "TV Ads May Be Driving Children to Drink," *CNN*, January 29, 2013, http://thechart.blogs.cnn.com/2013/01/29/tv-ads-may-be-driving-children-to-drink/ (Accessed February 5, 2013).
37. Elizabeth Wilson, "Using the Dollar-metric Scale," in 1987 AMA Educator's Proceedings, ed. Susan Douglas et al. (Chicago, IL: American Marketing Association, 1987), 107.
38. Matthew Lynley, "Ouya Finds a Friend with Amazon," *Wall Street Journal*, February 5, 2013, http://blogs.wsj.com/digits/2013/02/05/ouya-finds-a-friend-with-amazon/ (Accessed February 5, 2013).
39. "Arby's and 8 Other Dramatic Rebranding Campaigns," *The Week*, October 2, 2012, http://theweek.com/article/slide/228241/spam-and-7-other-dramatic-rebranding-campaigns# (Accessed February 5, 2013).
40. Ibid.
41. Jyothi Datta, "Aspartame: Bitter Truth in Artificial Sweeteners?" *Business Line*, October 3, 2005, www.thehindubusinessline.com/2005/10/04/stories/2005100404220300.htm (Accessed April 18, 2012).

7

1. Brad Smith, "The Two Primary Goals of a Business Website," *FixCourse*, http://fixcourse.com/website-goals/ (Accessed February 5, 2013).
2. Michael D. Hutt and Thomas W. Speh, *Business Marketing Management: B2B*, 11th ed. (Cincinnati: Thomson, 2013), 4.
3. Ibid.
4. Christopher Hosford, "BtoB Study Shows Surge in Social Media Marketing," *BtoB*, May 14, 2012, p.1.
5. Ashley Zeckman, "Make the Most of Your Social Media Interactions: 9 Tips," *Search Engine Watch*, January 29, 2013, http://searchenginewatch.com/article/2239610/Make-the-Most-of-Your-Social-Media-Interactions-9-Tips (Accessed February 5, 2013).
6. TJ Raphael, "B-to-B Content Marketing Is Up, Despite Mixed Effectiveness," *Folio*, December 18, 2012, www.foliomag.com/2012/b-b-content-marketing-spend-despite-mixed-effectiveness (Accessed February 5, 2013).
7. "Make the Most of Your Social Media Interactions: 9 Tips."
8. "BtoB 2012 Social Media Marketing Awards," *BtoB Magazine*, www.btobonline.com/section/social-media-awards2012 (Accessed February 6, 2013).
9. "Top 10 B2B Websites," *TradeFord*, June 26, 2012, http://forum.tradeford.com/topic-354/top-10-b2b-websites.html (Accessed February 6, 2013).
10. Michelle Jones, "Apple Inc. (AAPL) Setting Itself Apart from Competitors," *ValueWalk*, February 4, 2013, www.valuewalk.com/2013/02/apple-inc-aapl-setting-itself-apart-from-competitors/ (Accessed February 6, 2013).
11. Sasthi Sarma, "Measuring Stickiness with Basic Google Analytics' Key Performance Indicators," *Position²*, June 3, 2010, http://blogs.position2.com/measuring-stickiness-with-basic-google-analytics-key-performance-indicators (Accessed February 6, 2013).
12. Jean Gianfagna, "Four Lessons Big Direct Marketers Can Learn from Small Mailers," *Smart Marketing Strategy*, May 24, 2011, www.gianfagnamarketing.com/blog/2011/05/24/4-lessons-big-direct-marketers-can-learn-from-small-mailers (Accessed May 21, 2012).
13. "Leading Brands Start Measuring Online Ad Performance with Revolutionary Nielsen Online Campaign Ratings as it Launches in UK," *Nielsen*, October 16, 2012, www.nielsen.com/us/en/insights/press-room/2012/leading-brands-measuring-online-ad-performance-with-nielsen-online-campaign-ratings-in-uk.html (Accessed February 6, 2013).
14. Chris Lee, "Why Online Marketing Is as Simple as Five-a-side Football," *Econsultancy*, February 1, 2013, http://econsultancy.com/us/blog/62018-why-online-marketing-is-as-simple-as-five-a-side-football (Accessed February 6, 2013).
15. "Emerging Trends in B-to-B Social Media Marketing: Insights from the Field," *BtoB*, April 2011, 6–9.
16. "The Best Repeat Business Practices," *eLocal.com*, March 8, 2012, www.elocal.com/content/home-expert-network/repeat-business-practices-2547 (Accessed February 6, 2013).
17. Daisuke Wakabayashi, "Softbank: In Strategic Alliance to Create PayPal Japan," *Wall Street Journal*, May 8, 2012, http://online.wsj.com/article/BT-CO-20120508-724913.html (Accessed May 21, 2012).
18. Ethan Smith, "Ticket Firm AEG, StubHub to Align," *Wall Street Journal*, November 12, 2012, B6.
19. "H&R Block Saluted for Partnership with Arizona Catholic Schools," *Ahwatukee Foothills News*, February 6, 2013, http://www.ahwatukee.com/money/article_bb3dc05e-6f26-11e2-b270-001a4bcf887a.html (Accessed February 6, 2013).
20. Robert M. Morgan and Shelby D. Hunt, "The Commitment-Trust Theory of Relationship Marketing," *Journal of Marketing*, 58, no. 3, 1994, 23.
21. Ibid.
22. Zach Bowman, "Suzuki Gets Legal with VW over Troubled Partnership," *Autoblog*, July 7, 2012, www.autoblog.com/2012/07/07/suzuki-gets-legal-with-vw-over-troubled-partnership (Accessed February 6, 2013).
23. Ibid.
24. Jamie Yap, "Maps, LBS Bolster Google Enterprise's Asia Roadmap," *ZDNet*, February 1, 2013, www.zdnet.com/maps-lbs-bolster-google-enterprises-asia-roadmap-7000010671/ (Accessed February 6, 2013).
25. "6 Steps to Doing Business with the Government," *Black Enterprise*, February 16, 2012, www.blackenterprise.com/small-business/6-steps-to-doing-business-with-the-government/ (Accessed February 6, 2013).
26. Hutt and Speh, 7.
27. Ibid.
28. Ibid.
29. Justin Scheck, "Timber Sales Cultivate Jobs," *Wall Street Journal*, August 13, 2012, A3.
30. Jon Hilkevitch, "CTA to Spend $2 Billion for 846 New Rail Cars," *Chicago Tribune*, February 6, 2013, www.chicagotribune.com/news/local/breaking/chi-cta-to-spend-2-billion-for-846-new-rail-cars-20130206,0,1482382.story (Accessed February 7, 2013).
31. Alan Levin and Susanna Ray, "Boeing 878 Dreamliner Is Grounded Worldwide by Regulators," *Bloomberg*, January 17, 2013, www.bloomberg.com/news/2013-01-16/boeing-787-dreamliner-fleet-grounded-by-u-s-after-emergency.html (Accessed February 7, 2013).
32. Hutt and Speh, 6.
33. "Exostar's Global Customer Base," Exostar, www.exostar.com/Exostar_Customers.aspx (Accessed May 21, 2012).
34. David Barboza, "Foxconn Plant Closed after Riot, Company Says," *New York Times*, September 24, 2012, www.nytimes.com/2012/09/25/technology/foxconn-plant-in-china-closed-after-worker-riot.html (Accessed February 7, 2013); "Foxconn Technology," *New York Times*, December 27, 2012, http://topics.nytimes.com/top/news/business/companies/foxconn_technology/index.html (Accessed February 7, 2013); "Foxconn's Plant Reopens, Says No Impact on Supply," *CNBC*, September 24, 2012, www.cnbc.com/id/49157143/Foxconn039s_Plant_Reopens_Says_No_Impact_on_Supply (Accessed February 7, 2013).
35. Cameron McWhirter, "Chinese Diapers Save U.S. Paper Mill," *Wall Street Journal*, August 13, 2012, B1.
36. Hutt and Speh, 52.
37. Ibid.
38. Nicholas Read, "How to Sell to the C-Suite," *Forbes*, May 8, 2010, www.*Forbes*.com/2010/05/08/selling-to-the-c-suite-entrepreneurs-sales-management-nicholas-read.html (Accessed February 7, 2013).
39. Ibid.
40. Hutt and Speh, 231.
41. Ibid.

8

1. Sue Shellenbarger, "American Dads Get into Gear," *Wall Street Journal*, February 6, 2013, http://blogs.wsj.com/juggle/2013/02/06/american-dads-get-into-gear (Accessed February 11, 2013).
2. Sarah Nassauer, "A Season [or 13] For Shopping," *Wall Street Journal*, August 17, 2011, D5.
3. Andrea Petersen, "Tots Invade Luxury Hotels," *Wall Street Journal*, July 26, 2012, D1.
4. "Teenage Consumer Spending Statistics," *Statistic Brain*, September 8, 2012, www.statisticbrain.com/teenage-consumer-spending-statistics (Accessed February 11, 2013).
5. Lauren Edwards, "Millennials Shape Adult Beverage Digital Marketing Efforts," August 21, 2012, http://blogs.technomic.com/millennials-shape-digital-marketing-efforts (Accessed February 11, 2013).
6. Aquino, Judith, "Gen Y: The Next Generation of Spenders," *Customer Relationship Management*, February 2012, 20–23.
7. Matt Townsend, Ashley Lutz, and Christopher Palmeri, "A Star Customer Falls Back to Earth," *Bloomberg Businessweek*, March 26–April 1, 2012, 19–20.
8. Charles S. Madden, "Three Generations and the Real Estate Marketer," *Baylor University*, www.baylor.edu/business/kellercenter/index.php?id=85849 (Accessed February 11, 2013).
9. Leonard Klie, "Gen X: Stuck in the Middle," *Customer Relationship Management*, February 2012, 24–29.
10. Lena Sin, "Dine Out Vancouver Cooks Up New Culinary Experience," *The Province*, January 17, 2013, www.theprovince.com/entertainment/Dine+Vancouver+cooks+culinary+experience/7822661/story.html (Accessed February 11, 2013).
11. Pamela Yip, "Baby Boomers Make a Plum Marketing Target," *Dallas News*, August 10, 2012, www.dallasnews.com/business/columnists/pamela-yip/20120810-baby-boomers-make-a-plum-marketing-target.ece (Accessed February 11, 2013).

12. Paul Hyman, "Baby Boomers: Every Silver Lining Has a Touch of Gray," *Customer Relationship Management*, February 2012, 30–34.

13. "Founder of Nestle-Acquired Company Joins Prismic Pharmaceuticals," *MarketWatch*, February 12, 2013, www.marketwatch.com/story/founder-of-nestle-acquired-company-joins-prismic-pharmaceuticals-2013-02-12 (Accessed February 12, 2013).

14. S. E. Smith, "What Is the Silent Generation?" *wiseGEEK*, January 23, 2013, www.wisegeek.com/what-is-the-silent-generation.htm (Accessed February 12, 2013).

15. Ibid.

16. Stephen M. Golant, "Aging in the American Suburbs: A Changing Population," *AgingWell*, www.agingwellmag.com/news/ex_06309_01.shtml (Accessed February 12, 2013).

17. Lauren Stiller Rikleen, "Not Buying Offensive Super Bowl Ads," *Boston Globe*, February 4, 2013, http://bostonglobe.com/opinion/2013/02/04/not-buying-offensive-super-bowl-ads/1eNEMBDxLyLWFnHS7jKI2I/story.html (Accessed February 12, 2013).

18. Ruthie Ackerman, "Clients from Venus," *Wall Street Journal*, April 30, 2012, http://online.wsj.com/article/SB10001424059702041905045770404020069714264 (Accessed February 12, 2013.

19. Robert Klara, "Perspective: A Whole Different Hog," *Adweek*, July 26, 2012, www.adweek.com/news/advertising-branding/perspective-whole-different-hog-142058 (Accessed February 12, 2013.

20. Rosemary Feitelberg, "Russell Simmons to Launch Yoga Brand Tantris," *Women's Wear Daily*, March 29, 2012, www.wwd.com/markets-news/intimates-activewear/russell-simmons-to-launch-tantris-brand-5835915 (Accessed April 18, 2012).

21. Emma Lacey-Bordeaux and Gavin Godfrey, "Dieting Companies Now Targeting Men," *CNN*, March 23, 2012, www.cnn.com/2012/03/23/health/beauty-dieting-men (Accessed February 12, 2013).

22. Barbara Thau, "Why Dollar Stores Are Hotter than Ever (Even among the Rich)," *DailyFinance*, January 7, 2012, www.dailyfinance.com/2012/01/07/why-dollar-stores-are-hotter-than-ever-even-among-the-rich (Accessed February 12, 2013).

23. Erin Shea, "How Luxury Retailers Can Take On Showrooming Threat," *Luxury Daily*, January 29, 2013, www.luxurydaily.com/how-luxury-retailers-can-take-on-threat-of-showrooming (Accessed February 12, 2013).

24. Eric Bellman, "Multinationals Market to the Poor," *Wall Street Journal*, July 24, 2012, B8.

25. Breanne L. Heldman, "Adam Levine and Nicki Minaj Designing Clothes for Kmart," *Yahoo!*, January 15, 2013, http://omg.yahoo.com/blogs/celeb-news/adam-levine-nicki-minaj-designing-clothes-kmart-194136723.html (Accessed February 12, 2013).

26. "Fashion Fair Cosmetics Introduces Its First Makeup Collection from Legendary Makeup Artist Sam Fine," January 11, 2013, *Yahoo!*, http://finance.yahoo.com/news/fashion-fair-cosmetics-introduces-first-211900575.html (Accessed February 12, 2013).

27. Katherine Rosman, "Big Marketers on Campus," *Wall Street Journal*, April 4, 2012, http://online.wsj.com/article/SB10001424052702303816504577321594090033560.html (Accessed February 12, 2013).

28. Emily Steel, "Exploring Ways to Build a Better Consumer Profile," *Wall Street Journal*, March 15, 2010, http://online.wsj.com/article/SB10001424052748703447104575117972284656374.html (Accessed April 18, 2012).

29. Julie Jargon, "Starbuck's Gives Single-Serve a Shot," *Wall Street Journal*, September 20, 2012, B9, B10.

30. Joseph F. Kovar, "Actfio Looks to Simplify Storage Product Line, Channel Program," *CRN*, February 1, 2013, www.crn.com/news/storage/240147697/actifio-looks-to-simplify-storage-product-line-channel-program.htm (Accessed February 12, 2013).

31. Kasey Wehrum, "Comic Books for Entrepreneurs," *Inc.*, May 2011, www.inc.com/magazine/20110501/comic-books-for-entrepreneurs.html (Accessed April 18, 2012).

32. Eric Wilson, "Social Shopping: Everybody Wants In," *New York Times*, March 25, 2012, www.nytimes.com/imagepages/2012/03/25/fashion/25SOCIALSHOP_GRAPHIC.html (Accessed April 18, 2012).

33. Yannick Lejacq, "Nintendo's Wii U Aims to Court Casual and Hardcore Gamers," *Wall Street Journal*, November 18, 2012, http://blogs.wsj.com/speakeasy/2012/11/18/nintendos-wii-u-aims-to-court-casual-and-hardcore-gamers (Accessed February 13, 2013).

34. Janice Bitters, "Mpls. To Expand Car Sharing," *Minnesota Daily*, February 13, 2013, www.mndaily.com/2013/02/13/mpls-expand-car-sharing (Accessed February 13, 2013).

35. Erik Sherman, "Is iPad Mini Cannibalizing its Bigger Sibling?" *CBS*, January 18, 2013, www.cbsnews.com/8301-505124_162-57564708/is-ipad-mini-cannibalizing-its-bigger-sibling (Accessed February 13, 2013).

36. Josh Constine, "Facebook Lets Businesses Plug In CRM Email Addresses to Target Customers with Hyper-Relevant Ads," *TechCrunch*, September 20, 2012, http://techcrunch.com/2012/09/20/facebook-crm-ads/ (Accessed February 13, 2013).

37. "All Brands," *Coca-Cola*, www.thecoca-colacompany.com/brands/brandlist.html (Accessed February 13, 2013).

38. Jeanine Poggi, "Can Esquire's Brand Make a TV Channel a Hit?" *AdAge*, http://adage.com/article/media/nbc-universal-rebrands-g4-esquire-network/239727/ (Accessed February 13, 2013).

39. "Nutrition Guide," *Kentucky Fried Chicken*, January 22, 2013, www.kfc.com/nutrition/pdf/kfc_nutrition.pdf (Accessed February 13, 2013).

40. "Our Brands," *Gap Inc.*, www.gapinc.com/content/gapinc/html/aboutus/ourbrands.html (Accessed April 18, 2012).

41. Lara O'Reilly, "Vertu Shifts from Bling to Emotional Positioning," *MarketingWeek*, February 12, 2013, www.marketingweek.co.uk/news/vertu-shifts-from-bling-to-emotional-positioning/4005671.article (Accessed February 13, 2013).

42. "Timex to Reposition Brand as Fashion Accessory," *WatchPro*, May 25, 2012, www.watchpro.com/13495-timex-to-reposition-brand-as-fashion-accessory/ (Accessed February 13, 2013).

9

1. "MCommerce Satisfaction Is Best Achieved by Amazon," *Mobile Commerce News*, February 13, 2013, www.qrcodepress.com/mcommerce-satisfaction-is-best-achieved-by-amazon/8517102 (Accessed February 15, 2013).

2. Luigi Lugmayr, "75% of Consumers Would Buy an Alternative Fuel Car Next Says Consumer Reports Survey," *I4U News*, May 22, 2012, www.i4u.com/50608/75-consumers-would-buy-alternative-fuel-car-next-says-consumer-reports-survey#full_story (Accessed February 15, 2013).

3. Emily Glazer, Ellen Byron, Dennis K. Berman, and Joann S. Lublin, "P&G's Stumbles Put CEO on Hot Seat for Turnaround," *Wall Street Journal*, September 27, 2012, http://online.wsj.com/article/SB10000872396390444813104578016191845779524.html (Accessed February 15, 2013).

4. Tim Lynch, "FocusVision Releases 15th Annual Focus Group Index," *PRWeb*, May 18, 2012, www.prweb.com/releases/2012/5/prweb9497403.htm (Accessed February 15, 2013).

5. "From Details to Desires: The Power of Big Data," IBM advertisement, *Fortune*, October 8, 2012, 79.

6. "Big Data – What Is It?" *SAS Institute*, www.sas.com/big-data/index.html?gclid=CIy5rOyy4rICFVGd4AodqSAAyA (Accessed February 15, 2013).

7. "Facebook Sells More Access to Members," *Wall Street Journal*, October 2, 2012, B1, B7.

8. Erik Milster, "The Coalition for Innovative Media Measurement Completes Consumer Survey Phase of Its 'USA TouchPoints' Cross-Media Research Study," *CIMM*, June 14, 2011, http://cimmusorg.startlogic.com/the-coalition-for-innovative-media-measurement-completes-consumer-survey-phase-of-its-usa-touchpoints-cross-media-research-study/ (Accessed February 15, 2013).

9. Raymond R. Burke, "Virtual Shopping: Breakthrough in Marketing Research," *Harvard Business Review*, March/April 1996, 120–131; Valla Roth, "Winning at Retail with Virtual Shopping Research," *Quirk's Marketing Research Review*, June 2011, 46.

10. "New Products," *USDA Economic Research Service*, February 6, 2013, www.ers.usda.gov/topics/food-markets-prices/processing-marketing/new-products.aspx (Accessed February 15, 2013).

11. Richard Rizzo, "Virtual Shopping Research Beyond CPG and Retail," *Vision Critical*, October 21, 2012, www.visioncritical.com/blog/virtual-shopping-research-beyond-cpg-and-retail (Accessed February 15, 2013).

12. Leslie Townsend, "Flowing with the Mainstream" *Quirk's Marketing Research Review,* July 2012, 36-41.

13. Ibid.

14. Emily Goon, "Animated Responses," *Quirk's Marketing Research Review,* July 2012, 32–35.

15. "Internet Users in the World Distribution by World Regions – 2012 Q2," *Internet World Stats,* January 17, 2013, www.internetworld stats.com/stats.htm (Accessed February 15, 2013).

16. "Internet Users in North America," *Internet World Stats,* December 16, 2012, www .internetworldstats.com/stats14.htm (Accessed February 15, 2013).

17. Conversation with Roger Gates, President of DSS Marketing Research, October 3, 2012.

10

1. Karen Weise, "Patagonia Swims Upstream with New Salmon Jerky," *Bloomberg Businessweek,* April 11, 2012, www.business week.com/articles/2012-04-11/patagonia -swims-upstream-with-new-salmon-jerky (Accessed March 4, 2013).

2. Ray Smith, "For Men, New Swimsuits with Drawstrings and Dignity," *Wall Street Journal,* April 11, 2012, http://online.wsj.com /article/SB1000142405270230444460457 7337750372504374.html (Accessed March 4, 2013).

3. Keach Hagey, "Rebuilding Playboy: Less Smut, More Money," *Wall Street Journal,* February 20, 2013, http://online.wsj.com /article/SB1000142412788732443200457 8304102041831988.html (Accessed March 4, 2013).

4. Bruce Einhorn and Ashlee Vance, "HTC Pins Its Hopes on Music and Software," *Bloomberg Businessweek,* April 5, 2012, www.businessweek.com/articles/2012-04 -05/htc-pins-its-hopes-on-music-and -software (Accessed March 4, 2013).

5. Elaine Watson, "General Mills: Our Greek Yogurt Sales Are Significantly Outpacing Growth of the Segment," *FoodNavigator USA,* February 19, 2013, www.foodnavigator-usa.com/Business /General-Mills-Our-Greek-yogurt-sales -are-significantly-outpacing-growth-of-the -segment (Accessed March 4, 2013); "Yoplait Product List," *General Mills,* www .generalmills.com/Home/Brands/Yogurt /Yoplait/Brand%20Product%20List%20 Page.aspx (Accessed March 4, 2013).

6. Sam Laird, "Yahoo Killing Message Boards Site and Other Products," *Mashable,* March 2, 2013, http://mashable.com/2013/03/01 /yahoo-kills-properties (Accessed March 4, 2013).

7. Ashraf Eassa, "Google Stole Apple's Mojo," *Seeking Alpha,* March 3, 2013, http:// seekingalpha.com/article/1242371-google -stole-apple-s-mojo (Accessed March 4, 2013); Darcy Travlos, "Is Apple Losing Its Brand Equity?" *Forbes,* January 19, 2013, www.*Forbes*.com/sites/darcytravlos /2013/01/19/is-apple-losing-its-brand-equity (Accessed March 4, 2013).

8. Pat Reynolds, "Shoppers Believe Private Label = National Brands in Different Packaging," *Packaging World,* February 26, 2013, www.packworld.com/venue/private-label /shoppers-believe-private-label-national -brands-different-packaging (Accessed March 5, 2013).

9. Hannah Karp, "Store Brands Step Up Their Game," *Wall Street Journal,* January 31, 2012, B1–B2.

10. Ibid.

11. "Brands & Products: Brand Browser," *Church & Dwight,* www.churchdwight.com /brands-and-products/brand-browser.aspx (Accessed March 5, 2013).

12. Robin Sidel, "Prepaid Enters Mainstream," *Wall Street Journal,* October 9, 2012, C1, C2.

13. Anthony Garreffa, "ASUS Co-branded the Nexus 7 to Increase Brand Value," *TweakTown,* July 2, 2012, www.tweaktown .com/news/24762/asus_co_branded_the _nexus_7_to_increase_brand_value/index .html (Accessed March 5, 2013).

14. T. Thompson, "What Is the Difference between a Copyright, Trademark, and Patent?" *WiseGEEK,* February 9, 2013, www.wisegeek.com/what-is-the-difference -between-a-copyright-trademark-and-patent .htm (Accessed March 5, 2013).

15. Edward Wyatt, "F.C.C. Backs Consumers in Unlocking of Cellphones," *New York Times,* March 4, 2013, www.nytimes .com/2013/03/05/technology/fcc-urges-a -right-to-unlock-cellphones.html (Accessed March 5, 2013).

16. Monte Burke, "Under Armour Files Lawsuit against Nike for Trademark Infringement," *Forbes,* February 21, 2013, www.*Forbes* .com/sites/monteburke/2013/02/21/under -armour-files-lawsuit-against-nike-for -trademark-infringement (Accessed March 5, 2013).

17. "Bridgestone Wins Trademark Infringement Lawsuit against Chinese Manufacturer," *Bridgestone,* February 1, 2013, www .bridgestone.com/corporate/news/2013 020101.html (Accessed March 5, 2013); Michael C. Dorf, "A Federal Appeals Court Upholds Louboutin's Trademark for Red-Soled Shoes," *Justia,* September 12, 2012, http://verdict.justia.com/2012/09/12/a -federal-appeals-court-upholds-louboutins -trademark-for-red-soled-shoes (Accessed March 2, 2013).

18. Steven Lee Lewis, "11 Ridiculous Fast Food Chain Ripoffs in China," *Very Nanchang,* August 25, 2012, http://verynanchang.com /forum/topics/11-ridiculous-fast-food-chain -ripoffs-in-china (Accessed March 5, 2013).

19. Lisa McTigue Pierce, "GE Brings Good Packaging Design to Light," *Packaging Digest,* April 11, 2012, www.packagingdigest .com/article/521468-GE_brings_good _packaging_design_to_light.php (Accessed April 18, 2012).

20. Gemma Charles, "Brotyhers Cider Unveils Premium Packaging," *Marketing,* February 28, 2013, www.marketingmagazine.co.uk /news/1172938/Brothers-Cider-unveils-new -premium-packaging (Accessed March 5, 2013).

21. Rebecca J. Rosen, "Plastic Clamshell Packaging Is the Worst," *The Atlantic,* May 31, 2012, www.theatlantic.com/technology /archive/2012/05/plastic-clamshell -packaging-is-the-worst/257936 (Accessed March 5, 2013).

22. Rieva Lesonsky, "Do Consumers Care about Buying Green?" *Grow Smart Biz,* July 18, 2012, www.networksolutions.com /smallbusiness/2012/07/do-consumers -care-about-buying-green (Accessed March 5, 2013).

23. Adele Peters, "The Disappearing Package: From Dissolving Wrappers to Products that Package Themselves," *GOOD,* January 31, 2013, www.good.is/posts/the-disappearing -package-from-dissolving-wrappers-to -products-that-package-themselves (Accessed March 5, 2013).

24. "New Packaging to Monitor Food Freshness," *Health24,* February 28, 2013, www.health24.com/Diet-and-nutrition /News/New-packaging-to-monitor-food -freshness-20130228 (Accessed March 5, 2013).

25. "About Green Seal," *Green Seal,* www .greenseal.org/AboutGreenSeal.aspx (Accessed March 5, 2013).

11

1. "The World's 50 Most Innovative Companies," *Fast Company,* March 2012, 70–149.

2. "At P&G, the Innovation Well Runs Dry," *Bloomberg Businessweek,* September 10–16, 2012, 23–26.

3. Ibid.

4. Jon Ostrower, "777 Makeover Agitates Boeing," *Wall Street Journal,* September 24, 2012, B1.

5. Amar Toor. "Has the Transparent Smartphone Finally Arrived?" *The Verge,* February 15, 2013, www.theverge .com/2013/2/15/3966950/will-we-see-a -transparent-phone-polytron-prototype -display (Accessed February 18, 2013).

6. "Moleskine World," *Moleskine,* www .moleskine.com/moleskine_world (Accessed April 19, 2012).

7. Ben Popken, "Taco Bell's Cool Ranch Tacos: Co-branding Genius," *Today,* January 10, 2013, http://lifeinc.today.com /_news/2013/01/10/16430586-taco-bells -cool-ranch-tacos-co-branding-genius (Accessed February 18, 2013).

8. "At P&G, the Innovation Well Runs Dry," 23–26

9. Mike Ramsey, "Old Mustang Is Put Out to Pasture", *Wall Street Journal,* April 16, 2012, B1

10. "John Deere Designs 655K Crawler Loader with Customer Input," *SitePrep,* October 30, 2012, www.siteprepmag.com/Articles /Products/2012/10/30/John-Deere-Designs -655K-Crawler-Loader-with-Customer-Input (Accessed February 18, 2013).

11. Rachel Emma Silverman, "For Bright Ideas, Ask the Staff," *Wall Street Journal,* October 17, 2011, B7.

12. Ibid.

13. Brad Farris, "Leaders Encourage Risk Taking, Innovation," *EnMast,* December 10, 2012, www.enmast.com/2012/12 /leaders-encourage-risk-innovation/ (Accessed February 18, 2013).

14. "Fuld & Company Is the World's Preeminent Research and Consulting Firm in the Field of

Competitive Intelligence," *Fuld & Company*, www.fuld.com/company (Accessed February 18, 2013).

15. Kim Bhasin, "Nike Has Gone All-in on its Game-changing Flyknit Racer," *Business Insider*, February 14, 2013, www .businessinsider.com/nike-has-gone-all-in -on-its-game-changing-flyknit-racer-2013-2 (Accessed February 18, 2013).

16. Ray A. Smith, "Can New Products and Techniques Make Sharing Better? Calling Out the Myths," *Wall Street Journal*, August 29, 2012, D1, D3.

17. "Company Profile," *Continuum*, http:// continuuminnovation.com/about/company -profile (Accessed February 18, 2013).

18. James R. Hagerty, "Tapping Crowds for Military Design," *Wall Street Journal*, August 17, 2012, A3.

19. Ibid.

20. Andrew Marton, "2006: A Face Odyssey," *Fort Worth Star-Telegram*, February 16, 2006, E1, E8.

21. "Can New Products and Techniques Make Sharing Better? Calling Out the Myths."

22. Michael D. Hutt and Thomas W. Speh, *Business Marketing Management*, 11th ed. (Cincinnati: Cengage Learning, 2013), p. 155.

23. "About Ryz," *RYZ*, www.ryz.com/about (Accessed February 18, 2013); "Threadless Graphic T-shirt Designs," *Threadless*, www .threadless.com (Accessed February 18, 2013).

24. "Adventures in Test Marketing," *CBS News*, March 25, 2012, www.cbsnews.com/video /watch/?id=7403144n (Accessed February 18, 2013).

25. John Reid Blackwell, "Altria to Test Market New Nicotine Product in Virginia," *Richmond Times-Dispatch*, May 23, 2012, www .timesdispatch.com/business/altria-to-test -market-new-nicotine-product-in-virginia /article_9b138a72-7d9c-5668-8266 -656f0ad5cf35.html (Accessed February 18, 2013).

26. "P&G Everyday," *Procter & Gamble*, www .pgeveryday.com/pgeds/index.jsp (Accessed February 18, 2013).

27. Copernicus Marketing Consulting and Research, "Top 10 Reasons for New Product Failure," *GreenBook*, www.greenbook.org /marketing-research.cfm/top-10-reasons -for-new-product-failure (Accessed February 18, 2013).

28. "Major Product Flops in 2012," *Yahoo!*, http://finance.yahoo.com/news/major -product-flops-in-2012.html (Accessed February 18, 2013).

29. Alex Pigliucci, "Wealth Management for China's Richest: An Industry with a Great Future," *Forbes*, January 28, 2013, www .Forbes.com/sites/Forbesleadershipforum /2013/01/28/wealth-management-for-chinas -richest-an-industry-with-a-great-future/ (Accessed February 18, 2013).

30. Marisa Grimes, "Nielsen: Global Consumers' Trust in 'Earned' Advertising Grows in Importance," *Nielsen*, April 10, 2012, www .nielsen.com/us/en/insights/press-room/2012 /nielsen-global-consumers-trust-in-earned -advertising-grows.html (Accessed February 18, 2013).

31. Ibid.

32. Mercedes Cardona, "Word-of-mouth Drives Teen Conversations," *Direct Marketing News*, July 1, 2012, www.dmnews.com /word-of-mouth-drives-teen-conversions /article/247170 (Accessed February 19, 2013).

33. Ibid.

34. "Women's Influence on Purchase Decisions on the Rise," *eMarketer*, February 1, 2012, www.emarketer.com/Articles/Print.aspx ?R=1008807 (Accessed February 19, 2013).

35. Tracey E. Schelmetic, "32 Percent of Customers Share Customer Service Experiences via Social Media," *LiveOps*, November 20, 2012, http://news.liveops.com/articles /share/48294/ (Accessed February 19, 2013).

36. David Moin, "Madewell Ready for Ramp Up," *Women's Wear Daily*, April 13, 2012, 1, 8.

37. David Goldman, "Are Landlines Doomed?" *CNN Money*, April 10, 2012, http://money .cnn.com/2012/04/10/technology/att -verizon-landlines/index.htm (Accessed February 19, 2013).

12

1. "Revenue Grew in Most Service Sectors in 2011, Census Bureau Reports," *United States Census Bureau*, January 29, 2013, www .census.gov/newsroom/releases/archives /service_industries/cb13-18.html (Accessed March 5, 2013); "Services," *Office of the United States Trade Representative*, www .ustr.gov/trade-topics/services-investment /services (Accessed March 5, 2013).

2. Andrea Petersen, "Checking In? Hidden Ways Hotels Court Guests Faster," *Wall Street Journal*, April 11, 2012, http://online .wsj.com/article/SB1000142405270230435 6604577337671375500872.html (Accessed March 6, 2013).

3. "Top 10 IT Certifications for IT Professionals in 2013," *Certification Camps*, January 22, 2013, www.certificationcamps.com/blog /index.php/microsoft-certification/top-10 -it-certifications-of-2013 (Accessed March 6, 2013).

4. Dwayne Gremler, Mary Jo Bitner and Valarie Zeithaml, *Services Marketing* (New York: McGraw-Hill, 2012).

5. Ibid.

6. Simon Dumenco, "Venti, Venti Annoying: So How Does Starbucks Misspell Your Name?" *Ad Age*, March 5, 2013, http://adage.com /article/the-media-guy/starbucks-pop-song -head/240104 (Accessed March 6, 2013).

7. Jim Harger, "New App Lets Fifth Third Bank Customers Deposit Checks via their Smartphones," *Michigan Live*, February 7, 2013, www.mlive.com/business/west-michigan /index.ssf/2013/02/new_app_lets_fifth_third _bank.html (Accessed March 6, 2013).

8. Karen Aho, "2012 Customer Service Hall of Fame," *MSN*, http://money.msn.com /investing/2012-customer-service-hall-of -fame-1 (Accessed March 6, 2013).

9. Much of the material in this section is based on Christopher H. Lovelock and Jochen Wirtz, *Services Marketing*, 7th ed. (Upper Saddle River, NJ: Prentice Hall, 2010).

10. Frank T. Piller, "Interview: Glubal: A Configurator for University-level Education to Solve the Complexity of Choice of Study Programs," *Mass Customization & Open Innovation News*, September 28, 2012, http:// mass-customization.de/service _customization, September 28, 2012 (Accessed March 5, 2013).

11. Florence Fabricant, "Kitchit, for Chef-Made Meals at Home," *New York Times*, May 7, 2012, http://dinersjournal.blogs.nytimes .com/2012/05/07/kitchit-for-chef-made -meals-at-home (Accessed March 6, 2013).

12. Lovelock and Wirtz, *Services Marketing*.

13. Ibid.

14. Much of the material in this section is based on Leonard L. Berry and A. Parasuraman, *Marketing Services* (New York: Free Press, 1991), 132–150.

15. Petersen, "Checking In?"

16. "100 Best Companies to Work For," *CNN*, http://money.cnn.com/magazines/fortune /best-companies (Accessed March 5, 2013).

13

1. James Murray, "Ford Focus Electric will Use 'Build-to-order' Sales Model," *The Guardian*, March 29, 2012, www.guardian .co.uk/environment/2012/mar/29/ford-focus -electric-dell-build (Accessed February 20, 2013).

2. Heather Clancy, "Kimberly-Clark Makes Sense of Demand," *Consumer Goods Technology*, October 11, 2012, http://consumer goods.edgl.com/case-studies/Kimberly-Clark -Makes-Sense-of-Demand82520 (Accessed February 20, 2013).

3. Chad W. Autry, "Balancing Demand and Supply in a Rapidly Changing World," *Logistics Management*, February 23, 2012, www.logisticsmgmt.com/view/balancing _demand_and_supply_in_a_rapidly _changing_world/education (Accessed February 20, 2013).

4. Much of this section is based on material adapted from Donald J. Bowersox, David J. Closs, and Theodore P. Stank, *21st Century Logistics: Making Supply Chain Integration a Reality* (Oak Brook, IL: Council of Logistics Management, 1999).

5. "Häagen-Dazs and General Mills to Help Smallholder Vanilla Farmers Increase Yields and Improve Sustainability Practices in Madagascar," *CSRwire*, February 20, 2013, www.csrwire.com/press_releases/35228 -H-agen-Dazs-and-General-Mills-to-Help -Smallholder-Vanilla-Farmers-Increase -Yields-and-Improve-Sustainability -Practices-in-Madagascar (Accessed February 20, 2013).

6. Much of this and the following sections is based on material adapted from the edited volume Douglas M. Lambert, ed., *Supply Chain Management: Processes, Partnerships, Performance* (Sarasota, FL: Supply Chain Management Institute, 2004).

7. "C.H. Briggs Builds a Better Relationship with its Customers," *IBM*, October 16, 2012, www-01.ibm.com/software/success /cssdb.nsf/CS/STRD-8YWGWZ (Accessed February 20, 2013).

8. James A. Cooke, "Inside Dell's Global Command Centers," *DC Velocity*, September 24, 2012, www.dcvelocity.com

/articles/20120924-inside-dells-global -command-centers (Accessed February 20, 2013).

9. "Nissan: Planning for Quality and Productivity," *The Times 100*, www .thetimes100.co.uk/downloads/nissan /nissan_9_full.pdf (Accessed February 20, 2013).

10. John Letzing, "Amazon Adds That Robotic Touch," *Wall Street Journal*, March 20, 2012, http://online.wsj.com/article/SB10001 4240527023047244045772919032447962 14.html (Accessed April 24, 2012).

11. Yasuhiro Monden, *Toyota Production System, An Integrated Approach to Just-In-Time*, 3rd ed. (Norcross, GA: Engineering & Management Press, 1998).

12. Justin Brown, "4 Steps to Rebuilding Customer-Supplier Relationships," *Supply Chain Quarterly*, February 20, 2013, www.supplychainquarterly.com/topics /Procurement/scq201003supplier/ (Accessed February 20, 2013).

13. Kenneth J. Petersen, Robert Handfield, and Gary Ragatz, "Supplier Integration into New Product Development: Coordinating Product, Process, and Supply Chain Design," *Journal of Operations Management*, 23, no. 3–4, (2005): 371–388.

14. Curtis Greve and Jerry Davis, "Recovering Lost Profits by Improving Reverse Logistics," *UPS*, www.ups.com/media/en/Reverse _Logistics_wp.pdf (Accessed February 20, 2013).

15. "RFID News: JC Penney CEO says Retailer Going All In on RFID, Perhaps with Significant Impact on Industry," *Supply Chain Digest*, August 15, 2012, www .scdigest.com/ontarget/12-08-15-1 .php?cid=6106&ctype=content (Accessed February 20, 2013).

16. Claire Swedburg, "American Apparel Adopting RFID at Every Store," *RFID Journal*, February 8, 2012, www.rfidjournal .com/article/view/9202 (Accessed February 20, 2013).

17. Suzanne Marques, "Fit Like a Glove: Levi's Making Customized Jeans for a Reasonable Price," *CBS*, March 29, 2012, http:// losangeles.cbslocal.com/2012/03/29/fit-like -a-glove-levis-now-makes-customized -jeans-for-reasonable-price/ (Accessed February 20, 2013).

18. Thomas J. Goldsby, Stanley E. Griffis, and Anthony S. Roath, "Modeling Lean, Agile, and Leagile Supply Chain Strategies," *Journal of Business Logistics*, 27, no. 1, (2006): 57–80.

19. "PepsiCo's CEO Discusses Q4 2012 Results – Earnings Call Transcript," *Seeking Alpha*, February 14, 2013, http://seekingalpha.com /article/1183771-pepsico-s-ceo-discusses -q4-2012-results-earnings-call-transcript (Accessed February 20, 2013).

20. "DollarTree's CEO Discusses Q3 2012 Results – Earnings Call Transcript," *Seeking Alpha*, November 15, 2012, http:// seekingalpha.com/article/1010791-dollar -tree-s-ceo-discusses-q3-2012-results -earnings-call-transcript (Accessed February 20, 2013).

21. William Kremer, "How Much Bigger Can Container Ships Get?" *BBC*, February 18,

2013, www.bbc.co.uk/news/magazine -21432226 (Accessed February 20, 2013).

22. UPS, "Logistics of Sustainability," *Compass*, Spring 2012, 10.

23. Steve Szilagyi, keynote address, *Warehousing Education and Research Council* Annual Conference, Atlanta GA, May 2012.

24. Martin Christopher, *Logistics and Supply Chain Management*, 4th ed. (New York: Prentice Hall/Financial Times, 2010).

25. Kate Vitasek, "10 Essentials of a Vested Outsourcing Agreement," *Global Delivery Report*, September 19, 2012, http:// globaldeliveryreport.com/10-essentials-of -a-vested-outsourcing-agreement (Accessed February 20, 2013).

26. Dinah Wisenberg Brin, "Need Technology Experts? Try Rural America," *CNBC*, February 20, 2013, www.cnbc.com/id/100470457 (Accessed February 20, 2013).

27. Chang-Ran Kim, "Toyota Says Supply Chain Will Be Ready by Autumn for Next Quake," *Reuters*, March 2, 2012, http://uk.reuters .com/article/2012/03/02/uk-toyota-supply -chain-idUKTRE8210BW20120302 (Accessed February 20, 2013).

28. "Printing Titanium Bicycle Parts. A Charge Bikes Collaboration with EADS," *Vimeo*, August 14, 2012, http://vimeo .com/47522348 (Accessed February 21, 2013).

29. Ibid.

14

1. Eric Savitz, "Apple Screens for iPad3 in Short Supply," *Forbes*, March 1, 2012, 9.

2. James Hagerty, "Whirlpool Expands in China," *Wall Street Journal*, March 20, 2012, B4.

3. Anna Ringstrom and Veronica Ek, "Fashion Retailer H&M Aims to Set Up Shop in India," *Reuters*, February 19, 2013, http:// in.reuters.com/article/2013/02/19/hm-india -idINDEE91I06420130219 (Accessed February 22, 2013).

4. Jason Busch, "Amazon: A Supply Chain Look Beyond the Numbers," *Spend Matters*, February 5, 2013, http://spendmatters .com/2013/02/05/amazon-a-supply-chain -look-beyond-the-numbers (Accessed February 22, 2013).

5. John Cassidy, "Six Reasons to Discount the G.D.P. Shocker," *New Yorker*, January 30, 2013, www.newyorker.com/online /blogs/johncassidy/2013/01/six-reasons-to -discount-the-gdp-shocker.html (Accessed February 22, 2013).

6. "Retail Job Growth," *National Retail Federation*, www.nrf.com/modules .php?name=Pages&sp_id=1243#3 (Accessed February 22, 2013).

7. C. Brett Lockard and Michael Wolf, "Occupational Employment Projections to 2020," *Bureau of Labor Statistics Monthly Labor Review*, 135, no. 1, (2012): 84–108.

8. "Retail Firms by Employment Size," *National Retail Federation*, www.nrf .com/modules.php?name=Pages&sp _id=1252 (Accessed February 22, 2013).

9. "In the Wake of Sandy Hook Shooting, a Rush on Guns and Armored Backpacks," *Al.com*, December 20, 2012, http://blog

.al.com/wire/2012/12/after_sandy_hook _shooting_a_ru.html (Accessed February 22, 2013); Melissa Herbert, "Poll: Dick's, Walmart Halt Gun Sales after Sandy Hook Shootings," *Westlake Patch*, December 18, 2012, http://westlake.patch.com/articles /poll-dick-s-walmart-halt-guns-sales-after -sandy-hook-shootings (Accessed February 22, 2013).

10. "Man Cave – Home Parties for Men," *Man Cave*, www.mancaveworldwide.com (Accessed February 22, 2013).

11. "Telemarketing in the 21st Century," *BusinessTM*, http://businesstm.com/home -based/telemarketing-in-the-21st-century .html (Accessed February 22, 2013).

12. "DMA Releases New 'Power of Direct' Report; DM-Driven Sales Growth Outpace Overall Economic Growth," *Direct Marketing Association*, October 2, 2011, www .the-dma.org/cgi/dispannouncements ?article=1590 (Accessed February 22, 2013).

13. Stu Woo, "Online-retail Spending at $200 Billion Annually and Growing," *Wall Street Journal*, February 27, 2012, http://blogs .wsj.com/digits/2012/02/27/online-retail -spending-at-200-billion-annually-and -growing/ (Accessed February 22, 2013).

14. Tracy Stapp, "Top 10 New Franchises," *Entrepreneur*, February 19, 2013, www .entrepreneur.com/article/225830 (Accessed February 22, 2013).

15. Ina Jaffe, "Baby Boomers Return to the Multiplex, and Hollywood Notices," *NPR*, February 21, 2013, www.npr .org/2013/02/21/172605098/baby-boomers -return-to-the-multiplex-and-hollywood -notices (Accessed February 23, 2013).

16. "NYC Gets First Natural Gas–powered Food Truck," *Wall Street Journal*, February 21, 2013, http://online.wsj.com/article /APc93d8df0454e4e88b836a9dd802f4708 .html (Accessed February 22, 2013).

17. Tiffany Hsu, "Toys R Us to Open Holiday Pop-up Shops in Macy's," *Los Angeles Times*, October 10, 2012, www.latimes.com /business/money/la-fi-mo-toys-r-us-holiday -popup-macys-20121010,0,5423349.story (Accessed February 22, 2013).

18. Louis Bedigian, "Amazon's Lockers Coming to Staples," *Forbes*, November 7, 2012, www.Forbes.com/sites/benzingainsights /2012/11/07/amazons-lockers-coming-to -staples (Accessed February 22, 2013).

19. Grant Arnott, "eBay Opens QR Code Store on London High Street," *Power Retail*, November 18, 2012, www.powerretail .com.au/news/ebay-opens-qr-code-store -on-london-high-street (Accessed February 22, 2013).

20. "Industry Statistics," *Digsby*, www.digby .com/mobile-statistics (Accessed February 22, 2013).

21. Joanna Brenner, "Pew Internet: Mobile," *Pew Mobile*, January 31, 2013, http:// pewinternet.org/Commentary/2012 /February/Pew-Internet-Mobile.aspx (Accessed February 22, 2013).

22. Ibid.

23. Aaron Smith, "In-store Mobile Commerce during the 2012 Holiday Shopping Season," *Pew Internet*, January 31, 2013, http:// pewinternet.org/Reports/2013/in-store

-mobile-commerce.aspx (Accessed February 22, 2013).

24. Ibid.

25. Jack Uldrich, "The Future of Retail Isn't So Foreign," *Jump the Curve*, January 30, 2013, http://jumpthecurve.net/retail-marketing /the-future-of-retail-isnt-so-foreign/ (Accessed February 22, 2013).

15

1. Brendan Byrnes, "How Zillow's Culture Is a Competitive Advantage," *The Motley Fool*, February 18, 2013, www.fool.com/investing /general/2013/02/18/how-zillows-culture -is-a-competitive-advantage.aspx (Accessed March 7, 2013).

2. Pratima Singh, "Nestle Confirms Horsemeat DNA in Food, Apologises to Consumers," *Pardaphash*, February 19, 2013, www .pardaphash.com/news/nestle-confirms -horsemeat-dna-in-food-apologises-from -consumers/706106.html (Accessed March 7, 2013).

3. Michael Blaustein, "Watch: Ad for Colin Farrell Movie Goes Too Far with 'Elevator Murder' Video," *New York Post*, March 5, 2013, www.nypost.com/p/entertainment /movies/watch_marketing_elevator_collin _NOOBhxqXYHO3QXW8W4SjII (Accessed March 7, 2013).

4. Ibid.

5. "Elevator Murder Experiment," *YouTube*, March 4, 2013, www.youtube.com /watch?v=qo6Jzh7SHRA (Accessed March 7, 2013).

6. Steve Dent, "Google Glass' Now-like UI Finally Revealed, Just Accept and Say 'Ok,'" *Engadget*, February 20, 2013, www .engadget.com/2013/02/20/google-glass -how-it-feels-video (Accessed March 7, 2013).

7. Jared Newman, "Ouya Ships March 28 to Kickstarter Backers, More Exclusives Coming," *TIME*, March 1, 2013, http://techland .time.com/2013/03/01/ouya-ships-march -28-to-kickstarter-backers-more-exclusives -coming (Accessed March 7, 2013).

8. Andrew Johnson, "As Card Firms Try Social Media, Critics Keep Watch," *Wall Street Journal*, March 23, 2012, http://online.wsj .com/article/SB10001424052702304724404577297860607013698.html (Accessed March 7, 2013); "Chase Freedom," *Facebook*, www.facebook.com/ChaseFreedom (Accessed March 7, 2013).

9. Emily Glazer, "Avon Is Late to Social Media's Party," *Wall Street Journal*, April 23, 2012, B1–2.

10. The AIDA concept is based on the classic research of E. K. Strong Jr. as theorized in *The Psychology of Selling and Advertising* (New York: McGraw-Hill, 1925) and "Theories of Selling," *Journal of Applied Psychology*, 9, 1925, 75–86.

11. Zachary Lutz, "Pew Research Finds 22 Percent of Adults in US Own Tablets, Low-cost Android on the Rise," *Engadget*, October 2, 2012, www.engadget.com/2012/10/02 /pew-research-center-tablet-ownership-report (Accessed March 7, 2013).

12. Thomas E. Barry and Daniel J. Howard, "A Review and Critique of the Hierarchy of Effects in Advertising," *International Journal of Advertising*, 9, 1990, 121–135.

13. "Teva Launches Global Marketing Campaign 'Unfollow,'" *MarketWatch*, www .marketwatch.com/story/teva-launches -global-marketing-campaign-unfollow -2013-03-04 (Accessed March 7, 2013).

14. Diana Reese, "Why Is Michelle Obama Praising Wal-Mart in Springfield, Mo.?" *Washington Post*, www.washingtonpost .com/blogs/she-the-people/wp/2013/03/01 /why-is-michelle-obama-praising-walmart -in-springfield-mo (Accessed March 7, 2013).

16

1. Bradley Johnson, "100 Leading National Advertisers," *Adage*, June 25, 2012, http:// adage.com/article/news/advertising-age-100 -leading-national-advertisers/235573/ (Accessed March 8, 2013); Natalie Zmuda, "Ad Spending Rises 3% in 2012; Kantar Media Report Retail, Auto Categories Lead Outlays, as Financial Services, Insurance Make Cuts," *Advertising Age*, March 11, 2013, http://adage.com/article/media/kantar-media -report-ad-spending-rises-3-2012/240271 (Accessed April 10, 2013).

2. Darryl K. Taft, "IBM's Not-so-secret Weapon: Big Data," *eWeek*, February 26, 2013, www.eweek.com/database/ibms -not-so-secret-weapon-big-data-marketing (Accessed March 8, 2013).

3. "Fortune 500: Top Companies: Most Profitable," *CNN*, May 21, 2012, http://money .cnn.com/magazines/fortune/fortune500 /2012/performers/companies/profits/ (Accessed March 8, 2013).

4. Harvey Chipkin, "Hilton, 'Onion' Create Humorous, Effective Campaign," *MediaPost*, February 19, 2013, www.mediapost.com /publications/article/193693/hilton-onion -create-humorous-effective-campaig.html (Accessed March 8, 2013); Lauren Cleave, "What Do We Really Think about Humour in Advertising?" *AdGrad*, May 17, 2012, http://adgrad.co.uk/blog/2012/05/17/what -do-we-really-think-about-humour-in -advertising (Accessed March 11, 2013).

5. Bruce Jones, "Brand Loyalty: Applying Disney's Formula for Long-Lasting Success," *Gardner Business Media*, August 8, 2012, www.gardnerweb.com/blog/post/brand -loyalty-applying-disneys-formula-for-long -lasting-success- (Accessed March 8, 2013).

6. Christina Austin, "The Billionaires' Club: Only 36 Companies Have $1,000 Million-plus Ad Budgets," *Business Insider*, November 11, 2012, www.businessinsider .com/the-35-companies-that-spent-1-billion -on-ads-in-2011-2012-11?op=1 (Accessed March 8, 2013).

7. David Griner, "Oreo Surprises 26 Million Facebook Fans with Gay Pride Post," *Adweek*, June 25, 2012, www.adweek.com /adfreak/oreo-surprises-26-million-facebook -fans-gay-pride-post-141440 (Accessed March 8, 2013).

8. "Samsung Smart TV for the New 2012 TVs," *YouTube*, March 1, 2012, www .youtube.com/watch?v=JV6JLcjVJiA (Accessed March 8, 2013).

9. "'Shopping Carts' Commercial—21st Century Auto Insurance: Same Great Coverage for Less," *YouTube*, February 22, 2012, www.youtube.com/watch?v=CDoAmgIfj_U (Accessed March 8, 2013).

10. Ibid.

11. John Babish, "Ithaca, NY Company, Bionexus, Introduces First Natural Skin Care Lotion for Dogs Containing Standardized Nigella Sativa Extracts," *PRNewswire*, April 17, 2012, www.prnewswire.com /news-releases/ithaca-ny-company-bionexus -introduces-first-natural-skin-care-lotion-for -dogs-containing-standardized-nigella-sativa -extracts-147811745.html (Accessed March 11, 2013).

12. "The Saddleback Story," *Saddleback Leather*, www.saddlebackleather.com/Saddleback -Story (Accessed March 11, 2013).

13. Vincent Friedewald, "The Tobacco Brown Backpack by Saddleback Leather Co., San Antonio," *The Diego Files*, October 5, 2012, http://thediegofiles.com/blog/2012/10/5/the -tobacco-brown-backpack-by-saddleback -leather-co-san-antonio (Accessed March 11, 2013).

14. Lauren Cleave, "What Do We Really Think about Humour in Advertising?"

15. Neil King Jr., "Anti-Obama Ads Take Elegiac Tone," *Wall Street Journal*, May 4, 2012, http://online.wsj.com/article/SB100014240527023038776045773839503396568540052 .html (Accessed March 11, 2013).

16. Press release, "TNS Media Intelligence Forecasts 4.2 Percent Increase in U.S. Advertising Spending for 2008," www.tns-mi.com/news /01072008 (Accessed February 20, 2008).

17. "US Ad Spend Reported Up in '11, Forecast to Grow 2.2% in '12," *Marketing Charts*, May 3, 2012, www.marketingcharts.com /television/politics-olympics-to-drive-almost -half-of-12-us-ad-revenue-growth-20894 (Accessed March 11, 2013).

18. Suzanne Vranica, "Costly Super Bowl Ads Pay Publicity Dividend," *Wall Street Journal*, February 3, 2013, http://online.wsj.com /article/SB100014241278873249002045782823600080857752.html (Accessed March 11, 2013).

19. Robert Hof, "Online Ad Spending Tops $100 Billion in 2012," *Forbes*, January 9, 2013, www.*Forbes*.com/sites/roberthof /2013/01/09/online-ad-spending-tops-100 -billion-in-2012 (Accessed March 11, 2013).

20. David Kaplan, "For Turner Digital, Audience Buying Risk Outweighs Reward," *AdExchanger*, October 9, 2012, www.adexchang er.com/online-advertising/for-turner-digital -audience-buying-risk-outweighs-reward (Accessed March 11, 2013).

21. "IAB Internet Advertising Revenue Report: 2012 First Six Months' Results," *PricewaterhouseCoopers*, October 2012, www.iab.net /media/file/IAB_Internet_Advertising _Revenue_Report_HY_2012.pdf (Accessed March 11, 2013).

22. Mike Thompson, "The Top 25 Facebook Games of February 2013," *Inside Social Games*, February 1, 2013, www.insidesocial games.com/2013/02/01/the-top-25-facebook -games-of-february-2013 (Accessed March 11, 2013).

23. Mike Thompson, "Social Games News Roundup: Lots of People Play Facebook

Games, Social Casino Games Will Make Lots More Money Soon and Wooga is Updating Diamond Dash for iOS," *Inside Social Games*, September 14, 2012, www.insidesocialgames.com/2012/09/14/social-games-news-roundup-lots-of-people-play-facebook-games-social-casino-games-will-make-lots-more-money-soon-and-wooga-is-updating-diamond-dash-for-ios (Accessed March 11, 2013).

24. Joanna Brenner, "Pew Internet: Mobile," *Pew Research Center*, January 31, 2013, http://pewinternet.org/Commentary/2012/February/Pew-Internet-Mobile.aspx (Accessed March 11, 2013).

25. Owen Thomas, "New Marissa Mayer's Complaint about Yahoo's Hold Music Has Turned into a Music Video," *Business Insider*, February 4, 2013, www.businessinsider.com/yahoo-earnings-hold-music-video-snow-rapper-2013-2 (Accessed March 11, 2013).

26. Andrew Hampp, "Cross-Platform Ads: What's Working?" *Advertising Age*, June 26, 2008, http://adage.com/article/media/cross-platform-ads-working/128029/ (Accessed June 21, 2012).

27. Kathy Crosett, "Online Product Placement to Increase," *Ad-ology*, January 10, 2013, www.marketingforecast.com/archives/22200 (Accessed March 12, 2013).

28. "2013 Sponsorship Outlook: Spending Increase Is Double-edged Sword," *IEG Sponsorship Report*, January 7, 2013, www.sponsorship.com/iegsr/2013/01/07/2013-Sponsorship-Outlook--Spending-Increase-Is-Dou.aspx (Accessed March 12, 2013).

29. Ibid.

30. Jennifer Wang, "10 Marketing Masterworks," *Entrepreneur*, February 18, 2013, www.entrepreneur.com/article/225462 (Accessed March 12, 2013).

31. Philip Caulfield, "Web Pranksters Hijack Restaurant's Mountain Dew Naming Contest," *New York Daily News*, August 15, 2012, www.nydailynews.com/news/national/web-pranksters-hijack-mountain-dew-online-crowdsourced-naming-effort-new-green-apple-flavored-soda-article-1.1136204 (Accessed March 12, 2013).

32. Amy Dunn, "Coupon Use Plummets, and Some Wonder Whether it's the End of an Era," *News Observer*, March 9, 2013, www.newsobserver.com/2013/03/09/2735590/coupon-use-plummets-and-some-wonder.html (Accessed March 12, 2013).

33. Andrew R. Johnson, "@AmericanExpress Tries #Deals via Twitter," *Wall Street Journal*, March 7, 2012, http://online.wsj.com/article/SB10001424052970204781804577267402969728444.html (Accessed March 12, 2013).

34. Donna L. Montaldo, "How to Avoid the Rebate Rip-off," *About.com*, http://couponing.about.com/od/bargainshoppingtips/a/hub_rebate.htm (Accessed March 12, 2013).

35. Martin Moylan, "Retailers' Loyalty Programs Popular with Consumers," *Minnesota Public Radio*, January 2, 2013, http://minnesota.publicradio.org/display/web/2013/01/02/business/retail-rewards-programs (Accessed March 12, 2013).

36. Elizabeth Holmes, "At Bloomies, Loyalty for All," *Wall Street Journal*, February 24, 2012, B5.

37. Kelly Short, "Study Shows In-store Sampling Events Outperform Other Top In-store Marketing Tactics," *Interactions*, February 28, 2013, www.interactionsmarketing.com/news/?p=352 (Accessed March 12, 2013).

38. "POPAI: 76% of Decisions Made In-store," *Supermarket News*, May 8, 2012, http://supermarketnews.com/consumer-trends/popai-76-decisions-made-store (Accessed March 12, 2013).

39. "May 7, 2012: Coupon Redemption Up, Distribution Down in 2011," *Supermarket News*, May 8, 2012, http://supermarketnews.com/datasheet/may-7-2012-coupon-redemption-distribution-down-2011 (Accessed March 12, 2013).

40. Rachel King, "Google Trying out Real-time, Targeted Digital Coupons with Zavers," *ZDNet*, January 11, 2013, www.zdnet.com/google-trying-out-real-time-targeted-digital-coupons-with-zavers-7000009722 (Accessed March 12, 2013).

17

1. Sue Webber, "Arc Offering Free Personal Shopper Service," *Sun Current*, June 2, 2012, http://current.mnsun.com/2012/06/arc-offering-free-personal-shopper-service (Accessed March 13, 2013).

2. Juliet Fanny Poujol, Beatrice Siadou-Martin, David Vidal, and Ghislaine Pellat, "Examining the Impact of Salespeople's Relational Behavior and Organizational Fairness on Customer Loyalty," *The 12th International Research Converence in Service Management*, May 29 – June 1, 2012, www.cerog.org/lalondeCB/SM/2012_lalonde_seminar/papers/21-P118-2012-POUJOL-SIADOU%20MARTIN-VIDAL-PELLAT-REV%2003.04-2012%20RC.pdf (Accessed March 13, 2013).

3. Stephanie Clifford, "Browsing While Browsing," *New York Times*, March 9, 2012, B1.

4. "CNN Uses Facebook Conversations as a Barometer to Visualize Election Trends," *Mass Relevance*, February 19, 2013, www.massrelevance.com/case-study/cnn-uses-facebook-conversations-barometer-visualize-election-trends (Accessed March 13, 2013).

5. Paul Greenberg, "CRM Watchlist 2013 Winners: Social Is as Social Does the Mainstream, Part 1," *ZDNet*, March 7, 2013, www.zdnet.com/crm-watchlist-2013-winners-social-is-as-social-does-the-mainstream-part-1-7000012230 (Accessed March 13, 2013).

6. Matt Mansfield, "Customer Retention: Keep Customers by Growing Relationships Online," *Pitney Bowes*, June 12, 2012, www.pbsmartessentials.com/customer-satisfaction/customer-retention-keep-customers-by-growing-relationships-online (Accessed March 13, 2013).

7. Jessica Bruder, "A Customer Loyalty Program (From Some of the Folks Who Brought You Groupon)," *New York Times*, February 21, 2012, http://boss.blogs.nytimes.com/2012/02/21/a-customer-loyalty-program-from-some-of-the-folks-who-brought-you-groupon (Accessed March 13, 2013).

8. Loren McDonald, "Birthday Emails: Analysis and Samples from My Inbox," *Silverpop*, June 6, 2012, www.silverpop.com/blogs/email-marketing/birthday-emails-analysis.html (Accessed March 12, 2013).

9. "Discover Financial Services' CEO Hosts Financial Community Briefing Conference (Transcript)," *Seeking Alpha*, March 12, 2013, http://seekingalpha.com/article/1267761-discover-financial-services-ceo-hosts-financial-community-briefing-conference-transcript (Accessed March 13, 2013).

10. Allison Schiff, "DMA: Direct Mail Response Rates Beat Digital," *Direct Marketing News*, June 14, 2012, www.dmnews.com/dma-direct-mail-response-rates-beat-digital/article/245780 (Accessed March 13, 2013); Jason Webster, "What's Your LinkedIn InMail Response Rate," *Ongig*, August 26, 2012, http://ongig.com/blog/hiring/whats-your-linkedin-inmail-response-rate (Accessed March 13, 2013); Natasha Lomas, "LinkedIn Hits 200 Million Registered Users Worldwide – Adding New Users at Rate of Two per Second," *TechCrunch*, January 9, 2013, http://techcrunch.com/2013/01/09/linkedin-hits-200-million-users-worldwide-adding-new-users-at-rate-of-two-per-second (Accessed March 13, 2013).

11. Barton Weitz, Stephen Castleberry, and John Tanner, *Selling: Building Partnerships* (Burr Ridge, IL: McGraw-Hill/Irwin, 2004), 184–185.

12. Fred Perrotta, "How to Use Social Media for Customer Research," *Social Media Examiner*, September 12, 2012, www.socialmediaexaminer.com/social-media-for-customer-research (Accessed March 13, 2013).

13. "Leadership Program," *General Electric*, www.ge.com/careers/students/clp/index.html (Accessed March 13, 2013).

14. Weitz, Castleberry, and Tanner, *Selling*, 17–22.

15. "Oracle PeopleSoft Applications," *Oracle*, www.oracle.com/us/products/applications/peoplesoft-enterprise/overview/index.htm (Accessed March 12, 2013).

16. Kathleen M. Joyce, "In the Cards," *Chief Marketer*, September 1, 2003, http://chiefmarketer.com/mag/marketing_cards_3 (Accessed March 13, 2013).

18

1. "Social Media and the New Reality for Law Practice," *LegalWire*, February 24, 2013, www.legalwire.co.uk/?dt_portfolio=legal-profession-2-0-social-media-and-the-new-reality-for-law-firms (Accessed March 14, 2013).

2. Shanyndi Raice, Mike Ramsey, and Sam Schechner, "Facebook Gains Two Big Advertisers' Support," *Wall Street Journal*, June 20, 2012, B6.

3. Suzanne Vranica, "Knights, Pirates, Trees Flock to Facebook," *Wall Street Journal*, March 26, 2012, B1.

4. "4 Ways to Use Google Hangouts in Your Business," *U.S. Small Business Administra-*

tion, February 13, 2013, www.sba.gov /community/blogs/4-ways-use-google -hangouts-your-business (Accessed March 13, 2013).

5. Tessa Stuart, "Secrets of a Celebrity Twitter Coach," *BuzzFeed*, February 19, 2013, www .buzzfeed.com/tessastuart/secrets-of-a -celebrity-twitter-coach (Accessed March 14, 2013).

6. Matthew Radmanovich, "A Social Media Plan for the Ultimate Fighting Championship," *University of Nevada, Las Vegas*, October 1, 2012, http://digitalscholarship .unlv.edu/cgi/viewcontent.cgi?article=2476 &context=thesesdissertations (Accessed March 14, 2013).

7. Daniel Terdiman, "Report: Twitter Hits Half a Billion Tweets a Day," *CNET*, October 26, 2012, http://news.CNET.com/8301-1023_3 -57541566-93/report-twitter-hits-half -a-billion-tweets-a-day (Accessed March 14, 2013); "Infographic: 24 Hours on the Internet," *Digital Buzz Blog*, March 13, 2012, www.digitalbuzzblog.com/infographic -24-hours-on-the-internet (Accessed March 14, 2013).

8. "SBANC Newsletter – June 5th, 2012," *International Council for Small Business*, June 5, 2012, www.icsb.org/article .asp?messageID=983 (Accessed March 14, 2013).

9. Joanna Brenner, "Pew Internet: Mobile," *Pew Research Center*, January 31, 2013, http:// pewinternet.org/Commentary/2012 /February/Pew-Internet-Mobile.aspx (Accessed March 14, 2013).

10. Steven Musil, "U.S. Tablet Usage Hits 'Critical Massn' ComScore Reports," *CNET*, June 10, 2012, http://news.cnet.com/8301 -13579_3-57450079-37/u.s-tablet-usage -hits-critical-mass-comscore-reports (Accessed March 14, 2013).

11. Ibid.

12. Sid Gandotra, "Why Social Commerce Matters," *Social Media Today*, November 6, 2012, http://socialmediatoday.com/sid -gandotra/974961/social-commerce -socialmedia-ecommerce (Accessed March 14, 2013).

13. Samantha Murphy, "50% of Web Sales to Occur via Social Media by 2015," *Mashable*, November 1, 2012, http:// mashable.com/2012/11/01/facebook-sales (Accessed March 14, 2013).

14. "Giveaway!!! Pin it to Win it! An iPad Mini for Two Lucky Winners!!!" *Favorite Family Recipes*, March 10, 2013, www.favfamily recipes.com/2013/03/giveaway-pin-it-to -win-it-an-ipad-mini-for-two-lucky-winners .html (Accessed March 14, 2013); Lauren Indvik, "How Brands Are Using Promotions to Market on Pinterest," *Mashable*, March 7, 2012, http://mashable.com/2012/03/07 /pinterest-brand-marketing (Accessed March 14, 2013).

15. Ibid.

16. "Complimentary White Paper: Forrester's US Interactive Marketing Forecast through 2016," *Adobe Marketing Cloud*, http:// success.adobe.com/en/na/programs/products /digitalmarketing/migration12/1208_21408 _forrester_interactive_marketing_forecast .html (Accessed March 14, 2013).

17. Eric Mosley, "Crowdsource your Performance Reviews," *Harvard Business Review*, June 15, 2013, http://blogs.hbr.org /cs/2012/06/crowdsource_your _performance_r.html (Accessed March 14, 2013).

18. "Photograph for Ellie Goulding with HP Connected Music," *Talenthouse*, www .talenthouse.com/photograph-for-ellie -goulding-and-hp-connected-music #description (Accessed March 14, 2013).

19. "Paid Media Marketing," *Greenlight*, www .greenlightdigital.com/paid-media (Accessed March 14, 2013).

20. Ibid.

21. Russell Working, "Most Unhappy with Social Media Measurement, Survey Says," *Ragan Communications*, December 10, 2012, www.ragan.com/Main/Articles /Most_unhappy_with_social_media _measurement_survey_45919.aspx (Accessed March 14, 2013).

22. Jon Mehlman, "How to Stalk Your Competitors in Social Media (So You Can Crush Them)," *HubSpot*, July 19, 2012, http://blog .hubspot.com/blog/tabid/6307/bid/33347 /How-to-Stalk-Your-Competitors-in-Social -Media-So-You-Can-Crush-Them.aspx (Accessed March 14, 2013).

23. Andy Williams, "How Social Media Has Changed the Way We Complain," *Koozai*, February 25, 2013, www.koozai.com /blog/branding/reputation-management /how-social-media-has-changed-the-way -we-complain (Accessed March 14, 2013); Bob Fine, "How Social Media Has Changed Politics: It's Not Just Tactics," *The Social Media Monthly*, January 18, 2013, http:// thesocialmediamonthly.com/how-social -media-has-changed-politics-its-not-just -tactics (Accessed March 14, 2013); "How Social media Has Changed the Way We Communicate," *Information Gateway*, January 24, 2013, www.informationgateway .org/social-media-changed-communicate (Accessed March 14, 2013).

24. Charlene Li and Josh Bernoff, *Groundswell: Winning in a World Transformed by Social Technologies*, revised ed. (Boston: Harvard Business Press, 2011).

25. Gina Sverdlov, "Global Social Technographics Update 2011: US and EU Mature, Emerging Markets Show Lots of Activity," *Forrester*, January 4, 2012, http://blogs .forrester.com/gina_sverdlov/12-01-04 -global_social_technographics_update_2011 _us_and_eu_mature_emerging_markets _show_lots_of_activity (Accessed April 10, 2013); "What's the Social Technographics Profile of Your Customer?" *Forrester Empowered*, http://empowered.forrester.com /tool_consumer.html (Accessed March 14, 2013).

26. Gina Sverdlov, "Global Social Technographics Update 2011: US and EU Mature, Emerging Markets Show Lots of Activity."

27. Crystal Schauf, "Why Employees Should Contribute to the Company Blog," *Intrapromote*, August 15, 2012, http://blog .intrapromote.com/employees-contribute -company-blog (Accessed March 15, 2013).

28. Roger Yu, "More Companies Quit Blogging, Go With Facebook Instead," *USA Today*, April 20, 2012, www.usatoday.com /tech/news/story/2012-04-19/corporate -blogging/54419982/1 (Accessed March 15, 2013).

29. Lauren Drell, "The Quick and Dirty Guide to Tumblr for Small Business," *Mashable*, February 18, 2012, http://mashable.com /2012/02/18/tumblr-small-biz-guide (Accessed March 15, 2013).

30. Olga Khazan, "How Do You Use Twitter and Facebook for Marketing," *Washington Post*, April 22, 2012, www.washingtonpost .com/blogs/on-small-business/post/how-do -you-use-twitter-and-facebook-for-marketing /2012/04/20/gIQA7NXwZT_blog.html (Accessed March 15, 2013).

31. Josh Bersin, "Facebook Vs. LinkedIn – What's the Difference?" *Forbes*, May 21, 2012, www.*Forbes*.com/sites/joshbersin /2012/05/21/facebook-vs-linkedin-whats-the -difference (Accessed March 15, 2013).

32. "Top Sites," *Alexa*, www.alexa.com/topsites (Accessed March 15, 2013).

33. Tony Nguyen, "The Importance of Social Bookmarking and RSS in SEO," *Business Review Center*, October 18, 2012, http:// businessreviewcenter.com/social -bookmarking-and-rss (Accessed March 15, 2013).

34. Rob Walker, "How Reddit's Ask Me Anything Became Part of the Mainstream Media Circuit," *Yahoo!*, March 13, 2013, http:// news.yahoo.com/how-reddit-s-ask-me -anything-became-part-of-the-mainstream -media-circuit--130755591.html (Accessed March 15, 2013); "Top Scoring Links: IAmA," *Reddit*, www.reddit.com/r/IAmA /top/ (Accessed March 15, 2013).

35. "Foursquare as a Powerful Customer Loyalty Tool," *Customer Insight Group*, April 15, 2012, www.customerinsightgroup.com /marketinglibrary/foursquare-as-a-powerful -customer-loyalty-tool (Accessed March 15, 2013).

36. "The Yelp Elite P Party @ Pies & Pints," *Yelp*, www.yelp.com/biz/the-yelp-elite-p -party-pies-and-pints-worthington (Accessed March 15, 2013).

37. "Second Life Grid Survey – Economic Metrics," *GridSurvey*, March 15, 2013, http:// gridsurvey.com/economy.php (Accessed March 15, 2013).

38. Mike Thompson, "The Top 25 Facebook Games of February 2013," *Inside Social Games*, February 1, 2013, www.insidesocial games.com/2013/02/01/the-top-25-facebook -games-of-february-2013 (Accessed March 15, 2013)

39. Stuart Dredge, "Angry Birds Maker Rovio Reports £60.8m Revenues for 2011," *The Guardian*, May 7, 2013, www.guardian .co.uk/technology/appsblog/2012/may/07 /angry-birds-rovio-revenues-2011 (Accessed March 15, 2013).

40. "Global Mobile Statistics 2013 Part A: Mobile Subscribers; Handset Market Share; Mobile Operators," *mobiThinking*, March 2013, http://mobithinking.com/mobile -marketing-tools/latest-mobile-stats/a (Accessed March 15, 2013).

41. Robert Hof, "Mobile Ad Spending Doubles in 2012's First Half," *Forbes*, October 11, 2012, www.Forbes.com/sites/roberthof /2012/10/11/mobile-ad-spending-doubles

-in-2012s-first-half (Accessed March 15, 2013).

42. "Modify QR Code Watch – Because Simply Reading Time on Your Watch Is Soooo 2011," *Modify Watches*, February 23, 2012, www.modifywatches.com/blog/qr-code-watch (Accessed March 15, 2013).

43. JP Mangalindan, "Barnes & Noble CEO: NFC Coming to the Nook," *CNN*, May 1, 2012, http://tech.fortune.cnn.com/2012/05/01/nook (Accessed March 15, 2013).

44. David Pierce, "Samsung Galaxy S4 Preview: A Bigger, Faster Upgrade to the World's Most Popular Android Phone," *The Verge*, March 14, 2013, www.theverge.com/2013/3/14/4104650/samsung-galaxy-s4-announced-upgrade (Accessed March 15, 2013).

45. Beth Kanter, "Screencast: Using Widgets to Build Community on Blogs Featured on NTEN Blog," *Beth's Blog*, March 20, 2007, http://beth.typepad.com/beths_blog/2007/03/screncast_using.html (Accessed June 23, 2012).

19

1. Patrick Lefler, "Five Rules for Pricing Excellence: Getting the Most for Your Services," *ChangeThis*, April 11, 2012, http://changethis.com/manifesto/93.06.PricingRules/pdf/93.06.PricingRules.pdf (Accessed February 26, 2013).

2. Franziska Volckner, "The Dual Role of Price: Decomposing Consumers' Reactions to Price," *Journal of the Academy of Marketing Science*, 36, no. 3, Fall 2008, 359–377.

3. Ibid.

4. Patrick Lefler, "Five Rules for Pricing Excellence: Getting the Most for Your Services."

5. "Rise of the Barter Economy," *Bloomberg Businessweek*, April 30–May 6, 2012, 75–77.

6. Aaron Brough and Mathew Isaac, "Finding a Home for Products We Love: How Buyer Usage Intent Affects the Pricing of Used Goods," *Journal of Marketing*, July 2012, 78–91.

7. Salvador Rodriguez, "Shipments of 'Phablets,' or large smartphones, to double in 2013," *Los Angeles Times*, January 16, 2013, www.latimes.com/business/technology/la-fi-tn-phablet-shipments-double-2013-20130116,0,6706144.story (Accessed February 26, 2013).

8. Tammo H. A. Bijmolt, Harald J. Van Heerde, and Rik G. M. Pieters, "New Empirical Generalizations on the Determinants of Price Elasticity," *Journal of Marketing Research*, 42, May 2005, 141–156; Christian Homburg, Wayne Hoyer, and Nicole Koschate, "Customers' Reactions to Price Increases: Do Customer Satisfaction and Perceived Motive Fairness Matter?" *Journal of the Academy of Marketing Science*, 33, no. 1, Winter 2005, 35–49; Gadi Fibich, Arieh Gavious, and Oded Lowengart, "The Dynamics of Price Elasticity of Demand in the Presence of Reference Price Effects," *Journal of the Academy of Marketing Science*, 33, no. 1, Winter 2005, 66–78.

9. Catherine Valenti, "Concert Ticket Prices Rise, Sales Fall," *ABC*, July 9, 2012, http://abcnews.go.com/Business/story?id=87981 (Accessed February 26, 2013).

10. Thorin Klosowski, "How Web Sites Vary Prices Based on Your Information (and What You Can Do About It)," *Lifehacker*, January 7, 2013, http://lifehacker.com/5973689/how-web-sites-vary-prices-based-on-your-information-and-what-you-can-do-about-it (Accessed February 26, 2013).

11. Lisa Benson and Steve Watkins, "Cincinnati Reds Make Move to Dynamic Pricing," *Business Courier*, February 25, 2013, www.bizjournals.com/cincinnati/news/2013/02/25/cincinnati-reds-make-move-to-dynamic.html (Accessed February 26, 2013); Pedro Moura, "Angels Switch to 'Dynamic Pricing' for Tickets," *Orange County Register*, February 22, 2013, www.ocregister.com/sports/ticket-497067-angels-tickets.html (Accessed February 26, 2013); Rob Low, "Royals Add Curve Ball to Ticket Prices," *Fox 4 Kansas City*, February 18, 2013, http://fox4kc.com/2013/02/18/royals-add-curve-ball-to-ticket-prices (Accessed February 26, 2013).

12. Dan Rascon, "West Valley City Gas Stations Engage in Price War," *KUTV*, February 5, 2013, www.kutv.com/news/top-stories/stories/vid_3720.shtml (Accessed February 5, 2013).

13. Erik Sherman, "Why Amazon May Have Killed the Golden Goose," *CBS*, April 18, 2012, www.cbsnews.com/8301-505124_162-57415335/why-amazon-may-have-killed-the-golden-goose (Accessed February 26, 2013).

14. "Successful Companies Master Positioning and Distribution," *BizFilings*, May 24, 2012, www.bizfilings.com/toolkit/sbg/marketing/overview/positioning-and-distribution-for-success.aspx (Accessed February 26, 2013).

15. Andrew Davis, "The 10 Best Shopping Engines," *Search Engine Watch*, June 19, 2012, http://searchenginewatch.com/article/2097413/The-10-Best-Shopping-Engines (Accessed February 26, 2013); Yun Wan and Nan Hu, "Comparison Shopping Channel Selection by Small Online Vendors: An Exploratory Study (Abstract)," *IGI Global*, 2009, www.igi-global.com/bookstore/Chapter.aspx?TitleId=6735 (Accessed February 26, 2013).

16. "Online Bot Traffic Spikes During Q4 2012 Holiday Shopping Season," *Business Wire*, February 7, 2013, www.businesswire.com/news/home/20130207005131/en/Online-Bot-Traffic-Spikes-Q4-2012-Holiday (Accessed February 26, 2013).

17. Charisma Madarang, "Subway Bringing Back $5 Footlongs for FebruANY," *Foodbeast*, February 1, 2013, http://foodbeast.com/content/2013/02/01/subway-bringing-back-5-footlongs-for-februany/ (Accessed February 27, 2013).

18. "Early Price Breaks Spur Worry that Industry Is Shifting from Full-price Model," Outdoor Industry Association, February 7, 2013, www.outdoorindustry.org/news/ceobrief.php?newsId=17924&newsletterId=327 (Accessed February 27, 2013).

19. Martinne Geller and Jessica Wohl, "Analysis: Walmart's Price Push Tests Manufacturers' Prowess," *Reuters*, March 6, 2012, www.reuters.com/article/2012/03/06/us-usa-consumer-walmart-idUSTRE8250GM20120306 (Accessed February 27, 2013).

20. Brad Tuttle, "Does a Low Price Mean Good Value or Bad Quality?" *TIME*, November 14, 2012, http://business.time.com/2012/11/14/does-a-low-price-mean-good-value-or-bad-quality (Accessed February 27, 2013).

21. Ibid.

22. Volckner, "The Dual Role of Price."

23. Ibid; Marco Bertini, Luc Wathieu, and Sheena Iyengar, "The Discriminating Consumer: Product Proliferation and Willingness to Pay for Quality," *Journal of Marketing Research*, February 2012, 39–49.

24. Courtney Subramanian, "Maker's Mark Reverses Decision to Water Down Whiskey," *TIME*, February 17, 2013, http://newsfeed.time.com/2013/02/17/makers-mark-reverses-decision-to-water-down-whiskey (Accessed February 27, 2013); Rob Samuels and Bill Samuels, Jr., "You Spoke. We Listened." *Maker's Mark*, www.makersmark.com/#!/live-feed/news/34-you-spoke-we-listened (Accessed February 27, 2013).

25. Merrie Brucks, Valarie Zeithaml, and Gillian Naylor, "Price and Brand Name as Indicators of Quality Dimensions for Consumer Durables," *Journal of the Academy of Marketing Science*, 28, no. 3, Summer 2000, 359–374; Wilford Amaldoss and Sanjay Jain, "Pricing of Conspicuous Goods: A Competitive Analysis of Social Effects," *Journal of Marketing Research*, 42, February 2005, 30–42; also see Margaret Campbell, "Says Who?! How the Source of Price Information and Affect Influence Perceived Price (UN) fairness," *Journal of Marketing Research*, 44, no. 2, May 2007, 261–271.

20

1. Andreas Hinterhuber and Stephan Liozu, "Do You Even Have a Pricing Strategy?" *Build*, January 4, 2013, http://thebuildnetwork.com/innovation/pricing-strategy (Accessed February 27, 2013).

2. Ibid.

3. "Store Brands Step Up Their Games and Prices," *Wall Street Journal*, January 31, 2012, B1-B2; Jan–Benedict Steenkamp, Harald VanHeerde, and Inge Geyskens, "What Makes Consumers Willing to Pay a Price Premium for National Brands over Private Labels?" *Journal of Marketing Research*, December 2010, 1011–1024.

4. Ibid.

5. Scott McCartney, "Olympic-Sized Fare Hikes This Summer Make It Important to Book Early," *Wall Street Journal*, April 12, 2012, http://blogs.wsj.com/middleseat/2012/04/12/olympic-sized-fare-hikes-this-summer-make-it-important-to-book-early (Accessed February 27, 2012).

6. "2014 Mustang: 10 Models Priced from $21,995 - $60,445," *Ford*, www.ford.com/cars/mustang/pricing/ (Accessed February 28, 2013).

7. "A Stingy Spirit Lifts Airlines' Profit," *Wall Street Journal*, May 12–13, 2012.

8. Joe Cahill, "How McDonald's Is Losing the Burger Brawl," *Crain's Chicago Business*, December 3, 2013, www.chicagobusiness

.com/article/20121201/ISSUE10/312019983/how-mcdonalds-is-losing-the-burger-brawl (Accessed February 28, 2013).

9. Jeb Boone, "Nokia Targets Developing World with Cheap, Simple Phones," *CNBC*, February 26, 2013, www.cnbc.com/id/100494024 (Accessed February 28, 2013); "Nokia Lumina 920 4G Windows Phone, Black (AT&T)," *Amazon Wireless*, http://wireless.amazon.com/Nokia-Lumia-920-Windows-Phone/dp/B00A2V7BA4 (Accessed February 28, 2013).

10. Thomas Catan, Jeffrey A. Trachtenberg, and Chad Bray, "U.S. Alleges E-Book Scheme," *Wall Street Journal*, April 12, 2012, A1.

11. Kate Linebaugh, "GE Sues Whirlpool on Cartel," *Wall Street Journal*, February 20, 2013, http://online.wsj.com/article/SB10001424127887323864304578316581632464570.html (Accessed February 28, 2013).

12. "How Driving Prices Lower Can Violate Antitrust Statutes," *Wall Street Journal*, January 24, 2004, A1, A11.

13. Evan Clark and Kristi Ellis, "Price-Fixing Plays Out in Supreme Court," *Women's Wear Daily*, June 19, 2008.

14. "A Powerful Law Has Been Losing a Lot of Its Punch," *Wall Street Journal*, May 21, 2012, R2.

15. Ibid.

16. Bruce Alford and Abhijit Biswas, "The Effects of Discount Level, Price Consciousness, and Sale Proneness on Consumers' Price Perception and Behavioral Intention," *Journal of Business Research*, 55, no. 9, September 2002, 775–778; also see V. Kumar, Vibhas Madan, and Srinin Srinivasan, "Price Discounts or Coupon Promotions: Does It Matter?" *Journal of Business Research*, 57, no. 9, September 2004, 933–941.

17. Martinne Geller and Jessica Wohl, "Analysis: Walmart's Price Push Tests Manufacturers' Prowess," *Reuters*, March 6, 2012, www.reuters.com/article/2012/03/06/us-usa-consumer-walmart-idUSTRE8250GM20120306 (Accessed May 3, 2012).

18. Brad Tuttle, "Is There a Future for Same-Day Delivery? How About Online Grocery Shopping?" *TIME*, January 29, 2013, http://business.time.com/2013/01/29/is-there-a-future-for-same-day-delivery-how-about-online-grocery-shopping (Accessed February 28, 2013).

19. Richard Lawler, "DirecTV 'Price Adjustment' Will Raise Rates About 4.5 Percent in February," *Engadget*, December 27, 2012, www.engadget.com/2012/12/27/directv-price-adjustment-will-raise-prices-about-4-5-percent-i (Accessed February 28, 2013).

20. Felix Salmon, "Matter's Vision for Long-Form Journalism," *Reuters*, February 23, 2012, http://blogs.reuters.com/felix-salmon/2012/02/23/matters-vision-for-long-form-journalism (Accessed February 28, 2013).

21. Brad Tuttle, "Is Airline-style Variable Pricing Coming to Theme Park Tickets?" *TIME*, December 5, 2013, http://business.time.com/2012/12/05/is-airline-style-variable-pricing-coming-to-theme-park-tickets (Accessed February 28, 2013).

22. Jim Gorzelany, "Five Reasons to Buy a New Car in 2012," *Forbes*, January 2, 2012, www.*Forbes*.com/sites/jimgorzelany/2012/01/02/five-reasons-to-buy-a-new-car-in-2012 (Accessed February 28, 2013).

23. Tara Baukus Mello, "Why Sell a Used Car Instead of Trade It?" *Bankrate.com*, February 15, 2013, www.bankrate.com/finance/auto/sell-used-car-instead-trade.aspx (Accessed February 28, 2013).

24. Rui (Juliet) Zhu, Xinlei (Jack) Chen, and Srabana Dasgupta, "Can Trade-ins Hurt You? Exploring the Effect of a Trade-in on Consumers' Willingness to Pay for a New Product," *American Marketing Association*, www.marketingpower.com/AboutAMA/Pages/AMA%20Publications/AMA%20Journals/Journal%20of%20Marketing%20Research/TOCs/summary%20apr%202008/CanTradejmrapr08.aspx (Accessed March 1, 2013).

25. Mary Jo Foley, "Microsoft Office 2013: What to Expect on the Pricing Front," *ZD-Net*, January 16, 2013, www.zdnet.com/microsoft-office-2013-what-to-expect-on-the-pricing-front-7000009591 (Accessed March 1, 2013).

26. David Freedman, "Is SaveLocal a Better Deal Than Groupon?" *New York Times*, March 14, 2012, http://boss.blogs.nytimes.com/2012/03/14/would-you-consider-using-a-groupon-alternative (Accessed March 1, 2013).

27. Martin Lindstrom, "The Psychology behind the Sweet Spots of Pricing," *Fast Company*, March 27, 2012, www.fastcompany.com/1826172/martin-lindstrom-buyology-marketing-psychology-pricing-sweet-spot (Accessed March 1, 2013).

28. Ibid.

29. Russell Adams, "Many Formats, One Price," *Wall Street Journal*, May 15, 2011, http://online.wsj.com/article/SB10001424052748703421204576325600834789440.html (Accessed March 1, 2013).

30. Dilip Soman and John Gourville, "Transaction Decoupling: The Effects of Price Bundling on the Decision to Consume," *MSI Report*, 2002, 98–131; Stefan Stremersch and Gerard J. Tellis, "Strategic Bundling of Products and Prices: A New Synthesis for Marketing," *Journal of Marketing*, 66, no. 1, January 2002, 55–71; "Forget Prices and Get People to Use the Stuff," *Wall Street Journal*, June 3, 2004, A2; Rashmi Adaval and Robert Wyer, Jr., "Conscious and Non-conscious Comparisons with Price Anchors: Effects on Willingness to Pay for Related and Unrelated Products," *Journal of Marketing Research*, April 2011, 355–365.

31. Hugo Martin, "Airlines Report Combined Profit of $152 Million in 2012," *Los Angeles Times*, February 21, 2013, www.latimes.com/business/money/la-fi-mo-airlines-report-profit-20130221,0,6289295.story (Accessed March 1, 2013).

32. Rebecca Hamilton and Joydeep Srivastava, "When 2+2 Is Not the Same as 1+3: Variations in Price Sensitivity across Components of Partitioned Prices," *Journal of Marketing Research*, 45, no. 4, August 2008, 450–461.

33. Sinan Kubba, "Humble Indie Bundle 7 Culminates in Sales of $2.65 Million," *Joystiq*, January 3, 2013, www.joystiq.com/2013/01/03/humble-indie-bundle-7-culminates-in-sales-of-2-65-million (Accessed March 1, 2013).

34. Paul Hunt and Greg Thomas, "Scoring Birdies Instead of Bogies," *Pricing Solutions Newsletter*, 2, no. 2, Winter 2009, www.pricingsolutions.com/index.php/en/more-about-joomla/45-newsletters/125-newsletter2 (Accessed on March 1, 2013).

35. Kelli B. Grant, "Just Relax, Then Buy More and Pay More For It," *Wall Street Journal*, November 2, 2011, 04.

36. Ibid.

KEY TERMS

LO 1-1

marketing the activity, set of institutions, and processes for creating, communicating, delivering, and exchanging offerings that have value for customers, clients, partners, and society at large

exchange people giving up something in order to receive something else they would rather have

LO 1-2

production orientation a philosophy that focuses on the internal capabilities of the firm rather than on the desires and needs of the marketplace

sales orientation the belief that people will buy more goods and services if aggressive sales techniques are used and that high sales result in high profits

marketing concept the idea that the social and economic justification for an organization's existence is the satisfaction of customer wants and needs while meeting organizational objectives

market orientation a philosophy that assumes that a sale does not depend on an aggressive sales force but rather on a customer's decision to purchase a product; it is synonymous with the marketing concept

societal marketing orientation the idea that an organization exists not only to satisfy customer wants and needs and to meet organizational objectives but also to preserve or enhance individuals' and society's long-term best interests

KEY CONCEPTS

LO 1-1 Define the term *marketing*. Marketing is the activity, set of institutions, and processes for creating, communicating, delivering, and exchanging offerings that have value for customers, clients, partners, and society at large. Marketing also requires all facets of a company to work together to pool ideas and resources. One major goal of marketing is to create an exchange. An exchange has five conditions, as listed below. Even if all five conditions are met, however, an exchange might not occur. People engage in marketing whether or not an exchange happens.

Five conditions of exchange
1. There must be at least two parties.
2. Each party has something that might be of value to the other party.
3. Each party is capable of communication and delivery.
4. Each party is free to accept or reject the exchange offer.
5. Each party believes it is appropriate or desirable to deal with the other party.

LO 1-2 Describe four marketing management philosophies. The role of marketing and the character of marketing activities within an organization are strongly influenced by the organization's marketing philosophy and orientation. A production-oriented organization focuses on the internal capabilities of the firm rather than on the desires and needs of the marketplace. A sales orientation is based on the beliefs that people will buy more products and services if aggressive sales techniques are used and that high sales volumes produce high profits. A market-oriented organization focuses on satisfying customer wants and needs while meeting organizational objectives. A societal marketing orientation goes beyond a market orientation to include the preservation or enhancement of individuals' and society's long-term best interests.

LO 1-3 Discuss the differences between sales and market orientations.
First, sales-oriented firms focus on their own needs; market-oriented firms focus on customers' needs and preferences. Second, sales-oriented companies consider themselves to be deliverers of goods and services, whereas market-oriented companies view themselves as satisfiers of customers. Third, sales-oriented firms direct their products to everyone; market-oriented firms aim at specific segments of the population. Fourth, sales-oriented organizations place a higher premium on making a sale, while market-oriented businesses seek a long-term relationship with the customer. Finally, sales-oriented businesses pursue maximum sales volume through intensive promotion, whereas market-oriented businesses pursue customer satisfaction through coordinated activities.

LO 1-3

customer value the relationship between benefits and the sacrifice necessary to obtain those benefits

customer satisfaction customers' evaluation of a good or service in terms of whether it has met their needs and expectations

relationship marketing a strategy that focuses on keeping and improving relationships with current customers

empowerment delegation of authority to solve customers' problems quickly—usually by the first person the customer notifies regarding a problem

teamwork collaborative efforts of people to accomplish common objectives

customer relationship management (CRM) a company-wide business strategy designed to optimize profitability, revenue, and customer satisfaction by focusing on highly defined and precise customer groups

LO 1-4 Describe several reasons for studying marketing. First, marketing affects the allocation of goods and services that influence a nation's economy and standard of living. Second, an understanding of marketing is crucial to understanding most businesses. Third, career opportunities in marketing are diverse, profitable, and expected to increase significantly during the coming decade. Fourth, understanding marketing makes consumers more informed.

Using the correct tool for the job will help an organization ACHIEVE ITS GOALS. *Marketing tools are covered throughout this book!*

© Seregam/Shutterstock.com

© iStockphoto.com/OSTILL / © iStockphoto.com/billnoll

KEY TERMS

LO 2-1

strategic planning the managerial process of creating and maintaining a fit between the organization's objectives and resources and the evolving market opportunities

LO 2-2

strategic business unit (SBU) a subgroup of a single business or collection of related businesses within the larger organization

LO 2-3

market penetration a marketing strategy that tries to increase market share among existing customers

market development a marketing strategy that entails attracting new customers to existing products

product development a marketing strategy that entails the creation of new products for present markets

diversification a strategy of increasing sales by introducing new products into new markets

portfolio matrix a tool for allocating resources among products or strategic business units on the basis of relative market share and market growth rate

star in the portfolio matrix, a business unit that is a fast-growing market leader

cash cow in the portfolio matrix, a business unit that generates more cash than it needs to maintain its market share

problem child (question mark) in the portfolio matrix, a business unit that shows rapid growth but poor profit margins

dog in the portfolio matrix, a business unit that has low growth potential and a small market share

planning the process of anticipating future events and determining strategies to achieve organizational objectives in the future

marketing planning designing activities relating to marketing objectives and the changing marketing environment

KEY CONCEPTS

LO 2-1 Understand the importance of strategic planning. Strategic planning is the basis for all marketing strategies and decisions. These decisions affect the allocation of resources and ultimately the financial success of the company.

LO 2-2 Define strategic business units (SBUs). Each SBU should have these characteristics: a distinct mission and a specific target market, control over its resources, its own competitors, a single business, and plans independent from other SBUs in the organization. Each SBU has its own rate of return on investment, growth potential, and associated risks, and requires its own strategies and funding.

LO 2-3 Identify strategic alternatives and know a basic outline for a marketing plan. Ansoff's opportunity matrix presents four options to help management develop strategic alternatives: market penetration, market development, product development, and diversification. In selecting a strategic alternative, managers may use a portfolio matrix, which classifies strategic business units as stars, cash cows, problem children (or question marks), and dogs, depending on their present or projected growth and market share. Alternatively, the GE model suggests that companies determine strategic alternatives based on the comparisons between business position and market attractiveness.

A marketing plan should define the business mission, perform a situation analysis, define objectives, delineate a target market, and establish components of the marketing mix. Other elements that may be included in a plan are budgets, implementation timetables, required marketing research efforts, or elements of advanced strategic planning.

LO 2-4 Develop an appropriate business mission statement. The firm's mission statement establishes boundaries for all subsequent decisions, objectives, and strategies. A mission statement should focus on the market(s) the organization is attempting to serve rather than on the good or service offered.

LO 2-5 Describe the components of a situation analysis. In the situation (or SWOT) analysis, the firm should identify its internal strengths (S) and weaknesses (W) and also examine external opportunities (O) and threats (T). When examining external opportunities and threats, marketing managers must analyze aspects of the marketing environment in a process called *environmental scanning*. The six macroenvironmental forces studied most often are social, demographic, economic, technological, political and legal, and competitive.

LO 2-6 Identify sources of competitive advantage. There are three types of competitive advantage: cost, product/service differentiation, and niche. Sources of cost competitive advantage include experience curves, efficient labor, no-frills goods and services, government subsidies, product design, reengineering, production innovations, and new methods of service delivery. A product/service differentiation competitive advantage exists when a firm provides something unique that is valuable to buyers beyond just low price. Niche competitive advantages come from targeting unique segments with specific needs and wants. The goal of all these sources of competitive advantage is to be sustainable.

LO 2-7 Explain the criteria for stating good marketing objectives. Objectives should be realistic, measurable, time specific, and compared to a benchmark. They must also be consistent and indicate the priorities of the organization. Good marketing objectives communicate marketing management philosophies, provide management direction, motivate employees, force executives to think clearly, and form a basis for control.

marketing plan a written document that acts as a guidebook of marketing activities for the marketing manager

LO 2-4

mission statement a statement of the firm's business based on a careful analysis of benefits sought by present and potential customers and an analysis of existing and anticipated environmental conditions

marketing myopia defining a business in terms of goods and services rather than in terms of the benefits customers seek

LO 2-5

SWOT analysis identifying internal strengths (S) and weaknesses (W) and also examining external opportunities (O) and threats (T)

environmental scanning collection and interpretation of information about forces, events, and relationships in the external environment that may affect the future of the organization or the implementation of the marketing plan

LO 2-6

competitive advantage a set of unique features of a company and its products that are perceived by the target market as significant and superior to those of the competition

cost competitive advantage being the low-cost competitor in an industry while maintaining satisfactory profit margins

experience curves curves that show costs declining at a predictable rate as experience with a product increases

product/service differentiation competitive advantage the provision of something that is unique and valuable to buyers beyond simply offering a lower price than that of the competition

niche competitive advantage the advantage achieved when a firm seeks to target and effectively serve a small segment of the market

LO 2-8 Discuss target market strategies. Targeting markets begins with a market opportunity analysis (MOA), which describes and estimates the size and sales potential of market segments that are of interest to the firm. In addition, an assessment of key competitors in these market segments is performed. After the market segments are described, one or more may be targeted by the firm.

LO 2-9 Describe the elements of the marketing mix. The marketing mix is a blend of product, place, promotion, and pricing strategies (the four Ps) designed to produce mutually satisfying exchanges with a target market. The starting point of the marketing mix is the product offering—tangible goods, ideas, or services. Place (distribution) strategies are concerned with making products available when and where customers want them. Promotion includes advertising, public relations, sales promotion, and personal selling. Price is what a buyer must give up in order to obtain a product and is often the most flexible of the four marketing mix elements.

LO 2-10 Explain why implementation, evaluation, and control of the marketing plan are necessary. Before a marketing plan can work, it must be implemented—that is, people must perform the actions in the plan. The plan should also be evaluated to see if it has achieved its objectives. Poor implementation can be a major factor in a plan's failure, but working to gain acceptance can be accomplished with task forces. Once implemented, one major aspect of control is the marketing audit and ultimately continuing to apply what the audit uncovered through postaudit tasks.

LO 2-11 Identify several techniques that help make strategic planning effective. First, management must realize that strategic planning is an ongoing process and not a once-a-year exercise. Second, good strategic planning involves a high level of creativity. The last requirement is top management's support and participation.

sustainable competitive advantage an advantage that cannot be copied by the competition

LO 2-7

marketing objective a statement of what is to be accomplished through marketing activities

LO 2-8

marketing strategy the activities of selecting and describing one or more target markets and developing and maintaining a marketing mix that will produce mutually satisfying exchanges with target markets

market opportunity analysis (MOA) the description and estimation of the size and sales potential of market segments that are of interest to the firm and the assessment of key competitors in these market segments

LO 2-9

marketing mix (four Ps) a unique blend of product, place (distribution), promotion, and pricing strategies designed to produce mutually satisfying exchanges with a target market

LO 2-10

implementation the process that turns a marketing plan into action assignments and ensures that these assignments are executed in a way that accomplishes the plan's objectives

evaluation gauging the extent to which the marketing objectives have been achieved during the specified time period

control provides the mechanisms for evaluating marketing results in light of the plan's objectives and for correcting actions that do not help the organization reach those objectives within budget guidelines

marketing audit a thorough, systematic, periodic evaluation of the objectives, strategies, structure, and performance of the marketing organization

KEY TERMS

LO 3-1

ethics the moral principles or values that generally govern the conduct of an individual or a group

LO 3-2

deontological theory ethical theory that states that people should adhere to their obligations and duties when analyzing an ethical dilemma

utilitarian ethical theory ethical theory that is founded on the ability to predict the consequences of an action

casuist ethical theory ethical theory that compares a current ethical dilemma with examples of similar ethical dilemmas and their outcomes

moral relativism an ethical theory of time-and-place ethics; that is, the belief that ethical truths depend on the individuals and groups holding them

virtue a character trait valued as being good

LO 3-3

morals the rules people develop as a result of cultural values and norms

code of ethics a guideline to help marketing managers and other employees make better decisions

Foreign Corrupt Practices Act (FCPA) a law that prohibits U.S. corporations from making illegal payments to public officials of foreign governments to obtain business rights or to enhance their business dealings in those countries

LO 3-4

corporate social responsibility (CSR) a business's concern for society's welfare

stakeholder theory ethical theory stating that social responsibility is paying attention to the interest of every affected stakeholder in every aspect of a firm's operation

KEY CONCEPTS

LO 3-1 Explain the determinants of a civil society. Societal order is created through the six modes of social control. Ethics are the moral principles or values that generally govern the conduct of an individual or a group. Laws come into being when ethical rules and guidelines are codified into law. Formal and informal groups have codes of conduct that prescribe acceptable and desired behaviors of their members. Self-regulation involves the voluntary acceptance of standards established by nongovernmental entities. The media play a key role in informing the public about the actions of individuals and organizations—both good and bad. An informed and engaged society can help mold individual and corporate behavior.

LO 3-2 Explain the concept of ethical behavior. Ethics are the standards of behavior by which conduct is judged. Standards that are legal may not always be ethical. An ethics violation offends a person's sense of justice or fairness. Ethics basically constitute the unwritten rules developed to guide interactions. Many ethical questions arise from balancing a business's need to produce profit for shareholders against its desire to operate honestly and with concern for environmental and social issues.

Several ethical theories apply to marketing. Deontological theory states that people should adhere to their obligations and duties when analyzing an ethical dilemma. Utilitarian ethical theory says that the choice that yields the greatest benefit to the most people is the choice that is ethically correct. The casuist ethical theory compares a current ethical dilemma with examples of similar ethical dilemmas and their outcomes. Moral relativists believe in time-and-place ethics, that is, ethical truths depend on the individuals and groups holding them. Virtue ethics suggests that individuals become able to solve ethical dilemmas when they develop and nurture a set of virtues.

LO 3-3 Describe ethical behavior in business. Business ethics may be viewed as a subset of the values of society as a whole, with a foundation based on the cultural values and norms that constitute a culture's morals. The ethical conduct of businesspeople is shaped by societal elements, including family, education, and religious institutions. Morals are the rules people develop as a result of cultural values and norms. As members of society, businesspeople are morally obligated to consider the ethical implications of their decisions. Ethical decision making can be grouped into three basic approaches. The first approach examines the consequences of decisions. The second approach relies on rules and laws to guide decision making. The third approach is based on a theory of moral development that places individuals or groups in one of three developmental stages: preconventional morality, conventional morality, or postconventional morality.

In addition to personal influences, there are many business influences on ethical decision making. Some of the most influential include the extent of ethical problems within the organization, top management's actions on ethics, potential magnitude of the consequences, social consensus, probability of a harmful outcome, length of time between the decision and the onset of consequences, and the number of people affected.

Many companies develop a code of ethics to help their employees make ethical decisions. A code of ethics can help employees identify acceptable business practices, be an effective internal control on behavior, help employees avoid confusion when determining whether decisions are ethical, and facilitate discussion about what is right and wrong.

3 ETHICS AND SOCIAL RESPONSIBILITY

pyramid of corporate social responsibility a model that suggests corporate social responsibility is composed of economic, legal, ethical, and philanthropic responsibilities and that the firm's economic performance supports the entire structure

LO 3–5

sustainability the idea that socially responsible companies will outperform their peers by focusing on the world's social problems and viewing them as opportunities to build profits and help the world at the same time

green marketing the development and marketing of products designed to minimize negative effects on the physical environment or to improve the environment

LO 3–6

cause-related marketing the cooperative marketing efforts between a for-profit firm and a nonprofit organization

Studies show that ethical beliefs vary little from country to country. However, there are enough cultural differences, such as the practice of bribery or gift giving, that laws such as the Foreign Corrupt Practices Act (FCPA) have been put in place to discourage and attempt to modify the current acceptance of such practices.

LO 3-4 Discuss corporate social responsibility. Corporate social responsibility (CSR) is a business's concern for society's welfare. Responsibility in business refers to a firm's concern for the way its decisions affect society. Stakeholder theory says that social responsibility means paying attention to the interest of every affected stakeholder in every aspect of a firm's operation, including employees, management, customers, the local community, suppliers, and owners. According to the pyramid of corporate social responsibility, CSR has four components: economic, legal, ethical, and philanthropic. These are intertwined, yet the most fundamental is earning a profit. If a firm does not earn a profit, the other three responsibilities are moot.

EXHIBIT 3: PYRAMID OF CORPORATE SOCIAL RESPONSIBILITY

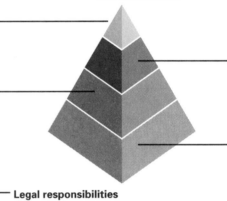

Philanthropic responsibilities
Be a good corporate citizen.
Contribute resources to the community; improve the quality of life.

Ethical responsibilities
Be ethical.
Do what is right, just, and fair. Avoid harm.

Legal responsibilities
Obey the law.
Law is society's codification of right and wrong. Play by the rules of the game.

Economic responsibilities
Be profitable.
Profit is the foundation on which all other responsibilities rest.

© Cengage Learning

LO 3-5 Describe the arguments for and against social responsibility. Most businesspeople believe they should do more than pursue profits. Although a company must consider its economic needs first, it must also operate within the law, do what is ethical and fair, and be a good corporate citizen. Sustainability is the concept that socially responsible companies will outperform their peers by focusing on the world's social problems and viewing them as an opportunity to earn profits and help the world at the same time. Social responsibility is growing, but it can be costly and the benefits are not always immediate. In addition, some surveys report that consumer desire to purchase responsible products does not always translate to actually purchasing those products. One branch of social responsibility is green marketing, which aids the environment and often the bottom line of a business.

LO 3-6 Explain cause-related marketing. Cause-related marketing is the cooperative effort between a for-profit firm and a nonprofit organization. It is different from philanthropy, which is a specific, tax-deductible donation. Cause-related marketing is very popular because it can enhance the reputation of the corporation and also make additional profit for the company. However, consumers sometimes come to believe that every company is tied to a cause, resulting in consumer cause fatigue.

KEY TERMS

LO 4-1

target market a group of people or organizations for which an organization designs, implements, and maintains a marketing mix intended to meet the need of that group, resulting in mutually satisfying exchanges

environmental management when a company implements strategies that attempt to shape the external environment within which it operates

LO 4-2

component lifestyles the practice of choosing goods and services that meet one's diverse needs and interests rather than conforming to a single, traditional lifestyle

LO 4-3

demography the study of people's vital statistics, such as age, race and ethnicity, and location

Generation Y people born between 1979 and 1994

Generation X people born between 1965 and 1978

baby boomers people born between 1946 and 1964

LO 4-5

purchasing power a comparison of income versus the relative cost of a standard set of goods and services in different geographic areas

inflation a measure of the decrease in the value of money, expressed as the percentage reduction in value since the previous year

recession a period of economic activity characterized by negative growth, which reduces demand for goods and services

LO 4-6

basic research pure research that aims to confirm an existing theory or to learn more about a concept or phenomenon

KEY CONCEPTS

LO 4-1 Discuss the external environment of marketing and explain how it affects a firm. The external marketing environment consists of social, demographic, economic, technological, political and legal, and competitive variables. Marketers generally cannot control the elements of the external environment. Instead, they must understand how the external environment is changing and the impact of that change on the target market. Then marketing managers can create a marketing mix to effectively meet the needs of target customers.

LO 4-2 Describe the social factors that affect marketing. Within the external environment, social factors are perhaps the most difficult for marketers to anticipate. Several major social trends are currently shaping marketing strategies. First, people of all ages have a broader range of interests, defying traditional consumer profiles. Second, social media, Web-based, and mobile technology change how people and marketers interact by allowing one-to-one, one-to-many, and many-to-many communications. Because Facebook is about human-to-human interaction, companies are turning to it and other forms of social media with ever-increasing speed.

LO 4-3 Explain the importance to marketing managers of current demographic trends. Today, several basic demographic patterns are influencing marketing mixes. The world population hit 7 billion in 2012, but growth was unevenly distributed. Marketers are also faced with increasingly experienced consumers among the younger generations such as tweens and teens. And because the population is also growing older, marketers are offering more products that appeal to middle-aged and older consumers.

LO 4-4 Explain the importance to marketing managers of growing ethnic markets. About one in three U.S. residents is a member of a minority group. By 2050, about one in three U.S. residents will be Hispanic. Many companies are creating departments and product lines to target multicultural market segments effectively. Companies have quickly found that ethnic markets are not homogeneous.

LO 4-5 Identify consumer and marketer reactions to the state of the economy. In recent years, U.S. incomes have fallen around 8 percent. During a time of inflation, marketers generally attempt to maintain level pricing to avoid losing customer brand loyalty. During times of recession, many marketers maintain or reduce prices to counter the effects of decreased demand; they also concentrate on increasing production efficiency and improving customer service. The Great Recession was the largest economic downturn since the Great Depression. While the causes of recession are very complex, this one began with the collapse of inflated housing prices.

LO 4-6 Identify the impact of technology on a firm. Monitoring new technology and encouraging research and development (R&D) of new technology are essential to keeping up with competitors in today's marketing environment. Innovation through R&D needs to be stimulated by upper management and fostered in creative environments. Although developing new technology internally is a key to creating and maintaining a long-term competitive advantage, external technology is also important to managers.

LO 4-7 Discuss the political and legal environment of marketing. All marketing activities are subject to state and federal laws and the rulings of regulatory agencies. Marketers are responsible for remaining aware of and abiding by such regulations. Some key federal agencies that affect marketing are the Consumer Product Safety Commission, the Food and Drug Administration, and the Federal Trade

applied research research that attempts to develop new or improved products

LO 4-7

Consumer Product Safety Commission (CPSC) a federal agency established to protect the health and safety of consumers in and around their homes

Food and Drug Administration (FDA) a federal agency charged with enforcing regulations against selling and distributing adulterated, misbranded, or hazardous food and drug products

Federal Trade Commission (FTC) a federal agency empowered to prevent persons or corporations from using unfair methods of competition in commerce

Commission. Many laws, including privacy laws, have been passed to protect the consumer as well. In 2012, the FTC called for online data collectors to adopt better privacy policies and asked Congress to pass comprehensive privacy legislation. Despite federal efforts, online tracking has become widespread and pervasive.

EXHIBIT 2: PRIMARY U.S. LAWS PROTECTING CONSUMERS

Legislation	Impact on Marketing
Federal Food and Drug Act of 1906	Prohibits adulteration and misbranding of foods and drugs involved in interstate commerce; strengthened by the Food, Drug, and Cosmetic Act (1938) and the Kefauver-Harris Drug Amendment (1962).
Federal Hazardous Substances Act of 1960	Requires warning labels on hazardous household chemicals.
Kefauver-Harris Drug Amendment of 1962	Requires that manufacturers conduct tests to prove drug effectiveness and safety.
Consumer Credit Protection Act of 1968	Requires that lenders fully disclose true interest rates and all other charges to credit customers for loans and installment purchases.
Child Protection and Toy Safety Act of 1969	Prevents marketing of products so dangerous that adequate safety warnings cannot be given.
Public Health Smoking Act of 1970	Prohibits cigarette advertising on television and radio and revises the health hazard warning on cigarette packages.
Poison Prevention Labeling Act of 1970	Requires safety packaging for products that may be harmful to children.
National Environmental Policy Act of 1970	Established the Environmental Protection Agency to deal with various types of pollution and organizations that create pollution.
Public Health Cigarette Smoking Act of 1971	Prohibits tobacco advertising on radio and television.
Consumer Product Safety Act of 1972	Created the Consumer Product Safety Commission, which has authority to specify safety standards for most products.
Child Protection Act of 1990	Regulates the number of minutes of advertising on children's television.
Children's Online Privacy Protection Act of 1998	Empowers the FTC to set rules regarding how and when marketers must obtain parental permission before asking children marketing research questions.
Aviation Security Act of 2001	Requires airlines to take extra security measures to protect passengers, including the installation of stronger cockpit doors, improved baggage screening, and increased security training for airport personnel.
Homeland Security Act of 2002	Protects consumers against terrorist acts; created the Department of Homeland Security.
Do Not Call Law of 2003	Protects consumers against unwanted telemarketing calls.
CAN-SPAM Act of 2003	Protects consumers against unwanted e-mail, or spam.
Credit Card Act of 2009	Provides many credit card protections.
Restoring American Financial Stability Act of 2010	Created the Consumer Financial Protection Bureau to protect consumers against unfair, abusive, and deceptive financial practices.

© Cengage Learning

LO 4-8 Explain the basics of foreign and domestic competition. The competitive environment encompasses the number of competitors a firm must face, the relative size of the competitors, and the degree of interdependence within the industry. Declining population growth, rising costs, and shortages of resources have heightened domestic competition.

KEY TERMS

LO 5-1

global marketing marketing that targets markets throughout the world

global vision recognizing and reacting to international marketing opportunities, using effective global marketing strategies, and being aware of threats from foreign competitors in all markets

gross domestic product (GDP) the total market value of all final goods and services produced in a country for a given time period

job outsourcing sending U.S. jobs abroad

LO 5-2

multinational corporation a company that is heavily engaged in international trade, beyond exporting and importing

capital intensive using more capital than labor in the production process

global marketing standardization production of uniform products that can be sold the same way all over the world

multidomestic strategy when multinational firms enable individual subsidiaries to compete independently in domestic markets

LO 5-3

Mercosur the largest Latin American trade agreement; includes Argentina, Bolivia, Brazil, Chile, Colombia, Ecuador, Paraguay, Peru, Uruguay, and Venezuela

Uruguay Round a trade agreement to dramatically lower trade barriers worldwide; created the World Trade Organization

World Trade Organization (WTO) a trade organization that replaced the old General Agreement on Tariffs and Trade (GATT)

KEY CONCEPTS

LO 5-1 Discuss the importance of global marketing. Businesspeople who adopt a global vision are better able to identify global marketing opportunities, understand the nature of global networks, create effective global marketing strategies, and compete against foreign competition in domestic markets. Large corporations have traditionally been the major global competitors, but more and more small businesses are entering the global marketplace. Despite fears of job losses to other countries with cheaper labor, there are many benefits to globalization, including the reduction of poverty and increased standards of living.

LO 5-2 Discuss the impact of multinational firms on the world economy. Multinational corporations are international traders that regularly operate across national borders. Because of their vast size and financial, technological, and material resources, multinational corporations have great influence on the world economy. They have the ability to overcome trade problems, save on labor costs, and tap new technology. There are critics and supporters of multinational corporations, and the critics question the actual benefits of bringing capital-intensive technology to impoverished nations. Many countries block foreign investment in factories, land, and companies to protect their economies.

Some companies presume that markets throughout the world are more and more similar, so some global products can be standardized across global markets.

LO 5-3 Describe the external environment facing global marketers. Global marketers face the same environmental factors as they do domestically: culture, economic and technological development, political structure and actions, demography, and natural resources. Cultural considerations include societal values, attitudes and beliefs, language, and customary business practices. A country's economic and technological status depends on its stage of industrial development, which, in turn, affects average family incomes. The political structure is shaped by political ideology and such policies as tariffs, quotas, boycotts, exchange controls, trade agreements, and market groupings. Demographic variables include the size of a population and its age and geographic distribution. A shortage of natural resources also affects the external environment by dictating what is available and at what price.

LO 5-4 Identify the various ways of entering the global marketplace. Firms use the following strategies to enter global markets, in descending order of risk and profit: direct investment, joint venture, contract manufacturing, licensing and franchising, and exporting.

EXHIBIT 3: RISK LEVELS FOR FIVE METHODS OF ENTERING THE GLOBAL MARKETPLACE

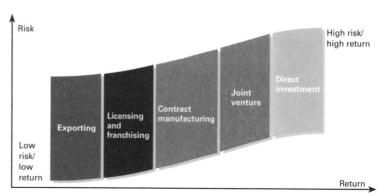

© Cengage Learning

General Agreement on Tariffs and Trade (GATT) a trade agreement that contained loopholes enabling countries to avoid trade-barrier reduction agreements

North American Free Trade Agreement (NAFTA) an agreement between Canada, the United States, and Mexico that created the world's then-largest free trade zone

Dominican Republic-Central America Free Trade Agreement (CAFTA-DR) a trade agreement instituted in 2005 that includes Costa Rica, the Dominican Republic, El Salvador, Guatemala, Honduras, Nicaragua, and the United States

European Union (EU) a free trade zone encompassing twenty-eight European countries

World Bank an international bank that offers low-interest loans, advice, and information to developing nations

International Monetary Fund (IMF) an international organization that acts as a lender of last resort, providing loans to troubled nations, and also works to promote trade through financial cooperation

Group of Twenty (G-20) a forum for international economic development that promotes discussion between industrial and emerging-market countries on key issues related to global economic stability

LO 5-4

exporting selling domestically produced products to buyers in other countries

buyer for export an intermediary in the global market that assumes all ownership risks and sells globally for its own account

export broker an intermediary who plays the traditional broker's role by bringing buyer and seller together

LO 5-5 List the basic elements involved in developing a global marketing mix. A firm's major consideration is how much it will adjust the four Ps—product, promotion, place (distribution), and price—within each country. One strategy is to use one product and one promotion message worldwide. A second strategy is to create new products for global markets. A third strategy is to keep the product basically the same but alter the promotional message. A fourth strategy is to slightly alter the product to meet local conditions.

GLOBAL MARKETING MIX

Product + Promotion	Place (Distribution)	Price
One product, one message	Channel choice	Dumping
Product invention	Channel structure	Countertrade
Product adaptation	Country infrastructure	Exchange rates
Message adaptation	Purchasing power	

© Cengage Learning

LO 5-6 Discover how the Internet is affecting global marketing. Simply opening an e-commerce site can open the door for international sales. International carriers, such as UPS, can help solve logistics problems. Language translation software can help an e-commerce business become multilingual. Yet cultural differences and old-line rules, regulations, and taxes hinder rapid development of e-commerce in many countries. Not only do global marketers use social media for understanding consumers but also to build their brands as they expand internationally.

export agent an intermediary who acts like a manufacturer's agent for the exporter; the export agent lives in the foreign market

licensing the legal process whereby a licensor allows another firm to use its manufacturing process, trademarks, patents, trade secrets, or other proprietary knowledge

contract manufacturing private label manufacturing by a foreign company

joint venture when a domestic firm buys part of a foreign company or joins with a foreign company to create a new entity

direct foreign investment active ownership of a foreign company or of overseas manufacturing or marketing facilities

LO 5-5

exchange rate the price of one country's currency in terms of another country's currency

floating exchange rates a system in which prices of different currencies move up and down based on the demand for and the supply of each currency

dumping the sale of an exported product at a price lower than that charged for the same or a like product in the "home" market of the exporter

countertrade a form of trade in which all or part of the payment for goods or services is in the form of other goods or services

blog a publicly accessible Web page that functions as an interactive journal, where readers can post comments on the author's entries

KEY TERMS

LO 6-1

consumer behavior processes a consumer uses to make purchase decisions, as well as to use and dispose of purchased goods or services; also includes factors that influence purchase decisions and product use

LO 6-2

consumer decision-making process a five-step process used by consumers when buying goods or services

need recognition result of an imbalance between actual and desired states

want recognition of an unfulfilled need and a product that will satisfy it

stimulus any unit of input affecting one or more of the five senses: sight, smell, taste, touch, hearing

internal information search the process of recalling past information stored in the memory

external information search the process of seeking information in the outside environment

nonmarketing-controlled information source a product information source that is not associated with advertising or promotion

marketing-controlled information source a product information source that originates with marketers promoting the product

evoked set (consideration set) a group of brands resulting from an information search from which a buyer can choose

LO 6-3

cognitive dissonance inner tension that a consumer experiences after recognizing an inconsistency between behavior and values or opinions

KEY CONCEPTS

LO 6-1 Explain why marketing managers should understand consumer behavior. An understanding of consumer behavior reduces marketing managers' uncertainty when they are defining a target market and designing a marketing mix.

LO 6-2 Analyze the components of the consumer decision-making process. The consumer decision-making process begins with need recognition, when stimuli trigger awareness of an unfulfilled want. If additional information is required to make a purchase decision, the consumer may engage in an internal or external information search. The consumer then evaluates the alternatives using the additional information and establishes purchase guidelines. Finally, a purchase decision is made.

LO 6-3 Explain the consumer's postpurchase evaluation process. Consumer postpurchase evaluation is influenced by prepurchase expectations, the prepurchase information search, and the consumer's general level of self-confidence. When a purchase creates cognitive dissonance, consumers tend to react by seeking positive reinforcement for the purchase decision, avoiding negative information about the purchase decision, or revoking the purchase decision by returning the product.

LO 6-4 Identify the types of consumer buying decisions and discuss the significance of consumer involvement. Consumer decision making falls into three broad categories: routine response behavior, limited decision making, and extensive decision making. High-involvement decisions usually include an extensive information search and a thorough evaluation of alternatives. In contrast, low-involvement decisions are characterized by brand loyalty and a lack of personal identification with the product. The main factors affecting the level of consumer involvement are previous experience, interest, perceived risk of negative consequences (financial, social, and psychological), and social visibility. A purchase decision can be highly involved due to a wide range of factors, including product involvement, situational involvement, shopping involvement, enduring involvement, and emotional involvement.

LO 6-5 Identify and understand the cultural factors that affect consumer buying decisions. Cultural influences on consumer buying decisions include culture and values, subculture, and social class. Culture is the essential character of a society that distinguishes it from other cultural groups. The underlying elements of every culture are the values, language, myths, customs, rituals, laws, and the artifacts, or products, that are transmitted from one generation to the next. The most defining element of a culture is its values. A culture can be divided into subcultures on the basis of demographic characteristics, geographic regions, national and ethnic background, political beliefs, and religious beliefs.

LO 6-6 Identify and understand the social factors that affect consumer buying decisions. Social factors include such external influences as reference groups, opinion leaders, and family. Consumers seek out others' opinions for guidance on new products or services and products with image-related attributes or because attribute information is lacking or uninformative. Consumers may use products or brands to identify with or become a member of a reference group, or to follow an opinion leader. Family members also influence purchase decisions; children tend to shop in similar patterns as their parents.

LO 6-7 Identify and understand the individual factors that affect consumer buying decisions. Individual factors that affect consumer buying decisions include gender; age and family life cycle stage; and personality, self-concept, and lifestyle. Beyond obvious physiological differences, men and women differ in their social and

LO 6-4

involvement the amount of time and effort a buyer invests in the search, evaluation, and decision processes of consumer behavior

routine response behavior the type of decision making exhibited by consumers buying frequently purchased, low-cost goods and services; requires little search and decision time

limited decision making the type of decision making that requires a moderate amount of time for gathering information and deliberating about an unfamiliar brand in a familiar product category

extensive decision making the most complex type of consumer decision making, used when buying an unfamiliar, expensive product or an infrequently bought item; requires use of several criteria for evaluating options and much time for seeking information

LO 6-5

culture the set of values, norms, attitudes, and other meaningful symbols that shape human behavior and the artifacts, or products, of that behavior as they are transmitted from one generation to the next

value the enduring belief that a specific mode of conduct is personally or socially preferable to another mode of conduct

subculture a homogeneous group of people who share elements of the overall culture as well as unique elements of their own group

social class a group of people in a society who are considered nearly equal in status or community esteem, who regularly socialize among themselves both formally and informally, and who share behavioral norms

LO 6-6

reference group all of the formal and informal groups in society that influence an individual's purchasing behavior

economic roles, and that affects consumer buying decisions. A consumer's age generally indicates what products he or she may be interested in purchasing. Marketers often define their target markets in terms of consumers' life cycle stage, following changes in consumers' attitudes and behavioral tendencies as they mature. Finally, certain products and brands reflect consumers' personality, self-concept, and lifestyle.

LO 6-8 Identify and understand the psychological factors that affect consumer buying decisions. Psychological factors include perception, motivation, learning, values, beliefs, and attitudes. These factors allow consumers to interact with the world around them, recognize their feelings, gather and analyze information, formulate thoughts and opinions, and take action. Perception allows consumers to recognize their consumption problems. Motivation is what drives consumers to take action to satisfy specific consumption needs. Almost all consumer behavior results from learning, which is the process that creates changes in behavior through experience. Consumers with similar beliefs and attitudes tend to react alike to marketing-related inducements.

primary membership group a reference group with which people interact regularly in an informal, face-to-face manner, such as family, friends, and coworkers

secondary membership group a reference group with which people associate less consistently and more formally than a primary membership group, such as a club, professional group, or religious group

aspirational reference group a group that someone would like to join

norm a value or attitude deemed acceptable by a group

nonaspirational reference group a group with which an individual does not want to associate

opinion leader an individual who influences the opinions of others

socialization process how cultural values and norms are passed down to children

LO 6-7

personality a way of organizing and grouping the consistencies of an individual's reactions to situations

self-concept how consumers perceive themselves in terms of attitudes, perceptions, beliefs, and self-evaluations

ideal self-image the way an individual would like to be perceived

real self-image the way an individual actually perceives himself or herself

LO 6-8

perception the process by which people select, organize, and interpret stimuli into a meaningful and coherent picture

selective exposure the process whereby a consumer notices certain stimuli and ignores others

selective distortion a process whereby a consumer changes or distorts information that conflicts with his or her feelings or beliefs

selective retention a process whereby a consumer remembers only that information that supports his or her personal beliefs

motive a driving force that causes a person to take action to satisfy specific needs

Maslow's hierarchy of needs a method of classifying human needs and motivations into five categories in ascending order of importance: physiological, safety, social, esteem, and self-actualization

learning a process that creates changes in behavior, immediate or expected, through experience and practice

stimulus generalization a form of learning that occurs when one response is extended to a second stimulus similar to the first

stimulus discrimination a learned ability to differentiate among similar products

belief an organized pattern of knowledge that an individual holds as true about his or her world

attitude a learned tendency to respond consistently toward a given object

KEY TERMS

LO 7-1

business marketing (industrial marketing) the marketing of goods and services to individuals and organizations for purposes other than personal consumption

LO 7-2

business-to-business electronic commerce (B-to-B or B2B e-commerce) the use of the Internet to facilitate the exchange of goods, services, and information between organizations

stickiness a measure of a Web site's effectiveness; calculated by multiplying the frequency of visits by the duration of a visit by the number of pages viewed during each visit (site reach)

LO 7-3

strategic alliance (strategic partnership) a cooperative agreement between business firms

relationship commitment a firm's belief that an ongoing relationship with another firm is so important that the relationship warrants maximum efforts at maintaining it indefinitely

trust the condition that exists when one party has confidence in an exchange partner's reliability and integrity

keiretsu a network of interlocking corporate affiliates

LO 7-4

original equipment manufacturers (OEMs) individuals and organizations that buy business goods and incorporate them into the products they produce for eventual sale to other producers or to consumers

LO 7-5

North American Industry Classification System (NAICS) a detailed numbering system developed by the United States, Canada, and Mexico to classify North American business establishments by their main production processes

KEY CONCEPTS

LO 7-1 Describe business marketing. Business marketing provides goods and services that are bought for use in business rather than for personal consumption. Intended use, not physical characteristics, distinguishes a business product from a consumer product.

LO 7-2 Describe the role of the Internet in business marketing. The rapid expansion and adoption of the Internet have made business markets more competitive than ever before. Businesses are integrating content marketing into their B-to-B marketing campaigns, and online measurements such as a Web site's stickiness are increasingly important to B-to-B marketers. Many marketers use social media to create awareness and build relationships and community. Some metrics that are particularly useful for increasing the success of a social media campaign are awareness, engagement, and conversion. These Web-based tools help B-to-B marketers generate more valuable leads and pull customers into their Web sites.

LO 7-3 Discuss the role of relationship marketing and strategic alliances in business marketing. Relationship marketing entails seeking and establishing long-term alliances or partnerships with customers. A strategic alliance is a cooperative agreement between business firms. Firms form alliances to leverage what they do well by partnering with others that have complementary skills. Although the concepts of relationship marketing and strategic alliances are relatively new to American marketers, these ideas have long been used by marketers in other cultures.

LO 7-4 Identify the four major categories of business market customers. Producer markets consist of for-profit individuals and organizations that buy products to use in producing other products, as components of other products, or in facilitating business operations. Reseller markets consist of wholesalers and retailers that buy finished products to resell for profit. Government markets include federal, state, county, and city governments that buy goods and services to support their own operations and serve the needs of citizens. Institutional markets consist of very diverse nonbusiness institutions whose main goals do not include profit.

LO 7-5 Explain the North American Industry Classification System. The North American Industry Classification System (NAICS) provides a way to identify, analyze, segment, and target business and government markets. Organizations can be identified and compared by a numeric code indicating business sector, subsector, industry group, industry, and industry subdivision. NAICS is a valuable tool for analyzing, segmenting, and targeting business markets.

LO 7-6 Explain the major differences between business and consumer markets. In business markets, demand is derived, inelastic, joint, and fluctuating. Purchase volume is much larger than in consumer markets, customers are fewer and more geographically concentrated, and distribution channels are more direct. Buying is approached more formally using professional purchasing agents, more people are involved in the buying process, negotiation is more complex, and reciprocity and leasing are more common. And, finally, selling strategy in business markets normally focuses on personal contact rather than on advertising.

Characteristic	Business Market	Consumer Market
Demand	Organizational	Individual
Purchase volume	Larger	Smaller

7 BUSINESS MARKETING

LO 7-6

derived demand the demand for business products

joint demand the demand for two or more items used together in a final product

multiplier effect (accelerator principle) phenomenon in which a small increase or decrease in consumer demand can produce a much larger change in demand for the facilities and equipment needed to make the consumer product

business-to-business online exchange an electronic trading floor that provides companies with integrated links to their customers and suppliers

reciprocity a practice whereby business purchasers choose to buy from their own customers

LO 7-7

major equipment (installations) capital goods such as large or expensive machines, mainframe computers, blast furnaces, generators, airplanes, and buildings

accessory equipment goods, such as portable tools and office equipment, that are less expensive and shorter-lived than major equipment

raw materials unprocessed extractive or agricultural products, such as mineral ore, lumber, wheat, corn, fruits, vegetables, and fish

component parts either finished items ready for assembly or products that need very little processing before becoming part of some other product

processed materials products used directly in manufacturing other products

supplies consumable items that do not become part of the final product

business services expense items that do not become part of a final product

Characteristic	Business Market	Consumer Market
Number of customers	Few	Many
Location of buyers	Geographically concentrated	Dispersed
Distribution structure	More direct	More indirect
Nature of buying	More professional	More personal
Nature of buying influence	Multiple	Single
Type of negotiations	More complex	Simpler
Use of reciprocity	Yes	No
Use of leasing	Greater	Lesser
Primary promotional method	Personal selling	Advertising

LO 7-7 Describe the seven types of business goods and services. Major equipment includes capital goods such as heavy machinery. Accessory equipment is typically less expensive and shorter lived than major equipment. Raw materials are extractive or agricultural products that have not been processed. Component parts are finished or near-finished items to be used as parts of other products. Processed materials are used to manufacture other products. Supplies are consumable and not used as part of a final product. Business services are intangible products that many companies use in their operations.

LO 7-8 Discuss the unique aspects of business buying behavior. Business buying behavior is distinguished by five fundamental characteristics. First, buying is normally undertaken by a buying center consisting of many people who range widely in authority level.

Second, business buyers typically evaluate alternative products and suppliers based on quality, service, and price—in that order. Third, business buying falls into three general categories: new buys, modified rebuys, and straight rebuys. Fourth, the ethics of business buyers and sellers are often scrutinized. Fifth, customer service before, during, and after the sale plays a big role in business purchase decisions.

LO 7-8

buying center all those people in an organization who become involved in the purchase decision

new buy a situation requiring the purchase of a product for the first time

modified rebuy a situation in which the purchaser wants some change in the original good or service

straight rebuy a situation in which the purchaser reorders the same goods or services without looking for new information or investigating other suppliers

KEY TERMS

LO 8-1

market people or organizations with needs or wants and the ability and willingness to buy

market segment a subgroup of people or organizations sharing one or more characteristics that cause them to have similar product needs

market segmentation the process of dividing a market into meaningful, relatively similar, and identifiable segments or groups

LO 8-4

segmentation bases (variables) characteristics of individuals, groups, or organizations

geographic segmentation segmenting markets by region of a country or the world, market size, market density, or climate

demographic segmentation segmenting markets by age, gender, income, ethnic background, and family life cycle

family life cycle (FLC) a series of stages determined by a combination of age, marital status, and the presence or absence of children

psychographic segmentation segmenting markets on the basis of personality, motives, lifestyles, and geodemographics

geodemographic segmentation segmenting potential customers into neighborhood lifestyle categories

benefit segmentation the process of grouping customers into market segments according to the benefits they seek from the product

usage-rate segmentation dividing a market by the amount of product bought or consumed

80/20 principle a principle holding that 20 percent of all customers generate 80 percent of the demand

KEY CONCEPTS

LO 8-1 Describe the characteristics of markets and market segments. A market is composed of individuals or organizations with the ability and willingness to make purchases to fulfill their needs or wants. A market segment is a group of individuals or organizations with similar product needs as a result of one or more common characteristics.

LO 8-2 Explain the importance of market segmentation. Before the 1960s, few businesses targeted specific market segments. Today, segmentation is a crucial marketing strategy for nearly all successful organizations. Market segmentation enables marketers to tailor marketing mixes to meet the needs of particular population segments. Segmentation helps marketers identify consumer needs and preferences, areas of declining demand, and new marketing opportunities.

LO 8-3 Discuss the criteria for successful market segmentation. Successful market segmentation depends on four basic criteria: (1) a market segment must be substantial and have enough potential customers to be viable; (2) a market segment must be identifiable and measurable; (3) members of a market segment must be accessible to marketing efforts; and (4) a market segment must respond to particular marketing efforts in a way that distinguishes it from other segments.

LO 8-4 Describe the bases commonly used to segment consumer markets. Five bases are commonly used for segmenting consumer markets. Geographic segmentation is based on region, size, density, and climate characteristics. Demographic segmentation is based on age, gender, income level, ethnicity, and family life cycle characteristics. Psychographic segmentation includes personality, motives, and lifestyle characteristics. Benefits sought is a type of segmentation that identifies customers according to the benefits they seek in a product. Finally, usage segmentation divides a market by the amount of product purchased or consumed.

LO 8-5 Describe the bases for segmenting business markets. Business markets can be segmented on two general bases. First, businesses may segment markets based on company characteristics, such as customers' geographic location, type of company, company size, and product use. Second, companies may segment customers based on the buying processes those customers use.

LO 8-6 List the steps involved in segmenting markets. Six steps are involved when segmenting markets: (1) selecting a market or product category for study; (2) choosing a basis or bases for segmenting the market; (3) selecting segmentation descriptors; (4) profiling and evaluating segments; (5) selecting target markets; and (6) designing, implementing, and maintaining appropriate marketing mixes.

LO 8-7 Discuss alternative strategies for selecting target markets. Marketers select target markets using three different strategies: undifferentiated targeting, concentrated targeting, and multisegment targeting. An undifferentiated targeting strategy assumes that all members of a market have similar needs that can be met with a single marketing mix. A concentrated targeting strategy focuses all marketing efforts on a single market segment. Multisegment targeting is a strategy that uses two or more marketing mixes to target two or more market segments.

LO 8-5

satisficers business customers who place an order with the first familiar supplier to satisfy product and delivery requirements

optimizers business customers who consider numerous suppliers (both familiar and unfamiliar), solicit bids, and study all proposals carefully before selecting one

LO 8-7

target market a group of people or organizations for which an organization designs, implements, and maintains a marketing mix intended to meet the needs of that group, resulting in mutually satisfying exchanges

undifferentiated targeting strategy a marketing approach that views the market as one big market with no individual segments and thus uses a single marketing mix

concentrated targeting strategy a strategy used to select one segment of a market for targeting marketing efforts

niche one segment of a market

multisegment targeting strategy a strategy that chooses two or more well-defined market segments and develops a distinct marketing mix for each

cannibalization a situation that occurs when sales of a new product cut into sales of a firm's existing products

LO 8-9

positioning developing a specific marketing mix to influence potential customers' overall perception of a brand, product line, or organization in general

position the place a product, brand, or group of products occupies in consumers' minds relative to competing offerings

product differentiation a positioning strategy that some firms use to distinguish their products from those of competitors

LO 8-8 Explain how CRM can be used as a targeting tool. Companies that successfully implement CRM tend to customize the goods and services offered to their customers based on data generated through interactions between carefully defined groups of customers and the company. CRM relies on four things to be successful: personalization, time savings, loyalty, and technology. Although mass marketing will probably continue to be used, the advantages of CRM cannot be ignored.

LO 8-9 Explain how and why firms implement positioning strategies and how product differentiation plays a role. Positioning is used to influence consumer perceptions of a particular brand, product line, or organization in relation to competitors. The term *position* refers to the place that the offering occupies in consumers' minds. To establish a unique position, many firms use product differentiation, emphasizing the real or perceived differences between competing offerings. Products may be differentiated on the basis of attribute, price and quality, use or application, product user, product class, competitor, or emotion. Some firms, instead of using product differentiation, position their products as being similar to competing products or brands. Sometimes products or companies are repositioned in order to sustain growth in slow markets or to correct positioning mistakes.

EXHIBIT 3: PERCEPTUAL MAP AND POSITIONING STRATEGY FOR SAKS DEPARTMENT STORES

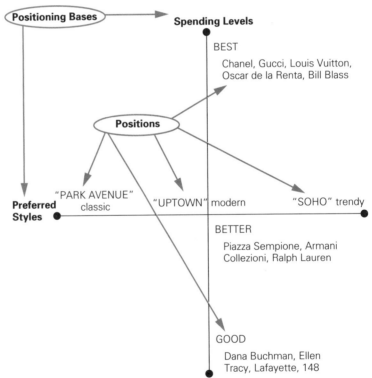

Source: Adapted from Vanessa O'Connell, "Park Avenue Classic or Soho Trendy?" *Wall Street Journal*, April 20, 2007, B1.

perceptual mapping a means of displaying or graphing, in two or more dimensions, the location of products, brands, or groups of products in customers' minds

repositioning changing consumers' perceptions of a brand in relation to competing brands

KEY TERMS

LO 9-1

marketing research the process of planning, collecting, and analyzing data relevant to a marketing decision

LO 9-2

marketing research problem determining what information is needed and how that information can be obtained efficiently and effectively

marketing research objective the specific information needed to solve a marketing research problem; the objective should be to provide insightful decision-making information

management decision problem a broad-based problem that uses marketing research in order for managers to take proper actions

secondary data data previously collected for any purpose other than the one at hand

research design specifies which research questions must be answered, how and when the data will be gathered, and how the data will be analyzed

primary data information that is collected for the first time; used for solving the particular problem under investigation

survey research the most popular technique for gathering primary data, in which a researcher interacts with people to obtain facts, opinions, and attitudes

mall intercept interview a survey research method that involves interviewing people in the common areas of shopping malls

computer-assisted personal interviewing an interviewing method in which the interviewer reads questions from a computer screen and enters the respondent's data directly into the computer

KEY CONCEPTS

LO 9-1 Define marketing research and explain its importance to marketing decision making. Marketing research is a process of collecting and analyzing data for the purpose of solving specific marketing problems. Practically speaking, marketers use marketing research to improve the decision-making process, trace problems, serve customers, gauge the value of goods and services, and measure customer service efforts.

LO 9-2 Describe the steps involved in conducting a marketing research project. The marketing research process involves several basic steps. First, the researcher and the decision maker must agree on a problem statement or set of research objectives. The researcher then creates an overall research design to specify how primary data will be gathered and analyzed. Before collecting data, the researcher decides whether the group to be interviewed will be a probability or nonprobability sample. Field service firms are often hired to carry out data collection. Once data have been collected, the researcher analyzes them using statistical analysis. The researcher then prepares and presents oral and written reports, with conclusions and recommendations, to management. As a final step, the researcher determines whether the recommendations were implemented and what could have been done to make the project more successful.

LO 9-3 Discuss the profound impact of the Internet on marketing research. The Internet has simplified the secondary data search process. Internet survey research is surging in popularity. Internet surveys can be created rapidly, are reported in real time, are relatively inexpensive, and are easily personalized. Often, researchers use the Internet to contact respondents who are difficult to reach by other means. The Internet can also be used to conduct focus groups, to distribute research proposals and reports, and to facilitate collaboration between the client and the research supplier. Consumer-generated media (CGM) comes from various sources, such as blogs, message boards, review sites, and podcasts. Because it is consumer based, CGM is trusted more than traditional forms of advertising and promotion.

LO 9-4 Discuss the growing importance of scanner-based research. A scanner-based research system enables marketers to monitor a market panel's exposure and reaction to such variables as advertising, coupons, store displays, packaging, and price. By analyzing these variables in relation to the panel's subsequent buying behavior, marketers gain useful insight into sales and marketing strategies.

LO 9-5 Explain when marketing research should be conducted. Because acquiring marketing information can be time-consuming and costly, deciding to acquire additional decision-making information depends on managers' perceptions of its quality, price, and timing. Research, therefore, should be undertaken only when the

Probability Samples	
Simple Random Sample	Every member of the population has a known and equal chance of selection.
Stratified Sample	The population is divided into mutually exclusive groups (such as gender or age); then random samples are drawn from each group.
Cluster Sample	The population is divided into mutually exclusive groups (such as geographic areas); then a random sample of clusters is selected. The researcher then collects data from all the elements in the selected clusters or from a probability sample of elements within each selected cluster.
Systematic Sample	A list of the population is obtained—e.g., all persons with a checking account at XYZ Bank—and a skip interval is obtained by dividing the sample size by the population size. If the sample size is 100 and the bank has 1,000 customers, then the skip interval is 10. The beginning number is randomly chosen within the skip interval. If the beginning number is 8, then the skip pattern would be 8, 18, 28, and so on.
Nonprobability Samples	
Convenience Sample	The researcher selects the easiest population members from which to obtain information.
Judgment Sample	The researcher's selection criteria are based on personal judgment that the elements (persons) chosen will likely give accurate information.
Quota Sample	The researcher finds a prescribed number of people in several categories—e.g., owners of large dogs versus owners of small dogs. Respondents are not selected on probability sampling criteria.
Snowball Sample	Additional respondents are selected on the basis of referrals from the initial respondents. This method is used when a desired type of respondent is hard to find—e.g., persons who have taken round-the-world cruises in the last three years. This technique employs the old adage "Birds of a feather flock together."

computer-assisted self-interviewing an interviewing method in which a mall interviewer intercepts and directs willing respondents to nearby computers where each respondent reads questions off a computer screen and directly keys his or her answers into the computer

central-location telephone (CLT) facility a specially designed phone room used to conduct telephone interviewing

executive interview a type of survey that involves interviewing businesspeople at their offices concerning industrial products or services

focus group seven to ten people who participate in a group discussion led by a moderator

open-ended question an interview question that encourages an answer phrased in the respondent's own words

closed-ended question an interview question that asks the respondent to make a selection from a limited list of responses

scaled-response question a closed-ended question designed to measure the intensity of a respondent's answer

observation research a research method that relies on four types of observation: people watching people, people watching an activity, machines watching people, and machines watching an activity

mystery shoppers researchers posing as customers who gather observational data about a store

behavioral targeting (BT) a form of observation marketing research that combines a consumer's online activity with psychographic and demographic profiles compiled in databases

social media monitoring the use of automated tools to monitor online buzz, chatter, and conversations

expected value of the information is greater than the cost of obtaining it. A customer relationship management system is integral to analyzing, transforming, and leveraging customer data.

LO 9-6 Explain the concept of competitive intelligence. Intelligence is analyzed information, and it becomes decision-making intelligence when it has implications for the organization. By helping managers assess their competition and vendors, (CI) leads to fewer surprises. CI is part of a sound marketing strategy, helps companies respond to competitive threats, and helps reduce unnecessary costs.

big data the exponential growth in the volume, variety, and velocity of information and the development of complex, new tools to analyze and create meaning from such data

ethnographic research the study of human behavior in its natural context; involves observation of behavior and physical setting

experiment a method of gathering primary data in which the researcher alters one or more variables while observing the effects of those alterations on another variable

sample a subset from a larger population

universe the population from which a sample will be drawn

probability sample a sample in which every element in the population has a known statistical likelihood of being selected

random sample a sample arranged in such a way that every element of the population has an equal chance of being selected as part of the sample

nonprobability sample any sample in which little or no attempt is made to get a representative cross section of the population

convenience sample a form of nonprobability sample using respondents who are convenient or readily accessible to the researcher—for example, employees, friends, or relatives

measurement error an error that occurs when there is a difference between the information desired by the researcher and the information provided by the measurement process

sampling error an error that occurs when a sample somehow does not represent the target population

frame error an error that occurs when a sample drawn from a population differs from the target population

random error an error that occurs when the selected sample is an imperfect representation of the overall population

field service firm a firm that specializes in interviewing respondents on a subcontracted basis

cross-tabulation a method of analyzing data that lets the analyst look at the responses to one question in relation to the responses to one or more other questions

LO 9-3

consumer-generated media (CGM) media that consumers generate and share among themselves

LO 9-4

scanner-based research a system for gathering information from a single group of respondents by continuously monitoring the advertising, promotion, and pricing they are exposed to and the things they buy

BehaviorScan a scanner-based research program that tracks the purchases of 3,000 households through store scanners in each research market

InfoScan a scanner-based sales-tracking service for the consumer packaged-goods industry

neuromarketing a field of marketing that studies the body's responses to marketing stimuli

LO 9-6

competitive intelligence (CI) an intelligence system that helps managers assess their competition and vendors in order to become more efficient and effective competitors

KEY TERMS

LO 10-1

product everything, both favorable and unfavorable, that a person receives in an exchange

LO 10-2

business product (industrial product) a product used to manufacture other goods or services, to facilitate an organization's operations, or to resell to other customers

consumer product a product bought to satisfy an individual's personal wants or needs

convenience product a relatively inexpensive item that merits little shopping effort

shopping product a product that requires comparison shopping because it is usually more expensive than a convenience product and is found in fewer stores

specialty product a particular item for which consumers search extensively and are very reluctant to accept substitutes

unsought product a product unknown to the potential buyer or a known product that the buyer does not actively seek

LO 10-3

product item a specific version of a product that can be designated as a distinct offering among an organization's products

product line a group of closely related product items

product mix all products that an organization sells

product mix width the number of product lines an organization offers

product line depth the number of product items in a product line

product modification changing one or more of a product's characteristics

KEY CONCEPTS

LO 10-1 Define the term *product*. A product is anything, desired or not, that a person or organization receives in an exchange. The basic goal of purchasing decisions is to receive the tangible and intangible benefits associated with a product. Tangible aspects include packaging, style, color, size, and features. Intangible qualities include service, the retailer's image, the manufacturer's reputation, and the social status associated with a product. An organization's product offering is the crucial element in any marketing mix.

LO 10-2 Classify consumer products. Consumer products are classified into four categories: convenience products, shopping products, specialty products, and unsought products. Convenience products are relatively inexpensive and require limited shopping effort. Shopping products are of two types: homogeneous and heterogeneous. Because of the similarity of homogeneous products, they are differentiated mainly by price and features. In contrast, heterogeneous products appeal to consumers because of their distinct characteristics. Specialty products possess unique benefits that are highly desirable to certain customers. Finally, unsought products are either new products or products that require aggressive selling because they are generally avoided or overlooked by consumers.

LO 10-3 Define the terms *product item*, *product line*, and *product mix*. A product item is a specific version of a product that can be designated as a distinct offering among an organization's products. A product line is a group of closely related products offered by an organization. An organization's product mix includes all the products it sells. Product mix width refers to the number of product lines an organization offers. Product line depth is the number of product items in a product line. Firms modify existing products by changing their quality, functional characteristics, or style. Product line extension occurs when a firm adds new products to existing product lines.

LO 10-4 Describe marketing uses of branding. A brand is a name, term, or symbol that identifies and differentiates a firm's products. Established brands encourage customer loyalty and help new products succeed. Branding strategies require decisions about individual, family, manufacturers', and private brands.

LO 10-5 Describe marketing uses of packaging and labeling. Packaging has four functions: containing and protecting products; promoting products; facilitating product storage, use, and convenience; and facilitating recycling and reducing environmental damage. As a tool for promotion, packaging identifies the brand and its features. It also serves the critical function of differentiating a product from

Product Category	Dominant Brand Name
Children's Entertainment	Disney
Laundry Detergent	Tide
Tablet Computer	Apple
Toothpaste	Crest
Microprocessor	Intel
Soup	Campbell's
Bologna	Oscar Meyer
Ketchup	Heinz
Bleach	Clorox
Greeting Cards	Hallmark
Overnight Mail	FedEx
Copiers	Xerox
Gelatin	Jell-O
Hamburgers	McDonald's
Baby Lotion	Johnson & Johnson
Tissues	Kleenex
Acetaminophen	Tylenol
Coffee	Starbucks
Information Search	Google

Used with the permission of Chris Moorman. All Rights Reserved.

planned obsolescence the practice of modifying products so those that have already been sold become obsolete before they actually need replacement

product line extension adding additional products to an existing product line in order to compete more broadly in the industry

LO 10-4

brand a name, term, symbol, design, or combination thereof that identifies a seller's products and differentiates them from competitors' products

brand name that part of a brand that can be spoken, including letters, words, and numbers

brand mark the elements of a brand that cannot be spoken

brand equity the value of a company or brand name

global brand a brand that obtains at least a one-third of its earnings from outside its home country, is recognizable outside its home base of customers, and has publicly available marketing and financial data

brand loyalty consistent preference for one brand over all others

manufacturer's brand the brand name of a manufacturer

private brand a brand name owned by a wholesaler or a retailer

captive brand a brand manufactured by a third party for an exclusive retailer, without evidence of that retailer's affiliation

individual branding using different brand names for different products

family branding marketing several different products under the same brand name

co-branding placing two or more brand names on a product or its package

trademark the exclusive right to use a brand or part of a brand

competing products and linking it with related products from the same manufacturer. The label is an integral part of the package, with persuasive and informational functions. In essence, the package is the marketer's last chance to influence buyers before they make a purchase decision.

LO 10-6 Discuss global issues in branding and packaging. In addition to brand piracy, international marketers must address a variety of concerns regarding branding and packaging, including choosing a brand name policy, translating labels and meeting host-country labeling requirements, making packages aesthetically compatible with host-country cultures, and offering the sizes of packages preferred in host countries.

Global Branding Considerations	Global Packaging Considerations
One name	Labeling
Modify or adapt one name	Aesthetics
Different names in different markets	Climate

LO 10-7 Describe how and why product warranties are important marketing tools. Just as a package is designed to protect the product, a warranty protects the buyer and gives essential information about the product. A warranty confirms the quality or performance of a good or service. An express warranty is a written guarantee. Express warranties range from simple statements—such as "100-percent cotton" (a guarantee of quality) and "complete satisfaction guaranteed" (a statement of performance)—to extensive documents written in technical language. In contrast, an implied warranty is an unwritten guarantee that the good or service is fit for the purpose for which it was sold. All sales have an implied warranty under the Uniform Commercial Code.

Express warranty = written guarantee

Implied warranty = unwritten guarantee

service mark a trademark for a service

generic product name identifies a product by class or type and cannot be trademarked

LO 10-5

persuasive labeling a type of package labeling that focuses on a promotional theme or logo, and consumer information is secondary

informational labeling a type of package labeling designed to help consumers make proper product selections and lower their cognitive dissonance after the purchase

universal product codes (UPCs) a series of thick and thin vertical lines (bar codes) readable by computerized optical scanners that represent numbers used to track products

LO 10-7

warranty a confirmation of the quality or performance of a good or service

express warranty a written guarantee

implied warranty an unwritten guarantee that the good or service is fit for the purpose for which it was sold

KEY TERMS

LO 11-1

new product a product new to the world, the market, the producer, the seller, or some combination of these

LO 11-2

new-product strategy a plan that links the new-product development process with the objectives of the marketing department, the business unit, and the corporation

product development a marketing strategy that entails the creation of marketable new products; the process of converting applications for new technologies into marketable products

brainstorming the process of getting a group to think of unlimited ways to vary a product or solve a problem

screening the first filter in the product development process, which eliminates ideas that are inconsistent with the organization's new-product strategy or are obviously inappropriate for some other reason

concept test a test to evaluate a new-product idea, usually before any prototype has been created

business analysis the second stage of the screening process where preliminary figures for demand, cost, sales, and profitability are calculated

development the stage in the product development process in which a prototype is developed and a marketing strategy is outlined

simultaneous product development a team-oriented approach to new-product development

test marketing the limited introduction of a product and a marketing program to determine the reactions of potential customers in a market situation

KEY CONCEPTS

LO 11-1 Explain the importance of developing new products and describe the six categories of new products. New products are important to sustain growth and profits and to replace obsolete items. New products can be classified as new-to-the-world products (discontinuous innovations), new product lines, additions to existing product lines, improvements or revisions of existing products, repositioned products, or lower-priced products. To sustain or increase profits, a firm must innovate.

LO 11-2 Explain the steps in the new-product development process. First, a firm forms a new-product strategy by outlining the characteristics and roles of future products. Then new-product ideas are generated by customers, employees, distributors, competitors, vendors, and internal research and development personnel. Once a product idea has survived initial screening by an appointed screening group, it undergoes business analysis to determine its potential profitability. If a product concept seems viable, it progresses into the development phase, in which the technical and economic feasibility of the manufacturing process is evaluated. The development phase also includes laboratory and use testing of a product for performance and safety. Following initial testing and refinement, most products are introduced in a test market to evaluate consumer response and marketing strategies. Finally, test market successes are propelled into full commercialization. The commercialization process involves starting up production, building inventories, shipping to distributors, training a sales force, announcing the product to the trade, and advertising to consumers.

EXHIBIT 1: NEW-PRODUCT DEVELOPMENT PROCESS

1. New-product strategy
2. Idea generation
3. Idea screening
4. Business analysis
5. Development
6. Test marketing
7. Commercialization

New product

© Cengage Learning

simulated (laboratory) market testing the presentation of advertising and other promotional materials for several products, including a test product, to members of the product's target market

commercialization the decision to market a product

LO 11-5

innovation a product perceived as new by a potential adopter

diffusion the process by which the adoption of an innovation spreads

LO 11-6

product life cycle (PLC) a concept that provides a way to trace the stages of a product's acceptance, from its introduction (birth) to its decline (death)

product category all brands that satisfy a particular type of need

introductory stage the full-scale launch of a new product into the marketplace

growth stage the second stage of the product life cycle when sales typically grow at an increasing rate, many competitors enter the market, large companies may start to acquire small pioneering firms, and profits are healthy

maturity stage a period during which sales increase at a decreasing rate

decline stage a long-run drop in sales

LO 11-3 Understand why some products succeed and others fail. Despite the amount of time and money spent on developing and testing new products, a large proportion of new-product introductions fail. Products fail for a number of reasons. Failure can be a matter of degree—absolute failure occurs when a company cannot recoup its development, marketing, and production costs, while relative product failure occurs when the product returns a profit but fails to achieve sales, profit, or market share goals.

LO 11-4 Discuss global issues in new-product development. A marketer with global vision seeks to develop products that can easily be adapted to suit local needs. The goal is not simply to develop a standard product that can be sold worldwide. Smart global marketers also look for good product ideas worldwide.

LO 11-5 Explain the diffusion process through which new products are adopted. The diffusion process is the spread of a new product from its producer to ultimate adopters. Adopters in the diffusion process belong to five categories: innovators, early adopters, the early majority, the late majority, and laggards. Product characteristics that affect the rate of adoption include product complexity, compatibility with existing social values, relative advantage over existing substitutes, visibility, and "trialability." The diffusion process is facilitated by word-of-mouth communication and communication from marketers to consumers.

LO 11-6 Explain the concept of product life cycles. All brands and product categories undergo a life cycle with four stages: introduction, growth, maturity, and decline. The rate at which products move through these stages varies dramatically. Marketing managers use the product life cycle concept as an analytical tool to forecast a product's future and devise effective marketing strategies.

EXHIBIT 4: RELATIONSHIP BETWEEN THE DIFFUSION PROCESS AND THE PRODUCT LIFE CYCLE

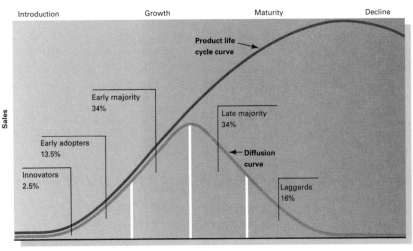

SERVICES AND NONPROFIT ORGANIZATION MARKETING

12

KEY TERMS

LO 12-1

service the result of applying human or mechanical efforts to people or objects

LO 12-2

intangibility the inability of services to be touched, seen, tasted, heard, or felt in the same manner that goods can be sensed

search quality a characteristic that can be easily assessed before purchase

experience quality a characteristic that can be assessed only after use

credence quality a characteristic that consumers may have difficulty assessing even after purchase because they do not have the necessary knowledge or experience

inseparability the inability of the production and consumption of a service to be separated; consumers must be present during the production

heterogeneity the variability of the inputs and outputs of services, which causes services to tend to be less standardized and uniform than goods

perishability the inability of services to be stored, warehoused, or inventoried

LO 12-3

reliability the ability to perform a service dependably, accurately, and consistently

responsiveness the ability to provide prompt service

assurance the knowledge and courtesy of employees and their ability to convey trust

empathy caring, individualized attention to customers

tangibles the physical evidence of a service, including the physical facilities, tools, and equipment used to provide the service

KEY CONCEPTS

LO 12-1 Discuss the importance of services to the economy. The service sector plays a crucial role in the U.S. economy. In 2012, service industries accounted for 68 percent of U.S. GDP and four out of five U.S. jobs. Services have unique characteristics that distinguish them from goods, and marketing strategies need to be adjusted for these characteristics.

LO 12-2 Discuss the differences between services and goods. Services are distinguished by four characteristics. Services are intangible performances in that they lack clearly identifiable physical characteristics, making it difficult for marketers to communicate their specific benefits to potential customers. The production and consumption of services occurs simultaneously. Services are heterogeneous because their quality depends on such elements as the service provider, individual consumer, location, and the like. Finally, services are perishable in the sense that they cannot be stored or saved. As a result, synchronizing supply with demand is particularly challenging in the service industry.

LO 12-3 Describe the components of service quality and the gap model of service quality. Service quality has five components: reliability (ability to perform the service dependably, accurately, and consistently), responsiveness (providing prompt service), assurance (knowledge and courtesy of employees and their ability to convey trust), empathy (caring, individualized attention), and tangibles (physical evidence of the service).

The gap model identifies five key discrepancies that can influence customer evaluations of service quality. When the gaps are large, service quality is low. As the gaps shrink, service quality improves. Gap 1 is found between customers' expectations and management's perceptions of those expectations. Gap 2 is found between management's perception of what the customer wants and specifications for service quality. Gap 3 is found between service quality specifications and delivery of the service. Gap 4 is found between service delivery and what the company promises to the customer through external communication. Gap 5 is found between customers' service expectations and their perceptions of service performance.

EXHIBIT 1: GAP MODEL OF SERVICE QUALITY

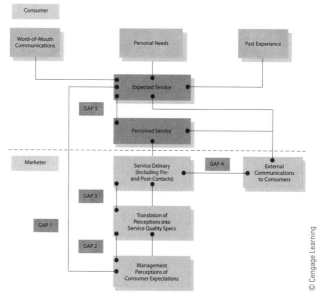

© Cengage Learning

The gap analysis model measures consumer perceptions of service quality. Managers use the model to analyze sources of quality problems and to understand how service quality can be improved.

Source: From Valarie A. Zeithaml, Mary Jo Bitner, and Dwayne Gremler, *Services Marketing*, 6/e, © 2013 (New York: McGraw-Hill, 2012). Used by permission.

gap model a model identifying five gaps that can cause problems in service delivery and influence customer evaluations of service quality

LO 12-4

core service the most basic benefit the consumer is buying

supplementary services a group of services that support or enhance the core service

mass customization a strategy that uses technology to deliver customized services on a mass basis

LO 12-6

internal marketing treating employees as customers and developing systems and benefits that satisfy their needs

LO 12-7

nonprofit organization an organization that exists to achieve some goal other than the usual business goals of profit, market share, or return on investment

nonprofit organization marketing the effort by nonprofit organizations to bring about mutually satisfying exchanges with target markets

public service advertisement (PSA) an announcement that promotes a program of a federal, state, or local government or of a nonprofit organization

LO 12-4 Develop marketing mixes for services. "Product" (service) strategy issues include what is being processed (people, possessions, mental stimulus, information), core and supplementary services, customization versus standardization, and the service mix. Distribution (place) decisions involve convenience, number of outlets, direct versus indirect distribution, and scheduling. Stressing tangible cues, using personal sources of information, creating strong organizational images, and engaging in postpurchase communication are effective promotion strategies. Pricing objectives for services can be revenue oriented, operations oriented, patronage oriented, or any combination of the three.

LO 12-5 Discuss relationship marketing in services. Relationship marketing in services involves attracting, developing, and retaining customer relationships. There are three levels of relationship marketing: level 1 focuses on pricing incentives; level 2 uses pricing incentives and social bonds with customers; and level 3 uses pricing, social bonds, and structural bonds to build long-term relationships.

LO 12-6 Explain internal marketing in services. Internal marketing means treating employees as customers and developing systems and benefits that satisfy their needs. Employees who like their jobs and are happy with the firm they work for are more likely to deliver good service.

LO 12-7 Describe nonprofit organization marketing. Nonprofit organizations pursue goals other than profit, market share, and return on investment. Nonprofit organization marketing facilitates mutually satisfying exchanges between nonprofit organizations and their target markets. Several unique characteristics distinguish nonbusiness marketing strategy, including a concern with services and social behaviors rather than manufactured goods and profit; a difficult, undifferentiated, and in some ways marginal target market; a complex product that may have only indirect benefits and elicit very low involvement; distribution that may or may not require special facilities depending on the service provided; a relative lack of resources for promotion; and prices only indirectly related to the exchange between the producer and the consumer of services.

LO 12-8 Discuss global issues in services marketing. The United States has become the world's largest exporter of services. Although competition is keen, the United States has a competitive advantage because of its vast experience in many service industries. To be successful globally, service firms must adjust their marketing mix for the environment of each target country.

EXHIBIT 2: CORE AND SUPPLEMENTARY SERVICES FOR A UNIVERSITY

© Cengage Learning

KEY TERMS

LO 13-1

supply chain the connected chain of all of the business entities, both internal and external to the company, that perform or support the logistics function

supply chain management a management system that coordinates and integrates all of the activities performed by supply chain members into a seamless process, from the source to the point of consumption, resulting in enhanced customer and economic value

supply chain agility an operational strategy focused on inducing inventory velocity and operational flexibility simultaneously in the supply chain

LO 13-2

supply chain integration when multiple firms or business functions in a supply chain coordinate their activities and processes so that they are seamlessly linked to one another in an effort to satisfy the customer

demand-supply integration (DSI) a supply chain operational philosophy focused on integrating the supply-management and demand-generating functions of an organization

LO 13-3

business processes bundles of interconnected activities that stretch across firms in the supply chain

customer relationship management (CRM) process allows companies to prioritize their marketing focus on different customer groups according to each group's long-term value to the company or supply chain

customer service management process presents a multi-company, unified response system to the customer whenever complaints, concerns, questions, or comments are voiced

demand management process seeks to align supply and demand throughout the supply chain by anticipating customer requirements at each level and creating demand-related plans of action prior to actual customer purchasing behavior

KEY CONCEPTS

LO 13-1 Define the terms *supply chain* and *supply chain management*, and discuss the benefits of supply chain management. Management coordinates and integrates all of the activities performed by supply chain members into a seamless process from the source to the point of consumption. The benefits of supply chain management include reduced inventory, transportation, warehousing, and packaging costs; greater supply chain flexibility; improved customer service; and higher revenues.

LO 13-2 Discuss the concepts of internal and external supply chain integration, and explain why each of these types of integration is important. In the modern supply chain, integration can be either internal or external. Internally, the very best companies develop a managerial orientation toward demand-supply integration. Externally, five types of integration are sought by firms interested in providing top-level service to customers: relationship integration, measurement integration, technology and planning integration, material and service supplier integration, and customer integration.

LO 13-3 Identify the eight key processes of excellent supply chain management, and discuss how each of these processes affects the end customer. The key processes that leading supply chain companies focus on are (1) customer relationship management, (2) customer service management, (3) demand management, (4) order fulfillment, (5) manufacturing flow management, (6) supplier relationship management, (7) product development and commercialization, and (8) returns management. When firms practice excellent supply chain management, each of these processes is integrated from end to end in the supply chain.

LO 13-4 Understand which supply chain functions affect business success, and how. The supply chain team, in concert with the logistics information system, orchestrates the movement of goods, services, and information from the source to the consumer. Supply chain teams typically cut across organizational boundaries, embracing all parties who participate in moving product to market. The supply chain consists of several interrelated and integrated logistical components. The logistics information system integrates and links all of the logistics functions of the supply chain.

LO 13-5 Understand the importance of sustainable supply chain management to modern business operations. Sustainable supply chain management involves the integration and balancing of environmental, social, and economic thinking into all phases of the supply chain management process.

LO 13-6 Discuss new technology and emerging trends in supply chain management. Several emerging trends are changing the job of today's supply chain manager. Some of the business trends affecting supply chain management include outsourcing logistics, maintaining a secure supply chain and minimizing supply chain risk, and maintaining a sustainable supply chain. While these changes exert pressure on managers to change the way their supply chains function, electronic distribution is being used and changed frequently to help make supply chain management more integrated and easier to track.

order fulfillment process a highly integrated process, often requiring persons from multiple companies and multiple functions to come together and coordinate to create customer satisfaction at a given place and time

manufacturing flow management process concerned with ensuring that firms in the supply chain have the needed resources to manufacture with flexibility and to move products through a multi-stage production process

supplier relationship management process supports manufacturing flow by identifying and maintaining relationships with highly valued suppliers

product development and commercialization process includes the group of activities that facilitates the joint development and marketing of new offerings among a group of supply chain partner firms

returns management process enables firms to manage volumes of returned product efficiently while minimizing returns-related costs and maximizing the value of the returned assets to the firms in the supply chain

LO 13-4

supply chain team an entire group of individuals who orchestrate the movement of goods, services, and information from the source to the consumer

inventory control system a method of developing and maintaining an adequate assortment of materials or products to meet a manufacturer's or a customer's demand

stockout a situation where a customer demand for an inventory item goes unfulfilled because the requested item is unavailable at the needed time and place

cycle stock inventory held temporarily for the purpose of fulfilling predicted demand in a period

safety (buffer) stock extra inventory held in addition to cycle stock as insurance against unexpected demand increases

in-transit inventory inventory that is currently moving within a transportation network to or from the company's facilities (plant, warehouse, or sales location)

work-in-process inventory materials inventory that is currently in the process of being converted into finished goods

seasonal inventory an extra inventory buffer that is held in response to predictable demand increases that occur annually

materials requirement planning (MRP or materials management) an inventory control system that manages the replenishment of raw materials, supplies, and components from the supplier to the manufacturer

distribution resource planning (DRP) an inventory control system that manages the replenishment of goods from the manufacturer to the final consumer

automatic replenishment program a real-time inventory system that triggers shipments only when a good is sold to the end user

order processing system a system whereby orders are entered into the supply chain and filled

electronic data interchange (EDI) information technology that replaces the paper documents that usually accompany business transactions, such as purchase orders and invoices, with electronic transmission of the needed information to reduce inventory levels, improve cash flow, streamline operations, and increase the speed and accuracy of information transmission

smart RFID (radio-frequency identification) an inventory handling and tracking system that employs radio-frequency electromagnetic fields to transfer and read product data via an electronic tag

build-to-stock a production method whereby products are made in advance of demand based on forecasts and are stored until customer orders arrive

mass customization (build-to-order) a production method whereby products are not made until an order is placed by the customer; products are made according to customer specifications

postponement a hybrid production method whereby basic units of a finished good are manufactured in advance of actual demand and held in strategic form or location until demand occurs, when final customization takes place

materials-handling system a method of moving inventory into, within, and out of a warehouse

logistics information system the link that connects all the logistics functions of the supply chain

LO 13-5

sustainable supply chain management a supply chain management philosophy that embraces the need for optimizing social and environmental costs in addition to financial costs

LO 13-6

outsourcing (contract logistics) a manufacturer's or supplier's use of an independent third party to manage an entire function of the logistics system, such as transportation, warehousing, or order processing

third-party logistics company (3PL) a firm that provides functional logistics services to others

fourth-party logistics company (4PL or logistics integrator) a consulting-based organization that assesses another's entire logistical service needs and provides integrated solutions, often drawing on multiple 3PLs for actual service

offshoring the outsourcing of a business process from one country to another for the purpose of gaining economic advantage

nearshoring the transfer of an offshored activity from a distant to a nearby country

supply chain risk any potential disruption that threatens the supply chain's efficient and effective operations

supply chain security efforts made by companies to protect their in-transit inventory or value-transforming assets from external or internal threats

supply chain resiliency the ability of a supply chain to return to its ideal operational state after being disrupted

electronic distribution a distribution technique that includes any kind of product or service that can be distributed electronically, whether over traditional forms such as fiber-optic cable or through satellite transmission of electronic signals

three-dimensional printing (3DP) the creation of three-dimensional objects via an additive manufacturing (printing) technology that layers raw material into desired shapes

© iStockphoto.com/OSTILL / © iStockphoto.com/billnoll

KEY TERMS

LO 14-1

marketing channel (channel of distribution) a set of interdependent organizations that eases the transfer of ownership as products move from producer to business user or consumer

channel members all parties in the marketing channel who negotiate with one another, buy and sell products, and facilitate the change of ownership between buyer and seller in the course of moving the product from the manufacturer into the hands of the final consumer

form utility the elements of the composition and appearance of a product that make it desirable

time utility the increase in customer satisfaction gained by making a good or service available at the appropriate time

place utility the usefulness of a good or service as a function of the location at which it is made available

exchange utility the increased value of a product that is created as its ownership is transferred

retailer a channel intermediary that sells mainly to consumers

merchant wholesaler an institution that buys goods from manufacturers and resells them to businesses, government agencies, and other wholesalers or retailers and that receives and takes title to goods, stores them in its own warehouses, and later ships them

agents and brokers wholesaling intermediaries who do not take title to a product but facilitate its sale from producer to end user by representing retailers, wholesalers, or manufacturers

LO 14-2

direct channel a distribution channel in which producers sell directly to consumers

dual distribution (multiple distribution) the use of two or more channels to distribute the same product to target markets

nontraditional channels nonphysical (often electronic) channels that facilitate the unique market access of products and services

KEY CONCEPTS

LO 14-1 Explain what marketing channels and channel intermediaries are, and describe their functions and activities. A marketing channel is a business structure of interdependent organizations that reach from the point of production to the consumer. Intermediaries negotiate with one another, buy and sell products, and facilitate the change of ownership between buyer and seller. Retailers are those firms in the channel that sell directly to consumers.

LO 14-2 Describe common channel structures and strategies, and the factors that influence their choice. When possible, producers use the direct channel to sell directly to consumers. When one or more channel members are small companies, an agent/broker channel may be the best solution. Most consumer products are sold through distribution channels similar to the retailer channel and the wholesaler channel. Dual distribution may be used to distribute the same product to target markets, and companies often form strategic channel alliances to use already-established channels.

LO 14-3 Discuss channel relationship types and roles, and their unique benefits and drawbacks. Marketing managers should carefully consider the types of relationships they choose to foster between their company and other companies (integrated, cooperative, arm's-length, co-opetition).

LO 14-4 Explain the importance of the retailer within the channel and within the national economy. The retailing industry is one of the largest employers in the United States. Though most retailers are quite small, a few giant organizations dominate the industry.

LO 14-5 List and understand the different classifications and types of retailers, as well as their different operational models. Retail establishments can be classified according to ownership, level of service, product assortment, and price. Because consumers demand convenience, non-store retailing is currently growing faster than in-store retailing.

LO 14-6 Explain the major tasks involved in developing a retail marketing strategy. Retailers must develop marketing strategies based on their periodic goals and overall strategic plans. The key tasks in strategic retailing are defining and selecting a target market and developing the retailing mix to successfully meet the needs of the chosen target market.

LO 14-7 Discuss the role of customer data in retailer decision making. Retailers decide what to sell on the basis of what their target market wants to buy. Data mining uses complex mathematical models to help retailers make better product mix decisions. The data manufacturers and retailers collect in databases allow them to gain better insight into who is buying their products.

LO 14-8 Describe trends in retail and channel management. M-commerce enables consumers using wireless mobile devices to connect to the Internet and shop, social shopping allows multiple retailers to sell products to customers through social media sites, and facial recognition technology allows market researchers to record consumers' nonverbal reactions to products and advertisements.

14 MARKETING CHANNELS AND RETAILING

strategic channel alliance a cooperative agreement between business firms to use the other's already established distribution channel

intensive distribution a form of distribution aimed at having a product available in every outlet where target customers might want to buy it

selective distribution a form of distribution achieved by screening dealers to eliminate all but a few in any single area

exclusive distribution a form of distribution that establishes one or a few dealers within a given area

LO 14-3

arm's-length relationship a relationship between companies that is loose, characterized by low relational investment and trust, and usually taking the form of a series of discrete transactions with no or low expectation of future interaction or service

cooperative relationship a relationship between companies that takes the form of informal partnership with moderate levels of trust and information sharing as needed to further each company's goals

integrated relationship a relationship between companies that is tightly connected, with linked processes across and between firm boundaries and high levels of trust and interfirm commitment

co-opetition a relationship that mixes elements of cooperation and competition between two partners

channel power the capacity of a particular marketing channel member to control or influence the behavior of other channel members

channel control a situation that occurs when one marketing channel member intentionally affects another member's behavior

channel captain a member of a marketing channel that exercises authority and power over the activities of other channel members

channel conflict a clash of goals and methods between distribution channel members

horizontal conflict a channel conflict that occurs among channel members on the same level

vertical conflict a channel conflict that occurs between different levels in a marketing channel, most typically between the manufacturer and wholesaler or between the manufacturer and retailer

channel partnering the joint effort of all channel members to create a channel that serves customers and creates a competitive advantage

LO 14-4

retailing all the activities directly related to the sale of goods and services to the ultimate consumer for personal, nonbusiness use

LO 14-5

independent retailer a retailer owned by a single person or partnership and not operated as part of a larger retail institution

chain store a store that is part of a group of the same stores owned and operated by a single organization

franchise a relationship in which the business rights to operate and sell a product are granted by the franchisor to the franchisee.

gross margin the amount of money the retailer makes as a percentage of sales after the cost of goods sold is subtracted

department store a store housing several departments under one roof

specialty store a retail store specializing in a given type of merchandise

supermarket a large, departmentalized, self-service retailer that specializes in food and some nonfood items

scrambled merchandising the tendency to offer a wide variety of nontraditional goods and services under one roof

drugstore a retail store that stocks pharmacy-related products and services as its main draw

convenience store a miniature supermarket, carrying only a limited line of high-turnover convenience goods

discount store a retailer that competes on the basis of low prices, high turnover, and high volume

specialty discount store a retail store that offers a nearly complete selection of single-line merchandise and uses self-service, discount prices, high volume, and high turnover

off-price retailer a retailer that sells at prices 25 percent or more below traditional department store prices because it pays cash for its stock and usually doesn't ask for return privileges

factory outlet an off-price retailer that is owned and operated by a manufacturer

used goods retailer a retailer whereby items purchased from one of the other types of retailers are resold to different customers

non-store retailing shopping without visiting a store

automatic vending the use of machines to offer goods for sale

direct retailing the selling of products by representatives who work door-to-door, office-to-office, or at home sales parties

direct marketing (direct response marketing) techniques used to get consumers to make a purchase from their home, office, or other nonretail setting

telemarketing the use of the telephone to sell directly to consumers

shop-at-home television network a specialized form of direct response marketing whereby television shows display merchandise, with the retail price, to home viewers

online retailing (e-tailing) a type of shopping available to consumers with personal computers and access to the Internet

franchisor the originator of a trade name, product, methods of operation, and the like that grants operating rights to another party to sell its product

franchisee an individual or business that is granted the right to sell another party's product

LO 14-6

retailing mix a combination of the six Ps—product, place, promotion, price, presentation, and personnel—to sell goods and services to the ultimate consumer

destination store a store that consumers purposely plan to visit

atmosphere the overall impression conveyed by a store's physical layout, décor, and surroundings

layout the internal design and configuration of a store's fixtures and products

LO 14-7

data mining the process of discovering patterns in large data sets for the purposes of extracting knowledge and understanding human behavior

LO 14-8

m-commerce the ability to conduct commerce using a mobile device for the purpose of buying or selling goods or services

KEY TERMS

LO 15-1

promotion communication by marketers that informs, persuades, and reminds potential buyers of a product in order to influence an opinion or elicit a response

promotional strategy a plan for the optimal use of the elements of promotion: advertising, public relations, personal selling, sales promotion, and social media

competitive advantage one or more unique aspects of an organization that cause target consumers to patronize that firm rather than competitors

LO 15-2

communication the process by which we exchange or share meaning through a common set of symbols

interpersonal communication direct, face-to-face communication between two or more people

mass communication the communication of a concept or message to large audiences

sender the originator of the message in the communication process

encoding the conversion of a sender's ideas and thoughts into a message, usually in the form of words or signs

channel a medium of communication—such as a voice, radio, or newspaper—for transmitting a message

noise anything that interferes with, distorts, or slows down the transmission of information

receiver the person who decodes a message

decoding interpretation of the language and symbols sent by the source through a channel

feedback the receiver's response to a message

KEY CONCEPTS

LO 15-1 Discuss the role of promotion in the marketing mix. Promotional strategy is the plan for using the elements of promotion—advertising, public relations, sales promotion, personal selling, and social media—to meet the firm's overall objectives and marketing goals. Based on these objectives, the elements of the promotional strategy become a coordinated promotion plan. The promotion plan then becomes an integral part of the total marketing strategy for reaching the target market along with product, distribution, and price.

LO 15-2 Describe the communication process. The communication process has several steps. When an individual or organization has a message it wishes to convey to a target audience, it encodes that message using language and symbols familiar to the intended receiver and sends the message through a channel of communication. Noise in the transmission channel distorts the source's intended message. Reception occurs if the message falls within the receiver's frame of reference. The receiver decodes the message and usually provides feedback to the source. Normally, feedback is direct for interpersonal communication and indirect for mass communication. Social media has increased the amount of feedback received by marketers.

LO 15-3 Explain the goals and tasks of promotion. The fundamental goals of promotion are to induce, modify, or reinforce behavior by informing, persuading, reminding, and connecting. *Informative promotion* explains a good's or service's purpose and benefits. Promotion that informs the consumer is typically used to increase demand for a general product category or to introduce a new good or service. *Persuasive promotion* is designed to stimulate a purchase or an action. Promotion that persuades the consumer to buy is essential during the growth stage of the product life cycle, when competition becomes fierce. *Reminder promotion* is used to keep the product and brand name in the public's mind. Promotions that remind are generally used during the maturity stage of the product life cycle. *Connection promotion* is designed to form relationships with customers and potential customers using social media. Connecting encourages customers to become brand advocates and share their experiences via social media.

LO 15-4 Discuss the elements of the promotional mix. The elements of the promotional mix include advertising, public relations, sales promotion, personal selling, and social media. *Advertising* is a form of impersonal, one-way mass communication paid for by the source. *Public relations* is the function of promotion concerned with a firm's public image. *Sales promotion* is typically used to back up other components of the promotional mix by stimulating immediate demand. *Personal selling* typically involves direct communication, in person or by telephone; the seller tries to initiate a purchase by informing and persuading one or more potential buyers. Finally, social media are promotion tools used to facilitate conversations among people online.

LO 15-5 Discuss the AIDA concept and its relationship to the promotional mix. The AIDA model outlines the four basic stages in the purchase decision-making process, which are initiated and propelled by promotional activities: (1) attention, (2) interest, (3) desire, and (4) action. The components of the promotional mix have varying levels of influence at each stage of the AIDA model. Advertising is a good tool for increasing awareness and knowledge of a good or service. Sales promotion is effective when consumers are at the purchase stage of the decision-making process. Personal selling is most effective in developing customer interest and desire.

LO 15-4

promotional mix the combination of promotional tools—including advertising, public relations, personal selling, sales promotion, and social media—used to reach the target market and fulfill the organization's overall goals

advertising impersonal, one-way mass communication about a product or organization that is paid for by a marketer

public relations the marketing function that evaluates public attitudes, identifies areas within the organization the public may be interested in, and executes a program of action to earn public understanding and acceptance

publicity public information about a company, product, service, or issue appearing in the mass media as a news item

sales promotion marketing activities—other than personal selling, advertising, and public relations—that stimulate consumer buying and dealer effectiveness

personal selling a purchase situation involving a personal, paid-for communication between two people in an attempt to influence each other

paid media a category of promotional tactic based on the traditional advertising model, whereby a brand pays for media space

earned media a category of promotional tactic based on a public relations or publicity model that gets customers talking about products or services

owned media a new category of promotional tactic based on brands becoming publishers of their own content in order to maximize the brands' value to customers

LO 15-5

AIDA concept a model that outlines the process for achieving promotional goals in terms of stages of consumer involvement with the message; the acronym stands for attention, interest, desire, and action

LO 15-6

integrated marketing communications (IMC) the careful coordination of all promotional messages for a product or a service to ensure the consistency of messages at every contact point at which a company meets the consumer

LO 15-6 Discuss the concept of integrated marketing communications. Integrated marketing communications is the careful coordination of all promotional messages for a product or service to ensure the consistency of messages at every contact point where a company meets the consumer—advertising, sales promotion, personal selling, public relations, and social media, as well as direct marketing, packaging, and other forms of communication. Marketing managers carefully coordinate all promotional activities to ensure that consumers see and hear one message. Integrated marketing communications has received more attention in recent years due to the proliferation of media choices, the fragmentation of mass markets into more segmented niches, and the decrease in advertising spending in favor of promotional techniques that generate an immediate sales response.

LO 15-7 Describe the factors that affect the promotional mix. Promotion managers consider many factors when creating promotional mixes. These factors include the nature of the product, product life-cycle stage, target market characteristics, the type of buying decision involved, availability of funds, and feasibility of push or pull strategies. As products move through different stages of the product life cycle, marketers will choose to use different promotional elements. Characteristics of the target market, such as geographic location of potential buyers and brand loyalty, influence the promotional mix, as does whether the buying decision is complex or routine. The amount of funds a firm has to allocate to promotion may also help determine the promotional mix. Last, if a firm uses a push strategy to promote the product or service, the marketing manager might choose to use aggressive advertising and personal selling to wholesalers and retailers. If a pull strategy is chosen, then the manager often relies on aggressive mass promotion, such as advertising and sales promotion, to stimulate consumer demand.

LO 15-7

push strategy a marketing strategy that uses aggressive personal selling and trade advertising to convince a wholesaler or a retailer to carry and sell particular merchandise

pull strategy a marketing strategy that stimulates consumer demand to obtain product distribution

KEY TERMS

LO 16-1

advertising response function a phenomenon in which spending for advertising and sales promotion increases sales or market share up to a certain level but then produces diminishing returns

LO 16-2

institutional advertising a form of advertising designed to enhance a company's image rather than promote a particular product

product advertising a form of advertising that touts the benefits of a specific good or service

advocacy advertising a form of advertising in which an organization expresses its views on controversial issues or responds to media attacks

pioneering advertising a form of advertising designed to stimulate primary demand for a new product or product category

competitive advertising a form of advertising designed to influence demand for a specific brand

comparative advertising a form of advertising that compares two or more specifically named or shown competing brands on one or more specific attributes

LO 16-3

advertising campaign a series of related advertisements focusing on a common theme, slogan, and set of advertising appeals

advertising objective a specific communication task that a campaign should accomplish for a specified target audience during a specified period

advertising appeal a reason for a person to buy a product

unique selling proposition a desirable, exclusive, and believable advertising appeal selected as the theme for a campaign

KEY CONCEPTS

LO 16-1 Discuss the effects of advertising on market share and consumers. Advertising helps marketers increase or maintain brand awareness and, subsequently, market share. Typically, more is spent to advertise new brands with a small market share than to advertise older brands. Brands with a large market share use advertising mainly to maintain their share of the market. Advertising affects consumers' daily lives as well as their purchases. Although advertising can seldom change strongly held consumer attitudes and values, it may transform a consumer's negative attitude toward a product into a positive one. Finally, advertising can also change the importance of a brand's attributes to consumers. By emphasizing different brand attributes, advertisers can change their appeal in response to consumers' changing needs or try to achieve an advantage over competing brands.

LO 16-2 Identify the major types of advertising. Advertising is any form of nonpersonal, paid communication in which the sponsor or company is identified. The two major types of advertising are institutional advertising and product advertising. *Institutional advertising* is not product oriented; rather, its purpose is to foster a positive company image among the general public, investment community, customers, and employees. *Product advertising* is designed mainly to promote goods and services, and it is classified into three main categories: pioneering, competitive, and comparative. A product's place in the product life cycle is a major determinant of the type of advertising used to promote it.

LO 16-3 Discuss the creative decisions in developing an advertising campaign. Before any creative work can begin on an advertising campaign, it is important to determine what goals or objectives the advertising should achieve. The objectives of a specific advertising campaign often depend on the overall corporate objectives and the product being advertised and are often determined using the DAGMAR approach. Once objectives are defined, creative work can begin (e.g., identifying the product's benefits, developing possible advertising appeals, evaluating and selecting the advertising appeals, executing the advertising message, and evaluating the effectiveness of the campaign).

LO 16-4 Describe media evaluation and selection techniques. Media evaluation and selection make up a crucial step in the advertising campaign process. Major types of advertising media include newspapers, magazines, radio, television, the Internet, and outdoor media such as billboards and bus panels. Recent trends in advertising media include shopping carts, computer screen savers, DVDs, CDs, interactive kiosks, advertisements run before movies, posters on bathroom stalls, and "advertainments." Promotion managers choose the advertising campaign's media mix on the basis of the following variables: cost per contact, reach, frequency, characteristics of the target audience, flexibility of the medium, noise level, and the life span of the medium. After choosing the media mix, a media schedule designates when the advertisement will appear and the specific vehicles in which it will appear.

LO 16-5 Discuss the role of public relations in the promotional mix. Public relations is a vital part of a firm's promotional mix. A company fosters good publicity to enhance its image and promote its products. Popular public relations tools include new-product publicity, product placement, consumer education, sponsorship, and company Web sites. An equally important aspect of public relations is managing unfavorable publicity in a way that is least damaging to a firm's image.

LO 16-6 Define and state the objectives of sales promotion and the tools used to achieve them. Marketing managers can use sales promotion to increase the effectiveness of their promotional efforts. Sales promotion can target either trade

LO 16-4

medium the channel used to convey a message to a target market

media planning the series of decisions advertisers make regarding the selection and use of media, allowing the marketer to optimally and cost-effectively communicate the message to the target audience

cooperative advertising an arrangement in which the manufacturer and the retailer split the costs of advertising the manufacturer's brand

infomercial a thirty-minute or longer advertisement that looks more like a television talk show than a sales pitch

advergaming placing advertising messages in Web-based, mobile, console, or handheld video games to advertise or promote a product, service, organization, or issue

media mix the combination of media to be used for a promotional campaign

cost per contact (cost per thousand or CPM) the cost of reaching one member of the target market

cost per click the cost associated with a consumer clicking on a display or banner ad

reach the number of target consumers exposed to a commercial at least once during a specific period, usually four weeks

frequency the number of times an individual is exposed to a given message during a specific period

audience selectivity the ability of an advertising medium to reach a precisely defined market

media schedule designation of the media, the specific publications or programs, and the insertion dates of advertising

continuous media schedule a media scheduling strategy in which advertising is run steadily throughout the advertising period; used for products in the later stages of the product life cycle

flighted media schedule a media scheduling strategy in which ads are run heavily every other month or every two weeks to achieve a greater impact with an increased frequency and reach at those times

pulsing media schedule a media scheduling strategy that uses continuous scheduling throughout the year coupled with a flighted schedule during the best sales periods

seasonal media schedule a media scheduling strategy that runs advertising only during times of the year when the product is most likely to be used

LO 16-5

public relations the element in the promotional mix that evaluates public attitudes, identifies issues that may elicit public concern, and executes programs to gain public understanding and acceptance

publicity an effort to capture media attention, often initiated through press releases that further a corporation's public relations plans

product placement a public relations strategy that involves getting a product, service, or company name to appear in a movie, television show, radio program, magazine, newspaper, video game, video or audio clip, book, or commercial for another product; on the Internet; or at special events

sponsorship a public relations strategy in which a company spends money to support an issue, cause, or event that is consistent with corporate objectives, such as improving brand awareness or enhancing corporate image

crisis management a coordinated effort to handle all the effects of unfavorable publicity or another unexpected unfavorable event

LO 16-6

sales promotion marketing communication activities other than advertising, personal selling, and public relations, in which a short-term incentive

or consumer markets. Trade promotions may push a product through the distribution channel using sales contests, premiums, P-O-P displays, trade allowances, push money, training, free merchandise, store demonstrations, and business meetings. Consumer promotions may push a product through the distribution channel using coupons, rebates, premiums, loyalty marketing programs or frequent buyer programs, contests, sweepstakes, sampling, and P-O-P displays. The biggest trend in sales promotion on both the trade and consumer sides has been the increased use of the Internet.

motivates consumers or members of the distribution channel to purchase a good or service immediately, either by lowering the price or by adding value

trade sales promotion promotion activities directed to members of the marketing channel, such as wholesalers and retailers

consumer sales promotion promotion activities targeted to the ultimate consumer market

trade allowance a price reduction offered by manufacturers to intermediaries such as wholesalers and retailers

push money money offered to channel intermediaries to encourage them to "push" products—that is, to encourage other members of the channel to sell the products

coupon a certificate that entitles consumers to an immediate price reduction when the product is purchased.

rebate a cash refund given for the purchase of a product during a specific period

premium an extra item offered to the consumer, usually in exchange for some proof of purchase of the promoted product

loyalty marketing program a promotional program designed to build long-term, mutually beneficial relationships between a company and its key customers

frequent buyer program a loyalty program in which loyal consumers are rewarded for making multiple purchases of a particular good or service

sampling a promotional program that allows the consumer the opportunity to try a product or service for free

point of purchase (P-O-P) display a promotional display set up at the retailer's location to build traffic, advertise the product, or induce impulse buying

KEY TERMS

LO 17-2

relationship selling (consultative selling) a sales practice that involves building, maintaining, and enhancing interactions with customers in order to develop long-term satisfaction through mutually beneficial partnerships

LO 17-3

customer-centric a philosophy under which the company customizes its product and service offering based on data generated through interactions between the customer and the company

learning an informal process of collecting customer data through customer comments and feedback on product or service performance

knowledge management the process by which customer information is centralized and shared in order to enhance the relationship between customers and the organization

interaction the point at which a customer and a company representative exchange information and develop learning relationships

touch points areas of a business where customers have contact with the company and data might be gathered

point-of-sale interactions a touch point in stores or information kiosks that uses software to enable customers to easily provide information about themselves without feeling violated

campaign management developing product or service offerings customized for the appropriate customer segment and then pricing and communicating these offerings for the purpose of enhancing customer relationships

KEY CONCEPTS

LO 17-1 Describe personal selling. Personal selling is direct communication between a sales representative and one or more prospective buyers in an attempt to influence each other in a purchase situation. Broadly speaking, all businesspeople use personal selling to promote themselves and their ideas. Personal selling offers several advantages over other forms of promotion. Personal selling allows salespeople to thoroughly explain and demonstrate a product. Salespeople have the flexibility to tailor a sales proposal to the needs and preferences of individual customers. Personal selling is more efficient than other forms of promotion because salespeople target qualified prospects and avoid wasting efforts on unlikely buyers. Personal selling affords greater managerial control over promotion costs. Finally, personal selling is the most effective method of closing a sale and producing satisfied customers.

LO 17-2 Discuss the key differences between relationship selling and traditional selling. *Relationship selling* is the practice of building, maintaining, and enhancing interactions with customers to develop long-term satisfaction through mutually beneficial partnerships. *Traditional selling*, on the other hand, is transaction focused. That is, the salesperson is most concerned with making a one-time sale and moving on to the next prospect. Salespeople practicing relationship selling spend more time understanding a prospect's needs and developing solutions to meet those needs.

EXHIBIT 2: KEY DIFFERENCES BETWEEN TRADITIONAL SELLING AND RELATIONSHIP SELLING

Traditional Personal Selling	Relationship or Consultative Selling
Sell products (goods and services)	Sell advice, assistance, and counsel
Focus on closing sales	Focus on improving the customer's bottom line
Limited sales planning	Consider sales planning as top priority
Spend most contact time telling customers about product	Spend most contact time attempting to build a problem-solving environment with the customer
Conduct product-specific needs assessment	Conduct discovery in the full scope of the customer's operations
Lone wolf approach to the account	Team approach to the account
Proposals and presentations based on pricing and product features	Proposals and presentations based on profit impact and strategic benefits to the customer
Sales follow-up is short term, focused on product delivery	Sales follow-up is long term, focused on long-term relationship enhancement

Source: Robert M. Peterson, Patrick Schul, and George H. Lucas Jr., "Consultative Selling: Walking the Walk in the New Selling Environment," *National Conference on Sales Management Proceedings*, March 1996.

LO17-3 Describe customer relationship management. Companies that have a CRM system have a customer-centric model, learn ways to enhance their product and service, and often use knowledge management systems to centralize customer information. When managing interactions between customers, companies manage touch points. Interactions between the company and the customer facilitate the collection of large amounts of data. Companies can obtain contact information and data pertaining to the customer's current relationship with the organization. Companies that leverage customer information use that information for campaign management, retaining loyal customers, cross-selling other products and services, and designing targeted marketing communications.

LO 17-4

sales process (sales cycle) the set of steps a salesperson goes through in a particular organization to sell a particular product or service

lead generation (prospecting) identification of those firms and people most likely to buy the seller's offerings

referral a recommendation to a salesperson from a customer or business associate

networking a process of finding out about potential clients from friends, business contacts, coworkers, acquaintances, and fellow members in professional and civic organizations

cold calling a form of lead generation in which the salesperson approaches potential buyers without any prior knowledge of the prospects' needs or financial status

lead qualification determination of a sales prospect's (1) recognized need, (2) buying power, and (3) receptivity and accessibility

preapproach a process that describes the "homework" that must be done by a salesperson before he or she contacts a prospect

needs assessment a determination of the customer's specific needs and wants and the range of options the customer has for satisfying them

sales proposal a formal written document or professional presentation that outlines how the salesperson's product or service will meet or exceed the prospect's needs

sales presentation a formal meeting in which the salesperson presents a sales proposal to a prospective buyer

negotiation the process during which both the salesperson and the prospect offer special concessions in an attempt to arrive at a sales agreement

LO 17-4 List the steps in the selling process. The selling process is composed of seven basic steps: (1) generating leads, (2) qualifying leads, (3) approaching the customer and probing needs, (4) developing and proposing solutions, (5) handling objections, (6) closing the sale, and (7) following up.

LO 17-5 Describe the functions of sales management. The sales manager's basic job is to maximize sales at a reasonable cost while also maximizing profits. The sales manager's responsibilities include (1) defining sales goals and the sales process, (2) determining the sales force structure, (3) recruiting and training the sales force, (4) compensating and motivating the sales force, and (5) evaluating the sales force.

EXHIBIT 4: COMMON CRM MARKETING DATABASE APPLICATIONS

© Cengage Learning

EXHIBIT 5: RELATIVE AMOUNT OF TIME SPENT IN THE KEY STEPS OF THE SELLING PROCESS

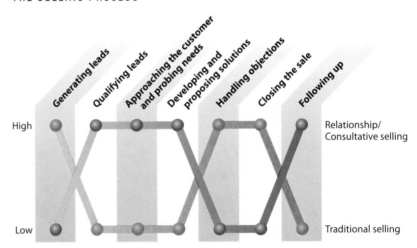

Source: Robert Peterson, Patrick Schul, and George H. Lucas Jr., "Consultative Selling: Walking the Walk in the New Selling Environment," *National Conference on Sales Management Proceedings*, March 1996.

follow-up the final step of the selling process, in which the salesperson ensures delivery schedules are met, goods or services perform as promised, and the buyers' employees are properly trained to use the products

quota a statement of the salesperson's sales goals, usually based on sales volume

SOCIAL MEDIA AND MARKETING

18

KEY TERMS

LO 18-1

social media any tool or service that uses the Internet to facilitate conversations

social commerce a subset of e-commerce that involves the interaction and user contribution aspects of social online media to assist online buying and selling of products and services

crowdsourcing using consumers to develop and market products

LO 18-2

social media monitoring the process of identifying and assessing what is being said about a company, individual, product, or brand

LO 18-5

blog a publicly accessible Web page that functions as an interactive journal, whereby readers can post comments on the author's entries

corporate blogs blogs that are sponsored by a company or one of its brands and maintained by one or more of the company's employees

noncorporate blogs independent blogs that are not associated with the marketing efforts of any particular company or brand

microblogs blogs with strict post length limits

social networking sites Web sites that allow individuals to connect—or network—with friends, peers, and business associates

media sharing sites Web sites that allow users to upload and distribute multimedia content like videos and photos

social news sites Web sites that allow users to decide which content is promoted on a given Web site by voting that content up or down

KEY CONCEPTS

LO 18-1 Describe social media, how they are used, and their relation to integrated marketing communications. Social media, commonly thought of as digital technology, offer a way for marketers to communicate one-on-one with consumers and measure the effects of those interactions. Social media include social networks, microblogs, and media sharing sites, all of which are used by the majority of adults. Smartphones and tablet computers have given consumers greater freedom to access social media on the go, which is likely to increase usage of social media sites. Many advertising budgets are allotting more money to online marketing, including social media, mobile marketing, and search marketing.

LO 18-2 Explain how to create a social media campaign. A social media campaign should take advantage of owned media, earned media, and paid media. To use these types of media in a social media campaign, first implement an effective listening system. Marketers can interact with negative feedback, make changes, and effectively manage their online presence. Paying attention to the ways that competing brands attract and engage with their customers can be particularly enlightening for both small businesses and global brands. Second, develop a list of objectives that reflects how social media dynamically communicate with customers and build relationships.

EXHIBIT 1: EIGHT STAGES OF EFFECTIVE LISTENING

Stage	Description	Resources Required	Purpose
Stage 1: Without objective	The organization has established a listening system but has no goals.	Social media notification tools (Google Alerts)	Keep up with brand and competitor information.
Stage 2: Tracking brand mentions	The organization tracks mentions in social space but has no guidance on next steps.	A listening platform with key word report capabilities (Radian6)	Track discussions, understand sentiment, and identify influencers to improve overall marketing strategy.
Stage 3: Identifying market risks and opportunities	The organization seeks discussions online that may result in identification of problems and opportunities.	A listening platform with a large staff dedicated to the client (Converseon)	Staff seeks out discussions and reports to other teams, like product development and sales. These teams then engage the customers directly or conduct further research.
Stage 4: Improving campaign efficiency	The organization uses tools to get real-time data on marketing efficiency.	Web analytics software (Google Analytics)	See a wealth of information about consumers' behavior on their Web sites (and social media).
Stage 5: Measuring customer satisfaction	The organization collects information about satisfaction, including measures of sentiment.	Insight platforms that offer online focus-group solutions	Measure impact of satisfaction or frustration during interaction.
Stage 6: Responding to customer inquiry	The organization identifies customers where they are (e.g., Twitter).	A customer service team is allowed to make real-time responses.	Generate a high sense of satisfaction for customer but generates public complaints.
Stage 7: Better understanding of customers	The organization adds social information to demographics and psychographics to gain a better profile.	Social customer relationship management (CRM) systems to sync data	Social CRM marries database and social media to create a powerful analytical tool. (See Chapters 9 and 17 for more on CRM.)
Stage 8: Being proactive and anticipating customer demands	The organization examines previous patterns of data and social behavior to anticipate needs.	Advanced customer database with predictive application (yet to be created)	Modify social media strategy to preempt consumer behavior modifications based on trends.

Sources: Jeremiah Owyang, "Web Strategy Matrix: The Eight Stages of Listening," *Web Strategy*, November 10, 2009, www.web-strategist.com/blog/2009/11/10/evolution-the-eight-stages-of-listening/; Jim Sterne, *Social Media Metrics* (Hoboken, NJ: John Wiley & Sons, 2010).

LO 18-3 Evaluate the various methods of measurement for social media. Most marketers have not been able to figure out how to measure the benefits of social media. Hundreds of metrics have been developed to measure social media's value, but

location-based social networking sites Web sites that combine the fun of social networking with the utility of location-based GPS technology

review sites Web sites that allow consumers to post, read, rate, and comment on opinions regarding all kinds of products and services

these metrics are meaningless unless they are tied to key performance indicators. Some social media metrics to consider include buzz, interest, participation, search engine rank and results, influence, sentiment analysis, and Web site metrics.

LO 18-4 Explain consumer behavior on social media. To effectively leverage social media, marketers must understand who uses social media and how they use it. If a brand's target market does not use social media, a social media campaign might not be useful. There are six categories of social media users: creators, critics, collectors, joiners, spectators, and inactives. A new category is emerging called "conversationalists," who post status updates on social networking sites or microblogs.

LO 18-5 Describe the social media tools in a marketer's toolbox and how they are useful. A marketer has many tools to implement a social media campaign. However, new tools emerge daily, so these resources will change rapidly. Some of the strongest social media platforms are blogs, microblogs, social networks, media creation and sharing sites, social news sites, location-based social networking sites, and virtual worlds and online gaming. Blogs allow marketers and consumers to create content in the form of posts, which ideally build trust and a sense of authenticity in customers. Microblogs allow brands to follow, repost, respond to potential customers, and post content that inspires customers to engage the brand, laying a foundation for meaningful two-way conversation. Social networks allow marketers to increase awareness, target audiences, promote products, forge relationships, attract event participants, perform research, and generate new business. Media sharing sites give brands an interactive channel to disseminate content. Social news sites are useful to marketers to promote campaigns, create conversations, and build Web site traffic. Location-based social networking sites can forge lasting relationships and loyalty in customers. Review sites allow marketers to respond to customer reviews and comments about their brand. Virtual worlds are fertile ground for branded content, and online gaming allows marketers to integrate their message onto a game platform.

LO 18-6 Describe the impact of mobile technology on social media. There are five reasons for the popularity of mobile marketing: (1) mobile platforms are standardized, (2) fewer consumers are concerned about privacy and pricing policies, (3) advertising can be done in real time, (4) mobile marketing is measurable, and (5) there is a higher response rate than with traditional advertising. Because of the rapid growth of smartphones, well-branded, integrated apps allow marketers to create buzz and generate customer engagement. Widgets allow customers to post a company's information to its site, are less expensive than apps, and broaden that company's exposure.

LO 18-7 Understand the aspects of developing a social media plan. The social media plan should fit into the overall marketing plan and help marketers meet the organization's larger goals. There are six stages in creating an effective social media plan; (1) listening, (2) setting social media objectives, (3) defining strategies, (4) identifying the target audience, (5) selecting the appropriate tools and platforms, and (6) implementing and monitoring the strategy. Listening and revising the social media plan to accommodate changing market trends and needs is key to an effective social media plan.

CHAPTER REVIEW

KEY TERMS

LO 19-1

price that which is given up in an exchange to acquire a good or service

revenue the price charged to customers multiplied by the number of units sold

profit revenue minus expenses

LO 19-2

return on investment (ROI) net profit after taxes divided by total assets

market share a company's product sales as a percentage of total sales for that industry

status quo pricing a pricing objective that maintains existing prices or meets the competition's prices

LO 19-3

demand the quantity of a product that will be sold in the market at various prices for a specified period

supply the quantity of a product that will be offered to the market by a supplier at various prices for a specified period

price equilibrium the price at which demand and supply are equal

elasticity of demand consumers' responsiveness or sensitivity to changes in price

elastic demand a situation in which consumer demand is sensitive to changes in price

inelastic demand a situation in which an increase or a decrease in price will not significantly affect demand for the product

unitary elasticity a situation in which total revenue remains the same when prices change

LO 19-4

dynamic pricing a strategy whereby prices are adjusted over time to maximize a company's revenues

yield management systems (YMS) a technique for adjusting prices that uses complex mathematical software to profitably fill unused capacity by discounting early purchases, limiting early sales at these discounted prices, and overbooking capacity

KEY CONCEPTS

LO 19-1 Discuss the importance of pricing decisions to the economy and to the individual firm. Pricing plays an integral role in the U.S. economy by allocating goods and services among consumers, governments, and businesses. Pricing is essential in business because it creates revenue, which is the basis of all business activity. In setting prices, marketing managers strive to find a level high enough to produce a satisfactory profit. Profit drives growth, salary increases, and corporate investment.

$$\text{Price} \times \text{Sales Units} = \text{Revenue}$$
$$\text{Revenue} - \text{Costs} = \text{Profit}$$

LO 19-2 List and explain a variety of pricing objectives. Establishing realistic and measurable pricing objectives is a critical part of any firm's marketing strategy. Pricing objectives are commonly classified into three categories: profit oriented, sales oriented, and status quo. Profit-oriented pricing is based on profit maximization, a satisfactory level of profit, or a target *return on investment (ROI)*. The goal of profit maximization is to generate as much revenue as possible in relation to cost. Often, a more practical approach than profit maximization is setting prices to produce profits that will satisfy management and stockholders. The most common profit-oriented strategy is pricing for a specific ROI relative to a firm's assets. The second type of pricing objective is sales oriented, and it focuses on either maintaining a percentage share of the market or maximizing dollar or unit sales. The third type of pricing objective aims to maintain the status quo by matching competitors' prices.

LO 19-3 Explain the role of demand in price determination. *Demand* is a key determinant of price. When establishing prices, a firm must first determine demand for its product. A typical demand schedule shows an inverse relationship between quantity demanded and price: when price is lowered, sales increase; when price is increased, the quantity demanded falls. For prestige products, however, there may be a direct relationship between demand and price: the quantity demanded will increase as price increases.

Marketing managers must also consider demand elasticity when setting prices. *Elasticity of demand* is the degree to which the quantity demanded fluctuates with changes in price. If consumers are sensitive to changes in price, demand is elastic; if they are insensitive to price

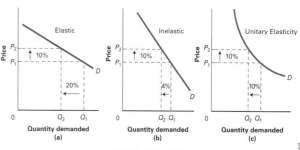

LO 19-5

variable cost a cost that varies with changes in the level of output

fixed cost a cost that does not change as output is increased or decreased

average variable cost (AVC) total variable costs divided by quantity of output

average total cost (ATC) total costs divided by quantity of output

average fixed cost (AFC) total fixed costs divided by quantity of output

marginal cost (MC) the change in total costs associated with a one-unit change in output

markup pricing the cost of buying the product from the producer, plus amounts for profit and for expenses not otherwise accounted for

keystoning the practice of marking up prices by 100 percent, or doubling the cost

profit maximization a method of setting prices that occurs when marginal revenue equals marginal cost

marginal revenue (MR) the extra revenue associated with selling an extra unit of output or the change in total revenue with a one-unit change in output

break-even analysis a method of determining what sales volume must be reached before total revenue equals total costs

LO 19-6

selling against the brand stocking well-known branded items at high prices in order to sell store brands at discounted prices

extranet a private electronic network that links a company with its suppliers and customers

prestige pricing charging a high price to help promote a high-quality image

---

changes, demand is inelastic. Thus, an increase in price will result in lower sales for an elastic product and little or no loss in sales for an inelastic product.

LO 19-4 Understand the concepts of dynamic pricing and yield management systems. When competitive pressures are high, a company must know when it can raise prices to maximize its revenues. *Dynamic pricing* allows companies to adjust prices on the fly to meet demand. *Yield management systems* use complex mathematical software to fill unused capacity profitably. The software uses techniques such as discounting early purchases, limiting early sales at these discounted prices, and overbooking capacity. These systems are used in service and retail businesses and are substantially raising revenues.

LO 19-5 Describe cost-oriented pricing strategies. The other major determinant of price is *cost*. Marketers use several cost-oriented pricing strategies. To cover their own expenses and obtain a profit, wholesalers and retailers commonly use *markup pricing*: they tack an extra amount on to the manufacturer's original price. Another pricing technique is to maximize profits by setting the price where marginal revenue equals marginal cost. Still another pricing strategy determines how much a firm must sell to break even; this amount in turn is used as a reference point for adjusting price.

Markup: Cost + x% = Price
Profit maximization: Price set at point where MR = MC

Break-even: Price set at point where total costs = total revenue

LO 19-6 Demonstrate how the product life cycle, competition, distribution and promotion strategies, customer demands, the Internet and extranets, and perceptions of quality can affect price. The price of a product normally changes as it moves through the life cycle and as demand for the product and competitive conditions change. Management often sets a high price at the introductory stage, and the high price tends to attract competition. The competition usually drives prices down because individual competitors lower prices to gain market share. Adequate distribution for a new product can sometimes be obtained by offering a larger-than-usual profit margin to wholesalers and retailers. The Internet enables consumers to compare products and prices quickly and efficiently. Price is also used as a promotional tool to attract customers. Special low prices often attract new customers and entice existing customers to buy more. Large buyers can extract price concessions from vendors. Such demands can squeeze the profit margins of suppliers. Perceptions of quality can also influence pricing strategies. A firm trying to project a prestigious image often charges a premium price for a product. Consumers tend to equate high prices with high quality.

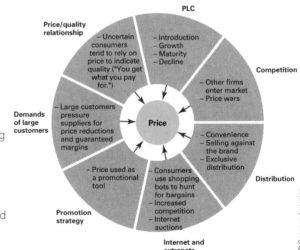

CHAPTER REVIEW

KEY TERMS

LO 20-1

price strategy a basic, long-term pricing framework that establishes the initial price for a product and the intended direction for price movements over the product life cycle

price skimming a pricing policy whereby a firm charges a high introductory price, often coupled with heavy promotion

penetration pricing a pricing policy whereby a firm charges a relatively low price for a product initially as a way to reach the mass market

status quo pricing charging a price identical to or very close to the competition's price

LO 20-2

unfair trade practice acts laws that prohibit wholesalers and retailers from selling below cost

price fixing an agreement between two or more firms on the price they will charge for a product

predatory pricing the practice of charging a very low price for a product with the intent of driving competitors out of business or out of a market

LO 20-3

base price the general price level at which the company expects to sell the good or service

quantity discount a price reduction offered to buyers buying in multiple units or above a specified dollar amount

cumulative quantity discount a deduction from list price that applies to the buyer's total purchases made during a specific period

noncumulative quantity discount a deduction from list price that applies to a single order rather than to the total volume of orders placed during a certain period

KEY CONCEPTS

LO 20-1 Describe the procedure for setting the right price. The process of setting the right price on a product involves four major steps: (1) establishing pricing goals; (2) estimating demand, costs, and profits; (3) choosing a price policy to help determine a base price; and (4) fine-tuning the base price with pricing tactics. A price strategy establishes a long-term pricing framework for a good or service. The three main types of price policies are price skimming, penetration pricing, and status quo pricing.

LO 20-2 Identify the legal constraints on pricing decisions. Government regulation helps monitor four major areas of pricing: unfair trade practices, price fixing, price discrimination, and predatory pricing. Many states have enacted unfair trade practice acts that protect small businesses from large firms that operate efficiently on extremely thin profit margins; the acts prohibit charging below-cost prices. The Sherman Act and the Federal Trade Commission Act prohibit both price fixing, which is an agreement between two or more firms on a particular price, and predatory pricing, in which a firm undercuts its competitors with extremely low prices to drive them out of business. Finally, the Robinson-Patman Act makes it illegal for firms to discriminate between two or more buyers in terms of price.

LO 20-3 Explain how discounts, geographic pricing, and other pricing tactics can be used to fine-tune the base price. Several techniques enable marketing managers to adjust prices within a general range in response to changes in competition, government regulation, consumer demand, and promotional and positioning goals. Techniques for fine-tuning a price can be divided into three main categories: discounts, allowances, rebates, and value-based pricing; geographic pricing; and other pricing tactics.

The first type of tactic gives lower prices to those who pay promptly, order a large quantity, or perform some function for the manufacturer. Additional tactics in this category include seasonal discounts, promotion allowances, and rebates (cash refunds).

Geographic pricing tactics—such as FOB origin pricing, uniform delivered pricing, zone pricing, freight absorption pricing, and basing-point pricing—are ways of moderating the impact of shipping costs on distant customers.

A variety of other pricing tactics stimulate demand for certain products, increase store patronage, and offer more merchandise at specific prices.

More and more customers are paying price penalties, which are extra fees for violating the terms of a purchase contract. The perceived fairness or unfairness of a penalty may affect some consumers' willingness to patronize a business in the future.

Charging customers shipping fees based on the zone in which they are located is a popular GEOGRAPHIC PRICING *tactic.*

20 SETTING THE RIGHT PRICE

cash discount a price reduction offered to a consumer, an industrial user, or a marketing intermediary in return for prompt payment of a bill

functional discount (trade discount) a discount to wholesalers and retailers for performing channel functions

seasonal discount a price reduction for buying merchandise out of season

promotional allowance (trade allowance) a payment to a dealer for promoting the manufacturer's products

rebate a cash refund given for the purchase of a product during a specific period

value-based pricing setting the price at a level that seems to the customer to be a good price compared to the prices of other options

FOB origin pricing a price tactic that requires the buyer to absorb the freight costs from the shipping point ("free on board")

uniform delivered pricing a price tactic in which the seller pays the actual freight charges and bills every purchaser an identical, flat freight charge

zone pricing a modification of uniform delivered pricing that divides the United States (or the total market) into segments or zones and charges a flat freight rate to all customers in a given zone

freight absorption pricing a price tactic in which the seller pays all or part of the actual freight charges and does not pass them on to the buyer

basing-point pricing a price tactic that charges freight from a given (basing) point, regardless of the city from which the goods are shipped

single-price tactic a price tactic that offers all goods and services at the same price (or perhaps two or three prices)

LO 20-4 Discuss product line pricing. Product line pricing maximizes profits for an entire product line. When setting product line prices, marketing managers determine what type of relationship exists among the products in the line: complementary, substitute, or neutral. Managers also consider joint (shared) costs among products in the same line.

LO 20-5 Describe the role of pricing during periods of inflation and recession. Marketing managers employ cost-oriented and demand-oriented tactics during periods of economic inflation. Cost-oriented tactics include dropping products with a low profit margin, using delayed-quotation pricing and escalator pricing, and adding fees. Demand-oriented pricing methods include price shading and increasing demand through cultivating selected customers, creating unique offerings, changing the package size, and heightening buyer dependence.

To stimulate demand during a recession, marketers use value-based pricing, bundling, and unbundling. Recessions are also a good time to prune unprofitable items from product lines. Managers strive to cut costs during recessions in order to maintain profits as revenues decline. Implementing new technology, renegotiating contracts, and pressuring suppliers for reduced prices are common techniques used to cut costs.

flexible pricing (variable pricing) a price tactic in which different customers pay different prices for essentially the same merchandise bought in equal quantities

price lining the practice of offering a product line with several items at specific price points

leader pricing (loss-leader pricing) a price tactic in which a product is sold near or even below cost in the hope that shoppers will buy other items once they are in the store

bait pricing a price tactic that tries to get consumers into a store through false or misleading price advertising and then uses high-pressure selling to persuade consumers to buy more expensive merchandise

odd–even pricing (psychological pricing) a price tactic that uses odd-numbered prices to connote bargains and even-numbered prices to imply quality

price bundling marketing two or more products in a single package for a special price

unbundling reducing the bundle of services that comes with the basic product

two-part pricing a price tactic that charges two separate amounts to consume a single good or service

consumer penalty an extra fee paid by the consumer for violating the terms of the purchase agreement

LO 20-4
product line pricing setting prices for an entire line of products

joint costs costs that are shared in the manufacturing and marketing of several products in a product line

LO 20-5
delayed-quotation pricing a price tactic used for industrial installations and many accessory items in which a firm price is not set until the item is either finished or delivered

escalator pricing a price tactic in which the final selling price reflects cost increases incurred between the time the order is placed and the time delivery is made

price shading the use of discounts by salespeople to increase demand for one or more products in a line